MJLT

Messianic Jewish Literal Translation

of the

כִּתְבֵי הַבְּרִית הַחֲדָשָׁה

New Covenant Scriptures

———⁓———

MJLT

Messianic Jewish Literal Translation

of the

כִּתְבֵי הַבְּרִית הַחֲדָשָׁה

New Covenant Scriptures

Based on
The Holy Bible consisting of the Old and New Covenants translated according to the letter and idioms of the original languages, also known as
"Young's Literal Translation"
by
Robert Young, LL.D.

Updated, edited and revised
by
Kevin Geoffrey

A ministry of Perfect Word Ministries

©2018 by Kevin Geoffrey. All rights reserved.

The MJLT text may be quoted in any form (written, visual, electronic, or audio) up to and inclusive of two hundred and fifty (250) verses without express written permission of the publisher, provided that the verses quoted do not constitute a complete book of Scripture, nor account for 25 percent or more of the total text of the work in which they are quoted.

Full attribution must be given on the copyright page as follows:

> Scripture taken from the Sacred Scriptures, Messianic Jewish Literal Translation (MJLT). ©2018 by Kevin Geoffrey. Used by permission of Perfect Word Publishing.

When verses are used non-commercially, no copyright notice is necessary, but the letters MJLT must appear following each quotation.

Permission requests that exceed the above guidelines must be sent to the publisher:

A ministry of Perfect Word Ministries

PO Box 82954 • Phoenix, AZ 85071
www.perfectword.org
1-888-321-PWMI

Paperback ISBN #: 978-0-9837263-3-3
Hardcover ISBN #: 978-0-9837263-4-0

Library of Congress Control Number: 2018944554

Cover art by Esther Geoffrey
Cover design elements ©kowit paikhamnam/123RF.COM

הָאֵל תָּמִים דַּרְכּוֹ אִמְרַת־יהוה צְרוּפָה
מָגֵן הוּא לְכֹל הַחֹסִים בּוֹ

God! His way *is* perfect, The word of A<small>DONAI</small> is tried *and true*,
A shield *is* He to all those trusting in Him.

תְּהִלִּים *T'hiliym* 18:31(30)

Contents

Preface i

Introduction v

The Scriptures Written to Messianic Jews 1

    מַתִּתְיָהוּ Matit'yahu (Matthew) 3

    יַעֲקֹב Ya'aqov (Jacob/"James") 42

    1 Timothy 46

    2 Timothy 50

    כֵּיפָא א 1 Keifa (1 Peter) 53

    עִבְרִים Iv'riym (Hebrews) 58

The Scriptures Written to both Messianic Jews and the Reconciled from among the Nations 71

    Mark 73

    Luke 98

    Acts 139

    Galatians 181

    1 Thessalonians 187

    2 Thessalonians 190

    1 Corinthians 192

    2 Corinthians 208

    Romans 218

    Colossians 235

    Philemon 239

    Ephesians 240

    Philippians 245

    Titus 249

    כֵּיפָא ב 2 Keifa (2 Peter) 251

    יְהוּדָה Y'hudah (Jude) 254

    יוֹחָנָן Yochanan (John) 256

    יוֹחָנָן א Yochanan (1 John) 287

    יוֹחָנָן ב Yochanan (2 John) 291

    יוֹחָנָן ג Yochanan (3 John) 291

    Revelation 292

Glossary of Transliterated Terms 313

About the Editor 323

Preface

When I first began working on MJLT, I had three children—my oldest about to become a teenager—and I wanted desperately to be able to hand them a Bible that would not only nurture their growing Messianic Jewish faith, but also be an utterly reliable, trustworthy and to-the-letter accurate translation of the Scriptures. So, in my spare time, about half an hour each morning, I set out to update and revise Robert Young's Literal Translation—the version of the Scriptures I had been using in my teachings for many years—in a way that was compatible with and supportive of the language, understanding and identity with which I was raising my kids. At first, whittling away at MJLT was a pleasurable discipline—spending time in my Father's Word; laboring on behalf of my sons. Had I known, though, what a time-intensive, energy-siphoning, stress-inducing undertaking this translation would eventually become, I may very well have never started down this road in the first place—and that would have been a shame. Because now—a fourth child later, with my first teenager exiting his teens—I can finally hand my boys that Bible that I dreamed of… and I am so proud, and oh so grateful.

For me, the *Messianic Jewish Literal Translation of the New Covenant Scriptures* represents my children's future, their children's future, and my hope and expectations for the greater Messianic Jewish Movement. As such, the MJLT NCS is for anyone who wants not only a translation that preserves the authentic Messianic Jewish perspective of God's Word, but also endeavors to supply the truest, most complete representation of the original languages of Scripture in English… the very same reason Young originally undertook his seminal translation two centuries ago.

There is no doubt that I feel a kindred spirit with brother Robert, as his love for God's Word abounds in each wonderfully precise, beautifully awkward phrase and figure of speech throughout his translation. I would like to think that he would approve of many of the changes I've made to his text, and not be too unhappy with me for some of the others, but that overall he would see my unending admiration for his work, as well as my passion for preserving and faithfully retransmitting the Word as purely as possible. I have to admit, I do feel some level of guilt that, in modifying the MJLT to make it more accessible than Young's, I had to do a certain amount of damage to the concept and execution of the "literal translation." In the end, however, I believe with my whole heart that this "slightly-less-than-literal" literal translation is the right one for the time and season in which we presently find ourselves.

I also realize that, in undertaking this current project, I have left the MJLT NCS with one glaring omission—namely, the first three-quarters of the Bible. Let me be clear that I in no way consider the Hebrew Scriptures—the "Tanakh" or "Old Testament"—to be merely a faded background for the vastly more important New Covenant Scriptures. On the contrary, the Hebrew Scriptures are the eminent and immeasurably valuable foundation of God's Word, and while that foundation is embedded in the New Covenant Scriptures, the New Covenant Scriptures cannot be fully understood apart from them. To read the New Covenant writings alone is to come in at the middle of the story, and thereby miss the point completely. While the two may be separable by book binding or ignorance, they can never be separated by their eternal bond as the beginning and the end of God's one, great story.

The reason, then, for publishing only the New Covenant Scriptures *at this time* was purely practical—with limited time and resources, I needed to prioritize my efforts. As a first-generation Messiah-following Jew (both my parents are Jewish, and all my grandparents), I felt that, for the sake of my children, I had to first deal with the confusion and difficulty that often surrounds the New Covenant writings as it concerns Jewish believers and Jewish issues—not the least of which is Torah-keeping under the Messiah. It is in the New Covenant Scriptures, not the Hebrew Scriptures, where most of the misunderstanding resides regarding how to live as a Messianic Jew. I therefore did not feel the same urgency to start with the Hebrew Scriptures, since there is no question that they naturally apply to Jews; and with so many decent translations already in existence, I felt I could endure the delay.

My heart for the MJLT reflects my heart for how today's followers of Messiah should read and understand the Scriptures. It is my contention that the Book has its fullest meaning when it is read and understood in its original language and context; therefore, the most meaningful and life-changing Bible translation will not be the one that "speaks" to us and "touches our heart," but the one that is most faithful to the original, inspired Word of God. When we try to apply Scripture to modern issues without considering its original context (which is the way Scripture is primarily applied in today's Body of Messiah), this makes Scripture far too susceptible to interpretation. A literal translation, on the other hand—like the MJLT—cements the meaning of the text, and therefore gives us a firm foundation upon which to apply the word. My hope, then, is that people will choose the MJLT not because it's Messianic, and not even because they like the unique way it reads, but because they so love and cherish the Word of God that they must get as close as they possibly can to the authors' original language, expression and intended meaning.

Before I conclude, I would like to acknowledge all those without whom this work would not have been possible. First and foremost, I want to thank my incredible family for their love and support, and especially the countless, unending hours of editorial work done by my amazing wife Esther, and my brilliant son Isaac. You two elevated this translation to transcend anything I could have ever imagined it would be. I would also like to thank the Messianic Jewish Movement International (MJMI), Jewish Voice Ministries International (JVMI), and the Perfect Word Ministries board of directors for their overwhelming support in furtherance of this important work. And last, but far from least, the MJLT NCS would not exist today without the faithful prayers and support of our generous Perfect Word partners, donors and friends. Thank you for holding up my arms, and seeing me through to this day—this translation is yours. I would also like to dedicate the MJLT NCS in memory of our dear friends and

Preface

supporters Sandra Kelley and Kay Wonderley, whom we lost before this volume could be published. Thank you for your years of love and encouragement—I miss you.

To my Jewish brothers and sisters, I pray that the MJLT NCS will help you to embrace your identity and calling as Israel, and to deepen your understanding of what it truly means to be a Jew in Messiah. I exhort you to not allow any preconceived ideas—positive or negative—about Christianity, God, Torah, Jewish tradition, or Jewishness in general to affect the way you see yourself in the plain, simple text of Scripture. Allow the pure Word of God to speak the truth, that you may find the purpose in who you truly are.

And to my Gentile brothers and sisters in Messiah, I pray that the MJLT NCS will also help you to embrace your identity as the Reconciled from among the Nations—that it will increase your burden for the salvation of the Jewish people, and deepen your understanding of what it means to be a child of God. I exhort you also to set aside any preconceived ideas about what you expect or want the Scriptures to say, and instead read the Word with brand new eyes. Let the Scriptures reform you and renew you, teaching you what it truly means to be a disciple of Messiah, and showing you your inherent, eternal value just the way God made you.

May the peace of God, which is surpassing all understanding, guard your hearts and your thoughts in Messiah יֵשׁוּעַ, Yeshua. May you find your life's meaning, purpose and passion as you submit your will to God's perfect Word.

Kevin Geoffrey
June 1, 2018

Introduction

The Messianic Jewish Literal Translation of the New Covenant Scriptures (MJLT NCS)—Matit'yahu (Matthew) through Revelation—is a fresh, vibrant translation of the "New Testament" unlike any other. Based on the groundbreaking *Young's Literal Translation (YLT)*, which is in the public domain, the MJLT NCS is an exhaustive update and re-rendering of the YLT for the modern, Messianic reader. It is designed not only to provide a reliable 21st century version of the text, but also to further restore the true, Messianic Jewish perspective of Scripture that is often obscured by deeply ingrained anti-Jewish, anti-Torah preconceptions.

This distinctive Bible version contains several uncommon features that set it apart from other translations:

- **Literal translation.** The MJLT is built on the word-for-word translation framework of the YLT, which faithfully preserves word order, idioms, tense, and other figures of speech in order to transport the reader back into the time and mindset of the ancient writer.

- **Hebrew embedded within the English text.** For the beginning and intermediate Hebrew reader, the actual Hebrew—with vowel points, as well as transliteration—for various names, places and terms is printed in line with the English text of the MJLT, accentuating the Jewishness of Scripture.

- **Reordering of books.** The sequence of books has been rearranged, first, according to the author's original, intended audience (either Jewish, or both Jewish and Gentile together), and second, chronologically, according to the order in which they were written.

- **Acts timeline synced with Paul.** The accounts recorded in the book of Acts have been integrated with dates for Paul's writings, so that the reader may jump from Acts to the corresponding Pauline letter to see exactly what Paul was writing about in relation to the surrounding historical events.

- **Additions to the text made obvious.** Every word not found in the original Greek text that has been added to the translation for the sake of clarity is clearly marked so that the changes are evident and unhidden from the reader.

- **Messianic Jewish understanding.** Emphasis is placed on bringing clarity to passages that are often misunderstood and misapplied as they relate to Jewish believers, Torah, and other closely related topics.

- **Alternative manuscripts represented.** Extensive use of footnotes allows for the most important variant readings from other manuscripts to be included along with the main text of the MJLT.

Messianic Jewish Literal Translation

Ideal for Jewish believers in Yeshua, the MJLT NCS also uniquely provides Gentile believers and Jewish seekers with an accurate and faithful rendering of the original biblical text that helps to reveal and make better sense of the Messianic Jewish message of the New Covenant Scriptures.

Introduction to "Young's Literal Translation"

The MJLT NCS is built on the foundation of the "New Testament" portion of the previously published work, *The Holy Bible consisting of the Old and New Covenants translated according to the letter and idioms of the original languages*. Commonly known as Young's Literal Translation (YLT), the aforementioned volume—being both unique and revolutionary—is the providential accomplishment of self-taught, nineteenth century linguist Robert Young, LL.D.

Born in Scotland in 1822, Young became proficient in several oriental languages. A printer by trade, he began printing and selling his own works in 1847, specifically those related to his studies of the Hebrew Scriptures. The first edition of his translation of the Sacred Scriptures—a work that took him nearly twenty years to complete—was published by Pickering & Inglis in 1862. His *Analytical Concordance of the Bible*, perhaps his best-known work, was published in 1879. Young died in 1888, leaving behind two sons and four daughters.

Though Young's new translation of the Scriptures stood in stark contrast to the "commonly received English Version" of the day—the King James Version (KJV)—it was not Young's intention that his work be considered "competition" for the KJV, per se. Rather, he hoped that his translation would be seen for what it is: "a strictly literal and idiomatic rendering of the Original Hebrew and Greek Texts"—"literal" in the sense that it follows the original writings word for word without imposing upon the text (as opposed to "literal" in the sense of taking a metaphorical or hyperbolic passage literally), and "idiomatic" in the sense that it seeks to preserve the peculiar expressions and idioms of the original authors.

In his preface to the first edition, Young championed this literal and idiomatic mode of translation, comparing the goals of two very different kinds of translators: the one who brings the original text *forward* into a modern mindset, and the other who seeks to transport the reader *back* into the time and mindset of the ancient writer. He writes,

> There are two modes of translation which may be adopted in rendering into our own language the writings of an ancient author; the one is, to bring him before us in such a manner as that we may *regard him as our own*; the other, to *transport ourselves*, on the contrary, *over to him*, adopting his situation, modes of speaking, thinking, acting,—peculiarities of age and race, air, gesture, voice, &c. Each of these plans has its advantages, but the latter is incomparably the better of the two, being suited—not for the ever-varying modes of thinking and acting of the men of the fifth, or the tenth, or the fifteenth, or some other century, but—for all ages alike. All attempts to make Moses or Paul act, or speak, or reason, as if they were Englishmen of the nineteenth century, must inevitably tend to change the translator into a paraphrast [a person who paraphrases] or a commentator… characters which,

Introduction

however useful, stand altogether apart from [the translator], who, with a work before him in one language, seeks only to transfer it into another.

In prosecuting the plan thus adopted, a literal translation was indispensable. No other kind of rendering could place the reader in the position contemplated, side by side with the writer—prepared to think as *he* does, to see as *he* sees, to reason, to feel, to weep, and to exult along with him.

So, Young saw the necessity of a literal translation as being tied to the work of responsible translating: that is, the preservation and recommunication of only the original sense and meaning of the text. He considered any other mode of translation as needing to incorporate and impose *interpretation* upon the text, thereby straying from the author's original message, and thus exceeding the essential work of the translator. In the preface to the revised edition, published in 1887, Young further expounded upon why a literal translation is not only superior, but also indispensable for safeguarding the Sacred Scriptures, as well as championing the foundational belief in divine, verbal inspiration of the written Word of God.

[This] Translation of the New Testament is based upon the belief that every word of the original is "God-breathed," as the Apostle Paul says in his Second Epistle to Timothy, chap. 3.16....

This inspiration extends only to the original text, *as it came from the pens of the writers*, not to any translations ever made by man, however aged, venerable, or good; and only in so far as any of these adhere to the original—neither adding to nor omitting from it one particle—are they of any *real value*, for, to the extent that they vary from the original, the doctrine of verbal inspiration is lost, so far as that version is concerned.

[For example, if] a translation gives a *present tense* [part of speech] when the original gives a *past*, or a *past* when it has a *present*;... an *a* for a *the*, or a *the* for an *a*;... a *verb* for a *noun*, or a *noun* for a *verb*, it is clear that verbal inspiration is as much overlooked as if it had no existence. **THE WORD OF GOD IS MADE VOID BY THE TRADITIONS OF MEN.**

Young goes so far as to say that a translation that glosses over even the smallest part of speech in pursuit of a smoother translation—or worse, to make a difficult passage make more sense—nullifies God's Word. While there are certainly instances when such strictly literal translation rules need to be broken (for example, if a literal translation renders an idea nonsensical in the receiving language), the overall intention and execution of a *literal* translation best fulfills verbal inspiration.

Because of this exceedingly reverent approach to Bible translation, the result can be quite dynamic. While a literal translation often yields a "lively, picturesque, dramatic style, by which the inimitable beauty of the Original Text is more vividly brought out than by any previous Translation," Young admits that, at times, a literal approach to Bible translation can also have its aesthetic drawbacks. Nevertheless, in Young's view, foregoing easy readability is a small price to pay when the eternal, unabridged truth of the Scriptures is at stake. Young concludes,

A *strictly literal* rendering may not be so pleasant to the ear as one where the *apparent sense* is chiefly aimed at, yet it is not *euphony* [pleasantness of sound] but *truth* that ought to be sought....

Modern scholarship is beginning to be alive to the inconsistency of thus gratuitously obscuring, and really changing, the meaning, of the sacred writers by subjective notions of what they *ought* to have written, rather than what they *did* write, for if we admit that in a single case it can be lawful to render a *past* tense by a *present*, where shall we end? who is to be judge? if we do so in one passage, to bring out what may appear to us might, could, would, or should, be the Scriptural meaning, we cannot deny the same privilege to others who may twist other passages in like manner.

Young's translation, therefore—and, by extension, the MJLT—affords the reader an unparalleled opportunity to peer through the words of the modern English language with a confidence that he will catch the purest possible reflection of the words, thoughts and mindset of the ancient authors. By retaining direct one-to-one word translations, word order, colloquialisms, and literal phrase renderings, Young avoids the trap of subjective interpretation that is fundamentally encoded into more liberal, seemingly more "readable" Bible translations.

Ultimately at issue is this: when one reads the Bible, he will inevitably apply the words to himself and to his own situation, thereby taking the meaning of certain texts one step further into his experience, while simultaneously removing it one step farther from the original context. A *non-literal* Bible translation has necessarily already gone that first step in an effort to make the translation more readable and relatable, thus granting the reader greater liberty to travel even further from the original meaning. A *literal* translation on the other hand will hopefully provide a tighter tether on the reader. For sure, this often results in a rendering that takes a little more mental effort to comprehend. But in the time it takes the reader to do this, he loses the ability to step too far from the text as he makes his application. A literal translation, then, *limits* the understanding, interpretation and application of the Word in a profoundly healthy way, keeping the reader closer to God's Word, and not as easily able to wander off into the fields of his own spiritual imagination.

In the end, the goal of Young's literal translation—as also the MJLT—is to provide the truth-seeking disciple of Messiah with a valuable and reliable transmission of God's Word that reveals the original text in the most unfiltered form possible within the limitations and dynamic range of the modern English language.

Translation Elements

MJLT Literalness Compared to Young's

The act of translation is often as much art as it is science. In addition to having to know how to correctly and exactly use the tools of the translation trade, it takes intuition and creativity to correctly represent a word or thought from another time and another tongue in our language of today. Because of the natural limitations of linguistics, then, the unabridged truth of an original text is always obscured, at least in part, by the receiving language itself. The goal of a *literal* translation, then, is to minimize this inherent difficulty by preserving as many aspects of the original language as possible—even at the expense of ease of readability. The results of this approach, in terms of style and readability, are immediately apparent.

For example, most translations *smooth out* the text to the point that the entire Bible sounds as if it was written by a single human author. A literal translation, on the other hand, not only keeps extremely difficult-to-translate passages intact, but it retains each individual author's distinct writing style—and some biblical authors are, from a strictly grammatical standpoint, better writers than others! Even within the range of Paul's writings, for instance, the differences between books with varying co-authors are clearly evident in a literal translation like the MJLT. This effect is quite advantageous, as a not-entirely-smoothed-out rendering of the Scriptures constantly reminds the reader that he is not just reading some ordinary piece of English-language literature; but, in actuality, he is peering through a lens at an ancient, spiritual text composed in an unfamiliar and quite foreign language. This is the beauty and power of the literal approach to Scripture translation.

But despite these benefits, and with great respect and admiration for Young's method and the absoluteness to which he held his standard for translation, it was nevertheless determined that a certain level of literalness needed to be sacrificed in order for the MJLT to achieve its goals for the modern, Messianic reader. Several factors went into making this decision.

First, contrary to the MJLT, Young's original intention for his translation was more as a companion study tool than as a standalone translation for everyday reading. The strictness he kept with regard to literalness necessarily erected a barrier for any reader, almost requiring him to read the YLT at least alongside another English translation (which would have been the King James Version in Young's day), if not in parallel with a copy in the original languages.

Second—and sadly—today's average reader has a far worse grasp of the English language than Young's nineteenth century audience. Therefore, even minor changes in word order, for example, proved beneficial in greatly increasing the readability of the MJLT. Where Mark 1:15 reads in the YLT, "fulfilled has been the time," the MJLT reads, "the time has been fulfilled," and understanding becomes instantaneous. Though Young's word order holds closely to that of the original Greek, the slightly-less-literal version of the MJLT keeps the reader from unnecessarily stumbling through the phrase, while, at the same time, not altering the meaning of the text in the least. These changes were made on an as-needed basis.

Third, Young himself at times bent his own translation rules, slightly reordering words where the original order resulted in a meaningless translation, and even sparingly adding italicized words to the text for clarity. This practice implicitly granted some liberties for the MJLT, while still keeping with the spirit of the literal translation. Indeed, changes of any kind were cautiously considered, and only when deemed absolutely necessary for the clearest transmission of the text were they utilized.

Lastly, such less-than-literal changes were offset to a certain degree by places where the MJLT is *even more literal* than Young's. In every case, these were the result of going deeper into the Greek, with the resulting lexical research revealing a more literal rendering to be the most beneficial to the text. Such cases were often prompted by the need to re-render Young's obsolete English words in modern English, and study ensued.

On balance, the MJLT still falls on the very far end of the literal/idiomatic translation spectrum—perhaps not as literal as Young's incredible translation, but certainly very close.

Methodology for Revising Young's

The MJLT is a very transparent translation, showing all but some of the most minor editorial changes made to Young's. From the beginning of the revision process, it was deemed of great importance that the MJLT reader be able to not only see changes to Young's, but every addition to or modification of the translation of the Greek. This was accomplished through the use of extensive footnotes and creative formatting of the type.

Perhaps the most significant issue affecting the updating of Young's was the underlying Greek text that he used for his translation. At the time the YLT was published in the late 1800s, the Textus Receptus or Received Text—the compilation of Greek manuscripts published by Erasmus in 1516, used to translate the King James Version New Testament—was still the most widely used and accepted text. Over the last two centuries, however, more reliable Greek manuscripts dating from earlier periods have not only been discovered, but authenticated and incorporated into Greek manuscript compilations known as Critical Text versions. A Critical Text, then, will have numerous differences from the Textus Receptus—most of them significantly minor, with only a few of them quite major. So, a translation based on the Textus Receptus, while containing many differences in the original Greek from nearly every other modern English translation, is *not* significantly different in substance from those other translations. Their agreement far outweighs their differences. Nevertheless, because of the utmost importance placed on the accuracy and reliability of the MJLT NCS, it was decided to search Young's verse by verse, word by word, and replace every single Textus Receptus difference with the presumably more accurate corresponding passage from a Critical Text version. While several Greek manuscript versions were consulted in the course of this work—including the Textus Receptus—we ultimately settled on using the Critical Text as found in the United Bible Societies' Fourth, Corrected Edition of the *Greek New Testament* (Nestle-Aland).

Throughout the MJLT NCS, wherever the Critical Text is rendered in place of the Textus Receptus such that a change of any significance is made, the alternate Textus Receptus renderings—as represented by Young's—are preserved as *footnotes*. Therefore, where a footnote reads, "some mss" (mss = manuscripts), this is usually referring to the less reliable, later manuscripts, specifically the Textus Receptus. There are, however, a few instances when the Textus Receptus is represented in the body of the

Introduction

MJLT instead, in which case a footnote may say, "earlier mss," indicating that the alternate rendering included in the footnote is from an earlier manuscript, as found in the Critical Text.

It is important to note that while great pains were taken to include these changes in order to faithfully represent the YLT, the inclusion of these particular "some mss/earlier mss" footnotes is not to suggest a legitimate optional reading—nor should these footnotes ever be used to formulate some secondary or alternate understanding of the passage in question. What is in the main text of the MJLT is what ought to be considered not merely the primary, but the likely and most reliable, rendering. (Occasionally, a footnote *will* offer a legitimate alternate reading with a simple "or," indicating a high degree of equality with what was selected for the body of the text—i.e., "eagles" or "vultures." Nevertheless, the word or phrase in the main body should still be considered the most accurate translation.)

Other information contained in footnotes ranges from citations of the Hebrew Scriptures to notes from other outside works. All Hebrew Scripture chapter and verse numbers are the same as those found in the Jewish Tanakh; however, when these numbers differ from those found in the Christian Old Testament, the Old Testament numbers are included in parentheses, i.e., מַלְאָכִי *Mal'akhiy* 3:24(4:6). Abbreviations or names found in these footnotes include: *Stern* (David Stern's *Jewish New Testament Commentary*), *CJB* (David Stern's *Complete Jewish Bible*), *Thayer* (Thayer's *Greek English Lexicon of the New Testament*), *Friberg* (Friberg's *Analytical Lexicon to the Greek New Testament*) and *LXX* (an abbreviation for the Septuagint—the Greek translation of the Hebrew Scriptures completed in the mid-3rd century B.C.). Other resources consulted in the course of this work include the Bauer-Danker-Arndt-Gingrich (BDAG) Greek Lexicon, the United Bible Societies' Greek Dictionary, the Salkinson-Ginsburg Hebrew New Testament, the Trinitarian Bible Society's Hebrew New Testament, and the following additional Bible versions: the English Standard Version (ESV), the New American Standard Bible (NAS), the New International Version (NIV), the King James Version (KJV), and the Tree of Life Version (TLV).

It should especially be noted that the work of Messianic Jewish scholar David Stern was inspirational and instrumental to the creation of the MJLT. His influence will be most readily seen in the usage of such terms as "Keifa" and "emissary," as well as critical theological concepts, such as, "a goal of תּוֹרָה, Torah is Messiah" (Romans 10:4, MJLT).

Finally, the most obvious and statistically significant changes that the MJLT makes to Young's are in the over 2,000 individual English words (which are, themselves, repeated numerous times throughout the text) that have been updated or retranslated. Many of these words have been changed because the word in Young's was archaic or obsolete—it may have fallen out of usage, or its meaning may have changed significantly over the last two centuries. Other words were changed simply for the sake of consistency; for example, to sometimes make the translation of a given Greek word uniform across the whole MJLT, rather than using different English words in different passages. Still other words were changed because our lexical research revealed there were more accurate translation choices available. While there is insufficient space to print all 2,000 changes here, a complete list of all YLT to MJLT word replacements is available on the MJLT website (mjlt.org).

Other miscellaneous word and grammar changes made to Young's include:

- Updates reflecting grammatical differences between Greek and English. For example, "where He Himself was about to **come**" becomes "where He Himself was about to **go**."
- Simplification of verb forms. For example, "did love" becomes "loved," "may be" becomes "is."
- Changing the tense (past, present, future, etc.) when preserving the Greek tense would be unnecessarily confusing, and when changing the tense does not change the contextual meaning. For example, "as he is praying" becomes "as he was praying."
- Addition, subtraction, or modification of punctuation to assist with reading and understanding.
- Personal pronouns ("He," "Him," "Me," etc.) ascribed to Messiah and Deity, and also other titles, are capitalized. (Messiah's personal pronouns are *not* capitalized in certain instances—specifically, in long passages that also refer to the Father—since the capitalization would cause confusion for the reader. Yeshua's personal pronouns are also not capitalized when the speaker referring to Him is an unbeliever, or someone who fails to recognize His authority.) Also, "Heaven" is capitalized when the text is referring to the abode of God, and it is uncapitalized when simply referring to the sky. "Heaven" is also uncapitalized when the context is ambiguous.

Organization and Order

One of the most revolutionary characteristics of the MJLT is in the organization and sequence of its books. While every jot and tittle of the traditionally accepted "New Testament" is present in the MJLT, the traditional "New Testament" structure (which was still fluctuating as late as the 4th century A.D., and has little to no theological significance, much less any divine authority) has been replaced by an arrangement that is, first, according to the author's original, intended **audience**—that is, either Jewish, or both Jewish and Gentile together—and, second, **chronologically**; that is, according to the order that the books were written (with a few notable exceptions). By challenging the traditional structure and rearranging the books according to these criteria, it not only presents the New Covenant writings in a way that makes logical, common sense, but it also helps to combat Christian Replacement Theology and anti-Semitism through the restoration of the Jewish perspective and identity of Scripture.

Introduction

The books of the MJLT, then, appear in the following order:

Year A.D. (Approximate)	The Scriptures Written to Messianic Jews	The Scriptures Written to both Messianic Jews and the Reconciled from among the Nations
(40's - 60's)	Matit'yahu (Matthew)	
(50's - 60's)		Mark
(57 - 62)		Luke
(60 - 62)		Acts
40	Ya'aqov (Jacob/"James")	
51		Galatians
52		1 Thessalonians
52		2 Thessalonians
54		1 Corinthians
54		2 Corinthians
56		Romans
59		Colossians
60		Philemon
60		Ephesians
61		Philippians
62	1 Timothy	
62		Titus
63	2 Timothy	
63	1 Keifa (1 Peter)	
67		2 Keifa (2 Peter)
69	Iv'riym (Hebrews)	
70's		Y'hudah (Jude)
80's		Yochanan (John)
80's		1 Yochanan (1 John)
80's		2 Yochanan (2 John)
80's		3 Yochanan (3 John)
90's		Revelation

The Scriptures Written to Messianic Jews

The first main section of the MJLT NCS is called, "The Scriptures written to Messianic Jews," and is comprised of just 6 of the 27 books of the New Covenant Scriptures. Each book in this section is placed in chronological order, with the exception of Matit'yahu, which may have been written as late as the A.D. 60's. Despite this fact, it was necessary to keep Matit'yahu at the beginning of the MJLT NCS in order to adequately introduce Yeshua and provide context for the rest of the writings—and, certainly, the historical events that Matit'yahu recorded preceded the writing of all the other books in this section. In deciding which books to include here, the selection was limited to only those where it could be confidently determined that the authors' original, primary, intended audiences were Jewish believers in Yeshua.

Messianic Jewish Literal Translation

Matit'yahu (Matthew), while not explicitly identifying a Jewish audience, contains a great deal of internal evidence indicating that this is the case—not the least of which is the author's heavy reliance upon and interest in the fulfillment of the Hebrew Scriptures. He also does not explain Jewish culture to his readers like the other Good News reporters do, which implies his audience's Jewishness.

Ya'aqov (Jacob/"James") explicitly identifies his Jewish audience in the very first verse of his letter as "the Twelve Tribes *of Yis'rael* who are in the Dispersion." This "Dispersion" may be referring to that which came after the massive persecution of the Jewish believers in Jerusalem, when "they were all scattered abroad [dispersed] throughout the regions of יְהוּדָה, Y'hudah and שֹׁמְרוֹן, Shom'ron" (see Acts 8:1-4). Alternatively, Ya'aqov may be referring to Jewish believers who were already living outside the Land of Israel in places where the Jewish people had been dispersed as a result of persecution in earlier eras.

1 & 2 Timothy—which, despite their early appearance in the MJLT, are actually among Paul's last letters chronologically—were written to his disciple Timothy, who Luke tells us in Acts 16:1 was the "son of a believing יְהוּדִי, Y'hudiy [Jewish] woman." Paul clearly considered Timothy to be Jewish, and treated him as such, having him circumcised before bringing him on his travels (see Acts 16:3).

1 Keifa (1 Peter), like Ya'aqov, initially identifies his Jewish audience in his opening address ("to the chosen temporary residents of the Dispersion"). Then the "emissary of the Circumcision" (Galatians 2:7-9) most fully addresses his readers in 1 Keifa 2:9-10, where he identifies them with the unmistakable Hebrew Scripture references to divinely chosen Israel, and then immediately juxtaposes them with the Gentiles among whom they are dispersed (see 1 Keifa 2:11-12).

And finally, **Iv'riym** (Hebrews). As the name implies, the content of the book is clearly addressed to Hebrews (Jews) who are having difficulty maintaining the Messianic faith. Like Matit'yahu, however, Iv'riym does not explicitly identify its obviously implied Jewish audience.

As a point of interest, other books were considered for this first section of the MJLT NCS, but were ultimately not included. **2 Keifa** (2 Peter) was obviously considered because it was the second letter written by the "emissary of the Circumcision" (Galatians 2:7-9) who had clearly written previously to a primarily Jewish audience; however, 2 Keifa 3:15 indicates that, in his second letter, he is writing to the same group as Paul, which would have certainly been of mixed ethnic background. **Y'hudah** (Jude) was considered because of its similarity to 2 Keifa, especially regarding the manner in which both authors cite Jewish sources; however, there was ultimately not enough evidence to place Y'hudah's letter squarely within a Jewish audience. **Luke-Acts** were considered for the first section because of Luke's very Jewish perspective, along with the possibility that Theophilus—Luke's stated audience-of-one for both books—may have actually been a *cohen* (priest). Nevertheless, without clearer evidence from the Scriptures, a determination for a Jewish audience could not be confidently made. Finally, Paul's letter to **Philemon** was briefly considered for this section, but since Philemon's lineage could not be determined, the book bearing his name was also not included.

The Scriptures Written to both Messianic Jews and the Reconciled from among the Nations

The second section of the MJLT NCS, containing the remaining twenty-one books, is called, "The Scriptures written to both Messianic Jews and the Reconciled from among the Nations." As in the first section, the books appear in purely chronological order, with the exception of Mark, Luke and Acts, which, like Matit'yahu, were moved to the beginning of the section to provide proper historical context. A sub-section of sorts comprises the last quarter of this section containing all the works of Yochanan (John), which were actually composed considerably later than the rest of the New Covenant writings. This made for a fortuitous grouping and an unexpectedly exciting climax to the end of the MJLT.

The majority of the New Covenant Scriptures, then, as evidenced by the books in this section, were written to a mixed Jewish and Gentile audience, with the exception of Titus (and possibly Luke-Acts and Philemon). Since it seemed unnecessarily complicated to create a section for a strictly Gentile audience that would contain only one book—four at most—it made the most sense to keep Titus (and the others) where they were. For the rest of the books, most of them Paul's, the audience was undoubtedly the Body of Messiah at large, which was comprised of both Jewish and Gentile believers. Still, there are definitely instances when the author—for example, Paul in his letter to the Roman believers—is clearly addressing Jews and Gentiles *separately and in turn* within the scope of a single letter, with both groups hearing what the author has to say to the other.

The term "Reconciled from among the Nations" is perhaps a more verbose, but certainly a more accurate and respectful, description for our brothers and sisters in Yeshua who are not of Jewish descent. The concept of the Reconciled comes from passages such as 2 Corinthians 5:18-20, Romans 5:10, Colossians 1:21-22, and Ephesians 2:16. Regarding these from among the nations who have been reconciled to God through Yeshua, Ya'aqov clearly says, "God looked after the גּוֹיִם, Goyim [nations] to take out from them a people for His Name" (Acts 15:14, MJLT).

As for the word גּוֹיִם, Goyim (or the singular form גּוֹי, Goy, or even the English word "Gentile," for that matter): while there are some believers who are not of Jewish descent who take offense at these words—especially given that certain Jews use them in a derogatory fashion—from a Scriptural standpoint, they simply mean "nation" or "ethnic-group" (ἔθνος, ethnos in Greek) with no further characterization attached to them. Context, however, will often reveal that the group being referred to is of non-Jewish descent, which is how "גּוֹיִם, Goyim" is used in the MJLT NCS—with no intended, implied, or accidentally derogatory overtones, whatsoever.

Does the Order of Books in the MJLT NCS Re-erect the Middle Wall of Partition?

Some may be concerned that dividing the New Covenant Scriptures according to Jewish and mixed Jewish and Gentile audiences in some way re-erects the middle wall of partition that Yeshua Himself destroyed (see Ephesians 2:14-15). This, of course, is not the intent of the MJLT NCS, nor does it, in actuality, do so.

Far from creating any kind of division or separation between Jewish and Gentile believers, reordering the Scriptures in this manner instead *recognizes and celebrates the unity* we have *despite* the natural distinctions already created by our God-given, immutable *ethnicity* (people-grouping based on lineage/ancestry/physical descent)—in the same way, for example, that the Scriptures recognize and celebrate the unity we have despite the distinctions created by our God-given, immutable *gender*. God glorifies Himself through men and women *equally*, but not *identically*. In the same way, He glorifies Himself through Jews and Gentiles equally, but not identically—and to obscure or lose these distinctions is to pervert the work of God, and rob Him of the fullness of His glory.

Foreign (and uncomfortable) as this concept may be to most believers in Yeshua—a concept that the MJLT NCS was specifically designed to help promote—the Scriptures demonstrate that, within the spiritual unity and equality of the members of the Body of Messiah, there are unique and important differences between groups of believers—and because of those differences, we necessarily have different roles and functions. By distinguishing between audiences according to no other criterion but ethnicity—and in no way implying a hierarchy or more-favored status for one group over another—the MJLT provides a more complete context for what is written, which in turn effects practical application. In short, things spoken to a Jewish audience will have a somewhat different application than if a general audience is assumed, and vice versa.

Therefore, to glean the fullest understanding and meaning of the Scriptures as the authors originally intended, the first section of the MJLT NCS should be read as through the eyes of one who is ethnically Jewish; the second section, as one sitting among an ethnically diverse group of people—both Messianic Jews and the Reconciled from among the Nations. Much more can and should be said about this topic, but for now, let it be understood that this approach ought to be seen as one that promotes health and unity in the Body by restoring the glorious perspective that should accompany our respective identities as Jews and Gentiles in Messiah, as only God could make us.

Acts Timeline and Synchronization with Paul

Another important feature of the way the MJLT is organized centers on the book of Acts and the writings of Paul. Of the twenty-seven books comprising the New Covenant Scriptures, essentially half of them were written by the emissary Paul. It is certainly, then, no understatement to say that to misunderstand Paul is to misunderstand the majority of the Scriptural teachings about the Messianic faith. One of the major aspects of Paul's writings that is obscured by the traditional "New Testament" organization is the natural progression of Paul's theology. When approached chronologically instead—as they have been restored in the MJLT—previously confusing theological concepts can begin to take on a more logical and coherent form.

Introduction

Another obscured aspect of Paul's writings is uncovered in the MJLT by the synchronization of Paul's chronology with the events of the book of Acts. In God's wisdom, the book of Acts supplies us with a detailed record following Paul from his persecution of Messianic Jews through his lifetime of service to the Messiah. By overlaying these events with Paul's chronology, the MJLT dynamically reveals Paul's history—more specifically, the timing, circumstances, conditions and mindset under which he penned his Scriptural letters.

Inlaid within the text of the book of Acts, then, the MJLT periodically notes approximate dates to mark important events, and to demonstrate the long passage of time that actually takes place over the course of the entire book—30 years! Many of these notations also identify the letter(s) written by Paul during that same time period (there is one entry for Ya'aqov as well).

While, at first, one would most likely read the MJLT by going straight through Acts and Paul sequentially, as an alternative reading, one may begin in Acts, then stop at each date with an accompanying book notation, skip to the corresponding letter in Paul and read it, and then return to Acts, continue, and repeat. This provides the most hyper-chronological reading, and is sure to add to the depth of understanding of both the events of Acts, and the teachings of Paul.

It is important to note that the purpose of including actual dates was not to offer exact points in time, but merely a fairly accurate, yet approximate, representation for the timeline of events—hence, the use of "circa," as in "c. A.D. 30." Beginning with compilations by H. Wayne House in his *Chronological and Background Charts of the New Testament* (Zondervan, 2009), a certain amount of firsthand calculation based on the biblical texts themselves was also necessary in an attempt to fill in some of the blanks, and maintain a helpful chronology. Where the order of books is concerned, Young actually has his own chronological list printed in his Bible. However, since it was derived from sources considerably older than those available to modern scholarship, Young's list often differs with today's range of more commonly accepted dates. While the exact dates are disputed among scholars, and no two chronological lists of and dates associated with the New Covenant writings are identical, the reader may be assured that great care was taken to provide as faithful and accurate a chronology as possible—both for the order of books, and for the dates of events as indicated in Acts.

Formatting Styles

As mentioned previously, the MJLT is a very transparent translation, and great effort was taken to show as many editorial changes as possible, keeping nothing hidden from the reader. To that end, certain formatting choices were made to indicate different types of changes and various aspects of the text that are being represented in the MJLT. Of primary importance,

- Words in *italics* or *CAPITAL ITALICS* indicate MJLT clarifying additions. They do not have corresponding words in the underlying Greek. While every Bible translation necessarily (and some Bible translations unnecessarily) adds words to the original text, rarely are even the most important additions made obvious to the reader, much less the smallest ones. This has been remedied in the MJLT.

- Words in *ITALIC SMALL CAPS* are Young's clarifying additions. They also do not have corresponding words in the underlying Greek. Young makes far fewer clarifying additions to the text than the MJLT does.

- Words in ALL CAPS are in line quotations of Hebrew Scripture. Hebrew Scripture quotations may also be set off from the surrounding text as right and left indented paragraphs (as are poetic sections, and the words of Yeshua in Revelation 22). When the author expressly indicates that he is quoting Scripture, the indented paragraph is the usual format of choice. Otherwise, the ALL CAPS formatting is used.

It would be most advantageous to the reader to familiarize himself with these formatting styles in order to make the most of his MJLT understanding.

Use of Hebrew

The MJLT is not the first English Bible version to incorporate Hebrew names and terminology within the text. It is the first, however, to go beyond the use of Hebrew transliteration (the rendering of corresponding characters from one alphabet into another) to also include the actual Hebrew lettering. For example, "Yeshua" is a transliteration of the Hebrew, "יֵשׁוּעַ", and appears in the MJLT as "יֵשׁוּעַ, Yeshua."

The decision to incorporate Hebrew initially came from a place of personal expression, in which the regular use of Hebrew is a natural part of Messianic Jewish identity. However, it also serves as a visual and phonic reminder of the overall Jewish authorship of the New Covenant Scriptures. Though the authors clearly wrote and spoke in Greek, they were, first and foremost (with the probable exception of Luke), Jews, with Jewish names, born in Jewish places, speaking Jewish dialects, practicing a Jewish faith in the Jewish Messiah. It did not make sense, then, to unnecessarily anglicize Hebrew names and places, when they could naturally be rendered in Hebrew. Then, following suit, other terms could also be rendered in Hebrew, especially when it benefitted the unique perspective of this translation. Overall, the use of Hebrew in the MJLT has both a practical and aesthetic purpose which serves to reinforce and emphasize the underlying Jewish character and origin of the Scriptures.

While it would have been far easier from a formatting standpoint to include just transliterated Hebrew without Hebrew lettering, just as other translations have previously done, in practice, the transliteration alone often leads the reader to actually *mispronounce* the Hebrew. (In addition, the use of transliteration can be quite awkward for a reader who is also familiar with Hebrew.) It was therefore decided to incorporate a middle-of-the-road solution. Rather than only including the transliteration, the actual Hebrew lettering immediately precedes each transliterated term. Additionally, the Hebrew text is pointed with *n'qudot* (dots and dashes used to indicate vowel sounds), which will be helpful for beginning and intermediate Hebrew readers, although somewhat annoying and completely redundant for the advanced Hebrew reader. Nevertheless, this seemed like the most reasonable and useful course, considering the MJLT's primarily English-speaking audience.

It is worth mentioning that there are also a few places in the MJLT NCS where neither English nor Hebrew seemed the best choice to translate the Greek, out of concern that a nuance of the Greek word would be lost in translation. Therefore, on rare occasions, the MJLT also incorporates the original Greek term along with its transliteration. Footnotes and glossary entries have been provided to assist the reader in understanding these words.

The Name

One of the more difficult decisions for the MJLT translation as a whole was how to best represent the Tetragrammaton—what is commonly referred to as God's sacred name, יהוה. In the MJLT New Covenant Scriptures, the Greek word κύριος, kurios is most often translated as "Master." However, when the context demands it, and it is a clear reference to God, this word can also represent the Tetragrammaton.

But while the Name ought to command reverence and respect, there are also cultural attitudes toward the use of the Name—both in Judaism and in some corners of the Hebraic and Messianic worlds—that can lead to a great deal of rhetoric and divisiveness. The controversy surrounds the audible pronunciation of the Name—whether it can or should be spoken aloud, and, if so, what does it sound like?

In ancient (and orthodox) Jewish tradition, it was forbidden to audibly pronounce the Name. Unfortunately, with various substitutions being regularly employed to avoid saying the Name, the true pronunciation eventually fell out of use and was lost to antiquity. Though some scholars and others assert that the pronunciation of the Name has indeed been preserved, or is capable of being derived, the arguments are ultimately unconvincing, especially considering that the surviving manuscripts of Scripture do not clearly communicate to us how the Name is to be pronounced.

And therein lies the problem. If an exact, accurate pronunciation were able to be reliably ascertained, it would have been an almost automatic decision to simply transliterate the Hebrew as had been done with every other Hebrew word in the MJLT—pausing only to consider the risk of offending and alienating Jewish readers. However, with no such pronunciation available to us, and any sort of approximation being wholly insufficient, it was deemed necessary—through a considerable amount of thoughtful deliberation—to arrive at an alternative.

Selecting the Best Representation of the Name for the MJLT

Young's choice for representing יהוה in the Hebrew Scriptures is "Jehovah," but this was never considered as an option for the MJLT, since it comes from a Christian misunderstanding of the Hebrew vowel pointing that early-medieval Judaism designed to avoid the pronunciation of the Name.

There was also never any serious consideration for co-opting Judaism's "HaShem," which literally means "The Name." This transliteration of a circumlocution invented by Judaism to further a practice not found in Scripture also did not seem an appropriate solution for the MJLT.

Messianic Jewish Literal Translation

Our first real choice, then, was to simply use יהוה alone, with no transliteration. As favorable as this option was, we ultimately decided against it, realizing how extremely difficult it would then be for most readers to quote MJLT passages in writing, and read MJLT passages aloud. Without an accompanying transliteration, it would unnecessarily increase the degree of difficulty for readers who had not yet made up their minds about how to properly address the issue of the Name.

Next, we considered representing the Name as YHVH in transliterated English. Unfortunately, this presented similar problems as the above, in addition to there being concern that, like the Hebrew-only option, it might feed into the misuse of the Name in modern Sacred Name movements.

So finally, taking a cue from David Stern, we settled on representing יהוה with ADONAI in small caps, in the same way that most English language Bibles differentiate יהוה with LORD in small caps. Since "Adonai" is its own Hebrew word (אֲדֹנָי), distinct from and unrelated to יהוה, it was decided not to pair "ADONAI" with the Hebrew for יהוה. The MJLT reader would simply need to be aware that when He sees "ADONAI" in the text, it is referring to יהוה; and, like Mosheh did when he heard God speak the Name to him in Exodus 33:19-34:9, the reader may enunciate "Adonai" as written. For readers who prefer to utter some other semblance of יהוה—at the risk of mispronouncing God's Name, and offending and alienating others—they, too, may be so prompted by "ADONAI," thus, satisfying the needs (though perhaps not the preferences) of all camps.

In a few instances in the MJLT, in the context of more extensive titles for God (i.e., יהוה צְבָאוֹת, ADONAI Tz'vaot), the use of Hebrew did warrant the inclusion of the actual Hebrew for יהוה without vowel pointing. In these situations, "ADONAI" is used in the transliteration, even though it does not represent the actual Hebrew characters.

Specific Translation Choices Unique to the MJLT

Though a fundamental goal of the MJLT was merely to update and revise Young's 19th century English, it seemed wise to also take advantage of the opportunity to revisit words that are still in regular use, but carry with them a considerable amount of theological baggage. It was actually Young himself who opened the door to this reexamination by never using the word "church," but rather "assembly" to translate the Greek "ἐκκλησία, ekklesia." Working with Young's translation, then, there seemed to be an implicit invitation to reconsider any word that Christianity—over time, and through various church traditions—had loaded with meaning.

This, then, is why the following words do not exist in the MJLT: sanctify, grace, minister, fellowship, church, apostle, repent, preach, cross, angel, supplication, parable, tribulation, transfiguration, justified, predestined, evangelist and lord (when translating κύριός, kurios). Each of these words was carefully reconsidered both in context, and also according to lexical and modern dictionary definitions.

Although some readers may be especially concerned by the absence of "Lord" and its replacement in the MJLT with "Master," both words are actually *neutral* on the matter of deity. There may be a perception that the word "Lord" necessarily connotes deity, but linguistically, it simply does not. Despite its widespread, modern-day religious usage, "Lord" is actually an archaic term; and it is not a synonym for "God," but rather, "Master." Therefore, it is theologically equivalent to say that Yeshua is either "Lord" or "Master," as the words themselves do not confirm or convey His deity (in whose body, indeed, "all the fullness of the Deity dwells"), but only His authority.

In addition to the various exclusions and retranslations already mentioned, this re-examination of theologically loaded terms also resulted in the coining of a few brand new hyphenates specifically and originally for the MJLT. These terms include *world-ethnicities, stopping-place, Messiah-follower* and, most notably, *the Called-Forth*.

The concept of *the Called-Forth* is one of the most distinctive and paradigm-challenging translation choices of the MJLT. The term comes from the definitions of the root words of ἐκκλησία, ekklesia (that is, "called out" or "called forth"), which is often translated ambiguously as "church," and, in modern Messianic contexts, vaguely as "congregation," "community," or *kehilah* (see the MJLT footnote at Matit'yahu 16:18 for more about this topic). By hyper-literally translating ἐκκλησία, ekklesia as "Called-Forth," and its plural forms as "Called-Forth-Communities" or "Called-Forth-Gatherings" depending upon context, it immediately forces the reader out of the religious building/service mentality usually associated with "church" or "congregation," and makes him rethink the concept of the Scriptural ἐκκλησία, ekklesia in terms of what significant, meaningful way he, as a disciple of Messiah, has been "called forth" as a part of it.

In the end, each of these strategic word retranslations accomplishes a similar task—not so much by challenging the theologically loaded words themselves, but the widespread, long-held, deep-seated, preconceived ideas that are associated with those words. As a result, the reader is driven back to the context of Scripture for his understanding, and compelled to allow God's Word alone to re-teach him from the plain, simple words of the text. This is, ultimately, the reason the MJLT exists—for the faithful reader of God's Sacred Scriptures to clearly see and comprehend His pure, holy, and perfect Word.

The Scriptures
written to
Messianic Jews

בְּשׂוֹרַת יֵשׁוּעַ עַל־פִּי THE GOOD NEWS OF YESHUA ACCORDING TO

מַתִּתְיָהוּ Matit'yahu

1 ¹A scroll of the birth of יֵשׁוּעַ, Yeshua the Messiah,[a] son of דָּוִד, David, son of אַבְרָהָם, Av'raham.

²אַבְרָהָם, Av'raham brought forth יִצְחָק, Yitz'chaq; and יִצְחָק, Yitz'chaq brought forth יַעֲקֹב, Ya'aqov; and יַעֲקֹב, Ya'aqov brought forth יְהוּדָה, Y'hudah and his brothers; ³and יְהוּדָה, Y'hudah brought forth פֶּרֶץ, Peretz and זֶרַח, Zerach by תָּמָר, Tamar; and פֶּרֶץ, Peretz brought forth חֶצְרוֹן, Chetz'ron; and חֶצְרוֹן, Chetz'ron brought forth רָם, Ram; ⁴and רָם, Ram brought forth עַמִּינָדָב, Amiynadav; and עַמִּינָדָב, Amiynadav brought forth נַחְשׁוֹן, Nach'shon; and נַחְשׁוֹן, Nach'shon brought forth שַׂלְמוֹן, Sal'mon; ⁵and שַׂלְמוֹן, Sal'mon brought forth בֹּעַז, Boaz by רָחָב, Rachav; and בֹּעַז, Boaz brought forth עוֹבֵד, Oved by רוּת, Rut; and עוֹבֵד, Oved brought forth יִשַׁי, Yishai; ⁶and יִשַׁי, Yishai brought forth דָּוִד, David the king.

And דָּוִד, David brought forth שְׁלֹמֹה, Sh'lomoh by her WHO HAD BEEN the wife of אוּרִיָּה, Uriyah; ⁷and שְׁלֹמֹה, Sh'lomoh brought forth רְחַבְעָם, R'chav'am; and רְחַבְעָם, R'chav'am brought forth אֲבִיָּה, 'Aviyah; and אֲבִיָּה, 'Aviyah brought forth אָסָא, Asa; ⁸and אָסָא, Asa brought forth יְהוֹשָׁפָט, Y'hoshafat; and יְהוֹשָׁפָט, Y'hoshafat brought forth יְהוֹרָם, Y'horam; and יְהוֹרָם, Y'horam brought forth עֻזִיָּהוּ, Uziyahu; ⁹and עֻזִיָּהוּ, Uziyahu brought forth יוֹתָם, Yotam; and יוֹתָם, Yotam brought forth אָחָז, Achaz; and אָחָז, Achaz brought forth חִזְקִיָּהוּ, Chiz'qiyahu; ¹⁰and חִזְקִיָּהוּ, Chiz'qiyahu brought forth מְנַשֶּׁה, M'nasheh; and מְנַשֶּׁה, M'nasheh brought forth אָמוֹן, Amon; and אָמוֹן, Amon brought forth יֹאשִׁיָּהוּ, Yoshiyahu; ¹¹and יֹאשִׁיָּהוּ, Yoshiyahu brought forth יְכָנְיָהוּ, Y'khan'yahu and his brothers at the Babylonian expulsion.

¹²And after the Babylonian expulsion, יְכָנְיָהוּ, Y'khan'yahu brought forth שְׁאַלְתִּיאֵל, Sh'al'tiyel; and שְׁאַלְתִּיאֵל, Sh'al'tiyel brought forth זְרֻבָּבֶל, Z'rubavel; ¹³and זְרֻבָּבֶל, Z'rubavel brought forth אֲבִיהוּד, 'Aviyhud; and אֲבִיהוּד, 'Aviyhud brought forth אֶלְיָקִים, El'yaqiym; and אֶלְיָקִים, El'yaqiym brought forth עַזּוּר, Azur; ¹⁴and עַזּוּר, Azur brought forth צָדוֹק, Tzadoq; and צָדוֹק, Tzadoq brought forth יָכִין, Yakhiyn; and יָכִין, Yakhiyn brought forth אֱלִיהוּד, 'Eliyhud; ¹⁵and אֱלִיהוּד, 'Eliyhud brought forth אֶלְעָזָר, El'azar; and אֶלְעָזָר, El'azar brought forth מַתָּן, Matan; and מַתָּן, Matan brought forth יַעֲקֹב, Ya'aqov; ¹⁶and יַעֲקֹב, Ya'aqov brought forth יוֹסֵף, Yosef—the husband of מִרְיָם, Mir'yam, of whom was brought forth יֵשׁוּעַ, Yeshua, who is declared Messiah.

¹⁷All the generations, therefore, from אַבְרָהָם, Av'raham to דָּוִד, David ARE fourteen generations; and from דָּוִד, David to the Babylonian expulsion, fourteen generations; and from the Babylonian expulsion to the Messiah, fourteen generations.

¹⁸And the birth of יֵשׁוּעַ, Yeshua the Messiah was this way: when His mother מִרְיָם, Mir'yam had been pledged to יוֹסֵף, Yosef, before their coming together she was found to have conceived from the רוּחַ הַקֹּדֶשׁ, Ruach HaQodesh. ¹⁹And יוֹסֵף, Yosef her husband, being righteous and not wanting to make her a spectacle,[b] intended to privately send her away.

---

[a] "the Messiah"—הַמָּשִׁיחַ, HaMashiyach

[b] "spectacle"—some mss say, "public example"

²⁰But on his thinking of these things, look! a Messenger of ADONAI appeared to him in a dream, saying, "יוֹסֵף, Yosef, son of דָּוִד, David, do not fear to take מִרְיָם, Mir'yam *as* your wife, for that which was brought forth in her IS of the רוּחַ הַקֹּדֶשׁ, Ruach HaQodesh! ²¹And she will bring forth a son, and you will call his name יֵשׁוּעַ, Yeshua, for He will save His people from their sins!"

²²And all this has come to pass so that it may be fulfilled—that *which* was spoken by ADONAI through the prophet, saying,

²³"Look! The virgin will conceive, and she will bring forth a son, and they will call his name עִמָּנוּאֵל, Imanuel,"[a]

which means, being interpreted, "With us HE IS God."

²⁴And יוֹסֵף, Yosef, having awoken from sleep, did as the Messenger of ADONAI directed him, and took his wife, ²⁵and did not know her until she brought forth a son[b]—and he called His name יֵשׁוּעַ, Yeshua.

2 ¹And when יֵשׁוּעַ, Yeshua had been born in בֵּית־לֶחֶם, Beit-Lechem of יְהוּדָה, Y'hudah, in the days of Herod the king, look! mages[c] from the east came to יְרוּשָׁלַיִם, Y'rushalayim, ²saying, "Where is He who was born king of the יְהוּדִים, Y'hudiym? For we saw His star in the east, and we came to bow to him." ³And Herod the king, having heard *this*, was stirred, and all יְרוּשָׁלַיִם, Y'rushalayim with him. ⁴And having gathered all the chief כֹּהֲנִים, Ko'haniym and סוֹפְרִים, Sof'riym of the people, he was inquiring from them where the Messiah is *to be* born. ⁵And they said to him, "In בֵּית־לֶחֶם, Beit-Lechem of יְהוּדָה, Y'hudah, for it has been so written through the prophet,

⁶'And you, בֵּית־לֶחֶם, Beit-Lechem *in* the land of יְהוּדָה, Y'hudah: you are by no means the least among the leaders of יְהוּדָה, Y'hudah, for out of you will come One leading, who will feed My people יִשְׂרָאֵל, Yis'rael.'[d]

⁷Then Herod, having privately called the mages, inquired exactly from them the time of the appearing star. ⁸And sending them to בֵּית־לֶחֶם, Beit-Lechem, he said, "Having gone, search diligently for the child. And whenever you have found *him*, bring word back to me, *so* that, having come, I also may bow to him."

⁹And having heard the king, they went away, and look! the star that they saw in the east went in front of them until, having come, it stood *still* over where the child was. ¹⁰And having seen the star, they rejoiced with exceedingly great joy!

¹¹And having come to the house, they saw the child with מִרְיָם, Mir'yam His mother. And having fallen down *in worship*, they bowed to Him. And having opened their treasures, they presented gifts to Him: gold, and frankincense, and myrrh. ¹²And having been divinely warned in a dream not to return to Herod, *the mages* withdrew to their own region through another road.

¹³And upon their having withdrawn, look! a Messenger of ADONAI appeared in a dream to יוֹסֵף, Yosef, saying, "Having risen, take the child and His mother and flee to מִצְרַיִם, Mitz'rayim, and be there until I speak to you, for Herod is about to look for the child to destroy Him." ¹⁴And he, having risen, took the child and his mother by night and withdrew to מִצְרַיִם, Mitz'rayim, ¹⁵and he was there until the death of Herod, so that it might be fulfilled—that *which* was spoken by ADONAI through the prophet, saying,

"Out of מִצְרַיִם, Mitz'rayim I called my son."[e]

¹⁶Then Herod was enraged, having seen that he was deceived by the mages. And having sent *orders*, he put to death all the male children in בֵּית־לֶחֶם, Beit-Lechem

---

[a] יְשַׁעְיָהוּ *Y'sha'yahu* 7:14
[b] Some mss insert, "—her first-born"
[c] "mages"—μάγοι, magoi; that is, astrologers; trad. "wise men"; also in vss. 7 and 16
[d] מִיכָה *Miykhah* 5:2
[e] הוֹשֵׁעַ *Hoshea* 11:1

and in all its borders, from two years *old* and under, according to the time that he inquired exactly of the mages.

[17] Then was fulfilled that which was spoken through יִרְמְיָהוּ, Yir'm'yahu the prophet, saying,

[18] "A voice in רָמָה, Ramah was heard, weeping[a] and much mourning—רָחֵל, Rachel weeping FOR her children. And she would not be comforted because they are no *more*."[b]

[19] And when Herod had died, look! a Messenger of ADONAI appeared in a dream to יוֹסֵף, Yosef in מִצְרַיִם, Mitz'rayim, [20] saying, "Having risen, take the child and His mother and be going to the land of יִשְׂרָאֵל, Yis'rael, for those seeking the life of the child—they have died."

[21] And he, having risen, took the child and His mother and went into the land of יִשְׂרָאֵל, Yis'rael. [22] But having heard that Archelaus reigned in יְהוּדָה, Y'hudah instead of his father Herod, *Yosef* was afraid to go there. And having been divinely warned in a dream, he withdrew to the parts of the גָּלִיל, Galiyl; [23] and coming *there*, he lived in a city named נְצֶרֶת, N'tzaret, *so* that it might be fulfilled—that *which* was said through the prophets, that He will be called a נָצְרָתִי, Natz'ratiy.

3 [1] And in those days came יוֹחָנָן, Yochanan the Immerser, proclaiming in the desert of יְהוּדָה, Y'hudah, [2] saying, "Reform! for the Reign of the Heavens has come near!" [3] For this is he who was spoken of through יְשַׁעְיָהוּ, Y'sha'yahu the prophet, saying,

"A voice of one calling, 'In the desert, prepare the way of ADONAI! Make His paths straight!'"[c]

[4] (And this יוֹחָנָן, Yochanan had his clothing *made* of camel's hair, and a belt of leather around his waist, and his nourishment was locusts and honey of the field.) [5] Then *people* were going out to him *from* יְרוּשָׁלַיִם, Y'rushalayim and all יְהוּדָה, Y'hudah, and all the region around the יַרְדֵּן, Yar'den, [6] and they were immersed in the יַרְדֵּן, Yar'den River by him, confessing their sins.

[7] And having seen many of the פְּרוּשִׁים, P'rushiym and the צַדּוּקִים, Tzaduqiym coming for immersion, he said to them, "*You* brood of *venomous* snakes! Who showed you to flee from the coming wrath? [8] Therefore, make fruits worthy of the reformation! [9] And do not think to say to yourselves, 'We have a father: אַבְרָהָם, Av'raham.' For I say to you that God is able to raise *up* children to אַבְרָהָם, Av'raham out of these stones. [10] And now the axe is laid to the root of the trees; therefore, every tree *that is* not making good fruit is cut down and is thrown into *the* fire. [11] I indeed immerse you with water toward reformation. But He who is coming after me—of whom I am not worthy to carry the sandals—is mightier than I. He will immerse you with the רוּחַ הַקֹּדֶשׁ, Ruach HaQodesh and with fire—[12] *He* whose *winnowing* fan IS in His hand. And He will thoroughly cleanse His *threshing* floor and will gather His wheat into the storehouse, but He will burn the chaff with fire unquenchable!"

[13] Then יֵשׁוּעַ, Yeshua came from the גָּלִיל, Galiyl to the יַרְדֵּן, Yar'den to יוֹחָנָן, Yochanan, to be immersed by him, [14] but יוֹחָנָן, Yochanan was preventing Him, saying, "I need to be immersed by You—and You come to me?" [15] But יֵשׁוּעַ, Yeshua, answering, said to him, "Let it be so now, for it is appropriate for us to fulfill all righteousness this way." Then *Yochanan* let Him. [16] And having been immersed, יֵשׁוּעַ, Yeshua came up immediately from the water, and look! the heavens were opened,[d] and he saw the רוּחַ אֱלֹהִים, Ruach 'Elohiym descending as a dove coming upon Him. [17] And look! *there was* a voice out of the heavens, saying, "This is My Son—the Beloved, in whom I delighted."

---

[a] "weeping"—some mss say, "lamentation and weeping"
[b] יִרְמְיָהוּ *Yir'm'yahu* 31:15
[c] יְשַׁעְיָהוּ *Y'sha'yahu* 40:3
[d] Some mss insert, "to Him"

מַתִּתְיָהוּ Matit'yahu 4:1 — Messiah's temptation.

4 ¹Then יֵשׁוּעַ, Yeshua was led up to the desert by the רוּחַ, Ruach to be tempted by the Accuser. ²And having fasted forty days and nights, afterwards He hungered.

³And the Tempter, having come, said to Him, "If you are *the* Son of God, speak! that these stones may become loaves *of bread.*" ⁴But He, answering, said, "It has been written,

'Not upon bread alone does man live, but upon every word coming forth from the mouth of God.'"ᵃ

⁵Then the Accuser took Him to the HOLY city, and set Him on the pinnacle of the Temple, ⁶and said to Him, "If you are *the* Son of God, throw yourself down, for it has been written that,

'He will command His Messengers concerning you, and they will raise you up on *their* hands, *so that* you will not strike your foot on a stone.'"ᵇ

⁷יֵשׁוּעַ, Yeshua said to him again, "It has been written,

'You must not test ADONAI your God.'"ᶜ

⁸Again the Accuser took Him to a very high mountain, and showed to Him all the kingdoms of the world and the glory of them, ⁹and said to Him, "All these I will give to you, if—falling down—you will bow to me *in worship.*" ¹⁰Then יֵשׁוּעַ, Yeshua said to him, "Go *away*, הַשָּׂטָן, Ha-Satan! For it has been written,

'You will bow to ADONAI your God, and you will serve only Him.'"ᵈ

¹¹Then the Accuser left Him, and look! Messengers came and were attending to Him.

¹²And יֵשׁוּעַ, Yeshua, having heard that יוֹחָנָן, Yochanan was handed over *and put in prison*, withdrew to the גָּלִיל, Galiyl. ¹³And having left נְצֶרֶת, N'tzaret, having come, He lived at כְּפַר־נַחוּם, K'far-Nachum (that *which* is by the sea, in the borders of זְבֻלוּן, Z'vulun and נַפְתָּלִי, Naf'taliy) ¹⁴so that it might be fulfilled—that *which* was spoken through יְשַׁעְיָהוּ, Y'sha'yahu the prophet, saying,

¹⁵"Land of זְבֻלוּן, Z'vulun and land of נַפְתָּלִי, Naf'taliy, way of the sea, beyond the יַרְדֵּן, Yar'den, גָּלִיל, G'liyl of the גּוֹיִם, Goyim! ¹⁶The people that are sitting in darkness saw a great light. And to those sitting in a region and shadow of death—light arose to them."ᵉ

¹⁷From that time, יֵשׁוּעַ, Yeshua began to proclaim and to say, "Reform! for the Reign of the Heavens has come near!"

¹⁸And יֵשׁוּעַ, Yeshua, walking by the sea of the גָּלִיל, Galiyl, saw two brothers—שִׁמְעוֹן, Shim'on, called כֵּיפָא, Keifa,ᶠ and Andrew his brother—casting a net into the sea, for they were fishers; ¹⁹and He said to them, "Come *follow* after Me, and I will make you fishers of men." ²⁰And they immediately, having left the nets, followed Him.

²¹And having gone forward from that place, He saw two other brothers—יַעֲקֹב, Ya'aqov of זַבְדִּי, Zav'diy, and יוֹחָנָן, Yochanan his brother—in the boat with זַבְדִּי, Zav'diy their father, refitting their nets. And He called them, ²²and they immediately, having left the boat and their father, followed Him.

²³And יֵשׁוּעַ, Yeshua was going around in all the גָּלִיל, Galiyl teaching in their synagogues, and proclaiming the Good News of the Reign, and healing every disease and every debility among the people. ²⁴And news of Him went forth to all Syria, and they brought to Him all *those* having illnesses—*those* suffering with various diseases and pains, and *the* demon-possessed, and *the* moon-struck, and *the* paralytics—and He healed them. ²⁵And many crowds followed Him from the

---

ᵃ דְּבָרִים *D'variym* 8:3 (LXX)
ᵇ תְּהִלִּים *T'hiliym* 91:11-12
ᶜ דְּבָרִים *D'variym* 6:16
ᵈ דְּב׳ *D'v.* 6:13 says "fear," rather than "bow to"
ᵉ יְשַׁעְיָהוּ *Y'sha'yahu* 9:1-2
ᶠ כֵּיפָא, Keifa—Gk: Πέτρος, Petros; see יוֹחָנָן *Yn.* 1:42

Messiah's discourse on the mountain.

גָּלִיל, Galiyl, and Decapolis, and יְרוּשָׁלַיִם, Y'rushalayim, and יְהוּדָה, Y'hudah, and beyond the יַרְדֵּן, Yar'den.

5 ¹And having seen the crowds, He went up to the mountain; and when He sat down, His disciples came to Him.

²And having opened His mouth, He was teaching them, saying,

³ "Happy *are* the poor in רוּחַ, ruach—because theirs is the Reign of the Heavens.
⁴ Happy *are* those *who are* mourning—because they will be comforted.
⁵ Happy *are* THE HUMBLE—because they WILL INHERIT THE LAND.ᵃ
⁶ Happy *are* those *who are* hungering and thirsting for righteousness—because they will be filled.
⁷ Happy *are* the *ones showing loving-*kindness—because they will be shown *loving-*kindness.
⁸ Happy *are* the clean in heart—because they will see God.
⁹ Happy *are* the peace-makers—because they will be called sons of God.
¹⁰ Happy *are* those persecuted for righteousness' sake—because theirs is the Reign of the Heavens.
¹¹ Happy are you whenever *people* denounce you and persecute *you* and say every *kind of* evil against you falsely for My sake. ¹²Rejoice and be extremely joyful, for your reward IS great in the Heavens—for *it was* in this way *that* they persecuted the prophets who were before you.

¹³"You are the salt of the land, but if the salt loses savor, in what way will it be salted *again*? It is now good for nothing, except being thrown out to be trampled underfoot by men. ¹⁴You are the light of the world—a city set upon a mountain is not able to be hidden; ¹⁵nor do *people* light a lamp and put it under the measuring basket, but on the lampstand, and it shines to all those in the house. ¹⁶In this way, let your light shine in front of men, *so that* they may see your good actions and may glorify your Father who IS in the Heavens.

¹⁷"Do not suppose that I came to throw down the תּוֹרָה, Torah or the Prophets—I did not come to throw down, but to fulfill. ¹⁸אָמֵן, Amen, for I say to you: until *the time* that the heaven and the earth pass away, not one יʹᵇ or one stroke will pass away from the תּוֹרָה, Torah—until *the time* that all comes to pass. ¹⁹Whoever, therefore, unbinds one of these commands—the least *of them*—and teaches men *to do* so, he will be called least in the Reign of the Heavens. But whoever will do and will teach THEM, he will be called great in the Reign of the Heavens. ²⁰For I say to you that if your righteousness does not abound above that of the סוֹפְרִים, Sof'riym and פְּרוּשִׁים, P'rushiym, you will not enter into the Reign of the Heavens.

²¹"You heard that it was said to the ancients, 'YOU MUST NOT MURDER,'ᶜ and whoever murders will be in danger of the judgment. ²²But I—I say to you that everyone who is angry at his brotherᵈ will be in danger of the judgment. And whoever says to his brother, 'Empty fellow!' will be in danger of the Sanhedrin. And whoever says, 'Rebel!' will be in danger of the גֵּיהִנֹּם, Geihinom of the fire. ²³If, therefore, you bring your gift to the altar, and there remember your brother has something against you, ²⁴leave your gift there before the altar, and go—first be reconciled to your brother, and then, having come, bring your gift. ²⁵Be agreeing with your opponent quickly, while you are with him on the road, *so that* the opponent may not hand you over to the judge, and the judge to the officer, and you be thrown into prison. ²⁶אָמֵן, Amen, I say to you: you will not come forth from that

---
ᵃ תְּהִלִּים, T'hiliym 37:11
ᵇ the יוּד, yud (ʹ) is the smallest Hebrew letter
ᶜ שְׁמוֹת Sh'mot 20:13; דְּבָרִים D'variym 5:17
ᵈ Some mss insert, "without cause"

place until *the time* that you pay the last coin. ²⁷"You heard that it was said,ᵃ 'YOU MUST NOT COMMIT ADULTERY.'ᵇ ²⁸But I—I say to you that everyone who is looking on a woman to covet herᶜ has already committed adultery with her in his heart. ²⁹So if your right eye causes you to stumble, pluck it out and throw *it away* from you, for it is good for you that one of your body parts be destroyed and not your whole body be thrown into גֵּיהִנֹּם, Geihinom. ³⁰And if your right hand causes you to stumble, cut it off and throw *it away* from you, for it is good for you that one of your body parts be destroyed and not your whole body go into גֵּיהִנֹּם, Geihinom.

³¹"And it was said, 'Whoever sends away his wife, let him give to her a DOCUMENT OF DIVORCE.'ᵈ' ³²But I—I say to you that everyone who sends away his wife, except for the matter of sexual unfaithfulness,ᵉ makes her commit adultery; and whoever marries her who has been sent away *also* commits adultery.

³³"Again, you heard that it was said to the ancients, 'YOU MUST NOT SWEAR FALSELY,' but 'YOU WILL PAY YOUR OATHS TO ADONAI.'ᶠ ³⁴But I—I say to you not to swear at all; neither by the heaven (because it is the throne of God), ³⁵nor by the earth (because it is His footstool), nor by יְרוּשָׁלַיִם, Y'rushalayim (because it is a CITY OF THE GREAT KINGᵍ). ³⁶Nor may you swear by your head, because you are not able to make one hair white or black. ³⁷But let your word be, 'Yes, yes,' *or* 'No, no,' and *anything* which is more than these is of the evil.

³⁸"You heard that it was said, 'EYE FOR EYE, AND TOOTH FOR TOOTH,'ʰ ³⁹But I—I say to you not to resist the evil, but whoever slaps you on the right cheek, turn to him the other also. ⁴⁰And whoever is wanting to take you to trial and to take your shirt, let him also *take your* coat. ⁴¹And whoever forces you *to go* one mile, go with him two. ⁴²Be giving to him who asks *something* of you, and do not turn him away who is wanting to borrow from you.

⁴³"You heard that it was said, 'YOU MUST LOVE YOUR NEIGHBORⁱ and hate your enemy.' ⁴⁴But I—I say to you: love your enemies,ʲ and pray for thoseᵏ persecuting you, ⁴⁵*so* that you may be sons of your Father in the Heavens, for He causes His sun to rise on evil and good *alike*, and He sends rain on *both the* righteous and *the* unrighteous. ⁴⁶For, if you love *only* those loving you, what reward do you have? Do not the tax-gatherers also do the same? ⁴⁷And if you greet only your brothers, what more are you doing *than others*? Do not also the גּוֹיִם, Goyimˡ do the same? ⁴⁸You therefore are to be perfect, as your heavenly Father is perfect.

6 ¹"Be careful not to do your righteousnessᵐ in front of men, to be seen by them; otherwise, you *will* not have a reward from your Father, who *is* in the Heavens. ²Whenever you do charity, then, you should not sound a שׁוֹפָר, shofar before yourself as the hypocrites do in the synagogues and in the streets, *so* that they may have glory from men. אָמֵן, Amen, I say to you—they have their reward! ³But you, doing charity, let not your left hand know what your right hand does, ⁴*so* that your charity may be in se-

---

ᵃ Some mss insert, "to the ancients"
ᵇ שְׁמוֹת *Sh'mot* 20:13(14); דְּבָרִים *D'variym* 5:17(18)
ᶜ "to covet her" or "to desire her" or "to lust after her"
ᵈ דְּבָרִים *D'variym* 24:1
ᵉ "sexual unfaithfulness"—πορνεία, porneia
ᶠ וַיִּקְרָא *Vayiq'ra* 19:12; בְּמִדְבַּר *B'mid'bar* 30:2; דְּבָרִים *D'variym* 23:21&23
ᵍ תְּהִלִּים *T'hiliym* 48:3(2)

ʰ שְׁמוֹת *Sh'mot* 21:24; וַיִּקְרָא *Vayiq'ra* 24:20; דְּבָרִים *D'variym* 19:21
ⁱ וַיִּקְרָא *Vayiq'ra* 19:18
ʲ Some mss insert, "bless those cursing you, do good to those hating you"; cf. Luke 6:27-28
ᵏ Some mss insert, "accusing you falsely and"
ˡ "גּוֹיִם, Goyim"—some mss say, "tax-gatherers"
ᵐ "righteousness"—some mss say, "charity"

Prayer and fasting. מַתִּתְיָהוּ **Matit'yahu 6:30**

cret; and your Father, who is seeing in secret, will reward you.[a]

⁵"And when you pray, you must not be as the hypocrites, because they love to pray in the synagogues and standing on the street corners *so* that they may be seen by men. אָמֵן, Amen, I say to you, they have their reward. ⁶But you, when you pray, go into your *private* room and, having shut the door, pray to your Father who IS in secret. And your Father, who is seeing in secret, will reward you. ⁷And *when you are* praying, you should not use empty repetitions like the גּוֹיִם, Goyim, for they think that in their much-speaking they will be heard. ⁸Therefore, do not be like them—for your Father knows those things that you have need of before your asking Him. ⁹Therefore, pray this way:

'Our Father who IS in the Heavens! Set apart is Your Name.
¹⁰ Your Reign come: Your will come into being, as *it is* in Heaven, also on earth.
¹¹ Our apportioned bread, give us today.
¹² And forgive us our debts *of wrongdoing*, as we also have forgiven[b] those owing a debt to us[c] *because of wrongdoing.*
¹³ And may You not lead us to testing *through temptation*, but deliver us from the evil.'[d]

¹⁴For if you forgive men their missteps, He also will forgive you—your Father who IS in the Heavens. ¹⁵But if you do not forgive men their missteps, neither will your Father forgive your missteps.

¹⁶"And when you fast, be not as the hypocrites with gloomy expressions, for they disfigure their faces *so* that they may show to men *they are* fasting. אָמֵן, Amen, I say to you, they have their reward. ¹⁷But you—*when you are* fasting—anoint your head and wash your face, ¹⁸*so* that you will not show to men *you are* fasting, but to your Father who IS in secret. And your Father, who is seeing in secret, will reward you.

¹⁹"Store not up to yourselves treasures *here* on the earth—where moth and rust disfigure, and where thieves break through and steal—²⁰but store up to yourselves treasures in Heaven, where neither moth nor rust disfigure, and where thieves do not break through, nor steal. ²¹For where your treasure is, there your heart will be also. ²²The lamp of the body is the eye. If, therefore, your eye is perfect,[e] your whole body will be full of light. ²³But if your eye is evil,[f] your whole body will be dark. If, therefore, the light that IS in you is darkness—the darkness, how great *it is!* ²⁴No one is able to serve two masters, for either he will hate the one and love the other, or he will hold to the one and despise the other. You are not able to serve *both* God and wealth.[g]

²⁵"Because of this, I say to you: be not anxious for your life (what you will eat, or what you will drink) nor for your body (what you will wear). Is not the life more than the nourishment, and the body *more* than the clothing? ²⁶Look to the birds of the heaven, for they do not sow, nor reap, nor gather into storehouses, yet your heavenly Father nourishes them. Are you not much more valuable than they *are?* ²⁷And who of you, being anxious, is able to add one hour[h] to his age? ²⁸And why are you anxious about clothing? Consider well the lilies of the field: how do they grow? They do not labor, nor do they spin *thread*. ²⁹Yet I say to you that not even שְׁלֹמֹה, Sh'lomoh in all his glory was wrapped around as one of these. ³⁰And if God so clothes the grass of the field—which is *here* today and tomorrow is thrown into the furnace—*will He*

---

[a] Some mss conclude, "openly"; also in vss 6 and 18
[b] "have forgiven"—some mss say, "forgive"
[c] "those owing a debt to us" or "our debtors"
[d] Some late mss continue, "Because Yours is the Reign, and the power, and the glory—to the ages. אָמֵן, Amen."
[e] that is, if you are generous
[f] that is, if you are selfish
[g] "wealth"—lit. "μαμωνᾶ, mamona"; mammon
[h] "hour"—lit. "πῆχυν, pechun"; a unit of measurement, sp. cubit

9

not *clothe* you much more, O you of little faith? ³¹Therefore, you should not be anxious, saying, 'What will we eat?' or 'What will we drink?' or 'What will we wear?' ³²for the גּוֹיִם, Goyim seek all these *things*—indeed, your heavenly Father knows that you have need of all these *things*. ³³But seek first the Reign and His righteousness, and all these *things* will be added to you. ³⁴Therefore, be not anxious for tomorrow, for tomorrow will be anxious for itself. The wickedness of the day IS enough for it.

7

¹"Judge not, so that you may not be judged, ²for in what*ever* judgment you judge, you will be judged, and with what*ever* measure you measure, it will be measured to you. ³And why do you look at the speck *of sawdust* that IS in your brother's eye, yet the log that IS in your own eye, *you* do not *even* consider? ⁴Or how will you say to your brother, 'Let me remove[a] the speck from your eye,' and look! the log IS in your own eye? ⁵Hypocrite! First remove the log out of your own eye, and then you will see clearly to remove the speck out of your brother's eye.

⁶"Do not give that which is HOLY to the dogs, nor throw your pearls in front of the pigs, *so* that they will not trample them among their feet, and—having turned—may tear you *to pieces*.

⁷"Ask, and it will be given to you; seek, and you will find; knock, and it will be opened to you; ⁸for everyone who is asking receives, and he who is seeking finds, and to him who is knocking it will be opened. ⁹Or what man is among you, of whom his son asks *for* a loaf *of bread, who* will give to him a stone? ¹⁰Or *if* he also asks *for* a fish, will give to him a serpent? ¹¹If, therefore, you—being evil—have known *how* to give good gifts to your children, how much more will your Father, who IS in the Heavens, give good things to those asking Him? ¹²All things, therefore, whatever you want that men may be doing to you, so also do to them, for this is the תּוֹרָה, Torah and the Prophets.

¹³"Go in through the narrow gate, because wide IS the gate and broad the road that is leading to the destruction, and many are those going in through it. ¹⁴How narrow IS the gate and tight the road that is leading to the Life, and few are those finding it!

¹⁵"Be careful of the false prophets who come to you in sheep's clothing, but inwardly are ravenous wolves; ¹⁶from their fruits you will know them. Do MEN gather grapes from thorns? Or figs from thistles? ¹⁷So every good tree yields good fruits, but the bad tree yields evil fruits. ¹⁸A good tree is not able to yield evil fruits, nor a bad tree to yield good fruits. ¹⁹Every tree not yielding good fruit is cut down and is thrown into fire. ²⁰Therefore, from their fruits you will know them. ²¹Not everyone who is saying to Me, 'Master, Master!' will come into the Reign of the Heavens; but he who is doing the will of my Father, who is in the Heavens. ²²Many will say to Me in that day, 'Master, Master! Have we not prophesied in Your Name? and in Your Name cast out demons? and in Your Name done many powerful things?' ²³And then I will acknowledge to them that—'I never knew you. GO AWAY FROM ME, YOU WHO ARE DOING MISDEEDS.'[b] ²⁴Therefore, everyone who hears these words of Mine and does them, I will liken to a wise man who built his house upon the rock; ²⁵and the rain descended, and the streams came, and the winds blew, and they beat on that house, but it fell not, for it had been founded on the rock. ²⁶But everyone who is hearing these words of Mine and is not doing them will be likened to a foolish man who built his house upon the sand; ²⁷and the rain descended, and the streams came, and the winds blew, and they beat on the house, and it fell, and its fall was massive."

²⁸And it came to pass, when יֵשׁוּעַ, Yeshua finished these words, the crowds were astonished at His teaching, ²⁹for He was

---

[a] "remove"—lit. "cast out"; also in verse 5

[b] תְּהִלִּים T'hiliym 6:9(8)

Rebuking the winds. מַתִּתְיָהוּ Matit'yahu 8:29

teaching them as *one* having authority, and not as *the authority of* their סוֹפְרִים, Sof'riym.

8 ¹And when He came down from the mountain, large crowds followed Him, ²and look! a leper, having come, was bowing to Him *and* saying, "Sir, if you are willing, you are able to cleanse me." ³And having stretched out the hand, יֵשׁוּעַ, Yeshua touched him, saying, "I *do* will *it*—be cleansed"; and immediately, his leprosy was cleansed. ⁴And יֵשׁוּעַ, Yeshua said to him, "See *that* you tell no one. But go, show yourself to the כֹּהֵן, kohen, and bring the *sacrificial* gift that מֹשֶׁה, Mosheh commanded as a testimony to them."

⁵And when He had entered כְּפַר־נַחוּם, K'far-Nachum, there came to Him a centurion, pleading with Him ⁶and saying, "Sir, my servant-boy has been laid in the house—a paralytic—terribly afflicted." ⁷And He said to him, "I, having come, will heal him." ⁸But the centurion, answering, said, "Sir, I am not worthy that you may enter under my roof. But only say a word, and my servant-boy will be healed; ⁹for I also am a man under authority, having soldiers under myself. And I say to this one, 'Go,' and he goes; and to another, 'Be coming,' and he comes; and to my slave, 'Do this,' and he does *IT*."

¹⁰And יֵשׁוּעַ, Yeshua, having heard, marveled and said to those following Him, "אָמֵן, Amen, I say to you, with no one in יִשְׂרָאֵל, Yis'rael have I found such great faith. ¹¹And I say to you that many from east and west will come and recline (at mealtime) with אַבְרָהָם, Av'raham and יִצְחָק, Yitz'chaq and יַעֲקֹב, Ya'aqov in the Reign of the Heavens, ¹²but the sons of the Reign will be thrown out to the outer darkness, *where* there will be the weeping and the gnashing of the teeth." ¹³And יֵשׁוּעַ, Yeshua said to the centurion, "Go! As you believed, let it be to you," and the servant-boy was healed in that moment.

¹⁴And יֵשׁוּעַ, Yeshua, having come into the house of כֵּיפָא, Keifa,[a] saw his mother-in-law laid *down* and fevered, ¹⁵and He touched her hand, and the fever left her, and she arose and was attending to them.

¹⁶And *when* evening had come, they brought to Him many *who were* demon-possessed, and He cast out the רוּחוֹת, ruchot with a word, and healed all who were ill, *so* that it would be fulfilled—¹⁷that *which* was spoken through יְשַׁעְיָהוּ, Y'sha'yahu the prophet, saying, "HE HIMSELF TOOK OUR *SICKLY* WEAKNESSES, AND HE CARRIED THE diseases."[b]

¹⁸And having seen a crowd around Him, יֵשׁוּעַ, Yeshua gave command to go to the other side *of the sea*. ¹⁹And a certain סוֹפֵר, Sofer, having come, said to Him, "Teacher, I will follow You wherever You go." ²⁰And יֵשׁוּעַ, Yeshua said to him, "The foxes have holes, and the birds of the heaven *have* places to nest. But the Son of Man has nowhere He can lay the head."

²¹And another *one* of the disciples said to Him, "Master, first permit me to go and bury my father." ²²And יֵשׁוּעַ, Yeshua said to him, "Follow Me, and allow the dead to bury their own dead."

²³And when He entered into the boat, His disciples followed Him, ²⁴and look! a huge storm arose in the sea, so that the boat was being covered by the waves; but He was sleeping. ²⁵And having come to Him, they awoke Him, saying, "Master, save us! We are being destroyed!" ²⁶And He said to them, "Why are you fearful, O you of little faith?" Then, having arisen, He rebuked the winds and the sea, and there was a great calm. ²⁷And the men marveled, saying, "What kind *of thing* is this, that even the wind and the sea obey Him?"

²⁸And when He had come to the other side, to the region of the גַּדְרִיִּים, Gad'riyiym, two demon-possessed *men* met Him, coming forth out of the tombs—very fierce, so that no one was able to pass over by that way. ²⁹And look! they shouted, saying, "What do You *want* with us,[c] Son of God?

---

[a] כֵּיפָא, Keifa—Gk: Πέτρος, Petros; see יוֹחָנָן *Yn.* 1:42

[b] יְשַׁעְיָהוּ *Y'sha'yahu* 53:4
[c] "What do you *want* with us"—lit., "what to us and to you"; some mss also insert, "יֵשׁוּעַ, Yeshua"

Did you come here, before the *appointed* time, to torment us?" ³⁰And far off from them, there was a herd of many pigs *that were* feeding; ³¹and the demons were pleading with Him, saying, "If you cast us out, send usᵃ into the herd of the pigs."

³²And He said to them, "Go." And having come out, they went into the pigs, and look! the whole herd rushed down the steep *bank* to the sea and died in the waters. ³³And those feeding *the pigs* fled; and, having gone to the city, they declared all *they had seen*, and the *entire* matter of the demon-possessed *men*. ³⁴And look! the whole city came out to meet יֵשׁוּעַ, Yeshua, and having seen Him, they pleaded with *Him* that He might leave their borders.

9 ¹And having gone to the boat, He crossed over *the sea* and came to His own city. ²And look! they were bringing to Him a paralytic laid upon a cot; and יֵשׁוּעַ, Yeshua, having seen their faith, said to the paralytic, "Courage, child! Your sins are forgiven." ³And look! certain *ones* of the סוֹפְרִים, Sof'riym said within themselves, "This one speaks evil." ⁴And יֵשׁוּעַ, Yeshua, having known their thoughts, said, "Why do you think evil in your hearts? ⁵For which is easier: to say, 'Your sins are forgiven,' or to say, 'Rise *up*, and walk'? ⁶But so that you may know that the Son of Man has power upon the earth to forgive sins…" (then He said to the paralytic) "Rise, take up your cot, and go to your house." ⁷And he, having risen, went to his house. ⁸And the crowds, having seen, fearedᵇ and glorified God, who gave such power to men.

⁹And passing by there, יֵשׁוּעַ, Yeshua saw a man named מַתִּתְיָהוּ, Matit'yahu sitting at the tax-office, and said to him, "Be following Me." And he, having arisen, followed Him. ¹⁰And it came to pass, *as* He *was* reclining (at mealtime) in the house, that look! many tax-gatherers and sinners, having come, were reclining (at mealtime) with יֵשׁוּעַ, Yeshua and His disciples. ¹¹And the פְּרוּשִׁים, P'rushiym, having seen, said to His disciples, "Why does your teacher eat with the tax-gatherers and sinners?" ¹²And having heard, He said, "They who are whole have no need of a physician; rather, they who are ill. ¹³Now, having gone, learn what *this* is: 'I WANT LOVING-KINDNESS, AND NOT SACRIFICE.'ᶜ For I did not come to call righteous men, but sinners."ᵈ

¹⁴Then the disciples of יוֹחָנָן, Yochanan came to Him, saying, "Why do we and the פְּרוּשִׁים, P'rushiym fast much, and Your disciples fast not?" ¹⁵And יֵשׁוּעַ, Yeshua said to them, "Can the wedding guestsᵉ mourn as long as the bridegroom is with them? But days will come when the bridegroom will be taken from them, and then they will fast.

¹⁶"And no one puts a patch of *new*, unshrunk cloth on an old garment, for its fullnessᶠ pulls away from the garment, and a worse split is made. ¹⁷Nor do they put fresh wine into old skins; otherwise, the skins burst, and the wine pours out, and the skins are destroyed. Rather, they put fresh wine into new skins, and both are preserved together."

¹⁸While He was speaking these things to them, look! a ruler, having come, was bowing to Him, saying that, "My daughter just now died. But, having come, lay Your hand upon her, and she will live." ¹⁹And יֵשׁוּעַ, Yeshua, having arisen, followed Him—His disciples *followed* also —²⁰and look! a woman having a continuous flow of blood *for* twelve years, having come to Him *from* behind, touched the כָּנָף, kanafᵍ of His *outer* garments, ²¹for she said within herself, "If only I can touch His *outer* garment, I will be saved *from my affliction*." ²²And יֵשׁוּעַ, Yeshua, having

---

ᵃ "send us"—some mss say, "allow us to go away"
ᵇ "feared"—some mss say, "marveled"

ᶜ הוֹשֵׁעַ *Hoshea* 6:6
ᵈ Some mss insert, "to reformation"
ᵉ "wedding guests," lit. "sons of the bride-chamber"
ᶠ "fullness"—Young's says, "filling up"
ᵍ כָּנָף, kanaf—the Greek here is κρασπέδου, kraspedou, variations of which translate צִיצִת, tziytzit in בְּמִדְבַּר *B'mid'bar* 15:38-39, גְּדִלִים, g'diliym in דְּבָרִים *D'variym* 22:12, and כָּנָף, kanaf in זְכַרְיָה *Z'khar'yah* 8:23 in the LXX. The כָּנָף, kanaf is the area of the garment where one is to make the צִיצִת, tziytzit and גְּדִלִים, g'diliym.

10 ¹And having called His twelve disciples to Himself, He gave to them power over unclean רוּחוֹת, ruchot, so as to be casting them out, and to be healing every sickness and every debility. ²And of the twelve emissaries,[b] the names are these: first, שִׁמְעוֹן, Shim'on, who is called כֵּיפָא, Keifa,[c] and Andrew his brother; and יַעֲקֹב, Ya'aqov of זַבְדִּי, Zav'diy, and יוֹחָנָן, Yochanan his brother; ³Philip and בַּר-תַּלְמַי, Bar-Tal'mai; תּוֹמָא, Toma and מַתִּתְיָהוּ, Matit'yahu the tax-gatherer; יַעֲקֹב, Ya'aqov of חַלְפַי, Chal'fai, and[d] תַּדָּי, Tadai; ⁴שִׁמְעוֹן הַקַּנִּי, Shim'on HaQanai, and יְהוּדָה אִישׁ-קְרִיּוֹת, Y'hudah Iysh-Q'riyot, who also *betrayed and* handed Him over.

⁵These twelve יֵשׁוּעַ, Yeshua sent out, having given command to them, saying, "Do not go away to the road of the גּוֹיִם, Goyim, and do not go into a city of the שֹׁמְרֹנִים, Shom'roniym, ⁶but rather be going to the lost[e] sheep of the house of יִשְׂרָאֵל, Yis'rael. ⁷And going on, proclaim, saying that 'the Reign of the Heavens has come near!' ⁸*The* infirmed ones—be healing *them; the* dead—be raising *them; the* lepers—be cleansing *them; the* demons—be casting *them* out. Freely you received—freely give. ⁹Do not obtain gold, nor silver, nor brass in your *money* belts, ¹⁰nor *traveler's* bag for the road, nor two shirts, nor sandals, nor staff; for the workman is worthy of his nourishment.

¹¹"And into whatever city or village you enter, search *out* who in it is worthy, and remain there until you leave. ¹²And coming to the house, greet it; ¹³and if indeed the house is worthy, let your *blessing of* peace come upon it. But if it is not worthy, let your *blessing of* peace return to you. ¹⁴And whoever does not receive you nor hear your words: *as you are* coming out from that house or city, shake off the dust of your feet. ¹⁵אָמֵן, Amen, I say to you, it will be more tolerable for the land of סְדֹם,

---

Mission of the Twelve.

turned around and having seen her, said, "Courage, daughter! Your faith has saved you," and the woman was saved from that moment. ²³And יֵשׁוּעַ, Yeshua, having come to the house of the ruler and seen the flute-players and the crowds making a commotion, ²⁴said, "Go away, for the girl did not die, but *rather* sleeps"—and they were laughing at Him. ²⁵But when the crowd was sent away, having gone in, He took hold of her hand, and the girl arose, ²⁶and the news of this went forth to all the land.

²⁷And *while* יֵשׁוּעַ, Yeshua *was* passing on from there, two blind men followed Him, shouting and saying, "Deal kindly with us, Son of דָּוִד, David!" ²⁸And *when* He had come to the house, the blind men came to Him. And יֵשׁוּעַ, Yeshua said to them, "Do you believe that I am able to do this?" They said to Him, "Yes, sir." ²⁹Then He touched their eyes, saying, "According to your faith, let it be to you," ³⁰and their eyes were opened. And יֵשׁוּעַ, Yeshua sternly warned them, saying, "See *that you* let no one know." ³¹But having gone out, they spread news *of* Him in all that land.

³²And as they were leaving, look! they brought to Him a man *who was* mute *and* demon-possessed. ³³And *with* the demon having been cast out, the mute *man* spoke, and the crowd marveled, saying, "*Such a thing*—it was never so seen in יִשְׂרָאֵל, Yis'rael!" ³⁴But the פְּרוּשִׁים, P'rushiym said, "By the ruler of the demons he casts out the demons."

³⁵And going up and down *through* all the cities and villages, יֵשׁוּעַ, Yeshua was teaching in their synagogues, and proclaiming the Good News of the Reign, and healing every sickness and every debility. ³⁶And having seen the crowds, He was *deeply* moved with compassion for them—that they were harassed[a] and cast aside, as sheep not having a shepherd. ³⁷Then He said to His disciples, "The harvest indeed IS abundant, but the workmen *are* few. ³⁸Therefore, implore the Master of the Harvest, that He may send out workmen to His harvest."

---

[a] "harassed"—some mss say, "faint-*hearted*"
[b] "emissaries"—שְׁלִיחִים, sh'liychiym
[c] כֵּיפָא, Keifa—Gk: Πέτρος, Petros; see יוֹחָנָן *Yn*. 1:42
[d] Some mss insert, "לָבֵּי, Labai, who was also named"
[e] lose/lost—ἀπόλλυμι, apollumi, meaning "to kill or destroy"

מַתִּתְיָהוּ **Matit'yahu 10:16** — *Encouragement in persecution.*

S'dom and עֲמֹרָה, 'Amorah in the Day of judgment than for that city.

¹⁶"Look! I send you out as sheep in the middle of wolves. Therefore, be wise as the serpents, and simple as the doves. ¹⁷And be careful of men, for they will give you up to Sanhedrins, and in their synagogues they will flog you, ¹⁸and you will be brought before governors and kings for My sake, for a testimony to them and to the גּוֹיִם, Goyim. ¹⁹And whenever they hand you over, be not anxious *about* how or what you will say, for it will be given you in that moment what you will say; ²⁰for you are not the speakers, but *it is the* רוּחַ, Ruach of your Father that is speaking in you.

²¹"And brother will hand over brother—to death; and father, child; and children will rise up against parents and will put them to death; ²²and you will be hated by all because of My Name. But he who has endured to the end—he will be saved. ²³And whenever they persecute you in this city, flee to another, for, אָמֵן, amen, I say to you: you will not have completed *going to all* the cities of יִשְׂרָאֵל, Yis'rael until the Son of Man comes.

²⁴"A disciple is not above the teacher, nor a slave above his master; ²⁵*it is* sufficient for the disciple that he may be as his teacher, and the slave as his master. If they call the house-master בַּעַל־זְבוּב, Ba'al–Z'vuv, how much more *will they call* those of his household? ²⁶Therefore, you should not fear them, for there is nothing covered that will not be revealed, and *nothing* hidden that will not be known. ²⁷That which I tell you in the darkness, speak in the light; and that which you hear *whispered* at the ear, proclaim on the house-tops!

²⁸"And do not be afraid of those *who are* killing the body, yet are not able to kill the soul, but rather fear Him who is able to destroy both soul and body in גֵּיהִנֹּם, Geihinom. ²⁹Are not two sparrows sold for a coin? Yet one of them will not fall on the ground without your Father's *will*. ³⁰And of you—even the hairs of the head are all numbered. ³¹Therefore, be not afraid—you are more *valuable* than many sparrows!

³²"So then, everyone who professes Me in front of men, I also will profess him in front of My Father who is in the Heavens; ³³and whoever denies Me in front of men, I also will deny him in front of My Father who is in the Heavens. ³⁴You should not suppose that I came to put peace on the earth—I did not come to put peace, but a sword. ³⁵For I came to divide a man against his father, and a daughter against her mother, and a daughter-in-law against her mother-in-law—³⁶and THE ENEMIES OF A MAN ARE THOSE OF HIS HOUSEHOLD.ᵃ ³⁷He who is loving *his* father or mother above Me is not worthy of Me, and he who is loving *his* son or daughter above Me is not worthy of Me, ³⁸and whoever does not take his *execution* stake and follow after Me is not worthy of Me. ³⁹He who *has* found his life will loseᵇ it, and he who *has* lost his life for My sake will find it. ⁴⁰He who is receiving you receives Me, and he who is receiving Me receives Him who sent Me. ⁴¹He who is receiving a prophet in the name of a prophet will receive a prophet's reward, and he who is receiving a righteous man in the name of a righteous man will receive a righteous man's reward, ⁴²and whoever in the name of a disciple gives one of these little ones only a cup of cold water to drink—אָמֵן, amen, I say to you, he cannot lose his reward.

11 ¹And it came to pass, when יֵשׁוּעַ, Yeshua ended instructing His twelve disciples, He left from that place to teach and to proclaim in their cities. ²And יוֹחָנָן, Yochanan—*while* in the prison, having heard *about* the acts of the Messiah, having sent *word* by his disciples—³said to Him, "Are you He who is coming, or should we look for another?"

ᵃ מִיכָה *Miykhah* 7:6
ᵇ lose/lost—ἀπόλλυμι, apollumi, meaning "to kill or destroy"

Messiah's testimony of Yochanan. מַתִּתְיָהוּ **Matit'yahu 11:30**

⁴And יֵשׁוּעַ, Yeshua, answering, said to them, "Having gone, declare to יוֹחָנָן, Yochanan *all* the things that you hear and see: ⁵BLIND RECEIVE SIGHT,ᵃ and lame walk; lepers are cleansed, and deaf hear, and dead are raised, and *the* POOR HAVE GOOD NEWS PROCLAIMED.ᵇ ⁶And happy is he who is not stumbled in Me."

⁷And as they were going, יֵשׁוּעַ, Yeshua began to speak to the crowds regarding יוֹחָנָן, Yochanan, "What did you go out to the desert to look upon?—a reed shaken by the wind? ⁸*If not*, then what did you go out to see?—a man clothed in soft garments? Look! those wearing the soft things are in the kings' houses. ⁹Then what did you go out to see?—a prophet? Yes, I say to you—and more than a prophet. ¹⁰This is he of whom it has been written,

> 'Look! I send My messenger before your face who will prepare Your way before You.'ᶜ

¹¹אָמֵן, Amen, I say to you: among those born of women, there has not risen a greater *one* than יוֹחָנָן, Yochanan the Immerser, *and* yet he who is least in the Reign of the Heavens is greater than he! ¹²And, from the days of יוֹחָנָן, Yochanan the Immerser until now, the Reign of the Heavens comes violentlyᵈ—and violent men take it by force—¹³for all the Prophets and the תּוֹרָה, Torah prophesied until יוֹחָנָן, Yochanan. ¹⁴But if you are willing to receive *IT*, he is אֵלִיָּהוּ, Eliyahu who was about to come! ¹⁵He who is having earsᵉ—let him hear.

¹⁶"And to what will I liken this generation? It is like little children sitting in the market-places, who are calling to the others, ¹⁷and saying, 'We piped *the flute* to you, and *yet* you did not dance; we sang a dirge, and *yet* you did not beat your chest.' ¹⁸For יוֹחָנָן, Yochanan came neither eating bread nor drinking wine, and they say, 'He has a demon!' ¹⁹Yet the Son of Man came *both* eating *bread* and drinking *wine*, and they say, 'Look! A man *who is* a glutton and a wine-drinker, a friend of tax-gatherers and sinners!' But wisdom is justified by her actions."ᶠ

²⁰Then He began to denounce *all* the cities in which most of His powerful acts were done, because they did not reform. ²¹"אוֹי, Oy! to you, Chorazin! אוֹי, Oy! to you, בֵּית-צַיְדָה, Beit-Tzai'dah! Because if the powerful acts that were done in you had been done in צוֹר, Tzor and צִידוֹן, Tziydon, they *would* have reformed long ago in sackcloth and ashes! ²²But I say to you: it will be more tolerable to צוֹר, Tzor and צִידוֹן, Tziydon in the Day of Judgment than for you!

²³"And you, כְּפַר-נַחוּם, K'far-Nachum, will you not beᵍ exalted to the Heaven? *No— you* will be brought down to שְׁאוֹל, Sh'ol! Because if the powerful acts had been done in סְדֹם, S'dom that were done in you, it *would* have remained to this day. ²⁴But I say to you: it will be more tolerable to the land of סְדֹם, S'dom in the Day of Judgment than to you!"

²⁵At that time יֵשׁוּעַ, Yeshua, answering, said, "I confess to You, Father—Master of the heavens and of the earth—that You hid these things from wise and understanding ones, and *You* revealed them to little children. ²⁶Yes, Father—because this way, it was good pleasure in front of You.

²⁷"All things were handed over to Me by My Father. And no one knows the Son except the Father, nor does anyone know the Father except the Son and he to whom the Son intends to reveal *HIM*. ²⁸Come to Me, all you laboring and burdened ones, and I will give you rest. ²⁹Take up My yoke upon you and learn from Me, because I am humble and lowly in heart; and you will find rest to your souls, ³⁰for my yoke *is* easy, and my load is light."

ᵃ יְשַׁעְיָהוּ *Y'sha'yahu* 35:5
ᵇ יְשַׁעְיָהוּ *Y'sha'yahu* 61:1
ᶜ מַלְאָכִי *Mal'akhiy* 3:1
ᵈ "comes violently" or "suffers violence"
ᵉ Some mss insert, "to hear"

ᶠ "actions"—some mss say, "children"
ᵍ "will you not be"—some mss say, "which was"

מַתִּתְיָהוּ Matit'yahu 12:1 — P'rushiym refuted.

12 ¹At that time, on the שַׁבָּתוֹת, Shabatot, יֵשׁוּעַ, Yeshua went through the grain *fields*, and His disciples were hungry, and they began to pluck heads *of grain* and to eat *them*. ²And the פְּרוּשִׁים, P'rushiym, having seen, said to Him, "Look! Your disciples do that which is not permitted to do on the שַׁבָּת, Shabat." ³And He said to them, 'Did you not read what דָּוִד, David did[a] when he was hungry (and those with him)—⁴how he went into the House of God and ate the לֶחֶם הַפָּנִים, Lechem HaPaniym, which it is not permitted to him to eat (nor to those with him), except to the כֹּהֲנִים, Ko'haniym alone? ⁵Or did you not read in the תּוֹרָה, Torah that on the שַׁבָּתוֹת, Shabatot the כֹּהֲנִים, Ko'haniym in the Temple profane the שַׁבָּת, Shabat, yet are blameless? ⁶And I say to you that *One* greater than the Temple is here; ⁷and if you had known what *this* is—'I WANT LOVING-KINDNESS, AND NOT SACRIFICE'[b]—you *would* have not condemned the blameless. ⁸For the Son of Man is Master[c] *of the* שַׁבָּת, Shabat."

⁹And having left from that place, He went to their synagogue. ¹⁰And look! there was a man *who* had a withered hand. And they questioned Him, saying, "Is it permitted to heal on the שַׁבָּתוֹת, Shabatot?"—so that they might *find reason to* accuse Him. ¹¹And He said to them, "Which man is from *among* you who has one sheep, and, if this *sheep* falls into a ditch on the שַׁבָּתוֹת, Shabatot, will not take hold of it and raise IT out? ¹²How much more *valuable*, therefore, is a man than a sheep? So then, it is permitted on the שַׁבָּתוֹת, Shabatot to do good!" ¹³Then He said to the man, "Stretch out your hand," and he stretched IT out, and it was restored—whole, as the other.

¹⁴And the פְּרוּשִׁים, P'rushiym, having gone forth, held a council against Him, *considering* how they might destroy Him. ¹⁵And יֵשׁוּעַ, Yeshua, having perceived *this*, withdrew from that place.

And many followed Him, and He healed them all ¹⁶and warned them that they should not make His *identity* known, ¹⁷so that it might be fulfilled—that *which* was spoken through the prophet יְשַׁעְיָהוּ, Y'sha'yahu, saying,

¹⁸"Look! My servant, whom I chose; My beloved in whom My soul delighted! I will put My רוּחַ, Ruach upon Him, and He will declare judgment to the גּוֹיִם, Goyim. ¹⁹He will not strive nor cry *out*, nor will any hear His voice in the streets. ²⁰A bruised reed He will not break, and smoking flax He will not quench, until He brings forth judgment to victory. ²¹And in His Name will גּוֹיִם, Goyim hope."[d]

²²Then a demon-possessed *man*—blind and mute—was brought to Him, and He healed him, so that the mute *man both* spoke and saw. ²³And all the crowds were amazed, and said, "Is this the Son of דָּוִד, David?" ²⁴But the פְּרוּשִׁים, P'rushiym, having heard, said, "This one does not cast out demons except by בַּעַל־זְבוּב, Ba-al–Z'vuv, ruler of the demons!"

²⁵And knowing their thoughts, He said to them, "Every kingdom having been divided against itself is desolated, and no city or house having been divided against itself will stand; ²⁶and if הַשָּׂטָן, HaSatan casts out הַשָּׂטָן, HaSatan, he was divided against himself. How, then, does his kingdom stand? ²⁷And if I cast out the demons by בַּעַל־זְבוּב, Ba-al–Z'vuv, by whom do your sons cast *them* out? Because of this, they—they will be your judges. ²⁸But if by the רוּחַ אֱלֹהִים, Ruach 'Elohiym I cast out the demons, then the Reign of God has already come to you! ²⁹Or how is one able to go into the house of the strong man and to take away his property, if he does not first tie up the strong man? And then he will plunder his house.

³⁰"He who is not with Me is against Me, and he who is not gathering with Me, scatters. ³¹Because of this I say to you: all sin

---

[a] שְׁמוּאֵל א *Sh'muel Alef* 21:3-7(2-6)
[b] הוֹשֵׁעַ *Hoshea* 6:6
[c] Some mss insert, "even"

[d] יְשַׁעְיָהוּ *Y'sha'yahu* 42:1-4 (LXX)

and evil-speaking will be forgiven to men, but the evil-speaking against the רוּחַ, Ruach will not be forgiven. ³²And whoever speaks a word against the Son of Man, it will be forgiven to him, but whoever speaks against the רוּחַ הַקֹּדֶשׁ, Ruach Ha-Qodesh, it will not be forgiven him—neither in this age, nor in that which is coming.

³³"Either make the tree good and its fruit *will be* good, or make the tree bad and its fruit *will be* bad; for from the fruit is the tree known. ³⁴Brood of *venomous* snakes! How are you able to speak good things *with you* being evil? For out of the overflow of the heart the mouth speaks. ³⁵The good man, out of the good treasure,[a] sends out the good things, and the evil man, out of the evil treasure, sends out evil things. ³⁶And I say to you that every fruitless word that men speak, they will give an accounting for it in the Day of Judgment; ³⁷for from your words you will be declared righteous, and from your words you will be declared unrighteous."

³⁸Then certain *ones* from the סוֹפְרִים, Sof'-riym and *the* פְּרוּשִׁים, P'rushiym answered Him, saying, "Teacher, we want to see a sign from you." ³⁹And He, answering, said to them, "An evil and adulterous generation seeks a sign, but a sign will not be given to it, except the sign of יוֹנָה, Yonah the prophet; ⁴⁰for as יוֹנָה, YONAH WAS IN THE BELLY OF THE FISH THREE DAYS AND THREE NIGHTS,[b] so will the Son of Man be in the heart of the earth three days and three nights. ⁴¹Men of נִינְוֵה, Niyn'veh will stand up in the Judgment with this generation and will condemn it, for they reformed at the proclamation of יוֹנָה, Yonah, and look! *One* greater than יוֹנָה, Yonah *is* here! ⁴²A queen of the south will rise up in the Judgment with this generation and will condemn it, for she came from the ends of the earth to hear the wisdom of שְׁלֹמֹה, Sh'lomoh, and look! *One* greater than שְׁלֹמֹה, Sh'lomoh *is* here!

⁴³And when the רוּחַ הַטְּמְאָה, ruach ha-tum'ah[c] comes out from a man, it walks through dry places looking for rest, and does not find *it*. ⁴⁴Then it says, 'I will return to my house from which I came.' And having come *back*, it finds IT unoccupied, swept, and arranged. ⁴⁵Then it goes and takes with itself seven other רוּחוֹת, ruchot more evil than itself. And having gone in, they live there, and the final *condition* of that man becomes worse than the first. So will it be also to this evil generation."

⁴⁶While He was still speaking to the crowds, look! His mother and brothers stood outside, looking to speak to Him.[d] ⁴⁸And answering *the one* who told Him, He said, "Who is My mother? And who are My brothers?" ⁴⁹And stretching out His hand toward His disciples, He said, "Look! My mother and My brothers! ⁵⁰For whoever does the will of My Father who is in the Heavens, he is My brother, and sister, and mother."

13 ¹On that day, יֵשׁוּעַ, Yeshua, having gone out of the house, was sitting by the sea. ²And many crowds were gathered together to Him, so that He, having gone into the boat, sat down; and all the crowd stood on the beach. ³And He spoke many things to them in analogies, saying, "Look! The sower went out *to his field* to sow, ⁴and in his sowing, indeed, some *seeds* fell by the road, and the birds came and devoured them. ⁵And others fell on the rocky places where they did not have much ground, and they immediately sprang up because of not having depth of ground; ⁶but *upon* the sun having risen, they were scorched, and because of having no root, they withered. ⁷And others fell among the thorns, and the thorns came up and choked them. ⁸And others fell among the good ground, and were giving fruit—some, indeed, a

---

[a] Some mss insert, "of the heart"
[b] יוֹנָה *Yonah* 2:1(1:17)
[c] זְכַרְיָה *Z'khar'yah* 13:2
[d] Some mss insert verse 47, "And *some*one said to Him, 'Look! Your mother and your brothers are standing outside, looking to speak to You.'"

hundred-fold, and some sixty, and some thirty *times what was sown*. ⁹He who is having ears—let him hear."

¹⁰And the disciples, having come near, said to Him, "Why do you speak to them in analogies?" ¹¹And He, answering, said that "it has been given to you to know the mysteries of the Reign of the Heavens; but to these it has not been given. ¹²For whoever has, it will be given to him, and he will have overabundance; but whoever does not have, even that which he has will be taken from him. ¹³Because of this, I speak to them in analogies: because *while* seeing, they do not see, and *while* hearing, they do not hear, nor *do they* understand. ¹⁴And fulfilled by them is the prophecy of יְשַׁעְיָהוּ, Y'sha'yahu that says,

'With hearing you will hear, yet you will not understand; and *with* seeing you will see, yet you will not perceive. ¹⁵For the heart of this people was made thick, and they heard heavily with the ears, and they closed their eyes (otherwise, they would see with the eyes, and with the ears would hear, and with the heart understand, and return, and I would heal them).'ᵃ

¹⁶But happy are your eyes because they see, and your ears because they hear— ¹⁷for אָמֵן, amen, I say to you that many prophets and righteous men desired to see that which you look upon, and they did not see *it*, and to hear that which you hear, and they did not hear *it*. ¹⁸You, therefore, hear the analogy of the sower:

¹⁹"When anyone is hearing the word of the Reign and *is* not having understanding, the evil one comes and takes away that which has been sown in his heart— this is that *seed which was* sown by the road. ²⁰And that *seed* sown among the rocky places: this is he who is hearing the word, and immediately, with joy, is receiving it; ²¹but he has no root in himself— rather, *it* is temporary—and when persecution or oppression happen because of

the word, immediately, he is stumbled. ²²And that *seed* sown toward the thorns: this is he who is hearing the word, yet the anxiety of the age and the deceitfulness of the wealth choke the word, and it becomes unfruitful. ²³And that *seed* sown on the good ground: this is he who is hearing the word and is understanding *it*, who indeed bears fruit and produces *a crop*—some, indeed, a hundredfold, and some sixty, and some thirty *times what was sown.*"

²⁴Another analogy He set before them, saying, "The Reign of the Heavens was compared to a man sowing good seed in his field, ²⁵and while *he and his* men were sleeping, his enemy came and sowed weed *seeds* among the wheat *seeds*, and went away. ²⁶And when the plant sprang up and yielded fruit, then the weeds also appeared. ²⁷And the slaves of the householder, having come near, said to him, 'Sir, did you not sow good seed in your field? From where, then, does it have the weeds?' ²⁸And he said to them, 'A man— an enemy—did this.' And the slaves said to him, 'Do you want, then, THAT we should go away *and* gather it up?' ²⁹And he said, 'No. Otherwise, *while* gathering up the weeds, you will *also* uproot the wheat with it. ³⁰Allow both to grow together until the harvest, and in the time of the harvest I will say to the reapers, "First gather up the weeds, and bind it in bundles to burn it; and the wheat, gather up into my storehouse."'"

³¹Another analogy He set before them, saying, "The Reign of the Heavens is like a grain of mustard—which a man, having taken, sowed in his field—³²which is smaller, indeed, than all the *other* seeds, but when it is grown, is greatest of *all* the plants, and becomes a tree, so that the birds of the heaven come and rest in its branches."

³³Another analogy He spoke to them: "The Reign of the Heavens is like leaven, which a woman, having taken, hid in

---

ᵃ יְשַׁעְיָהוּ Y'sha'yahu 6:9-10

three measures of flour, until the whole batch was leavened."

34 יֵשׁוּעַ, Yeshua spoke all these things to the crowds in analogies, and He was saying nothing to them without an analogy, 35so that it would be fulfilled—that *which* was spoken through the prophet, saying,

"I will open my mouth in analogies; I will utter things having been hidden since the foundation of the world."[a]

36 Then, having sent away the crowds, He came to the house, and his disciples came near to Him, saying, "Explain to us the analogy of the weeds of the field." 37And He, answering, said, "He who is sowing the good seed is the Son of Man; 38and the field is the world; and the good seed, these are the sons of the Reign; and the weeds are the sons of the evil one; 39and the enemy who sowed them is the Accuser; and the harvest is the full end of the age; and the reapers are Messengers. 40Therefore, as the weed is gathered up and is burned with fire, so will it be in the full end of the age: 41the Son of Man will send forth His Messengers, and they will gather up out of His kingdom all the stumbling-blocks, and those doing the misdeeds, 42and will throw them into the furnace of the fire. There will be the weeping and the gnashing of the teeth. 43Then the righteous will shine forth as the sun in the Reign of their Father. He who is having ears—let him hear.

44"The Reign of the Heavens is like treasure hidden in the field, which a man, having found, hid. And from his joy, he goes and sells all—as much as he has—and buys that field.

45"Again, the Reign of the Heavens is like a man—a merchant—looking for fine pearls, 46and having found one pearl of great value, having gone away, *he* sold all —as much as he had—and bought it.

47"Again, the Reign of the Heavens is like a net that was cast into the sea and gathered together *fish* of every kind, 48*from* which, when it was filled—having drawn *it* up again onto the beach, and having sat down—they gathered the good *fish* into containers, and the bad *fish* they threw out. 49So will it be in the full end of the age: the Messengers will come forth and separate the evil out from among the righteous, 50and *they* will throw them into the furnace of the fire. There will be the weeping and the gnashing of the teeth.

51"Did you understand all these *things?*" They said to Him, "Yes.[b]" 52And He said to them, "Because of this, every סוֹפֵר, Sofer having been discipled to the Reign of the Heavens is like a man—a householder—who brings forth out of his treasure things new and old."

53 And it came to pass, when יֵשׁוּעַ, Yeshua had finished these analogies, He moved on from that place; 54and having come to His own homeland, He was teaching them in their synagogue so that they were astonished, and were saying, "From where *did* this wisdom and the powerful acts *come* to this one? 55Is this not the carpenter's son? *And* is not his mother called מִרְיָם, Mir'yam, and his brothers יַעֲקֹב, Ya'aqov, and יוֹסֵף, Yosef, and שִׁמְעוֹן, Shim'on, and יְהוּדָה, Y'hudah? 56And his sisters—are they not all *here* with us? From where, then, *did* all these *things come* to this one?" 57And they were stumbled at Him. And יֵשׁוּעַ, Yeshua said to them, "A prophet is not without honor except in his homeland, and in his own house." 58And He did not do many powerful acts there, because of their unbelief.

14 ¹At that time, Herod the tetrarch heard the news of יֵשׁוּעַ, Yeshua ²and said to his servants, "This is יוֹחָנָן, Yochanan the Immerser—he rose from the dead! And because of this, the mighty energies are working in him."

³For Herod, having arrested יוֹחָנָן, Yochanan, *had* bound him and put him in

---

[a] תְּהִלִּים T'hiliym 78:2

[b] Some mss insert, "Master"

מַתִּתְיָהוּ Matit'yahu 14:4   *Yochanan the Immerser beheaded.*

prison because of Herodias, his brother Philip's wife. ⁴For יוֹחָנָן, Yochanan was saying to him, "It is not permitted to you to have her."ᵃ ⁵And *he was* wanting to kill Yochanan, *but* he feared the crowds, because they were holding him *in esteem* as a prophet. ⁶But *with* the birthday of Herod having come,ᵇ the daughter of Herodias danced in the middle *of them*, and *it* pleased Herod, ⁷upon which he professed with an oath to give her whatever she might ask. ⁸And she (having been instigated by her mother)—she said, "Give me, here upon a plate, the head of יוֹחָנָן, Yochanan the Immerser." ⁹And the king was grieved, but because of the oaths and of those reclining with him, he commanded IT to be given. ¹⁰And having sent *orders*, he beheaded יוֹחָנָן, Yochanan in the prison, ¹¹and his head was brought on a plate and was given to the girl, and she brought IT near to her mother. ¹²And his disciples, having come, took up the body and buried it, and having come, they told יֵשׁוּעַ, Yeshua.

¹³And *when* יֵשׁוּעַ, Yeshua had heard, *He* withdrew from there in a boat to a deserted place by Himself. Yet the crowds, having heard, followed Him on land from the cities. ¹⁴And having come forth, He saw a large crowd, and was moved with compassion upon them, and healed their infirmed.

¹⁵And evening having come, His disciples came to Him, saying, "This place is *remote and* deserted, and the hour *for labor* has now passed. Send away the crowds so that, having gone to the villages, they may buy food for themselves." ¹⁶And יֵשׁוּעַ, Yeshua said to them, "They have no need to go away—you give them *something* to eat." ¹⁷And they said to Him, "We do not have *any food* here except five loaves *of bread* and two fish." ¹⁸And He said, "Bring them here to Me." ¹⁹And having commanded the crowds to recline on the grass, *and* having taken the five loaves and the two fish *and* having looked up to the heaven, He blessed *them*. And having broken *the* bread, He gave the loaves to the disciples, and the disciples *gave* to the crowds, ²⁰and they all ate and were filled. And they took up what was *left* over of the broken pieces: twelve hand-baskets full! ²¹And those eating were about five thousand men—apart from women and children.

²²And immediately He compelled the disciples to go into the boat, and *then* to go before Him to the other side until He could release the crowds. ²³And having released the crowds, He went up to the mountain by Himself to pray. And evening having come, He was there alone. ²⁴And the boat was now many miles distant from the land,ᶜ *and* tossed by the waves, for the wind was against *it*. ²⁵And in the fourth watch of the night, He cameᵈ to them, walking on the sea. ²⁶But the disciples, having seen Him walking on the sea, were troubled, saying, "It is a phantasm!" and they shouted from the fear. ²⁷And immediately, יֵשׁוּעַ, Yeshua spoke to them, saying, "Courage! I am HE! Be not afraid!" ²⁸And כֵּיפָא, Keifa,ᵉ answering Him, said, "Master, if it is You, *then* command me to come to You on the waters!" ²⁹And He said, "Come!" And having gone down from the boat, כֵּיפָא, Keifa walked on the waters, and *he* came to יֵשׁוּעַ, Yeshua. ³⁰But seeing the wind, *Keifa* was afraid; and having begun to sink, he shouted, saying, "Master! Save me!" ³¹Immediately יֵשׁוּעַ, Yeshua, having stretched out the hand, took hold of him and said to him, "Little faith! Why did you doubt?" ³²And *when* they had gone up into the boat, the wind stopped, ³³and those in the boat bowed *down* to Him, saying, "Truly You are God's Son."

³⁴And having crossed over, they came on the land to גְּנֵיסָרֶת, G'neisaret. ³⁵And hav-

---

ᵃ See וַיִּקְרָא *Vayiq'ra* 18:16 and 20:21
ᵇ "having come"—some mss say, "being kept"
ᶜ "many miles (lit. *stadia*) distant from the land"—some mss say, "in the middle of the sea"
ᵈ "He came"—some mss say, יֵשׁוּעַ, Yeshua went out"
ᵉ כֵּיפָא, Keifa—Gk: Πέτρος, Petros; see יוֹחָנָן *Yn.* 1:42; also in 14:29 and 15:15

ing recognized Him, the men of that place sent *word* to all that surrounding region, and they brought to Him all who were ill, ³⁶and were pleading with Him that they might only touch the כָּנָף, kanaf[a] of His *outer* garment. And as many as touched *it* were saved *from their illnesses*.

15 ¹Then פְּרוּשִׁים, P'rushiym and סוֹפְרִים, Sof'riym came to יֵשׁוּעַ, Yeshua from יְרוּשָׁלַיִם, Y'rushalayim, saying, ²"Why do your disciples sidestep the tradition of the זְקֵנִים, Z'qeniym? for they do not wash their hands when they eat bread!" ³So, answering, He said to them, "Why also do you sidestep the command of God because of your tradition? ⁴For God said, 'HONOR YOUR FATHER AND MOTHER,'[b] and 'HE WHO IS SPEAKING EVIL OF *HIS* FATHER OR MOTHER—LET HIM DIE THE DEATH.'[c] ⁵But you say, 'Whoever says to *his* father or mother, "An offering IS *being* made to God with whatever *good thing* you would have *otherwise* benefited from me," ⁶he will not *need* to honor his father.'[d] And *in so teaching*, you set aside the word of God because of your tradition. ⁷Hypocrites! יְשַׁעְיָהוּ, Y'sha'yahu prophesied well of you, saying,

⁸'This people[e] honors Me with the lips, but their heart is far off from Me; ⁹and in vain they reverence Me, teaching teachings *that are but* commands of men.'"[f]

¹⁰And having called the crowd near, He said to them, "Hear and understand: ¹¹that which is coming into the mouth does not defile the man, but that which is coming out of the mouth—this defiles the man."

¹²Then the disciples, having come near, said to Him, "Have You known that the פְּרוּשִׁים, P'rushiym, having heard the word,

were stumbled?" ¹³And answering *them*, He said, "Every plant that My heavenly Father did not plant will be uprooted. ¹⁴Leave them alone. They are blind guides of *the* blind; and if *the* blind may guide *the* blind, both will fall into a ditch."

¹⁵And כֵּיפָא, Keifa, answering, said to Him, "Explain the analogy to us." ¹⁶And He said, "Are you also still without understanding? ¹⁷Do you not understand that all that is going into the mouth passes into the stomach, and is *then* expelled into the latrine? ¹⁸But the things coming out from the mouth come out from the heart, and *it is* these *which* defile the man. ¹⁹For out of the heart come evil thoughts, murders, adulteries, sexual immorality, thefts, false witnessings, *and* evil speakings *against others:* ²⁰these are the things *which are* defiling the man. But to eat with unwashed hands does not defile the man."

²¹And *when* יֵשׁוּעַ, Yeshua had come forth from there, *He* withdrew to the parts of צוֹר, Tzor and צִידוֹן, Tziydon, ²²and look! a woman—a כְּנַעֲנִית, K'na'aniyt—having come forth from those borders, shouted, saying, "Deal kindly with me, sir—Son of דָּוִד, David; my daughter is severely demon-possessed!" ²³But He did not answer her a word. And His disciples, having come to Him, were asking Him, saying, "Send her away, for she *continually* shouts after us."

²⁴And He, answering, said, "I was not sent except to the lost[g] sheep of the house of יִשְׂרָאֵל, Yis'rael." ²⁵But having come, she was bowing to Him, saying, "Sir! Help me!" ²⁶And He, answering, said, "It is not good to take the children's bread and to throw *it* to the little dogs." ²⁷And she said, "Yes, sir, but even the little dogs eat of the crumbs that are falling from their masters' table." ²⁸Then answering, יֵשׁוּעַ, Yeshua said to her, "O woman—great IS your faith. Let it be to you as you want," and her daughter was healed from that moment.

---

[a] כָּנָף, kanaf—see מַתִּתְיָהוּ *Matit'yahu* 9:20
[b] שְׁמוֹת *Sh'mot* 20:12; דְּבָרִים *D'variym* 5:16
[c] שְׁמוֹת *Sh'mot* 21:17; וַיִּקְרָא *Vayiq'ra* 20:9
[d] Some mss insert, "or his mother"
[e] Some mss insert, "draws near to Me with their mouth, and"
[f] יְשַׁעְיָהוּ *Y'sha'yahu* 29:13

[g] lose/lost—ἀπόλλυμι, apollumi, meaning "to kill or destroy"

29And *when* יֵשׁוּעַ, Yeshua had left from there, *He* came near to the Sea of the גָּלִיל, Galiyl. And having gone up to the mountain, He was sitting there; 30and large crowds came to Him, having with them *the* lame, crippled, blind, mute, and many others. And they threw them at His feet, and He healed them, 31so that the crowd marveled, seeing mute ones speaking, crippled *made* whole, and lame walking, and blind seeing; and they glorified the God of יִשְׂרָאֵל, Yis'rael.

32And יֵשׁוּעַ, Yeshua, having called near His disciples, said, "I have compassion for the crowd, because they continue with Me three days now, but they have nothing they can eat. And I do not want to send them away hungry; otherwise, they *may* faint on the road." 33And His disciples said, "From where *will this come* to us in a wilderness—so many loaves as to fill so large a crowd?"

34And יֵשׁוּעַ, Yeshua said to them, "How many loaves do you have?" And they said, "Seven, and a few little fishes." 35And having given command to the crowd to sit down upon the ground, 36He took the seven loaves and the fishes; and having given thanks, He broke *the bread* and was giving to the disciples, and the disciples to the crowds. 37And they all ate and were filled. And they took up what was *left* over of the broken pieces: seven baskets full! 38And those eating were four thousand men, apart from women and children.

39And having sent away the crowds, He went into the boat, and came to the borders of מָגָדוֹן, Magadon.

16 1And the פְּרוּשִׁים, P'rushiym and צְדוּקִים, Tzaduqiym, having come *with the agenda of* tempting Yeshua, questioned Him, *challenging Him* to show to them a sign from the Heaven. 2And He, answering, said to them, "*With* evening having come you say, 'We will have fair weather, for the heaven is red,' 3and at morning, 'We will have foul weather today, for the heaven is red *and* gloomy.' You, indeed, know *how* to discern the face of the heavens, but the signs of the times you are not able *to discern!* 4A generation evil and adulterous searches for a sign, but a sign will not be given to it, except the sign of יוֹנָה, Yonah." And having left them, He went away.

5And the disciples, having come to the other side, forgot to take loaves *of bread*, 6and יֵשׁוּעַ, Yeshua said to them, "Watch out! and be careful of the leaven of the פְּרוּשִׁים, P'rushiym and צְדוּקִים, Tzaduqiym." 7And they were reasoning within themselves, saying, "*He said this* because we took no loaves *with us.*" 8And יֵשׁוּעַ, Yeshua, having known, said, "Why do you reason within yourselves—you of little faith—*that I said this* because you have no loaves? 9Do you not yet understand nor remember the five loaves of the five thousand, and how many hand-baskets you took up? 10nor the seven loaves of the four thousand, and how many baskets you took up? 11How do you not understand that I did not speak to you of bread? Rather, be careful of the leaven of the פְּרוּשִׁים, P'rushiym and צְדוּקִים, Tzaduqiym." 12Then they understood that He did not say to be careful of the leaven of the bread, but of the teaching of the פְּרוּשִׁים, P'rushiym and צְדוּקִים, Tzaduqiym.

13And יֵשׁוּעַ, Yeshua, having come to the parts of Cæsarea Philippi, was asking His disciples, saying, "Who do men say[a] the Son of Man to be?" 14And they said, "Some *say* יוֹחָנָן, Yochanan the Immerser; and others, אֵלִיָּהוּ, Eliyahu; and others, יִרְמְיָהוּ, Yir'm'yahu or one of the prophets." 15He said to them, "And you—who do you say Me to be?" 16And שִׁמְעוֹן כֵּיפָא, Shim'on Keifa,[b] answering, said, "You are the Messiah, the Son of the living God!" 17And יֵשׁוּעַ, Yeshua, answering, said to him, "Happy are you, שִׁמְעוֹן בַּר־יוֹנָה, Shim'on Bar-Yonah, because flesh and blood did not reveal IT to you, but My Father who is in the Heavens. 18And I also say to you that you are a rock, and upon this rock I will build My

---

[a] Some mss insert, "Me"
[b] כֵּיפָא, Keifa—Gk: Πέτρος, Petros; see יוֹחָנָן Yn. 1:42; also 16:22,23 and throughout chapter 17

Transformation of Messiah.   מַתִּתְיָהוּ **Matit'yahu 17:13**

Called-Forth,[a] and *the* gates *of* שְׁאוֹל, Sh'ol will not prevail against it. ¹⁹I will give to you the keys of the Reign of the Heavens, and whatever you bind on the earth will be having been bound in the heavens, and whatever you unbind on the earth will be having been unbound in the heavens." ²⁰Then He warned the disciples that they say to no one that He is[b] the Messiah.

²¹From that time, יֵשׁוּעַ, Yeshua began to show to His disciples that it is necessary for Him to go away to יְרוּשָׁלַיִם, Y'rushalayim, and to suffer many things from the זְקֵנִים, Z'qeniym and chief כֹּהֲנִים, Ko'haniym and סוֹפְרִים, Sof'riym, and to be put to death, and the third day to rise *to life*. ²²And having taken Him aside, כֵּיפָא, Keifa began to rebuke Him, saying, "Be kind to Yourself, Master! This will not happen to You!" ²³And He, having turned, said to כֵּיפָא, Keifa, "Get behind Me, שָׂטָן, Satan! You are a stumbling-block to Me, for you do not think the things of God, but the things of men!"

²⁴Then יֵשׁוּעַ, Yeshua said to His disciples, "If anyone wants to come after Me, let him deny himself, and take up his *execution* stake, and follow Me. ²⁵For whoever wants to save his life will lose[c] it, and whoever loses his life for My sake will find it. ²⁶For what will it benefit a man if he gains the whole world, but suffers *the* loss of his life? Or what will a man give as an exchange for his life? ²⁷For the Son of Man is about to come in the glory of His Father, with His Messengers, and then He will REWARD EACH MAN ACCORDING TO HIS PRACTICES.[d] ²⁸אָמֵן, Amen, I say to you that there are certain *ones* of those standing here who will not taste of death until they see the Son of Man coming in His Reign."

17 ¹And after six days, יֵשׁוּעַ, Yeshua took כֵּיפָא, Keifa and יַעֲקֹב, Ya'aqov and יוֹחָנָן, Yochanan his brother, and brought them up to a high mountain by themselves, ²and He was transformed in front of them. And His face shone as the sun, and His clothes became white as the light, ³and look! מֹשֶׁה, Mosheh and אֵלִיָּהוּ, Eliyahu appeared to them, talking together with Him. ⁴And כֵּיפָא, Keifa, answering, said to יֵשׁוּעַ, Yeshua, "Master, it is good for us to be here. If you want, I will make three סֻכּוֹת, sukot here—one for You, and one for מֹשֶׁה, Mosheh, and one for אֵלִיָּהוּ, Eliyahu." ⁵While he was still speaking, look! a bright cloud overshadowed them, and look! a voice *came* out of the cloud, saying, "This is My Son—the Beloved, in whom I delighted. Hear Him." ⁶And the disciples, having heard, fell upon their face, and were exceedingly afraid; ⁷and יֵשׁוּעַ, Yeshua came near, and having touched them, said, "Arise, be not afraid." ⁸And having lifted up their eyes, they saw no one except יֵשׁוּעַ, Yeshua Himself only. ⁹And as they were coming down from the mountain, יֵשׁוּעַ, Yeshua commanded them, saying, "Tell no one the vision until the Son of Man is raised out of the dead."

¹⁰And the disciples questioned Him, saying, "Why, then, do the סוֹפְרִים, Sof'riym say that אֵלִיָּהוּ, Eliyahu must come first?" ¹¹And, answering, He said, "אֵלִיָּהוּ, Eliyahu does indeed come, and will restore all things; ¹²and I say to you—אֵלִיָּהוּ, Eliyahu already came, and they did not know him, but did with him whatever they would. So also the Son of Man is about to suffer by them." ¹³Then the disciples understood that He spoke to them concerning יוֹחָנָן, Yochanan the Immerser.

---

[a] "Called-Forth"—ἐκκλησίαν, ekklesian, traditionally, "church" (which originates not from ἐκκλησία, ekklesia, but κυριακός, kuriakos; cf. 1Co.11:20 & Rev.1:10). In the Hebrew Scriptures, those who assemble before ADONAI for sacred purposes are the קָהָל, qahal or קְהִלָּה, q'hilah; however, while most occurrences of ἐκκλησία in its various forms in the LXX translate קָהָל, qahal, it is also translated numerous times by συναγωγῆς, sunagoges—"synagogue." There is no absolute correlation between קָהָל, qahal and ἐκκλησία, ekklesia.

[b] Some mss insert, "יֵשׁוּעַ, Yeshua"

[c] lose/lost—ἀπόλλυμι, apollumi, meaning "to kill or destroy"

[d] תְּהִלִּים T'hiliym 62:13(12); מִשְׁלֵי Mish'lei 24:12

¹⁴And when they came to the crowd, there *also* came to Him a man, kneeling down to Him ¹⁵and saying, "Sir, deal kindly with my son, for he is moon-struck and suffers miserably, for he often falls into the fire, and often into the water, ¹⁶and I brought him near to Your disciples, but they were not able to heal him." ¹⁷And יֵשׁוּעַ, Yeshua, answering, said, "O faithless and perverse generation, until when will I be with you? until when will I tolerate you? Bring him here to Me." ¹⁸And יֵשׁוּעַ, Yeshua rebuked him, and the demon went out of him, and the boy was healed from that moment. ¹⁹Then the disciples, having come to יֵשׁוּעַ, Yeshua *while He was* by Himself, said, "Why were we not able to cast him out?" ²⁰And He said to them, "*It is* through your littleness of faith. אָמֵן, Amen, for I say to you: if you have faith as a grain of mustard, you will *be able to* say to this mountain, 'Move from here to there,' and it will move—and nothing will be impossible to you."ᵃ

²²And while they were gatheringᵇ in the גָּלִיל, Galiyl, יֵשׁוּעַ, Yeshua said to them, "The Son of Man is about to be handed over into the hands of men, ²³and they will kill Him. But on the third day, He will rise *to life*," and they were exceedingly sorrowful.

²⁴And when they came to כְּפַר־נַחוּם, K'far-Nachum, those collecting the didrachms-*tax* came near to כֵּיפָא, Keifa and said, "Your teacher—does He not pay the didrachms-*tax*?" ²⁵He said, "Yes." And having come into the house, יֵשׁוּעַ, Yeshua anticipated him, saying, "What do you think, שִׁמְעוֹן, Shim'on? The kings of the earth—from whom do they take customs or poll-tax? From their sons, or from the others?" ²⁶And he having said, "From the others," יֵשׁוּעַ, Yeshua said to him, "Then the sons are free. ²⁷However, so that we do not cause them to stumble, having gone to the sea, cast a hook, and take up the fish that comes up first. And having opened its mouth, you will find a שֶׁקֶל, sheqel. Having taken that, give *it* to them for Me and you."

18

¹At that time, the disciples came near to יֵשׁוּעַ, Yeshua, saying, "Who, now, is greater in the Reign of the Heavens?" ²And He, having called near a child, set him in the middle of them ³and said, "אָמֵן, Amen, I say to you, if you will not be turned and become like the children, you will not enter into the Reign of the Heavens. ⁴Whoever, then, humbles himself as this child, he is the greater in the Reign of the Heavens. ⁵And he who receives one such child in My Name receives Me, ⁶but whoever causes one of those little ones who are believing in Me to stumble—it is better for him that a weighty millstone be hung around his neck, and he be sunk in the depth of the sea. ⁷אוֹי, Oy! to the world because of the stumbling-blocks! Indeed, there is a necessity for the stumbling-blocks to come, but אוֹי, oy! to the man through whom the stumbling-block comes!

⁸"And if your hand or your foot causes you to stumble, cut it off and throw *it* away from you! It is good for you to enter into the Life crippled or lame, rather than, having two hands or two feet, to be cast into the fire—the age-enduring. ⁹And if your eye causes you to stumble, pluck it out and throw *it* away from you! It is good for you to enter into the Life one-eyed, rather than, having two eyes, to be cast into the גֵּיהִנֹּם, Geihinom of the fire. ¹⁰Watch out! *that* you do not despise one of these little ones, for I say to you that their Messengers in the Heavens always see the face of My Father, who is in the Heavens.ᶜ

¹²"What do you think? If a man has a hundred sheep, and one of them goes astray, will he not leave the ninety-nine on the mountains and, having gone, look for the *one* gone astray? ¹³And if it comes

---

ᵃ Some mss continue with verse 21, "But this kind does not go out except in prayer and fasting."
ᵇ "gathering"—some mss say, "living"

ᶜ Some mss continue with vs. 11, "for the Son of Man came to save the lost."

to pass that he finds it, אָמֵן, amen, I say to you that he rejoices over it more than over the ninety-nine that have not gone astray. ¹⁴So it is not *the* will in front of your Father, who is in the Heavens, that one of these little ones be destroyed.

¹⁵"And if your brother sins against you,ᵃ go show him his fault between you and him alone. If he hears you, you gained your brother. ¹⁶But if he does not hear, take with you one or two more, so that BY THE MOUTH OF TWO WITNESSES, OR THREE, EVERY WORD WILL STAND.ᵇ ¹⁷And if he does not hear them, *then* say IT to the Called-Forth. And if he also does not hear the Called-Forth,ᶜ *then* let him be to you as the גּוֹי, Goy *foreigner* and the tax-gatherer.

¹⁸"אָמֵן, Amen, I say to you, whatever things you bind upon the earth will be having been bound in the Heavens, and whatever things you may unbind on the earth will be having been unbound in the Heavens.

¹⁹"Again, I say to you, that if two of you agree on the earth concerning anything, *then* whatever they ask, it will be done to them from My Father, who is in the Heavens. ²⁰For where there are two or three gathered together—to My Name—I am there in the middle of them."

²¹Then כֵּיפָא, Keifa,ᵈ having come, said to Him, "Master, how often will my brother sin against me, and I forgive him? Until seven times?" ²²יֵשׁוּעַ, Yeshua said to him, "I do not say to you 'Until seven times,' but 'Until seventy times seven.'

²³"Because of this, the Reign of the Heavens is likened to a man—a king—who wanted to settle accounts with his slaves; ²⁴and when he had begun to take account, one debtor was brought near to him *who owed* thousands *of decades' worth* of wages;ᵉ ²⁵and *when* he had nothing to pay *it*, the master commanded him to be sold—also the wife, and the children, and everything, whatever he had—and payment to be made. ²⁶The slave, then, having fallen down *before him*, was bowing to him, saying, 'Have patience with me, and I will pay you everything!' ²⁷And the master of that slave, having been moved with compassion, released him, and he forgave him the debt.

²⁸"And having come forth, that slave found one of his fellow-slaves who was owing him a hundred days' wages,ᶠ and having laid hold *of him*, he took him by the throat, saying, 'Pay what you owe!' ²⁹His fellow-slave then, having fallen down at his feet, was pleading with him, saying, 'Have patience with me, and I will pay you!'ᵍ ³⁰But he would not *listen*, and having gone away, he threw him into prison until he could pay what *he* was owing.

³¹"Therefore, having seen the things that were done, his fellow-slaves were grieved exceedingly. And having come, *they* explained fully to their master all the things that were done. ³²Then, having called *the slave*, his master said to him, 'Evil slave! All that debt I forgave you, since you pleaded with me, ³³did it not become necessary *for* you also to have dealt kindly with your fellow-slave, *just* as I also dealt kindly with you?' ³⁴And having been angered, his master handed him over to the torturers until he should pay all that was being owed.

³⁵"So also will My heavenly Father do to you, if each one *of* you does not forgive his brother from your hearts."ʰ

19 ¹And it came to pass *that*, when יֵשׁוּעַ, Yeshua finished *saying* these words, He moved on from the גָּלִיל, Galiyl and came to the borders of

---

ᵃ "against you"—this phrase in the Gk is disputed; cf. Lk. 17:3

ᵇ דְּבָרִים D'variym 19:15

ᶜ "Called-Forth"—ἐκκλησία, ekklesia and ἐκκλησίας, ekklesias, resp.; see מַתִּתְיָהוּ *Matit'yahu* 16:18

ᵈ כֵּיפָא, Keifa—Gk: Πέτρος, Petros; see יוֹחָנָן *Yn.* 1:42; also in 19:27

ᵉ "thousands *of decades' worth* of wages"—lit. "a myriad of talents"; see footnote for *Mt.* 25:15

ᶠ "a hundred days' wages"—lit. "a hundred denaries"

ᵍ Some mss insert, "everything"

ʰ Some mss insert, "their missteps"

מַתִּתְיָהוּ **Matit'yahu 19:2** *Rich young man's inquiry.*

יְהוּדָה, Y'hudah, beyond the יַרְדֵן, Yar'den, ²and large crowds followed Him, and He healed them there.

³And the פְּרוּשִׁים, P'rushiym came near to Him, tempting Him and saying, "Is it permitted for a man to send away his wife *in divorce* for every cause?" ⁴And He, answering, said, "Did you not read that He who created[a] THEM from the beginning MADE THEM A MALE AND A FEMALE,[b] ⁵and said, 'FOR THIS REASON WILL A MAN LEAVE FATHER AND MOTHER AND STICK TO HIS WIFE, AND THEY WILL BE—THE TWO—FOR ONE FLESH,'[c] ⁶so that they are no longer two, but one flesh? Whatever, therefore, God joined together, let no man separate." ⁷*So* they said to Him, "Why, then, did מֹשֶׁה, Mosheh command *him* to GIVE *her* A SCROLL OF DIVORCE, AND to SEND HER AWAY?"[d] ⁸*Then* He said to them, "מֹשֶׁה, Mosheh, for your stiffness of heart, allowed you to send away your wives; but from the beginning, it has not been so. ⁹And *now* I say to you that whoever sends away his wife (except for sexual unfaithfulness[e]) and marries another, commits adultery."[f] ¹⁰The disciples said to Him, "If the case of the man with the woman is this way, *then* it is not good to marry." ¹¹And He said to them, "Not all *can* receive this word, but *only* those to whom it has been given; ¹²for there are eunuchs who from the mother's womb were born so, and there are eunuchs who were made eunuchs by men, and there are eunuchs who kept themselves eunuchs[g] because of the Reign of the Heavens. He who is able to receive IT—let him receive."

¹³Then children were brought near to Him so that He might lay *His* hands on them and pray, and the disciples rebuked them. ¹⁴But יֵשׁוּעַ, Yeshua said, "Allow the children to come to Me and forbid them not, for of such is the Reign of the Heavens." ¹⁵And having laid *His* hands on them, He went away from that place.

¹⁶And look! one having come near said to Him, "Teacher,[h] what good thing should I do, so that I may have life age-enduring?" ¹⁷And He said to him, "Why do you ask Me about the good? There is *only* One who is good.[i] But if you want to enter into the Life, keep the commands." ¹⁸He said to Him, "What kind?" And יֵשׁוּעַ, Yeshua said, "YOU MUST NOT MURDER; YOU MUST NOT COMMIT ADULTERY; YOU MUST NOT STEAL; YOU MUST NOT GIVE FALSE TESTIMONY;[j] ¹⁹HONOR YOUR FATHER AND MOTHER;[k] and, YOU MUST LOVE YOUR NEIGHBOR AS YOURSELF.[l]" ²⁰The young man said to Him, "All these I have kept.[m] What do I still lack?" ²¹יֵשׁוּעַ, Yeshua said to him, "If you want to be perfect, go away, sell what you have, and give to the poor; and you will have treasure in Heaven. And come, follow Me." ²²And the young man, having heard the word, went away grieving, for he had many possessions.

²³And יֵשׁוּעַ, Yeshua said to His disciples, "אָמֵן, Amen, I say to you that a rich man will enter into the Reign of the Heavens with difficulty. ²⁴And again I say to you: it is easier for a camel to go through the eye of a needle than for a rich man to enter into the Reign of God." ²⁵And the disciples, having heard, were exceedingly amazed, saying, "Who, then, is able to be saved?" ²⁶And יֵשׁוּעַ, Yeshua, having looked straight at *them*, said to them, "With men

---

[a] "created"—some mss say, "made"
[b] בְּרֵאשִׁית *B'reshiyt* 1:27, 5:2
[c] בְּרֵאשִׁית *B'reshiyt* 2:24
[d] דְּבָרִים *D'variym* 24:1ff
[e] "sexual unfaithfulness"—πορνεία, porneia
[f] Some mss insert, "And he who marries her that has been sent away *also* commits adultery."; cf. 5:32
[g] "eunuchs who kept themselves eunuchs," prob. metaphorical
[h] "Teacher"—some mss say, "Good Teacher"
[i] "ask Me about the good? There is *only* One who is good."—some mss say, "call Me good? No one IS good except One: God."; cf. Mark 10:18 and Luke 18:19
[j] שְׁמוֹת *Sh'mot* 20:13(13-16); דְּבָרִים *D'variym* 5:17 (17-20)
[k] שְׁמוֹת *Sh'mot* 20:12; דְּבָרִים *D'variym* 5:16
[l] וַיִּקְרָא *Vayiq'ra* 19:18
[m] Some mss insert, "from my youth"

this is impossible, but with God, all things are possible."

²⁷Then כֵּיפָא, Keifa, answering, said to Him, "Look! We left everything and follow You. What, then, will we have?" ²⁸And יֵשׁוּעַ, Yeshua said to them, "אָמֵן, Amen, I say to you that you who have followed Me, in the Regeneration (when the Son of Man sits upon a throne of His glory) you also will sit upon twelve thrones, judging the twelve tribes of יִשְׂרָאֵל, Yis'rael; ²⁹and everyone who left houses, or brothers, or sisters, or father, or mother,ᵃ or children, or fields for My Name's sake, will receive a hundred times, and will inherit life age-enduring; ³⁰and many *who are* first will be last, and last, first.

20 ¹"Indeed, the Reign of the Heavens is like a man, a householder, who went out with the morning to hire workmen for his vineyard. ²And having agreed with the workmen on a day's wageᵇ *for* the day, he sent them into his vineyard.

³"And having gone out about the third hour *of the day*, he saw others standing *around* doing nothing in the marketplace, ⁴and *so* he said to these, 'You, go—you also—to the vineyard, and whatever *wage* is righteous, I will give you'; ⁵and *so* they went away *to the vineyard*. Again, having gone out about the sixth and the ninth hour, he did likewise.

⁶"And about the eleventh *hour*, having gone out, he found others standing *around*, and said to them, 'Why have you stood here all the day doing nothing?' They said to him, 'Because no one hired us.' He said to them, 'You go—you also—to the vineyard.'ᶜ

⁸"And evening having come, the master of the vineyard said to his foreman, 'Call the workmen, and pay them the wages, having begun from the last to the first.' ⁹And they—*the workers* of about the eleventh hour—having come, each received a day's wage.

¹⁰"And the first *workers, when they* had come, supposed that they would receive more, but they each received a day's wage —they also. ¹¹And having received IT, they were grumbling against the householder, ¹²saying, 'These—the last *workers*—worked *only* one hour, and you made them equal to us—*we* who were bearing the burden and the heat of the day.' ¹³And he, answering, said to one of them, 'Friend, I do no unrighteousness to you. Did you not agree with me for a day's wage? ¹⁴Take that which is yours and go, and I want to give to this *worker*—the last—also as to you. ¹⁵Is it not permitted for me to do what I want with *what is* my own? Or is your eye evil because I am good?ᵈ ¹⁶So the last will be first, and the first, last.'"ᵉ

¹⁷And going up to יְרוּשָׁלַיִם, Y'rushalayim, יֵשׁוּעַ, Yeshua took the twelve disciples by themselves, and said to them on the way, ¹⁸"Look! We are going up to יְרוּשָׁלַיִם, Y'rushalayim; and the Son of Man will be handed over to the chief כֹּהֲנִים, Ko'haniym and סֹפְרִים, Sof'riym; and they will condemn Him to death ¹⁹and will hand Him over to the גּוֹיִם, Goyim to mock, and to flog, and to crucify; and *on* the third day, He will be raised up."

²⁰Then the mother of the sons of זַבְדִּי, Zav'diy came near to Him with her sons, bowing and asking something from Him. ²¹And He said to her, "What do you want?" She said to Him, "Say that they may sit—these, my two sons—one on Your right hand, and one on Your left, in Your Reign." ²²And answering, יֵשׁוּעַ, Yeshua said, "You do not know what you ask for yourselves. Are you able to drink of the cup that I am about to drink?"ᶠ They

---

ᵃ Some mss insert, "or wife"

ᵇ "day's wage"—lit. "denary"; throughout chapter

ᶜ Some mss insert, "and whatever *wage* is righteous, you will receive"

ᵈ "is your eye evil because I am good?" or "are you selfish because I am generous?"

ᵉ Some mss insert, "for many are called, but few chosen"

ᶠ Some mss insert, "and to be immersed with the immersion that I am immersed with?"; cf. Mark 10:38

said to Him, "We are able." ²³He said to them, "Of My cup, indeed, you will drink.ᵃ But to sit at My right hand and on *My* left is not Mine to give, but *it is* for those for whom it has been prepared by My Father."

²⁴And the Ten, having heard, were much displeased with the two brothers, ²⁵and יֵשׁוּעַ, Yeshua, having called them near, said, "You have known that the rulers of the גּוֹיִם, Goyim lord it over them, and those great *in rank* exercise authority over them. ²⁶It will not be so among you! Rather, whoever among you wants to become great will be your servant, ²⁷and whoever among you wants to be first will be your slave; ²⁸even as the Son of Man did not come to be served, but to serve and to give His life *as* a ransom for many."

²⁹And as they were going out of יְרִיחוֹ, Y'riycho, a large crowd followed Him. ³⁰And look! two blind men sitting by the road, having heard that יֵשׁוּעַ, Yeshua *had* passed by, shouted, saying, "Sir, deal kindly with us—Son of דָּוִד, David!" ³¹And the crowd warned them that they should be silent, but they shouted out *all* the more, saying, "Sir, deal kindly with us—Son of דָּוִד, David!" ³²And having stood *still*, יֵשׁוּעַ, Yeshua called them and said, "What do you want THAT I should do to you?" ³³They said to Him, "Sir, that our eyes may be opened!" ³⁴And having been moved with compassion, יֵשׁוּעַ, Yeshua touched their eyes—and immediately they received sight, and they followed Him.

21

¹And when they came near to יְרוּשָׁלַיִם, Y'rushalayim, and came to בֵּית־פַּגֵּי, Beit-Pagei, to the Mountain of the Olives, then יֵשׁוּעַ, Yeshua sent two disciples, ²saying to them, "Go on to the village opposite you, and immediately, you will find a donkey tied *there*, and a colt with her. Having untied *her*, bring *them* to Me, ³and if anyone says anything to you, *then* you will say that the Master has need of them, and immediately, he will send them *with you*." ⁴And this came to pass so that it might be fulfilled—that which was spoken through the prophet, saying,

⁵"Tell the daughter of צִיּוֹן, Tziyon, 'Look! Your King comes to you: humble, and mounted on a donkey and on a colt, a foal of a beast of burden!'"ᵇ

⁶And the disciples, having gone and having done as יֵשׁוּעַ, Yeshua appointed them, ⁷brought the donkey and the colt, and put their coats on them; and He sat upon them. ⁸And the very large crowd spread their own coats in the road, and others were cutting branches from the trees, and were spreading *them out* in the road. ⁹And the crowds, who were going in front of Him and who were following, were shouting, saying, "הוֹשַׁע־נָא, Hosha-na to the Son of דָּוִד, David! BLESSED IS HE WHO IS COMING IN THE NAME OF ADONAI!ᶜ הוֹשַׁע־נָא, Hosha-na in the highest!" ¹⁰And when He had entered into יְרוּשָׁלַיִם, Y'rushalayim, the whole city was shaken, saying, "Who is this?" ¹¹And the crowds said, "This is the prophet יֵשׁוּעַ, Yeshua, who IS from נְצֶרֶת, N'tzaret of the גָּלִיל, Galiyl."

¹²And יֵשׁוּעַ, Yeshua entered into the Temple of God and threw out all those selling and buying in the Temple, and He overturned the tables of the money-changers and the seats of those selling the doves. ¹³And He said to them, "It has been written, 'MY HOUSE WILL BE CALLED A HOUSE OF PRAYER,'ᵈ but you make it a 'DEN OF ROBBERS!'ᵉ"

¹⁴And in the Temple, there came to Him blind and lame men, and He healed them. ¹⁵And the chief כֹּהֲנִים, Ko'haniym and the סוֹפְרִים, Sof'riym—having seen the wonderful things that He did, and the children shouting in the Temple and saying, "הוֹשַׁע־נָא, Hosha-na to the Son of דָּוִד, David!"—were much displeased. ¹⁶And

---

ᵃ Some mss insert, "and with the immersion that I am immersed with, you will be immersed"; cf. Mark 10:39
ᵇ יְשַׁעְיָהוּ Y'sha'yahu 62:11; זְכַרְיָה Z'khar'yah 9:9
ᶜ תְּהִלִּים T'hiliym 118:26
ᵈ יְשַׁעְיָהוּ Y'sha'yahu 56:7
ᵉ יִרְמְיָהוּ Yir'm'yahu 7:11

they said to Him, "Do you hear what they say?" And יֵשׁוּעַ, Yeshua said to them, "Yes! Did you never read that 'OUT OF THE MOUTH OF LITTLE CHILDREN AND INFANTS, YOU PREPARED PRAISE'[a]?"

¹⁷And having left them, He went out away from the city to בֵּית־עֲנִיָה, Beit-An'-yah, and spent the night there; ¹⁸and in the morning, returning to the city, He hungered. ¹⁹And having seen a certain fig-tree on the road, He came to it, and found nothing in it except only leaves. And He said to it, "No longer will fruit be from you—to the age," and instantly, the fig-tree withered. ²⁰And the disciples, having seen *this*, marveled, saying, "How did the fig-tree instantly wither?" ²¹And יֵשׁוּעַ, Yeshua, answering, said to them, "אָמֵן, Amen, I say to you: if you have faith, and do not doubt, not only will you do this of the fig-tree, but even if you say to this mountain, 'Be lifted up and thrown into the sea,' it will come to pass; ²²and everything—as much as you ask in the prayer—believing, you will receive."

²³And when He had come to the Temple, while *He was* teaching, there came to Him the chief כֹּהֲנִים, Ko'haniym and the זְקֵנִים, Z'qeniym of the people, saying, "By what authority do you do these things? and who gave you this authority?" ²⁴And יֵשׁוּעַ, Yeshua, answering, said to them, "I will ask you—I also—one word, which, if you tell me, I also will tell you by what authority I do these things. ²⁵The immersion of יוֹחָנָן, Yochanan: where was it from? —from Heaven, or from men?" And they were reasoning among themselves, saying, "If we should say, 'From Heaven,' He will say to us, 'Why, then, did you not believe him?' ²⁶And if we should say, 'From men,' we fear the crowd, for all hold יוֹחָנָן, Yochanan as a prophet." ²⁷And answering יֵשׁוּעַ, Yeshua, they said, "We do not know." He said to them—He also—"Neither do I tell you by what authority I do these things.

²⁸"And what do you think? A man had two children, and having come to the first *son*, he said, 'Child, go. Today, be working in the vineyard.' ²⁹And he, answering, said, "I will not"; but afterwards, having regretted *it*, he went. ³⁰And having come to the other *son*, he spoke in the same manner. And he, answering, said, 'I will GO, sir,' but went not. ³¹Which of the two did the will of the father?" They said, "The first." יֵשׁוּעַ, Yeshua said to them, "אָמֵן, Amen, I say to you that the tax-gatherers and the prostitutes go before you into the Reign of God, ³²for יוֹחָנָן, Yochanan came to you on the road of righteousness, and you did not believe him. But the tax-gatherers and the prostitutes did believe him. And you, having seen, afterwards did not regret, *so as* to believe him.

³³"Hear another analogy: there was a man, a householder, who planted a vineyard, and put a fence around it, and dug a wine-press in it, and built a tower, and rented it out to farmers, and went abroad. ³⁴And when the season of the fruits came near, he sent his slaves to the farmers to receive the fruits of it. ³⁵And the farmers took his slaves—one they beat, and one they killed, and one they stoned. ³⁶Again, he sent other slaves—more than the first—and they did to them in the same manner. ³⁷And at last, he sent his son to them, saying, "They will respect my son"; ³⁸but the farmers, having seen the son, said among themselves, "This is the heir. Come! We can kill him and possess his inheritance." ³⁹And having taken him, they threw HIM out of the vineyard and killed him. ⁴⁰Whenever, therefore, the master of the vineyard comes, what will he do to these farmers?" ⁴¹*And* they said to him, "Evil men—he will evilly destroy them, and the vineyard will *be* rented out to other farmers who will give back to him the fruits in their seasons." ⁴²יֵשׁוּעַ, Yeshua said to them, "Did you never read in the Scriptures,

'A stone that the builders disallowed, it became *the* head of a corner. From

---

[a] תְּהִלִּים T'hiliym 8:3(2)

ADONAI this has come to pass, and it is wonderful in our eyes'?[a]

⁴³Because of this, I say to you that the Reign of God will be taken from you and given to a גוֹי, Goy, bringing forth its fruit; ⁴⁴and he who is falling on this stone will be broken. And on whomever it falls, it will crush him to pieces." ⁴⁵And the chief כֹּהֲנִים, Ko'haniym and the פְּרוּשִׁים, P'rushiym, having heard His analogies, knew that He spoke of them. ⁴⁶But looking to take hold of Him, they feared the crowds, since they were holding Him *in esteem* as a prophet.

22 ¹And יֵשׁוּעַ, Yeshua, answering, again spoke to them in analogies, saying, ²"The Reign of the Heavens was likened to a man—a king —who made marriage-feasts for his son, ³and he sent out his slaves to call those having been called to the marriage-feasts, but they were not willing to come.

⁴"Again he sent out other slaves, saying, 'Say to those who have been called, "Look! I have prepared my dinner. My oxen and the fattened *calves* have been killed, and all things ARE ready. Come to the marriage-feasts!"' ⁵But they, having disregarded IT, went away, one to his own field, and the other to his *own* business; ⁶and the remainder, having taken hold of his slaves, insulted and killed THEM.

⁷"And the king was angered, and having sent out his soldiers, he destroyed those murderers, and he set their city on fire. ⁸Then he said to his slaves, 'The marriage-feast indeed is ready, and those called were not worthy. ⁹Be going, then, on to the crossroads, and as many as you find, call to the marriage-feasts!' ¹⁰And those slaves, having gone out to the streets, gathered all whom they found—both bad and good—and the marriage-feast[b] was filled with those reclining *to eat.*

¹¹"And the king, *when he* had come in to view those reclining, saw there a man not clothed with *the* clothing of the marriage-feast. ¹²And he said to him, 'Friend, how were you *able to* come in here, not having *the* clothing of the marriage-feast?'—and he was speechless. ¹³Then the king said to the servants, 'Having bound his feet and hands,[c] throw *him* out to the outer darkness—in that place will be the weeping and the gnashing of the teeth; ¹⁴for many are called, but few chosen.'"

¹⁵At that time, the פְּרוּשִׁים, P'rushiym, having gone, took counsel *as to* how they might ensnare Him in *His* words, ¹⁶and they sent their disciples to Him with the Herodians, saying, "Teacher, we have known that you are true, and you teach the way of God in truth, and you are not caring about any*one's opinion*, for you do not look at the face of men. ¹⁷Tell us, then, what do you think? Is it permitted to give census-taxes to Cæsar, or not?"

¹⁸But יֵשׁוּעַ, Yeshua, having known their wickedness, said, "Why do you tempt Me, hypocrites? ¹⁹Show Me the census-tax-coin!" and they brought a denary to Him. ²⁰And he said to them, "Whose IS this image, and the inscription?" ²¹They said to Him, "Cæsar's." Then He said to them, "Return, therefore, the things of Cæsar to Cæsar, and the things of God to God." ²²And having heard, they marveled; and having left Him, they went away.

²³In that day, there came near to Him צַדּוּקִים, Tzaduqiym who were saying there is not a Rising Again *from the dead*. And they questioned Him, saying, ²⁴"Teacher! מֹשֶׁה, Mosheh said,

'If anyone dies not having children, his brother will marry his wife, and will raise up seed to his brother.'[d]

²⁵And there were seven brothers with us; and the first, having married, died; and not having seed, he left his wife to his brother. ²⁶Likewise also the second, and the third, to the seventh; ²⁷and last of all, the woman also died. ²⁸Therefore, in the Rising Again, of which of the seven will

---

[a] תְּהִלִּים *T'hiliym* 118:22ff
[b] "marriage-feast" or possibly "wedding hall"
[c] Some mss insert, "lift him up and"
[d] דְּבָרִים *D'variym* 25:5

Substance of the Torah.   מַתִּתְיָהוּ **Matit'yahu 23:13**

she be wife—for all had her?" ²⁹And יֵשׁוּעַ, Yeshua, answering, said to them, "You go astray, not knowing the Scriptures, nor the power of God! ³⁰For in the Rising Again, they do not marry, nor are they given in marriage, but are as Messengers of God in Heaven. ³¹And concerning the Rising Again from the dead, did you not read that which was spoken to you by God, saying,

³²אָנֹכִי אֱלֹהֵי אַבְרָהָם אֱלֹהֵי יִצְחָק וֵאלֹהֵי יַעֲקֹב
Anokhiy 'Elohei Av'raham, 'Elohei Yitz'chaq, vElohei Ya'aqov'?ᵃ

God is not a God of dead men, but of *the* living!" ³³And having heard *this*, the crowds were astonished at His teaching.

³⁴And having heard that He silenced the צַדּוּקִים, Tzaduqiym, the פְּרוּשִׁים, P'rushiym gathered together to Him, ³⁵and one of them, a תּוֹרָה, Torah-expert,ᵇ questioned Him—tempting Himᶜ—³⁶"Teacher, which IS the great command in the תּוֹרָה, Torah?"

³⁷And He said to him, "'YOU WILL LOVE ADONAI YOUR GOD WITH ALL YOUR HEART, AND WITH ALL YOUR SOUL,ᵈ and with all your understanding'—³⁸this is the great and first command. ³⁹And the second IS like to it: 'YOU WILL LOVE YOUR NEIGHBOR AS YOURSELF.'ᵉ ⁴⁰On these—the two commands—all the תּוֹרָה, Torah and the Prophets hang."

⁴¹And while the פְּרוּשִׁים, P'rushiym were gathered together, יֵשׁוּעַ, Yeshua *also* questioned them *back*, ⁴²saying, "What do you think concerning the Messiah? Of whom is He *the* son?" They said to Him, "Of דָּוִד, David." ⁴³He said to them, "How, then, does דָּוִד, David—in the רוּחַ, Ruach—call Him 'Master,' saying,

⁴⁴'ADONAI said to my Master, "Sit at my right hand, until I put Your enemies under Your feet"'ᶠ?

⁴⁵If, then, דָּוִד, David calls Him 'Master,' how is He his son?" ⁴⁶And no one was able to answer Him a word, nor from that day did anyone dare question Him anymore.

23 ¹At that time, יֵשׁוּעַ, Yeshua spoke to the crowds and to His disciples, ²saying, "The סוֹפְרִים, Sof'riym and the פְּרוּשִׁים, P'rushiym sat down on the seat of מֹשֶׁה, Mosheh. ³All, then—as much as they say to you—do and guard; but according to their actions, do not—for they say *the word of Mosheh*, but *then* do not *keep it themselves*. ⁴And they bind together loads, heavy and hard to bear, and lay *them* upon the shoulders of men, but they themselves are not willing to move them *even* with their finger. ⁵And all their actions, they do to be seen by men; for they make their תְּפִלִּין, t'filiyn broad, and *they* enlarge the כַּנְפוֹת, kan'fotᵍ of their garments. ⁶And they love the prime seating at the supper *table*, and the most important seats in the synagogues, ⁷and the greetings in the market-places, and to be called 'רַבִּי, Rabiy' by men.

⁸"But you—you are not *to* be called 'רַבִּי, Rabiy,' for One is your Teacher,ʰ and you are all brothers; ⁹and do not call ANY on the earth your 'Father,' for One is your Father, who is in the Heavens; ¹⁰nor are you *to* be called 'Leaders,' for your Leader is Oneⁱ—the Messiah. ¹¹And the greater of you will be your servant, ¹²and whoever exalts himself will be humbled, and whoever humbles himself will be exalted.

¹³אוֹי, Oy! to you, סוֹפְרִים, Sof'riym and פְּרוּשִׁים, P'rushiym—hypocrites!—because you shut up the Reign of the Heavens in front of men; for you do not go in, nor do you allow those going in to enter!ʲ

ᵃ שְׁמוֹת *Sh'mot* 3:6, "I am the God of Abraham, and the God of Isaac, and the God of Jacob"; cf. שְׁמוֹת *Sh'mot* 3:15-16
ᵇ "Torah-expert"—νομικός, nomikos
ᶜ Some mss insert, "and saying"
ᵈ דְּבָרִים *D'variym* 6:5
ᵉ וַיִּקְרָא *Vayiq'ra* 19:18
ᶠ תְּהִלִּים *T'hiliym* 110:1
ᵍ כַּנְפוֹת, kan'fot—see note at מַתִּתְיָהוּ *Matit'yahu* 9:20
ʰ "Teacher"—some mss say, "Leader: the Messiah"
ⁱ "your Leader is One"—some mss say, "One is your Leader"
ʲ Some mss continue with verse 14, "אוֹי, Oy! to you,

¹⁵"אוֹי, Oy! to you, סוֹפְרִים, Sof'riym and פְּרוּשִׁים, P'rushiym—hypocrites!—because you go around *on* the sea and the dry land to make one proselyte, and whenever it happens, you make him a son of גֵיהִנֹם, Geihinom twofold more than yourselves!

¹⁶"אוֹי, Oy! to you—blind guides!—who are saying, 'Whoever swears by the Temple, it is nothing, but whoever swears by the gold of the Temple is indebted *to his oath!*' ¹⁷Fools and Blind! For which IS greater: the gold, or the Temple that set the gold apart *as sacred?* ¹⁸And *you also say,* 'Whoever swears by the altar, it is nothing, but whoever swears by the gift that is upon it is indebted *to his oath.*' ¹⁹Blind men!ª For which IS greater: the gift, or the altar that is setting the gift apart *as sacred?* ²⁰He, therefore, who swore by the altar swears by it, and by all things on it; ²¹and he who swore by the Temple swears by it, and by Him who is dwelling in it; ²²and he who swore by the heaven swears by the throne of God, and by Him who is sitting upon it!

²³"אוֹי, Oy! to you, סוֹפְרִים, Sof'riym and פְּרוּשִׁים, P'rushiym—hypocrites!—because you give a tenth of the mint and the dill and the cumin, but neglected the weightier things of the תּוֹרָה, Torah: the judgment, and the *loving-*kindness, and the faithfulness! But it was necessary *for* YOU to do these, and those *lighter things also* not to neglect. ²⁴Blind guides! who are straining out the gnat, but are swallowing the camel!

²⁵"אוֹי, Oy! to you, סוֹפְרִים, Sof'riym and פְּרוּשִׁים, P'rushiym—hypocrites!—because you make the outside of the cup and the plate clean, but within they are full of property-rape and lack of self-control! ²⁶Blind פָּרוּשׁ, Parush! First cleanse the inside of the cupᵇ so that the outside of it may also be clean!

²⁷"אוֹי, Oy! to you, סוֹפְרִים, Sof'riym and פְּרוּשִׁים, P'rushiym—hypocrites!—because you are like whitewashed tombs, which indeed appear beautiful outwardly, but within are full of bones of dead men, and of all uncleanness! ²⁸So also you indeed appear righteous outwardly to men, but within, you are full of hypocrisy and misdeeds.

²⁹"אוֹי, Oy! to you, סוֹפְרִים, Sof'riym and פְּרוּשִׁים, P'rushiym—hypocrites!—because you build the tombs of the prophets and adorn the grave-monuments of the righteous ³⁰and say, 'If we had been *alive* in the days of our fathers, we would not have been sharers with them in *spilling* the blood of the prophets'—³¹therefore, you testify against yourselves that you are *the* sons of them who murdered the prophets. ³²And you—fill up, *then,* the measure of your fathers' *wrongdoing!* ³³Serpents! Brood of *venomous* snakes! How can you escape from the judgment of the גֵיהִנֹם, Geihinom?

³⁴"Because of this, look! I send to you prophets, and wise men, and סוֹפְרִים, sof'-riym—and *some* of them you will kill and crucify, and *some* of them you will flog in your synagogues and will pursue from city to city, ³⁵so that on you will come all the righteous blood being poured out on the earth, from the blood of הֶבֶל, Hevel the righteous, to the blood of זְכַרְיָה, Z'khar'yah son of בֶּרֶכְיָה, Berekh'yah, whom you murdered between the Temple *holy place* and the altar: ³⁶אָמֵן, amen, I say to you *that* all these things will come upon this generation.

³⁷"יְרוּשָׁלַיִם יְרוּשָׁלַיִם, Y'rushalayim, Y'rushalayim! *You* that are killing the prophets and stoning those sent to you—how often I wanted to gather your children together, as a hen gathers her chicks under the wings, yet you did not want *it.* ³⁸Look! your House is left deserted to you, ³⁹for I say to you: you will not see Me from

---

ª "Blind *men!*"—some mss say, "Fools and Blind!"

ᵇ Some mss insert, "and the plate"

now on until you say, 'BLESSED IS HE WHO IS COMING IN THE NAME OF ADONAI.'ᵃ"

24 ¹And יֵשׁוּעַ, Yeshua, having gone out from the Temple, went away; and His disciples came near to show Him the buildings of the Temple. ²And answering, He said to them, "Do you not see all these? אָמֵן, Amen, I say to you *that* there will not be left here a stone upon a stone that will not be thrown down."

³And when He was sitting on the Mountain of the Olives, the disciples came near to Him privately, saying, "Tell us—when will these *things* be? and what IS the sign of Your *coming* presence, and of the full end of the age?" ⁴And answering, יֵשׁוּעַ, Yeshua said to them, "Watch out that no one leads you astray, ⁵for many will come in My Name, saying, 'I am the Messiah,' and they will lead many astray, ⁶and you will begin to hear of wars, and reports of wars. See—be not troubled—for it is necessary forᵇ THESE to come to pass. But the end is not yet.

⁷"For גּוֹי, Goy will rise against גּוֹי, Goy, and kingdom against kingdom, and there will be faminesᶜ and earthquakes in various places, ⁸and all these ARE the beginning of labor pains. ⁹Then they will hand you over to oppression, and *they* will kill you, and you will be hated by all the גּוֹיִם, Goyim because of My Name, ¹⁰and then many will be stumbled, and they will hand over one another and will hate one another.

¹¹"And many false prophets will arise and will lead many astray, ¹²and because of the abounding of the misdeeds, the love of the many will become cold; ¹³but he who endured to the end—he will be saved. ¹⁴And this Good News of the Reign will be proclaimed in all the world for a testimony to all the גּוֹיִם, Goyim; and then will the end arrive.

¹⁵"Whenever, therefore, you see the ABOMINATION OF THE DESOLATIONᵈ (that was spoken of through דָּנִיֵּאל, Daniyel the prophet) standing in the holy place (whoever is reading, let him understand), ¹⁶then those in יְהוּדָה, Y'hudah—let them flee to the mountains; ¹⁷he on the house-top—let him not come down to take up anything out of his house; ¹⁸and he in the field—let him not turn back to take his coat. ¹⁹And אוֹי, oy! to those pregnant *mothers*, and to those nursing in those days. ²⁰But pray that your flight may not be in winter, nor on a שַׁבָּת, Shabat, ²¹for there will be great oppression then, such as was not from the beginning of the world until now—no, nor may *ever* be again. ²²And if those days were not shortened, no flesh would have been saved; but because of The Chosen will those days be shortened.

²³"Then if anyone says to you, 'Look! Here IS the Messiah!' or 'Here *He* is!'—do not believe; ²⁴for there will arise false messiahs and false prophets, and they will give great signs and wonders, so as to lead *people* astray—if possible, even The Chosen. ²⁵Look! I told you beforehand. ²⁶If, therefore, they say to you, 'Look! He is in the desert,' do not go out *there*; or 'Look! *We saw Him* in the inner rooms,' do not believe; ²⁷for as the lightning comes forth from the east and appears to the west, so will be the *coming* presence of the Son of Man. ²⁸Wherever the carcass is, there will the eaglesᵉ be gathered together.

²⁹"And immediately after the oppression of those days, THE SUN WILL BE DARKENED, AND THE MOON WILL NOT GIVE HER LIGHT,ᶠ AND THE STARS WILL FALLᵍ from the heaven, and the powers of the heavens will be shaken; ³⁰and then the sign of the Son of Man will appear in the heaven; and then all the nations of the earth will beat the breast *in grief*, and they will see the SON

ᵃ תְּהִלִּים *T'hiliym* 118:26
ᵇ Some mss insert, "all"
ᶜ Some mss insert, "and pestilences"
ᵈ דָּנִיֵּאל *Daniyel* 9:27; 11:31; 12:11
ᵉ "eagles" or "vultures"
ᶠ יְשַׁעְיָהוּ *Y'sha'yahu* 13:10, 24:23; יְחֶזְקֵאל *Y'chez'qel* 32:7; יוֹאֵל *Yoel* 3:4, 4:15ff (2:31, 3:15ff); עָמוֹס *Amos* 5:20, 8:9; צְפַנְיָה *Tz'fan'yah* 1:15
ᵍ יְשַׁעְיָהוּ *Y'sha'yahu* 34:4

OF MAN COMING ON THE CLOUDS OF THE HEAVEN,[a] with power and much glory; [31]and He will send His Messengers with A GREAT שׁוֹפָר, SHOFAR, and THEY WILL GATHER TOGETHER[b] His Chosen from the four winds—from *one of* the ends of the heavens to *the other of* its ends.

[32]"Now from the fig-tree, learn this analogy: when its branch has already become tender, and it puts out the leaves, you know that summer IS near. [33]So also *with* you: when you see all these *things*, you know that it is near—at the doors. [34]אָמֵן, Amen, I say to you that this generation will not pass away until all these *things* come to pass. [35]The heaven and the earth will pass away, but My words will not pass away.

[36]"And concerning that day and hour, no one has known—not even the Messengers of the heavens, nor the Son[c]— except the Father only. [37]For as *were* the days of נֹחַ, Noach, so will be the *coming* presence of the Son of Man. [38]Indeed, as they were in those days before the Flood —eating and drinking, marrying and giving in marriage, until the day *that* נֹחַ, Noach entered into the ark, [39]and they did not understand until the Flood came and took everything away—so will be the *coming* presence of the Son of Man. [40]Then two men will be in the field—one is received, and one is left. [41]Two women will be grinding in the mill—one is received, and one is left. [42]Therefore, *stay* awake, because you have not known in what day[d] your Master will come. [43]But understand this: that if the householder had known during what *night*-watch the thief would come, he would have *stayed* awake and not allowed his house to be broken through. [44]Because of this, you also, become ready—because in whatever time you do not think *He will arrive*, the Son of Man comes.

[45]"Who, then, is the slave—faithful and wise—whom the master set over his household, to give them *all* the nourishment in season? [46]Happy *is* that slave, whom his master, having come, finds so doing. [47]אָמֵן, Amen, I say to you that *the master* will set him over all his possessions. [48]But if that evil slave says in his heart, 'My master delays,' [49]and begins to beat his fellow-slaves, and eats and drinks with the drunkards, [50]the master of that slave will arrive in a day when he does not expect, and in a time of which he does not know, [51]and will cut him in pieces, and will put his portion with the hypocrites. In that place will be the weeping and the gnashing of the teeth.

25 [1]"Then the Reign of the Heavens will be likened to ten virgins, who, having taken their *oil*-lamps, went out to meet the bridegroom; [2]and five of them were foolish, and five were prudent. [3]For the foolish, having taken their lamps, did not take with themselves *any* oil; [4]but the prudent took oil in containers with their lamps. [5]Now when the bridegroom *was* delaying *in coming*, they all became sleepy, and were sleeping. [6]And in the middle of the night, a cry was made: 'Look! The bridegroom! Go out to meet him!' [7]Then all those virgins awoke and trimmed their lamps. [8]And the foolish said to the prudent, 'Give us *some* of your oil, because our lamps are going out!' [9]But the prudent answered, saying, '*No*, otherwise there may not be enough for *both* us and you. Go instead to those selling *oil*, and buy *some* for yourselves.' [10]And while they were going away to buy, the bridegroom came, and those *who were* ready went in with him to the marriage-feasts, and the door was shut. [11]But afterwards, the rest of the virgins also came, saying, 'Sir! Sir! Open *up* to us!' [12]and he, answering, said, 'אָמֵן, Amen, I say to you: I have not known you.' [13]Therefore, *stay* awake, for you have not known the day nor the time.[e]

---

[a] דָּנִיֵּאל *Daniyel* 7:13
[b] שְׁמוֹת *Sh'mot* 19:16; דְּבָרִים *D'variym* 30:4; יְשַׁעְיָהוּ *Y'sha'yahu* 27:13; זְכַרְיָה *Z'khar'yah* 9:14
[c] Some mss omit, "nor the Son"; cf. Mark 13:32
[d] "day"—some mss say, "time"
[e] Some mss insert, "in which the Son of Man comes"

The sheep and the goats. מַתִּתְיָהוּ **Matit'yahu 25:40**

¹⁴"For *the Reign of the Heavens is* as a man going abroad, *who* called his own slaves and handed his possessions over to them. ¹⁵And to one he gave five *decades' worth of* wages;ᵃ and to another, two; and to another, one—to each according to his individual ability. And *he* went abroad immediately. ¹⁶He who received the five *decades' worth of* wages, having gone, worked with them and gained another five. ¹⁷Likewise, he who RECEIVED the two gained another two. ¹⁸But he who received the one, having gone away, dug *a hole* in the earth and hid his master's money.

¹⁹"And after a long time, the master of those slaves came and settled accounts with them. ²⁰And he who received the five *decades' worth of* wages, having come, brought another five *decades' worth of* wages, saying, 'Sir, you handed five *decades' worth of* wages over to me. Look! I gained another five *decades' worth of* wages!'ᵇ ²¹His master said to him, 'Well done, slave, good and faithful! You were faithful over a few things, *so now* I will set you over many things. Enter into the joy of your master!'

²²"He also who *received* the two *decades' worth of* wages, having come, said, 'Sir, you handed over to me two *decades' worth of* wages. Look! I gained another two *decades' worth of* wages!' ²³His master said to him, 'Well done, slave, good and faithful! You were faithful over a few things, *so now* I will set you over many things. Enter into the joy of your master!'

²⁴"And he also who had received the one *decade's* wage, having come, said, 'Sir, I know you, that you are a hard man, reaping where you did not sow, and gathering from where you did not scatter. ²⁵And having been afraid, having gone away, I hid your *one decade's* wage in the earth. Look! You have what *is* your own!' ²⁶And, answering, his master said to him, 'Evil slave, and lazy! You knew that I reap where I did not sow, and *that* I gather where I did not scatter! ²⁷It was necessary, then, *for* you to put my money with the money-lenders; and, having come, I *would* have received *what is* my own with interest! ²⁸Therefore, take the wage from him *who has the one decade's worth,* and give *it* to him *who is* having the ten *decades' worth of* wages! ²⁹For to everyone *who is* having, *more* will be given, and he will have overabundance. But he who is not having, even that which he has will be taken from him. ³⁰And throw out the unprofitable slave into the outer darkness. In that place will be the weeping and the gnashing of the teeth.'

³¹"And whenever the Son of Man comes in His glory, and all theᶜ Messengers with Him, then He will sit upon a throne of His glory; ³²and gathered together in front of Him will be all the world-ethnicities, and He will separate them from one another, as the shepherd separates the sheep from the goats; ³³and He will set the sheep on His right hand, and the goats on the left.

³⁴"Then the King will say to those on his right hand, 'Come, you, the blessed of My Father, inherit the Reign that has been prepared for you from the foundation of the world; ³⁵for I hungered, and you gave Me *food* to eat; I thirsted, and you gave Me *something* to drink; I was a stranger, and you received Me; ³⁶naked, and you put *clothes* around Me; I was infirmed, and you looked after Me; I was in prison, and you came to *visit* Me.'

³⁷"Then the righteous will answer Him, saying, 'Master, when did we see You hungering, and we nourished *You?* or thirsting, and we gave *You something* to drink? ³⁸And when did we see You a stranger, and we received *You?* or naked, and we put *clothes* around *You?* ³⁹And when did we see You infirmed, or in prison, and we came to You?' ⁴⁰And the King, answering, will say to them, 'אָמֵן, Amen, I say to you:

ᵃ "five *decades' worth of* wages"—lit. "five talents"; also in verses 16 and 20 (and similar in verses 22, 24, and 25). Different sources cite different monetary values for the Greek talent; ten years' laborer's wages is a conservative estimate.

ᵇ Some mss insert, "besides them"; also in vs 22

ᶜ Some mss insert, "holy"

in as much as you did IT to one of these, my brothers—the least—you did IT to Me.'

⁴¹"Then He will say also to those on the left hand, 'Go *away* from Me—*you*, the cursed—to the age-enduring fire that has been prepared for the Accuser and his messengers! ⁴²For I hungered, and you gave Me no*thing* to eat; I thirsted, and you gave Me no*thing* to drink; ⁴³I was a stranger, and you did not receive Me; naked, and you put no*thing* around Me; infirmed, and in prison, and you did not look after Me.' ⁴⁴Then they will answer also, saying, 'Master, when did we see You hungering, or thirsting, or a stranger, or naked, or infirmed, or in prison, and we did not attend to You?' ⁴⁵Then will He answer them, saying, 'אָמֵן, Amen, I say to you: in as much as you did IT not to one of these —the least—you did IT not to Me.' ⁴⁶And these will go away to punishment age-enduring; but the righteous, to life age-enduring."

26

¹And it came to pass, when יֵשׁוּעַ, Yeshua finished all these words, He said to His disciples, ²"You have known that after two days, the פֶּסַח, Pesach comes, and the Son of Man will be handed over to be crucified."

³At that time the chief כֹּהֲנִים, Ko'haniym[a] and the זְקֵנִים, Z'qeniym of the people were gathered together to the court of the כֹּהֵן הַגָּדוֹל, Kohen HaGadol, who was called קַיָּפָא, Qayafa; ⁴and they consulted together, that they might take *hold of* יֵשׁוּעַ, Yeshua by underhandedness, and kill HIM. ⁵But they said, "Not during the Feast, so that there will not be a riot among the people."

⁶And while יֵשׁוּעַ, Yeshua was in בֵּית־עַנְיָה, Beit-An'yah in the house of שִׁמְעוֹן, Shim'on the Leper, ⁷there came to Him a woman having an alabaster box of ointment— very expensive—and she poured *the ointment* on His head as He was reclining (at mealtime). ⁸And having seen THIS, the disciples were much displeased, saying, "For what purpose IS this waste? ⁹for this could have been sold for much, and given to the poor." ¹⁰And יֵשׁוּעַ, Yeshua, having known *what they were saying*, said to them, "Why do you give trouble to the woman? Indeed, she did a beautiful act for Me; ¹¹for the poor you *will* always have with you, but you *will* not always have Me. ¹²For she, having put this ointment on My body— she did IT for My burial. ¹³אָמֵן, Amen, I say to you, wherever this Good News is proclaimed in the whole world, what this ONE did will also be spoken of, for a memorial of her."

¹⁴Then one of the Twelve, *the one* who is called יְהוּדָה אִישׁ־קְרִיּוֹת, Y'hudah Iysh-Q'riyot, having gone to the chief כֹּהֲנִים, Ko'haniym, said, ¹⁵"What are you willing to give me, and *in exchange*, I will hand Him over to you?" And they weighed out to him thirty silver pieces, ¹⁶and from that time *on*, he was looking for an opportune moment to hand Him over.

¹⁷ Now, before[b] the first DAY of הַמַּצּוֹת, HaMatzot, the disciples came near to יֵשׁוּעַ, Yeshua, saying, "Where do you want THAT we should prepare for You to eat the פֶּסַח, Pesach?" ¹⁸And He said, "Go away to the city, to a certain person, and say to him, 'The Teacher says, "My time is near, *and I want to* keep the פֶּסַח, Pesach with you, *and* with my disciples."'" ¹⁹And the disciples did as יֵשׁוּעַ, Yeshua appointed them, and prepared the פֶּסַח, Pesach.

²⁰And when evening had come, He was reclining (at mealtime) with the Twelve; ²¹and while they were eating, He said, "אָמֵן, Amen, I say to you that one of you will hand Me over *in betrayal*." ²²And being grieved exceedingly, they began to say to Him, each one, "Is it I, Master?" ²³And He, answering, said, "He who dipped the hand in the dish with Me—he will hand Me over. ²⁴The Son of Man does indeed go, as it has been written regarding Him.

---

[a] Some mss insert, "and the סוֹפְרִים, Sof'riym"

[b] "before"—Young's says, "on"; cf. Mark 14:12, Luke 22:7, and וַיִּקְרָא *Vayiq'ra* 23:5-6

Agony in the garden.

But אוֹי, oy! to that man through whom the Son of Man is handed over! It would have been better for him if that man had not been born!" ²⁵And יְהוּדָה, Y'hudah (he who handed Him over) answering, said, "Is it I, רַבִּי, Rabiy?" *Yeshua* said to him, "*As you have said.*"

²⁶And as they were eating, יֵשׁוּעַ, Yeshua, having taken *some matzah* bread and having blessed *it*, broke *it* and, giving *it* to the disciples, said, "Take, eat—this is My body."

²⁷And having taken the cup and having given thanks, He gave to them, saying, "Drink of it, all *of you*, ²⁸for this is My blood of the בְּרִית, B'riyt[a] that for many is being poured out—for release from sins. ²⁹And I say to you *that* I will not drink this fruit of the vine from now on until that Day when I drink it with you new in the Reign of My Father."

³⁰And having sung a הַלֵּל, Halel, they went out to the Mountain of the Olives. ³¹Then יֵשׁוּעַ, Yeshua said to them, "You will all be stumbled over Me this night, for it has been written,

'I will strike the shepherd, and the sheep of the flock will be scattered abroad.'[b]

³²But after My having risen *from the dead*, I will go before you to the גָּלִיל, Galiyl."

³³And כֵּיפָא, Keifa,[c] answering, said to Him, "Even if everyone is stumbled over You, I will never be stumbled!" ³⁴יֵשׁוּעַ, Yeshua said to him, "אָמֵן, Amen, I say to you that this night, before *the* rooster-crowing, three times you will deny Me." ³⁵כֵּיפָא, Keifa said to Him, "Even if it is necessary for me to die with You, I will not deny you!" All the disciples also said likewise.

³⁶Then יֵשׁוּעַ, Yeshua came with them to a place called גַּת־שְׁמָנֶה, Gat-Sh'menah and said to the disciples, "Sit here while, having gone away, I will pray over there." ³⁷And having taken כֵּיפָא, Keifa and the two sons of זַבְדִּי, Zav'diy, He began to be sorrowful, and to be very heavy-*hearted*. ³⁸Then He said to them, "Exceedingly sorrowful is My soul—to death. Remain here and *stay* awake with Me." ³⁹And having gone forward a little, He fell on His face, praying and saying, "My Father! If it is possible, let this cup pass from Me! Nevertheless, not as I will, but as You *will*."

⁴⁰And He came to the disciples and found them sleeping. And He said to כֵּיפָא, Keifa, "So! You were not able to *stay* awake with Me *even for* one hour! ⁴¹*Stay* awake and pray, so that you do not enter into temptation: the רוּחַ, ruach, indeed, is willing, but the flesh *is* weak." ⁴²Again, a second time, having gone away, He prayed, saying, "My Father, if this cannot pass[d] unless I drink it—Your will be done!"

⁴³And again having come, He found them sleeping, for their eyes were heavy. ⁴⁴And having left them again—having gone away—He prayed a third time, saying the same word again.

⁴⁵Then He came *back* to the disciples and said to them, "Sleep from now on, and rest! Look! the hour has come near, and the Son of Man is handed over to the hands of sinners. ⁴⁶Rise, let us go! Look! he who is handing Me over *in betrayal* has come near."

⁴⁷And while He was still speaking, look! יְהוּדָה, Y'hudah (one of the Twelve) came, and with him a large crowd, with swords and sticks, from the chief כֹּהֲנִים, Ko'haniym and זְקֵנִים, Z'qeniym of the people. ⁴⁸And he who handed Him over gave them a sign, saying, "Whomever I kiss is He: take hold of Him." ⁴⁹And immediately having come to יֵשׁוּעַ, Yeshua, he said, "שָׁלוֹם לְךָ רַבִּי, Shalom l'kha,[e] Rabiy," and kissed Him. ⁵⁰And יֵשׁוּעַ, Yeshua said to him, "Friend, what have you come for?" Then, having come near, they laid hands on יֵשׁוּעַ, Yeshua and took hold of Him.

---

[a] Some mss insert, "הַחֲדָשָׁה, Ha'Chadashah"; cf. Mark 14:24, Luke 22:20, and 1 Corinthians 11:25
[b] זְכַרְיָה Z'khar'yah 13:7
[c] כֵּיפָא, Keifa—Gk: Πέτρος, Petros; see יוֹחָנָן Yn. 1:42, also throughout the chapter
[d] "if this cannot pass"—some mss say, "if this cup cannot pass away from Me"
[e] "שָׁלוֹם לְךָ, Shalom l'kha"—"Peace to you"; also see glossary entry for *shalom*

מַתִּתְיָהוּ Matit'yahu 26:51 *Messiah denied by Keifa.*

⁵¹And look! one of those with יֵשׁוּעַ, Yeshua, having stretched out the hand, drew his sword; and having struck the slave of the כֹּהֵן הַגָּדוֹל, Kohen HaGadol, he took off his ear! ⁵²Then יֵשׁוּעַ, Yeshua said to him, "Return your sword to its place, for all who take up the sword will be destroyed by the sword. ⁵³Do you think that I am not able to call upon My Father, and He will *even* now place beside Me more than twelve legions of Messengers? ⁵⁴How *else*, then, may the Scriptures be fulfilled that *say* it must happen this way?" ⁵⁵In that moment, יֵשׁוּעַ, Yeshua said to the crowd, "As *if you were coming* against a robber, you come out with swords and sticks to take Me! Daily I sat[a] in the Temple, teaching, yet you did not take hold of Me *then*! ⁵⁶But all this has come to pass, so that the Scriptures of the prophets might be fulfilled." Then all the disciples, having left Him, fled.

⁵⁷And those taking hold of יֵשׁוּעַ, Yeshua led *Him* away to קַיָפָא, Qayafa, the כֹּהֵן הַגָּדוֹל, Kohen HaGadol, where the סוֹפְרִים, Sof'riym and the זְקֵנִים, Z'qeniym were gathered together. ⁵⁸And כֵּיפָא, Keifa was following Him from afar to the courtyard of the כֹּהֵן הַגָּדוֹל, Kohen HaGadol, and having entered within, he was sitting with the attendants to see the outcome.

⁵⁹And the chief כֹּהֲנִים, Ko'haniym[b] and all the Sanhedrin were seeking false testimony against יֵשׁוּעַ, Yeshua so that they might put Him to death, ⁶⁰but they did not find *any, even* after many false witnesses had come near.[c] And at last, two[d] (having come near) ⁶¹said, "This *Yeshua* said, 'I am able to throw down the Temple of God, and after three days, to build it *back up!*'"

⁶²And having stood up, the כֹּהֵן הַגָּדוֹל, Kohen HaGadol said to Him, "You answer nothing!? What do these *people* testify against you?" ⁶³But יֵשׁוּעַ, Yeshua was silent. And the כֹּהֵן הַגָּדוֹל, Kohen HaGadol, answering, said to Him, "I charge you *under oath* by the living God, that you should say to us if you are the Messiah—the Son of God!" ⁶⁴יֵשׁוּעַ, Yeshua said to him, "*As* you have said. Nevertheless, I say to you: from now on you will see THE SON OF MAN SITTING AT THE RIGHT HAND OF THE POWER,[e] and COMING UPON THE CLOUDS OF THE HEAVEN."[f] ⁶⁵Then the כֹּהֵן הַגָּדוֹל, Kohen HaGadol tore his garments, saying, "He has spoken evil! What need have we of further witnesses? Look! now you *have* heard the evil-speaking! ⁶⁶What do you think?" And they, answering, said, "He is worthy of death." ⁶⁷Then they spit in His face and punched Him, and others slapped *Him*, ⁶⁸saying, "Prophesy to us, O Messiah: who is he that struck You?"

⁶⁹Now, כֵּיפָא, Keifa was sitting outside in the courtyard, and there came near to him a certain slave-girl, saying, "And you were with יֵשׁוּעַ הַגְּלִילִי, Yeshua HaGaliyliy!" ⁷⁰And he denied *it* in front of *them* all, saying, "I do not know *of* what you speak." ⁷¹And *when* he had gone out to the entrance, another female saw him, and said to those there, "This one was with יֵשׁוּעַ הַנָּצְרָתִי, Yeshua HaNatz'ratiy"; ⁷²and again he denied *it* with an oath—"I have not known the man." ⁷³And after a little *while*, those standing near, having come, said to כֵּיפָא, Keifa, "Truly you also are *one* of them, for even your *manner of* speech makes you evident." ⁷⁴Then he began to call down curses on himself, and to swear, "I have not known the man!" And immediately a rooster crowed, ⁷⁵and כֵּיפָא, Keifa remembered the spoken word of יֵשׁוּעַ, Yeshua, *when* He said, "Before *the* rooster-crowing, three times you will deny Me." And having gone outside, he wept bitterly.

27 ¹And when morning had come, all the chief כֹּהֲנִים, Ko'haniym and the זְקֵנִים, Z'qeniym of the people took counsel against יֵשׁוּעַ, Yeshua,

---

[a] Some mss insert, "with you"
[b] Some mss insert, "and the זְקֵנִים, Z'qeniym"
[c] Some mss insert, "they did not find *any*"
[d] Some mss insert, "false witnesses"
[e] תְּהִלִּים T'hiliym 110:1
[f] דָּנִיֵּאל Daniyel 7:13

so as to put Him to death. ²And having bound Him, they led *Him* away, and handed Him over to[a] Pilate, the governor.

³Then יְהוּדָה, Y'hudah—he who handed Him over—having seen that He was condemned, *and* having regretted *what had happened*, brought back the thirty silver pieces to the chief כֹּהֲנִים, Ko'haniym and זְקֵנִים, Z'qeniym, saying, ⁴"I *have* sinned, having handed over innocent blood!" And they said, "What *is that* to us? You will see *to that!*" ⁵And having thrown down the silver pieces into the Temple, he went away; and having gone away, he strangled himself.

⁶And the chief כֹּהֲנִים, Ko'haniym, having taken the silver pieces, said, "It is not permitted to put them into the treasury, since it is the price of blood"; ⁷and having taken counsel, they bought with them the field of the potter—for the burial of strangers. ⁸Therefore, that field is called "Field of Blood" to this day. ⁹Then *it* was fulfilled—that *which* was spoken through יִרְמְיָהוּ, Yir'm'yahu the prophet, saying, "AND I TOOK THE THIRTY SILVER PIECES—THE PRICE OF HIM WHO HAD BEEN PRICED, whom they of the sons of יִשְׂרָאֵל, Yis'rael priced—¹⁰AND GAVE THEM FOR the field of THE POTTER, as ADONAI appointed to me."[b]

¹¹And יֵשׁוּעַ, Yeshua stood before the governor, and the governor questioned Him, saying, "Are you the king of the יְהוּדִים, Y'hudiym?" And יֵשׁוּעַ, Yeshua said, "*As* you say." ¹²But in His being accused by the chief כֹּהֲנִים, Ko'haniym and זְקֵנִים, Z'qeniym, He did not answer anything. ¹³Then Pilate said to Him, "Do you not hear how many things they testify against You?" ¹⁴And He did not answer him, not even to one word *of accusation*, so that the governor marveled greatly.

¹⁵And at the Feast, the governor had been accustomed to releasing one to the crowd—a prisoner, whom they wanted —¹⁶and they had then a notorious prisoner, called בַּר-אַבָּא, Bar-Aba. ¹⁷Therefore, when they had gathered together, Pilate said to them, "Whom do you want me to release to you? בַּר-אַבָּא, Bar-Aba or יֵשׁוּעַ, Yeshua, who is called Messiah?" ¹⁸(for he had known that *it was* because of envy *that* they had handed Him over).

¹⁹And as he was sitting on the judgment seat, his wife sent *a message* to him, saying, "*Have* nothing to *do between* you and that righteous one, for I suffered many things today in a dream because of Him." ²⁰But the chief כֹּהֲנִים, Ko'haniym and the זְקֵנִים, Z'qeniym persuaded the crowds that they should request for themselves בַּר-אַבָּא, Bar-Aba, and should destroy יֵשׁוּעַ, Yeshua.

²¹And the governor, answering, said to them, "Which of the two do you want me *to* release to you?" And they said, "בַּר-אַבָּא, Bar-Aba!" ²²Pilate said to them, "What, then, will I do with יֵשׁוּעַ, Yeshua, who is called Messiah?" They all said, "Let *him* be crucified!" ²³And he said, "Why? What evil did He do?" And they were shouting *all* the more, saying, "Let *him* be crucified!" ²⁴And Pilate (having seen that it benefited nothing, but rather made a riot), having taken water, washed *his* hands in front of the crowd, saying, "I am innocent of the blood of this[c] one; you—you will see." ²⁵And all the people, answering, said, "His blood IS upon us, and upon our children!" ²⁶Then he released בַּר-אַבָּא, Bar-Aba to them, and having flogged יֵשׁוּעַ, Yeshua, he handed HIM over, so that He would be crucified.

²⁷Then the soldiers of the governor, having taken יֵשׁוּעַ, Yeshua to the Prætorium,[d] gathered the whole battalion *of soldiers* to Him. ²⁸And having stripped Him *of his clothes*, they put a crimson robe around Him; ²⁹and having braided a crown out of thorns, they put IT on His head, and a reed *staff* in His right hand; and having kneeled before Him, they were mocking Him, saying, "Hail, the king of the Jews!"

---

[a] Some mss insert, "Pontius"
[b] זְכַרְיָה Z'khar'yah 11:13; cf. יִרְמְיָהוּ Yir'm'yahu 19:1-13, 32:6-9
[c] Some mss insert, "righteous"
[d] "Prætorium"—the governor's headquarters

מַתִּתְיָהוּ Matit'yahu 27:30 — The crucifixion.

30 And having spit on Him, they took the reed *staff* and were striking *Him* on His head. 31 And when they had mocked Him, they stripped Him *of* the robe, and put His own clothes on Him, and led Him away to crucify HIM.

32 And coming out, they found a man—a Cyrenian by *the* name *of* שִׁמְעוֹן, Shim'on. They compelled him, so that he would take up His *execution* stake. 33 And having come to a place called גֻּלְגֻּלְתָּא, Gal'gal'ta (that is *to* say, "Place of a Skull"), 34 they gave Him wine[a] mixed with gall to drink; but having tasted *it*, He would not drink.

35 And having crucified Him, they divided *up* His clothes *by* casting a lot;[b] 36 and sitting down, they were watching Him there; 37 and they put up over His head His accusation, written, "This is יֵשׁוּעַ, Yeshua, the king of the Jews."

38 Then two robbers were crucified with Him—one on the right hand, and one on the left—39 and those passing by *there* were speaking evil of Him, wagging their heads 40 and saying, "You that are throwing down the Temple and *re*building IT in three days: save yourself! If you are *the* Son of God, come down from the stake!" 41 Likewise also the chief כֹּהֲנִים, Ko'haniym, mocking *Him* with the סוֹפְרִים, Sof'riym and זְקֵנִים, Z'qeniym, said, 42 "He saved others, *but* he is not able to save himself! He[c] is *the* King of יִשְׂרָאֵל, Yis'rael! Let him come down now from the stake, and we will believe in him! 43 He has trusted on God—LET HIM NOW DELIVER HIM[d] (if He wants him), because he said, 'I am *the* Son of God!'" 44 And with the same *words* also, the robbers who were crucified with Him were denouncing Him.

45 And from the sixth hour,[e] darkness came over all the Land until the ninth hour; 46 and about the ninth hour, יֵשׁוּעַ, Yeshua cried out with a loud voice, saying, "אֵלִי אֵלִי לָמָה עֲזַבְתָּנִי, Eliy! Eliy! Lamah 'azav'taniy?"[f]—that is, "MY GOD! MY GOD! WHY DID YOU ABANDON ME?" 47 And certain *ones* of those standing there, having heard, said, "He calls אֵלִיָּהוּ, Eliyahu!" 48 And immediately, one of them—having run and having taken a sponge, having filled IT with *wine* vinegar and having put IT on a reed—was giving *it to* Him to drink, 49 but the rest said, "Leave *him* alone; let us see if אֵלִיָּהוּ, Eliyahu comes to save him."

50 And יֵשׁוּעַ, Yeshua, having shouted again with a loud voice, yielded the רוּחַ, ruach. 51 And look! the curtain of the Temple was split in two—from top to bottom—and the earth quaked, and the rocks were split, 52 and the tombs were opened, and many bodies of the קְדוֹשִׁים, Q'doshiym who had fallen asleep arose *from the dead* 53 (and having come forth out of the tombs after His rising, they went into the Holy City and appeared to many). 54 And the centurion and those watching יֵשׁוּעַ, Yeshua with him, having seen the earthquake and the things that were done, were exceedingly afraid, saying, "Truly, this was God's Son."

55 And there were many women there looking *on* from afar, who followed יֵשׁוּעַ, Yeshua from the גָּלִיל, Galiyl, attending to Him, 56 among whom was מִרְיָם הַמַּגְדָּלִית, Mir'yam HaMag'daliyt, and מִרְיָם, Mir'yam the mother of יַעֲקֹב, Ya'aqov and of יוֹסֵף, Yosef, and the mother of the sons of זַבְדִּי, Zav'diy.

57 And when evening had come, there came a rich man from הָרָמָתַיִם, HaRamatayim named יוֹסֵף, Yosef, who himself also had become a disciple to יֵשׁוּעַ, Yeshua. 58 Having gone near to Pilate, he asked for the body of יֵשׁוּעַ, Yeshua. Then Pilate commanded *it* to be given *to* Yosef. 59 And having taken the body, יוֹסֵף, Yosef wrapped it in clean linen, 60 and *he* laid it in his new

---

[a] "wine"—some mss say, "sour wine" or "vinegar"
[b] Some mss insert, "that it might be fulfilled—that which was spoken by the prophet, 'They divided my clothes to themselves, and over my garment they cast a lot.'" תְּהִלִּים T'hiliym 22:19(18)
[c] "he"—some mss say, "If he"
[d] תְּהִלִּים T'hiliym 22:9(8)
[e] "the sixth hour"—six hours after dawn, i.e., noon
[f] תְּהִלִּים T'hiliym 22:2(1), though the Greek may be rendering Aramaic

The rising again. מַתִּתְיָהוּ **Matit'yahu 28:20**

tomb that he had cut in the rock. And having rolled a large stone to *cover* the door of the tomb, he went away; ⁶¹and מִרְיָם הַמַּגְדָּלִית, Mir'yam HaMag'daliyt and the other מִרְיָם, Mir'yam were there, sitting opposite the tomb.

⁶²And on the next day that is after the Preparation *Day,* the chief כֹּהֲנִים, Ko'haniym, and the פְּרוּשִׁים, P'rushiym were gathered together to Pilate, ⁶³saying, "Sir, we have remembered that that deceiver said while *He was* still alive, 'After three days, I will rise.' ⁶⁴Command, then, the tomb to be made secure until the third day; otherwise his disciples, having come,ᵃ might steal him away and say to the people, 'He rose from the dead!' and the last deceit will be worse than the first!" ⁶⁵Pilate said to them, "You have a guard—go away *and* make *it as* secure as you know how." ⁶⁶And they, having gone, made the tomb secure, having sealed the stone, together with *posting* the guard.

28 ¹Now afterᵇ the שַׁבָּתוֹת, Shabatot, at the dawn, toward the first of the week,ᶜ מִרְיָם הַמַּגְדָּלִית, Mir'yam HaMag'daliyt and the other מִרְיָם, Mir'yam came to see the tomb, ²and look! there came a massive earthquake! for a Messenger of ADONAI *was* having come down out of Heaven; and having come, *he* rolled away the stoneᵈ and was sitting on it; ³and his appearance was like lightning, and his clothing white as snow; ⁴and the guards shook from the fear of him, and they became as dead men.

⁵So, answering, the Messenger said to the women, "Fear not! for I have known that you *are* looking for יֵשׁוּעַ, Yeshua, who has been crucified. ⁶He is not here; for He rose, as He said. Come! See the place where Heᵉ was lying *down*; ⁷and having gone quickly, say to His disciples that He rose from the dead; and look! He goes be-

fore you to the גָּלִיל, Galiyl. There you will see Him. Look! I have told you." ⁸And having gone quickly from the tomb, with fear and great joy, they ran to tell His disciples.

⁹Andᶠ look! יֵשׁוּעַ, Yeshua met them, saying, "שָׁלוֹם, Shalom!"ᵍ And having come near, they took hold of His feet and bowed *down* to Him. ¹⁰Then יֵשׁוּעַ, Yeshua said to them, "Fear not. Go *and* declare to My brothers that they should go to the גָּלִיל, Galiyl, and they will see Me there."

¹¹And while they were going on, look! certain *ones* of the guard, having come to the city, declared to the chief כֹּהֲנִים, Ko'haniym all the things that happened. ¹²And having been gathered together with the זְקֵנִים, Z'qeniym—having also taken counsel—they gave much money to the soldiers, ¹³saying, "Say that his disciples, having come by night, stole him—we being asleep. ¹⁴And if this is heard by the governor, we will persuade him and keep you free from anxiety." ¹⁵And having received the money, they did as they were taught, and this word was spread abroad among the יְהוּדִים, Y'hudiym to this very day.

¹⁶And the eleven disciples went to the גָּלִיל, Galiyl, to the mountain where יֵשׁוּעַ, Yeshua appointed *for* them *to go*; ¹⁷and having seen Him, they bowed *in worship,* but some wavered *in their belief.*

¹⁸And having come near, יֵשׁוּעַ, Yeshua spoke to them, saying, "All authority in Heaven and on earth was given to Me. ¹⁹Having gone, then, disciple all *of* the world-ethnicities (immersing them—to the Name of the Father, and of the Son, and of the רוּחַ הַקֹּדֶשׁ, Ruach HaQodesh), ²⁰teaching them to guard everything, whatever I commanded you. And look! I am with you all the days—until the full end of the age!"ʰ

ᵃ Some mss insert, "by night"
ᵇ "after"—Young's says, "on the eve of"
ᶜ "week"—lit. σαββάτων, sabbaton, that is, שַׁבָּתוֹת, shabatot; Young's says, "sabbaths"
ᵈ Some mss insert, "from the door"
ᵉ "He"—some mss say, "the Master"

ᶠ Some mss insert, "as they were going to tell His disciples, then"
ᵍ χαίρω, chairo, a greeting—see glossary entry for שָׁלוֹם, shalom
ʰ Some mss conclude, "אָמֵן, Amen."

הַמִכְתָּב מִן The Letter from
יַעֲקֹב Ya'aqov

1 ¹*From* יַעֲקֹב, Ya'aqov, a slave of God and of the Master יֵשׁוּעַ, Yeshua *the* Messiah; to the Twelve Tribes *of* Yis'rael who are in the Dispersion: שָׁלוֹם, Shalom.ᵃ

²Count *it* all joy, my brothers, when you fall into various *ways of* testing, ³knowing that the proving of your faith brings about perseverance *in you*. ⁴And let the perseverance have a maturing work, so that you may be mature and complete, lacking in nothing. ⁵And if any of you lack wisdom, let him ask from God—who is giving to all, generously and not denouncing—and it will be given to him; ⁶and let him ask in faith, doubting nothing. For he who is doubting has been like a wave of the sea, driven by wind and tossed *about*. ⁷For let not that man suppose that he will receive anything from the Master—⁸a two-minded man *is* unstable in all his ways.

⁹And let the brother who is humble take pride in his exaltation, ¹⁰and the *one who is* rich, in his humiliation, because, as a flower of grass, he will pass away. ¹¹For *as* the sun rises with the burning heat, and THE GRASS WITHERS, AND THE FLOWER OF IT FALLS,ᵇ and the beauty of its appearance is destroyed, so also the rich *man* in his pursuits will fade away! ¹²Happy *is* the man who perseveres *through the ways of* testing, because, becoming proven *in his faith*, he will receive the crown of the Life, which the Master promised to those loving Him.

¹³Let no one being tempted say, "I am tempted from God," for God is not tempted by evil, and *so* He Himself tempts no one. ¹⁴Rather, each one is tempted, being led away and enticed by his own desires. ¹⁵Afterward, the desire (having conceived) gives birth to sin, and the sin (having become fully-grown) brings forth death. ¹⁶Be not led astray, my beloved brothers!

¹⁷Every good *act of* giving, and every perfect gift, is from above, coming down from the Father of the lights, with whom is no variation or turning shadows. ¹⁸Having *so* intended, He brought us forth with a word of truth, for us to be a certain *kind of* first-fruit of His created *things*.

¹⁹Know *this*, my beloved brothers, and let every man be swift to hear, slow to speak, *and* slow to anger, ²⁰for the anger of a man does not accomplish the righteousness of God.

²¹Therefore, having put aside all filthiness and superabundance of evil, in humility be receiving the ingrafted word that is able to save your souls, ²²and become doers of the word, and not hearers only, *thereby* deceiving yourselves. ²³Because if anyone is a hearer of the word and not a doer, this one has been likened to a man viewing his natural face in a mirror, ²⁴for he viewed himself, and went away, and immediately forgot what kind of *man* he was. ²⁵But he who looked into the perfect תּוֹרָה, Torah—that of liberty—and continued there, *was* not a forgetful hearer, but a doer of action. This one will be happy in his doing.

²⁶If anyone thinks *himself* to be devoutᶜ —not bridling his tongue, but *rather* deceiving his heart—the devotionᵈ of this one *is* vain. ²⁷Devotion pure and unde-

---

ᵃ χαίρω, chairo, a greeting—see glossary entry for שָׁלוֹם, shalom
ᵇ יְשַׁעְיָהוּ Y'sha'yahu 40:7-8
ᶜ "devout"—θρησκὸς, threskos; Young's says, "religious"; some mss insert, "among you"
ᵈ "devotion" (also in verse 27)—θρησκεία, threskeia; Young's says, "religion"

filed with the God and Father is this: to look after orphans and widows in their oppression, *and* to keep himself unspotted from the world.

2 ¹My brothers, do not hold the faith of the glory of our Master יֵשׁוּעַ, Yeshua *the* Messiah in favoritism. ²For if there comes into your synagogue a man with a gold ring, *dressed* in bright clothing, and there also comes in a poor man in shabby clothing, ³and you look upon him wearing the bright clothing and say, "You—sit here well-*situated*," and to the poor man say, "You—stand there," or "Sit under my footstool," ⁴did you not make distinctions fully among yourselves, and *so* become ill-reasoning judges? ⁵Listen, my beloved brothers: did not God choose the poor in the world *to be* rich in faith, and heirs of the Reign that He promised to those loving Him? ⁶But you dishonored the poor one. Do not the rich subjugate you, and themselves drag you into court? ⁷Do they themselves not speak evil of the good Name by which you have been called? ⁸If, indeed, you bring *the* King's תּוֹרָה, Torah to its goal according to the Scripture,

"You must love your neighbor as yourself,"ᵃ

you do well; ⁹but if you show favoritism, you enact sin, *and are* being convicted by the תּוֹרָה, Torah as sidesteppers.

¹⁰For whoever keeps the whole תּוֹרָה, Torah, and stumbles in one POINT, has become guilty *of breaking it* all. ¹¹For He who is saying, "YOU MUST NOT COMMIT ADULTERY,"ᵇ also said, "YOU MUST NOT MURDER."ᶜ And *so*, if you do not commit adultery, yet *you* commit murder, you have become a sidestepper of תּוֹרָה, Torah. ¹²*Therefore*, as *ones who are* about to be judged by a תּוֹרָה, Torah of liberty, so speak, and so do; ¹³for the judgment without *loving*-kindness IS *shown* to him who has not done *loving*-kindness *to oth-*

*ers; loving-*kindness triumphs over judgment.

¹⁴What IS the profit, my brothers, if anyone speaks of having faith, but he does not have actions? Is that faith able to save him? ¹⁵If a brother or sister is naked and lacking of the daily food, ¹⁶and anyone of you says to them, "Go in peace, be warmed and be filled," but gives not to them the things needful for the body, what IS the profit *to that person's life?* ¹⁷So also, the faith by itself, if it does not have actions, is dead.

¹⁸But someone might say, "You have faith, and I have actions." Show me your faith apart from theᵈ actions, and I will show you by my actions, the faith! ¹⁹You —you believe that God is One.ᵉ You do well *to believe so*, but *even* the demons believe *that*, and they shudder *at the thought!* ²⁰Now, O empty man, do you want to know *the evidence* that the faith apart from the actions is inactive?ᶠ

²¹אַבְרָהָם, Av'raham, our father—was he not declared righteous by actions, having brought up יִצְחָק, Yitz'chaq his son upon the altar? ²²Do you see that the faith was working with his actions, and by the actions the faith was perfected? ²³And fulfilled was the Scripture that is saying,

"And אַבְרָהָם, Av'raham believed God, and it was credited to him—to righteousness";ᵍ

and he was called "friend of God."ʰ ²⁴You see, then, that by actions is man declared righteous, and not by faith only.

²⁵And likewise, also, רָחָב, Rachav the prostitute—was she not, by *her* actions, declared righteous, having received the messengers and sent *them* out by another road? ²⁶For *just* as the body apart from the רוּחַ, ruach is dead, so also the faith apart from actions is dead!

ᵃ וַיִּקְרָא *Vayiq'ra* 19:18; מַתִּתְיָהוּ *Matit'yahu* 22:39
ᵇ שְׁמוֹת *Sh'mot* 20:13(14); דְּבָרִים *D'variym* 5:17(18)
ᶜ שְׁמוֹת *Sh'mot* 20:13; דְּבָרִים *D'variym* 5:17

ᵈ "apart from the"—some mss say, "by your"
ᵉ "God is One," perhaps a ref. to דְּבָרִים *D'variym* 6:4
ᶠ "inactive"—some mss say, "dead"
ᵍ בְּרֵאשִׁית *B'reshiyt* 15:6
ʰ "friend of God," see יְשַׁעְיָהוּ *Y'sha'yahu* 41:8; דִּבְרֵי הַיָּמִים בֵּית *Div'rei HaYamiym Beit* 20:7

3 ¹Many *of you should* not become teachers, my brothers—having known that we *who teach* will receive greater judgment—²for we all make many stumbles. If anyone does not stumble in word, this one IS a perfect man, able to also bridle the whole body.

³Now if we put the bits into the mouths of the horses for their being persuaded by[a] us, *then* we *can* also turn about their whole body. ⁴Look! also the ships *of the sea*—being so great, and being driven by fierce winds—are led about by a very small rudder, wherever the impulse of the helmsman wants. ⁵So also the tongue is a little member *of the body*, yet *it* boasts greatly. Look! such a little fire—*yet* how great a forest it sets aflame! ⁶And *so* the tongue IS a fire—the world of the unrighteousness.

In this manner, the tongue is set in our *body's* members *as that* which is polluting our whole body, and is setting on fire the course of *our fleshly* nature, and is *itself* set on fire by the גֵּיהִנֹּם, Geihinom. ⁷For every kind *of animal in* nature—both of beasts and of birds, both of creeping things and things of the sea—is subdued, and has been subdued, by the human's nature. ⁸But the tongue, no one of men is able to subdue. IT IS an uncontrollable evil, full of deadly poison. ⁹With it we bless the Master[b] and Father, and with it we curse the men *who have been* made according to the likeness of God; ¹⁰out of the same mouth comes forth blessing and cursing—it is not necessary, my brothers, *for* these things to happen this way! ¹¹Does the fountain—out of the same opening—pour out *both* the sweet and the bitter *water*? ¹²Is a fig-tree able, my brothers, to make olives? or a vine, figs? Nor *can* salt water make fresh.[c]

¹³Who IS wise and understanding among you? Let him show *it* by the good behavior—his actions in humility of wisdom. ¹⁴But if you have bitter jealousy and *selfish* ambition in your heart, boast not, nor lie against the truth: ¹⁵this "wisdom" is not descending from above, but IS earthly, physical, demon-like. ¹⁶For where jealousy and *selfish* ambition ARE, there is disorder and every evil practice. ¹⁷But the wisdom from above, first, indeed, is pure, then peaceable, gentle, cooperative, full of *loving*-kindness and good fruits, uncontentious,[d] and unhypocritical; ¹⁸and the fruit of righteousness in peace is sown to those making peace.

4 ¹From where DO wars and from where *do* fightings among you *come*? Are *they* not from that place *created* by your passions—which are like soldiers *at war* in your *body's* members? ²You desire, but you do not have, *so* you murder; and *you* are jealous, and are not able to get *what you want, so* you fight and war. But you have not, because of your not asking; ³or you ask, and you receive not, because you ask evilly—so that you can spend IT on your pleasures.

⁴Adulteresses![e] Have you not known that the world's friendship is hostility with God? Whoever, then, wants to be a friend of the world is made an enemy of God. ⁵Do you think that, emptily, the Scripture says *that* with envy the רוּחַ, Ruach that He caused to live in us earnestly desires *us*?[f] ⁶But greater *unmerited* favor He gives! Therefore, *the Scripture* says,

"God sets Himself against proud ones; but to humble ones, He gives *unmerited* favor."[g]

---

[a] "being persuaded by"—πείθω, peitho, most often translated "trust" or "persuade." Here, Young says, "obeying."

[b] "Master"—some mss say, "God"

[c] "Nor *can* salt water make fresh"—some mss say, "So no fountain IS ABLE to make *both* salt and sweet water."

[d] "uncontentious"—most translations use "impartial" or similar

[e] "Adulteresses!"—some mss say, "Adulterers and adulteresses!"

[f] "with envy the רוּחַ, Ruach that He caused to live in us earnestly desires *us*," or "to envy earnestly desireth the spirit that did dwell in us" (Young's), or "a spirit in us which longs to envy" (CJB), or "how He jealously desires the Spirit which He has made to dwell in us" (NAS)

[g] מִשְׁלֵי Mish'lei 3:34

Unrighteous riches. יַעֲקֹב Ya'aqov 5:16

⁷Be submitted, then, to God; stand up against the Accuser, and he will flee from you. ⁸Draw near to God, and He will draw near to you. Cleanse *your* hands, you sinners! and purify *your* hearts, you two-minded *ones!* ⁹Be exceedingly afflicted, and mourn, and weep; let your laughter be turned to mourning, and the joy to heaviness. ¹⁰Be made low before the Master, and He will exalt you.

¹¹Speak not one against another, brothers. He who is speaking against a brother, or is judging his brother, speaks against תּוֹרָה, Torah and judges *the* תּוֹרָה, Torah. And if you judge תּוֹרָה, Torah, you are not a doer of תּוֹרָה, Torah, but a judge *of it.* ¹²One *alone* is the Giver of תּוֹרָה, Torah and Judge[a] who is able to save and to destroy. But you—who are you *to be* judging the neighbor?

¹³Go, now, you who are saying, "Today or tomorrow we will go on to such-a-city, and *we* will pass *the time* there *for* a year, and do business, and make a profit"— ¹⁴*you* who do not *even* know the things of the next day! What is your life? For you are a vapor that is appearing for a little *while,* and then is vanishing. ¹⁵Instead of saying, "If the Master wants, we will live and do this or that," ¹⁶as it is, you boast in your pride. All such boasting is evil! ¹⁷To him, then, *who is* knowing *how* to do good, but *is* not doing *it,* it is sin to him.

5 ¹Go, now, you *who are* rich! Weep, howling over your miseries that are coming upon YOU! ²Your riches have rotted, and your garments have become moth-eaten. ³Your gold and silver have corroded, and the corrosion of them will be to you for a testimony, and will eat your flesh like fire. You stored up treasure *for yourselves, as if we were not* in the last days!

⁴Look! the wages of the workmen (of those who in-gathered your fields, *and* which had been fraudulently withheld by you) cry out; and the exclamations of those who reaped have entered in to the ears of יהוה צְבָאוֹת, ADONAI Tz'vaot. ⁵You lived in luxury upon the earth, and were self-indulgent; you fed your hearts in a day of slaughter. ⁶You condemned *and* you murdered the righteous *man;* he did not resist you.

⁷Be patient, then, brothers, until the *coming* presence of the Master. Look! the farmer awaits the precious fruit of the earth, being patient for it until he receives rain —יוֹרֶה וּמַלְקוֹשׁ, Yoreh uMalqosh. ⁸You also, be patient; stabilize your hearts, because the coming presence of the Master has drawn near.

⁹Do not grumble against one another, brothers, so that you may not be judged.[b] Look! the Judge is standing at the door! ¹⁰*As* an example, brothers, of the suffering of evil and of the patience, take the prophets who spoke in the Name of ADONAI. ¹¹Look! we call happy those who were enduring *with* the perseverance of אִיּוֹב, Iyov—which you *have* heard of—and you have seen ADONAI's goal: that ADONAI is very compassionate and pitying.

¹²But before all things, my brothers, do not swear[c]—neither "by the heaven," nor "by the earth," nor by any other oath— but let your "Yes" be "Yes," and the "No" *be* "No," so that under judgment you may not fall.

¹³Does anyone suffer hardship among you? Let him pray. Is anyone *of you* cheerful? Let him sing melodies *of praise.* ¹⁴Is anyone infirmed among you? Let him call for the זְקֵנִים, z'qeniym of the Called-Forth,[d] and let them pray over him, having anointed him with oil, in the Name of the Master. ¹⁵And the prayer of the faith will save the distressed one *from his affliction,* and the Master will raise him up; and if he has committed sins, they will be forgiven to him.

¹⁶So be confessing *your* sins[e] to one another, and be praying for one another, so

---

[a] Some mss omit, "and Judge"

[b] "judged"—some mss say, "condemned"

[c] cf. *Vy.* 19:12; *Mt.* 5:33-37, 23:20-22; *Iv.* 6:16; Ac. 2:29-30

[d] "Called-Forth"—ἐκκλησία, ekklesia; see *Mt.* 16:18

[e] "sins"—some mss say, "missteps"

that you may be healed; *for of* great power is a prayer from a righteous man—working *effectively*.[a] 17(אֵלִיָּהוּ, Eliyahu was a man, affected *just* like us, and with prayer he prayed *for it* not to rain, and it did not rain upon the Land *for* three years and six months. 18And again he prayed, and the heaven gave rain, and the Land brought forth her fruit.[b])

19My brothers, if any among you goes astray from the truth, and anyone turns him back, 20let him know that the one turning back a sinner from the straying of his way will save his soul from death—and will cover a great number of sins.

[a] "*for of* great power is a prayer from a righteous man—working *effectively*" better preserves the word order of the Gk, compared to Young, which says, "very strong is a working supplication of a righteous man."

[b] מְלָכִים א *M'lakhiym Alef* 17:1, 18:1, 18:42-45

PAUL'S FIRST LETTER TO TIMOTHY

1 Timothy

1 ¹*From* Paul,[a] an emissary of Messiah יֵשׁוּעַ, Yeshua, according to a command of God our Savior and of[b] Messiah יֵשׁוּעַ, Yeshua our hope; ²to Timothy, *my* genuine son[c] in *the* faith: *unmerited* favor, *loving*-kindness, *and* peace from God the Father, and *from* Messiah יֵשׁוּעַ, Yeshua our Master.

³As *when* I exhorted you to remain in Ephesus (*while* I *was* going on to Macedonia), *I continue to exhort you now:* that you command certain *men* not to teach anything other *than the truth*, ⁴nor to pay attention to fables and endless genealogies that cause questioning rather than the stewardship[d] of God—which is in faith. ⁵But the goal of this mandate is love out of a pure heart, and of a good conscience, and of faith unfeigned, ⁶from which certain *men*, having swerved, turned aside to fruitless discussion, ⁷wanting to be teachers of תּוֹרָה, Torah, not understanding either the things they say, nor regarding what they confidently assert.

⁸Rather, we have known that the תּוֹרָה, Torah IS good, provided one uses it lawfully, ⁹having known this: that תּוֹרָה, Torah is not set *in place* for a righteous man, but for *those who are* without תּוֹרָה, Torah and out-of-control, *the* ungodly and sinful, *the* unholy and profane, *those who* kill their fathers and kill their mothers, murderers, ¹⁰*the* sexually immoral, men who practice homosexual acts, slave-dealers, liars, perjurers, and if there be any other thing that is contrary to sound teaching ¹¹according to the Good News of the glory of the blessed God, with which I was entrusted.

¹²I give thanks to Him who strengthened me—Messiah יֵשׁוּעַ, Yeshua, our Master—that He considered me faithful, having put ME in *His* service, *though I* was previously speaking evil, and persecuting, and insulting. But I found *loving*-kindness, because (being ignorant) I did THESE THINGS in unbelief. ¹⁴So the *unmerited* fa-

[a] "Paul"—Παῦλος, Paulos, born a Roman citizen of Tarsus (Acts 21:39, 22:28), was also known as the פָּרוּשׁ, Parush-turned-Messianic-Emissary-to-the-גּוֹיִם, Goyim: שָׁאוּל, Shaul (Acts 13:9). Despite his impressive Jewish pedigree (Phil. 3:5), however, his letters—including those written to the Jewish disciple Timothy (Acts 16:1-3)—are clearly signed with his Roman name. The MJLT therefore faithfully renders the name "Paul," where it is warranted by the Greek text.

[b] Some mss insert, "the Master".

[c] "son"—lit. "child"; also in verse 18

[d] "stewardship"—some mss say, "building up"

vor of our Master exceedingly abounded with *the* faith and love that IS in Messiah יֵשׁוּעַ, Yeshua. ¹⁵Faithful IS the word, and worthy of all acceptance: that Messiah יֵשׁוּעַ, Yeshua came to the world to save sinners—*the* foremost of whom I am. ¹⁶But because of this, I found *loving-kindness*, so that in me foremost, Messiah יֵשׁוּעַ, Yeshua might show all patience as a pattern for those about to believe in Him to life age-enduring. ¹⁷Now, to the King of the ages—the immortal, invisible, only God[a]—IS honor and glory to the ages of the ages! אָמֵן, Amen.

¹⁸This mandate I commit to you, *my* son, Timothy, according to the prophecies that went before upon you, so that by them you may wage the good warfare, ¹⁹holding *to* faith and a good conscience (*without* which certain *ones*, having thrust away *these things*, suffered shipwreck regarding the faith—²⁰of whom are Hymenæus and Alexander, whom I handed over to הַשָּׂטָן, HaSatan so that they might be instructed not to speak evil).

2 ¹I exhort *you*, then, first of all, *that* there be made requests for help, prayers, petitions, *and* thanksgivings for all men, ²for kings and all who are in authority, so that we may lead a tranquil and peaceable life in all godliness and seriousness. ³This IS right and acceptable in the sight of God our Savior, ⁴who wants all men to be saved, and to come to the full knowledge of the truth. ⁵For God IS one; one also IS *the* mediator of God and of men: the man, Messiah יֵשׁוּעַ, Yeshua, ⁶who gave Himself *as* a ransom for all—the testimony *given* in its own times, ⁷in regard to which I was appointed *as* a proclaimer and emissary (I say[b] *the* truth—I do not lie), a teacher of ethnic-groups, in faithfulness and truth.

⁸I want, then, that *the* men pray in every place, lifting up undefiled hands, separated from anger and disputes.[c] ⁹Likewise, *I* also *want the* women to adorn themselves in respectable *manner of* dress, with modesty and soundness of mind—not in braided hair, and gold, or pearls, or expensive clothing,[d] ¹⁰but *with that* which is fitting for women *who are* professing godliness through *their* good actions.

¹¹Let a woman learn in quietness in all submission. ¹²I also do not allow a woman to teach, nor to exercise authority over[e] a husband,[f] but to be in quietness. ¹³For אָדָם, Adam was formed first, then חַוָּה, Chavah, ¹⁴and אָדָם, Adam was not deceived; rather, the woman (having been deceived) came into sidestepping, ¹⁵and she will be saved through the child-bearing, if they remain in faith, and love, and holiness, with soundness of mind.

3 ¹Faithful IS the word: if anyone longs for the *work of* oversight, a right work he desires. ²It is necessary, therefore, *for* the overseer to be above reproach, a husband of one wife, temperate, of sound mind, respectable, a friend of strangers, adept at teaching, ³not given to wine, not violent[g] but gentle, not contentious, not a lover of money, ⁴leading his own house well, having children in submission with all seriousness ⁵(for if anyone has not known HOW to lead his own house, how will he take care of the Called-Forth[h] of God?), ⁶not newly planted;[i] otherwise, having been puffed up, he might fall into a judgment of the Accuser. ⁷And it is also necessary *for* him to have a good testimony from those outside *the community*, so that he may not fall into disgrace and a snare of the Accuser.

⁸Servers in like manner *should be* serious, not double-tongued, not given to much wine, not given to dishonest gain,

---

[a] "only God"—some mss say, "only wise God"
[b] Some mss insert, "in Messiah"
[c] "disputes"—lit. "reasonings"
[d] "expensive clothing"—lit. "garments of great price"
[e] "exercise authority over"—Young's says, "rule"
[f] "husband" or "man"
[g] "violent"—some mss insert, "not given to dishonest gain"
[h] "Called-Forth"—ἐκκλησία, ekklesia; see *Mt.* 16:18
[i] "newly planted" either in the faith, or perhaps, as a parent

⁹having the mystery of the faith in a pure conscience. ¹⁰And let these also first be examined, then let them serve, being unblameable. ¹¹(*Their* wives[a] in like manner *should be* serious, not false accusers, temperate, *and* faithful in all things.) ¹²Servers—let them be husbands of one wife, leading their children and their own houses well. ¹³For those who served well obtain for themselves a good standing and much boldness in *the* faith that *is* in *the* Messiah יֵשׁוּעַ, Yeshua.

¹⁴These things I write to you, hoping to come to you soon, ¹⁵but so that if I delay, you may know how it is necessary *for* YOU to conduct yourself in the house of God, which is the Called-Forth[b] of the living God—a pillar and foundation of the truth.

¹⁶And, undeniably, great is the mystery of godliness—Who[c] was revealed in flesh, declared righteous in רוּחַ, ruach, seen by Messengers, proclaimed among ethnic-groups, believed on in the world, *and* taken up in glory!

4 ¹And the רוּחַ, Ruach specifically says that in latter times certain *ones* will fall away from the faith: paying attention to seducing רוּחוֹת, ruchot and *the* teachings of demons; ²speaking lies in hypocrisy, being seared *as with a hot iron* in their own conscience; ³forbidding *people* to marry; forcing them to abstain from foods created *by* God to be received with thanksgiving by those believing and acknowledging the truth ⁴(because every creature of God *is* good, and nothing *is* to be rejected *if* being received with thanksgiving—⁵for it is set apart through the word of God and petition).

⁶*By* pointing out these things to the brothers, you will be a good servant of Messiah יֵשׁוּעַ, Yeshua (being nourished by the words of the faith and of the good teaching which you followed after). ⁷And reject the profane and old women's myths,

and *instead* train yourself to godliness. ⁸For the training *of the* body is of little profit, yet the *training to* godliness is profitable to all things, having a promise of the life that is now, and of that which is coming. ⁹Faithful *is* this word, and worthy of all acceptance, ¹⁰because for this we labor and strive,[d] since we hope on the living God, who is Savior of all men—especially of those believing.

¹¹Command and teach these things. ¹²Let no one despise your youth; but in word, in behavior, in love,[e] in faith, *and* in purity, become a pattern for those believing. ¹³Until I come, pay attention to the reading,[f] to the exhortation, *and* to the teaching. ¹⁴Be not careless of the gift in you that was given you through prophecy with laying on of the hands of the Body of זְקֵנִים, Z'qeniym. ¹⁵Of these things, be careful; in these things, be, so that your advancement may be known to all. ¹⁶Pay close attention to yourself and to the teaching; remain in them, for *by* doing this thing, you will save both yourself and those hearing you.

5 ¹You should not rebuke an older man,[g] but appeal to *him* as a father; younger persons as brothers; ²older women as mothers; *and* younger ones as sisters—in all purity.

³Honor widows who are really widows, ⁴but if a widow has any children or grandchildren, let *those children* learn first to show godliness to their own house, and to give back a repayment to the parents, for this is acceptable in God's sight. ⁵(Now, she who is really a widow and *is* left all alone has hoped upon God and remains *faithful* in the requests for help and in the prayers night and day——⁶yet she who is given to luxury, *though* living, has died.

---

[a] "wives"—Young's says, "women"
[b] "Called-Forth"—ἐκκλησία, ekklesia; see מַתִּתְיָהוּ Matit'yahu 16:18; also in 5:16
[c] "Who"—some mss say, "God"
[d] "strive"—some mss say, "are reviled"
[e] Some mss insert, "in רוּחַ, ruach"
[f] "the reading" of Scripture, or perhaps, Paul's letters
[g] "older man" is a form of πρεσβύτερος, presbuteros, as also are "Body of זְקֵנִים, Z'qeniym" in 4:14, "older women" in 5:2, "older men" in 5:17, and "older one" in 5:19

⁷Command these things also, so that *the people* may be above reproach.)

⁸Now, if anyone does not provide for his own (and especially for those of the household), he has denied the faith, and he is worse than an unbeliever.

⁹A widow—let her be *so* listed *if she is* not under sixty years of age, having been a wife of one husband, ¹⁰*and* being testified to in good actions: if she brought up children; if she showed hospitality to strangers; if she washed *the* feet *of the* קְדוֹשִׁים, Q'doshiym; if she relieved those in oppression; if she followed after every good action.

¹¹But be refusing younger widows, for when they feel sensual desires *that compete* against the Messiah, they want to marry, ¹²*thus* bringing judgment on themselves because they put away the first faith. ¹³And at the same time also, they learn TO BE idle, going about the houses; and not only idle, but also tattlers and busybodies, speaking the things *that* they ought not. ¹⁴Therefore, I want *the* younger ones to marry, to bear children, to be keeper of the house, *and* to give no opportunity to the Opposer for slander, ¹⁵for certain *ones* already turned aside after הַשָׂטָן, HaSatan.

¹⁶If any[a] believing woman has *dependent* widows, let her[b] assist them, and let not the Called-Forth be burdened, so that they may assist those *who are* really widows.

¹⁷The older men[c] *who are* leading well—let them be counted worthy of double honor, especially those laboring in word and teaching, ¹⁸for the Scripture says, "YOU MUST NOT MUZZLE AN OX *WHILE HE IS* THRESHING OUT *THE* GRAIN,"[d] and "the workman IS worthy of his wages."[e] ¹⁹Receive not an accusation against an older *one* except upon *the testimony of* two or three witnesses. ²⁰Those *who are* sinning, rebuke in *the* sight of all, so that the others may also have fear.

²¹I testify fully before God, and[f] Messiah יֵשׁוּעַ, Yeshua, and the chosen Messengers, that you *are to* guard these things without prejudging—doing nothing by partiality. ²²Be laying hands quickly on no one, nor be sharing in *the* sins of others. Be keeping yourself pure.

²³No longer be drinking *only* water, but be using a little wine because of your stomach and of your frequent ailments.

²⁴The sins of certain men are evident beforehand, going before *them* to judgment; but certain *others, their sins* also follow after them. ²⁵Likewise also the right actions are evident beforehand, and those that are otherwise are not able to be hidden.

6 ¹As many as are slaves under a yoke—let them consider their own slave-masters *to be* worthy of all honor, so that the Name of God and the teaching may not be spoken evil of. ²And those having believing slave-masters, let them not slight THEM because they are brothers. But rather, let them slave *all the more*, because they who are taking part in the benefit are faithful and beloved.

Be teaching and exhorting these things. ³If anyone is teaching otherwise, and does not consent to sound words (those of our Master, יֵשׁוּעַ, Yeshua *the* Messiah) and to the teaching according to godliness, ⁴he is proud—knowing nothing, but having an unhealthy interest with *intentionally polarizing* questions and quarreling about words, out of which comes envy, infighting, evil-speakings, evil-suspicions, ⁵*and* constant irritations[g] of men wholly corrupted in mind and destitute of the truth, supposing the godliness to be *a means of* gain.[h]

⁶But it is great gain—the godliness *that comes* with contentment! ⁷For we brought

---

[a] Some mss insert, "believing man or"
[b] "her"—some mss say, "them"
[c] "older men" or "זְקֵנִים, z'qeniym"; similar in vs. 19
[d] דְּבָרִים D'variym 25:4; cf. 1Cor. 9:9ff, about emissaries
[e] Perhaps a modern proverb based on *Vy.* 19:13 and *Dv.* 24:15, or a saying of Yeshua; cf. *Mt.* 10:10, Luke 10:7.
[f] Some mss insert, "the Master"
[g] "constant irritations"—some mss say, "wranglings"
[h] Some mss insert, "Depart from such *people*."

nothing into the world, since we are able to carry nothing out. ⁸But having food and clothing—with these we will be content.

⁹But those wanting to be rich fall into temptation, and a snare, and many lusts—foolish and hurtful—that sink men into ruin and destruction. ¹⁰Indeed, a root of all the evils is the love of money, for which certain *ones* were longing, and *thereby* went astray from the faith, and pierced themselves through with many sorrows.

¹¹But you, O man of God, flee *from* these things, and pursue righteousness, godliness, faithfulness, love, perseverance, *and* humble behavior. ¹²Strive the good striving of the faith; be laying hold on the life age-enduring to which you were called and *to which you* professed the right profession in the presence of many witnesses. ¹³I command you in the sight of God (who is making all things alive) and Messiah יֵשׁוּעַ, Yeshua (who testified the right profession before Pontius Pilate): ¹⁴that you *must* pay attention to the command—unspotted *and* unblameable—until the appearing of our Master, יֵשׁוּעַ, Yeshua *the* Messiah, ¹⁵which He—the blessed and only lord, the King of the kings and Master of the masters—will show in His own times, ¹⁶who alone is having immortality, dwelling in light unapproachable; whom no one of men saw, nor is able to see; to whom *is* honor and power age-enduring! אָמֵן, Amen.

¹⁷Those *who are* rich in the present age: command *them* not to be high-minded, nor to hope in the uncertainty of riches, but in God,ᵃ who is giving to us all things richly for enjoyment. ¹⁸*Rather, command them* to do good, to be rich in good actions, to be ready to impart *and* willing to share, ¹⁹treasuring up to themselves a right foundation for the time to come, so that they may lay hold on the real life.ᵇ

²⁰O Timothy, guard the thing entrusted to you, *all the while* avoiding the profane vain-words and opposition of the falsely-named "knowledge" ²¹which certain *ones are* professing, *and thereby*, concerning the faith, *have* swerved.

The *unmerited* favor *is* with you.ᶜ

ᵃ "God"—some mss say, "the living God"
ᵇ "real life"—some mss say, "life age-enduring"
ᶜ Some mss conclude, "אָמֵן, Amen."

PAUL'S SECOND LETTER TO TIMOTHY

2 Timothy

1

¹*From* Paul,ᵃ an emissary of Messiah יֵשׁוּעַ, Yeshua, through the will of God, according to a promise of life that *is* in Messiah יֵשׁוּעַ, Yeshua; ²to Timothy, *my* beloved son:ᵇ *unmerited* favor, *loving*-kindness, *and* peace from God the Father, and Messiah יֵשׁוּעַ, Yeshua, our Master!

³I am thankful to God (whom I serve from *my* ancestors in a pure conscience) that unceasingly I have remembrance concerning you in my requests for help night and day, ⁴desiring greatly to see you (being mindful of your tears), so that with joy I may be filled, ⁵taking remembrance of the unfeigned faith that is in you, that dwelled first in your grandmother Lois and your mother Eunice, and I am persuaded that also *lives* in you.

⁶For this cause, I remind you to stir up the gift of God that is in you through the laying on of my hands. ⁷For God did not give us a רוּחַ, ruach of fear, but of power, and of love, and of a sound mind. ⁸Therefore, you should not be ashamed of the

ᵃ "Paul"—Παῦλος, Paulos; see 1 Timothy 1:1
ᵇ "son"—lit. "child"

testimony of our Master, nor of me, His prisoner. But suffer hardship along with *me for* the Good News according to the power of God, ⁹who saved us, and called *us* with a holy calling (not according to our actions, but according to His own purpose and *unmerited* favor) that was given to us in Messiah יֵשׁוּעַ, Yeshua before the times of the ages, ¹⁰and was made evident now through the appearing of our Savior, Messiah יֵשׁוּעַ, Yeshua—who indeed abolished death and enlightened life and immortality through the Good News ¹¹(to which I was placed *as* a proclaimer, and an emissary, and a teacher;ᵃ ¹²for which cause I also suffer these things). But I am not ashamed, for I have known in whom I have believed, and have been persuaded that He is able to guard that which I have committed to Him—to that Day. ¹³The pattern of sound words which you heard from me, hold in faith and love that *is* in Messiah יֵשׁוּעַ, Yeshua. ¹⁴Guard the good thing committed to you through the רוּחַ הַקֹּדֶשׁ, Ruach HaQodesh that is living in us.

¹⁵You have known this: that they turned from me—all those in Asia, of whom are Phygelus and Hermogenes. ¹⁶May the Master give *loving*-kindness to the house of Onesiphorus, because many times he refreshed me, and was not ashamed of my chain; ¹⁷but being in Rome, he sought diligently and found me ¹⁸(may the Master give to him to find *loving*-kindness from ADONAI in that Day); and you know very well how many things he served in Ephesus.

2 ¹You, therefore, my son,ᵇ be strong in the *unmerited* favor that *is* in Messiah יֵשׁוּעַ, Yeshua, ²and the things that you heard from me through many witnesses. *And* be committing these things to faithful men who will also be sufficient to teach others. ³You, therefore, suffer hardship *with me* as a good soldier of Messiah יֵשׁוּעַ, Yeshua.

ᵃ Some mss insert, "of גּוֹיִם, Goyim"
ᵇ "son"—lit. "child"

⁴No one serving as a soldier *gets* himself entangled with the affairs of life, so that he may please *the one* who enlisted him. ⁵And if, also, anyone strives *in competition*, he is not crowned *as the winner* unless he strives according to the laws *of the competition*. ⁶The laboring farmer must *be* first to share of the fruits. ⁷Be considering what things I say, for the Master will give to you understanding in all things.

⁸Remember יֵשׁוּעַ, Yeshua *the* Messiah (raised out of the dead, of the seed of דָּוִד, David) according to my Good News ⁹in which I suffer hardship as an evil-doer—*even* to bonds. But the word of God has not been bound! ¹⁰Because of this, I endure all things, because of the Chosen Ones, so that they also may obtain salvation with glory age-enduring that *is* in Messiah יֵשׁוּעַ, Yeshua.

¹¹Faithful *is* the word: for if we died together *with Him*, we will also live together *with Him*; ¹²if we endure together *with Him*, we will also reign together *with Him*; if we deny HIM, He also will deny us; ¹³if we are not faithful, He remains faithful, for He is not able to deny Himself. ¹⁴Remind THEM of these things (testifying fully before God ᶜ), *and* not to quarrel about words, *which leads* to nothing useful, but to the catastrophe of those hearing *it*.

¹⁵Be diligent to bring yourself near—proven to God, a workman irreproachable, straightly cuttingᵈ *a path for* the word of the truth—¹⁶and turn around from the profane, empty talkings, for they will advance to more ungodliness, ¹⁷and their word will have pasture as a gangrene—of whom is Hymenæus and Philetus, ¹⁸who swerved concerning the truth (saying the Rising Again has already been) and overthrow the faith of some.

¹⁹Nevertheless, the firm foundation of God has stood, having this seal: "ADONAI HAS KNOWN THOSE WHO ARE HIS,"ᵉ

ᶜ "God"—some mss say, "the Master"
ᵈ "straightly cutting" is the literal translation (cf. מִשְׁלֵי Mish'lei 3:6); other translations: "rightly dividing" (Young's), "rightly handling"
ᵉ בְּמִדְבַּר B'mid'bar 16:5

and "Let him go away from unrighteousness—everyone who is naming the Name of *the* Master.ᵃ" ²⁰And in a great house, there are not only things of gold and silver, but also of wood and of earth, and some to honor, and some to dishonor. ²¹If, then, anyone cleans himself from these, he will be a thing to honor: set apart, useful to the housemaster, having been prepared to *do* every good act.

²²So flee the youthful lusts, and *instead* pursue righteousness, faith, love *and* peace, with those calling upon the Master out of a pure heart.

²³And be avoiding the foolish and stupid *intentionally polarizing* questions, having known that they bring forth fights. ²⁴But *for* a slave of the Master, it is necessary not to be combative, but to be gentle to all; adept at teaching; patient under evil; ²⁵in humility, instructing those opposing *him, not knowing* if perhaps God may give to them reformation to an acknowledging of the truth, ²⁶and they may awake out of the Accuser's snare, having been caught by him at his will.

3 ¹And know this: that in the last days there will come difficult times. ²For men will be lovers of themselves, lovers of money, boasters, arrogant, evil-speakers, obstinateᵇ toward parents, unthankful, unholy,ᶜ ³without natural affection, unappeasable, false accusers, lacking self-control, brutal, not lovers of those who are good, ⁴traitors, reckless, swollen with conceit, lovers of pleasure more than lovers of God, ⁵having a form of godliness, yet having denied its power. But be turning away from these, ⁶for of these there are those creeping into the houses and leading captive the weak-*willed* women (*who are* loaded down with sins, *and* led away with various lusts, ⁷always learning, but never able to come to a knowledge of truth). ⁸And even as Jannes and Jambresᵈ stood against מֹשֶׁה, Mosheh, so also do these stand against the truth—men corrupted in mind; disqualified concerning the faith. ⁹But they will not advance any further, for their foolishness will be evident to all, as *Mosheh's opponents'* also became.

¹⁰But you—you have followed after my teaching, manner of life, purpose, faith, patience, love, perseverance, ¹¹*and* the persecutions (the sufferings that befell me in Antioch, in Iconium, *and* in Lystra—what persecutions I endured!—but out of *them* all, the Master delivered me).

¹²And all who also want to live godly *lives* in Messiah יֵשׁוּעַ, Yeshua will be persecuted, ¹³and evil men and impostors will advance *from the bad* to the worse—leading astray, and being led astray.

¹⁴But you—be remaining in the things you learned and with which *you* were entrusted, having known from whom you learned, ¹⁵and that from infancy you have known the Sacred Scriptures,ᵉ which are able to make you wise—to salvation, through faith that *is* in Messiah יֵשׁוּעַ, Yeshua. ¹⁶Every Scripture *is* God-breathed, and profitable for teaching, for refuting, for setting aright, *and* for instruction that *is* in righteousness, ¹⁷so that the man of God may be *fully* equipped—having been completed for every good act.

4 ¹I fully testify *to you* before God and Messiah יֵשׁוּעַ, Yeshuaᶠ (who is about to judge *those* living and dead) and *by*ᵍ His Appearing and His Reign: ²proclaim the Word; be standing ready in season *and* out of season; refute, rebuke, *and* exhort in all patience and teaching. ³For there will be a season when they will not tolerate the sound teaching, but according to their own lusts, they will heap up teachers to themselves (*who will gladly*

ᵃ "the Master"—some mss say, "Messiah"

ᵇ "obstinate"—ἀπειθής, apeithes, a negative of πείθω, peitho, which is most often translated "trust" or "persuade." Here, Young says "disobedient."

ᶜ "unholy"—Young's says, "unkind"

ᵈ Jannes and Jambres—"Targum Pseudo-Jonathan" (see Glossary) שְׁמוֹת *Sh'mot* 7:11ff

ᵉ "Scriptures" or "Writings"

ᶠ "Messiah Yeshua"—some mss say, "the Master יֵשׁוּעַ, Yeshua *the* Messiah"

ᵍ "dead) and *by*"—some mss say, "dead at"

Exhortation to Timothy.

scratch their itching in the hearing), ⁴and indeed, they will turn away the hearing from the truth, and to myths they will be turned aside. ⁵But you—be sober-minded in all things, suffer hardship, do the work of one proclaiming Good News, make yourself fully assured[a] of your service.

⁶For I am already being poured out *as a drink offering*, and the time of my release has arrived— ⁷the good striving I have striven; the course I have finished; the faith I have kept. ⁸From now *on* there is stored away for me the crown of righteousness that the Master— the Righteous Judge—will give to me in that Day; and not only to me, but also to all those loving His Appearing.

⁹Be diligent to come to me quickly, ¹⁰for Demas—having loved the present age— abandoned me and went on to Thessalonica, Crescens *has gone* to Galatia, *and* Titus to Dalmatia. ¹¹Only Luke is with me. Having taken Mark, bring *him* with yourself, for he is useful to me for service. ¹²(And Tychicus I sent to Ephesus.) ¹³The cloak that I left in Troas with Carpus: *when you are* coming, bring *it* and the books—especially the parchments. ¹⁴Alexander the coppersmith did me much evil (the Master will repay to him according to his actions)— ¹⁵you also *should* beware of him, for he stood greatly against our words.

¹⁶In my first defense, no one stood with me, but all *of them* abandoned me (may it not be counted against them!). ¹⁷But the Master stood by me and *He* strengthened me, so that through me the proclaiming would be fully assured, and all the ethnic-groups would hear. And *as* I was freed out of the mouth of a lion, ¹⁸the Master will free me from every evil act, and will save ME—to His heavenly kingdom; to whom IS the glory to the ages of the ages! אָמֵן, Amen!

¹⁹Greet Prisca and Aquila, and Onesiphorus' household. ²⁰(Erastus remained in Corinth, and Trophimus I left infirmed in Miletus.)

²¹Be diligent to come before winter. Eubulus greets you, and *so do* Pudens, and Linus, and Claudia, and all the brothers. ²²The Master[b] IS with your רוּחַ, ruach; the *unmerited* favor IS with you![c]

---

[a] "make yourself fully assured"—Young's says, "make full assurance"

[b] Some mss insert, "יֵשׁוּעַ, Yeshua *the* Messiah"

[c] Some mss conclude, "אָמֵן, Amen."

הַמִּכְתָּב הָרִאשׁוֹן מִן כֵּיפָא   THE FIRST LETTER FROM KEIFA

כֵּיפָא א 1 Keifa

¹From כֵּיפָא, Keifa,[a] an emissary of יֵשׁוּעַ, Yeshua *the* Messiah; to the chosen temporary residents of the Dispersion of Pontus, Galatia, Cappadocia, Asia, and Bithynia— ²*chosen* according to a foreknowledge of God the Father, in holiness of the רוּחַ, Ruach, to obedience and sprinkling of the blood of יֵשׁוּעַ, Yeshua *the* Messiah: *unmerited* favor to you and peace be multiplied!

³Blessed IS the God and Father of our Master יֵשׁוּעַ, Yeshua *the* Messiah—who, according to the abundance of His *loving*-kindness, brought us forth again to a living hope through the Rising Again of יֵשׁוּעַ, Yeshua *the* Messiah out of the dead, ⁴to an inheritance immortal and undefiled and unfading, reserved in the Heavens for you, ⁵who (in the power of God) are being guarded through faith to salvation, ready to be revealed in the Last Time.

---

[a] כֵּיפָא, Keifa—Gk: Πέτρος, Petros; see יוֹחָנָן Yn. 1:42

⁶In this you are *being* extremely joyful, *though for* a little *while* now, if it is necessary, *also* being made to grieve in various trials, ⁷so that the proof of your faith *(which is* more precious than gold that is being destroyed, and being proven through fire) may be found to *result in* commendation and glory and honor at the revelation of יֵשׁוּעַ, Yeshua *the* Messiah—⁸whom you love *(though* not having seen), *and* in whom *(though* not seeing now, and *yet, still* believing) you are extremely joyful with joy unspeakable and glorified, ⁹receiving the goal of your faith: salvation of *your* souls.

¹⁰Concerning this salvation, *the* prophets (who prophesied about the *unmerited* favor toward you) sought out and searched out—¹¹searching in regard to what or *at* what kind of time the רוּחַ, Ruach of Messiah that was in them was making *it* clear, testifying beforehand *of* the sufferings of Messiah and the glory *that would follow* after these *sufferings*. ¹²It was revealed to them that they were serving these *things* not to themselves, but to you—*things* which are now told to you through those who proclaimed Good News to you in the רוּחַ הַקֹּדֶשׁ, Ruach HaQodesh sent from Heaven—things into which Messengers desire to bend *down* looking.

¹³Therefore, having bound up *the* loose-hanging garment around the loins of your mind, being sober-minded, hope perfectly on the *unmerited* favor that is being brought to you in the revelation of יֵשׁוּעַ, Yeshua *the* Messiah ¹⁴as obedient children —not conforming yourselves to the former lusts in your ignorance. ¹⁵But as He who called you *is* holy, you also, become holy in all behavior, ¹⁶because it has been written,

"Become holy, because I am holy."ᵃ

¹⁷And if you call on the Father (who is judging without partiality, according to the action of each *person*), pass the time of your sojourn *in the* Dispersion with reverent fear, ¹⁸having known that not with perishable things—silver or gold—were you redeemed from your foolish behavior handed down *to you* by *your* fathers, ¹⁹but with precious blood, as of a lamb unblemished and unspotted—Messiah's! ²⁰*He was* foreknown, indeed, before the foundation of the world, and revealed in the Last Times because of you, ²¹who through Him are believers in God (who raised *Him* out of the dead, and gave glory to Him), so that your faith and hope may be in God.

²²Having purified your souls (in the obedience of the truthᵇ) to brotherly love unfeigned, love one another intensely from the heart,ᶜ ²³being born again (not out of mortal seed, but immortal) through a word of God—living and remainingᵈ—²⁴because,

"All flesh IS as grass, and all its glory *is* as *the* flower of grass. The grass withered, and the flower fell away, ²⁵but the saying of ADONAI remains—to the age."ᵉ

And this is the spoken word that was proclaimed *as* Good News to you.

2 ¹Having put aside, then, all evil, and all underhandedness, and hypocrisies, and envyings, and all evil speakings, ²as newborn babies, desire the word's pure milk, so that in it you may grow to salvation,ᶠ ³if you have tasted that the Master is kind. ⁴To *those* who *are* coming, He *is* a living stone, indeed, having been rejected by men, but chosen *and* precious with God; ⁵and you yourselves, as living stones, are built up *as* a spiritual house, to *be* a כְּהֻנַּת קֹדֶשׁ, K'hunat Qodesh, to offer up spiritual sacrifices acceptable to God through יֵשׁוּעַ, Yeshua *the* Messiah.

⁶Therefore, it is contained in Scripture:

"Look! I lay a chief cornerstone in צִיּוֹן, Tziyon—chosen *and* precious—and

---

ᵃ וַיִּקְרָא *Vayiq'ra* 11:44,45; 19:2; 20:7
ᵇ Some mss insert, "through the רוּחַ, Ruach"
ᶜ "from the heart"—some mss say, "out of a pure heart"
ᵈ Some mss insert, "—to the age"
ᵉ יְשַׁעְיָהוּ *Y'sha'yahu* 40:6ff
ᶠ Some mss omit, "to salvation"

he who is believing on Him may not be put to shame."[a]

[7] To you, then, who are believing, *He* IS the preciousness; but to the unbelieving,

"A stone that the builders rejected, this one became for the head of a corner,"[b]

[8] and

"a stone of stumbling and a rock of offense"[c]

to those who are stumbling at the word (being unbelieving, *a destiny* to which also they were set). [9] But you ARE a CHOSEN ANCESTRY,[d] a KINGDOM OF כֹּהֲנִים, KO'HANIYM,[e] A HOLY ETHNICITY,[f] A PEOPLE TREASURED *as God's own*,[g] *so* that you may proclaim the excellences of Him who called you out of darkness to His wondrous light—[10] *you* who WERE once NOT A PEOPLE, but ARE now THE PEOPLE OF GOD; who had NOT FOUND *LOVING*-KINDNESS, but now have FOUND *LOVING*-KINDNESS.[h]

[11] Loved ones, I call upon YOU—as sojourners and temporary residents *among the Goyim*—to keep from the fleshly desires that war against the soul, [12] having your behavior among the גּוֹיִם, Goyim right—so that in that which they speak against you as evil-doers (from seeing good actions), they may glorify God in the Day of Inspection. [13] Be submitted for the sake of the Master to every human creation—whether to a king (as the highest), [14] *or* whether to governors (as to those sent through him for punishment of evildoers, and *for* a commendation of those doing good)—[15] because this is the will of God: doing good (to put to silence the ignorance of foolish men) [16] as free *men* (and not having the freedom as the cloak of the evil, but as slaves of God), [17] give honor to all; love the brotherhood; fear God; honor the king.

[18] The house-servants! Be submitting yourselves in all fear to the housemasters—not only to the good and gentle, but also to the crooked—[19] for this IS favorable, *even* if (because of conscience toward God) anyone endures grief, suffering unjustly. [20] For what renown IS IT *for you* if *you are* sinning, and *then*, being beaten with fists, you endure it? But if you endure, doing good and suffering FOR IT, this IS favorable with God. [21] For you were called to this because Messiah also suffered for you, leaving *Himself* to you *as* an example, so that you may follow His steps—[22] *He* WHO DID NOT COMMIT SIN, NOR WAS UNDER-HANDEDNESS FOUND IN HIS MOUTH;[i] [23] who, *though* being spoken evil of, was not speaking evil again *in turn, and though* suffering was not threatening *in turn*, and was committing Himself to Him who is judging justly; [24] who Himself BORE OUR SINS[j] in His body upon the tree, so that having died to the sins, we may live to the righteousness; *and* BY WHOSE WOUNDS YOU WERE HEALED—[25] for you were AS SHEEP GOING ASTRAY,[k] but you returned now to the Shepherd and Overseer of your souls.

3

[1] Likewise, the wives—be submitted to your own husbands, so that even if certain *ones* are unpersuaded by[l] the word, they may be won without the word through the conduct of the wives, [2] having seen your pure behavior in fear. [3] *And* whose adorning—let it not be *of* that which is outward (of braiding of *the* hair, and of putting around of gold *jewel-*

---

[a] יְשַׁעְיָהוּ Y'sha'yahu 28:16
[b] תְּהִלִּים T'hiliym 118:22
[c] יְשַׁעְיָהוּ Y'sha'yahu 8:14
[d] דְּבָרִים D'variym 10:15; cf. דְּבָרִים D'variym 7:6; יְשַׁעְיָהוּ Y'sha'yahu 43:20; "ancestry"—γένος, genos—race, family, nation, people; offspring, descendants; sort; kind
[e] שְׁמוֹת Sh'mot 19:6; cf. יְשַׁעְיָהוּ Y'sha'yahu 61:6—Gk. "kingly כֹּהֲנִים, ko'haniym"
[f] שְׁמוֹת Sh'mot 19:6; cf. דְּבָרִים D'variym 14:2
[g] דְּבָרִים D'variym 7:6, 14:2, 26:18; שְׁמוֹת Sh'mot 19:5
[h] הוֹשֵׁעַ Hoshea 2:1&25(1:10, 2:23)

[i] יְשַׁעְיָהוּ Y'sha'yahu 53:9
[j] יְשַׁעְיָהוּ Y'sha'yahu 53:11-12
[k] יְשַׁעְיָהוּ Y'sha'yahu 53:5-6
[l] "unpersuaded by"—ἀπειθέω, apeitheo, a negative of πείθω, peitho, which is most often translated "trust" or "persuade." Young says "disobedient to."

ry, or of putting on of clothes) ⁴but *of* the hidden man of the heart, in the immortal thing of the humble and tranquil רוּחַ, ruach, which is of great price in *the* sight of God. ⁵For also at one time, the holy women who hoped in God were adorning themselves this way, being submitted to their own husbands, ⁶*just* as שָׂרָה, Sarah (of whom you became daughters, doing good, and not fearing any terror) was obedient to אַבְרָהָם, Av'raham, calling him "sir."ᵃ

⁷The husbands, likewise—living with THEM, *behave* toward the wife (according to knowledge) as toward a weaker instrument, imparting honor, as also being heirs together of the *unmerited* favor of life, *so* that your prayers *will* not be hindered.

⁸And finally, be all of one mind, sharing the same feeling,ᵇ loving as brothers, compassionate, humble-minded,ᶜ ⁹not giving back evil for evil or insult for insult, but on the contrary, blessing, because you were called to this so that you may inherit a blessing. ¹⁰For,

"he who is wanting to love life and to see good days, let him guard his tongue from evil, and his lips—not to speak underhandedness. ¹¹And let him turn aside from evil, and do good; let him seek peace and pursue it, ¹²because the eyes of ADONAI ARE on the righteous, and His ears—to their request for help. But the face of ADONAI IS on those doing evil."ᵈ

¹³And who IS he who will be doing you evil, if you become zealousᵉ for that *which* is good? ¹⁴But if you should also suffer because of righteousness, happy ARE YOU! And do not be afraid of their fear, nor be troubled, ¹⁵but set apart the Messiahᶠ in your hearts *as* Master.

And always BE ready for *making a verbal* defense to everyone who is asking you for an account regarding the hope that IS in you, but with humility and fear, ¹⁶having a good conscience, so that in that in which they speak against you,ᵍ they may be ashamed—*those* who are defaming your good behavior in Messiah. ¹⁷For IT IS better *to be* doing good *and* (if the will of God wants it) to suffer, than *to be* doing evil, ¹⁸because Messiah also sufferedʰ once for sin—righteous for unrighteous—so that He might lead you to God (having been put to death, indeed, in the flesh, and having been made alive in רוּחַ, ruach, ¹⁹in which, having gone, He also proclaimed to the רוּחוֹת, ruchot in prison ²⁰who some time *ago* disbelieved, when the patience of God waited in *the* days of נֹחַ, Noach, *as* an ark *was* being prepared, in which few—that is, eight souls—were saved through water—²¹a thing also pointing to *that* whichⁱ now saves you: immersion—not a putting away of the filth of *bodily* flesh, but the question of a good conscience in regard to God—through the Rising Again of יֵשׁוּעַ, Yeshua *the* Messiah, ²²who is at the right hand of God, having gone on to Heaven, *with all* Messengers, and authorities, and powers having been submitted to Him).

4 ¹As Messiah, then, has sufferedʲ in the flesh, also arm yourselves with the same thinking, since he who suffers in the flesh is done with sin, ²to no longer live the remainder of *his* time in the flesh in the lusts of men, but in the will of God. ³For the past timeᵏ WAS sufficient to have worked the will of the גּוֹיִם, Goyim, having walked in sensualities, lusts, drunkennesses, orgies, drinking-bouts, and illicit idolatries; ⁴in which they think it strange—your not running with them to the same excess of reckless living—*and* are speaking evil *of you*, ⁵and who will give an account to Him who is ready to judge *the* liv-

---

ᵃ "sir" or "master"
ᵇ "sharing the same feeling"—Young's says, "having fellow-feeling"
ᶜ "humble-minded"—some mss say, "courteous"
ᵈ תְּהִלִּים T'hilyim 34:13-17(12-16)
ᵉ "zealous"—some mss say, "imitators"
ᶠ "Messiah"—some mss say, "God"
ᵍ Some mss insert, "as evil-doers"
ʰ "suffered"—other texts say, "died"
ⁱ "a thing also pointing to *that* which"—Young's says, "also to which an antitype"
ʲ Some mss insert, "for us"; also after "sufficient" in vs. 3
ᵏ Some mss insert, "of life"

ing and *the* dead. ⁶(Indeed, for this *reason* also, Good News was proclaimed to dead men, so that they may indeed be judged as men *alive* in the flesh, and may live according to *the will of* God in the רוּחַ, ruach.)

⁷Now the end of all things has come near. Be of sound mind, then, and soberminded in *your* prayers. ⁸In front of all things, *be* having the intense love to one another, because love covers a great number of sins.

⁹*Be* hospitable to one another without murmuring. ¹⁰*For* each *person*, as he received a gift, *should be* serving it to one another as good managers of the various *forms of* God's *unmerited* favor.

¹¹If anyone speaks, *it should be* "as sayings of God"; if anyone serves, *it should be* "as of the ability which God supplies," so that God may be glorified in all things through יֵשׁוּעַ, Yeshua *the* Messiah, to whom is the glory and the power—to the ages of the ages. אָמֵן, Amen!

¹²Loved ones, think it not strange at the fiery suffering among you that is coming to test you, as if a strange thing were happening to you. ¹³Rather, as you share in the sufferings of the Messiah, rejoice! so that also in the revealing of His glory, you may rejoice *with* extreme joy! ¹⁴If you are denounced in the Name of Messiah, YOU ARE happy, because the רוּחַ, Ruach of glory and of God rests on you.ᵃ ¹⁵Indeed, let none of you suffer as a murderer, or thief, or evil-doer, or as a meddler in other men's matters; ¹⁶but if as a Messiah-follower,ᵇ let him not be ashamed; and let him glorify God in this Name,ᶜ ¹⁷because *now* is the time of the beginning of the judgment with the house of God! (And if *it* first begins with us, what *will be* the end of those unpersuaded byᵈ the Good News of God? ¹⁸And IF THE RIGHTEOUS MAN IS SAVED WITH DIFFICULTY, WHAT OF THE UNGODLY AND *THE* SINNER? WHERE WILL HE BE SHOWN TO BE?ᵉ) ¹⁹Therefore, those suffering according to the will of God, let them also commit their souls to a faithful Creator in good-doing.

5

¹Therefore, זְקֵנִים, z'qeniym who ARE among you, I (who AM a fellow-זָקֵן, zaqen, and a witness of the sufferings of the Messiah, and a sharer of the glory about to be revealed) exhort *you:* ²shepherd the flock of God that IS among you, overseeing not because you are forced to, but willingly according to God;ᶠ and not for dishonest gain, but eager *to serve;* ³and not as lording it over those allotted *to your* care, but becoming examples of the flock. ⁴And at the appearing of the Head Shepherd, you will receive the unfading crown of glory.

⁵Likewise, you younger *ones:* be submitted to *the* זְקֵנִים, z'qeniym and all to one another;ᵍ clothe yourselves with humblemindedness, because GOD RESISTS THE PROUD, BUT TO THE HUMBLE HE GIVES *UNMERITED* FAVOR.ʰ ⁶Be humbled, then, under the powerful hand of God, so that He may exalt you in good time, ⁷having cast all your care on Him, because He cares for you.

⁸Be sober-minded *and* vigilant—your opponent, the Accuser, walks about as a roaring lion, seeking whom he may swallow up. ⁹Resist him,ⁱ firm in the faith—

ᵃ Some mss insert, "Indeed, in regard to them, He is evil-spoken of, and in regard to you, He is glorified."

ᵇ "Messiah-follower"(or "Messianic"); lit. Χριστιανός, Christianos, that is, "Christian." Though the terms "Messiah" and "Christ" today are culturally and sociologically disparate, they are *theologically* equivalent, both meaning "anointed *one*."

ᶜ "in this Name"—some mss say, "in this respect"

ᵈ "unpersuaded by"—ἀπειθέω, apeitheo, a negative of πείθω, peitho, which is most often translated "trust" or "persuade." Here, Young says "disobedient to."

ᵉ מִשְׁלֵי Mish'lei 11:31 (LXX); according to the Hebrew, "Look! the righteous in the land *of the earth* receives his due; surely also the wicked and the sinner!"

ᶠ Some mss omit, "according to God"

ᵍ Some mss insert, "submitting yourselves." Though context implies this, the phrase is not in the text.

ʰ מִשְׁלֵי Mish'lei 3:34

ⁱ "Resist him"—lit. "whom resist"

having known *that* the same sufferings are being accomplished among your brotherhood throughout the world.

¹⁰And the God of all *unmerited* favor—who called you (having suffered a little *while*) to His age-enduring glory in Messiah[a]—will Himself restore, stabilize, strengthen, *and* settle YOU. ¹¹To Him IS[b] the power—to the ages and the ages! אָמֵן, Amen.

¹²Through Silvanus[c] (the faithful brother to you, as I consider *him*) I wrote *to you* through *a* few WORDS, exhorting *you* and testifying this to be the true *unmerited* favor of God—in which, stand! ¹³The co-chosen in Babylon,[d] and Mark, my son, greet you.

¹⁴Greet one another in a kiss of love. Peace to you all who ARE in Messiah![e]

---

[a] Some mss insert, "יֵשׁוּעַ, Yeshua"
[b] Some mss insert, "the glory, and"
[c] "Silvanus"—a variant of סִילָא, Siyla
[d] "the co-chosen in Babylon," in Young's reads, "the ASSEMBLY in Babylon jointly elected"
[e] Some mss conclude, "יֵשׁוּעַ, Yeshua, אָמֵן, Amen."

מִכְתָּב לִיהוּדִים מְשִׁיחִיִּים   A LETTER TO MESSIANIC JEWS

עִבְרִים Iv'riym

1 ¹In many parts and many ways, God, having spoken to the fathers in the prophets long ago, ²in these last days spoke to us in a Son (whom He appointed heir of all things; through whom He also made the ages), ³who—being the brightness of the glory, and the *exact* imprint of His substantive existence; also sustaining all the things by the spoken word of His power[a]—having made a cleansing of[b] sins, sat down at the right hand of the Greatness in the Highest, ⁴having become so much better than the Messengers, as He inherited a more excellent Name than they. ⁵For to which of the Messengers did He ever say,

"You are My Son—today, I have brought you forth"[c]?

And again,

"I will be to him for a father, and he will be to Me for a son"[d]

⁶and again, when He brings in the firstborn to the world, He says,

"And let them bow before him—all Messengers of God,"[e]

⁷and to the Messengers, indeed, He says,

"He is making His Messengers רוּחוֹת, ruchot, and His servants a flame of fire,"[f]

⁸but to the Son,

"Your throne, O God, IS to the age of the age; and the scepter of righteousness IS the scepter of your reign. ⁹You loved righteousness and hated wickedness. Because of this, God, your God, anointed you with *the* oil of rejoicing above your companions,"[g]

¹⁰and,

"At the beginning, Master, You laid the foundation *of* the earth, and the heavens are the work of your hands. ¹¹These will be destroyed, but You will remain, and all *else*, like a garment,

---

[a] Some mss insert, "through Himself"
[b] Some mss insert, "our"
[c] תְּהִלִּים T'hiliym 2:7
[d] שְׁמוּאֵל ב Sh'muel Beit 7:14, דִּבְרֵי־הַיָּמִים א Div'rei Ha-Yamiym Alef 17:13
[e] תְּהִלִּים T'hiliym 97:7
[f] תְּהִלִּים T'hiliym 104:4
[g] תְּהִלִּים T'hiliym 45:7-8(6-7)

The supremacy of the Son. עִבְרִים Iv'riym 2:18

will become old. ¹²And You will roll them together as a robe, and like a garment[a] they will be changed, but You are the same, and Your years will not fail."[b]

¹³And to which of the Messengers did He ever say,

"Sit at My right hand, until I make your enemies your footstool"[c]?

¹⁴Are they not all *just* רוּחוֹת, ruchot of service—being sent forth for serving for the sake of those about to inherit salvation?

2 ¹Because of this, it is more abundantly necessary *for* us to pay careful attention to the things *we* heard; otherwise, we may glide aside. ²Indeed, if the word being spoken through Messengers became reliable, and every sidestepping and disobedience received a just payment, ³how will we escape *punishment*, having neglected so great a salvation (which, *after* receiving a beginning to be spoken through the Master, was confirmed to us by those having heard, ⁴*and* God *was* also bearing joint-witness, both with signs and wonders, and various powers, and distributions of the רוּחַ הַקֹּדֶשׁ, Ruach HaQodesh, according to His will)?

⁵For not to Messengers did He submit the coming world of which we speak, ⁶but *some*one in a certain place testified fully, saying,

"What is man, that You are mindful of him—or a son of man, that You look after him? ⁷You made him a little lower than Messengers—with glory and honor You crowned him.[d] ⁸You put all things in submission under his feet."[e]

For in the submitting all the things to him, He left nothing unsubmitted to him. And now we do not yet see all the things submitted to him, ⁹but we see him who was made a little lower than Messengers—יֵשׁוּעַ, Yeshua—because of the suffering of the death, having been crowned with glory and honor, *so* that by the *unmerited* favor of God he might taste of death for everyone.

¹⁰For it was appropriate for Him (because of whom ARE all the things, and through whom ARE all the things) *who is* bringing many sons to glory, to make perfect through sufferings the author of their salvation. ¹¹For both he who is setting apart and those *who are* set apart ARE all of one *Father*, for which reason he is not ashamed to call them brothers, ¹²saying,

"I will declare Your Name to my brothers; in the middle of the קָהָל, qahal I will sing praise to You";[f]

and again,

"I will be trusting in Him";[g]

¹³and again,

"Look! I and the children that God gave to me..."[h]

¹⁴Seeing, then, *that* the children have shared in blood and flesh, He Himself likewise shared of the same, so that through death He might destroy him *who is* having the power of death—that is, the Accuser—¹⁵and might deliver those who, with fear of death, throughout all their life were enslaved to slavery.[i] ¹⁶For doubtless, it does not take hold of Messengers, but it takes hold of *the* seed of אַבְרָהָם, Av'raham. ¹⁷Therefore, it was necessary *for* Him to be made like the brothers in all things, so that He might become a merciful and faithful כֹּהֵן גָּדוֹל, Kohen Gadol in the things with God, to make appeasement for the sins of the people. ¹⁸For in that *which* He suffered, Himself being tempted, He is able to help those who are tempted.

---

[a] Some mss omit, "like a garment"
[b] תְּהִלִּים *T'hiliym* 102:26-28(25-27)
[c] תְּהִלִּים *T'hiliym* 110:1
[d] Some mss insert, "and set him over the works of Your hands"
[e] תְּהִלִּים *T'hiliym* 8:5-7(4-6)
[f] תְּהִלִּים *T'hiliym* 22:23(22)
[g] יְשַׁעְיָהוּ *Y'sha'yahu* 8:17
[h] יְשַׁעְיָהוּ *Y'sha'yahu* 8:18
[i] "enslaved to slavery"—Young's says, "subjects of bondage"

3 ¹Therefore, holy brothers, sharers in a heavenly calling, consider the Emissary and כֹּהֵן הַגָּדוֹל, Kohen HaGadol whom we profess:ᵃ יֵשׁוּעַ, Yeshua, ²*who is* being faithful to Him who appointed him, as also מֹשֶׁה, Mosheh *was faithful* in all His House. ³For this One has been counted worthy of more glory than מֹשֶׁה, Mosheh, inasmuch as he who builds *the house* has more honor than the house *itself*, ⁴for every house is built by someone, and He who built all things *is* God. ⁵And מֹשֶׁה, Mosheh, WAS indeed faithful in all His House as an attendant, for a testimony of those things that were to be spoken, ⁶but Messiah *is faithful* as a Son over His House, whose House we are if we hold fast until the end *to* the boldness and the rejoicing of the hope.

⁷Therefore, as the רוּחַ הַקֹּדֶשׁ, Ruach HaQodesh says,

"Today, if you hear His voice, ⁸do not harden your hearts, as in the Provocation—in the day of the testing in the desert,ᵇ ⁹in which your fathers tempted Me in trying Me, and saw My actions. ¹⁰*For* forty years, therefore, I was grieved with this generation and said, 'They always go astray in heart,' and 'These have not known My ways.' ¹¹So I swore *an oath* in My anger, 'They will notᶜ enter into My stopping-place!'"ᵈ

¹²See *this*, brothers; otherwise, there will be in any *one* of you an evil heart of unbelief *resulting* in the falling away from the living God. ¹³Rather, exhort one another every day—while *it* is called the Today—so that none of you may be hardened by the deceitfulness of the sin. ¹⁴For we have become sharers of the Messiah if *to* the beginning of the confidence we hold fast until the end, ¹⁵in its being said,

"Today, if you hear His voice, do not harden your hearts, as in the Provocation."

¹⁶For certain *ones*, having heard, provoked *Him*, though not all who came out of מִצְרַיִם, Mitz'rayim through מֹשֶׁה, Mosheh *did so*.

¹⁷But with whom was He grieved *those* forty years? Was it not with those who sinned—whose dead bodies fell in the desert?

¹⁸And to whom did He swear that they will not enter into His stopping-place, except to those who did not believe? ¹⁹And *so* we see that they were not able to enter in because of unbelief.

4 ¹We should fear, then; otherwise, the promise of entering into His stopping-place *is being left behind, and* any one of you seems to have come short of it. ²For we also are having Good News proclaimed *to us*, even as they *did*, but the word *they* heard did not benefit them, not being mixed with faith in those who heard. ³For we do enter into the stopping-place—we who believed—as He said,

"So I swore *an oath* in My anger, 'They will not enter into My stopping-place!'"

and yet the works were done from the foundation of the world. ⁴For He spoke this in a certain place concerning the seventh DAY:

"And God stopped from all His works in the seventh day."ᵉ

⁵but in this PASSAGE (again),

"They will not enter into My stopping-place!"

⁶Since, then, it remains for certain *ones* to enter into it, and those who first heard *the* Good News did not enter in because of unbelief, ⁷again, He limits *it to* a certain day: "Today" (in דָּוִד, David saying *it* after so long a time), as it has been *already* said,

---

ᵃ Some mss insert, "Messiah"
ᵇ see שְׁמוֹת *Sh'mot* 17:1-7
ᶜ "they will not"—lit. "if they will"; however, cf. vs. 18; also in 4:3 and 4:5
ᵈ תְּהִלִּים *T'hiliym* 95:7-11 (LXX), referring to the Promised Land
ᵉ בְּרֵאשִׁית *B'reshiyt* 2:2

"Today, if you hear His voice, do not harden your hearts."

⁸For if יְהוֹשֻׁעַ, Y'hoshua had caused them to stop,[a] God would not have spoken after these things regarding another "day." ⁹There remains, then, a שַׁבָּת, Shabat-keeping[b] to the people of God; ¹⁰for he who entered into His stopping-place, he also stopped from his works, as God *did* from His own.

¹¹Let us be diligent, then, to enter into that stopping-place, so that no one may fall by *following* the same example of unbelief. ¹²For the reckoning[c] of God is living, and active, and sharp above every two-edged sword, and piercing to the dividing apart of soul and רוּחַ, ruach, also of joints and marrow, and a discerner of thoughts and intents of the heart. ¹³And there is not a created thing hidden from His sight; rather, all things ARE naked and open to His eyes—with whom is our reckoning.

¹⁴Having, then, a great כֹּהֵן גָּדוֹל, Kohen Gadol passed through the heavens— יֵשׁוּעַ, Yeshua, the Son of God—let us hold fast *to* the profession *of faith*. ¹⁵For we have a כֹּהֵן גָּדוֹל, Kohen Gadol not unable to sympathize with our weaknesses, but ONE tempted in all things likewise *as we are*, *yet remaining* apart from sin. ¹⁶Let us come near, then—unhindered—to the throne of *unmerited* favor, so that we may receive *loving*-kindness and find *unmerited* favor—for timely help.

5

¹For every כֹּהֵן גָּדוֹל, Kohen Gadol— taken from *among* men on behalf of men—is set *in place* in things PERTAINING to God, so that he may offer both gifts and sacrifices for sins, ²*and be* able to be gentle to those ignorant and going astray (since *he* himself is also encompassed with weakness, ³and because of it, he *is* also so obligated to offer *sacrifices* for *his own* sins as *well as* for the people). ⁴And no one takes this honor to himself, but *only* if called by God, as אַהֲרֹן, A'haron also *was*. ⁵So also the Messiah did not glorify Himself to become כֹּהֵן גָּדוֹל, Kohen Gadol, but *rather* He who spoke to Him,

"You are My Son; today I have brought You forth";[d]

⁶as also in another PASSAGE He says,

"You ARE a כֹּהֵן, kohen to the age, according to the order of מַלְכִּי־צֶדֶק, Mal'kiy-Tzedeq";[e]

⁷who, in the days of His *being in the* flesh, having offered up both prayers and requests for help to Him who was able to save Him from death—with strong crying and tears—and having been heard with respect to that which He revered, ⁸though being a Son, learned the obedience by the things which He suffered.

⁹And having been made perfect, He became a cause of age-enduring salvation to all those obeying Him, ¹⁰having been addressed by God *as* a כֹּהֵן גָּדוֹל, Kohen Gadol according to the order of מַלְכִּי־צֶדֶק, Mal'kiy-Tzedeq.

¹¹About that *one* we have many words, and *they are* of hard explanation to say, since you have become dull of hearing. ¹²For even *though* (because of the time) *you* ought to be teachers, again you have need that one teach you what the fundamental basics of the sayings of God ARE, and you have become needing of milk, and not of solid food. ¹³For everyone who is partaking of milk IS unskilled in the word of righteousness—for he is an infant—¹⁴but the solid food is for mature ones, who, through practice, are having their senses trained to the discernment both of good and of evil.

6

¹Therefore, having moved on from[f] the fundamental word of the Messiah, let us go on to the maturity, not

---

[a] "caused them to stop"—Young's says, "given them rest"
[b] "a Shabat-keeping"—Young's says, "a sabbatical rest"
[c] "reckoning" (λόγος, logos) or "account-settling"; also in vs. 13
[d] תְּהִלִּים T'hiliym 2:7
[e] תְּהִלִּים T'hiliym 110:4
[f] "moved on from"—ἀφέντες, aphentes—"left" or "sent away"

laying again a foundation of reformation from dead actions, and of faith on God, ²of the teaching about immersions, also of laying on of hands, also of rising again of the dead, and of judgment age-enduring. ³And this we will do, if God permits, ⁴for IT IS impossible for those once enlightened (having tasted also of the heavenly gift, and having become sharers of the רוּחַ הַקֹּדֶשׁ, Ruach HaQodesh, ⁵and tasted the good saying of God, also the powers of the coming age) ⁶and having fallen away, to *be* renew*ed* again to reformation (having again crucified the Son of God to themselves, and exposed *Him* to public shame). ⁷For land that is drinking in the rain *that is* coming upon it many times, and is bringing forth vegetation fit for those because of whom it is also tilled, shares in blessing from God. ⁸But that *land* which is bearing thorns and thistles IS disapproved of, and near to *receiving* cursing. Its end WILL BE for burning.

⁹But we are persuaded concerning you, loved ones, *of* the things that are better and *are* accompanying salvation (even though we speak this way). ¹⁰For God is not unrighteous to forget your work and[a] the love that you showed to His Name, having served (and *continuing to* serve) the קְדוֹשִׁים, Q'doshiym. ¹¹And we desire *for* each one of you to show the same diligence, to the full assurance of the Hope until the end, ¹²so that you may not become sluggish, but imitators of those who —through faith and patient endurance— are inheriting the promises.

¹³For to אַבְרָהָם, Av'raham, God, having made *the* promise—seeing He was able to swear by no *one* greater—swore by Himself, ¹⁴saying,

"With blessing indeed I will bless you, and multiplying I will multiply you,"[b]

¹⁵and so, having patiently endured, he obtained the promise. ¹⁶For men swear by the *one* greater *than* themselves, and the oath for confirmation IS an end of all controversy to them. ¹⁷In that *manner*, God— more abundantly wanting to show to the heirs of the promise the immutability of His purpose—intervened by an oath. ¹⁸*He did this so* that through two immutable things in which IT IS impossible for God to lie, we who fled for refuge to take hold of the hope set before US may have a strong comfort—¹⁹which we have as an anchor of the soul, both sure and reliable —and entering into that within the veil, ²⁰where a forerunner entered for us: יֵשׁוּעַ, Yeshua, after the order of מַלְכִּי־צֶדֶק, Mal'-kiy-Tzedeq, having become כֹּהֵן גָּדוֹל, Kohen Gadol—to the age.

7 ¹For this מַלְכִּי־צֶדֶק, Mal'kiy-Tzedeq, כֹּהֵן לְאֵל עֶלְיוֹן מֶלֶךְ שָׁלֵם, Melekh Shalem, Kohen l'El El'yon (who met אַבְרָהָם, Av'raham *as he was* returning from the slaughter of the kings, and blessed him; ²to whom אַבְרָהָם, Av'raham also apportioned a tenth of all)[c]—first, indeed, being interpreted, *his name means,* "King of Righteousness," and then also מֶלֶךְ שָׁלֵם, Melekh Shalem, which means, "King of Peace." ³*He is* without father, without mother, without genealogy, having neither beginning of days nor end of life, and, being made like to the Son of God, *he* remains a כֹּהֵן, Kohen continually.

⁴And see how great this one IS, to whom אַבְרָהָם, Av'raham the patriarch also gave out a tenth of the best of the plunder! ⁵And indeed, those out of the sons of לֵוִי, Leviy *who are* receiving the כְּהֻנָּה, K'hunah have a command to take tenths from the people—that is, their brothers—according to the תּוֹרָה, Torah (even though they came forth out from the loins of אַבְרָהָם, Av'raham); ⁶but he who was not traced from their genealogy *nevertheless* received tenths from אַבְרָהָם, Av'raham, and he blessed him who was having the promises. ⁷And without any dispute,[d] the lesser is blessed by the better—⁸and here *in the one case,* in-

---

[a] Some mss insert, "the labor of"
[b] בְּרֵאשִׁית B'reshiyt 22:17
[c] see בְּרֵאשִׁית B'reshiyt 14:17-20
[d] "without any dispute"—Young's says, "apart from all controversy"

deed, men who die receive tenths; but there *in the other case, it is* HE of whom *it* is testified that he was living *forever.* ⁹And so, in a manner of speaking,ᵃ even לֵוִי, Leviy (who receives tenths) paid tenths through אַבְרָהָם, Av'raham, ¹⁰for he was still in the loins of his father when מַלְכִּי־צֶדֶק, Mal'kiy-Tzedeq met *Av'raham.*

¹¹If indeed, then, perfection were through the כְּהֻנָּה, K'hunah of לֵוִי, Leviy (for the people under it received the תּוֹרָה, Torah), what further need *had they* for another כֹּהֵן, kohen to arise—*one* according to the order of מַלְכִּי־צֶדֶק, Mal'kiy-Tzedeq—and not to be called according to the order of אַהֲרֹן, A'haron? ¹²For *in the event of* the כְּהֻנָּה, K'hunah being changed, of necessity also comes a change of the תּוֹרָה, Torah. ¹³For He of whom these things are said has had part in another tribe of whom no one gave attendance at the altar. ¹⁴For IT IS evident that out of יְהוּדָה, Y'hudah our Master has arisen, in regard to which tribe מֹשֶׁה, Mosheh spoke nothing concerning כֹּהֲנִים, ko'haniym.

¹⁵And it is yet more abundantly most evident if there arises another כֹּהֵן, kohen according to the likeness of מַלְכִּי־צֶדֶק, Mal'kiy-Tzedeq, ¹⁶who came not according to the תּוֹרָה, Torah of a command regarding the flesh,ᵇ but according to the power of an endless life. ¹⁷For it is testified *of Him,*

"You ARE a כֹּהֵן, kohen to the age, according to the order of מַלְכִּי־צֶדֶק, Mal'kiy-Tzedeq";ᶜ

¹⁸for a nullification of the former command indeed comes because of its weakness and uselessness—¹⁹for the תּוֹרָה, Torah *made* nothing perfect—and the bringing in of a better hope, through which we draw near to God.

²⁰And inasmuch as IT WAS not without an oath (for those without an oath did indeed become כֹּהֲנִים, ko'haniym, ²¹but *this One became a kohen* with an oath through Him who is saying to Him,

"ADONAI swears, and will not regret, You ARE a כֹּהֵן, kohen—to the age"ᵈ),

²²by so much *more* has יֵשׁוּעַ, Yeshua also become *the* guarantee of a better בְּרִית, b'riyt. ²³And those who have become כֹּהֲנִים, ko'haniym are indeed many, because they are hindered by death from remaining *in office*. ²⁴But *this One*, because of His remaining to the age, has the כְּהֻנָּה, K'hunah non-transient. ²⁵Therefore, He is also able to save to the very end those coming through Him to God *because He is* ever living to make intercession for them.

²⁶For such a כֹּהֵן גָּדוֹל, Kohen Gadol was also appropriate *for* us—pure, innocent, undefiled, separate from the sinners, and become higher than the heavens—²⁷who has no daily need (as the כֹּהֲנִים הַגְּדוֹלִים, Ko'haniym HaG'doliym) first to offer up sacrifice for His own sins, then for those of the people. For this He did once, having offered up Himself, ²⁸for the תּוֹרָה, Torah appoints *as* כֹּהֲנִים גְּדוֹלִים, Ko'haniym G'doliym men having weakness, but the word of the oath that COMES after the תּוֹרָה, Torah APPOINTS the Son, *who is* having been perfected to the age.

8 ¹And *so* the summary regarding the things spoken of IS *this:* we have such a כֹּהֵן גָּדוֹל, Kohen Gadol who sat down at the right hand of the throne of the greatness in the Heavens, ²a servant of the holy places and of the true מִשְׁכָּן, Mish'kan, which the Master set up, not man.

³For every כֹּהֵן גָּדוֹל, Kohen Gadol is appointed to offer both gifts and sacrifices; therefore, IT IS necessary for this One to also have something that He may offer. ⁴If indeed, then, He were upon earth, He would not be a כֹּהֵן, kohen (there *already* being those who are offering the gifts according to תּוֹרָה, Torah, ⁵who serve as an example and shadow of the heavenly things,

---

ᵃ "in a manner of speaking"—Young's says, "so to speak"
ᵇ "command regarding the flesh"—Young's says, "fleshly command"
ᶜ תְּהִלִּים T'hiliym 110:4
ᵈ תְּהִלִּים T'hiliym 110:4; also, some mss repeat here, "according to the order of מַלְכִּי־צֶדֶק, Mal'kiy-Tzedeq"

Iv'riym עִבְרִים 8:6 — HaB'riyt Ha'Chadashah.

just as מֹשֶׁה, Mosheh, being about to construct the מִשְׁכָּן, Mish'kan, had been divinely warned: for "SEE," He says, "THAT YOU MAKE ALL THINGS ACCORDING TO THE PATTERN THAT WAS SHOWN TO YOU ON THE MOUNTAIN"ᵃ). ⁶But now *that* He has obtained a more excellent service, how much is He also mediator of a better בְּרִית, b'riyt, which has been sanctioned *by Torah*ᵇ on better promises.

⁷For if that first *K'hunah* were faultless, a place would not have been sought for a second.ᶜ ⁸For finding fault with them, He said,

"'Look! Days come,' says ADONAI, 'and I will complete a בְּרִית חֲדָשָׁה, b'riyt 'chadashah with the house of יִשְׂרָאֵל, Yis'rael, and with the house of יְהוּדָה, Y'hudah, ⁹not according to the בְּרִית, b'riyt that I made with their fathers (in the day of My taking THEM by their hand to bring them out of the land of מִצְרַיִם, Mitz'rayim) because they did not remain in My בְּרִית, b'riyt, and I disregarded them,' says ADONAI. ¹⁰'Because this IS the בְּרִית, b'riyt that I will make with the house of יִשְׂרָאֵל, Yis'rael after those days,' says ADONAI, 'giving My תּוֹרָה, Torah into their mind, and upon their hearts I will write them, and I will be to them for a God, and they will be to Me for a people. ¹¹And they will not teach each *one* his neighbor, and each *one* his brother, saying, "Know ADONAI," because they will all know Me—from the small one, to the great one of them—¹²because I will be merciful to their unrighteousness, and their sinsᵈ I will remember no more.'"ᵉ

¹³In the saying "חֲדָשָׁה, 'chadashah," He has made the first *K'hunah* old, and what becomes obsolete and is old IS near disappearing.

⁹ ¹Indeed, then, even the first *K'HUNAH*ᶠ had regulations of service, *and* also an earthlyᵍ holy-place. ²For a מִשְׁכָּן, mish'kan was prepared: the first *mish'kan* (in which was both the מְנוֹרָה, m'norah and the table, and the לֶחֶם הַפָּנִים, Lechem HaPaniym) which is called, "קֹדֶשׁ, Qodesh"; ³and after the second curtain, a מִשְׁכָּן, mish'kan that is called, "קֹדֶשׁ הַקֳּדָשִׁים, Qodesh HaQodashiym" ⁴(having a golden incense-holder, and the אֲרוֹן הַבְּרִית, 'Aron HaB'riyt overlaid all around with gold, in which IS the golden pot having the מָן, mahn, and the rod of אַהֲרֹן, A'haron that budded,ʰ and the tablets of the בְּרִית, B'riyt, ⁵and over it, כְּרֻבִים, K'ruviym of the Glory, overshadowing the כַּפֹּרֶת, Kaporet, about which we are not to speak now in detail).

⁶And *with* these things having been prepared this way, indeed, the כֹּהֲנִים, Ko'haniym go in at all times into the first מִשְׁכָּן, mish'kan, performing the services, ⁷but only the כֹּהֵן הַגָּדוֹל, Kohen HaGadol *goes* into the second *mish'kan just* once in the year (not apart from blood—which he offers for himself and *for* the errors of the people), ⁸the רוּחַ הַקֹּדֶשׁ, Ruach HaQodesh *thus* making this clear: that *since* the first מִשְׁכָּן, mish'kan was still standing, the way of the holy PLACES had not been yet been revealed ⁹(which IS an analogy in regard to the present time, in which both gifts and sacrifices are offered which, in regard to conscience, are not able to make perfect him who is serving; ¹⁰*rather, these* only involve foods, and drinks, and different immersions—material regulations imposed on THEM until the time of restraightening).

¹¹But Messiah, כֹּהֵן גָּדוֹל, Kohen Gadol of the good things *that* have come,ⁱ having come through the greater and more perfect מִשְׁכָּן, mish'kan (not made with hands; that is, not of this creation) ¹²nor through *the* blood of goats and calves, but through His own blood, entered in once *for all* into

---

ᵃ שְׁמוֹת *Sh'mot* 25:40
ᵇ "sanctioned *by Torah*"—νενομοθέτηται, nenomothetetai; cf. 7:11, same word used
ᶜ cf. 7:11
ᵈ Some mss insert, "and their misdeeds"
ᵉ יִרְמְיָהוּ *Yir'm'yahu* 31:31-34

ᶠ "*K'HUNAH*"—Young says "tabernacle" here, though neither word appears in the text.
ᵍ "earthly"—from κοσμικός, kosmikos
ʰ see בְּמִדְבַּר *B'mid'bar* 17:23(8)
ⁱ "have come"—some mss say, "*are coming*"

the holy places, having obtained age-enduring redemption. ¹³For if sprinkling the blood of goats, and *of* bulls, and ashes of a heifer *upon* those *who are* defiled sets *them* apart to the purifying of the flesh, ¹⁴how much more, *then*, will the blood of the Messiah (who through the age-enduring רוּחַ, Ruach offered Himself unblemished to God) purify our conscience from dead actions to serve the Living God?

¹⁵And because of this, He is *the* mediator of a בְּרִית חֲדָשָׁה, b'riyt 'chadashah—*His* death having come for redemption for the sidesteps under the בְּרִית רִאשֹׁנָה, b'riyt rishonah—*so that* those *who are* called may receive the promise of the age-enduring inheritance. ¹⁶For *example*, where there IS a *will and* testament,[a] the death of the one who made the *will and* testament[b] is necessary to come in, ¹⁷because a *will and* testament IS *only* in effect[c] over *the* dead,[d] since it has no force at all when the one who made the *will and* testament lives.

¹⁸Therefore, not even the *b'riyt* רִאשֹׁנָה, rishonah has been initiated apart from blood. ¹⁹For *with* every command having been spoken by מֹשֶׁה, Mosheh to all the people according to the תּוֹרָה, Torah, having taken the blood of the calves and the goats with water, and scarlet wool, and hyssop, he sprinkled both the book itself and all the people, ²⁰saying, "This IS THE BLOOD OF THE בְּרִית, B'RIYT THAT God *has* enjoined to you."[e] ²¹And likewise, he sprinkled both the מִשְׁכָּן, mish'kan and all the things of the service with blood.

²²And with blood, almost all things are purified according to the תּוֹרָה, Torah; and apart from blood-shedding, forgiveness does not come.[f]

²³ IT IS therefore indeed necessary *for* the pattern of the things in the Heavens to be purified with these *sacrifices*, and *for* the heavenly things themselves *to be* purified with sacrifices better than these. ²⁴For Messiah did not enter into holy places made with hands (*which are mere* depictions of the true *holy place*) but into the Heaven itself, now to appear in the presence of God for us. ²⁵Nor *did He enter* Heaven so that He may offer Himself many times (as the כֹּהֵן הַגָּדוֹל, Kohen HaGadol enters into the holy places every year with *the* blood of others), ²⁶since it would *then* be necessary for Him to suffer many times from the foundation of the world. But now—once—at the full end of the ages, He has been revealed for *the* nullification of sin through His sacrifice. ²⁷And *just* as it is laid up *in store* for men to die once, and after this *to face* judgment, ²⁸so also the Messiah (having been offered once, to bear the sins of many) will appear a second time—apart from *being* a sin-offering, to those waiting for Him—to salvation!

10

¹For the תּוֹרָה, Torah (having a shadow of the coming good things, *but* not the very image of the matters *themselves*) is never able to make perfect those coming near by *way of* the same sacrifices that they continually offer every year. ²Otherwise, would not the *sacrifices* have ceased to be offered because of those *who are* serving (having once been purified) no longer having consciousness of sins? ³But in those SACRIFICES is a remembrance of sins every year, ⁴for it is impossible for *the* blood of bulls and goats to take away sins.

⁵Therefore—coming into the world—He says, "YOU DID NOT WANT SACRIFICE AND OFFERING, but You prepared a body for me; ⁶in BURNT-OFFERINGS, AND REGARDING SIN-OFFERINGS, YOU DID NOT delight. ⁷THEN I SAID, 'LOOK! I COME (IT HAS BEEN WRITTEN ABOUT ME IN A SCROLL OF THE BOOK) TO DO YOUR WILL, O GOD."[g] ⁸*By* saying *the* above *statement* ("SACRI-

---

[a] "testament"—Young's says, "covenant"; also in vs 17

[b] "one who made the *will and* testament"—Young's says, "covenant-victim"; also in verse 17

[c] "in effect"—Young's says, "steadfast," meaning "reliable"

[d] "dead"—Young's says, "dead victims"

[e] שְׁמוֹת *Sh'mot* 24:8

[f] cf. וַיִּקְרָא *Vayiq'ra* 17:11

[g] תְּהִלִּים *T'hiliym* 40:7-9(6-8); cf. LXX

FICES, AND OFFERINGS, AND BURNT-OFFERINGS, AND REGARDING SIN-OFFERING"—which are offered according to תּוֹרָה, Torah—"YOU DID NOT WANT, nor delight in," ⁹then He said, "LOOK! I COME TO DO YOUR WILL"ᵃ), He takes away the first *K'hunah*, so that He may establish the second—¹⁰in whose will we are having been set apart through the offering of the body of יֵשׁוּעַ, Yeshua *the Messiah, once for all.*

¹¹And every כֹּהֵן, kohen, indeed, has stood daily, serving, and *is* offering many times the same sacrifices that are never able to take away sins. ¹²But this One, having offered one sacrifice for sin to the end *of time,* sat down at the right hand of God. ¹³As to the remainder, *He waits,* expecting, UNTIL HE PLACES HIS ENEMIES AS HIS FOOTSTOOL.ᵇ ¹⁴For by one offering, He has perfected to the end those *who are* set apart; ¹⁵and to us the רוּחַ הַקֹּדֶשׁ, Ruach HaQodesh also testifies. For after that, He says,

¹⁶"This IS the בְּרִית, b'riyt that I will make with them after those days," says ADONAI, "giving My תּוֹרָה, Torah on their hearts, and upon their mind I will write them,"ᶜ

¹⁷and,

"their sins and their misdeeds I will remember no more."ᵈ

¹⁸And where forgiveness of these IS, there is no longer *any* offering for sin.

¹⁹Therefore, brothers, having boldness for *approaching* the entrance into the holy places by the blood of יֵשׁוּעַ, Yeshua, ²⁰*we have a* way which He initiated for us—new and living, through the curtain (that is, His flesh)—²¹and a כֹּהֵן גָּדוֹל, Kohen Gadol over the House of God.

²²Let us draw near with a true heart, in full assurance of faith, having the hearts sprinkled from an evil conscience, and having the body bathed with pure water. ²³May we hold fast *to* the unwavering profession of the hope (for He who promised IS faithful). ²⁴And let us consider *how* to provoke one another to love and to good actions, ²⁵not forsaking the gathering of ourselves together, as IS the custom of certain *people,* but exhorting *one another,* and so much the more as you see the Day coming near.

²⁶For *if* we *keep* willfully sinning after the receiving *of* the full knowledge of the truth, *then* there no longer remains a sacrifice for sins, ²⁷but a certain *kind of* fearful expectationᵉ of judgment and fiery zeal, about to devour the opposers. ²⁸Anyone who has made a תּוֹרַת, Torah of מֹשֶׁה, Mosheh as nothing,ᶠ dies apart from compassion by *the testimony of* two or three witnesses. ²⁹Of how much sorer punishment, *then,* will he be counted worthy—he who trampled on the Son of God, and counted *as* a common thing the blood of the בְּרִית, b'riyt (in which he was set apart), and brought insult to the רוּחַ, Ruach of the *unmerited* favor? ³⁰For we have known Him who is saying,

"Vengeance IS Mine; I will repay,"ᵍ

and again,

"ADONAI will judge His people."ʰ

³¹A fearful *thing* IS the falling into the hands of a living God.

³²And call to your remembrance the former days, in which, having been enlightened, you endured much conflict of sufferings, ³³partly both with disgraces and oppressions (*you* being made objects of ridicule), and partly having become sharers of those so living. ³⁴For you also sympathized with prisoners,ⁱ and the robbery of your property you received with joy, knowing that you yourselves have a

---

ᵃ Some mss insert, "O GOD"
ᵇ תְּהִלִּים *T'hiliym* 110:1
ᶜ יִרְמְיָהוּ *Yir'm'yahu* 31:33
ᵈ יִרְמְיָהוּ *Yir'm'yahu* 31:34
ᵉ "expectation"—Young's says, "looking for"
ᶠ "made... as nothing"—Young's says, "set at nought"
ᵍ דְּבָרִים *D'variym* 32:35; some mss insert, "says ADONAI"
ʰ דְּבָרִים *D'variym* 32:36
ⁱ "prisoners"—some mss say, "my bonds"

Triumphs of faith. עִבְרִים Iv'riym 11:18

better possession,[a] and an enduring one. [35]You must not throw away, then, your boldness, which has great payment of reward, [36]for you have need of perseverance, so that you—having done the will of God —will receive the promise. [37]For *in yet a very little while*, He who is coming will come, and will not delay;[b] [38]and,

"my righteous *one* will live by faith,"[c]

and,

"if he draws back, My soul has no pleasure in him,"[d]

[39]but we are not of those *who are* drawing back to destruction, but of those believing to a preserving of *the* soul.

11 [1]Now faith is a confidence of things hoped for, a conviction regarding matters not seen, [2]for in this were those of old[e] testified of. [3]By faith we understand the ages to have been prepared by a saying of God (in regard to the thing *that is* seen having not come out of *the* things *that are* appearing).

[4]By faith, הֶבֶל, Hevel offered a better sacrifice to God than קַיִן, Qayin, through which he was testified to be righteous— God testifying of his gifts—and through it, he being dead still speaks.

[5]By faith, חֲנוֹךְ, 'Chanokh was changed (to not see death—and *he* was not found) because God changed him. Indeed before the change, he had been testified about— that he had pleased God well [6](and apart from faith it is impossible to please *God* well, for it is necessary for him who is coming to God to believe that He is, and to those seeking Him, He becomes a rewarder).

[7]By faith, נֹחַ, Noach—having been divinely warned concerning the things not yet seen, having feared—prepared an ark to the salvation of his house, through which he condemned the world and became heir of the righteousness according to faith.

[8]By faith, אַבְרָהָם, Av'raham, being called, obeyed to go out to a place that he was about to receive for an inheritance, and he went out, not knowing where he was going. [9]By faith, he sojourned in the Land of the promise as a strange country, having lived in tents with יִצְחָק, Yitz'chaq and יַעֲקֹב, Ya'aqov, fellow-heirs of the same promise. [10]For he was looking for the city *which* has the foundations, whose craftsman and constructor *is* God.

[11]By faith, שָׂרָה, Sarah herself—*a* barren *one*—also received power to conceive seed, even[f] after she *was* past the time of life. Seeing *this*, she judged Him who promised *as* faithful. [12]Therefore, also from *this* one (and of that one who had become *as good as* dead) were brought forth in GREAT NUMBER AS MANY AS THE STARS OF THE HEAVEN, AND AS THE SAND— THE INNUMERABLE—THAT *IS* BY THE SEA-SHORE.[g]

[13]In faith, all these died not having received the promises, but having seen them from afar,[h] and having greeted THEM, and having confessed that they are strangers and temporary residents upon the earth. [14]For those saying such things make *it* apparent that they seek a homeland. [15]And if, indeed, they had been mindful of that from which they went out, *then* they might have had an opportunity to return; [16]but now they long for a better *homeland*—that is, a heavenly *one*. Therefore, God is not ashamed of them—to be called their God —for He prepared for them a city.

[17]By faith, אַבְרָהָם, Av'raham, being tested, offered up יִצְחָק, Yitz'chaq (and he offered up the one and only[i] son, who received the promises, [18]of whom it was said,

"In יִצְחָק, Yitz'chaq will a seed be called to you"[j]),

---

[a] Some mss insert, "in the Heavens"
[b] cf. חֲבַקּוּק 'Chavaquq 2:3
[c] חֲבַקּוּק 'Chavaquq 2:4
[d] cf. חֲבַקּוּק 'Chavaquq 2:4 (LXX)
[e] "those of old"—Young's says, "the elders"
[f] "even"—some mss say, "and gave birth"
[g] בְּרֵאשִׁית B'reshiyt 22:17
[h] Some mss insert, "and having been persuaded"
[i] "one and only" or "only begotten"—μονογενῆ, monogene—lit. "one-of-a-kind"
[j] בְּרֵאשִׁית B'reshiyt 21:12

¹⁹considering that even out of the dead, God is able to raise up. Therefore, he similarly also received HIM back.

²⁰By faith also, regarding coming things, יִצְחָק, Yitz'chaq blessed יַעֲקֹב, Ya'aqov and עֵשָׂו, Esav.

²¹By faith, יַעֲקֹב, Ya'aqov, dying, blessed each of the sons of יוֹסֵף, Yosef, and bowed down upon the top of his staff.

²²By faith, יוֹסֵף, Yosef, dying, made mention regarding the outgoing of the sons of יִשְׂרָאֵל, Yis'rael, and gave command regarding his bones.

²³By faith, מֹשֶׁה, Mosheh, having been born, was hidden *for* three months by his parents, because they saw *that* the child *was* beautiful, and were not afraid of the decree of the king.

²⁴By faith, מֹשֶׁה, Mosheh, having become great, refused to be called a son of the daughter of פַּרְעֹה, Par'oh, ²⁵having chosen rather to be afflicted *along* with the people of God, than to have sin's pleasure for a season, *and* ²⁶having counted the disgrace of the Messiah greater wealth than the treasures of מִצְרַיִם, Mitz'rayim; for he looked to the payment of *the* reward.

²⁷By faith he left מִצְרַיִם, Mitz'rayim behind, not having been afraid of the rage of the king. For, as seeing the Invisible One —he endured.

²⁸By faith he kept the פֶּסַח, Pesach and the sprinkling of the blood, so that He who was destroying the first-born might not touch them.

²⁹By faith they passed through the יַם־סוּף, Yam-Suf as through dry land, *by* which the מִצְרַיִם, Mitz'rayim, having received an experience of *it*, were swallowed up.

³⁰By faith the walls of יְרִיחוֹ, Y'riycho fell, having been surrounded for seven days.

³¹By faith, רָחָב, Rachav the prostitute was not destroyed with those who disbelieved, having received the spies with peace.

³²And what more can I say? For the time will fail me *if I begin* recounting about גִּדְעוֹן, Gid'on, בָּרָק, Baraq also, and שִׁמְשׁוֹן, Shim'shon, and יִפְתָּח, Yif'tach, דָּוִד, David also, and שְׁמוּאֵל, Sh'muel, and the prophets— ³³who through faith conquered kingdoms, worked righteousness, obtained promises, stopped mouths of lions, ³⁴quenched the power of fire, escaped the mouth of the sword, were made powerful out of *their* weaknesses, became strong in battle, *and* caused camps of the other *armies* to give way. ³⁵Women received *back* their dead by a rising-again, and others were tortured, not accepting the redemption, so that they might receive a better rising-again, ³⁶and others received an experience of mockings and floggings, and yet *others an experience* of bonds and imprisonment. ³⁷They were stoned; they were sawn apart;ᵃ they died in the killing of the sword; they went about in sheepskins *and* in goatskins—lacking, being afflicted, injuriously treated—³⁸(*ones* of whom the world was not worthy) wandering in deserts, and IN mountains, and IN caves, and IN the holes of the earth.

³⁹And all these having been testified of through the faith did not receive the promise—⁴⁰God having provided something better for us, that apart from us, *these faithful ones* might not be made perfect.

12 ¹Therefore, *since* we also *are* having so great a cloud of witnesses set around us, having put off every weight and the closely-surrounding sin, through perseverance let us run the race that is set before us, ²fixing *our* eyes on the author and perfecter of faith—יֵשׁוּעַ, Yeshua —who, over-against the joy set before Him, endured an *execution* stake *and*, having despised *the* shame, also sat down at the right hand of the throne of God.

³For consider again Him who endured such opposition from the sinners to Himself, so that you may not be wearied in your souls—giving up. ⁴You did not yet resist to *the point of shedding your* blood *in your* struggling with the sin; ⁵and you have forgotten the exhortation that speaks fully with you as sons:

"My son—be not despising *the* discipline of ADONAI, nor giving up, being rebuked by Him; ⁶for whom ADONAI

ᵃ some mss insert, "they were tested"

Design of afflictions.

loves He disciplines, and He punishes every son whom He receives."[a]

⁷*It is* for discipline *that* you endure, *for* God behaves toward you as toward sons. Indeed, what son *is there* whom a father does not discipline? ⁸And if you are apart from discipline (of which all have become sharers), then you are illegitimate, and not sons.

⁹Then indeed, we have had fathers of our flesh disciplining *us*, and we were respecting THEM; will we not much rather be submitted to the Father of the רוּחוֹת, ruchot, and live? ¹⁰For they, indeed, for a few days, according to what seemed good to them, were disciplining; but He *disciplines us* for *our* good, to be sharers of His separateness. ¹¹And all discipline for the present *time*, indeed, does not seem to be of joy, but of grief. Yet afterward, it yields the peaceable fruit of righteousness to those trained through it.

¹²Therefore, straighten up the hanging-down hands and loosened knees, ¹³and make straight paths for your feet,[b] so that that which is lame may not be turned aside, but rather be healed. ¹⁴Pursue peace with all *people*, and *also* the separateness (apart from which no one will see the Master), ¹⁵diligently overseeing *one another*, so that no one will be failing *to partake* of the unmerited favor of God, so that no root of bitterness springing up may cause trouble—and many become defiled through it—¹⁶*and* so that no one *will* be sexually immoral, or a profane person (like עֵשָׂו, Esav, who, in exchange for one morsel of food, sold his birthright; ¹⁷for you know that also afterwards—wanting to inherit the blessing—he was rejected, for he found not a place of reformation, though having sought it with tears).

¹⁸For you *have* not come near to *what is*[c] *being* touched and scorched with fire, and to blackness, and gloom,[d] and windstorm, ¹⁹and a sound of a שׁוֹפָר, shofar, and a voice of sayings (to which those having heard did appeal, *so that* a word might not be added to them, ²⁰for they were not bearing that which was commanded:

"And if a beast touches the mountain, it must be stoned"[e]);

²¹and so terrible was the sight *that* מֹשֶׁה, Mosheh said,

"I am exceedingly fearful, and trembling."[f]

²²But you *have* come to הַר צִיּוֹן, Har Tziyon, and to a city of the living God; to the heavenly יְרוּשָׁלַיִם, Y'rushalayim, and to tens of thousands of Messengers; to the feast-gathering, ²³and to the assembly of the first-born enrolled in Heaven; and to God the judge of all; and to רוּחוֹת, ruchot of righteous men made perfect; ²⁴and to a mediator of a fresh בְּרִית, b'riyt—יֵשׁוּעַ, Yeshua—and to a blood of sprinkling *that is* speaking better things than that of הֶבֶל, Hevel!

²⁵See *that* you do not refuse Him who is speaking. For if those having refused him who was divinely-speaking upon earth did not escape, *how* much less *will* we who turn away from Him who SPEAKS from Heaven?—²⁶Him whose voice shook the earth at that time, but now He has promised, saying,

"Yet once *more* I will shake not only the earth, but also the heaven";[g]

²⁷and this "Yet once *more*" makes clear *that* the removal of the things shaken *are* as of things having been made, so that the things not shaken may remain. ²⁸Therefore—receiving a kingdom that cannot be shaken—may we have *unmerited* favor, through which we may serve God well-pleasingly, with reverence and awe; ²⁹for also our GOD IS A CONSUMING FIRE.[h]

---

[a] מִשְׁלֵי *Mish'lei* 3:11-12
[b] cf. מִשְׁלֵי *Mish'lei* 4:26
[c] "*what is*"—some mss say, "the mountain"
[d] "gloom"—some mss say, "darkness"
[e] שְׁמוֹת *Sh'mot* 19:12-13; some mss insert, "or shot through with an arrow"
[f] דְּבָרִים *D'variym* 9:19
[g] חַגַּי *Chagai* 2:6
[h] דְּבָרִים *D'variym* 4:24

13 ¹Let brotherly love remain. ²Be not forgetful of *showing* hospitality *to strangers*, for through this—unaware—certain *ones have* entertained Messengers.

³Be mindful of those *who are* in bonds, as *if* having been bound with them; *and* of those *who are* maltreated, as *if you* yourselves *are* also being maltreated in the body.

⁴Marriage *is to be* honored by all, and the *marriage* bed undefiled; for *those who are* sexually immoral and adulterers, God will judge.

⁵*Let* the behavior *be* without love of money,ᵃ being content with the present things. For He has said,

"No, I will not leave, no, nor abandon you";ᵇ

⁶so that we boldly say,

"ADONAI *IS* a helper to me, and I will not fear what man will do to me."ᶜ

⁷Be mindful of those leading you, who spoke the word of God to you, whose faith —considering the issue of the behavior —be imitating.

⁸יֵשׁוּעַ, Yeshua *the* Messiah *is* the same yesterday, and today, and to the ages; ⁹be not carried away by various and strange teachings.

For *IT IS* good that the heart be strengthened by *unmerited* favor—not with foods, in which they who are *so* occupied were not benefited. ¹⁰Indeed, we have an altar from which they who are serving the מִשְׁכָּן, Mish'kan have no authority to eat, ¹¹for of those beasts whose blood is brought for sin into the holy places through the כֹּהֵן הַגָּדוֹל, Kohen HaGadol, of these the bodies are burned outside the camp.

¹²Therefore, יֵשׁוּעַ, Yeshua also—so that He might set the people apart through *HIS* own blood—suffered outside the gate. ¹³Now, then, may we go out to Him outside the camp, bearing His disgrace, ¹⁴for we do not have an abiding city here, but we search *for* the coming one. ¹⁵Through Him, then, let us offer up a sacrifice of praise always to God—that is, the fruit of lips: giving thanks to His Name.

¹⁶And be not forgetful of doing good, and of sharing, for with such sacrifices God is well-pleased.

¹⁷Be persuaded byᵈ those leading you, and be submitted—for these *keep* alert for your souls, as *ones* about to give account —so that they may do this with joy, and not groaning, for this *IS* unprofitable to you.

¹⁸Pray for us, for we are persuadedᵉ that we have a good conscience, *and that* in all things *we are* willing to behave well, ¹⁹but more abundantly do I call on YOU to do this, so that I may be restored to you more quickly.

²⁰And *now, may* the God of peace (who brought up the great Shepherd of the sheep out of the dead in the blood of an age-enduring בְּרִית, b'riyt—our Master יֵשׁוּעַ, Yeshua) ²¹make you perfect in every good thingᶠ to do His will, doing in us that which is well-pleasing in His sight, through יֵשׁוּעַ, Yeshua *the* Messiah, to whom *IS* the glory —to the ages of the ages! אָמֵן, Amen.

²²And I appeal to you, brothers: bear with the word of the exhortation, for also I have written to you through *a* few words.

²³Know that our brother Timothy is released, with whom (if he may come more shortly) I may see you.

²⁴Greet all those leading you, and *also* all the קְדוֹשִׁים, Q'doshiym. Those from Italy greet you.

²⁵The *unmerited* favor *IS* with you all!ᵍ

ᵃ "love of money"—Young's says, "covetousness"
ᵇ דְּבָרִים D'variym 31:6
ᶜ תְּהִלִּים T'hiliym 118:6
ᵈ "Be persuaded by"—Young's says, "Be obedient to" (the Gk. form can warrant this); however, all other occurrences of πείθω, peitho in this letter are translated as some form of "persuaded by" or "trust"; cf. 2:12(13), 6:9, and the next verse (18).
ᵉ "are persuaded"—some mss say, "trust"
ᶠ "thing"—some mss say, "work"
ᵍ Some mss conclude, "אָמֵן, Amen."

The Scriptures
written to both
Messianic Jews
and
the Reconciled from among the Nations

———≈———

The Good News of Yeshua According to

Mark

1 ¹The beginning of the Good News of יֵשׁוּעַ, Yeshua *the* Messiah, Son of God: ²as it has been written in יְשַׁעְיָהוּ, Y'sha'yahu the prophet,[a]

"Look! I send My messenger before your face, who will prepare your way[b] —³a voice of one calling, 'In the desert, prepare the way of ADONAI! Make His paths straight!'"[c]

⁴יוֹחָנָן, Yochanan came immersing in the desert, and proclaiming an immersion of reformation for release from sins. ⁵And there were *people* going out to him *from* all the region of יְהוּדָה, Y'hudah, and all those of יְרוּשָׁלַיִם, Y'rushalayim *as well*, and they were immersed by him in the river יַרְדֵּן, Yar'den, confessing their sins.

⁶And יוֹחָנָן, Yochanan was clothed with camel's hair, and a belt of leather around his waist, and *was* eating locusts and honey of the field; ⁷and he proclaimed, saying, "After me, He comes! *One* who is mightier than I, of whom I am not worthy, having stooped down, to untie the strap of His sandals. ⁸I immersed you with water, but He will immerse you with the רוּחַ הַקֹּדֶשׁ, Ruach HaQodesh!"

⁹And it came to pass in those days *that* יֵשׁוּעַ, Yeshua came from נְצֶרֶת, N'tzaret of the גָּלִיל, Galiyl, and was immersed in the יַרְדֵּן, Yar'den by יוֹחָנָן, Yochanan. ¹⁰And immediately coming up from the water, He saw the heavens dividing, and the רוּחַ, Ruach as a dove coming down upon Him.

¹¹And a voice came out of the heavens, "You are My Son, the Beloved—in You I delighted."

¹²And immediately the רוּחַ, Ruach drove Him out into the desert, ¹³and He was in the desert *for* forty days, being tempted by הַשָּׂטָן, HaSatan. And He was with the beasts, and the Messengers were attending to Him.

¹⁴And after the handing over of יוֹחָנָן, Yochanan *to prison*, יֵשׁוּעַ, Yeshua came to the גָּלִיל, Galiyl, proclaiming the Good News[d] of God, ¹⁵and saying, "The time has been fulfilled, and the Reign of God has come near! Reform, and believe in the Good News!"

¹⁶And, passing by יָם־הַגָּלִיל, Yam HaGaliyl, He saw שִׁמְעוֹן, Shim'on and Andrew (the brother of שִׁמְעוֹן, Shim'on), casting a net into the sea, for they were fishers. ¹⁷And יֵשׁוּעַ, Yeshua said to them, "Come *follow* after Me, and I will make you to become fishers of men"; ¹⁸and immediately, having left the nets, they followed Him.

¹⁹And having gone on from there a little, He saw יַעֲקֹב בֶּן־זַבְדִּי, Ya'aqov Ben-Zav'diy and יוֹחָנָן, Yochanan his brother, and they were in the boat refitting the nets. ²⁰And immediately He called them, and, having left their father זַבְדִּי, Zav'diy in the boat with the hired servants, they went away *following* after Him.

²¹And they went on to כְּפַר־נַחוּם, K'far-Nachum, and immediately, on the שַׁבָּתוֹת, Shabatot, having gone into the synagogue, He was teaching. ²²And they were astonished at His teaching, for He was teach-

---

[a] "יְשַׁעְיָהוּ, Y'sha'yahu the prophet"—some mss "the prophets"
[b] מַלְאָכִי, *Mal'akhiy* 3:1
[c] יְשַׁעְיָהוּ, Y'sha'yahu 40:3

[d] Some mss insert, "of the Reign"

Mark 1:23   *Yeshua heals.*

ing them as *one* having authority, and not as *that of* the סוֹפְרִים, Sof'riym. 23 And immediately, in their synagogue was a man with an unclean רוּחַ, ruach, and he cried out, 24 saying, "What do You *want* with us,[a] יֵשׁוּעַ הַנָּצְרָתִי, Yeshua HaNatz'ratiy? Did You come to destroy us? I have known You —who You are: the Holy One of God!" 25 And יֵשׁוּעַ, Yeshua rebuked him, saying, "Be silenced, and come out of him!" 26 And the רוּחַ הַטֻּמְאָה, ruach ha-tum'ah having convulsed him, and having called out with a loud voice, came out of him, 27 and they were all amazed, so as to reason among themselves, saying, "What is this? a new teaching with authority! He even commands the unclean רוּחוֹת, ruchot, and they obey Him!" 28 And the news of Him immediately went out everywhere to all the surrounding region of the גָּלִיל, Galiyl. 29 And immediately, having come out of the synagogue, they went to the house of שִׁמְעוֹן, Shim'on and Andrew, with יַעֲקֹב, Ya'aqov and יוֹחָנָן, Yochanan. 30 And the mother-in-law of שִׁמְעוֹן, Shim'on was lying fevered, and they immediately told Him about her. 31 And having come near, He raised her up, having taken hold of her hand, and the fever left her, and she *began* attending to them.

32 And evening having come, when the sun set, they brought to Him all who were ill and demon-possessed, 33 and the whole city was gathered together near the door. 34 And He healed many who were ill from various diseases, and He cast out many demons, and was not allowing the demons to speak, because they knew Him.

35 And very early *before morning*, it still being night, having arisen, He left and went away to a deserted place, and was praying there. 36 And שִׁמְעוֹן, Shim'on and those with him went searching for Him. 37 And they found Him and said to Him, "Everyone *is* looking *for* You." 38 And He said to them, "Let us go elsewhere——to the next towns—so that I may proclaim there also. For *it was* for this *that* I came forth."

39 And He went in all the גָּלִיל, Galiyl, proclaiming in their synagogues, and was casting out the demons. 40 And there came to Him a leper, pleading with Him, and kneeling, and saying to Him, "If You are willing, You are able to cleanse me."

41 And having been moved with compassion, having stretched out His hand, He touched him and said to him, "I am willing. Be cleansed." 42 And[b] immediately, the leprosy went away from *the man*, and he was cleansed.

43 And having sternly warned him, He immediately sent him away 44 and said to him, "See *that* you say nothing to anyone, but go away, show yourself to the כֹּהֵן, Kohen, and bring near for your cleansing the offerings[c] מֹשֶׁה, Mosheh directed, for a testimony to them."

45 And he, having gone out, *instead* began to proclaim much, and to spread abroad the thing *that happened to him*, so that *Yeshua* was no longer able to openly enter into the city, but He *remained* outside *the city* in deserted places. And *the people* were coming to Him from every quarter *of the city*.

2 1 And when He entered again into כְּפַר־נַחוּם, K'far-Nachum after SOME days, it was heard that He was in the house. 2 And many *people* were gathered together so that there was no more room—not even at the door. And He was speaking the word to them.

3 And they came, bringing to Him a paralytic, lifted by four *men*. 4 And not being able to bring *him* near to *Yeshua* because of the crowd, they uncovered the roof where He was. And having broken IT up, they let down *through the opening* the mat on which the paralytic was lying. 5 And יֵשׁוּעַ, Yeshua, having seen their faith, said to the paralytic, "Child, your sins are forgiven."

---

[a] "What do You *want* with us"—lit., "what to us and to you"
[b] Some mss insert, "*when* He had spoken"
[c] "offerings"—lit. "things"

Calling of Leviy.   Mark 3:2

⁶And there were certain *ones* of the סוֹפְרִים, Sof'riym sitting there, and reasoning in their hearts, ⁷"Why does this one speak this way? He is speaking evil! Who is able to forgive sins except One—God?"

⁸And immediately, יֵשׁוּעַ, Yeshua, having known in His רוּחַ, ruach that they *were* reasoning this way within themselves, said to them, "Why do you reason these things in your hearts? ⁹*For* which is easier: to say to the paralytic, 'Your sins are forgiven,' or to say, 'Rise *up* and take up your mat, and walk'? ¹⁰And so that you may know that the Son of Man has authority on the earth to forgive sins..." (He said to the paralytic,) ¹¹"I say to you, rise *up*, take up your mat, and go away to your house!" ¹²and he arose. And having immediately taken up the mat, he went out in front of everyone, so that all were astonished. And *they* glorified God, saying, "Never *before* did we see *anything done* this way!"

¹³And He went out again by the sea, and all the crowd was coming to Him, and He was teaching them. ¹⁴And passing by, He saw לֵוִי בֶּן־חַלְפַי, Leviy Ben-Chal'fai sitting at the tax-office, and said to him, "Be following me." And *Leviy*, having risen, followed Him.

¹⁵And He came to recline (at mealtime) in *Leviy's* house, and many tax-gatherers and sinners were reclining (at mealtime) *along* with יֵשׁוּעַ, Yeshua and His disciples, for there were many, and they were following Him. ¹⁶And the סוֹפְרִים, Sof'riym of the פְּרוּשִׁים, P'rushiym, having seen that He was eating with the sinners and tax-gatherers, said to His disciples, "He eats[a] with the tax-gatherers and sinners!" ¹⁷And יֵשׁוּעַ, Yeshua, having heard, said to them, "They who are strong have no need of a physician, but *only* those who are ill. I came not to call righteous men, but sinners."[b]

¹⁸And the disciples of יוֹחָנָן, Yochanan and the פְּרוּשִׁים, P'rushiym were fasting,

and they came and said to Him, "Why do the disciples of יוֹחָנָן, Yochanan and the disciples of the פְּרוּשִׁים, P'rushiym fast, but your disciples do not fast?" ¹⁹And יֵשׁוּעַ, Yeshua said to them, "Are the wedding guests[c] able to fast while the bridegroom is with them? *For* so long a time as they have the bridegroom with them, they are not able to fast. ²⁰But days will come when the bridegroom may be taken from them, and then they will fast in that day.

²¹"No one will sew a patch of *new*, unshrunk cloth onto an old garment; otherwise, the new *cloth that is* filling it up pulls away from the old *cloth*, and the split becomes worse. ²²And no one puts fresh wine into old skins; otherwise, the wine will burst the skins, and the wine is destroyed, and the skins *also*;[d] rather, fresh wine is to be put into new skins."

²³And it came to pass on the שַׁבָּתוֹת, Shabatot *that* He was going along through the grain-fields, and His disciples began to make a path, plucking the heads. ²⁴And the פְּרוּשִׁים, P'rushiym said to Him, "Look! why do they do on the שַׁבָּתוֹת, Shabatot that which is not permitted?" ²⁵And He said to them, "Did you never read what דָּוִד, David did, when he had need and was hungry—he and those with him? ²⁶how he went into the House of God (at *the time of* אֶבְיָתָר, Ev'yatar the כֹּהֵן הַגָּדוֹל, Kohen Ha-Gadol) and ate the לֶחֶם הַפָּנִים, Lechem Ha-Paniym—which it is not permitted *for any-one* to eat, except the כֹּהֲנִים, Ko'haniym—and he gave also to those who were with him?" ²⁷And He said to them, "The שַׁבָּת, Shabat was made for man, and not man for the שַׁבָּת, Shabat, ²⁸so that the Son of Man is Master also of the שַׁבָּת, Shabat."

3 ¹And He entered again into the synagogue, and there was a man there having the withered hand, ²and they were watching Him, *to see* whether He would

---

[a] Some mss insert, "and drinks"
[b] Some mss insert, "to reformation"

[c] "wedding guests"—lit. "sons of the bride-chamber"
[d] "destroyed, and the skins *also*"—some mss say, "poured out, and the skins will be destroyed"

heal him on the שַׁבָּתוֹת, Shabatot, so that they might accuse Him. ³And He said to the man having the withered hand, "Rise up in the middle *of everyone.*" ⁴And He said to them, "Is it permitted on the שַׁבָּתוֹת, Shabatot to do good, or to do evil? to save a life, or to kill?" but they were silent. ⁵And having looked around upon them with anger, being grieved for the hardness of their heart, He said to the man, "Stretch out the hand," and he stretched *it* out, and his hand was restored!ᵃ ⁶And the פְּרוּשִׁים, P'rushiym, having gone out immediately with the Herodians, were giving counsel against Him —how they might destroy Him.

⁷And יֵשׁוּעַ, Yeshua withdrew with His disciples to the sea, and a large crowd from the גָּלִיל, Galiyl followed *them.* And *many* from יְהוּדָה, Y'hudah, ⁸and from יְרוּשָׁלַיִם, Y'rushalayim, and from אֱדוֹם, 'Edom, and beyond the יַרְדֵּן, Yar'den, and around צֹר, Tzor and צִידוֹן, Tziydon—a great number —hearing what great things He was doing, came to Him. ⁹And He said to His disciples that a little boat should stand ready for Himᵇ because of the crowd, so that they would not press *in* upon Him, ¹⁰for He healed many, so that they threw themselves on Him in order to touch Him —as many as had afflictions. ¹¹And the unclean רוּחוֹת, ruchot, when they were seeing Him, were falling down before Him and were shouting, saying, "You are the Son of God!" ¹²and many times He was warning them so that they would not make Him known.

¹³And He went up to the mountain and called near *those* whom He wanted; and they went away to Him; ¹⁴and He appointed twelve (whom He also named *as* emissariesᶜ), that they may be with Him, and so that He might send them out to proclaim, ¹⁵and to have powerᵈ to cast out the demons.

¹⁶And He appointed the Twelve;ᵉ and He put on שִׁמְעוֹן, Shim'on the name כֵּיפָא, Keifa;ᶠ ¹⁷and *He called* יַעֲקֹב, Ya'aqov of זַבְדִּי, Zav'diy, and יוֹחָנָן, Yochanan the brother of יַעֲקֹב, Ya'aqov, and He put names on them: בְּנֵי־רֶגֶשׁ, B'nei Ragesh (that is, "Sons of Thunder"); ¹⁸and *He called* Andrew, and Philip, and בַּר־תַּלְמַי, Bar-Tal'mai, and מַתִּתְיָהוּ, Matit'yahu, and תּוֹמָא, Toma, and יַעֲקֹב, Ya'aqov of חַלְפַי, Chal'fai, and תַּדַּי, Tadai, and שִׁמְעוֹן הַקַּנִּי, Shim'on HaQanai, ¹⁹and יְהוּדָה אִישׁ־קְרִיּוֹת, Y'hudah Iysh-Q'riyot— who also *betrayed and* handed Him over.

²⁰And He came into a house, and again a crowd came together, so that they were not able even to eat bread. ²¹And having heard *of this,* His familyᵍ went out to take hold of Him, for they said that He was beside Himself.ʰ ²²And the סוֹפְרִים, Sof'riym who ARE from יְרוּשָׁלַיִם, Y'rushalayim, having come down, said, "He has בַּעַל־זְבוּב, Ba-al-Z'vuv," and, "By the ruler of the demons he casts out the demons."

²³And having called them near, He said to them in analogies, "How is הַשָּׂטָן, HaSatan able to cast out הַשָּׂטָן, HaSatan? ²⁴And if a kingdom is divided against itself, that kingdom cannot be made to stand; ²⁵and if a house is divided against itself, that house cannot be made to stand; ²⁶and if הַשָּׂטָן, HaSatan rose against himself, and has been divided, he cannot be made to stand, but has an end. ²⁷But no one, having entered into the house of the strong man, is able to plunder his property if he does not first bind the strong man; and then he will plunder his house. ²⁸אָמֵן, Amen, I say to you that all the sins and evil speakings with which they might speak evil will be forgiven to the sons of men, ²⁹but whoever speaks evil in regard to the רוּחַ הַקֹּדֶשׁ, Ruach HaQodesh does not have forgiveness —to the age—but is guilty of age-enduring sin."ⁱ ³⁰*He said this* because they said,

---

ᵃ Some mss insert, "whole as the other"
ᵇ "should stand ready for Him"—Young's says, "may wait on him"
ᶜ Some mss omit, "whom He also named *as* emissaries"
ᵈ Some mss insert, "to heal the sicknesses, and"
ᵉ Some mss omit, "And He appointed the Twelve"
ᶠ כֵּיפָא, Keifa—Gk: Πέτρος, Petros; see יוֹחָנָן Yn. 1:42
ᵍ "family"—Young's says, "friends"
ʰ "was beside Himself," or "is out of his mind" or "has lost his senses"
ⁱ "sin"—some mss say, "judgment"

Analogy of the sower.   **Mark 4:24**

"He has an unclean רוּחַ, ruach." ³¹And His mother and brothers arrived; and standing outside, they sent *word* to Him, calling Him. ³²And a crowd was sitting around Him, and they said to Him, "Look! Your mother and your brothers *are* outside looking *for* you." ³³And having answered them, He said, "Who is My mother, and My brothers?" ³⁴And having looked around in a circle to those sitting around Him, He said, "Look! My mother and My brothers! ³⁵For whoever does the will of God, he is My brother, and sister, and mother."

4 ¹And again He began to teach by the sea; and a large crowd gathered to Him, so that (having gone into the boat) He sat in the sea; and the whole crowd was near the sea, on the land; ²and He taught them many things in analogies. And He said to them in His teaching:

³"Listen! Look! The sower went out to sow. ⁴And it came to pass in the sowing, *that* some *seed* fell by the road, and the birds came and devoured it. ⁵And other *seed* fell upon the rocky ground, where it did not have much *deep* ground; and it immediately sprang forth, because of not having depth of ground; ⁶and when the sun had risen, *the seedling* was scorched; and because of not having root, it withered.

⁷"And other *seed* fell toward the thorns, and the thorns came up and choked it, and it gave no fruit. ⁸But other *seed* fell to the good ground and was giving fruit, coming up and increasing; and it brought *crops:* one thirty-fold, and one sixty, and one a hundred *times what was sown.*" ⁹And He said, "He who has ears to hear—let him hear."

¹⁰And when He was alone, those around Him, *along* with the Twelve, asked Him about the analogies, ¹¹and He said to them, "To you has been given the mystery of the Reign of God, but to those who are outside, all the things are done in analogies, ¹²so that 'WHILE SEEING THEY MAY SEE BUT NOT PERCEIVE, AND WHILE HEARING THEY MAY HEAR BUT NOT UNDERSTAND; OTHERWISE, THEY MAY TURN, AND BE FORGIVEN.'"ᵃ ¹³And He said to them, "Have you not known this analogy? And how *then* will you understand all the analogies?

¹⁴"He who is sowing sows the word. ¹⁵And *some of* these *people* are they *who are* by the road where the word is sown: and whenever they hear *the word,* הַשָּׂטָן, HaSatan immediately comes, and he takes away the word that has been sown in them.ᵇ ¹⁶And *others of* these are they who are sown on the rocky ground: who, whenever they hear the word, immediately receive it with joy, ¹⁷but *since they do* not have root in themselves but are temporary, afterward—*with* oppression or persecution having come because of the word—they are immediately stumbled. ¹⁸And *still* others *of these* are they who are sown toward the thorns: these are they having heard the word, ¹⁹but *then* the anxieties of the age, and the deceitfulness of the riches, and the desires concerning the other things, once entering in, choke the word, and it becomes unfruitful. ²⁰But those *remaining* are they who have been sown on the good ground: who hear the word, and receive *it,* and bear fruit—one thirty-fold, and one sixty, and one a hundred *times what was sown.*"

²¹And He said to them, "Does the *oil-*lamp come so that it may be put under the measur*ing basket,* or under the bed? *Is it* not so that it may be put on the lampstand? ²²For there is not anything hidden, except that *it* may be revealed; nor was anything kept secret,ᶜ but that it may come to light. ²³If anyone has ears to hear—let him hear."

²⁴And He said to them, "Look *carefully* at what you hear. In whatever measure you measure, it will be measured to you—

ᵃ יְשַׁעְיָהוּ *Y'sha'yahu* 6:9-10; cf. יִרְמְיָהוּ *Yir'm'yahu* 5:21, יְחֶזְקֵאל *Y'chez'qel* 12:2
ᵇ "them"—some mss say, "their hearts"
ᶜ "secret"—Young's says "hidden" a second time

and to you[a] it will be added. ²⁵For whoever has, there will be *more* given to him, and whoever does not have, that which he has will also be taken from him."

²⁶And He said, "The Reign of God is this way: as a man *who* casts the seed on the ground, ²⁷and sleeps, and rises night and day, and the seed springs up and grows, *though* he has not known how; ²⁸by itself the ground bears fruit—first a blade, afterwards a head, afterwards full grain in the head. ²⁹And whenever the fruit yields itself, immediately he sends forth the sickle, because the harvest has come."

³⁰And He said, "How may we liken the Reign of God—or in what analogy may we put[b] it? ³¹*It is* like a grain of mustard, which, whenever it may be sown on the ground, is smaller than any of the seeds that are on the earth; ³²but whenever it may be sown, it comes up, and becomes greater than any of the herbs, and makes huge branches, so that the birds of the heaven are able to nest under its shade."

³³And with many such analogies He was speaking the word to them, as they were able to hear; ³⁴and He was not speaking to them without an analogy. But privately, to His own disciples, He was explaining all.

³⁵And He said to them on that day, *the* evening having come, "Let us pass over to the other side"; ³⁶and having sent the crowd away, they took Him up in the boat *just* as He was, and other boats were with Him. ³⁷And there came a massive storm of wind, and the waves were beating on the boat so that the boat was now being filled, ³⁸but He Himself was in the stern, sleeping upon the pillow. And they woke Him up and said to Him, "Teacher! are You not caring that we are being destroyed?" ³⁹And having woken up, He rebuked the wind, and said to the sea, "Peace, be stilled"; and the wind stopped, and there was a great calm. ⁴⁰And He said to them, "Why are you so fearful? Do you not yet have faith?" ⁴¹And they feared a great fear, and said to one another, "Who, then, is this, that even the wind and sea obey Him?"

5 ¹And they came to the other side of the sea, to the region of the גֵּרָזִיִּים, Geraziyiym, ²and when He had come out of the boat, immediately there met Him from out of the tombs a man with an unclean רוּחַ, ruach, ³who had his home in the tombs. And not even with chains was anyone able to bind him anymore ⁴(because *of the fact* that he had been bound many times with shackles and chains, and *yet* the chains had been pulled in pieces by him, and the shackles broken in pieces), and no one was able to tame him. ⁵And always, night and day, he was in the tombs and in the mountains, shouting and cutting himself with stones. ⁶And, having seen יֵשׁוּעַ, Yeshua from afar, he ran and bowed before Him; ⁷and having shouted with a loud voice, he said, "What do You *want* with me,[c] יֵשׁוּעַ בֶּן־אֵל עֶלְיוֹן, Yeshua Ben-El El'yon? I command you by God: may you not torment me!" ⁸(For He said to him, "Come out, unclean רוּחַ, ruach—out of the man.") ⁹And He was questioning him, "What *is* your name?" and he said to Him, "Legion *is* my name, because we are many"; ¹⁰and he was pleading with Him many *times*, that He would not send them out of the region. ¹¹And there near the mountain, there was a large herd of pigs feeding; ¹²and all the demons pleaded with Him, saying, "Send us to the pigs, so that we may enter into them"; ¹³and He gave them permission. And having come out, the unclean רוּחוֹת, ruchot entered into the pigs, and the herd rushed down the steep place to the sea—about two thousand *of them*—and they were choked in the sea.

¹⁴And those feeding the pigs fled and told *people* in the city and in the fields, and they came to see what it was that had been

---

[a] Some mss insert, "who hear"
[b] "put"—some mss say, "compare"

[c] "What do You *want* with me"—lit., "what to me and to You"

done. ¹⁵And they came to יֵשׁוּעַ, Yeshua, and saw the demon-possessed *man* (him having had the legion) sitting, clothed and right-minded, and they were afraid. ¹⁶And those having seen IT *all* described to them how it had come to pass to the demon-possessed *man*, and about the pigs. ¹⁷And they began to plead with Him to go away from their borders. ¹⁸And as He was getting into the boat, the demon-possessed *man* was pleading with Him, *asking* that he may be *allowed to go* with Him. ¹⁹And He did not allow him, but said to him, "Go away to your house, to your own FRIENDS, and tell them what great things ADONAI[a] has done to you, and *how He* dealt kindly with you"; ²⁰and he went away, and began to proclaim in the Decapolis what great things יֵשׁוּעַ, Yeshua did to him; and all were in wonder.

²¹And when יֵשׁוּעַ, Yeshua had passed over in the boat again to the other side, there was gathered to Him a large crowd. And He was near the sea, ²²and there came one of the leaders of the synagogue (by *the* name יָאִיר, Yaiyr), and having seen Him, he fell at His feet. ²³And he was pleading with Him much, saying, "My little daughter is at the last extremity *of life! I am asking* that, having come, you may lay YOUR hands on her, so that she may be saved, and she will live!" ²⁴And He went away with him.

And there was a large crowd following Him, and they were pressing in on Him. ²⁵And a woman having a continuous flow of blood *for* twelve years ²⁶(and having suffered many things under many physicians, and having spent all that she had, and having benefitted nothing, but rather having come to the worse), ²⁷having heard about יֵשׁוּעַ, Yeshua, *and* having come in the crowd *from* behind *Him*, touched His *outer* garment ²⁸(for she said *to herself*, "If I may touch even His *outer* garments, I will be saved *from my affliction*"); ²⁹and immediately, the well-spring of her blood was dried up, and she knew in the body that she had been healed of the affliction.

³⁰And immediately, יֵשׁוּעַ, Yeshua, having known in Himself that power had gone out of Him, having turned around in the crowd, said, "Who touched my *outer* garments?" ³¹And His disciples said to Him, "You see the crowd pressing in on You, and You say, 'Who touched me'!"

³²And He was looking around to see her who did this; ³³and the woman, having been afraid and trembling, and knowing what was done to her, came and fell down before Him and told Him all the truth. ³⁴And He said to her, "Daughter, your faith has saved you; go away in peace, and be whole from your affliction."

³⁵As He was still speaking, there came CERTAIN *ones* from the synagogue leader's HOUSE, saying, "Your daughter died; why do you still harass the Teacher?" ³⁶And יֵשׁוּעַ, Yeshua, having overheard the word that was spoken, said to the leader of the synagogue, "Do not be afraid, only believe." ³⁷And He did not allow anyone to follow with Him, except כֵּיפָא, Keifa,[b] and יַעֲקֹב, Ya'aqov, and יוֹחָנָן, Yochanan the brother of יַעֲקֹב, Ya'aqov.

³⁸And they came to the house of the leader of the synagogue, and saw a commotion *with* much weeping and wailing. ³⁹And having gone in, He said to them *all*, "Why do you make a commotion and weep? The child did not die, but sleeps"; ⁴⁰and they were laughing at Him. And He, having put *them* all out *of the house*, took the father of the child, and the mother, and those with Him, and went in where the child was.[c] ⁴¹And having taken the hand of the child, He said to her, "טַלִיתָא קוּמִי, Tal'y'ta qumiy," which is, being interpreted, "Girl (I say to you), arise." ⁴²And the girl immediately arose and was walking—for she was twelve years OLD—and they were immediately amazed with great amazement!

⁴³And He commanded them much, that no one should know *about* this thing, and

---

[a] "ADONAI" or "the Master"; Gk. κύριός, kurios
[b] כֵּיפָא, Keifa—Gk: Πέτρος, Petros; see יוֹחָנָן Yochanan 1:42
[c] Some mss insert, "lying"

He said that there *should* be *food* given to her to eat.

6 ¹And He went out from that place and came to His own homeland, and His disciples followed Him. ²And when שַׁבָּת, Shabat had come, He began to teach in the synagogue, and many hearing *Him* were astonished, saying, "From where has this one *learned* these things? and what *is* the wisdom that was given to him, and such powerful acts being done through his hands? ³Is this not the carpenter—the son of מִרְיָם, Mir'yam, and brother of יַעֲקֹב, Ya'aqov, and יוֹסֵי, Yosei, and יְהוּדָה, Y'hudah, and שִׁמְעוֹן, Shim'on? and are not his sisters here with us?"—and they were being stumbled at Him. ⁴And יֵשׁוּעַ, Yeshua said to them, "A prophet is not without honor, except in his own homeland, and among his relatives, and in his own house"; ⁵and He was not able to do any powerful act there, except, having put hands on a few infirmed people, He healed THEM. ⁶And He was in wonder because of their unbelief.

And He was going around teaching from village to village.ᵃ ⁷And He called near the Twelve, and He began to send them out two by two, and He was giving them power over the unclean רוּחוֹת, ruchot. ⁸And He commanded them that they may take nothing for the road, except a staff only—no bread, no bag, no brass *coins* in the belt, ⁹but having been bound under *foot* with sandals, "And you may not put on two shirts." ¹⁰And He said to them, "Whenever you enter into a house, remain there until you go away from that place. ¹¹And whatever place may not receive you nor hear you, going out from that place, shake off the dust that is under your feet, for a testimony to them."ᵇ ¹²And having gone out, they proclaimed that MEN should reform,

¹³and they were casting out many demons, and they were anointing with oil many *who were* infirmed, and they were healing THEM.

¹⁴And Herod the king heard (for *Yeshua's* name had become public); and *some* were saying, "יוֹחָנָן, Yochanan the Immerser has been raised out of the dead, and because of this, the powerful acts are working in Him." ¹⁵But others said, "It is אֵלִיָּהוּ, Eliyahu," and others said, "*He is* a prophet, like one of the prophets." ¹⁶But Herod, having heard, said, "He whom I beheaded—יוֹחָנָן, Yochanan—this one has risen."

¹⁷For Herod himself, having sent forth *a command*, took hold of יוֹחָנָן, Yochanan and bound him in prison because of Herodias, the wife of Philip his brother, because *Herod* married her. ¹⁸For יוֹחָנָן, Yochanan said to Herod, "It is not permitted for you to have the wife of your brother." ¹⁹So Herodias was having a grudge against *Yochanan*, and was wanting to kill him, but was not able, ²⁰for Herod was fearing יוֹחָנָן, Yochanan, knowing him *as* a righteous and holy man, and was keeping watch over him; and having heard him *speak, Herod* was much perplexed,ᶜ but *was* gladly listening to him. ²¹And when a timely day had come, on his birthday Herod made a supper for his great men, and for the chiefs of thousands, and for the elite men of the גָּלִיל, Galiyl; ²²and the daughter of Herodias, having come in and having danced, pleased Herod and those reclining (at mealtime) with him. The king said to the girl, "Ask of me whatever you want, and I will give *it* to you"; ²³and he swore to her, "Whatever you may ask me, I will give to you—*up* to the half of my kingdom." ²⁴And having gone out, she said to her mother, "What should I ask for myself?" and she said, "The head of יוֹחָנָן, Yochanan the Immerser." ²⁵And having come in immediately with haste to the king, she asked *it*, saying, "I want you to give me at once, upon a plate, the head of

---

ᵃ "from village to village"—Young's says, "round the villages, in a circle"
ᵇ Some mss continue, "אָמֵן, Amen, I say to you, it will be more tolerable for סְדֹם, S'dom or עֲמֹרָה, 'Amorah in the Day of Judgment than for that city."
ᶜ "much perplexed"—some mss say, "doing many things"

Death of Yochanan the Immerser.   Mark 6:55

יוֹחָנָן, Yochanan the Immerser." ²⁶And the king—though very sorrowful—because of the oaths and of those reclining (at mealtime) with him, did not want to put her away. ²⁷And immediately, the king, having sent a guardsman, commanded *him* to bring *Yochanan's* head. ²⁸And having gone, *the guard* beheaded him in the prison, and brought his head upon a plate, and gave it to the girl; and the girl gave it to her mother; ²⁹and having heard, his disciples came and lifted up his corpse and laid it in a tomb.

³⁰And the emissaries were gathered together to יֵשׁוּעַ, Yeshua, and they told Him everything—how many things they did, and how many things they taught. ³¹And He said to them, "Come *away by* yourselves, privately, to a deserted place, and rest a little," for those coming and going were many, and they had not even had *the* opportunity to eat. ³²So they went away in the boat to a deserted place by themselves.

³³And many saw them going away and recognized *them*; and they ran there by land from all the cities, and went ahead of them, and came together to Him. ³⁴And having come out *of the boat*, He saw a large crowd, and was moved with compassion on them—that they were as sheep not having a shepherd—and He began to teach many things.

³⁵And now, the hour being advanced, His disciples, having come near to Him, said, "The place is deserted, and the hour is now advanced. ³⁶Send them away, so that, having gone away to the surrounding fields and villages, they may buy for themselves what *they need* to eat."ᵃ ³⁷And answering, He said to them, "You give them *something* to eat." And they said to Him, "Having gone away, should we buy two hundred days' wagesᵇ worth of loaves, and give *it* to them to eat?" ³⁸And He said to them, "How many loaves do you have?

Go *and* see." And having *come to* know, they said, "Five—and two fishes." ³⁹And He commanded them to make all *the people sit down and* recline in groups on the green grass. ⁴⁰So they sat down in squares, by hundreds and by fifties. ⁴¹And having taken the five loaves and the two fishes, having looked up to the heaven, He blessed *them*, and broke the loaves, and was giving to His disciples, that they may set *them* before *the people*—and the two fishes He divided to all. ⁴²And they all ate and were filled, ⁴³and *afterward*, they took up twelve hand-baskets full of broken pieces, and of the fishes. ⁴⁴And those *who were* eating of the loaves were five thousand men.

⁴⁵And immediately, He compelled His disciples to go into the boat, and to go before *Him* to the other side, to בֵּית צַיְדָה, Beit Tzai'dah, until He could send the crowd away. ⁴⁶And having left them, He went away to the mountain to pray. ⁴⁷And evening having come, the boat was *already* in the middle of the sea, and He alone *was* on the land. ⁴⁸And having seen them tormented in the rowing—for the wind was against them—about the fourth watch of the night He came to them, walking on the sea, and wanted to pass by them. ⁴⁹But they, having seen Him walking on the sea, thought that ɪᴛ was a phantasm; and *they* cried out, ⁵⁰for they all saw Him and were troubled. But He immediately spoke with them, and said to them, "Take courage, I am ʜᴇ; do not be afraid." ⁵¹And He went up to them—to the boat—and the wind stopped. And they were amazed in themselves greatly beyondᶜ measure,ᵈ ⁵²for they did not understand concerning the loaves; rather, their heart had been hard.

⁵³And having passed over, they came upon the land of גְּנֵיסָרֶת, G'neisaret, and drew to the shore. ⁵⁴And when they had come out of the boat, immediately *the people*, having recognized Him, ⁵⁵ran about through all that region; and they began to

---

ᵃ "what *they* need to eat"—some mss say, "loaves, for what they may eat they have not"
ᵇ "days' wages"—lit. "denaries"

ᶜ "beyond"—Young's says, "out of"
ᵈ Some mss insert, "and were in wonder"

carry about upon the mats those *who were ill, to* wherever they were hearing that He was. ⁵⁶And wherever He was going—to villages, or to cities, or to fields, *or* in the market-places—they were laying the infirmed, and were pleading with Him that they may touch *Him, even* if it were just the כָּנָף, kanaf[a] of His *outer* garment. And as many as touched Him were saved *from their illnesses.*

7 ¹And gathered together to Him were the פְּרוּשִׁים, P'rushiym and certain *ones* of the סוֹפְרִים, Sof'riym, having come from יְרוּשָׁלַיִם, Y'rushalayim ²and having seen certain *ones* of His disciples: that with impure hands—that is, unwashed—they eat the bread[b] ³(for the פְּרוּשִׁים, P'rushiym and all the יְהוּדִים, Y'hudiym do not eat if they do not *first* wash the hands to the wrist, holding *to* the tradition of the זְקֵנִים, Z'qeniym; ⁴and COMING from the market-place, they do not eat if they do not *first* immerse themselves; and there are many other things that they received *from the Z'qeniym to which they* hold: immersions of cups, of pots, and *of* copper things, and *of* beds).

⁵And *so* the פְּרוּשִׁים, P'rushiym and the סוֹפְרִים, Sof'riym questioned Him, "Why do your disciples not walk according to the tradition of the זְקֵנִים, Z'qeniym, but eat the bread with impure[c] hands?" ⁶And He said to them, "יְשַׁעְיָהוּ, Y'sha'yahu prophesied well concerning you, hypocrites, as it has been written,

'This people honor Me with the lips, but their heart is far from Me; ⁷and in vain do they worship Me, teaching teachings *that are merely the* commands of men.'[d]

⁸Having put away the command of God, you hold *to* the tradition of men."[e]

⁹And He said to them, "You put away the command of God *very* well so that you may keep your tradition. ¹⁰For מֹשֶׁה, Mosheh, said, 'HONOR YOUR FATHER AND YOUR MOTHER';[f] and 'HE WHO IS SPEAKING EVIL OF *HIS* FATHER OR MOTHER—LET HIM DIE THE DEATH.'[g] ¹¹But you say *that* if a man says to *his* father or to *his* mother, 'Whatever you may be benefitted out of *what is* mine *IS already promised as* קָרְבָּן, qor'ban' (that is, a gift *to* God), ¹²no longer do you allow him to do anything for his father or mother, ¹³thus setting aside the word of God for your tradition that you handed down; and you do many such things like *this.*"

¹⁴And having called the crowd near again, He said to them, "Listen to me, all *of* you, and understand: ¹⁵there is nothing from outside the man entering into him that is able to defile him, but the things coming out from the man are the things defiling the man."[h]

¹⁷And when He entered into a house, *having gone away* from the crowd, His disciples were questioning Him about the analogy. ¹⁸And He said to them, "In this way, you are also without understanding! Do you not see that nothing from outside, entering into the man, is able to defile him? ¹⁹because it does not enter into his heart, but into the belly, and *then* it goes out into the latrine, cleansing all the foods."[i]

²⁰And He said, "That which is coming out from the man: that *is what* defiles the man. ²¹For from within, out of the heart of men, come forth the evil reasonings, sexual immoralities, thefts, murders, adulteries, ²²covetous desires, wickedness, deceit, arrogance, an evil eye,[j] evil speaking, pride *and* foolishness. ²³All *of* these evils come

---

[a] כָּנָף, kanaf—see מַתִּתְיָהוּ *Matit'yahu* 9:20
[b] Some mss insert, "they found fault"
[c] "impure"—some mss say, "unwashed"
[d] יְשַׁעְיָהוּ *Y'sha'yahu* 29:13 (LXX)
[e] Some mss insert, "immersions of pots and cups; and you do many other such things like *these*"

[f] שְׁמוֹת *Sh'mot* 20:12, דְּבָרִים *D'variym* 5:16
[g] שְׁמוֹת *Sh'mot* 21:17, וַיִּקְרָא *Vayiq'ra* 20:9
[h] Some mss continue with verse 16, "If anyone has ears to hear—let him hear."
[i] cf. דְּבָרִים *D'variym* 23:13-15(12-14), מִשְׁלֵי *Mish'lei* 30:11-12
[j] "evil eye"—that is, selfishness

Messiah feeds the crowd.

forth from within, and they *are what* defile the man."

²⁴And having risen from that place, He went away to the borders of צוֹר, Tzor;ᵃ and having entered into a house, He wanted no one to know, yet He was not able to be hidden. ²⁵But immediately, a woman having heard about Him, whose little daughter had an unclean רוּחַ, ruach, having come, fell at His feet. ²⁶And the woman was a Greek, a Syro-Phoenician by ancestry,ᵇ and was asking Him that He would cast the demon out of her daughter.

²⁷And He said to her, "First allow the children to be filled *with food*, for it is not good to take the children's bread, and to throw IT to the little dogs." ²⁸And she answered and said to Him, "Sir, even the little dogs under the table eat of the children's crumbs." ²⁹And He said to her, "Because of this word, go; the demon has gone out of your daughter."

³⁰And having gone away to her house, she found the child laid upon the bed, and the demon gone.

³¹And again, having gone out from the boundaries of צוֹר, Tzor, He came through צִידוֹן, Tziydon to יָם־הַגָּלִיל, Yam HaGaliyl, through the middle of the boundaries of Decapolis; ³²and they brought to Him a man *who was* deaf and *had* difficulty speaking, and they pleaded with Him that He might lay the hand on him. ³³And having taken him away from the crowd by himself, He put His fingers to his ears; and having spit, He touched his tongue. ³⁴And having looked to the heaven, He groaned, and said to him, "אֶתְפַּתַּח, Et'patach!" that is, "Be opened!" ³⁵And immediately his ears were opened, and the binding of his tongue was released, and he was speaking correctly. ³⁶And He commanded them that they may tell no one, but the more He was commanding them, the more abundantly they were proclaiming IT, ³⁷and *the people* were being astonished

---

ᵃ Some mss insert, "and צִידוֹן, Tziydon"
ᵇ "ancestry"—γένος, genos—race, family, nation, people; offspring, descendants; sort, kind

---

beyond measure, saying, "He has done all things well: He makes both the deaf to hear and the mute to speak."

8 ¹In those days (the crowd again being very large, and having nothing they could eat), having called His disciples near, He said to them, ²"I have compassion on the crowd, because they continue with Me three days now, and they have nothing they may eat; ³and if I send them away fasting to their home, they will faint on the way—and certain *ones* of them have come from far *away*." ⁴And His disciples answered Him, "From where will anyone be able to *find enough* bread to feed *all* these here in *this* wilderness?"

⁵And He was questioning them, "How many loaves *do* you have?" and they said, "Seven." ⁶And he commanded the crowd to sit down upon the ground; and having taken the seven loaves, *and* having given thanks, He broke *them*, and was giving *the pieces* to His disciples so that they may set *them* before THE PEOPLE; and they set *them* before the crowd. ⁷And they *also* had a few small fishes, and having blessed them, He said to set these also before THE PEOPLE. ⁸And they ate and were filled, and *the disciples* took up *the* broken pieces of that which was *left* over—seven baskets *full*. ⁹And there were about four thousand *people*, and He sent them away.

¹⁰And immediately, having entered into the boat with His disciples, He came to the parts of Dalmanutha, ¹¹and the פְּרוּשִׁים, P'rushiym came out and began to dispute with Him, looking for a sign from Him from the Heaven, tempting Him. ¹²And having sighed deeply in His רוּחַ, ruach, He said, "Why does this generation seek after a sign? אָמֵן, Amen, I say to you: no sign will be given to this generation."

¹³And having left them, having again entered into the boat, He went away to the other side. ¹⁴And they forgot to take loaves *of bread* with them, and except *for* one loaf, they had nothing in the boat.

¹⁵And He was commanding them, saying, "Watch out! Look *carefully* at the leaven of the פְּרוּשִׁים, P'rushiym, and the leaven of Herod." ¹⁶And they were reasoning with one another *that He said this* because they had no loaves. ¹⁷And having known *what they were saying*, He said to them, "Why do you reason *that it is* because you have no loaves? Do you not yet see? nor understand? Have you hardened your heart? ¹⁸Having eyes, do you not see? and having ears, do you not hear? And do you not remember ¹⁹when I broke the five loaves *and gave the pieces* to the five thousand? How many hand-baskets full of broken pieces did you take up?" They said to Him, "Twelve." ²⁰"When *I broke and gave* the seven to the four thousand, how many hand-baskets full of broken pieces did you take up?" And they said to Him, "Seven." ²¹And He said to them, "Do you not yet understand?"

²²And they came to בֵּית צַיְדָה, Beit Tzai'- dah, and brought to Him one *who was* blind, and pleaded with Him that He would touch him. ²³And having taken the hand of the blind man, He brought him outside the village. And having spit on his eyes, *and* having put H**IS** hands on him, He was questioning him, "Do you see anything?" ²⁴And he, having looked up, said, "I see men, *but* I see *them* as trees, walking." ²⁵Afterwards again, He put H**IS** hands on his eyes, and he saw clearly, and was restored, and discerned all things clearly. ²⁶And He sent him away to his house, saying, "You may not go to the village."ᵃ

²⁷And יֵשׁוּעַ, Yeshua and His disciples went out to the villages of Cæsarea Philippi, and on the way He was questioning His disciples, saying to them, "Who do men say Me to be?" ²⁸And they told Him, saying, "*Some say You are* יוֹחָנָן, Yochanan the Immerser, and others *say* אֵלִיָּהוּ, Eliyahu, but others *say You are* one of the prophets." ²⁹And He was questioning them, "And you —who do you say Me to be?" כֵּיפָא, Keifa,ᵇ answering, said to Him, "You are the Messiah." ³⁰And He sternly warned them that they should tell no one about it, ³¹and began to teach them that it was necessary for the Son of Man to suffer many things, and to be rejected by the זְקֵנִים, Z'qeniym, and the chief כֹּהֲנִים, Ko'haniym, and the סוֹפְרִים, Sof'riym, and to be killed, and after three days to rise again; ³²and He was speaking the word openly. And כֵּיפָא, Keifa, having taken Him aside, began to rebuke Him. ³³But He, having turned, and having looked on His disciples, rebuked כֵּיפָא, Keifa and said, "Get behind Me, שָׂטָן, Satan! because you do not think the things of God, but the things of men!"

³⁴And having called the crowd near with His disciples, He said to them, "If anyone wants to follow after Me, let him deny himself, and take up his *execution* stake, and follow Me; ³⁵for whoever wants to save his lifeᶜ will loseᵈ it; and whoever loses his life for My sake and the Good News' sake, will save it. ³⁶For what does it benefit a man to gain the whole world, yet to suffer loss *of* his life? ³⁷For what may a man give as an exchange for his life? ³⁸For whoever may be ashamed of Me and of My words in this adulterous and sinful generation, the Son of Man will also be ashamed of him when He comes in the glory of His Father, with the holy Messengers."

9 ¹And He said to them, "אָמֵן, Amen, I say to you, that there are certain *ones* of those standing here who may not taste of death until they see the Reign of God having come in power."

²And after six days, יֵשׁוּעַ, Yeshua took כֵּיפָא, Keifa and יַעֲקֹב, Ya'aqov and יוֹחָנָן, Yochanan and brought them up to a high mountain by themselves, alone. And He was transformed in front of them, ³and his garments became glittering—exceed-

---

ᵃ Some mss insert, "nor tell *of* I**T** to any*one* in the village"

ᵇ כֵּיפָא, Keifa—Gk: Πέτρος, Petros; also in 8:32-33; 9:2&5; see יוֹחָנָן *Yochanan* 1:42

ᶜ "life"—ψυχή, psuche—lit. "soul"; through vs. 7

ᵈ lose/lost—ἀπόλλυμι, apollumi, meaning "to kill or destroy"

The transformation.   Mark 9:31

ingly white[a]—so *white* as one upon the earth who bleaches cloth[b] is not able to whiten THEM. ⁴And there appeared to them אֵלִיָּהוּ, Eliyahu with מֹשֶׁה, Mosheh, and they were talking with יֵשׁוּעַ, Yeshua. ⁵And כֵּיפָא, Keifa, answering, said to יֵשׁוּעַ, Yeshua, "רַבִּי, Rabiy, it is good to us to be here; and *so* we will make three סֻכּוֹת, sukot—one for You, and one for מֹשֶׁה, Mosheh, and one for אֵלִיָּהוּ, Eliyahu" ⁶(for he was not knowing what he might say, for they were greatly afraid). ⁷And there came a cloud overshadowing them, and there came a voice out of the cloud: "This is My Son—the Beloved. Listen to Him." ⁸And suddenly, having looked around, they saw no one with themselves anymore—but only יֵשׁוּעַ, Yeshua. ⁹And as they were coming down from the mountain, He commanded them that they may describe to no one the things that they saw, until the Son of Man rises out of the dead. ¹⁰And they kept the thing to themselves, questioning together what "the Rising out of the Dead" is.

¹¹And they were questioning Him, saying that the סוֹפְרִים, Sof'riym say that it is necessary for אֵלִיָּהוּ, Eliyahu to come first. ¹²And He said to them, "אֵלִיָּהוּ, Eliyahu indeed, having come first, restores all things; but how has it been written concerning the Son of Man—that He will suffer many things, and *will* be treated with contempt? ¹³But I say to you that אֵלִיָּהוּ, Eliyahu has also come, and they did to him what they wanted, as it has been written of him."

¹⁴And having come to the disciples, they saw a large crowd around them, and סוֹפְרִים, Sof'riym questioning with them.

¹⁵And immediately, the whole crowd, having seen Him, were amazed; and, running near, *they* were greeting Him. ¹⁶And He questioned them, "What *are* you disputing with them?" ¹⁷And one out of the crowd answered, "Teacher, I brought to You my son, *who* has a mute רוּחַ, ruach;

¹⁸and wherever it seizes him, it tears *into* him, and he foams *at the mouth* and gnashes his teeth, and withers away. And I spoke to your disciples *hoping* that they would cast it out, but they were not able." ¹⁹And He, answering them, said, "O unbelieving generation, until when will I be with you? until when will I tolerate you? Bring him to Me." ²⁰And they brought him to Him; and *when* he had seen Him, immediately the רוּחַ, ruach convulsed him; and he, having fallen upon the ground, was rolling *and* foaming *at the mouth*.

²¹And He questioned his father, "How long *of* a time is it since this came to him?" and he said, "From childhood, ²²and many times it also threw him into fire, and into water, so that it might destroy him. But if You are able to do anything, help us, having compassion on us!" ²³And יֵשׁוּעַ, Yeshua said to him, "If you are able![c] all things are possible to the one that is believing." ²⁴Immediately the father of the child, having cried out, said, "I believe![d] Be helping my unbelief."

²⁵*Then* יֵשׁוּעַ, Yeshua, having seen that a crowd was running together *toward them*, rebuked the רוּחַ הַטֻּמְאָה, ruach ha-tum'ah, saying to it, "Mute and deaf רוּחַ, ruach, I command you: come out of him, and no longer may you enter into him!" ²⁶And having shouted and convulsed him much, it came out; and he became as dead, so that many said that he was dead. ²⁷But יֵשׁוּעַ, Yeshua, having taken him by the hand, lifted him up, and he arose.

²⁸And when He had come into the house, His disciples were questioning Him privately, "Why were we not able to cast it out?" ²⁹And He said to them, "This kind is able to come out with nothing except with prayer."[e]

³⁰And having gone out from that place, they were passing through the גָּלִיל, Galiyl, but He did not want that any might know *about it*, ³¹for He was teaching His

---

[a] Some mss insert, "as snow"
[b] "one… who bleaches cloth"—Young's says, "a fuller"
[c] Some mss insert, "to believe"
[d] Some mss insert, "sir" or "Master"
[e] Some mss insert, "and fasting"

disciples. And He said to them, "The Son of Man is being handed over into the hands of men, and they will kill Him; but having been killed, He will rise after three days";[a] ³²but they were not understanding the saying, and they were afraid to question Him.

³³And they came to כְּפַר־נַחוּם, K'far-Nachum, and being in the house, He was questioning them, "What were you reasoning *about* along the way?" ³⁴And they were silent, for along the way they reasoned with one another *about* who *among them* was greater. ³⁵And having sat down, He called the Twelve, and said to them, "If anyone wants to be first, he will be last of all, and servant of all."

³⁶And having taken a child, He set him in the middle of them; and taking him in His arms, said to them, ³⁷"Whoever receives one of such children in My Name receives Me; and whoever receives Me does not receive Me, but Him who sent Me." ³⁸יוֹחָנָן, Yochanan said to Him, "Teacher, we saw a certain one[b] casting out demons in Your Name, and we forbade him, since he does not follow us." ³⁹And יֵשׁוּעַ, Yeshua said, "Forbid him not, for there is no one who will do a powerful act in My Name, and will be able quickly to speak evil of Me; ⁴⁰for he who is not against us is for us. ⁴¹For whoever gives you a cup of water to drink in My Name, because you are Messiah's—אָמֵן, amen, I say to you that he will not lose his reward. ⁴²And whoever causes one of these little ones believing in Me to stumble—it is better for him if a weighty millstone is hung around his neck, and he has been thrown into the sea.

⁴³And if your hand causes you to stumble, cut it off—it is better for you to enter into the Life crippled than, having the two hands, to go away to the גֵּיהִנֹּם, Geihinom, to the fire, the unquenchable.[c]

⁴⁵And if your foot causes you to stumble, cut it off—it is better for you to enter into the Life lame than, having the two feet, to be thrown to the גֵּיהִנֹּם, Geihinom.[d]

⁴⁷"And if your eye causes you to stumble, throw it out—it is better for you to enter into the Reign of God one-eyed than, having two eyes, to be thrown to the גֵּיהִנֹּם, Geihinom[e]—⁴⁸where THEIR WORM IS NOT DYING, AND THE FIRE IS NOT BEING QUENCHED[f]—⁴⁹for everyone will be salted with fire.[g] ⁵⁰The salt IS good, but if the salt becomes saltless, with what will you season IT? Have salt in yourselves, and have peace in one another."

10

¹And *when He* had arisen from there, He came to the boundaries of יְהוּדָה, Y'hudah and beyond the יַרְדֵּן, Yar'den; and again the crowds came together to Him; and, as He had been accustomed, He was teaching them.

²And the פְּרוּשִׁים, P'rushiym, having come near, questioned Him, *asking* if it is permitted for a husband to send away a wife (*they were* tempting Him). ³And He, answering, said to them, "What did מֹשֶׁה, Mosheh command you?" ⁴And they said, "מֹשֶׁה, Mosheh allowed *a* man to WRITE A DOCUMENT OF DIVORCE, AND TO SEND HER AWAY."[h] ⁵And יֵשׁוּעַ, Yeshua said to them, "He wrote you this command for the stiffness of your heart, ⁶but from the beginning of the creation,

God made them a male and a female.[i]
⁷On this account will a man leave his father and mother, and will be joined to his wife, ⁸and they—the two—will be for one flesh;[j]

so that they are no longer two, but one flesh. ⁹Therefore, what God joined together, let not man separate."

---

[a] "after three days"—some mss say, "the third day"
[b] Some mss insert, "who does not follow us"
[c] Verses 44 and 46 are inserted in some mss, and are identical to verse 48.
[d] Some mss insert, "to the fire, the unquenchable"
[e] Some mss insert, "of the fire"
[f] יְשַׁעְיָהוּ Y'sha'yahu 66:24
[g] Some mss insert, "and every sacrifice will be salted with salt"
[h] דְּבָרִים D'variym 24:1
[i] בְּרֵאשִׁית B'reshiyt 1:27, 5:2
[j] בְּרֵאשִׁית B'reshiyt 2:24

He foretells His death.   **Mark 10:35**

¹⁰And *when they were* in the house again, the disciples questioned Him about this; ¹¹and He said to them, "Whoever sends his wife away, and marries another, commits adultery against her; ¹²and if she, sending away her husband, marries another, she commits adultery."

¹³And they were bringing children to Him so that He might touch them, and the disciples rebuked them. ¹⁴And יֵשׁוּעַ, Yeshua, having seen, was much displeased; and He said to them, "Allow the children to come to Me; forbid them not, for of such is the Reign of God. ¹⁵אָמֵן, Amen, I say to you: whoever does not receive the Reign of God as a child—he may not enter into it"; ¹⁶and having taken them in His arms, He was blessing them, having put *His* hands upon them.

¹⁷And as He was going out to the road, *a certain* one, having run and having kneeled to Him, was questioning Him, "Good teacher, what may I do, so that I may inherit life age-enduring?" ¹⁸And יֵשׁוּעַ, Yeshua said to him, "Why do you call Me good? No one *is* good except One—God.

¹⁹"You have known the commands: DO NOT MURDER, DO NOT COMMIT ADULTERY, DO NOT STEAL, DO NOT GIVE FALSE TESTIMONY, do not defraud, HONOR YOUR FATHER AND MOTHER."ᵃ ²⁰And he said to Him, "Teacher, I have kept all these from my youth." ²¹And יֵשׁוּעַ, Yeshua, having looked upon him, loved him; and *He* said to him, "One thing you lack: go away, *and* whatever you have, sell, and give to the poor, and you will have treasure in Heaven. And come, be following Me."ᵇ ²²And he—gloomy at the word—went away grieving, for he was having many possessions.

²³And יֵשׁוּעַ, Yeshua, having looked around, said to His disciples, "How difficultly will they who have riches enter into the Reign of God!" ²⁴And the disciples were astonished at His words.

And יֵשׁוּעַ, Yeshua, answering again, said to them, "Children, how difficult it isᶜ to enter into the Reign of God! ²⁵It is easier for a camel to go through the eye of the needle, than for a rich man to enter into the Reign of God." ²⁶And they were astonished beyond measure, saying among themselves, "And who is able to be saved?" ²⁷יֵשׁוּעַ, Yeshua, having looked upon them, said, "With men it is impossible, but not with God; for all things are possible with God."

²⁸And כֵּיפָא, Keifaᵈ began to say to Him, "Look! We left everything, and we followed You." ²⁹יֵשׁוּעַ, Yeshua said, "אָמֵן, Amen, I say to you: there is no one who left house or brothers or sisters or mother or fatherᵉ or children or fields for My sake, and for the sake of the Good News, ³⁰who will not receive a hundredfold now in this time (*in* houses and brothers and sisters and mothers and children and fields, with persecutions), and in the age that is coming, life age-enduring; ³¹and many *who are* first will be last, and the last first."

³²And they were on the road going up to יְרוּשָׁלַיִם, Y'rushalayim, and יֵשׁוּעַ, Yeshua was going before them, and they were amazed, but those following were afraid. And having again taken the Twelve, He began to tell them the things about to happen to Him—³³"Look! We go up to יְרוּשָׁלַיִם, Y'rushalayim, and the Son of Man will be handed over to the chief כֹּהֲנִים, Ko'haniym and to the סוֹפְרִים, Sof'riym; and they will condemn Him to death, and will hand him over to the גּוֹיִם, Goyim; ³⁴and they will mock Him, and spit on Him, and flog Him, and kill Him; but after three days,ᶠ He will rise again."

³⁵And there came near to Him יַעֲקֹב, Ya'aqov and יוֹחָנָן, Yochanan, the sons of זַבְדִּי, Zav'diy, saying to Him, "Teacher, we want

---

ᵃ שְׁמוֹת *Sh'mot* 20:12-13(12-16); דְּבָרִים *D'variym* 5:16-17(16-20)
ᵇ Some mss insert, "having taken up the *execution* stake"
ᶜ Some mss insert, "for those trusting on the riches"
ᵈ כֵּיפָא, Keifa—Gk: Πέτρος, Petros; see יוֹחָנָן *Yn.* 1:42
ᵉ Some mss insert, "or wife"
ᶠ "after three days"—some mss say, "the third day"

that whatever we may ask for ourselves, You may do for us"; ³⁶and He said to them, "What do you want Me to do for you?" ³⁷and they said to Him, "Give *this* to us: that—one *of us* on Your right hand, and one *of us* on Your left—we may sit in Your glory."

³⁸And יֵשׁוּעַ, Yeshua said to them, "You do not know what you ask. Are you able to drink of the cup that I drink of, or to be immersed with the immersion I am immersed with?" ³⁹And they said to Him, "We are able." And יֵשׁוּעַ, Yeshua said to them, "Of the cup that I drink of, you will drink; and with the immersion with which I am immersed, you will be immersed; ⁴⁰but to sit on My right or on My left is not Mine to give, but *belongs* to those for whom it has been prepared."

⁴¹And the Ten, having heard, began to be much displeased at יַעֲקֹב, Ya'aqov and יוֹחָנָן, Yochanan; ⁴²and having called them near, יֵשׁוּעַ, Yeshua said to them, "You have known that they who are considered to rule the גּוֹיִם, Goyim lord it over them, and their high-*ranked* ones exercise authority upon them. ⁴³But it is not so among you; rather, whoever wants to become great among you, he will be your servant; ⁴⁴and whoever among you wants to be first, he will be slave of all; ⁴⁵for even the Son of Man came not to be served, but to serve, and to give His life *as* a ransom for many."

⁴⁶And they came to יְרִיחוֹ, Y'riycho, and as He was going out from יְרִיחוֹ, Y'riycho with His disciples and a large crowd, the son of טִימַי, Tiymai—בַּרְטִימַי, Bar'tiymai, a blind beggar—was sitting beside the road. ⁴⁷And having heard that it was יֵשׁוּעַ הַנָּצְרָתִי, Yeshua HaNatz'ratiy, he began to shout, and to say, "Son of דָּוִד, David—יֵשׁוּעַ, Yeshua! deal kindly with me!" ⁴⁸And many were rebuking him—that he might keep silent—but he shouted *all* the more abundantly, "Son of דָּוִד, David, deal kindly with me!" ⁴⁹And יֵשׁוּעַ, Yeshua, having stood *still*, said, "Call him." And they called the blind man, saying to him, "Take courage. Rise.

He calls you." ⁵⁰And having thrown off his coat, having jumped up, he came to יֵשׁוּעַ, Yeshua. ⁵¹And answering him, יֵשׁוּעַ, Yeshua said, "What would you have Me do to you?" And the blind man said to Him, "רַבִּי, Rabiy[a]—that I may see again." ⁵²And יֵשׁוּעַ, Yeshua said to him, "Go, your faith has saved you"; and immediately he saw again, and was following Him on the road.

11

¹And when they came near to יְרוּשָׁלַיִם, Y'rushalayim, to בֵּית־פַּגֵּי, Beit-Pagei, and בֵּית־עַנְיָה, Beit-An'yah, He sent two of His disciples to the mountain of the Olives, ²and said to them, "Go away to the village that is opposite you, and immediately, entering into it, you will find a colt tied *there* on which no one of men has yet sat. Untie it and bring *it*; ³and if anyone says to you, 'Why do you do this?' say, 'The Master has need of it,' and immediately, he will send it back here." ⁴And they went away and found a colt tied outside at a door, by the two roads, and they untied it. ⁵And certain *ones* of those standing there said to them, "What are you doing—untying the colt?" ⁶and they said to them as יֵשׁוּעַ, Yeshua said, and they allowed them *to go*.

⁷And they brought the colt to יֵשׁוּעַ, Yeshua and threw their coats upon it, and He sat upon it, ⁸and many *people* spread their coats in the road, and others *spread* branches having been cut from the fields. ⁹And those going in front and those following were shouting, "הוֹשַׁע־נָא, Hosha-na! BLESSED *IS* HE WHO IS COMING IN THE NAME OF ADONAI![b] ¹⁰Blessed is the coming Reign[c] of our father דָּוִד, David! הוֹשַׁע־נָא, Hosha-na in the highest!"

¹¹And He entered into יְרוּשָׁלַיִם, Y'rushalayim, into the Temple, and having looked around on all *the* things (it being now evening), He went to בֵּית־עַנְיָה, Beit-An'yah with the Twelve. ¹²And on the next day, when they had come out from בֵּית־עַנְיָה, Beit-An'yah, He hungered. ¹³And having seen from

---
[a] "רַבִּי, Rabiy"—the Gk says ῥαββουνί, rabbouni
[b] תְּהִלִּים T'hiliym 118:26
[c] Some mss insert, "in the Name of ADONAI"

afar a fig-tree having leaves, He came *to see* if perhaps He would find anything *to eat* in it. And having come to it, He found nothing except leaves, for it was not the time *of year* for figs. ¹⁴And answering, He said to it, "No more—to the age—may any eat fruit from you"; and His disciples were listening.

¹⁵And they came to יְרוּשָׁלַיִם, Y'rushalayim, and having gone into the Temple, He began to drive out those selling and those buying in the Temple. He also overthrew the tables of the money-changers and the seats of those selling the doves, ¹⁶and He did not let anyone carry a container *of merchandise* through the Temple. ¹⁷And He was teaching, and was saying to them, "Has it not been written: 'MY HOUSE WILL BE CALLED A HOUSE OF PRAYER FOR ALL THE PEOPLES'[a]? But you have made it a DEN OF ROBBERS[b]!" ¹⁸And the chief כֹּהֲנִים, Ko'haniym and the סוֹפְרִים, Sof'riym heard *Him*, and they were looking for how they could destroy Him, for they were afraid of Him, because all the crowds were astonished at His teaching.

¹⁹And when evening came, He was going outside the city. ²⁰And passing by, in the morning, they saw the fig-tree having been dried up from the roots. ²¹And כֵּיפָא, Keifa,[c] having remembered, said to Him, "רַבִּי, Rabiy, look! the fig-tree that you cursed is dried up." ²²And יֵשׁוּעַ, Yeshua, answering, said to them, "Have faith of God.

²³"אָמֵן, Amen, I say to you that whoever says to this mountain, 'Be taken up, and be thrown into the sea,' and does not doubt in his heart, but believes that the things that he says will come to pass, it will be to him.[d] ²⁴Because of this I say to you: all *things*, whatever you pray and ask *for*, believe that you have received, and it will be to you. ²⁵And whenever you stand praying, if you have anything against anyone, forgive, so that your Father who is in the Heavens will also forgive you your missteps."[e]

²⁷And they came again to יְרוּשָׁלַיִם, Y'rushalayim, and as He was walking in the Temple, there came to Him the chief כֹּהֲנִים, Ko'haniym, and the סוֹפְרִים, Sof'riym, and the זְקֵנִים, Z'qeniym, ²⁸and they were saying to Him, "By what authority do you do these things? Or who gave you this authority that you may do these things?" ²⁹And יֵשׁוּעַ, Yeshua said to them, "I will question you one word, and *you must first* answer Me, and *then* I will tell you by what authority I do these things: ³⁰the immersion of יוֹחָנָן, Yochanan—was it from Heaven? or from men? Answer Me." ³¹And they were reasoning with themselves, saying, "If we should say, 'from Heaven,' he will say, 'Why, then, did you not believe him?' ³²But should we say, 'From men'? (They were fearing the crowd, for all were holding that יוֹחָנָן, Yochanan was indeed a prophet.) ³³And answering יֵשׁוּעַ, Yeshua, they said, "We do not know"; and יֵשׁוּעַ, Yeshua said to them, "Neither do I tell you by what authority I do these things."

12

¹And He began to speak to them in analogies: "A man planted a vineyard, and put a fence around *it*, and dug an under-wine*press*-vat, and built a tower, and gave it out *for rent* to farmers, and went abroad *on a journey*. ²And at the due time, he sent a slave to the farmers so that from the farmers he might receive from the fruit of the vineyard. ³And they, having taken him, severely beat HIM, and sent him away empty-*handed*. ⁴And again he sent to them another slave, and that one they wounded in the head, and dishonored. ⁵And he sent another, and that one they killed; and *they did the same to* many others—some beating, and some killing. ⁶He still had one *other*—a beloved son. He sent him to

---

[a] יְשַׁעְיָהוּ Y'sha'yahu 56:7; "peoples"—Gk. ἔθνεσιν, ethnesin
[b] יִרְמְיָהוּ Yir'm'yahu 7:11
[c] כֵּיפָא, Keifa—Gk: Πέτρος, Petros; see יוֹחָנָן Yn. 1:42
[d] Some mss insert, "whatever he says"
[e] Some mss continue with verse 26, "And if you do not forgive, neither will your Father who is in the Heavens forgive your missteps."; cf. Mt.6:15, 18:35

them, last *of all*, saying, 'They will respect my son.' ⁷But those farmers said among themselves, 'This is the heir. Come—we should kill him, and the inheritance will be ours'; ⁸and having taken *him*, they killed him, and threw him outside the vineyard. ⁹What, therefore, will the master of the vineyard do? He will come and destroy the farmers, and will give the vineyard to others. ¹⁰And did you not read this Scripture?

'A stone that the builders rejected, it became the head of a corner. ¹¹This was from ADONAI, and it is wonderful in our eyes.'ª

¹²And they were looking to lay hold on Him, but they feared the crowd, for they knew that He spoke the analogy against them.

And having left Him, they went away; ¹³and they sent to Him certain *ones* of the פְּרוּשִׁים, P'rushiym and of the Herodians, so that they might ensnare Him in *His* words. ¹⁴And having come, they said to Him, "Teacher, we have known that you are true, and you are not caring for anyone's *opinion*, for you do not look to the face of men, but teach the way of God in truth. Is it permitted to give *the* census-tax to Cæsar, or not? May we give, or may we not give?" ¹⁵And knowing their hypocrisy, He said to them, "Why do you tempt Me? Bring Me a denary, that I may see *it*"; ¹⁶and they brought *Him the coin*, and He said to them, "Whose image IS this, and the inscription?" and they said to Him, "Cæsar's"; ¹⁷and יֵשׁוּעַ, Yeshua said to them, "Give back the things of Cæsar to Cæsar, and the things of God to God"; and they marveled greatly at Him.

¹⁸And the צְדוּקִים, Tzaduqiym, who say there is not a Rising Again, came to Him; and they were questioning Him, saying, ¹⁹"Teacher, מֹשֶׁה, Mosheh wrote to us that if anyone's brother dies and leaves *behind* a wife, but leaves no child, that his brother should take the wife, and raise up seed to his brother.ᵇ ²⁰*Now* there were seven brothers, and the first took a wife, but dying, he left no seed; ²¹and the second took her, and died, not leaving *any* seed; and the third likewise. ²²And the seven *all* left no seed. Last of all, the woman also died. ²³*So* then, in the Rising Again, whenever they *all* rise, of which of them will she be *the* wife (for *each of* the seven had her as *a* wife)?" ²⁴יֵשׁוּעַ, Yeshua said to them, "Do you not go astray because of this, not knowing the Scriptures, nor the power of God? ²⁵For when they rise out of the dead, they neither marry, nor are they given in marriage, but are as Messengers in the Heavens.

²⁶"And concerning the dead—that they rise: have you not read in the Book of מֹשֶׁה, Mosheh how, at The Bush, God spoke to him, saying,

אָנֹכִי אֱלֹהֵי אַבְרָהָם אֱלֹהֵי יִצְחָק וֵאלֹהֵי יַעֲקֹב
Anokhiy 'Elohei Av'raham, 'Elohei Yitz'chaq, vElohei Ya'aqov'?ᶜ

²⁷He is not a God of dead men, but of living men. You go greatly astray!"

²⁸And one of the סוֹפְרִים, Sof'riym having come near, having heard them disputing, *and* having seen that He answered them well, questioned Him, "Which command is the first of all?" ²⁹יֵשׁוּעַ, Yeshua answered, "The first IS:

שְׁמַע יִשְׂרָאֵל יהוה אֱלֹהֵינוּ יהוה אֶחָד
Sh'ma Yis'rael, ADONAI 'Eloheinu, ADONAI echad;ᵈ

³⁰AND YOU WILL LOVE ADONAI YOUR GOD OUT OF ALL YOUR HEART, AND OUT OF ALL YOUR SOUL, and out of all your understanding, AND OUT OF ALL YOUR STRENGTH.ᵉ ³¹The second ISᶠ this:

ª תְּהִלִּים T'hiliym 118:22-23
ᵇ דְּבָרִים D'variym 25:5-6
ᶜ שְׁמוֹת Sh'mot 3:6, "I am the God of Abraham, and the God of Isaac, and the God of Jacob"; cf. שְׁמוֹת Sh'mot 3:15-16
ᵈ דְּבָרִים D'variym 6:4, "Hear, O Israel, ADONAI is our God, ADONAI is one."
ᵉ דְּבָרִים D'variym 6:5; some mss insert, "—this IS the first command"
ᶠ Some mss insert, "like IT"

The sign of things fulfilled.

'You will love your neighbor as yourself.'[a]

There is no other command greater than these." ³²And the סוֹפֵר, Sofer said to Him, "Teacher, in truth you have spoken well that He is one, AND THERE IS NONE OTHER BUT HE;[b] ³³ and to LOVE HIM OUT OF ALL THE HEART, and out of all the understanding,[c] AND OUT OF ALL THE STRENGTH,[d] and to love one's neighbor as one's self[e] is more than all the whole burnt-offerings and sacrifices." ³⁴And יֵשׁוּעַ, Yeshua, having seen him, that he answered with understanding, said to him, "You are not far from the Reign of God"; and no one dared question Him anymore.

³⁵And answering, יֵשׁוּעַ, Yeshua said—teaching in the Temple—"How *is it that* the סוֹפְרִים, Sof'riym say that the Messiah is *the* son of דָּוִד, David? ³⁶ דָּוִד, David himself said in the רוּחַ הַקֹּדֶשׁ, Ruach HaQodesh,

'ADONAI said to my Master, "Sit at My right hand, until I place your enemies under your feet."'[f]

³⁷*If* דָּוִד, David himself said of Him, 'Master,' then how is He his son?"

And the large crowd was hearing Him gladly, ³⁸and in His teaching He was saying, "Beware of the סוֹפְרִים, Sof'riym, who want to walk *around* in long robes; and *who* love greetings in the market-places, ³⁹and *the* most important seats in the synagogues, and *the* prime seating at supper *tables;* ⁴⁰who are devouring the widows' houses, and—for a pretense—are making long prayers. These will receive more abundant judgment."

⁴¹And He, having sat down opposite the treasury, was looking *at* how the crowd put brass *coins* into the treasury, and many rich *people* were putting in much. ⁴²And having come, a poor widow put in two very small coins which are *worth* barely a penny.[g] ⁴³And having called near His disciples, He said to them, "אָמֵן, Amen, I say to you that this poor widow put in more than all those putting into the treasury; ⁴⁴for all *of them* put in out of their abundance, but she, out of her want, put in all that she had—her whole living."

13

¹And as He was going out of the Temple, one of His disciples said to Him, "Teacher, see! what stones! and what buildings!" ²and יֵשׁוּעַ, Yeshua said to him, "Do you see these massive buildings? There will not be left here a stone upon a stone that will not be thrown down."

³And as He was sitting at the mountain of the Olives opposite the Temple, כֵּיפָא, Keifa[h] and יַעֲקֹב, Ya'aqov and יוֹחָנָן, Yochanan and Andrew were questioning Him privately, ⁴"Tell us when these things will be? and what IS the sign when all these things are about to be fulfilled?" ⁵And יֵשׁוּעַ, Yeshua began to say to them, "Watch out so that no one leads you astray. ⁶Many will come in My Name, saying, 'I am HE,' and they will lead many astray.

⁷"And when you hear of wars and reports of wars, be not troubled; these need to be, but the end IS not yet; ⁸for ethnic-group will rise against ethnic-group, and kingdom against kingdom; there will be earthquakes in different places; there will be famines.[i] These ARE *the* beginning of labor pains.

⁹"But watch out for yourselves! They will hand you over to *the* Sanhedrins and *the* synagogues, you will be beaten, and you will stand before governors and kings for My sake, for a testimony to them ¹⁰(but it is first necessary that the Good News be proclaimed to all the world-ethnicities).

---

[a] וַיִּקְרָא *Vayiq'ra* 19:18
[b] דְּבָרִים *D'variym* 4:35
[c] Some mss insert, "AND OUT OF ALL THE SOUL"
[d] דְּבָרִים *D'variym* 6:5
[e] וַיִּקְרָא *Vayiq'ra* 19:18
[f] תְּהִלִּים *T'hiliym* 110:1

[g] "barely a penny"—Young's says, "a farthing," though neither "penny" nor "farthing" exactly equal the true amount.
[h] כֵּיפָא, Keifa—Gk: Πέτρος, Petros; see יוֹחָנָן *Yn.* 1:42
[i] Some mss insert, "and troubles"

¹¹And when they lead you *to trial*—handing *you* over—be not anxious beforehand *about* what you will speak,ᵃ but whatever may be given to you in that moment, speak that, for it is not you who are speaking, but the רוּחַ הַקֹּדֶשׁ, Ruach HaQodesh.

¹²"And brother will hand over brother to death, and a father *his* child; and children will rise up against *their* parents, and *they* will put them to death; ¹³and you will be hated by all because of My Name; but he who has endured to the end—he will be saved.

¹⁴"And when you see the abomination of the desolationᵇ standing where it ought not" (whoever is reading *this*, let him understand) "then those in יְהוּדָה, Y'hudah, let them flee to the mountains; ¹⁵and he upon the house-top, let him not come down, nor go in to take anything out of his house; ¹⁶and he who is in the field, let him not turn to the things behind, *even* to pick up his coat. ¹⁷And אוֹי, oy! to those pregnant *mothers*, and to those *who* are nursing in those days; ¹⁸and pray that itᶜ may not be in winter. ¹⁹Indeed, those days will be oppression, such as has not been from the beginning of the creation that God created until now, and may not be *again*. ²⁰And if ADONAI did not shorten the days, no flesh would have been saved, but because of The Chosen, whom He chose to Himself, He shortened the days.

²¹"And then, if anyone says to you, 'Look! here IS the Messiah! Look! There!' do not believe; ²²for there will rise *up* false messiahs and false prophets, and they will give signs and wonders to seduce, if possible, The Chosen; ²³so watch out.

"I have foretold *to* you all things. ²⁴But in those days—after that oppression—THE SUN WILL BE DARKENED, AND THE MOON WILL NOT GIVE HER LIGHT,ᵈ ²⁵AND THE STARS WILL BE FALLING,ᵉ from the heaven, and the powers that are in the heavens will be shaken. ²⁶And then they will see THE SON OF MAN COMING IN CLOUDSᶠ with much power and glory, ²⁷and then He will send the Messengers and gather together His Chosen from the four winds, from the end of the earth to the end of heaven.

²⁸"Now learn the analogy from the figtree: when its branch has already become tender and has produced the leaves, you know that the summer is near; ²⁹so, also, when you see these *things* coming to pass, you know that it is near, at the doors. ³⁰אָמֵן, Amen, I say to you that this generation will not pass away until these things all come to pass; ³¹the heaven and the earth will pass away, but My words will not pass away.

³²"So concerning that Day or the hour, no one has known—not even the Messengers in Heaven, not even the Son—except the Father. ³³Watch out; *keep* alert;ᵍ for you have not known when the time is. ³⁴*It is* like a man who has gone abroad, having left his house and given the authority to his slaves—to each one his *assigned* work—and commanded the doorkeeper that he must *stay* awake. ³⁵*Stay* awake, therefore, for you have not known when the master of the house will come: either at evening, or at midnight, or at *the* rooster-crowing, or at the morning; ³⁶so that, having come suddenly, he may not find you sleeping. ³⁷And what I say to you, I say to all: *stay* awake!"

14 ¹And the פֶּסַח, Pesach and *the Feast of* הַמַּצּוֹת, HaMatzot were *coming* after two days, and the chief כֹּהֲנִים, Ko'haniym and the סוֹפְרִים, Sof'riym were looking for how—by underhandedness—having taken hold of Him, they might kill Him; ²for they said, "Not on the Feast; otherwise, there will be a commotion among the people."

ᵃ Some mss insert, "nor premeditate"
ᵇ Some mss insert, "that was spoken of by דָּנִיֵּאל, Daniyel the prophet"
ᶜ "it"—some mss say, "your flight"
ᵈ יְשַׁעְיָהוּ Y'sha'yahu 13:10, 24:23; יְחֶזְקֵאל Y'chez'qel 32:7; יוֹאֵל Yoel 3:4(2:31), 4:15ff(3:15ff); עָמוֹס Amos 5:20, 8:9; צְפַנְיָה Tz'fan'yah 1:15
ᵉ יְשַׁעְיָהוּ Y'sha'yahu 34:4
ᶠ דָּנִיֵּאל Daniyel 7:13
ᵍ Some mss insert, "and pray"

Messiah fulfills the Passover.

³And while He was in בֵּית־עַנְיָה, Beit-An'yah in the house of שִׁמְעוֹן, Shim'on the leper, during His reclining (at mealtime), there came a woman having an alabaster box of ointment—of spikenard, very precious. And having broken the alabaster box, *she* poured *the ointment* on His head. ⁴And there were certain *ones* much displeased within themselves, and saying, "For what *purpose* has this waste of the ointment been made? ⁵Indeed, this ointment could have been sold for more than three hundred days' wages,[a] and given to the poor"; and they were speaking sternly at her. ⁶And יֵשׁוּעַ, Yeshua said, "Leave her alone; why are you giving her trouble? She did a beautiful act to Me. ⁷For you *will* always have the poor with you; and whenever you want, you are able to do them good; but you *will* not always have Me. ⁸She did what she could: she anticipated to anoint My body for the burial preparation. ⁹And אָמֵן, amen, I say to you, wherever the Good News may be proclaimed in the whole world, what this woman did will also be spoken of, for a memorial of her."

¹⁰And יְהוּדָה אִישׁ־קְרִיּוֹת, Y'hudah Iysh-Q'riyot, one of the Twelve, went away to the chief כֹּהֲנִים, Ko'haniym so that he might hand Him over to them. ¹¹And having heard, they were glad, and promised to give him money. And he was looking for how he might hand Him over when the time was right.

¹²And *before* the first day of *the Feast of* הַמַּצּוֹת, HaMatzot, when they were killing the פֶּסַח, Pesach, His disciples said to Him, "Where do You want THAT, having gone, we may prepare the פֶּסַח, Pesach, so that You may eat *it*?"

¹³And He sent out two of His disciples, and said to them, "Go away to the city, and a man carrying a pitcher of water will meet you there. Follow him, ¹⁴and wherever he goes in, say to the master of the house, 'The Teacher says, "Where is My guest-room, where I may eat the פֶּסַח, Pesach with My disciples?"' ¹⁵and he will show you a large upper room, furnished *and* prepared. And make ready for us there." ¹⁶And the disciples went out, and came to the city, and found *everything* as He said to them, and they made ready the פֶּסַח, Pesach.

¹⁷And evening having come, He came with the Twelve; ¹⁸and as they were reclining and eating, יֵשׁוּעַ, Yeshua said, "אָמֵן, Amen, I say to you: one of you who is eating with Me will hand me over *in betrayal*." ¹⁹They began to be sorrowful, and to say to Him, one by one, "Is it I?"[b] ²⁰And He said to them, "*It is* one of the Twelve who is dipping with Me in the dish. ²¹For the Son of Man does indeed go, as it has been written concerning Him. But אוֹי, oy! to that man through whom the Son of Man is handed over! It would have been better to him if that man had not been born!"

²²And as they were eating, having taken *matzah* bread, having blessed *it*, He broke *it*, and gave *it* to them, and said, "Take;[c] this is My body." ²³And having taken a cup, *and* having given thanks *to God*, He gave *it* to them, and they drank of it—all *of them*; ²⁴and He said to them, "This is My blood of the בְּרִית, B'riyt,[d] which is being poured out for many. ²⁵אָמֵן, Amen, I say to you that I will no longer drink of the fruit of the vine until that Day when I will drink it new in the Reign of God."

²⁶And having sung the הַלֵּל, Halel, they went out to the Mountain of the Olives, ²⁷and יֵשׁוּעַ, Yeshua said to them, "You will all be stumbled,[e] because it has been written,

'I will strike the shepherd, and the sheep will be scattered abroad,'[f]

²⁸but after My having risen *from the dead*, I will go before you to the גָּלִיל, Galiyl."

---

[a] "days' wages"—lit. "denaries"
[b] Some mss insert, "and another, 'Is it I?'"
[c] Some mss insert, "eat"; cf. מַתִּתְיָהוּ *Matit'yahu* 26:26
[d] "בְּרִית, B'riyt"—some mss say, בְּרִית הַחֲדָשָׁה, B'riyt Ha'Chadashah"; cf. מַתִּתְיָהוּ *Mat.* 26:28, Luke 22:20, and 1 Corinthians 11:25.
[e] Some mss insert, "at Me this night"
[f] זְכַרְיָה *Z'khar'yah* 13:7

²⁹And כֵּיפָא, Keifaª said to Him, "Even if all will be stumbled, yet I *will* not!" ³⁰And יֵשׁוּעַ, Yeshua said to him, "אָמֵן, Amen, I say to you that today—this night—before a rooster crows twice, three times you will deny Me." ³¹And *Keifa* spokeᵇ vehemently, "If it is necessary for me to die with You, I will never ever deny You!" and they all also said likewise.

³²And they came to a spot, the name of which IS גַּת־שְׁמָנֶה, Gat-Sh'menah, and He said to His disciples, "Sit here until I have prayed." ³³And he took כֵּיפָא, Keifa and יַעֲקֹב, Ya'aqov and יוֹחָנָן, Yochanan with Him, and began to be overwhelmed and very heavy-hearted, ³⁴and He said to them, "Exceedingly sorrowful is My soul—to death; remain here, and *stay* awake." ³⁵And having gone forward a little, He was falling upon the ground, and was praying that, if it were possible, the hour might pass from Him. ³⁶And He said, "אַבָּא, Abba! Father! All things are possible to You; make this cup pass from Me—but not what I will; rather, what You *will*."

³⁷And He came and found them sleeping, and said to כֵּיפָא, Keifa, "שִׁמְעוֹן, Shim'on! You are asleep! You were not able to *stay* awake *for* one hour! ³⁸*Stay* awake and pray, so that you may not come into temptation. The רוּחַ, ruach indeed is willing, but the flesh *is* weak." ³⁹And again, having gone away, He prayed, saying the same word *as before*. ⁴⁰And again having come, He found them sleeping, for their eyes were very heavy; and *when they awoke*, they did not know what they could answer Him. ⁴¹And He came the third time, and said to them, "Sleep from now on, and rest—it is over. The hour has come. Look! the Son of Man is handed over to the hands of the sinful. ⁴²Rise, let us go! Look! he who is handing me over *in betrayal* has come near."

⁴³And immediately, while He was still speaking, יְהוּדָה, Y'hudah came near (one of the Twelve); and with him, *armed* with swords and sticks, *was* a crowd from the chief כֹּהֲנִים, Ko'haniym and the סוֹפְרִים, Sof'riym and the זְקֵנִים, Z'qeniym. ⁴⁴And he who was handing Him over had given a signal to them, saying, "Whomever I kiss, it is He. Take hold of Him, and lead Him away under guard." ⁴⁵Having come and immediately having gone near *to* Him, he said, "רַבִּי, Rabiy,"ᶜ and kissed Him.

⁴⁶And they laid their hands on Him, and kept hold on Him. ⁴⁷And a certain one of those standing by, having drawn the sword, struck the slave of the כֹּהֵן הַגָּדוֹל, Kohen HaGadol and took off his ear. ⁴⁸And יֵשׁוּעַ, Yeshua, answering, said to them, "*It is* as *if you were going* against a robber *that* you came out, with swords and sticks, to take Me! ⁴⁹Daily I was with you in the Temple, teaching, yet you did not take hold of Me *then!* But *all this has come to pass*, so that the Scriptures may be fulfilled." ⁵⁰And having left Him, all *the disciples* fled. ⁵¹And a certain young man was following Him, having put a linen cloth around HIS naked body, and theyᵈ took hold of him; ⁵²but he, having left the linen cloth, fled naked.

⁵³And they led יֵשׁוּעַ, Yeshua away to the כֹּהֵן הַגָּדוֹל, Kohen HaGadol, and all the chief כֹּהֲנִים, Ko'haniym and the זְקֵנִים, Z'qeniym and the סוֹפְרִים, Sof'riym came together. ⁵⁴And כֵּיפָא, Keifa followed Him from afar, to the inside of the courtyard of the כֹּהֵן הַגָּדוֹל, Kohen HaGadol, and was sitting with the attendants and warming himself near the fire.

⁵⁵And the chief כֹּהֲנִים, Ko'haniym, and all the Sanhedrin, were looking for testimony against יֵשׁוּעַ, Yeshua—to put Him to death—but they were not finding *any*, ⁵⁶for many were giving false testimony against Him, and their testimonies were not alike.

⁵⁷And certain *ones* having risen up were giving false testimony against Him, saying, ⁵⁸"We heard Him saying, 'I will throw

---

ª כֵּיפָא, Keifa—Gk: Πέτρος, Petros; also verse 33, 37, 54, 66, 67, 70 and 72; see יוֹחָנָן *Yochanan* 1:42
ᵇ Some mss insert, "*all* the more"
ᶜ Some mss say "רַבִּי, Rabiy" twice.
ᵈ "they"—some mss say, "the young men"

down this Temple made with hands, and by three days, I will build another made without hands'"; ⁵⁹but not even *in* this way was their testimony alike.

⁶⁰And the כֹּהֵן הַגָּדוֹל, Kohen HaGadol, having risen up in the middle *of them*, questioned יֵשׁוּעַ, Yeshua, saying, "You do not answer anything! What do these *people* testify against you?" ⁶¹But He was keeping silent, and did not answer anything. Again the כֹּהֵן הַגָּדוֹל, Kohen HaGadol was questioning Him, and said to Him, "Are you the Messiah—the Son of the Blessed One?" ⁶²And יֵשׁוּעַ, Yeshua said, "I am. And you will see THE SON OF MAN SITTING AT THE RIGHT HAND OF THE POWER,ᵃ and COMING WITH THE CLOUDS OF THE HEAVEN."ᵇ ⁶³And the כֹּהֵן הַגָּדוֹל, Kohen HaGadol, having torn his garments, said, "What need have we of further witnesses? ⁶⁴You heard the evil-speaking—how does it appear to you?" and they all condemned Him to be worthy of death. ⁶⁵And certain *ones* began to spit on Him, and to cover His face, and to beat Him with *their* fists, and to say to Him, "Prophesy!" and the assistants took Him with slaps.

⁶⁶And as כֵּיפָא, Keifa was beneath in the courtyard, one of the slave-girls of the כֹּהֵן הַגָּדוֹל, Kohen HaGadol came by. ⁶⁷And having seen כֵּיפָא, Keifa warming himself, having looked on him, she said, "And you were with הַנָּצְרָתִי, HaNatz'ratiy, יֵשׁוּעַ, Yeshua!" ⁶⁸and he denied *it*, saying, "I neither know Hɪᴍ, nor do I understand what you say," and he went outside to the entrance—and a rooster crowed.

⁶⁹And the slave-girl, having seen him, began again to say to those standing near, "This is *one* of them"; ⁷⁰and he was again denying *it*. And after a little *while*, again, those standing near to כֵּיפָא, Keifa said, "Truly you are *one* of them, for you also are a גְּלִילִי, G'liyliy."ᶜ ⁷¹And he began to bind curses on himself, and to swear *an oath*, "I have not known this man of whom you speak."

⁷²And immediately,ᵈ a rooster crowed a second time; and כֵּיפָא, Keifa remembered the saying, how יֵשׁוּעַ, Yeshua *had* said to him, "Before a rooster crows twice, you will deny me three times." And having thrown himself down,ᵉ he was weeping.

15

¹And immediately, in the morning, the chief כֹּהֲנִים, Ko'haniym (having made a council with the זְקֵנִים, Z'qeniym and *the* סוֹפְרִים, Sof'riym and the whole Sanhedrin), having bound יֵשׁוּעַ, Yeshua, led *Him* away and handed Hɪᴍ over to Pilate. ²And Pilate questioned Him, "Are you the king of the Jews?" And answering him, He said, "*As* you say ɪᴛ." ³And the chief כֹּהֲנִים, Ko'haniym were accusing Him of many things, ʙᴜᴛ ʜᴇ ᴀɴsᴡᴇʀᴇᴅ ɴᴏᴛʜɪɴɢ. ⁴And Pilate was questioning Him again, saying, "You do not answer anything! See how many accusations they bring against you!" ⁵But יֵשׁוּעַ, Yeshua no longer answered anything, so that Pilate *was* in wonder.

⁶And at every Feast, he was releasing one prisoner to them whom they were asking for. ⁷(And there was ᴏɴᴇ named בַּר־אַבָּא, Bar-Aba, *who was* bound with the insurrectionists, who had committed murder in the insurrection.) ⁸And the crowd, having gone up,ᶠ began to ask *Pilate to do* as he was *accustomed to* doing for them *at the Feasts.* ⁹And Pilate answered them, saying, "Do you want me to release to you the king of the Jews?" ¹⁰for he knew the chief כֹּהֲנִים, Ko'haniym had handed Him over because of envy. ¹¹But the chief כֹּהֲנִים, Ko'haniym stirred up the crowd so that *Pilate* might instead release בַּר־אַבָּא, Bar-Aba to them.

¹²And Pilate, answering again, said to them, "What, then, do you want me to do to him whom you call king of the Jews?"

ᵃ תְּהִלִּים T'hilyim 110:1
ᵇ דָּנִיֵּאל Daniyel 7:13
ᶜ Some mss insert, "and your *manner of* speech is similar"
ᵈ Some mss omit, "immediately"
ᵉ "thrown himself down"—Young's says, "thought thereon"
ᶠ "gone up"—some mss say, "cried out"

¹³And they shouted again, "Crucify him!" ¹⁴And Pilate said to them, "Why? What evil did he do?" and they shouted all the more, "Crucify him!" ¹⁵And Pilate, wanting to satisfy the crowd, released בַּר־אַבָּא, Bar-Aba to them, and handed over יֵשׁוּעַ, Yeshua—having flogged HIM—so that He might be crucified.

¹⁶And the soldiers led Him away into the courtyard (which is *the* Prætorium[a]), and called together their whole battalion. ¹⁷And *they* clothed Him with purple; and having braided a crown of thorns, they put IT on Him ¹⁸and began to salute Him: "Hail, King of the Jews!" ¹⁹And they were striking Him on the head with a reed, and were spitting on Him, and, having bent the knee, were bowing to Him. ²⁰And when they HAD mocked Him, they took the purple *garment* off Him and clothed Him in His garments, and they led Him out, so that they might crucify Him.

²¹And they forced a certain one passing by—שִׁמְעוֹן, Shim'on, a Cyrenian, the father of Alexander and Rufus, *who was* coming from the field—that he should take up His *execution* stake. ²²And they brought Him to the place גֻּלְגָּלְתָּא, Gal'gal'-ta (which is, being interpreted, "Place of a skull"), ²³and they were giving Him wine mingled with myrrh, but He did not take *it*. ²⁴And they crucified Him, and divided His garments, casting a lot upon them *to determine* what each *one* might take.

²⁵And it was the third hour,[b] and they crucified Him, ²⁶and the inscription of His accusation was written above—"The King of the Jews." ²⁷And they crucified two robbers with Him—one on the right hand, and one on His left.[c]

²⁹And those passing by were speaking evil of Him, shaking their heads and saying, "Ah! the Thrower-down of the Temple, and the Builder in Three Days! ³⁰Save yourself, having come down from the stake!"

³¹And likewise, the chief כֹּהֲנִים, Ko'ha-niym, also mocking with one another, *along* with the סוֹפְרִים, Sof'riym, said, "He saved others, *but* he is not able to save himself! ³²The Messiah! The king of יִשְׂרָאֵל, Yis'rael! Let him come down now from the stake, so that we may see and believe"; and those crucified with Him were denouncing Him *also*.

³³And when the sixth hour had come, darkness came over the whole land until the ninth hour; ³⁴and at the ninth hour, יֵשׁוּעַ, Yeshua cried *out* with a loud voice, "אֵלִי אֵלִי לָמָה עֲזַבְתָּנִי, Eliy! Eliy! Lamah 'azav'-taniy?"[d] which is, being interpreted, "MY GOD! MY GOD! WHY DID YOU ABANDON ME?" ³⁵And certain *ones* of those standing by, having heard *this*, said, "See! He calls אֵלִיָּהוּ, Eliyahu!" ³⁶And someone, having run and having filled a sponge with *wine* vinegar, having put IT on a reed, was giving *it to* Him to drink, saying, "Leave Him alone—let us see if אֵלִיָּהוּ, Eliyahu comes to take Him down."

³⁷And יֵשׁוּעַ, Yeshua, having let go a loud sound, breathed His last.[e] ³⁸And the curtain of the Temple was split in two, from top to bottom; ³⁹and the centurion who was standing opposite Him, having seen the way that[f] He breathed His last, said, "Truly this man was *the* Son of God."

⁴⁰And there were also women looking *on* from afar, among whom were מִרְיָם הַמַּגְדָּלִית, Mir'yam HaMag'daliyt, and מִרְיָם, Mir'yam *the mother* of יַעֲקֹב, Ya'aqov the less and of יוֹסֵי, Yosei, and שְׁלֹמִית, Sh'lomiyt ⁴¹(who were following Him, and were serving Him when He was in the גָּלִיל, Galiyl), and many other women who came up with Him to יְרוּשָׁלַיִם, Y'rushalayim.

---

[a] "Prætorium"—the governor's headquarters
[b] "the third hour"—presumably, three hours after dawn, i.e., 9 a.m.
[c] Some mss continue with verse 28, "and the Scripture was fulfilled that is saying, 'And he was numbered with wrongdoing ones.'"
[d] תְּהִלִּים T'hiliym 22:2(1), though the Gk is apparently rendering Aramaic.
[e] "breathed His last" or, as in Young's, "yielded the spirit"; also in verse 39; cf. Mt. 27:50
[f] Some mss insert, "having shouted"

⁴²And now *with* evening having come, since it was the Preparation *Day* (that is, *the day* before שַׁבָּת, Shabat), ⁴³יוֹסֵף מִן־הָרָמָתַיִם, Yosef Min-HaRamatayim—an honorable Councilman who himself was also waiting for the Reign of God—having come, boldly entered in to Pilate, and asked for the body of יֵשׁוּעַ, Yeshua. ⁴⁴And Pilate *was* in wonder that[a] He was already dead; and having called near the centurion, *he* questioned him *as to know* if He were long dead. ⁴⁵And having *come to* know IT from the centurion, he granted the body to יוֹסֵף, Yosef. ⁴⁶And *Yosef*, having brought fine linen, having taken Him down *from the stake*, wrapped Him in the linen and laid Him in a tomb that had been cut out of a rock. And he rolled a stone over the door of the tomb, ⁴⁷and מִרְיָם הַמַּגְדָּלִית, Mir'yam HaMag'daliyt and מִרְיָם, Mir'yam *the mother* of יוֹסֵי, Yosei were seeing where He was laid.

16

¹And when the שַׁבָּת, Shabat had past, מִרְיָם הַמַּגְדָּלִית, Mir'yam HaMag'daliyt, and מִרְיָם, Mir'yam *the mother* of יַעֲקֹב, Ya'aqov, and שְׁלֹמִית, Sh'lomiyt bought spices, so that, having come, they might anoint Him. ²And very early in the morning on the first *day* of the week,[b] they came to the tomb at the rising of the sun, ³and they said among themselves, "Who will roll away the stone for us from the door of the tomb?" ⁴And having looked, they saw that the stone had been rolled away (for it was very large).

⁵And having entered into the tomb, they saw a young man sitting on the right side, wrapped around in a long white robe; and they were amazed. ⁶And he said to them, "Be not amazed. You seek יֵשׁוּעַ הַנָּצְרָתִי, Yeshua HaNatz'ratiy, the Crucified. He rose *from the dead!* He is not here. See! *Here is* the place where they laid Him! ⁷But go, say to His disciples and כֵּיפָא, Keifa[c] that He goes before you to the גָּלִיל, Galiyl. There you will see Him, as He said to you." ⁸And, having come out, they fled from the tomb, for trembling and amazement had seized them. And they said nothing to anyone, for they were afraid.

The most reliable early manuscripts do not have Mark 16:9-20.

⁹And *when* He had risen in the morning of the first of the week, *He* appeared first to מִרְיָם הַמַּגְדָּלִית, Mir'yam HaMag'daliyt, out of whom He had cast out seven demons. ¹⁰She, having gone, told those who had been with Him, *as they were* mourning and weeping. ¹¹But they, having heard that He was alive and was seen by her, did not believe.

¹²And after these things, He was revealed in another form to two of them, as they were going into a field, walking. ¹³And they, having gone, told *it* to the rest; they did not even believe them.

¹⁴And afterwards, as they were reclining (at mealtime), He was revealed to the Eleven, and denounced their unbelief and stiffness of heart, because they did not believe those having seen Him being raised *from the dead.*

¹⁵And He said to them, "Having gone to all the world, proclaim the Good News to all the creation. ¹⁶He who has believed, and has been immersed, will be saved. But he who has not believed will be condemned. ¹⁷And signs will accompany those believing these things: in my Name, they will cast out demons; they will speak with new languages;[d] ¹⁸and with the hands[e] they will take up serpents; and if they drink any deadly thing, it will not hurt them; they will lay hands on the infirmed, and they will be well."

¹⁹The Master יֵשׁוּעַ, Yeshua, then, indeed, after speaking to them, was received up to the heaven, and sat at the right side of God. ²⁰And they, having gone out, proclaimed everywhere, *and* the Master *was* working with THEM, and confirming the word through the signs *that were* following.

---

[a] "that"—Young's and some other trans. say "if"
[b] "week"—lit. σαββάτου, sabbatou, that is, שַׁבָּת, shabat; also in verse 9; Young's says, "sabbaths"
[c] כֵּיפָא, Keifa—Gk: Πέτρος, Petros; see יוֹחָנָן Yn. 1:42

[d] "languages"—lit. "tongues"
[e] Some mss omit, "and with the hands"

The Good News of Yeshua According to

Luke

1 ¹Seeing that many put their hand to setting in order a narration of the matters that have been fully assured among us—²*just* as they *were* delivered to us *by those* who, from the beginning, became eye-witnesses and attendants of the word—³it also seemed good to me, having exactly followed after all things from the first, to write *an account* to you in *successive* order, most noble Theophilus, ⁴so that you may know the certainty of the words which you were told.

⁵In the days of Herod, the king of יְהוּדָה, Y'hudah, there was a certain כֹּהֵן, kohen by *the* name זְכַרְיָה, Z'khar'yah, of the division of אֲבִיָּה, 'Aviyah; and his wife *was* of the daughters of אַהֲרֹן, A'haron, and her name *was* אֱלִישֶׁבַע, 'Eliysheva; ⁶and they were both righteous before God, going on blamelessly in all the commands and righteousnesses of ADONAI. ⁷And they had no child, since אֱלִישֶׁבַע, 'Eliysheva was barren, and both were advanced in their days.

⁸And it came to pass, in his acting as כֹּהֵן, kohen in the order of his division before God, ⁹according to the custom of the כְּהֻנָּה, K'hunah, his lot was to make *offerings of* incense, having gone into the Temple of ADONAI. ¹⁰And all the crowds of the people were praying outside at the hour of the incense *offering*.

¹¹And there appeared to him a Messenger of ADONAI, standing on the right side of the altar of the incense. ¹²And זְכַרְיָה, Z'khar'yah, having seen *this*, was troubled, and fear fell on him. ¹³And the Messenger said to him, "Fear not, זְכַרְיָה, Z'khar'yah, for your request for help was heard; and your wife אֱלִישֶׁבַע, 'Eliysheva will bear a son to you; and you will call his name יוֹחָנָן, Yochanan; ¹⁴and there will be joy and rejoicing to you, and many will rejoice at his birth, ¹⁵for he will be great before ADONAI. And he may not drink wine and strong drink, but he will be full of the רוּחַ הַקֹּדֶשׁ, Ruach HaQodesh, even from his mother's womb. ¹⁶And he will turn many of the sons of יִשְׂרָאֵל, Yis'rael to ADONAI their God, ¹⁷and he will go before Him, in the רוּחַ, ruach and power of אֵלִיָּהוּ, Eliyahu, TO TURN *THE* HEARTS OF FATHERS TO *THEIR* CHILDREN,[a] and obstinate[b] ones to the wisdom of righteous ones, to make ready for ADONAI a people prepared."

¹⁸And זְכַרְיָה, Z'khar'yah said to the Messenger, "How will I know this? for I am aged, and my wife is advanced in her days." ¹⁹And the Messenger, answering, said to him, "I am גַּבְרִיאֵל, Gav'riyel, who has been standing near in the presence of God, and I was sent to speak to you, and to proclaim this Good News to you. ²⁰And look! you will be silent and not able to speak until the day that these things come to pass, because you did not believe my words, which will be fulfilled in their season."

²¹And the people were waiting for זְכַרְיָה, Z'khar'yah, and wondering at his delay in the Temple. ²²And having come out, he was not able to speak to them, and they perceived that he had seen a vision in the Temple. And he was motioning to them, but remained mute.

²³And it came to pass when the days of his service were fulfilled *that* he went away to his house. ²⁴And after those days, his wife אֱלִישֶׁבַע, 'Eliysheva conceived, and *she* hid herself *for* five months, saying, ²⁵"ADONAI has done so to me, in days

---

[a] מַלְאָכִי *Mal'akhiy* 3:24(4:6)
[b] "obstinate"—ἀπειθής, apeithes, a negative of πείθω, peitho, which is most often translated "trust" or "persuade." Here, Young says "disobedient."

The Messenger of God.

in which He looked upon ME, to take away my disgrace among men."

²⁶And in the sixth month, the Messenger גַּבְרִיאֵל, Gav'riyel was sent from God to a city of the גָּלִיל, Galiyl (the name of which IS נְצֶרֶת, N'tzaret), ²⁷to a virgin *who was* pledged to a man whose name WAS יוֹסֵף, Yosef, of the house of דָּוִד, David; and the name of the virgin WAS מִרְיָם, Mir'yam. ²⁸And having come in to her, he said, "שָׁלוֹם, Shalom,ᵃ favored one; ADONAI IS with you.ᵇ" ²⁹And she was troubled at the word, and was considering what kind of greeting this might be. ³⁰And the Messenger said to her, "Fear not, מִרְיָם, Mir'yam, for you have found favor with God. ³¹And look! you will conceive in the womb, and will bring forth a son and call His Name יֵשׁוּעַ, Yeshua. ³²He will be great, and He will be called Son of the Highest. And יהוה אֱלֹהִים, ADONAI 'Elohiym will give Him the throne of דָּוִד, David His father, ³³and He will reign over the house of יַעֲקֹב, Ya'aqov to the ages, and of His reign there will be no end."

³⁴And מִרְיָם, Mir'yam said to the Messenger, "How will this be, since I do not know a husband?"

³⁵And the Messenger, answering, said to her, "The רוּחַ הַקֹּדֶשׁ, Ruach HaQodesh will come upon you, and the power of the Highest will overshadow you. Therefore, also, the holy-born thing will be called Son of God. ³⁶And look! אֱלִישֶׁבַע, 'Eliysheva, your relative: in her old age, she has also conceived a son—and this is the sixth month to her who was called barren—³⁷because nothing will be impossible with God."

³⁸And מִרְיָם, Mir'yam said, "Look! *I am* the slaveᶜ of ADONAI; let it be to me according to your spoken word." And the Messenger went away from her.

³⁹And מִרְיָם, Mir'yam, having arisen in those days, went to the hill-country with haste, to a city of יְהוּדָה, Y'hudah, ⁴⁰and entered into the house of זְכַרְיָה, Z'khar'yah, and greeted אֱלִישֶׁבַע, 'Eliysheva. ⁴¹And it came to pass, when אֱלִישֶׁבַע, 'Eliysheva heard the greeting of מִרְיָם, Mir'yam, the baby leapt in her womb. And אֱלִישֶׁבַע, 'Eliysheva was filled with the רוּחַ הַקֹּדֶשׁ, Ruach HaQodesh, ⁴²and spoke out with a loud voice, and said, "Blessed ARE you among women, and blessed IS the fruit of your womb! ⁴³And how IS this *happening* to me, that the mother of my Master might come to me? ⁴⁴For, look! when the voice of your greeting came to my ears, the baby in my womb leapt with rejoicing. ⁴⁵And happy IS she who believed, for there will be a completion to the things spoken to her from ADONAI."

⁴⁶And מִרְיָם, Mir'yam said, "My soul magnifies ADONAI,

⁴⁷And my רוּחַ, ruach is extremely joyful in God my Savior,

⁴⁸Because He looked on the humble-mindedness of His slave.ᵈ

For, look! from now on, all the generations will call me happy.

⁴⁹For He who is mighty did great things to me,

And holy IS His Name,

⁵⁰AND HIS *LOVING*-KINDNESS IS TO GENERATIONS AND GENERATIONS, TO THOSE FEARING HIM.ᵉ

⁵¹He did powerfully with His arm:

He scattered abroad the proud *ones* in the thought of their heart;

⁵²He brought down the mighty from *their* thrones,

And He exalted the humble-minded;

⁵³THE HUNGRY HE FILLED WITH GOOD,ᶠ

And the rich He sent away empty;

⁵⁴He received again יִשְׂרָאֵל, Yis'rael His servant,

To remember *loving*-kindness,

⁵⁵As He spoke to our fathers,

ᵃ "שָׁלוֹם, shalom"—see מַתִּתְיָהוּ *Matit'yahu* 26:49
ᵇ Some mss insert, "Blessed ARE you among women."
ᶜ "slave"—Young's says, "maid-servant"
ᵈ "slave"—Young's says, "maid-servant"
ᵉ cf. תְּהִלִּים *T'hiliym* 103:17
ᶠ cf. תְּהִלִּים *T'hiliym* 107:9

To אַבְרָהָם, Av'raham and to his seed—to the age."

⁵⁶And מִרְיָם, Mir'yam remained with her *for* about three months, and *then* returned to her house.

⁵⁷And the time was fulfilled to אֱלִישֶׁבַע, 'Eliysheva for her bringing forth *her baby*, and she bore a son, ⁵⁸and the neighbors and her relatives heard that ADONAI was making His *loving*-kindness great with her, and they were rejoicing with her.

⁵⁹And it came to pass, on the eighth day, they came to circumcise the child, and they were calling him by the name of his father, זְכַרְיָה, Z'khar'yah, ⁶⁰but his mother, answering, said, "No. Rather, he will be called יוֹחָנָן, Yochanan." ⁶¹And they said to her, "*But* there is no one from your relatives who is called by this name," ⁶²and they were making signs to his father, *as to* what he would want him to be called. ⁶³And having asked for a tablet, he wrote *on it*, saying, "יוֹחָנָן, Yochanan is his name"; and they all marveled. ⁶⁴And instantly, his mouth was opened, and *also* his tongue, and he was speaking, praising God. ⁶⁵And fear came upon all those dwelling around them, and in all the hill-country of יְהוּדָה, Y'hudah all these sayings were spoken of. ⁶⁶And all who heard laid them up in their hearts, saying, "What, then, will this child be?" For the hand of ADONAI was also with him.

⁶⁷And זְכַרְיָה, Z'khar'yah his father was filled with the רוּחַ הַקֹּדֶשׁ, Ruach HaQodesh, and prophesied, saying,

⁶⁸"Blessed IS ADONAI, the God of יִשְׂרָאֵל, Yis'rael,
Because He looked upon *us*,
And worked redemption for His people,
⁶⁹And raised a horn of salvation to us,
In the house of דָּוִד, David His servant,
⁷⁰As He spoke by the mouth of His holy prophets,
Which have been from the age,
⁷¹Salvation FROM OUR ENEMIES, AND OUT OF THE HAND OF ALL *THOSE* HATING US,ᵃ
⁷²To do *loving*-kindness with our fathers,
And to be mindful of His holy בְּרִית, b'riyt,
⁷³An oath that He swore to אַבְרָהָם, Av'raham our father,
To give to us, ⁷⁴without fear,
Having been delivered out of the hand of our enemies,
⁷⁵To serve Him in holiness and righteousness
In His presence, for all our days.
⁷⁶And you also, child, you will be called Prophet of the Highest;
For you will go in the presence of ADONAI,
To prepare His ways.
⁷⁷To give knowledge of salvation to His people
In release from their sins,
⁷⁸Through the tender *loving*-kindness of our God,
In which the rising *sun* from on high will look upon us
⁷⁹TO GIVE LIGHT TO THOSE SITTING IN DARKNESS AND DEATH-SHADOW,ᵇ
To guide our feet to a road of peace."

⁸⁰And the child grew, and was strengthened in רוּחַ, ruach, and he was in the deserts until the day of his *public* appearance to יִשְׂרָאֵל, Yis'rael.

2 ¹And it came to pass in those days *that* there went out a decree from Cæsar Augustus, that all the world be enrolled ²(this enrollment first came to pass when Cyrenius was governor of Syria). ³And all were going *on their way* to be enrolled, each to his own city.

⁴And יוֹסֵף, Yosef also went up from the גָּלִיל, Galiyl, out of the city of נְצֶרֶת, N'tzaret, to יְהוּדָה, Y'hudah, to the city of דָּוִד, David (that is called בֵּית־לֶחֶם, Beit-Lechem), because of his being of the house and *the* family of דָּוִד, David, ⁵to enroll himself

---
ᵃ תְּהִלִּים T'hiliym 106:10
ᵇ יְשַׁעְיָהוּ Y'sha'yahu 9:1(2)

with מִרְיָם, Mir'yam his pledged *one*[a]—*she* being with child. ⁶And it came to pass, in their being there, *that* the days were fulfilled for her bringing forth *her baby*, ⁷and she brought forth her son—the firstborn—and wrapped him up and laid him down in a stable,[b] because there was not a place for them in the guest-room.

⁸And there were shepherds in the same region, living in the field and guarding over their flock *during* the night-watches. ⁹And a Messenger of ADONAI stood over them, and the glory of ADONAI shone around them, and they feared a great fear. ¹⁰And the Messenger said to them, "Fear not, for, look! I bring you Good News of great joy, that will be to all the people, ¹¹because there was born to you today a Savior—who is Messiah, the Master—in the city of דָּוִד, David. ¹²And this IS the sign to you: you will find a baby wrapped up, and lying in a stable."

¹³And suddenly, there came with the Messenger a great number of the heavenly army, praising God, and saying,

¹⁴"Glory in the highest to God;
and upon earth, peace among men of good will."

¹⁵And it came to pass, when the Messengers were gone away from them to the heavens, the shepherds were saying to one another, "Let us go over, indeed, to בֵּית־לֶחֶם, Beit-Lechem and see this thing that has come to pass—which ADONAI made known to us."

¹⁶And having hurried, they came and found both מִרְיָם, Mir'yam and יוֹסֵף, Yosef and the baby lying in the stable. ¹⁷And having seen *them*, they made *it* known about the saying spoken to them regarding the child. ¹⁸And all who heard *were in* wonder about the things spoken to them by the shepherds, ¹⁹but מִרְיָם, Mir'yam was preserving all these things—pondering *them* in her heart. ²⁰And the shepherds returned, glorifying and praising God for all those things they heard and saw, *just* as it was spoken to them.

²¹And when eight days were fulfilled *and it was time* to circumcise him, then his name was called יֵשׁוּעַ, Yeshua, having been called so by the Messenger before his being conceived in the womb.

²²And when the days of their purification were fulfilled according to the תּוֹרָה, Torah of מֹשֶׁה, Mosheh, they brought him up to יְרוּשָׁלַיִם, Y'rushalayim to present *him* to ADONAI ²³(as it has been written in the תּוֹרָה, Torah of ADONAI,

"Every male *that is* opening a womb will be called holy to ADONAI"[c]),

²⁴and to give a sacrifice according to that *which is* said in the תּוֹרָה, Torah of ADONAI,

"A pair of turtle-doves, or two young pigeons."[d]

²⁵And look! there was a man in יְרוּשָׁלַיִם, Y'rushalayim whose name WAS שִׁמְעוֹן, Shim'on, and this man was righteous and God-fearing, looking for the Comforting of יִשְׂרָאֵל, Yis'rael, and the רוּחַ הַקֹּדֶשׁ, Ruach HaQodesh was upon him. ²⁶And it had been divinely told *to* him by the רוּחַ הַקֹּדֶשׁ, Ruach HaQodesh *that he was* not to see death before he saw the Messiah of ADONAI. ²⁷And he came in the רוּחַ, Ruach to the Temple, and when the parents brought in the child יֵשׁוּעַ, Yeshua (for their doing according to the custom of the תּוֹרָה, Torah regarding him), ²⁸then *Shim'on* took Him in his arms and blessed God, and he said,

²⁹"Now, Sovereign *Master*, You send away Your slave in peace, according to Your word,
³⁰because my eyes saw Your salvation,

---

[a] "*one*"—some mss say, "wife"
[b] "stable" or "stall" (see Luke 13:15)—thus referring to an available shelter for Yosef's family, as juxtaposed with the unavailable "guest-room" at the end of the verse. Traditionally rendered "manger," the Gk. may alternatively mean something more precise, i.e., "feeding-trough." Also in verses 11 and 16.
[c] שְׁמוֹת *Sh'mot* 13:2, 12
[d] וַיִּקְרָא *Vayiq'ra* 12:8

³¹which You prepared before the face of all the peoples, ³²a light for the uncovering of *the* גּוֹיִם, Goyim,[a] and the glory of Your people יִשְׂרָאֵל, Yis'rael."

³³And His father and[b] mother were in wonder at *all* the things spoken about Him; ³⁴and שִׁמְעוֹן, Shim'on blessed them, and said to מִרְיָם, Mir'yam His mother, "Look! this ONE is set for the falling and rising again of many in יִשְׂרָאֵל, Yis'rael, and for a sign *that will be* spoken against ³⁵(and also a sword will pass through your own soul), *so that* the reasonings of many hearts may be revealed."

³⁶And there was a prophetess, חַנָּה, Chanah, daughter of פְּנוּאֵל, P'nuel, of the tribe of אָשֵׁר, Asher (she was much advanced in days, having lived with a husband *only* seven years from her virginity, ³⁷and *then* she WAS a widow until *she was* eighty-four years *of age*), who did not leave the Temple, *but was* serving with fasts and requests for help, night and day. ³⁸And she, having come in at that time, was likewise giving thanks to God,[c] and was speaking about Him to all those looking for the redemption of[d] יְרוּשָׁלַיִם, Y'rushalayim.

³⁹And when they finished all *the* things according to the תּוֹרָה, Torah of ADONAI, they returned to the גָּלִיל, Galiyl, to their city, נְצֶרֶת, N'tzaret. ⁴⁰And the child grew, and was strengthened,[e] being filled with wisdom. And the favor of God was upon Him.

⁴¹And His parents were going to יְרוּשָׁלַיִם, Y'rushalayim yearly at the Feast of the פֶּסַח, Pesach. ⁴²And when He became twelve years old—when they had gone up according to the custom of the Feast, ⁴³and had finished the days—in their returning, His parents[f] did not know the child יֵשׁוּעַ, Yeshua had remained behind in יְרוּשָׁלַיִם, Y'rushalayim.

⁴⁴And having supposed Him to be in the caravan, they went a day's journey, and were looking for Him among *all* the relatives and the acquaintances. ⁴⁵And not having found Him, they returned to יְרוּשָׁלַיִם, Y'rushalayim, looking for Him.

⁴⁶And it came to pass *that* after three days, they found Him in the Temple, sitting in the middle of the teachers, both hearing them and questioning them. ⁴⁷And all those hearing Him were astonished at His understanding and answers. ⁴⁸And having seen Him, they were amazed, and His mother said to him, "Child, why did you do this to us? Look! your father and I, deeply anguished, were looking for you!" ⁴⁹And He said to them, "Why IS IT that you were looking for Me? Did you not know that I must be in the things of My Father?" ⁵⁰And they did not understand the spoken word that He spoke to them.

⁵¹And He went down with them, and *they* came to נְצֶרֶת, N'tzaret, and He was submitted to them, and His mother was keeping all these sayings in her heart. ⁵²And יֵשׁוּעַ, Yeshua was advancing in wisdom, and in stature, and in favor with God and men.

3 ¹And in the fifteenth year of the government of Tiberius Cæsar (Pontius Pilate being governor of יְהוּדָה, Y'hudah; and Herod, tetrarch of the גָּלִיל, Galiyl; and Philip his brother, tetrarch of יְטוּר, Y'tur and of the region of Trachonitis; and Lysanias, tetrarch of Abilene; ²*and* חָנָן, Chanan and קַיָּפָא, Qayafa being chief כֹּהֲנִים, Ko'haniym), there came a word of God to יוֹחָנָן, Yochanan, the son of זְכַרְיָה, Z'khar'yah, in the desert. ³And he came to all the region around the יַרְדֵּן, Yar'den, proclaiming an immersion of reformation—for *the* release of sins—⁴as it has been written in the scroll of the words of יְשַׁעְיָהוּ, Y'sha'yahu the prophet,

"A voice of one calling, 'In the desert, prepare the way of ADONAI! Make His

---

[a] cf. יְשַׁעְיָהוּ Y'sha'yahu 49:6, 51:4, 60:3
[b] "His father and"—some mss: "יוֹסֵף, Yosef and His"
[c] "God"—some mss say, "the Master"
[d] "of"—some mss say, "in"
[e] Some mss insert, "in רוּחַ, ruach"
[f] "His parents"—some mss say, "יוֹסֵף, Yosef and His mother"

Genealogy of Yeshua.

paths straight! ⁵Every valley will be filled, and every mountain and hill will be made low, and the crooked will become straightness, and the rough roads *will* become smooth; ⁶and all flesh will see the salvation of God!'"ᵃ

⁷ Then he said to the crowds coming to be immersed by him, "Brood of vipers! Who prompted you to flee from the coming wrath? ⁸Therefore, make fruits worthy of the reformation, and do not begin to say within yourselves, 'We have a father: אַבְרָהָם, Av'raham.' For I say to you that God is able—out of these stones—to raise *up* children to אַבְרָהָם, Av'raham. ⁹And the axe is already also laid to the root of the trees. Therefore, every tree not making good fruit is cut down, and it is thrown into fire."

¹⁰And the crowds were questioning him, saying, "What, then, should we do?" ¹¹And answering, he said to them, "He *who is* having two coats—let him give a share to him *who is* having none. And he *who is* having food—let him do likewise."

¹²And there came also *some* tax-gatherers to be immersed, and they said to him, "Teacher, what should we do?" ¹³And he said to them, "Collect no more than that directed you."

¹⁴And soldiers were also questioning him, saying, "And we—what should we do?" And he said to them, "Do violence to no one, nor accuse falsely; and be content with your wages."

¹⁵And the people were looking forward *in expectation*, and all were reasoning in their hearts about יוֹחָנָן, Yochanan, whether or not he might be the Messiah. ¹⁶יוֹחָנָן, Yochanan answered, saying to all, "I, indeed, immerse you with water, but He is coming who is mightier than I, of whom I am not worthy to untie the strap of His sandals. He will immerse you with the רוּחַ הַקֹּדֶשׁ, Ruach HaQodesh and with fire —¹⁷*He* whose winnowing shovel *is* in His hand to thoroughly cleanse His threshing floor and to gather the wheat into His storehouse—and He will burn the chaff with fire unquenchable." ¹⁸And therefore, indeed, exhorting *them* with many other things, he was proclaiming Good News to the people.

¹⁹But Herod the tetrarch, being rebuked by him regarding Herodias (the wife of his brother) and regarding all the evils that Herod did, ²⁰also added this to *them* all: that he locked up יוֹחָנָן, Yochanan in prison.

²¹And it came to pass, in all the people being immersed, *that* יֵשׁוּעַ, Yeshua *was* also being immersed. And *while He was* praying, the heaven was opened, ²²and the רוּחַ הַקֹּדֶשׁ, Ruach HaQodesh came down upon Him in a bodily form, as if a dove. And a voice came out of heaven: "You are My Son—the Beloved. In You I delighted."

²³And יֵשׁוּעַ, Yeshua Himself was beginning to be about thirty years of age, being (as was supposed) *the* son of יוֹסֵף, Yosef, the son of עֵלִי, Eliy,
²⁴the son of מַתָּת, Matat,
the son of לֵוִי, Leviy,
the son of מַלְכִּי, Mal'kiy,
the son of יַנַּי, Yanai,
the son of יוֹסֵף, Yosef,
²⁵the son of מַתִּתְיָה, Matit'yah,
the son of אָמוֹץ, Amotz,
the son of נַחוּם, Nachum,
the son of חֶסְלִי, Ches'liy,
the son of נַגַּי, Nagai,
²⁶the son of מַחַת, Machat,
the son of מַתִּתְיָה, Matit'yah,
the son of שִׁמְעִי, Shim'iy,
the son of יוֹסֵף, Yosef,ᵇ
the son of יוֹדָה, Yodah,
²⁷the son of יוֹחָנָן, Yochanan,
the son of רֵישָׁא, Reisha,
the son of זְרֻבָּבֶל, Z'rubavel,
the son of שְׁאַלְתִּיאֵל, Sh'al'tiyel,
the son of נֵרִי, Neriy,
²⁸the son of מַלְכִּי, Mal'kiy,
the son of אַדִּי, Adiy,
the son of קוֹסָם, Qosam,

ᵃ יְשַׁעְיָהוּ *Y'sha'yahu* 40:3-5

ᵇ "יוֹסֵף, Yosef"—earlier mss say, "Ἰωσήχ, Iosech (Josech)"

the son of אֶלְמוֹדָם, El'modam,
the son of עֵר, Er,
²⁹the son of יֵשׁוּעַ, Yeshua,ᵃ
the son of אֱלִיעֶזֶר, 'Eliyezer,
the son of יוֹרִים, Yoriym,
the son of מַתָּת, Matat,
the son of לֵוִי, Leviy,
³⁰the son of שִׁמְעוֹן, Shim'on,
the son of יְהוּדָה, Y'hudah,
the son of יוֹסֵף, Yosef,
the son of יוֹנָם, Yonam,
the son of אֶלְיָקִים, El'yaqiym,
³¹the son of מַלְיָא, Mal'ya,
the son of מִינָא, Miyna,
the son of מַתַּתָּה, Matatah,
the son of נָתָן, Natan,
the son of דָּוִד, David,
³²the son of יִשַׁי, Yishai,
the son of עוֹבֵד, Oved,
the son of בֹּעַז, Boaz,
the son of שַׂלְמוֹן, Sal'mon,ᵇ
the son of נַחְשׁוֹן, Nach'shon,
³³the son of עַמִּינָדָב, Amiynadav,
the son of רָם, Ram,ᶜ
the son of חֶצְרוֹן, Chetz'ron,
the son of פֶּרֶץ, Peretz,
the son of יְהוּדָה, Y'hudah,
³⁴the son of יַעֲקֹב, Ya'aqov,
the son of יִצְחָק, Yitz'chaq,
the son of אַבְרָהָם, Av'raham,
the son of תֶּרַח, Terach,
the son of נָחוֹר, Nachor,
³⁵the son of שְׂרוּג, S'rug,
the son of רְעוּ, R'u,
the son of פֶּלֶג, Peleg,
the son of עֵבֶר, Ever,
the son of שֶׁלַח, Shalach,
³⁶the son of קֵינָן, Qeinan,ᵈ
the son of אַרְפַּכְשַׁד, Ar'pakh'shad,
the son of שֵׁם, Shem,
the son of נֹחַ, Noach,
the son of לֶמֶךְ, Lamekh,
³⁷the son of מְתוּשֶׁלַח, M'tushelach,
the son of חֲנוֹךְ, 'Chanokh,
the son of יֶרֶד, Yered,

the son of מַהֲלַלְאֵל, Ma'halal'el,
the son of קֵינָן, Qeinan,
³⁸the son of אֱנוֹשׁ, 'Enosh,
the son of שֵׁת, Shet,
the son of אָדָם, Adam,
the son of God.

Temptation in the desert.

4 ¹And יֵשׁוּעַ, Yeshua, full of the רוּחַ הַקֹּדֶשׁ, Ruach HaQodesh, returned from the יַרְדֵּן, Yar'den and was brought in the רוּחַ, Ruach into the desert, ²being tempted *for* forty days by the Accuser. And He did not eat anything in those days; and when they had ended, He hungered.

³And the Accuser said to Him, "If You are *the* Son of God, speak to this stone so that it may become bread." ⁴And יֵשׁוּעַ, Yeshua answered him, "It has been written, that,

'Not on bread only will man live.'"ᵉ

⁵And having brought Him up,ᶠ he showed to Him all the kingdoms of the world in a moment of time. ⁶And the Accuser said to Him, "I will give to You all this authority, and their glory, because it has been delivered to me, and I give it to whomever I want. ⁷You, then, if You bow before me *in worship*, all will be Yours." ⁸And answering, יֵשׁוּעַ, Yeshua said to him,ᵍ "It has been written,

'You will bow before ADONAI your God *in worship*, and Him only you will serve.'"ʰ

⁹And he brought Him to יְרוּשָׁלַיִם, Y'rushalayim, and set Him on the pinnacle of the Temple, and said to Him, "If You are the Son of God, throw yourself down from here, ¹⁰for it has been written,

'He will give command concerning you to His messengers, to *carefully* guard over you,'ⁱ

ᵃ "יֵשׁוּעַ, Yeshua"—some mss say, "יוֹסֵי, Yosei"
ᵇ "שַׂלְמוֹן, Sal'mon"—early mss say, "שֶׁלַח, Shalach"
ᶜ "רָם, Ram"—mss vary widely here; however, "רָם, Ram" is supported by א *Div'rei HaYamiym Alef* 2:5, 9-10.
ᵈ "קֵינָן, Qeinan"—not in ברא *B'reshiyt* 11 genealogy

ᵉ דְּבָרִים *D'variym* 8:3; some mss insert, "but on every saying of God"
ᶠ Some mss insert, "to a high mountain"
ᵍ Some mss insert, "Get behind me, הַשָּׂטָן, HaSatan, for"
ʰ דְּבָרִים *D'variym* 6:13 says "fear" rather than "bow before"
ⁱ תְּהִלִּים *T'hiliym* 91:11

¹¹and,

> 'they will raise you up on *their* hands, so that you will not strike your foot on a stone.'"ᵃ

¹²And יֵשׁוּעַ, Yeshua, answering, said to him, "It has been said,

> 'You must not test ADONAI your God.'"ᵇ

¹³And having ended all temptation, the Accuser went away from Him until an opportune time.

¹⁴And יֵשׁוּעַ, Yeshua returned in the power of the רוּחַ, Ruach to the גָּלִיל, Galiyl, and news about Him went through all the surrounding region, ¹⁵and He was teaching in their synagogues, being glorified by all.

¹⁶And He came to נָצְרַת, N'tzaret where He had been brought up, and on יוֹם הַשַּׁבָּת, Yom HaShabat, according to His custom, He went into the synagogue and stood up to read. ¹⁷And a scroll of the prophet יְשַׁעְיָהוּ, Y'sha'yahu was given over to Him. And having unrolled the scroll, He found the place where it has been written:

> ¹⁸"The רוּחַ אֲדֹנָי, Ruach 'Adonai *IS* upon me,
> Because He anointed me
> To proclaim Good News to the poor;
> Sent meᶜ to proclaim release to captives,
> And receiving of sight to *the* blind;
> To send out the bruised with release;
> ¹⁹To proclaim the acceptable year of ADONAI."ᵈ

²⁰And having folded the scroll, having given *IT* back to the attendant, He sat down; and the eyes of all in the synagogue were fixed on Him. ²¹And He began to say to them, "Today this Scripture has been fulfilled in your ears." ²²And all were giving testimony *as* to Him, and were in wonder at the favorable words that were coming out of His mouth. And they said, "Is this not the son of יוֹסֵף, Yosef?"

²³And He said to them, "Certainly, you will say this analogy to Me: 'Physician, heal yourself; as we heard *you had* done great things in כְּפַר־נַחוּם, K'far-Nachum, do so here as well in your homeland!'" ²⁴And He said, "אָמֵן, Amen, I say to you: no prophet is accepted in his own homeland. ²⁵And in truth I say to you: many widows were in יִשְׂרָאֵל, Yis'rael in the days of אֵלִיָּהוּ, Eliyahu (when the heaven was shut for three years and six months, *and* when great famine came on all the Land), ²⁶and אֵלִיָּהוּ, Eliyahu was sent to none of them, but *only* to צָרְפַת, Tzar'fat of צִידוֹן, Tziydon—to a woman, a widow. ²⁷And many lepers were in יִשְׂרָאֵל, Yis'rael in the time of אֱלִישָׁע, 'Eliysha the prophet, and none of them were cleansed except נַעֲמָן, Na'aman the Syrian."

²⁸And *upon* hearing these things, all *the* people in the synagogue were filled with rage, ²⁹and having risen *up*, they drove Him outside the city and brought Him to the brow of the hill on which their city had been built, in order to throw Him down headlong. ³⁰But He, having gone through the middle of them, went away.

³¹And He came down to כְּפַר־נַחוּם, K'far-Nachum, a city of the גָּלִיל, Galiyl, and was teaching them on the שַׁבָּתוֹת, Shabatot; ³²and they were astonished at His teaching, because His word was with authority.

³³And in the synagogue, *there* was a man having a רוּחַ, ruach of an unclean demon, and he cried out with a loud voice, ³⁴"Away! What do You *want* with us,ᵉ יֵשׁוּעַ הַנָּצְרָתִי, Yeshua HaNatz'ratiy? Did you come to destroy us? I have known You—who You are: the Holy One of God!" ³⁵And יֵשׁוּעַ, Yeshua rebuked him, saying, "Be silenced, and come out of him!" And the demon, having thrown him into the middle *of the synagogue*, came out from him, having hurt him in no way. ³⁶And amazement came upon all *the people*, and they were speaking together with one another,

---

ᵃ תְּהִלִּים T'hiliym 91:12
ᵇ דְּבָרִים D'variym 6:16
ᶜ Some mss insert, "to heal the broken of heart;"
ᵈ יְשַׁעְיָהוּ Y'sha'yahu 61:1-2 (LXX); cf. 42:7
ᵉ "What do you *want* with us"—lit., "what to us and to you"

saying, "What is this word, that he commands the unclean רוּחוֹת, ruchot with authority and power, and they come out?" ³⁷And the news regarding Him was going out to every place of the surrounding region.

³⁸And having risen *and gone* out of the synagogue, He entered into the house of שִׁמְעוֹן, Shim'on; and the mother-in-law of שִׁמְעוֹן, Shim'on was suffering with a high fever; and they asked Him about her. ³⁹And having stood over her, He rebuked the fever, and it left her—and instantly, having arisen, she was serving them.

⁴⁰And at the setting of the sun, all *the* people—as many as had any *who were* sick with various diseases—brought them to Him. And putting *His* hands on each one of them, He was healing them.

⁴¹And demons were also coming out of many *of the people*, shouting and saying, "You are[a] the Son of God!" And rebuking *them*, He did not allow them to speak, because they knew Him to be the Messiah.

⁴²And when day had come, He, having gone out, went on to a deserted place; but the crowds were looking for Him. And they came to Him and were holding Him *back*, not *allowing Him* to go on from them. ⁴³And He said to them, "It is necessary *for* Me to proclaim Good News of the Reign of God also to the other cities, because *it is* for this *that* I was sent." ⁴⁴And He was proclaiming in the synagogues of יְהוּדָה, Y'hudah.[b]

5 ¹And it came to pass, with the crowd pressing on Him to hear the word of God, that He was standing beside the lake of גְּנֵיסָרֶת, G'neisaret; ²and He saw two boats standing beside the lake; and the fishers, having gone away from them, were washing the nets. ³And having entered into one of the boats, *the one* that was *of* שִׁמְעוֹן, Shim'on, He asked him to put out a little from the land. And having sat down, *He* was teaching the crowds from the boat.

⁴And when He stopped speaking, He said to שִׁמְעוֹן, Shim'on, "Put out to the deep *water*, and let down your nets for a catch." ⁵And שִׁמְעוֹן, Shim'on, answering, said, "רַבִּי, Rabiy,[c] through the whole night, *though* having labored, we have taken nothing *in*, but at Your saying, I will let down the nets."

⁶And having done this, they enclosed a great number of fishes, but their nets were breaking. ⁷And they motioned to their companions in the other boat to come help them, and they came and filled both the boats so *full* that they were sinking!

⁸And שִׁמְעוֹן כֵּיפָא, Shim'on Keifa,[d] having seen *this*, fell down at the knees of יֵשׁוּעַ, Yeshua, saying, "Go from me, because I am a sinful man, O Master!" ⁹For, *seeing* the catch of the fishes that they took *in*, astonishment seized him and all those with him, ¹⁰and likewise also יַעֲקֹב, Ya'aqov and יוֹחָנָן, Yochanan, sons of זַבְדִּי, Zav'diy, who were partners with שִׁמְעוֹן, Shim'on. And יֵשׁוּעַ, Yeshua said to שִׁמְעוֹן, Shim'on, "Fear not. From now *on*, you will be catching men." ¹¹And they, having brought the boats upon the land, having left all *they had*, followed Him.

¹²And it came to pass, while He was in one of the cities, that look! a man full of leprosy *came*. Having seen יֵשׁוּעַ, Yeshua, and having fallen on *His* face, he implored Him, saying, "Sir, if you are willing, you are able to cleanse me." ¹³And having stretched out *His* hand, He touched him, saying, "I am willing. Be cleansed." And immediately the leprosy went away from him.

¹⁴And He commanded him to tell no one, "but, having gone away, show yourself to the כֹּהֵן, kohen, and bring near *an offering* for your cleansing as מֹשֶׁה, Mosheh directed, for a testimony to them." ¹⁵But *all* the more, the report regarding Him was going abroad, and large crowds were coming together to hear *Him* and to be

---

[a] Some mss insert, "the Messiah!"
[b] "Y'hudah"—some mss say, "the גָּלִיל, Galiyl"
[c] רַבִּי, Rabiy—Greek ἐπιστάτα, epistata, meaning "overseer"; usually translated "Master." Occurring only in Luke, the word is apparently used to translate רַבִּי, rabiy. See Thayer; Stern.
[d] כֵּיפָא, Keifa—Gk: Πέτρος, Petros; see יוֹחָנָן *Yn.* 1:42

Calling of Leviy.   Luke 6:2

healed[a] of their weaknesses. ⁱ⁶And He was withdrawing Himself in the deserted places and was praying.

¹⁷And on one of the days, it came to pass that He was teaching. And there were פְּרוּשִׁים, P'rushiym and teachers of the תּוֹרָה, Torah sitting nearby who had come out of every village of the גָּלִיל, Galiyl and יְהוּדָה, Y'hudah and יְרוּשָׁלַיִם, Y'rushalayim. And the power of ADONAI was *present* for Him to heal.[b]

¹⁸And look! men *were* bringing upon a cot a man who had been stricken with paralysis, and they were looking to bring him in and to place him in sight of Him. ¹⁹But not having found what way they might bring him in (because of the crowd) having gone up on the house-top, they let him down through the *roof* tiles, with the little mat, into the middle *of the crowd*, *right* in front of יֵשׁוּעַ, Yeshua. ²⁰And He, having seen their faith, said, "Man, your sins have been forgiven you."

²¹And the סוֹפְרִים, Sof'riym and the פְּרוּשִׁים, P'rushiym began to reason *among themselves*, saying, "Who is this that speaks evil words? Who is able to forgive sins, except God only?" ²²And having known their reasonings, יֵשׁוּעַ, Yeshua, answering, said to them, "What do you reason in your hearts? ²³Which is easier? To say, 'Your sins have been forgiven you,' or to say, 'Arise, and walk'? ²⁴But so that you may know that the Son of Man has authority upon the earth to forgive sins…" (He said to the one stricken with paralysis,) "I say to you arise, and having taken up your little mat, be going on to your house." ²⁵And instantly, having risen in front of them, having taken up THAT on which he was lying, he went away to his house, glorifying God. ²⁶And astonishment took *hold of* all *the people*, and they were glorifying God and were filled with fear, saying, "We saw strange things today."

²⁷And after these things, He went out and noticed a tax-gatherer by *the* name לֵוִי, Leviy, sitting at the tax-office, and said to him, "Be following Me." ²⁸And he, having left *it* all, having arisen, was following Him.

²⁹And לֵוִי, Leviy made a great banquet to Him in his house, and there was a large crowd of tax-gatherers and others who were *there* with them reclining (at mealtime). ³⁰And the פְּרוּשִׁים, P'rushiym and the סוֹפְרִים, Sof'riym among them were grumbling at His disciples, saying, "Why do you eat and drink with the tax-gatherers and sinners?" ³¹And יֵשׁוּעַ, Yeshua, answering, said to them, "They who are well have no need of a physician; rather, they that are ill. ³²I came not to call righteous men, but sinners, to reformation."

³³And they said to Him, "The disciples of יוֹחָנָן, Yochanan fast often and make requests for help *to God* (likewise, also those of the פְּרוּשִׁים, P'rushiym), but yours eat and drink?" ³⁴And יֵשׁוּעַ, Yeshua said to them, "Are you able to make the wedding guests[c] fast while the bridegroom is being with them? ³⁵But days will come when the bridegroom is taken away from them, and then they will fast in those days."

³⁶And He also spoke an analogy to them: "No one puts a patch torn from new clothing on old clothing; otherwise, then the new *cloth* will also make a tear, and the patch that IS from the new *cloth* will not agree with the old. ³⁷And no one puts fresh wine into old skins; otherwise, then the fresh wine will burst the skins, and itself will be poured out, and the skins will be destroyed. ³⁸But fresh wine is to be put into new skins,[d] ³⁹and no one having drunk old WINE wants fresh *wine*, for he says, 'The old is good.'"

6 ¹And it came to pass on the שַׁבָּת, Shabat,[e] as He was going through the grain fields, that His disciples were plucking and eating the heads *of grain*, rubbing *them* with the hands. ²And cer-

---

[a] Some mss insert, "by Him"
[b] "for Him to heal"—some mss say, "to heal them"
[c] "wedding guests"; lit. "sons of the bride-chamber"
[d] Some mss insert, "and both are preserved together"
[e] שַׁבָּת, Shabat—some mss say, "second-first שַׁבָּת, Shabat"

tain *ones* of the פְּרוּשִׁים, P'rushiym said, "Why do you do that which is not permitted on the שַׁבָּתוֹת, Shabatot?" ³And יֵשׁוּעַ, Yeshua, answering, said to them, "Did you not read even this: that *which* דָּוִד, David did when he hungered (himself and those who were with him)—⁴how he went into the House of God and, having taken the לֶחֶם הַפָּנִים, Lechem HaPaniym (which it is not permitted to eat, except only to the כֹּהֲנִים, Ko'haniym), *he* ate, and also gave *of the bread* to those with him?"ᵃ ⁵And He said to them, "The Son of Man is Master of the שַׁבָּת, Shabat."

⁶And it came to pass, on another שַׁבָּת, Shabat, that He went into the synagogue and taught. And there was a man there, and his right hand was withered, ⁷and the סוֹפְרִים, Sof'riym and the פְּרוּשִׁים, P'rushiym were watching Him, *to see* if He healed on the שַׁבָּת, Shabat, so that they might find *reason* to accuse Him. ⁸And He Himself had known their reasonings, and said to the man having the withered hand, "Rise, and stand in the middle *of the synagogue*," and he, having risen, stood. ⁹And יֵשׁוּעַ, Yeshua said to them, "I question you whether it is permitted on the שַׁבָּת, Shabat to do good, or to do evil? to save life, or to kill?" ¹⁰And having looked around on them all, He said to him, "Stretch out your hand"; and he did so, and his hand was restored!ᵇ ¹¹And they were filled with a mad rage, and were speaking with one another *concerning* what they might do to יֵשׁוּעַ, Yeshua.

¹²And it came to pass in those days, *that* He went to the mountain to pray, and was spending the night in the prayer to God. ¹³And when it became day, He called His disciples near; and having chosen twelve from them (whom He also named emissaries: ¹⁴שִׁמְעוֹן, Shim'on whom He also named כֵּיפָא, Keifa,ᶜ and Andrew his brother, and יַעֲקֹב, Ya'aqov, and יוֹחָנָן, Yochanan, and Philip, and בַּר־תַּלְמַי, Bar-Tal'mai, ¹⁵and מַתִּתְיָהוּ, Matit'yahu, and תּוֹמָא, Toma, and יַעֲקֹב, Ya-aqov of חַלְפַי, Chal'fai, and שִׁמְעוֹן, Shim'on called *the* Zealot, ¹⁶and יְהוּדָה, Y'hudah of יַעֲקֹב, Ya'aqov, and יְהוּדָה אִישׁ־קְרִיּוֹת, Y'hudah Iysh-Q'riyot who became *the* betrayer), ¹⁷and having come down with them, He stood upon a level spot. And *there was* a large crowd of His disciples, and a great number of the people from all יְהוּדָה, Y'hudah and יְרוּשָׁלַיִם, Y'rushalayim and the sea coast of צוֹר, Tzor and צִידוֹן, Tziydon, ¹⁸who came to hear Him and to be healed of their sicknesses; and those harassed by unclean רוּחוֹת, ruchot were healed. ¹⁹And the whole crowd was looking to touch Him because power was going forth from Him—and He was healing all.

²⁰And He, having lifted up His eyes to His disciples, said,

"Happy *are* the poor—because yours is the Reign of God.

²¹"Happy *are* those hungering now—because you will be filled.

"Happy *are* those weeping now—because you will laugh.

²²"Happy are you when men will hate you, and when they will separate *from* you and will denounce *you* and will cast out your name as evil, for the Son of Man's sake. ²³Rejoice in that day, and leap *for joy*, for look! your reward IS great in the Heaven—for according to these things were their fathers doing to the prophets.

²⁴"But אוֹי, oy! to you, the rich—because you have received your comfort.

²⁵"אוֹי, Oy! to you who have been filled *with food* now—because you will hunger.

"אוֹי, Oy! to you who are laughing now—because you will mourn and weep.

²⁶"אוֹי, Oy! to you when all men will speak well of you—for according to these things were their fathers doing to false prophets.

²⁷"But to you who are hearing *Me* I say *this:* love your enemies; do good to those hating you; ²⁸bless those cursing you; pray for those accusing you falsely. ²⁹And to him *who is* hitting you on the cheek, give the other also; and from him *who is* taking your coat away from you, you also may not keep back your shirt. ³⁰To everyone who

---

ᵃ שְׁמוּאֵל א *Sh'muel Alef* 21:3-7(2-6)
ᵇ Some mss insert, "whole as the other"
ᶜ כֵּיפָא, Keifa—Gk: Πέτρος, Petros; see יוֹחָנָן *Yn.* 1:42

is asking of you, be giving; and from him who is taking away your property, be not asking *for it back* again. ³¹And as you want that men may do to you, do also to them likewise.

³²"And if you love those loving you, what favor do you have? For the sinful *ones* also love those loving them. ³³And if you do good to those doing good to you, what favor do you have? The sinful *ones* also do the same. ³⁴And if you lend TO THOSE from whom you hope to receive, what favor do you have? For the sinful *ones* also lend to sinners so that they may receive as much in return. ³⁵But love your enemies, and do good, and lend, hoping for nothing in return, and your reward will be great, and you will be sons of the Highest, because He is kind to the ungrateful and evil.

³⁶"Be merciful, as your Father is also merciful;
³⁷and judge not, and you will not be judged;
and condemn not, and you will not be condemned;
release, and you will be released.
³⁸Give, and it will be given to you:
a good measure—pressed, shaken, running over—they will give into your arms;
for with the measure with which you measure, *so* it will be measured to you in return."

³⁹And He also spoke an analogy to them: "Is *the* blind able to lead *the* blind? Will they not both fall into a pit? ⁴⁰A disciple is not above his teacher, but everyone *who is* perfected will be as his teacher. ⁴¹And why do you look at the speck *of sawdust* that is in your brother's eye, but *you* do not *even* consider the log that IS in your own eye? ⁴²How are you able to say to your brother, 'Brother, let me take out the speck that IS in your eye,' *when you* yourself *are* not looking at the log in your own eye? Hypocrite! first take the log out of your own eye, and then you will see clearly to take out the speck that IS in your brother's eye.

⁴³"For there is not a good tree *that is* making bad fruit, nor again, a bad tree making good fruit, ⁴⁴for each tree is known from its own fruit. Certainly, they do not gather figs from thorns, nor from a bramble *bush* do they pick a grape. ⁴⁵The good man, out of the good treasure of the heart, brings forth that which IS good; and the evil *man*, out of the evil treasure of his heart,ᵃ brings forth that which IS evil—for out of the abounding of the heart, his mouth speaks.

⁴⁶"And why do you call Me, 'Master! Master!' but do not do what I say? ⁴⁷Everyone who is coming to Me, and is hearing My words, and is doing them, I will show you to whom he is like: ⁴⁸he is likened to a man building a house, who dug, and deepened, and laid a foundation upon the rock; and a flood having come, the stream broke forth on that house and was not able to shake it, because it had been well built.ᵇ ⁴⁹But he who heard *My word* and did not do *it* is likened to a man having built a house on the ground, without a foundation, against which the stream broke forth; and immediately it fell, and the ruin of that house became great."

7

¹When He completed all His sayings in the ears of the people, He went into כְּפַר־נַחוּם, K'far-Nachum. ²And a certain centurion's slave who was much valued by him, being ill, was about to die. ³And having heard about יֵשׁוּעַ, Yeshua, he sent זְקֵנִים, Z'qeniym of the יְהוּדִים, Y'hudiym to Him, asking Him that, having come, He might thoroughly save his slave. ⁴And having come near to יֵשׁוּעַ, Yeshua, they were appealing to Him earnestly, saying, "He is worthy, *the one* to whom you should do this, ⁵for he loves our ethnic-group, and he built the synagogue for us."

⁶So יֵשׁוּעַ, Yeshua was going on with them; but then, when He was not far away from the house, the centurion sent friends, saying to Him, "Sir, be not troubled, for I am not worthy that you should enter under

---

ᵃ "treasure of his heart" is not in the earliest mss
ᵇ "because it had been well built"—some mss say, "for it had been founded upon the rock"

my roof. ⁷Therefore, I did not think myself worthy even to come to you. But say *so* in a word, and let my boy be healed. ⁸For I also am a man placed under authority, having soldiers under myself. And I say to this ONE, 'Go,' and he goes; and to another, 'Be coming,' and he comes; and to my slave, 'Do this,' and he does IT."

⁹And having heard these things, יֵשׁוּעַ, Yeshua *was* in wonder at him. And having turned to the crowd following Him, He said, "I say to you, not even in יִשְׂרָאֵל, Yis'rael did I find so much faith." ¹⁰And those *who* had been sent, having returned to the house, found the[a] slave in health.

¹¹And it came to pass, on the next day, He went on to a city called נָעִין, Naiyn, and His disciples and a large crowd were going with Him. ¹²And as He came near to the gate of the city, then, look! one *who was* dead was being carried out—an only son of his mother (and she was a widow, and a large crowd of the city was with her). ¹³And the Master, having seen her, was moved with compassion towards her and said to her, "Be not weeping." ¹⁴And having come near, He touched the corpse-stand, and those carrying IT stood still. And He said, "Young man, I say to you: arise!" ¹⁵and the dead *man* sat up and began to speak, and He gave him to his mother. ¹⁶And fear took hold of all *the people*, and they were glorifying God, saying, "A great prophet has risen among us!" and "God has looked upon His people!" ¹⁷And this account about Him went out in all יְהוּדָה, Y'hudah and all the surrounding region.

¹⁸And the disciples of יוֹחָנָן, Yochanan told him about all these things, ¹⁹and יוֹחָנָן, Yochanan, having called near a certain two of his disciples, sent *word* to the Master,[b] saying, "Are You He who is coming, or do we look for another?"

²⁰And having come near to Him, the men said, "יוֹחָנָן, Yochanan the Immerser sent us to You, saying, 'Are You He who is coming, or do we look for another?'"

²¹In that hour, He cured many from sicknesses and afflictions and evil רוּחוֹת, ruchot, and He granted sight to many *who were* blind. ²²And answering, He said to them, "Having gone on, report *back* to יוֹחָנָן, Yochanan what you saw and heard: blind men see again, lame walk, lepers are cleansed and deaf hear, dead are raised, *the* poor have Good News proclaimed *to them*. ²³And happy is he, whoever is not stumbled in Me."

²⁴And when the messengers of יוֹחָנָן, Yochanan had gone away, He began to say to the crowds regarding יוֹחָנָן, Yochanan: "What did you go out to the desert to look upon? A reed shaken by the wind? ²⁵Rather, what did you go out to see? A man clothed in soft garments? Look! they *who are adorned* in splendid apparel and living in luxury are in the houses of kings! ²⁶Rather, what did you go out to see? A prophet? Yes, I say to you, and much more than a prophet: ²⁷this is he about whom it has been written,

'Look! I send my messenger in front of your face, who will prepare your way before you.'[c]

²⁸I say to you *that* among those born of women, there is not a greater *one*[d] than יוֹחָנָן, Yochanan;[e] *and* yet, the least in the Reign of God is greater than he."

²⁹And all the people (even the tax-gatherers), having heard, declared God righteous, having been immersed with the immersion of יוֹחָנָן, Yochanan. ³⁰But the פְּרוּשִׁים, P'rushiym and the תּוֹרָה, Torah-experts,[f] not having been immersed by him, rejected the purpose of God for themselves.

³¹And the Master said,[g] "To what, then, will I compare the men of this generation? and to what are they like? ³²They are like

---

[a] Some mss insert, "infirmed"
[b] "the Master"—some mss say, "יֵשׁוּעַ, Yeshua"
[c] מַלְאָכִי Mal'akhiy 3:1
[d] "*one*"—some mss say, "prophet"
[e] Some mss insert, "the Immerser"
[f] "Torah-experts"—νομικοὶ, nomikoi
[g] "And the Master said" is not in the earliest mss

Analogy of the sower.

children—those sitting in a market-place, and calling one to another—who say, 'We piped *the flute* to you, and you did not dance; we mourned, and you did not weep!' ³³For יוֹחָנָן, Yochanan the Immerser came neither eating bread nor drinking wine, and you say, 'He has a demon!' ³⁴Yet the Son of Man came *both* eating and drinking, and you say, 'Look! a man *who is* a glutton and a wine drinker——a friend of tax-gatherers and sinners!' ³⁵But the Wisdom is justified by all her children."ᵃ

³⁶And a certain one of the פְּרוּשִׁים, P'rushiym was asking Him that He might eat with him, and having gone into the house of the פָּרוּשׁ, Parush, He reclined (at mealtime). ³⁷And look! a woman in the city, who was a sinner, *came to Him*. And having known that He was reclining (at mealtime) in the house of the פָּרוּשׁ, Parush, having provided an alabaster box of ointment ³⁸and having stood behind *Him* at His feet—weeping—she began to wet His feet with the tears. And she was wiping *them* with the hairs of her head, and was kissing His feet, and anointing *them* with the ointment.

³⁹And the פָּרוּשׁ, Parush who called Him, having seen *this*, spoke within himself, saying, "This one, if he were a prophet, would have known who, and of what kind *of person*, the woman who touches him *is*—that she is a sinner." ⁴⁰And יֵשׁוּעַ, Yeshua, answering, said to him, "שִׁמְעוֹן, Shim'on, I have something to say to you." And he replied, "Teacher, say on." ⁴¹"Two debtors were *in debt* to a certain creditor——the one was owing five hundred days' wages,ᵇ and the other fifty. ⁴²They *were* not having THE MEANS to give *it* back, *so* he forgave both *debts*. So then, which of them will love him more?" ⁴³שִׁמְעוֹן, Shim'on, answering, said, "I suppose that *one* to whom he forgave the most." And He said to him, "Rightly did you judge."

⁴⁴And having turned to the woman, He said to שִׁמְעוֹן, Shim'on, "*Do* you see this woman? I entered into your house, *but* you did not give *Me* water for My feet; yet this woman wet My feet with tears and wiped *them* with her hair. ⁴⁵You did not give a kiss to Me; yet this woman, from what TIME I came in, did not stop kissing My feet. ⁴⁶You did not anoint my head with oil, but this woman anointed my feet with ointment. ⁴⁷Therefore, I say to you, her many sins have been forgiven, because she loved much; but to whom little is forgiven, little does he love." ⁴⁸And He said to her, "Your sins have been forgiven." ⁴⁹And those reclining with Him (at mealtime) began to say within themselves, "Who is this, who also forgives sins?" ⁵⁰And He said to the woman, "Your faith has saved you; be going on to peace."

8 ¹And it came to pass thereafter that He was going through every city and village, proclaiming and bringing Good News of the Reign of God. And the Twelve WERE with Him, ²and *also* certain women who were healed of evil רוּחוֹת, ruchot and weaknesses: *there were* מִרְיָם, Mir'yam who is called מַגְדָּלִית, Mag'daliyt (from whom seven demons had gone out), ³and יוֹחָנָה, Yochanah (*the* wife of כּוּזָא, Kuza, *household* manager of Herod), and שׁוֹשַׁנָּה, Shoshanah, and many others who were serving them from their possessions.

⁴And when a large crowd had gathered, and those who *were* from every cityᶜ were coming to Him, He spoke by an analogy: ⁵"The sower went out to sow his seed, and in his sowing, some indeed fell beside the road, and it was trampled underfoot, and the birds of the heaven devoured it. ⁶And other *seed* fell upon the rock, and having sprung up, it withered, because of not having moisture. ⁷And other *seed* fell among the thorns, and the thorns, having sprung up with it, choked it. ⁸And other *seed* fell into the good ground, and having sprung up, it made fruit a hundred times *what was sown*." Saying these things, He was calling *out*, "He *who is* having ears to hear—let him hear!"

ᵃ cf. מַתִּתְיָהוּ *Matit'yahu* 11:19
ᵇ "days' wages"—lit. "denaries"
ᶜ "every city"—Young's says, "city and city"

⁹And *so* His disciples were questioning Him, "What might this analogy be?" ¹⁰And He said, "It has been given to you to know the mysteries of the Reign of God, but to the rest *of the people, the mysteries are* in analogies, so that SEEING THEY MAY NOT SEE, AND HEARING THEY MAY NOT UNDERSTAND.[a]

¹¹"And this is *the meaning of* the analogy: the seed is the word of God. ¹²And those *sown* beside the road are those having heard *the word, but* then the Accuser comes and takes up the word from their heart; otherwise, having believed, they might be saved. ¹³And those *sown* upon the rock *are* they who, when they hear the word, receive *it* with joy. But these, who believe for a time, have no root, and in time of temptation *they* fall away. ¹⁴And that *seed* which fell to the thorns: these are they who have heard *the word* but, going *on their way*, are choked through anxieties and riches and pleasures of life, and bring no *fruit* to completion. ¹⁵But that *seed sown* in the good ground: these are they who, with an upright and good heart, having heard the word, retain IT and, with perseverance, bear fruit.

¹⁶"And no one, having lit a lamp, covers it with a container or puts IT under a bed. Rather, he puts IT upon a lamp-stand, so that those coming in may see the light. ¹⁷For nothing is secret that will not become unconcealed, nor hidden that will not be known, and become unconcealed. ¹⁸Look *carefully*, therefore, at how you hear. For whoever has, there will be *more* given to him; and whoever does not have, even what he seems to have will be taken from him."

¹⁹And His mother and brothers came to Him, but they were unable to get to Him because of the crowd; ²⁰and it was told *to* Him, "Your mother and your brothers stand outside, wanting to see You." ²¹And He, answering, said to them, "My mother and my brothers! they are those who are hearing and doing the word of God."

²²And it came to pass, on one of the days, that He Himself went into a boat with His disciples, and He said to them, "Let us go over to the other side of the lake." And they set out, ²³and as they were sailing, He fell deeply asleep. And a storm of wind came down to the lake, and they were filling *up with water*, and were in jeopardy. ²⁴And having come near, the *disciples* awoke Him, saying, "רַבִּי רַבִּי, Rabiy! Rabiy![b] We are destroyed!" And having awoken, He rebuked the wind and the raging of the water, and they stopped, and there came a calm. ²⁵And He said to them, "Where is your faith?" And they, being afraid, *were* in wonder, saying to one another, "Who, then, is this, that He commands even the winds and the water, and they obey Him?"

²⁶And they sailed down to the region of the גְרָזִיִּים, Geraziyiym that is opposite the גָלִיל, Galiyl; ²⁷and *when* He had gone out onto the land, there met Him a certain man out of the city, having demons; and for a long time, *he* was not clothed with a garment and was not staying in a house, but in the tombs. ²⁸And having seen יֵשׁוּעַ, Yeshua, having cried out, he fell before Him and, with a loud voice, said, "What do You *want* with me,[c] יֵשׁוּעַ בֶּן־אֵל עֶלְיוֹן, Yeshua Ben-El El'yon? I implore You: may You not afflict me!" ²⁹for He had commanded the רוּחַ הַטֻּמְאָה, ruach ha-tum'ah to come out from the man. (Indeed, many times it had caught him, and he was being bound with chains and shackles, *and he was* guarded, but, breaking apart the bonds, he was driven by the demon to the deserted *places*.)

³⁰So יֵשׁוּעַ, Yeshua questioned him, "What is your name?" and he said, "Legion" (because many demons were entered into him); ³¹and they were calling on Him, that He might not command them to go away to the abyss. ³²And there was a herd of many pigs feeding in the mountain

---

[a] יְשַׁעְיָהוּ Y'sha'yahu 6:9

[b] רַבִּי, Rabiy—Greek ἐπιστάτα, epistata; see Luke 5:5; also in Luke 8:45

[c] "What do You *want* with me"—lit., "what to me and to you"

there, and *the demons* called on Him, *begging* that He might allow them to enter into these. And He allowed them; ³³and the demons, having gone out from the man, entered into the pigs; and the herd rushed down the steep *bank* to the lake and were choked *in the water*.

³⁴And those feeding THEM, having seen what had come to pass, fled and told IT to the city and to the fields. ³⁵And they came out to see what had come to pass, and they came to יֵשׁוּעַ, Yeshua and found the man from whom the demons had gone out, sitting clothed and right-minded at the feet of יֵשׁוּעַ, Yeshua, and they were afraid. ³⁶And those having seen IT told them how the demon-possessed *man* was saved. ³⁷And all the great number *of people* of the surrounding region of the גֵּרְזִיִּים, Geraziyiym asked Him to go away from them, because they were pressed with great fear.

And He, having entered into the boat, turned back. ³⁸And the man from whom the demons had gone out was imploring Him to go with Him, but He sent him away, saying, ³⁹"Return to your house and tell what great things God did to you," and he went away through all the city proclaiming what great things יֵשׁוּעַ, Yeshua did to him.

⁴⁰And at the returning of יֵשׁוּעַ, Yeshua, the crowd received Him *in welcome*, for they were all looking for Him. ⁴¹And look! there came a man, whose name WAS יָאִיר, Yaiyr, and he was a leader of the synagogue. And having fallen at the feet of יֵשׁוּעַ, Yeshua, *he* was calling on Him to come to his house ⁴²because he had an only daughter, about twelve years OLD, and she was dying.

And as He was going away, the crowds were choking Him; ⁴³and a woman having a continuous flow of blood for twelve years (who, having spent all her living on physicians, was not able to be healed by anyone), ⁴⁴having come near behind Him, touched the כָּנָף, kanaf ᵃ of His outer garment; and instantly, the flow of her blood stood *still*. ⁴⁵And יֵשׁוּעַ, Yeshua said, "Who IS it that touched Me?" And when *they were* all denying *it*, כֵּיפָא, Keifa ᵇ said, "רַבִּי, Rabiy, the crowds surround You and press *against You*." ᶜ ⁴⁶And יֵשׁוּעַ, Yeshua said, "Someone touched Me, for I knew *that* power had gone out from Me." ⁴⁷And the woman, having seen that she was not hidden, came *out* trembling; and having fallen before Him, *she* declared in the sight of all the people for what reason she touched Him, and how she was healed instantly. ⁴⁸And He said to her, "Daughter, ᵈ your faith has saved you. Be going on in peace."

⁴⁹While He was still speaking, there came a certain one from the synagogue leader's HOUSE, saying, "Your daughter has died. Do not harass the Teacher anymore." ⁵⁰And יֵשׁוּעַ, Yeshua, having heard *this*, answered him, "Be not afraid; only believe, and she will be saved." ⁵¹And having come to the house, He did not allow anyone to go in except כֵּיפָא, Keifa, יוֹחָנָן, Yochanan and יַעֲקֹב, Ya'aqov, and the father of the child, and the mother. ⁵²And they were all weeping and beating themselves for her, but He said, "Weep not, for she did not die, but *merely* sleeps." ⁵³And they were laughing at Him, knowing that she died. ⁵⁴And He, ᵉ having taken hold of her hand, called *out*, saying, "Child, arise!" ⁵⁵and her רוּחַ, ruach came back, and she arose instantly, and He directed that *something* be given to her to eat. ⁵⁶And her parents were amazed, but He commanded them to tell no one what had come to pass.

9 ¹And having called together the Twelve, He gave them power and authority over all the demons, and to cure diseases; ²and He sent them to proclaim the Reign of God, and to heal the infirmed. ³And He said to them, "Take

---

ᵃ כָּנָף, kanaf—see מַתִּתְיָהוּ *Matit'yahu* 9:20

ᵇ כֵּיפָא, Keifa—Gk: Πέτρος, Petros; see יוֹחָנָן *Yn.* 1:42; also in 8:51

ᶜ Some mss insert, "and You say, 'Who IS it that touched Me?'"

ᵈ Some mss insert, "take courage"

ᵉ Some mss insert, "having put *them* all outside, and"

nothing for the road: neither staff, nor bag, nor bread, nor money; nor have two shirts each. ⁴And whatever house you enter into, remain there, and *then* go from that place *when you leave*. ⁵And *for* as many as do not receive you: going out from that city, shake off the dust from your feet for a testimony against them." ⁶And going out, they were going through the several villages, proclaiming Good News, and healing everywhere.

⁷And Herod the tetrarch heard of all the things being done and was perplexed, because it was said by certain *ones* that *it was* יוֹחָנָן, Yochanan *who* had been raised out of the dead, ⁸and by certain *others* that אֵלִיָּהוּ, Eliyahu had appeared, and by others *still* that a prophet was risen—one of the ancients. ⁹And Herod said, "I beheaded יוֹחָנָן, Yochanan, so who is this about whom I hear such things?" and he was looking to see Him.

¹⁰And the emissaries, having returned, described to Him what great things they did. And having taken them *with Him*, He withdrew privately to[a] a city called בֵּית־צָיְדָה, Beit-Tzai'dah; ¹¹but the crowds, having known, followed Him. And having received them *in welcome*, He was speaking to them about the Reign of God, and those having need of *medical* service, He cured.

¹²And the day began to decline; and the Twelve, having come near, said to Him, "Send away the crowd, so that, having gone to the villages and the surrounding fields, they may settle down *for the night* and find provision, because we are here in a deserted place." ¹³And He said to them, "You give them *something* to eat." And they said, *"But* we have no more than five loaves *of bread* and two fishes, unless we *ourselves*, having gone, buy food for all these people." ¹⁴(Indeed, they were about five thousand men.) And He said to His disciples, "Cause them to recline in eating-groups, about fifty in each"; ¹⁵and they did so, and caused all *of them* to recline.

¹⁶And having taken the five loaves and the two fishes, having looked up to the heaven, He blessed them, and broke *them*, and was giving *the pieces* to the disciples to set before the crowds. ¹⁷And they ate, and all were filled; and there was taken up to them what was *left* over of *the* broken pieces—twelve baskets.

¹⁸And it came to pass, as He was praying alone, *that* the disciples were with Him; and He questioned them, saying, "Who do the crowds say Me to be?" ¹⁹And they, answering, said, "*Some say* יוֹחָנָן, Yochanan the Immerser, and others אֵלִיָּהוּ, Eliyahu, and others *still* that a prophet—one of the ancients—has risen *from the dead*." ²⁰And He said to them, "And you—who do you say Me to be?" And כֵּיפָא, Keifa,[b] answering, said, "The Messiah of God." ²¹And having warned them, He commanded THEM to say this to no one, ²²saying, "It is necessary *for* the Son of Man to suffer many things, and to be rejected by the זְקֵנִים, Z'qeniym and chief כֹּהֲנִים, Ko'haniym and סוֹפְרִים, Sof'riym, and to be killed, and the third day to be raised *from the dead.*"

²³And He said to all *of them*, "If anyone wants to come after Me, let him deny himself, and take up his *execution* stake daily, and follow Me; ²⁴for whoever wants to save his life will lose[c] it, and whoever loses his life for My sake, he will save it; ²⁵for what is a man benefited, having gained the whole world, yet having lost or having forfeited himself? ²⁶For whoever is ashamed of Me and of My words, of this one will the Son of Man be ashamed when He comes in His glory, and the Father's *glory*, and *the glory* of the holy Messengers. ²⁷And אָמֵן, amen, I say to you: there are certain *ones* of those standing here who will not taste of death until they see the Reign of God."

²⁸And it came to pass, about eight days after these words, that, having taken כֵּיפָא, Keifa and יוֹחָנָן, Yochanan and יַעֲקֹב, Ya'a-

---

[a] Some mss insert, "a deserted place of"

[b] כֵּיפָא, Keifa—Gk: Πέτρος, Petros; see יוֹחָנָן *Yn*. 1:42; also in verses 28, 32, and 33

[c] lose/lost—ἀπόλλυμι, apollumi, meaning "to kill or destroy"; also in verse 25

qov, He went up to the mountain to pray. ²⁹And it came to pass, in His praying, *that* the appearance of His face became altered and His garment *became* sparkling white *like a flash of lightning.* ³⁰And look! two men were speaking together with Him, who were מֹשֶׁה, Mosheh and אֵלִיָּהוּ, Eliyahu—³¹who, having appeared in glory, spoke of His exodusª that He was about to fulfill in יְרוּשָׁלַיִם, Y'rushalayim. ³²But כֵּיפָא, Keifa and those with him were heavy with sleep.

And having woken, they saw His glory and the two men standing with Him. ³³And in their departing from Him, it came to pass *that* כֵּיפָא, Keifa said to יֵשׁוּעַ, Yeshua, "רַבִּי, Rabiy,ᵇ it is good for us to be here; and *so*, let us make three סֻכּוֹת, sukot—one for You, and one for מֹשֶׁה, Mosheh, and one for אֵלִיָּהוּ, Eliyahu," not knowing what he *was* saying. ³⁴And as he was speaking these things, a cloud came and was overshadowing them, and they feared in their entering into the cloud. ³⁵And a voice came out of the cloud, saying, "This is My Son—the Chosen.ᶜ Hear Him." ³⁶And when the voice was past, יֵשׁוּעַ, Yeshua was found alone. And they stopped talking and declared to no one in those days anything of what they had seen.

³⁷And the next day, when they had come down from the mountain, it came to pass *that* a large crowd met Him. ³⁸And look! a man from the crowd cried out, saying, "Teacher, I implore you to look upon my son, because he is my one and only.ᵈ ³⁹And look! a רוּחַ, ruach takes him, and suddenly he shouts, and it convulses him, with foaming *at the mouth,* and it hardly *ever* goes away from him, shattering him. ⁴⁰And I implored your disciples that they might cast it out, but they were not able." ⁴¹Then יֵשׁוּעַ, Yeshua, answering, said, "O generation, faithless and perverse, until when will I be with you and endure you? Bring your son here." ⁴²And as he was still coming near, the demon tore him and convulsed HIM; and יֵשׁוּעַ, Yeshua rebuked the רוּחַ הַטֻּמְאָה, ruach ha-tum'ah, and healed the boy, and gave him back to his father. ⁴³And they were all amazed at the greatness of God!

And while all *the people* were in wonder at all *the* things that He was doing, He said to His disciples, ⁴⁴"Lay these words to your ears, for the Son of Man is about to be handed over into the hands of men." ⁴⁵But they were not understanding this spoken word, and it was veiled from them so that they might not perceive it, and they were afraid to ask Him about this spoken word.

⁴⁶And *then they* entered *into* a reasoning among them*selves about* this: who of them is greater? ⁴⁷And יֵשׁוּעַ, Yeshua (knowing the reasoning of their heart), having taken a child, set him beside Himself ⁴⁸and said to them, "Whoever receives this child in My Name receives Me, and whoever receives Me receives Him who sent Me. For he who is least among you all—he is great." ⁴⁹And יוֹחָנָן, Yochanan, answering, said, "רַבִּי, Rabiy, we saw a certain one casting out demons in Your Name, and we were forbidding him, because he does not follow with us." ⁵⁰And יֵשׁוּעַ, Yeshua said to him, "Forbid not; for he who is not against you is for you."ᵉ

⁵¹And it came to pass, in the completing of the days *before* His being taken up, that He fixed His face to go on to יְרוּשָׁלַיִם, Y'rushalayim; ⁵²and He sent messengers before His face. And having gone on, they went into a village of שֹׁמְרוֹן, Shom'ron to make *things* ready for Him; ⁵³but they did not receive Him *in welcome,* because His face was going on to יְרוּשָׁלַיִם, Y'rushalayim. ⁵⁴And the disciples יַעֲקֹב, Ya'aqov and יוֹחָנָן, Yochanan, having seen *this,* said, "Master, do You want THAT we should tell fire to come down from the heaven and to con-

---

ª "exodus"—lit. ἔξοδον, exodon; Young's says, "outgoing"
ᵇ רַבִּי, Rabiy—Greek ἐπιστάτα, epistata; see Luke 5:5; also in 9:49
ᶜ "Chosen"—some mss say, "Beloved"
ᵈ "one and only" or "only begotten" (μονογενής, monogenes)—lit. "one-of-a-kind"
ᵉ "you... you"—some mss say, "us... us"

sume them?"ᵃ ⁵⁵And having turned, He rebuked them,ᵇ ⁵⁶and they went on to another village.

⁵⁷And as they were going on with the road, a certain one said to Him, "I will follow You wherever You go."ᶜ ⁵⁸And יֵשׁוּעַ, Yeshua said to him, "The foxes have holes, and the birds of the heaven *have* places to nest, but the Son of Man has nowhere He may recline *His* head."

⁵⁹And He said to another, "Be following Me." And he said, "Sir, permit me, having gone away, to first bury my father." ⁶⁰And He said to him, "Allow the dead to bury their own dead; but you, having gone away, publicize the Reign of God."

⁶¹And another also said, "I will follow you, sir, but first permit me to say goodbye to those in my house." ⁶²And יֵשׁוּעַ, Yeshua said to him, "No one having put the hand on a plow, and looking back, is fit for the Reign of God."

10

¹And after these things, the Master appointed seventy-twoᵈ others, and sent them by twos before His face, to every city and place where He Himself was about to go. ²And He said to them, "The harvest indeed *is* abundant, but the workmen *are* few. Therefore, implore the Master of the harvest, that He may send out workmen to His harvest.

³"Go away; look! I send you forth as lambs in the middle of wolves. ⁴Carry no money sack, no bag, no sandals; and greet no one on the way.

⁵"And into whatever house you enter, first say, 'Peace to this house'; ⁶and if there is a son of peace there, your peace will rest on it (and if not so, it will return on you). ⁷And remain in that house, eating and drinking the things they have, for the workman *is* worthy of his hire. Do not move around from house to house.

⁸"And into whatever city you enter, and they receive you *in welcome*, eat the things set before you, ⁹and heal the weak in it, and say to them, 'The Reign of God has come near to you.' ¹⁰But into whatever city you enter, and they do not receive you, having gone out to its streets, say, ¹¹'Even the dust from your city that sticks to our feet, we wipe off against you! But know this: that the Reign of God has come near.' ¹²I say to you that in that Day, it will be more tolerable for סְדֹם, S'dom than for that city.

¹³"אוֹי, Oy! to you, Chorazin! אוֹי, Oy! to you, בֵּית־צַיְדָה, Beit-Tzai'dah! For if the powerful acts that were done in you had been done in צוֹר, Tzor and צִידוֹן, Tziydon, they *would* have reformed long ago, sitting in sackcloth and ashes; ¹⁴but it will be more tolerable in the Judgment for צוֹר, Tzor and צִידוֹן, Tziydon than for you. ¹⁵And you, כְּפַר־נַחוּם, K'far-Nachum, will you not be exalted to heaven? *No*,ᵉ you will be brought down to שְׁאוֹל, Sh'ol.

¹⁶"He who is hearing you hears Me, and he who is putting you away puts Me away, and he who is putting Me away puts away Him who sent Me."

¹⁷And the Seventy-two returned with joy, saying, "Master, even the demons are being submitted to us in Your Name!" ¹⁸And He said to them, "I was seeing הַשָּׂטָן, HaSatan having fallen from the heaven as lightning. ¹⁹Look! I have given you the authority to tread upon serpents and scorpions, and on all the power of the enemy, and nothing by any means will hurt you. ²⁰But rejoice not in this—that the רוּחוֹת, ruchot are submitted to you—but rejoice that your names are written in the heavens."

²¹In that moment, He was extremely joyful in the רוּחַ הַקֹּדֶשׁ, Ruach HaQodeshᶠ and said, "I confess to You, Father—Master of the heaven and of the earth—that You hid these things from wise and understanding men, and revealed them to

---

ᵃ Some mss insert, "as אֵלִיָּהוּ, Eliyahu also did"
ᵇ Some mss insert, "and said, 'You have not known of what רוּחַ, ruach you are, ⁵⁶for the Son of Man did not come to destroy men's lives, but to save.'"
ᶜ Some mss insert, "Master"
ᵈ "seventy-two"—some mss say, "seventy"; also in verse 17
ᵉ "will you not be exalted to heaven? *No*"—some mss say, "which was exalted to the heaven"
ᶠ Some mss omit, "הַקֹּדֶשׁ, HaQodesh"

little children. Yes, Father, because this way became good pleasure in front of You.

²²"All things were handed over to Me by My Father; and no one knows who the Son is except the Father, and who the Father is except the Son, and he to whom the Son wants to reveal HIM." ²³And having turned to the disciples, He said privately, "Happy *are* the eyes that are seeing what you see; ²⁴for I say to you that many prophets and kings wanted to perceive what you see, but did not perceive, and to hear what you hear, but did not hear."

²⁵And look! a certain תּוֹרָה, Torah-expert[a] stood up, testing Him, saying, "Teacher! What, having done, will *cause* me *to* inherit life age-enduring?" ²⁶And He said to him, "In the תּוֹרָה, Torah, what has been written? How do you read *it*?"

²⁷And he, answering, said, "YOU MUST LOVE ADONAI YOUR GOD WITH ALL YOUR HEART, AND WITH ALL YOUR SOUL, AND WITH ALL YOUR STRENGTH,[b] and with all your understanding, AND YOUR NEIGHBOR AS YOURSELF.[c]"

²⁸And He said to him, "Rightly did you answer; do this, and you will live."

²⁹But he, wanting to declare himself righteous, said to יֵשׁוּעַ, Yeshua, "And who is my neighbor?" ³⁰And יֵשׁוּעַ, Yeshua, having taken up THE MATTER, said, "There was a certain man going down from יְרוּשָׁלַיִם, Y'rushalayim to יְרִיחוֹ, Y'riycho *who* fell among robbers. And having stripped him and inflicted wounds, they went away, leaving HIM half dead. ³¹And by a coincidence, a certain כֹּהֵן, kohen was going down on that road; and having seen him, he passed over on the opposite side. ³²And likewise, a לֵוִי, Leviy, also having been around the place, having come and seen, passed over on the opposite side. ³³But a certain journeying שֹׁמְרוֹנִי, Shom'roniy came upon him; and having seen him, he was moved with compassion; ³⁴and having come near, he bound up his wounds, pouring on oil and wine; and having lifted him up on his own beast *of burden*, he brought him to an inn and was taking care of him. ³⁵And on the next day,[d] taking out two days' wages,[e] he gave *it* to the innkeeper and said, 'Be taking care of him, and whatever more you may spend, in my coming again, I will give *it* back to you.' ³⁶Who, then, of these three seems to you to have become a neighbor of him who fell among the robbers?" ³⁷And he said, "He who did the *loving*-kindness with him." And יֵשׁוּעַ, Yeshua said to him, "Be going on, and be doing likewise."

³⁸And in their going on, He entered into a certain village, and a certain woman named מָרְתָא, Mar'ta received Him *in* welcome. ³⁹And she had a sister, called מִרְיָם, Mir'yam, who, having also seated herself beside the feet of the Master,[f] was hearing His word. ⁴⁰מָרְתָא, Mar'ta, however, was distracted about much serving; and having stood by Him, she said, "Sir, do you not care that my sister left me alone to serve? Tell her, then, that she should help along with me." ⁴¹And the Master, answering, said to her, "מָרְתָא מָרְתָא, Mar'ta, Mar'ta! You are anxious and bothered about many things, ⁴²but there is need of one thing *only*; indeed, מִרְיָם, Mir'yam chose the good part that will not be taken away from her."

11

¹And it came to pass *that*, in His being in a certain place praying, as He stopped, a certain one of His disciples said to Him, "Master, teach us to pray, as יוֹחָנָן, Yochanan also taught his disciples." ²And He said to them, "When you pray, say: Father,[g] set apart is Your Name; Your Reign come.[h] ³Our appointed bread, be giving us daily; ⁴and forgive us

---

[a] "Torah-expert"—νομικός, nomikos
[b] דְּבָרִים D'variym 6:5
[c] וַיִּקְרָא Vayiq'ra 19:18
[d] Some mss insert, "going out"
[e] "days' wages"—lit. "denaries"
[f] "the Master"—some mss say, "יֵשׁוּעַ, Yeshua"; also in vs. 41
[g] "Father"—some mss say, "Our Father who is in the Heavens"
[h] Some mss insert, "Your will come to pass, as in Heaven, also on earth"; cf. מַתִּתְיָהוּ Matit'yahu 6:10

our sins, for we ourselves also forgive everyone indebted to us; and may You not bring us into temptation."ᵃ

⁵And He said to them, "Who of you will have a friend, and will go on to him at midnight and say to him, 'Friend! Lend me three loaves *of bread*, ⁶since a friend of mine came off of the road to me, and I do not have what I will set before him *to eat*.' ⁷And he, answering from within *his home*, will say, 'Do not give me trouble! The door has already been shut, and my children are with me in the bed. I am not able, having risen, to give *anything* to you.' ⁸I say to you, even if, having risen, he will not give *anything* to him because of his being his friend, yet because of his *friend's* shameless persistence, having risen, he will give him as many *loaves* as he needs. ⁹And I say to you: ask, and it will be given to you; seek, and you will find; knock, and it will be opened to you; ¹⁰for everyone who is asking receives; and he who is seeking finds; and to him who is knocking, it will be opened.

¹¹"And which father from *among* you, if the son asks forᵇ a fish, will present to him a serpent instead of a fish? ¹²and if he asks *for* an egg, will present to him a scorpion? ¹³If, then, you (being evil) have known to be giving good gifts to your children, how much more will the Father (who is from Heaven) give the רוּחַ הַקֹּדֶשׁ, Ruach HaQodesh to those asking Him!"

¹⁴And *going on*, He was casting out a demon, and it was mute. And it came to pass, when the demon had gone out, *that* the mute man spoke, and the crowds *were* in wonder. ¹⁵And certain *ones* of them said, "By בַּעַל־זְבוּב, Ba-al–Z'vuv, the ruler of the demons, he casts out the demons"; ¹⁶and others, tempting *Him*, were asking *for* a sign out of heaven from Him.

¹⁷But He, knowing their thoughts, said to them, "Every kingdom having been di-

vided against itself is desolated; and house against house falls; ¹⁸and if הַשָּׂטָן, HaSatan was also divided against himself, how will his kingdom be made to stand (for you say My casting out the demons is by בַּעַל־זְבוּב, Ba-al–Z'vuv)? ¹⁹But if by בַּעַל־זְבוּב, Ba-al–Z'vuv I cast out the demons, *what about* your sons? By whom do they cast *them* out? Because of this, they will be your judges. ²⁰But if I cast out the demons by the finger of God, then the Reign of God has come upon you.

²¹"When the strong man, *fully* armed, guards his courtyard, his possessions are in peace; ²²but when *one* stronger than he, having come upon HIM, overcomes him, he takes away his whole-armor in which he had trusted, and distributes his plunder. ²³He who is not with Me is against Me, and he who is not gathering with me, scatters. ²⁴When the רוּחַ הַטֻּמְאָה, ruach hatum'ah goes out from the man, it walks through waterless places seeking rest. And not finding *any*, it then says, 'I will return to my house from which I came out'; ²⁵and having come, it finds *the house* swept and arranged. ²⁶Then it goes and takes *with* it seven other רוּחוֹת, ruchot more evil than itself; and, having entered, they live there; and the final *condition* of that man becomes worse than the first."

²⁷And it came to pass, in His saying these things, *that* a certain woman, having lifted up the voice out of *the middle of* the crowd, said to Him, "Happy *are* the womb that carried You and the breasts that nursed you!" ²⁸And He said, "Yes, rather, happy *are* those hearing the word of God and guarding IT!"

²⁹And the crowds *were* crowding together upon Him, *and* He began to say, "This generation is an evil generation; it seeks after a sign, but a sign will not be given to it, except *for* the sign of יוֹנָה, Yonah. ³⁰For as יוֹנָה, Yonah became a sign to the *men* of נִינְוֵה, Niyn'veh, so also will the Son of Man be to this generation. ³¹A queen of the south will rise up in the judgment with the men of this generation and will con-

---

ᵃ Some mss insert, "but deliver us from the evil"
ᵇ Some mss insert, "a loaf *of bread*, will present a stone to him? and if *the son asks for*"; cf. מַתִּתְיָהוּ Matit'yahu 7:9-10

demn them, because she came from the ends of the earth to hear the wisdom of שְׁלֹמֹה, Sh'lomoh; and look! *one* greater than שְׁלֹמֹה, Sh'lomoh *is* here! ³²Men of נִינְוֵה, Niyn'veh will stand up in the judgment with this generation and will condemn it, because they reformed at the proclamation of יוֹנָה, Yonah; and look! *one* greater than יוֹנָה, Yonah *is* here!

³³"No one having lit a lamp puts IT in a secret place, nor under the measur*ing bas-ket*, but on the lamp-stand, so that those coming in may see the light. ³⁴The lamp of the body is your eye. When your eye is perfect,[a] your whole body is also full of light, and when it is evil,[b] your body also is darkened. ³⁵Pay attention, then, so that the light that IS in you *may* not be darkness. ³⁶If your whole body is full of light—not having any part darkened—then the whole will be full of light, as when the lamp gives you light by the brightness."

³⁷And in HIS speaking, a פָּרוּשׁ, Parush was asking Him that He might eat with him. And having gone in, He reclined (at mealtime); ³⁸but the פָּרוּשׁ, Parush, having seen, was in wonder that He did not first immerse Himself before the meal. ³⁹And the Master said to him, "Now you, the פְּרוּשִׁים, P'rushiym, make the outside of the cup and of the plate clean, but your inward part is full of property-rape and wickedness. ⁴⁰Unthinking! Did not He who made the outside also make the inside? ⁴¹But give what is inside[c] AS charity, and look! all things are clean to you.

⁴²"But אוֹי, oy! to you, the פְּרוּשִׁים, P'rushiym, because you give a tenth *of* the mint and the rue *plant* and every *garden* herb, but you pass by the judgment and the love of God. So it is necessary to do these things, and not to neglect those.

⁴³"אוֹי, Oy! to you, the פְּרוּשִׁים, P'rushiym, because you love the most important seats in the synagogues, and the greetings in the market-places. ⁴⁴"אוֹי, Oy! to you,[d] because you are as the unseen tombs, and the men walking above have not known."

⁴⁵And one of the תּוֹרָה, Torah-experts,[e] answering, said to Him, "Teacher, *by* saying these things, you insult us also"; ⁴⁶and He said, "And to you, the תּוֹרָה, Torah-experts: אוֹי, oy! because you burden men with hardly bearable[f] burdens, and you yourselves do not touch the burdens with *even* one of your fingers. ⁴⁷אוֹי, Oy! to you, because you build the tombs of the prophets, and your fathers killed them. ⁴⁸You are therefore witnesses, and are well pleased with the actions of your fathers, because they indeed killed them, and you build their tombs. ⁴⁹Because of this the wisdom of God also said, 'I will send prophets and emissaries to them, and some of them they will kill and persecute,' ⁵⁰so that the blood of all the prophets that is having been poured out from the foundation of the world may be required of this generation ⁵¹(from the blood of הֶבֶל, Hevel to the blood of זְכַרְיָה, Z'khar'yah, who *was* destroyed between the altar and the House). Yes, I say to you, it will be required from this generation. ⁵²אוֹי, Oy! to you, the תּוֹרָה, Torah-experts, because you took away the key of the knowledge. *You* yourselves did not enter, and those coming in, you hindered."

⁵³And in His having gone out from there,[g] the סוֹפְרִים, Sof'riym and the פְּרוּשִׁים, P'rushiym began to have a grudge against *Him* with hostility, and to press Him to speak about many things, ⁵⁴laying in wait for Him, to catch something out of His mouth.[h]

---

[a] that is, to be generous; here, Young's says, "simple"; cf. מַתִּתְיָהוּ *Matit'yahu* 6:22
[b] that is, to be selfish
[c] "what is inside"—Young's says, "what you have"
[d] Some mss insert, "סוֹפְרִים, Sof'riym and פְּרוּשִׁים, P'rushiym—hypocrites!—"
[e] "Torah-experts"—νομικῶν, nomikon; also in verses 46 and 52 (νομικοῖς, nomikois)
[f] "hardly bearable"—Young's says, "grievous to be borne"
[g] "having gone out from there"—some mss say, "speaking these things to them"
[h] Some mss insert, "so that they might accuse Him"

12 ¹Meanwhile, *with* the crowd of the tens of thousands having been gathered together so as to trample upon one another, He began to say to His disciples foremost, "Be careful for yourselves of the leaven of the פְּרוּשִׁים, P'rushiym, which is hypocrisy. ²And there is nothing covered that will not be revealed, and *nothing* hidden that will not be known, ³because whatever you said in the darkness will be heard in the light, and what you spoke to the ear in the inner-rooms will be proclaimed upon the house-tops.

⁴"And I say to you, my friends: be not afraid of those *who are* killing the body, and after these things are not having anything more to do. ⁵But I will show you whom you should fear: fear Him who, after the killing *of the body*, is having authority to throw *you* to the גֵּיהִנֹּם, Geihinom. Yes, I say to you: fear Him.

⁶"Are not five sparrows sold for two coins? Yet not one of them is forgotten before God. ⁷Rather, even the hairs of your head have all been numbered. Fear not! You are of more value than many sparrows.

⁸"And I say to you: everyone who professes to Me in front of men, the Son of Man also will profess to him in front of the Messengers of God; ⁹but he who has denied Me in front of men will be denied in front of the Messengers of God. ¹⁰And everyone who says a word against[a] the Son of Man, it will be forgiven to him; but to him who spoke evil against the רוּחַ הַקֹּדֶשׁ, Ruach HaQodesh, it will not be forgiven.

¹¹"And when they bring you before the synagogues and the rulers and the authorities, be not anxious *about* how or what you may reply *in defense*, or what you may say, ¹²for the רוּחַ הַקֹּדֶשׁ, Ruach HaQodesh will teach you in that moment what YOU must say."

¹³And a certain one out of the crowd said to Him, "Teacher, tell my brother to divide the inheritance with me!" ¹⁴And He said to him, "Man, who set Me *as a* judge or a divider over you?" ¹⁵And He said to them, "See and beware of all covetousness, because one's life is not in the abundance of his possessions."

¹⁶And He spoke an analogy to them, saying, "The field of a certain rich man brought forth *crops* well; ¹⁷and he was reasoning within himself, saying, 'What should I do, because I do not have *a place* where I can gather together *all* my fruits?' ¹⁸And he said, 'I will do this: I will take down my storehouses, and I will build larger ones, and I will gather together there all my grain[b] and my good things. ¹⁹And I will say to my soul, "Soul, you have many good things laid up for many years. Be resting, eat, drink, rejoice!"' ²⁰And God said to him, 'Unthinking one! This *very* night they will require your soul from you, and what things did you prepare? To whom will they be *given*?' ²¹So *it is for* he who is treasuring up to himself, and is not rich toward God."

²²And He said to His disciples, "Because of this, I say to you: be not anxious for the life (what you will eat), nor for the body (what you will put on); ²³for the life is more than the nourishment, and the body *more* than the clothing. ²⁴Consider the ravens: that they sow not, nor reap, *and* to which there is no barn nor storehouse; yet God nourishes them. How much more *valuable* are you than the birds? ²⁵And who of you, being anxious, is able to add an hour[c] to his age? ²⁶If, then, you are not able *to do anything* for the least *of the things in life*, why are you anxious for the remainder *of them*? ²⁷Consider the lilies: how do they grow? They do not labor, nor do they spin *thread*. But I say to you: not even שְׁלֹמֹה, Sh'lomoh in all his glory was wrapped around as one of these. ²⁸And if God so clothes the grass in the field, that is *alive* today and tomorrow is thrown into an oven, how much more *will He clothe* you, you of little faith? ²⁹And you—look not for

---

[a] "against"—lit. "to"; both times in this sentence

[b] "grain"—some mss say, "products"

[c] "hour"—lit. "πῆχυν, pechun"—a unit of measurement, sp. cubit

what you will eat and what you will drink, and be not in suspense, ³⁰for all these things do the ethnic-groups of the world search after, and your Father has known that you have need of these things; ³¹but look for His Reign, and these things will be added to you. ³²Fear not, little flock, because your Father delighted to give you the Reign.

³³"Sell your possessions, and give charity; make money sacks for yourselves that do not become old—an unfailing treasure in the Heavens, where thief does not come near, nor moth destroy—³⁴for where your treasure is, there also your heart will be. ³⁵Let *the loose-hanging garment about* your loins be wrapped around *you,* and *keep* the lamps burning. ³⁶And *be* like men waiting for their master—*for* when he returns from the wedding feasts—so that *when* he has come and knocked, they may immediately open *the door* to him. ³⁷Happy *are* those slaves whom the master, having come, finds awake. אָמֵן, Amen, I say to you that he will wrap *the loose-hanging garment around* himself, and will cause them to recline (at mealtime), and, having come near, will serve them. ³⁸And if, in the second or in the third watch, he comes and finds *it* so, happy are those slaves. ³⁹And know this: that if the householder had known what time the thief comes, he[a] would not have allowed his house to be broken through. ⁴⁰You also, become ready, because at the moment you think *He is not coming,* the Son of Man comes."

⁴¹And כֵּיפָא, Keifa[b] said, "Master, do You speak this analogy *only* to us, or also to all?" ⁴²And the Master said, "Who, then, is the faithful and prudent steward whom the master will set over his household, to give *everyone* the portion of grain in *the proper* season? ⁴³Happy *is* that slave whom the master, having come, finds so doing. ⁴⁴Truly I say to you that he will set him over all his possessions. ⁴⁵But if that slave says in his heart, 'My master delays to come,' and begins to beat the slave-boys and the slave-girls—also to eat and to drink and to be drunk—⁴⁶the master of that slave will come (on a day in which he does not look for HIM, and in an hour that he does not know) and will cut him in pieces, and he will put his portion with the unfaithful. ⁴⁷And that slave who has known his master's will, and has not prepared or done according to his will, will be beaten with many strikes. ⁴⁸But he who has not known, yet has done things worthy of wounds, will be beaten with few. And everyone to whom much was given, much will be required from him; and *everyone* to whom they entrusted much, more abundantly they will ask of him.

⁴⁹"Fire I came to cast on the earth—and what if I wish it were already kindled? ⁵⁰But I have an immersion to be immersed with—and how I am pressed until it is completed! ⁵¹Do you think that I came to give peace in the earth? No, I say to you, but rather division! ⁵²For from now on there will be five in one house divided—three against two, and two against three. ⁵³They will be divided, a father against a son and a son against a father, a mother against the daughter and a daughter against the mother, a mother-in-law against her daughter-in-law and a daughter-in-law against the mother-in-law."

⁵⁴And He said also to the crowds, "When you see the cloud rising in the west, you immediately say, 'A *rain* shower comes,' and it is so; ⁵⁵and when *there is* a south wind blowing, you say that there will be heat, and it is. ⁵⁶Hypocrites! You have known *how* to interpret the face of the earth and of the heaven, but this *present* time—how have you not known *how* to interpret *it*? ⁵⁷And why, also, do you not judge of yourselves what is righteous? ⁵⁸For as you are going away with your opponent to *see* the ruler, on the way, be diligent to be released from him; otherwise, he might drag you to the judge, and the judge will hand you over to the officer, and the officer will throw you into prison. ⁵⁹I say to you: you

---

[a] Some mss insert, "would have *stayed* awake, and"
[b] כֵּיפָא, Keifa—Gk: Πέτρος, Petros; see יוֹחָנָן Yn. 1:42

will not come out from that place until you give back even the last very small coin."

13 ¹And there were certain *ones* present at that time, telling Him about the גְּלִילִים, G'liyliym whose blood Pilate mingled with their sacrifices. ²And answering, He said to them, "Do you think that these גְּלִילִים, G'liyliym are *worse* sinners beyond all the *other* גְּלִילִים, G'liyliym because they have suffered these things? ³No, I say to you. But if you do not reform, even you all will likewise be destroyed. ⁴Or those eighteen on whom the tower in שִׁלֹחַ, Shiloach fell, and *it* killed them: do you think that they are *worse* debtors beyond all the *other* men who are living in יְרוּשָׁלַיְם, Y'rushalayim? ⁵No, I say to you. But if you do not reform, you all will likewise be destroyed."

⁶And He spoke this analogy: "A certain one had a fig-tree planted in his vineyard, and he came looking for fruit in it, but he did not find *any*. ⁷And he said to the vinedresser, 'Look! for three years I have come looking for fruit in this fig-tree, but have not found *any*. Cut if off! Why should it also render the ground useless?' ⁸And he, answering, said to him, 'Sir, allow it also this year, until *such a time* that I may dig around it, and throw in *some* manure. ⁹And if indeed it makes fruit in the coming *year, good*; and if not so, *then* you will cut it off.'"

¹⁰And He was teaching in one of the synagogues on the שַׁבָּת, Shabat, ¹¹and look! there was a woman having a רוּחַ, ruach of weakness *for* eighteen years, and she was bent completely forward, and *was* not able to bend back at all. ¹²And יֵשׁוּעַ, Yeshua, having seen her, called HER near and said to her, "Woman, you have been released from your weakness"; ¹³and He laid HIS hands on her, and instantly she was set upright, and was glorifying God.

¹⁴And the head of the synagogue, answering (much displeased that יֵשׁוּעַ, Yeshua healed on the שַׁבָּת, Shabat), said to the crowd, "There are six days in which WE must be working, so come be healed during these—but not on יוֹם הַשַׁבָּת, Yom HaShabat!" ¹⁵And the Master answered him and said, "Hypocrite! Does not each of you untie his ox or donkey from the stall on the שַׁבָּת, Shabat, and having led *it* away, water IT? ¹⁶And this one, being a daughter of אַבְרָהָם, Av'raham whom הַשָׂטָן, HaSatan bound, look! *for* eighteen years, was it not necessary *for her* to be untied from this bond on יוֹם הַשַׁבָּת, Yom HaShabat?" ¹⁷And *as* He *was* saying these things, all who were opposed to Him were being ashamed, and the whole crowd was rejoicing over all the glorious things that were being done by Him.

¹⁸Then He said, "What is the Reign of God like? and to what will I liken it? ¹⁹It is like a grain of mustard, which a man, having taken, threw into his garden, and it increased and came to *be* a tree, and the birds of the heavens nested in its branches." ²⁰And again He asked, "To what will I liken the Reign of God? ²¹It is like leaven, which a woman, having taken, hid in three measures of flour, until that whole *batch* was leavened."

²²And He was going through cities and villages, teaching, and making progress toward יְרוּשָׁלַיְם, Y'rushalayim; ²³and a certain one said to Him, "Sir, are those *who are* saved *only* few *in number?*" And He said to them, ²⁴"Be striving to go in through the narrow door,[a] because many, I say to you, will look to go in and will not be able *to*, ²⁵from the time the householder has risen up and has shut the door. And you will begin to stand outside, and to knock at the door, saying, 'Sir, open *up* to us'; and he, answering, will say to you, 'I have not known you *or* where you are from.' ²⁶Then you will begin to say, 'We ate in your presence, and drank; and you taught in our streets.' ²⁷But he will say, 'I say to you: I have not known you *or* where you are from. Go away from me, all you workers of unrighteousness!'

²⁸"There will be in that place the weeping and the gnashing of teeth, when you

---

[a] "door"—some mss say, "gate"

see אַבְרָהָם, Av'raham and יִצְחָק, Yitz'chaq and יַעֲקֹב, Ya'aqov and all the prophets in the Reign of God, but yourselves being thrown outside. ²⁹And *others* will come from east and west, and from north and south, and will recline *at the feast-table* in the Reign of God. ³⁰And look! there are *those who are* last who will be first, and there are *those who are* first who will be last."

³¹At that time, there came near certain פְּרוּשִׁים, P'rushiym, saying to Him, "Go out, and be going on from here, for Herod wants to kill you." ³²And He said to them, "Having gone, say to that fox, 'Look! I *will* cast out demons and accomplish cures today and tomorrow, and *on* the third DAY I will be perfected.' ³³But today and tomorrow and the following DAY, I must go on, because it is not possible for a prophet to be destroyed out*side* of יְרוּשָׁלַיִם, Y'rushalayim.

³⁴"יְרוּשָׁלַיִם יְרוּשָׁלַיִם, Y'rushalayim, Y'rushalayim! *You* who are killing the prophets, and stoning those sent to her—how often I wanted to gather together your children, as a hen *gathers* her chicks under the wings, yet you did not want *it*. ³⁵Look! your house is being left deserted to you. And I say to you: you will not see Me until *the time* comes when you say, 'BLESSED IS HE WHO IS COMING IN THE NAME OF ADONAI.'"ª

14 ¹And it came to pass, on His going into the house of a certain one of the leaders of the פְּרוּשִׁים, P'rushiym on a שַׁבָּת, Shabat to eat bread, that they were watching Him. ²And look! there was a certain man in front of Him *who was* swollen with water *in his arms and legs*. ³And יֵשׁוּעַ, Yeshua, answering, spoke to the תּוֹרָה, Torah-expertsᵇ and פְּרוּשִׁים, P'rushiym, saying, "Is it permitted to heal on יוֹם הַשַּׁבָּת, Yom HaShabat, or not?" ⁴but they were silent. And having taken hold of HIM, He healed him and let HIM go. ⁵And He said to them, "Which *one* of you *sees* a sonᶜ or an ox fall into a well, and he does not immediately pull it up on יוֹם הַשַּׁבָּת, Yom HaShabat?" ⁶And to these things they were again not able to answer.

⁷And He spoke an analogy to those *who were* called *together to eat* (noticing how they were picking out the prime seating), saying to them, ⁸"When you are called by someone to *the* marriage-feasts, do not recline on the prime seating, in case a more honorable *guest* than you might have been called by him *who called you*; ⁹and he who called *both* you and him, having come, will say to you, 'Give *your* place to this one'; and then you will begin to occupy the last place with shame. ¹⁰But, when you are called *to marriage-feasts*, having gone on, recline in the last place, so that when he who called you comes, he will say to you, 'Friend! Come up higher!' Then you will have glory in front of all those reclining with you, ¹¹because everyone who is exalting himself will be humbled, and he who is humbling himself will be exalted." ¹²And He also said to him who called Him *to the feast*, "When you make a meal or supper, be not calling your friends, nor your brothers, nor your relatives, nor rich neighbors. Otherwise, they may invite you in return, and a repayment will come to you. ¹³But *instead*, when you make a banquet, be calling *the* poor, crippled, lame, *and* blind; ¹⁴and happy you will be, because they have no repayment *to give* you, for it will be repaid to you in the Rising Again of the righteous."

¹⁵And one of those reclining with Him, having heard these things, said to Him, "Happy IS he who will eat bread in the Reign of God!" ¹⁶And He said to him, "A certain man was making a huge meal, and *he* called many. ¹⁷And he sent his slave at the time of the meal to say to those having been called, 'Be coming, because it isᵈ ready now.' ¹⁸And they began to *make* excuse*s for* themselves, one after another. The first said to him, 'I bought a field,

---

ª תְּהִלִּים *T'hiliym* 118:26
ᵇ "Torah-experts"—νομικοί, nomikoi
ᶜ "son"—some mss say, "donkey"
ᵈ "it is"—some mss say, "all things are"

and I have need (having gone out) to see it; I ask of you, have me excused.' ¹⁹And another said, 'I bought five yoke of oxen, and I *need to* go on to examine them; I ask of you, have me excused.' ²⁰And another said, 'I married a wife, and because of this, I am not able to come.' ²¹And the slave, having come *back*, told these things to his master.

"Then the householder, having been angry, said to his slave, 'Go out quickly to the streets and lanes of the city, and bring in here the poor and crippled and blind and lame.' ²²And the slave said, 'Sir, what you commanded has been done, and there is still room.' ²³And the master said to the slave, '*Then* go out to the roads and fences, and make *anyone you find* come in, so that my house may be filled. ²⁴For I say to you, that none of those men who have been called will taste of my meal.'"

²⁵And there were large crowds going on with Him. And having turned, He said to them, ²⁶"If anyone comes to Me, and does not hate his own father and mother and wife and children and brothers and sisters—and yet even his own life—he is not able to be my disciple. ²⁷Whoever does not carry his own *execution* stake and come after Me is not able to be My disciple.

²⁸"Indeed, who of you, wanting to build a tower, does not, having sat down, first count the cost *to see* whether he has the things to complete *it*? ²⁹Otherwise, when he has laid the foundation and is not being able to finish, all who are looking *on* begin to mock him, ³⁰saying, 'This man began to build, and was not able to finish!' ³¹Or what king going on to engage with another king in war will not, having sat down, first consider if he is able with ten thousand *troops* to meet *in battle* him who is coming against him with twenty thousand? ³²And if not so—he being yet a long way off—having sent a delegation, he asks the terms[a] for peace. ³³So, then, every one of you who does not give up everything that he himself has is not able to be My disciple.

³⁴"The salt, then, *is* good, but if even the salt becomes tasteless, with what will it be seasoned? ³⁵It is fit neither for *the* ground, nor for *the* manure *pile*—they throw it out. He who is having ears to hear—let him hear."

15

¹And all the tax-gatherers and the sinners were coming near to Him to hear Him, ²and the פְּרוּשִׁים, P'rushiym and the סוֹפְרִים, Sof'riym were grumbling, saying, "This one receives sinners *in welcome* and eats with them!" ³And He spoke this analogy to them, saying, ⁴"What man among you, having a hundred sheep and having lost one out of them, does not leave behind the ninety-nine in the desert and go on after the lost one until he finds it? ⁵And having found *it*, he lays IT on his shoulders, rejoicing; ⁶and having come to the house, he calls together the friends and the neighbors, saying to them, 'Rejoice with me, for I found my sheep—the lost one!' ⁷I say to you that the same kind of[b] joy will be in the Heaven over one sinner reforming, rather than over ninety-nine righteous men who have no need of reformation.

⁸"Or what woman—having ten silver coins—if she loses one silver coin, does not light a lamp, and sweep the house, and look carefully until she finds it? ⁹And having found *it*, she calls together the female friends and neighbors, saying, 'Rejoice with me, for I found the silver coin that I lost!' ¹⁰So I say to you: joy comes in the presence of the Messengers of God over one sinner reforming."

¹¹And He said, "A certain man had two sons, ¹²and the younger of them said to the father, 'Father, give me the portion of the estate falling to ME,' and he divided the *sum of his* life to them. ¹³And not many days after, having gathered all *he had* together, the younger son went abroad to a far *away* country, and there he scattered *and squandered* his estate, living recklessly.

---

[a] "terms"—Young's says, "things"

[b] "the same kind of"—Young's says, "so"

¹⁴"And having spent all *of the estate*, there came a severe famine on that country, and he began to be in need. ¹⁵And having gone on, he joined himself to one of the citizens of that country, and he sent him to the fields to feed pigs. ¹⁶And he was covetous to be fed from the pods that the pigs were eating, but no one was giving *anything* to him. ¹⁷And having come to himself, he said, 'How many hired hands of my father have a superabundance of bread, yet here I am *being* destroyed with hunger! ¹⁸Having risen, I will go on to my father, and I will say to him, "Father, I sinned—to the Heaven, and in your sight. ¹⁹I am no longer worthy to be called your son. Make me as one of your hired hands."'

²⁰"And having risen, he went to his own father; and he still being far away, his father saw him and was moved with compassion. And having run *to his son*, he fell upon his neck and kissed him, ²¹and the son said to him, 'Father, I sinned—to the Heaven, and in your sight. I am no longer worthy to be called your son.' ²²And the father said to his slaves, 'Quickly! Bring out the prime robe and clothe him! And give a ring for his hand and sandals for the feet! ²³And bring the fatted calf! Kill ɪᴛ, and having eaten, let us rejoice, ²⁴because this, my son, was dead, and lived again; he was lost, and was found!' And they began to rejoice.

²⁵"And his elder son was in a field, and as *he was* coming, he drew near to the house, *and* he heard music and dancing. ²⁶"And having called near one of the servant-boys, he was asking what these things might be. ²⁷And he said to him, 'Your brother has arrived, and your father has killed the fatted calf, because he received him back in health.' ²⁸And he was angry and would not go in; and his father, having come out, was pleading with him. ²⁹And he, answering, said to his father, 'Look! I served you so many years, and never did I step past your command, but you never gave a young goat to me so that I might rejoice with my friends. ³⁰But when your son came—this one who devoured *the sum of* your life with prostitutes—you killed the fatted calf for him!' ³¹And he said to him, 'Child, you are always with me, and all my things are yours. ³²But it was needful to rejoice and to be joyful, because this, your brother, was dead, and lived again; he was lost, and was found.'"

16

¹And He also said to the disciples, "There was a certain rich man who had a manager *of his household*, and this *manager* was accused to him of scattering *and* squandering his possessions. ²And having called him, he said to him, 'What ɪs this I hear about you? Turn in the account of your stewardship, for you can no longer be *my* manager.' ³And the manager said within himself, 'What will I do, because my master takes away the stewardship from me? I am not able to dig; I am ashamed to beg. ⁴I know what I will do, so that when I am removed from the stewardship, *people* may receive me *with welcome* into their houses.' ⁵And having called near each one of his master's debtors, he said to the first, 'How much do you owe to my master?' ⁶and he said, 'A hundred baths of oil.' And he said to him, 'Take your bill, and having sat down quickly, write, "Fifty."' ⁷Afterward to another he said, 'And you, how much do you owe?' And he said, 'A hundred measures of wheat.' He said to him, 'Take your bill, and write, "Eighty."' ⁸And the master commended the unrighteous manager, that he did *this* astutely, because the sons of this age are more astute than the sons of the light, in respect to their generation. ⁹And I say to you: make friends to yourselves by *means of* the wealth of unrighteousness, so that when it fails,[a] they may receive you to the age-enduring dwellings.

¹⁰"He who is faithful in the least *of things* ɪs also faithful in much, and he who ɪs unrighteous in the least *of things* is also unrighteous in much. ¹¹If, then, you do not become faithful in the unrighteous wealth, who will entrust the true *wealth* to you? ¹²And if you do not become faith-

---

[a] "it fails"—some mss say, "you fail"

ful in the *possessions of* others, who will give to you your own? ¹³No house servant is able to serve two masters, for he will either hate the one and the other he will love, or he will hold to one and of the other he will be heedless. You are not able to serve *both* God and wealth."

¹⁴And the פְּרוּשִׁים, P'rushiym, being lovers of money, were hearing all these things and were sneering at Him. ¹⁵And He said to them, "You are those declaring yourselves righteous in the sight of men, but God knows your hearts; for that which is high among men IS an abomination before God. ¹⁶The תּוֹרָה, Torah and the prophets ARE *proclaimed* until יוֹחָנָן, Yochanan. Since then, the Reign of God is proclaimed as Good News, and everyone forces *his way* into it. ¹⁷But it is easier for the heaven and the earth to pass away, than for one stroke of the תּוֹרָה, Torah to fall.

¹⁸"Everyone who is sending away his wife and marrying another commits adultery; and he who is marrying her *who was* sent away from a husband commits adultery.

¹⁹"And there was a certain rich man, and *he* was clothed in purple and fine linen, rejoicing *in* sumptuous *living* every day. ²⁰And a certain poor man—אֶלְעָזָר, El'azar by name—was laid at his entrance, full of sores, ²¹and desiring to be filled from what wasª falling from the table of the rich man. Yes, even the dogs were coming *and* licking his sores.

²²"And it came to pass that the poor man died, and that he was carried away by the Messengers to the arms of אַבְרָהָם, Av'raham; and the rich man also died and was buried.

²³"And in שְׁאוֹל, Sh'ol, having lifted up his eyes—being in torments—*the rich man* saw אַבְרָהָם, Av'raham from afar, and אֶלְעָזָר, El'azar in his arms. ²⁴And having cried, he said, 'Father אַבְרָהָם, Av'raham, deal kindly with me and send אֶלְעָזָר, El'azar, so that he may dip the tip of his finger in water and cool my tongue, because I am deeply anguished in this flame.'

²⁵"But אַבְרָהָם, Av'raham said, 'Child, remember that during your life you received your good things, and אֶלְעָזָר, El'azar, likewise, the evil things. But now he is comforted here, and you are deeply anguished. ²⁶And besides all these things, a great chasm is fixed between us and you, so that they who are wanting to go over from here to you are not able, nor from that place do they cross over to us.'

²⁷"And he said, 'I ask you then, father, that you might send him to the house of my father, ²⁸for I have five brothers. *Send him* so that he might thoroughly testify to them, so that they will not also come to this place of torment.'

²⁹"But אַבְרָהָם, Av'raham said, 'They have מֹשֶׁה, Mosheh and the prophets—let them hear them.'

³⁰"And he said, 'No, father אַבְרָהָם, Av'raham, but if anyone from the dead goes to them, they will reform.

³¹"And he said to him, 'If they do not hear מֹשֶׁה, Mosheh and the prophets, neither will they be persuaded if one rises out of the dead.'"

17

¹And He said to His disciples, "It is impossible for the stumbling blocks not to come, but אוֹי, oy! TO HIM through whom they come. ²It is more profitable to him if a millstone is put around his neck and he has been cast into the sea, than that he causes one of these little ones to stumble. ³Be careful for yourselves. If your brother sins,ᵇ rebuke him; and if he reforms, forgive him; ⁴and if seven times in the day he sins against you, and seven times returns to you, saying, 'I reform,' you must forgive him."

⁵And the emissaries said to the Master, "Add faith to us!" ⁶And the Master said, "If you have faith as a grain of mustard, you would have said to this sycamine *tree*, 'Be uprooted and planted in the sea,' and it would have obeyed you.

⁷"But who of you is he—having a slave plowing or feeding *sheep*—who will say to him having come in out of the field,

---

ª "what was"—some mss say, "the crumbs that were"

ᵇ Some mss insert, "in regard to you"

'Having immediately come near, recline (at mealtime)'? ⁸But will *he* not INSTEAD say to him, 'Prepare what I may eat, and having bound clothes around yourself, serve me until I eat and drink, and after these things, you may eat and drink'? ⁹Does he have favor toward the slave because he did the things *he was* directed *to do*?ᵃ ¹⁰So also, when you have done all the things you are directed *to do*, you *should* say, 'We are worthless slaves; *only* that which we owed to do, we have done.'"

¹¹And in going on to יְרוּשָׁלַיִם, Y'rushalayim, it happened that He passed through the middle of שֹׁמְרוֹן, Shom'ron and *the* גָּלִיל, Galiyl. ¹²And *as* He *was* entering into a certain village, ten leprous men, who stood far off, met Him. ¹³And they lifted up the voice, saying, "יֵשׁוּעַ, Yeshua, רַבִּי, Rabiy,ᵇ deal kindly with us!" ¹⁴And He, having seen THEM, said to them, "Having gone on, show yourselves to the כֹּהֲנִים, Ko'haniym." And it came to pass, in their going, *that* they were cleansed.

¹⁵Now one of them, having seen that he was healed, returned *and was* glorifying God with a loud voice, ¹⁶and he fell on HIS face at *Yeshua's* feet, giving thanks to Him; and he was a שֹׁמְרוֹנִי, Shom'roniy. ¹⁷And יֵשׁוּעַ, Yeshua, answering, said, "Were not the ten cleansed? and where *are* the nine Y'hudiym? ¹⁸Were there not *any* found who returned to give glory to God, except this foreigner?" ¹⁹And He said to him, "Having risen, be going on; your faith has saved you."

²⁰And having been questioned by the פְּרוּשִׁים, P'rushiym *about* when the Reign of God will come, He answered them and said, "The Reign of God does not come with observation; ²¹nor will they say, 'Look, here!' or 'There!' for look! the Reign of God is within you."

²²And He said to His disciples, "Days will come when you will desire to see one of the days of the Son of Man, and you will not see IT. ²³And they will say to you, 'Look, there!' or 'Look, here!' *But* do not go away, nor follow. ²⁴For as the lightning flashing out of the one PART under heaven shines to the other part under heaven, so will be the Son of Man in His Day. ²⁵But first it is necessary for Him to suffer many things and to be rejected by this generation. ²⁶And, as it came to pass in the days of נֹחַ, Noach, so will it be also in the days of the Son of Man. ²⁷They were eating *and* they were drinking, they were marrying *and* they were given in marriage, until the day that נֹחַ, Noach entered into the ark and the Flood came and destroyed *them* all. ²⁸Likewise, as it came to pass in the days of לוֹט, Lot: they were eating *and* they were drinking, they were buying *and* they were selling, they were planting *and* they were building; ²⁹but on the day לוֹט, Lot went out from סְדֹם, S'dom, He rained fire and sulfur from heaven and destroyed *them* all. ³⁰According to these things will it be in the day *that* the Son of Man is revealed.

³¹"In that day, he who will be on the house-top, and his property in the house —let him not come down to take them away. And he in the field, likewise—let him not turn backward. ³²Remember the wife of לוֹט, Lot! ³³Whoever seeks to obtain his life will loseᶜ it, but whoever loses it will preserve it. ³⁴I say to you: in that night, there will be two men on one cot; the one will be taken, and the other will be left. ³⁵Two women will be grinding *grain* at the same place together; the one will be taken, and the other will be left."ᵈ

³⁷And answering, they said to Him, "Where, Master?" And He said to them, "Where the body IS, there also will the vulturesᵉ be gathered together."

18

¹And He spoke an analogy to them, *teaching* that they need to always pray and not lose heart, ²saying, "A certain judge was in a certain

---

ᵃ Some mss insert, "I think not."
ᵇ רַבִּי, Rabiy—Greek ἐπιστάτα, epistata; see Luke 5:5
ᶜ lose/loses—ἀπόλλυμι, apollumi, meaning "to kill or destroy"
ᵈ Some mss continue with verse 36, "Two men will be in the field; the one will be taken, and the other left."
ᵉ "vultures" or "eagles"

city—he was not fearing God, and he was not respecting man. ³And a widow was in that city, and she was coming to him, saying, 'Do me justice on my opponent.' ⁴And for a time, he was not willing; but after these things he said in himself, 'Even if I do not fear God nor respect man, ⁵yet because this widow gives me trouble, I will do her justice; otherwise, perpetually coming, she will beat me down.'" ⁶And the Master said, "Hear what the unrighteous judge says. ⁷And will not God execute the justice to His chosen ones who are crying *out* to Him day and night, having patience in regard to them? ⁸I say to you that He will execute the justice to them quickly. But the Son of Man, having come, will He find the faith upon the earth?"

⁹And also to certain *ones* who had been trusting in themselves that they were righteous, and had been treating the remainder with contempt, He spoke this analogy: ¹⁰"Two men went up to the Temple to pray, the one a פָּרוּשׁ, Parush, and the other a tax-gatherer. ¹¹The פָּרוּשׁ, Parush, having stood by himself, prayed this: 'God, I thank You that I am not as the remainder of men—predatory, unrighteous, adulterers—or even as this tax-gatherer. ¹²I fast twice in the week; I give tenths of all things —as many as I possess.' ¹³But the tax-gatherer, having stood far off, would not even lift up the eyes to the heaven, but was striking his chest, saying, 'God, be appeased toward me—the sinner!' ¹⁴I say to you: this one, rather than that *first* one, went down to his house declared righteous *by God*. For everyone who is exalting himself will be humbled, and he who is humbling himself will be exalted."

¹⁵And *the people* were also bringing the babies near to Him, so that He might touch them. And the disciples, having seen *this*, were rebuking *the people*. ¹⁶But יֵשׁוּעַ, Yeshua called *the disciples* near, saying, "Allow the little children to come to Me, and forbid them not, for of such is the Reign of God. ¹⁷אָמֵן, Amen, I say to you, whoever does not receive the Reign of God as a little child will not enter into it."

¹⁸And a certain ruler questioned Him, saying, "Good teacher, what *can I do so that* I will inherit life age-enduring?" ¹⁹And יֵשׁוּעַ, Yeshua said to him, "Why do you call Me good? No one *is* good, except One—God. ²⁰You have known the commands: DO NOT COMMIT ADULTERY, DO NOT MURDER, DO NOT STEAL, DO NOT GIVE FALSE TESTIMONY, HONOR YOUR FATHER AND MOTHER."ᵃ ²¹And he said, "All these I kept from my youth." ²²And having heard, יֵשׁוּעַ, Yeshua said to him, "Yet one thing is lacking to you: all things—as many as you have —sell *them* and distribute *the proceeds* to the poor, and you will have treasure in the Heavens. And come, be following Me." ²³And having heard these things, he became very sorrowful, for he was exceedingly rich.

²⁴Then יֵשׁוּעַ, Yeshua, having seen him,ᵇ said, "How difficultly those having riches enter into the Reign of God! ²⁵For it is easier for a camel to enter through the eye of a needle than for a rich man to enter into the Reign of God." ²⁶And those who heard said, "Then who is able to be saved?" ²⁷And He said, "The things impossible with men are possible with God." ²⁸And כֵּיפָא, Keifaᶜ said, "Look! we, having left our own things, followed You!" ²⁹And He said to them, "אָמֵן, Amen, I say to you that there is not one who left house, or wife, or brothers, or parents, or children for the sake of the Reign of God, ³⁰who will not receive back multifold more in this time, and in the coming age, life age-enduring."

³¹And having taken the Twelve aside, He said to them, "Look! we go up to יְרוּשָׁלַיִם, Y'rushalayim, and all things will be completed—*all things* that have been written through the prophets—to the Son of Man, ³²for He will be handed over to the גּוֹיִם,

---

ᵃ שְׁמוֹת *Sh'mot* 20:12-13(16); דְּבָרִים *D'variym* 5:16-17(20)
ᵇ Some early mss insert, "become very sorrowful"
ᶜ כֵּיפָא, Keifa—Gk: Πέτρος, Petros; see יוֹחָנָן *Yn.* 1:42

Goyim, and will be mocked and insulted and spit upon; ³³and having flogged *Him*, they will put Him to death; and on the third day, He will rise again." ³⁴But they understood none of these things, and this saying was hidden from them, and they were not knowing the things *He* said.

³⁵And it came to pass, in His coming near יְרִיחוֹ, Y'riycho, a certain blind man was sitting beside the road, begging. ³⁶And having heard a crowd going by, he was asking what this might be; ³⁷and they brought word to him that יֵשׁוּעַ הַנָּצְרָתִי, Yeshua Ha-Natz'ratiy passes by. ³⁸And he cried out, saying, "יֵשׁוּעַ, Yeshua, Son of דָּוִד, David! Deal kindly with me!" ³⁹And those going in front of *Him* were rebuking him, so that he would stop talking, but much more he was shouting, "Son of דָּוִד, David! Deal kindly with me!" ⁴⁰And יֵשׁוּעַ, Yeshua, having stood *still*, commanded him to be brought to Him. And having come near, He questioned him, ⁴¹"What do you want *that* I should do to you?" And he said, "Sir, that I may receive sight." ⁴²And יֵשׁוּעַ, Yeshua said to him, "Receive your sight; your faith has saved you." ⁴³And, instantly, he received sight and was following Him, glorifying God. And all the people, having seen, gave praise to God.

19

¹And having entered, He was passing through יְרִיחוֹ, Y'riycho; ²and look! *there was* a man, called by *the* name זַכַּי, Zakai; and he was a chief tax-gatherer; and he was rich. ³And he was looking to see יֵשׁוּעַ, Yeshua—who He was —but was not able because of the crowd, since he was small in stature. ⁴And having run forward to the *place* in front of *Him*, he went up on a sycamore *tree* so that he could see Him, because He was about to pass by that WAY. ⁵And as יֵשׁוּעַ, Yeshua came up to the place, having looked up, He said to him, "זַכַּי, Zakai! Having hurried, come down, for today I must stay in your house." ⁶And he, having hurried, came down and received Him *with* rejoicing.

⁷And having seen IT, all *the people* were grumbling, saying, "He went in to settle down *for the night* with a sinful man!" ⁸And זַכַּי, Zakai, having stood, said to the Master, "Look! The half of my possessions, sir, I *will* give to the poor; and if I took anything of anyone by false accusation, I *will* give back four times *as much*." ⁹And יֵשׁוּעַ, Yeshua said to him, "Today salvation came to this house, inasmuch as he also is a son of אַבְרָהָם, Av'raham; ¹⁰for the Son of Man came to seek and to save the lost."[a]

¹¹And as they were hearing these things, He added *more* and spoke an analogy, *both* because of his being near to יְרוּשָׁלַיִם, Y'rushalayim, and *also because* of their thinking that the Reign of God was about to be instantly brought out into the light. ¹²Therefore He said, "A certain man of *noble* birth went on to a far *away* country, to take to himself a kingdom, and *then* to return. ¹³And having called ten slaves of his own, he gave to them ten mina-coins and said to them, 'Do business *with this* until I come *back*.' ¹⁴*Meanwhile*, his citizens were hating him, and sent a delegation after him, saying, 'We do not want this one to reign over us.'

¹⁵"And having taken the kingdom, it came to pass that on his coming back, he commanded *for* these slaves to whom he had given the money to be called to him, so that he might know what they had done in business.

¹⁶"And the first came near, saying, 'Sir, your mina-coin gained ten mina-coins.' ¹⁷And he said to him, 'Well done, good slave! Because you became faithful in a very little *thing*, be having authority over ten cities.'

¹⁸"And the second came, saying, 'Sir, your mina-coin made five mina-coins.' ¹⁹And he said also to this one, 'And you! You become over five cities.'

²⁰"And another came, saying, 'Sir, look! *here is* your mina-coin that I had lying away in a piece of cloth, ²¹for I was afraid of you, because you are an austere man. You take up what you did not lay down,

---

[a] lost—ἀπόλωλός, apololos, meaning "to kill or destroy"

and reap what you did not sow.' ²²He said to him, 'Out of your *own* mouth I will judge you, evil slave, *for* you knew that I am an austere man, taking up what I did not lay down, and reaping what I did not sow! ²³And *so* why did you not give my money to the bank; and I, having come *back*, would have received it with interest?' ²⁴And to those standing by he said, 'Take the mina-coin from him and give *it* to him having the ten mina-coins,' ²⁵(and they said to him, 'Sir, he *already* has ten mina-coins!') ²⁶'I say to you that to everyone *who is* having, *more* will be given; and from him *who is* not having, also what he has will be taken. ²⁷But these *who are* my enemies, who do not want me to reign over them, bring *them* here and kill them in front of me.'"

²⁸And having said these things, He went on in front of *them*, going up to יְרוּשָׁלַיִם, Y'rushalayim. ²⁹And it came to pass, as He came near to בֵּית־פַּגֵּי, Beit-Pagei and בֵּית־עַנְיָה, Beit-An'yah, *that* He sent two of the disciples to the mountain called "of the Olives," ³⁰saying, "Go away to the opposite village, in which, entering into *it*, you will find a bound colt on which no one of men ever sat. And having untied it, bring IT; ³¹and if anyone questions you, *saying*, "Why do you untie IT?" you will say this: "The Master has need of it."

³²And those *who were* sent, having gone away, found *everything* as He said to them. ³³And while they were untying the colt, its owners said to them, "Why do you untie the colt?" ³⁴And they said, "The Master has need of it." ³⁵And they brought it to יֵשׁוּעַ, Yeshua, and having thrown their garments upon the colt, they set יֵשׁוּעַ, Yeshua upon it. ³⁶And as He was going, they were spreading their garments in the road.

³⁷And as He was now coming near, at the descent of the Mountain of the Olives, the whole crowd of the disciples began rejoicing to praise God with a loud voice for all the powerful acts they had seen, ³⁸saying, "BLESSED IS HE WHO IS COMING, the King, IN THE NAME OF ADONAI![a] Peace in Heaven, and glory in the highest!" ³⁹And certain *ones* of the פְּרוּשִׁים, P'rushiym from the crowd said to him, "Teacher, rebuke your disciples!" ⁴⁰And He, answering, said, "I say to you that if these will be silent, the stones will cry out!"

⁴¹And when He came near, having seen the city, He wept over it, ⁴²saying, "If you *only* knew, even you, in this day,[b] *about* the things for *bringing*[c] peace—but now they are hidden from your eyes. ⁴³For days will come upon you; and your enemies will set up a barricade around you and encompass you and press you on every side ⁴⁴and raze you to the ground, and your children within you; and they will not leave a stone upon a stone in you, because you did not know the time of your inspection."

⁴⁵And having entered into the Temple, He began to drive out those selling,[d] ⁴⁶saying to them, "It has been written, 'MY HOUSE WILL BE A HOUSE OF PRAYER[e]—but you made it a DEN OF ROBBERS!'"[f]

⁴⁷And He was teaching daily in the Temple, but the chief כֹּהֲנִים, Ko'haniym and the סוֹפְרִים, Sof'riym were looking to destroy Him (also the *most* prominent among the people), ⁴⁸but they were not finding what *way* they would do *it*, for all the people were hanging on *His words*, hearing Him.

20

¹And it came to pass on one of the days, as He was teaching the people in the Temple and proclaiming Good News, *that* the chief כֹּהֲנִים, Ko'haniym and the סוֹפְרִים, Sof'riym, *along* with the זְקֵנִים, Z'qeniym, came upon HIM ²and spoke, saying to Him, "Tell us by what authority you do these things? Or who is he that gave this authority to you?" ³And He, answering, said to them,

---

[a] תְּהִלִּים T'hiliym 118:26
[b] "in this day"—some mss say, "at least in this your day"
[c] Some mss insert, "your"
[d] Some mss insert, "in it, and those buying"
[e] יְשַׁעְיָהוּ Y'sha'yahu 56:7
[f] יִרְמְיָהוּ Yir'm'yahu 7:11

Analogy of the vineyard.   Luke 20:33

"I will ask you—I also—a word, and *then you* tell Me: ⁴the immersion of יוֹחָנָן, Yochanan—was it from Heaven, or from men?" ⁵And they reasoned with themselves, saying, "If we should say, 'From Heaven,' he will say, 'Why did you not believe him?' ⁶and if we should say, 'From men,' all the people will stone us, for they are having been persuaded *to believe* יוֹחָנָן, Yochanan to be a prophet." ⁷And they answered that they knew not where IT WAS from. ⁸And יֵשׁוּעַ, Yeshua said to them, "Neither do I say to you by what authority I do these things."

⁹And He began to speak this analogy to the people: "A certain man planted a vineyard, and gave it out to *tenant* farmers, and *then* went abroad for a long time. ¹⁰And at the *harvest* season, he sent a slave to the farmers, so that they would give to him from the fruit of the vineyard. But the farmers, having beat him, sent HIM away empty. ¹¹And he additionally sent another slave *to the farmers*; and they, having beaten and dishonored that one also, sent *him* away empty. ¹²And he additionally sent a third *slave*; and this one also, having wounded *him*, they threw out. ¹³And the owner of the vineyard said, 'What will I do? I will send my son—the beloved. Perhaps this one they will respect.' ¹⁴But having seen him, the farmers reasoned with one another, saying, 'This is the heir. We should kill him, so that the inheritance might become ours.' ¹⁵And having thrown him outside of the vineyard, they killed HIM. What, then, will the owner of the vineyard do to them? ¹⁶He will come and destroy these farmers, and will give the vineyard to others." And having heard *this*, they said, "Let it not be!" ¹⁷And He, having looked upon them, said, "What, then, is *the meaning of* this that has been written:

'A stone that the builders rejected—
this became head of a corner'ᵃ?

¹⁸Everyone who has fallen on that stone will be broken; and him on whom it falls, it will crush him to pieces."

¹⁹And the סוֹפְרִים, Sof'riym and the chief כֹּהֲנִים, Ko'haniym sought to lay hands on Him in that moment, but they feared the people, for they knew that He spoke this analogy against them.

²⁰And having watched HIM, they sent spies, themselves pretending to be righteous, so that they might take hold of His word, so as to deliver Him up to the rule and the authority of the governor. ²¹And they questioned Him, saying, "Teacher, we have known that you say and teach rightly, and do not show favoritism, but teach the way of God in truth: ²²is it permitted for us to give tribute to Cæsar or not?" ²³And He, having perceived their craftiness, said to them,ᵇ ²⁴"Show me a denary-*coin*. Of whom does it have an image and inscription?" And they said, "Of Cæsar." ²⁵And He said to them, "Therefore, give back the things of Cæsar to Cæsar, and the things of God to God." ²⁶And they were not able to seize upon His saying in front of the people; and having *been* in wonder at His answer, they stopped talking.

²⁷And certain *ones* of the צָדוֹקִים, Tzadu-qiym—who are denying that there is a Rising Again—having come near, questioned Him, ²⁸saying, "Teacher, מֹשֶׁה, Mosheh wrote to us, 'IF ANYONE'S BROTHER DIES, having a wife, AND THIS ONE IS CHILDLESS, IT MUST BE THAT HIS BROTHER TAKES THE WIFE, AND RAISES UP SEED TO HIS BROTHER.'ᶜ ²⁹There were, then, seven brothers; and the first, having taken a wife, died childless. ³⁰And the secondᵈ ³¹and the third took her, and likewise also the seven—they left no children, and they died. ³²And last, the woman also died. ³³The woman,

---

ᵃ תְּהִלִּים *T'hiliym* 118:22

ᵇ Some mss insert, "Why do you tempt me?"; cf. מַתִּתְיָהוּ *Matit'yahu* 22:18 and Mark 12:15
ᶜ דְּבָרִים *D'variym* 25:5
ᵈ Some mss insert, "took the wife, and he died childless"

then—in the Rising Again, of which of them does she become wife? for the seven *all* had her as a wife." ³⁴And יֵשׁוּעַ, Yeshua said to them, "The sons of this age marry and are given in marriage, ³⁵but those counted worthy to obtain that age, and the Rising Again that is out of the dead, neither marry, nor are they given in marriage. ³⁶For neither are they able to die anymore, for they are like Messengers; and they are sons of God, being sons of the Rising Again. ³⁷And even מֹשֶׁה, Mosheh showed at the Bush that the dead are raised, since he calls ADONAI the God of אַבְרָהָם, Av'raham, and the God of יִצְחָק, Yitz'chaq, and the God of יַעֲקֹב, Ya'aqov. ³⁸And He is not a God of dead men, but of living—for all live to Him." ³⁹And certain *ones* of the סוֹפְרִים, Sof'riym, answering, said, "Teacher, you said *it* well," ⁴⁰for they no longer dared question Him *on* anything.

⁴¹And He said to them, "How do they say the Messiah to be son of דָּוִד, David, ⁴²since[a] דָּוִד, David himself says in the Book of תְּהִלִּים, T'hiliym,

'ADONAI said to my Master, "Sit at my right hand ⁴³until I make your enemies your footstool."'[b]

⁴⁴דָּוִד, David, then, calls Him 'Master'—and how is He his son?"

⁴⁵And *with* all the people hearing, He said to His disciples, ⁴⁶"Be careful of the סוֹפְרִים, Sof'riym, who are wanting to walk *around* in long robes, and are loving greetings in the markets—also *the* most important seats in the synagogues, and *the* prime seating at the suppers—⁴⁷who devour the houses of the widows, and make long prayers for a pretense, *for* these will receive more abundant judgment."

21

¹And having looked up, He saw those rich men who threw their gifts into the *Temple* treasury, ²and He saw a certain poor widow throwing *in* two very small coins there. ³And He said, "אָמֵן, Amen, I say to you that this poor widow threw in more than all; ⁴for all these *people* threw in the gifts out of their superabundance, but this one threw in—out of her want—all the living that she had."

⁵And certain *ones were* saying about the Temple that it had been adorned with fine stones and devoted things. He said, ⁶"These things that you see—days will come in which there will not be a stone left upon a stone that will not be thrown down."

⁷And they questioned Him, saying, "Teacher, when, then, will these things be? And what IS the sign when these things will be about to happen?"

⁸And He said, "See *that* you are not led astray, for many will come in My Name saying, 'I am HE,' and, 'The time has come near.' Do not go after them. ⁹And when you hear of wars and uprisings, be not terrified, *for* it is necessary for these things to happen first—but the end IS not immediately." ¹⁰Then He said to them, "גּוֹי, Goy will rise against גּוֹי, goy, and kingdom against kingdom. ¹¹There will also be massive shakings, and in every place famines and pestilences; there will also be fearful things, and great signs from heaven.

¹²"But before all these *happen*, they will lay their hands on you and persecute *you*, handing *you* over to the synagogues and *the* prisons, *and* bringing *you* before kings and governors for My Name's sake. ¹³It will become a testimony for you. ¹⁴Settle, then, in your hearts, not to meditate beforehand *how* to reply, ¹⁵for I will give to you a mouth and wisdom that all your opposers will not be able to resist or refute.

¹⁶"And you will be handed over even by parents and brothers and relatives and friends, and they will put *some* of you to death. ¹⁷And you will be hated by all because of My Name. ¹⁸But not a hair out of your head will be destroyed; ¹⁹in your perseverance you obtain your souls.

²⁰"And when you see יְרוּשָׁלַיִם, Y'rushalayim surrounded by *army* encampments,

---

[a] "since"—some mss say, "and"
[b] תְּהִלִּים T'hiliym 110:1

then know that her desolation has come near. ²¹Then those in יְהוּדָה, Y'hudah, let them flee to the mountains; and those in her midst, let them depart from *there*; and those in the countrysides, let them not enter into her, ²²because these are days of vengeance, to fulfill all things that have been written.

²³"אוֹי, Oy! to those pregnant *mothers*, and to those nursing in those days, for there will be great distress upon the Land, and wrath to this people. ²⁴And they will fall by the mouth of the sword and will be led captive to all the גּוֹיִם, Goyim, and יְרוּשָׁלַיִם, Y'rushalayim will be trampled underfoot by גּוֹיִם, Goyim, until the times of גּוֹיִם, Goyim are fulfilled.

²⁵"And there will be signs in *the* sun and moon and stars; and on the Land WILL BE distress of גּוֹיִם, Goyim, with perplexity *at the* roaring of *the* sea and waves, ²⁶*and* men fainting at heart from fear and expectation of the things coming on the world, for the powers of the heavens will be shaken.

²⁷"And then they will see the Son of Man coming in a cloud with power and much glory; ²⁸and *when* these things *are* beginning to happen, bend yourselves back and lift up your heads, because your redemption draws near."

²⁹And He spoke an analogy to them: "See the fig-tree and all the trees. ³⁰When they now shoot forth, having seen, you know of yourselves that the summer is now near. ³¹So also you, when you see these things happening, you know that the Reign of God is near. ³²אָמֵן, Amen, I say to you: this generation will not pass away until all will have come to pass; ³³the heaven and the earth will pass away, but My words will not pass away.

³⁴"And be careful of yourselves, otherwise your hearts may be weighed down with crapulence[a] and drunkenness and *the* anxieties of life, and that day will come on you suddenly; ³⁵for it will come as a snare on all those dwelling on the face of all the land *of the earth*. ³⁶So be alert in every season, praying that you may have strength[b] to escape all these things that are about to come to pass, and to stand before the Son of Man."

³⁷And during the days, He was teaching in the Temple; and during the nights, going out, He was spending the night at the mountain called "of the Olives"; ³⁸and all the people were coming early *in the morning* to Him in the Temple to hear Him.

22

¹Now חַג הַמַּצּוֹת, Chag HaMatzot, which is *also widely* called פֶּסַח, Pesach, was coming near, ²and the chief כֹּהֲנִים, Ko'haniym and the סוֹפְרִים, Sof'riym were looking for how they might put Him to death, for they were afraid of the people.

³And הַשָּׂטָן, HaSatan entered into יְהוּדָה, Y'hudah, who is called אִישׁ־קְרִיּוֹת, Iysh-Q'riyot, being of the number of the Twelve. ⁴And having gone away, he spoke with the chief כֹּהֲנִים, Ko'haniym and captains *of the Temple guard about* how he might hand Him over to them. ⁵And they rejoiced and covenanted to give him money, ⁶and he agreed and was looking for an opportune moment to hand Him over to them without drawing a crowd.

⁷And the day *before the Feast* of הַמַּצּוֹת, HaMatzot came, in which it was necessary for the פֶּסַח, Pesach to be sacrificed,[c] ⁸and He sent כֵּיפָא, Keifa[d] and יוֹחָנָן, Yochanan, saying, "Having gone on, prepare the פֶּסַח, Pesach for us, so that we may eat *it*." ⁹And they said to Him, "Where would you *like* that we should prepare *it*?"

¹⁰And He said to them, "Look! in your entering into the city, a man carrying a pitcher of water will meet you. Follow him into the house into which he goes in; ¹¹and you will say to the master of the house, 'The Teacher says to you: where is the guestroom where I may eat the פֶּסַח, Pesach with

---

[a] "crapulence"—κραιπάλη, kraipale, that is, "the giddiness and headache caused by drinking wine to excess" (Thayer).
[b] "may have strength"—some mss "may be counted worthy"
[c] cf. וַיִּקְרָא *Vy.* 23:5-6, מַתִּתְיָהוּ *Mt.* 26:17, Mark 14:12
[d] כֵּיפָא, Keifa—Gk: Πέτρος, Petros; see יוֹחָנָן *Yn.* 1:42

my disciples?' ¹²and he will show you a large, furnished upper room. Make ready there." ¹³So having gone away, they found *everything* as He had said to them, and they made ready the פֶּסַח, Pesach.

¹⁴And when the time came, He reclined (at mealtime), and the emissaries with Him. ¹⁵And He said to them, "With desire I desired to eat this פֶּסַח, Pesach with you before My suffering, ¹⁶for I say to you that I will eat of it no more[a] until it is fulfilled in the Reign of God." ¹⁷And having taken a cup, having given thanks *to God*, He said, "Take this and divide *it* among yourselves, ¹⁸for I say to you that from now on[b] I will not drink of the fruit of the vine until the Reign of God comes." ¹⁹And having taken *matzah* bread, having given thanks *to God*, He broke *it* and gave *it* to them, saying, "This is My body that is being given for you; do this to *the* remembrance of Me." ²⁰He *did* likewise, also, *with* the cup after the eating, saying, "This cup *is* the בְּרִית הַחֲדָשָׁה, B'riyt Ha'Chadashah in My blood that is being poured out for you.

²¹"But look! the hand of him *who is* handing Me over *is* with Me on the table, ²²because, indeed, the Son of Man goes according to what has been determined, but אוֹי, oy! to that man through whom He is being handed over." ²³And they began to reason among themselves, *wondering* who of them, then, it might be who was about to do this thing.

²⁴And a dispute also happened among them: who of them is deemed to be greater. ²⁵And He said to them, "The kings of the גּוֹיִם, Goyim lord it over them, and those exercising authority on them are called 'benefactors,' ²⁶but you ARE not so. Rather, he who is greater among you—let him be as the younger; and he who is leading, as he who is serving. ²⁷For who is greater? He who is reclining (at mealtime), or he who is serving? Is it not he who is reclining (at mealtime)? And I—I am

in your midst as He who is serving; ²⁸and you—you are those who have remained with Me in my testings. ²⁹And I appoint to you, as My Father appointed to Me, a kingdom, ³⁰so that you may eat and drink at My table in My kingdom, and will sit on thrones, judging the twelve tribes of יִשְׂרָאֵל, Yis'rael.[c]

³¹"שִׁמְעוֹן שִׁמְעוֹן, Shim'on Shim'on, look! הַשָּׂטָן, HaSatan asked to sift you as the wheat for himself, ³²but I implored for you, so that your faith may not fail. And you, when you have turned, strengthen your brothers." ³³And he said to Him, "Master, I am ready to go with You both to prison and to death!" ³⁴And He said, "I say to you, כֵּיפָא, Keifa,[d] a rooster will not crow today, until you deny knowing me three times."

³⁵And He said to them, "When I sent you without money sack and bag and sandals, did you lack anything?" and they said, "Nothing." ³⁶And He said to them, "But now, he who is having a money sack, let him take IT up, and likewise also a bag; and he who is not having, let him sell his coat and buy a sword. ³⁷For I say to you that this that has been written must be fulfilled in Me:

'And he was counted with *the* wrongdoing ones.'[e]

For the things regarding Me also have a goal." ³⁸And they said, "Master, look! here ARE two swords," and He said to them, "It is sufficient."

³⁹And having gone out, He went on, according to *His* custom, to the Mountain of the Olives, and the disciples also followed Him. ⁴⁰And having come to the place, He said to them, "Pray to not enter into temptation."

⁴¹And He withdrew about a stone's throw from them; and having fallen on the knees,

---

[a] "eat of it no more"—earliest mss say, "not eat it"
[b] Some mss omit, "from now on"
[c] Some mss begin the next verse with "And the Master said,"
[d] כֵּיפָא, Keifa—Gk: Πέτρος, Petros; see יוֹחָנָן Yn. 1:42; also verses 54, 55, 58, 60, 61 and 62
[e] יְשַׁעְיָהוּ Y'sha'yahu 53:12

He was praying, ⁴²saying, "Father, if You are intending to, make this cup pass from me; yet, not my will, but Yours be done." [⁴³And there appeared to Him a Messenger from Heaven, strengthening Him. ⁴⁴And having been in agony, He was praying more intensely, and His sweat became like great drops of blood falling upon the ground.]ᵃ ⁴⁵And *when He* had risen up from the prayer, having come to the disciples, He found them sleeping from the sorrow, ⁴⁶and He said to them, "Why do you sleep? Having risen, pray that you may not enter into temptation!"

⁴⁷While He was speaking, look! a crowd *came*; and he who is called יְהוּדָה, Y'hudah, one of the Twelve, was coming ahead *of* them; and he came near to יֵשׁוּעַ, Yeshua to kiss Him. ⁴⁸And יֵשׁוּעַ, Yeshua said to him, "יְהוּדָה, Y'hudah, do you hand over the Son of Man with a kiss?"

⁴⁹And those around Him, having seen what was about to be, said, "Master, should we strike with the sword?" ⁵⁰And a certain one of them struck the slave of the כֹּהֵן הַגָּדוֹל, Kohen HaGadol and took off his right ear. ⁵¹But יֵשׁוּעַ, Yeshua, answering, said, "You *are only* allowed this far," and having touched the ear, He healed him.

⁵²And יֵשׁוּעַ, Yeshua said to those having come upon Him (*the* chief כֹּהֲנִים, Ko'haniym and captains of the Temple and זְקֵנִים, Z'qeniym), "Did you come out with swords and sticks as upon a robber? ⁵³While I was with you daily in the Temple, you stretched out no hands against Me, but this is your hour and the power of the darkness." ⁵⁴And having taken Him, they led *Him away* and brought Him to the house of the כֹּהֵן הַגָּדוֹל, Kohen HaGadol. And כֵּיפָא, Keifa was following from afar, ⁵⁵and when they had kindled a fire in the middle of the courtyard and had sat down together, כֵּיפָא, Keifa was sitting in the middle of them. ⁵⁶And a certain slave-girl, having seen him sitting in the light, and having fixed her gaze on him, said, "And this one was with Him!" ⁵⁷but he denied *it*,ᵇ saying, "I have not known Him, woman!" ⁵⁸And after a little *while*, another, having seen him, said, "And you are *one* of them!" and כֵּיפָא, Keifa said, "Man, I am not." ⁵⁹And *after* about one hour having passed, a certain other was confidently affirming, saying, "Of a truth, this one also was with Him, for he is also a גְּלִילִי, G'liyliy"; ⁶⁰and כֵּיפָא, Keifa said, "Man, I have not known what you say." And instantly, while he was speaking, a rooster crowed. ⁶¹And the Master, having turned, looked on כֵּיפָא, Keifa, and כֵּיפָא, Keifa remembered the saying of the Master, how He said to him, "Before a rooster crows today, you will deny Me three times." ⁶²And having gone outside, he wept bitterly.

⁶³And the men who were holding יֵשׁוּעַ, Yeshua were mocking Him, beating *Him*; ⁶⁴and having blindfolded Him, theyᶜ were questioning Him, saying, "Prophesy! Who is he who struck you?" ⁶⁵And they spoke many other things, speaking evilly, in regard to Him.

⁶⁶And when it became day, the Council of זְקֵנִים, Z'qeniym of the people were gathered together there—also *the* chief כֹּהֲנִים, Ko'haniym and סוֹפְרִים, Sof'riym—and they led Him away to their own Sanhedrin, ⁶⁷saying, "If you are the Messiah, tell us." And He said to them, "If I tell you, you will not believe; ⁶⁸and if I question *you*, you will not answer.ᵈ ⁶⁹But from now on, there will be the Son of Man SITTING AT THE RIGHT HAND of the power OF GOD."ᵉ ⁷⁰And they all said, "Are you, then, the Son of God?" And He said to them, "You say *it*, because I am"; ⁷¹and they said, "What further need have we for testimony? Indeed, we ourselves heard *it* from his mouth."

23
¹And having arisen, the whole crowd of them led Him to Pilate ²and began to accuse Him,

---

ᵃ bracketed text not in earliest, most reliable mss
ᵇ "*it*"—some mss say, "Him"
ᶜ Some mss insert, "were striking Him on the face, and"
ᵈ Some mss insert, "Me, or release Me"
ᵉ תְּהִלִּים T'hiliym 110:1

saying, "We found this one corrupting our ethnic-group, and forbidding *people* to give taxes to Cæsar, and saying himself to be Messiah, a king!"

³And Pilate questioned Him, saying, "Are you the king of the Jews?" and He, answering him, said, "*As you say IT*." ⁴And Pilate said to the chief כֹּהֲנִים, Ko'haniym and the crowd, "I find no fault in this man"; ⁵but they were *all* the more urgent, saying, "He stirs up the people, teaching throughout the whole of יְהוּדָה, Y'hudah—having begun from the גָּלִיל, Galiyl—even into this place." ⁶And Pilate, having heard,[a] questioned if the man is a גְּלִילִי, G'liyliy. ⁷And having known that he is from the jurisdiction of Herod, he sent him back to Herod, he also being in יְרוּשָׁלַיִם, Y'rushalayim in those days.

⁸And Herod, having seen יֵשׁוּעַ, Yeshua, rejoiced exceedingly. Indeed, he had been wanting for a long time to see Him because of hearing about Him, and he was hoping to see some *miraculous* sign done by Him. ⁹And *he* was questioning Him in many words, but He answered him nothing. ¹⁰And the chief כֹּהֲנִים, Ko'haniym and the סוֹפְרִים, Sof'riym stood *there* vehemently accusing Him, ¹¹but Herod—with his soldiers also—having treated Him with contempt, and having mocked *Him, and* having wrapped bright clothing around Him, sent Him back to Pilate. ¹²(And both Herod and Pilate became friends with one another on that day, for before *this* they were hostile between themselves.)

¹³And Pilate, having called together the chief כֹּהֲנִים, Ko'haniym and the rulers and the people, ¹⁴said to them, "You brought this man to me as *one* turning away the people, and look! having examined *him* in your sight, I found no fault in this man in *regard to* those things you brought forward against him. ¹⁵No, neither *did* Herod, for he sent him back to us;[b] and look! nothing worthy of death is having been done by him. ¹⁶Therefore, having disci-plined *him*, I will release him."[c] ¹⁸And they cried out—all together—saying, "Away with this one, and release בַּר־אַבָּא, Bar-Aba to us!" ¹⁹(who, because of a certain insurrection made in the city, and *because of* murder, had been thrown into prison).

²⁰And Pilate again, wanting to release יֵשׁוּעַ, Yeshua, called to them; ²¹but they were calling out, saying, "Crucify, crucify him!" ²²And he said to them a third time, "Why? What evil did he do? I find no cause for death in him. Having disciplined him, then, I will release *HIM*." ²³But they were pressing *him* with loud voices, asking *for* Him to be crucified, and their voices[d] were prevailing.

²⁴And *so* Pilate gave judgment for their request being done, ²⁵and he released him who, because of insurrection and murder, had been thrown into prison—*the one for* whom they were asking—and he gave up יֵשׁוּעַ, Yeshua to their will.

²⁶And as they led Him away, having taken hold on שִׁמְעוֹן, Shim'on—a certain Cyrenian coming from the field—they put the *execution* stake on him, to carry *IT* behind יֵשׁוּעַ, Yeshua.

²⁷And following Him was a large crowd of the people, and of women who were beating themselves and mourning Him. ²⁸And יֵשׁוּעַ, Yeshua, having turned to them, said, "Daughters of יְרוּשָׁלַיִם, Y'rushalayim, weep not for Me, but weep for yourselves and for your children; ²⁹for look! days will come in which they will say, 'Happy *are* the barren, and the wombs that did not bring forth, and breasts that did not nurse.' ³⁰Then they will begin to say to the mountains, 'Fall on us,' and to the hills, 'Cover us.' ³¹For, if they do these things *when the* tree *is* in the green, what will happen *when it is* in the dry?"

³²And there were also others—two evildoers—*brought* with Him to be put to

---

[a] Some mss insert, "of *the* גָּלִיל, Galiyl"

[b] "he sent him back to us"—some mss say, "I sent you back to him"

[c] Some mss continue with verse 17, "for it was necessary for him to release to them one *prisoner* at every Feast."

[d] Some mss insert, "and those of the chief כֹּהֲנִים, Ko'haniym"

death. ³³And when they came to the place that is called Skull, there they crucified Him (and *also* the evil-doers—one on the right hand, and one on the left). ³⁴And [יֵשׁוּעַ, Yeshua said, "Father, forgive them, for they have not known what they do"; and]ᵃ they cast lots, dividing up His garments.

³⁵And the people were standing *there* looking on. And the rulers also were sneering, saying, "He saved others, let him save himself—if this is the Messiah, the Chosen One of God!" ³⁶And the soldiers also mocked Him, coming near, and offering *wine* vinegar to Him, ³⁷and saying, "If you are the king of the Jews, save yourself!" ³⁸And there was also an inscription *written* over Him:ᵇ "This is the King of the Jews."

³⁹And one of the evil-doers who had been hung *there* was speaking evil of Him, saying, "Are you not the Messiah? Save yourself and us!" ⁴⁰But the other, answering *and* rebuking him, said, "Do you not even fear God, that you are in the same judgment? ⁴¹And we, indeed, righteously *so*, for we receive back things worthy of what we did. But this one did nothing out of place." ⁴²And he said, "יֵשׁוּעַ, Yeshua, remember meᶜ when You come into Your Reign"; ⁴³and He said to him, "אָמֵן, Amen, I say to you: today you will be with Me in the Paradise."

⁴⁴And it was now about the sixth hour; and darkness came over all the land until the ninth hour, ⁴⁵the sun having failed;ᵈ and the curtain of the Temple was split in the middle. ⁴⁶And having called out with a loud voice, יֵשׁוּעַ, Yeshua said, "Father, to Your hands I commit my רוּחַ, ruach!" And having said this, He breathed outᵉ *His last*.

⁴⁷And the centurion, having seen what was done, was glorifying God, saying, "Really, this man was righteous." ⁴⁸And all the crowds who had come together for this spectacle, having seen the things that came to pass, returned *home* hitting their chests. ⁴⁹And all His acquaintances, and *the* women who followed Him from the גָּלִיל, Galiyl, stood far off, seeing these things.

⁵⁰And look! *there was* a man by *the* name *of* יוֹסֵף, Yosef—being a Councilman, and a good and righteous man ⁵¹(he was not consenting to their decision and deed) from הָרָמָתַיִם, HaRamatayim (a city of the יְהוּדִים, Y'hudiym)—who was expecting the Reign of God. ⁵²This one, having gone near to Pilate, asked *for* the body of יֵשׁוּעַ, Yeshua. ⁵³And having taken it down, he wrapped it in fine linen and placed Him in a tomb cut out *of stone*, where no one had yet been laid.

⁵⁴And the day was a Preparation *Day*, and שַׁבָּת, Shabat was approaching, ⁵⁵and the women who had come with Him out of the גָּלִיל, Galiyl, having followed after *Him*, noticed the tomb and how His body was placed *in it*. ⁵⁶And having returned, they made ready spices and ointments; and on the שַׁבָּת, Shabat, indeed, they rested according to the command.

24

¹And on the first *day* of the week,ᶠ at early dawn, they came to the tomb, carrying the spices they made ready;ᵍ ²but they found the stone having been rolled away from the tomb! ³And having gone in, they did not find the body of the Master יֵשׁוּעַ, Yeshua.

⁴And while they were perplexed about this, it came to pass that look! two men stood by them in clothing gleaming like lightning. ⁵And upon their having become afraid and having inclined the faces to the ground, *the men* said to them, "Why do you look for the living among the dead? ⁶He is not here, but was raised! Remember how He spoke to you *while* still being in the גָּלִיל, Galiyl, ⁷saying, 'It is necessary for the Son of Man to be handed over to the hands of sinful men, and to be crucified, and the third day to rise again.'" ⁸And they remem-

---

ᵃ bracketed text not in earliest, most reliable mss
ᵇ Some mss insert, "in letters of Greek, and Latin, and Hebrew"
ᶜ Some mss insert, "Master"
ᵈ "having failed"—some mss say, "was darkened"
ᵉ "breathed out"—Young's says, "breathed forth the spirit"

ᶠ "week"—lit. שַׁבָּתוֹת, shabatot
ᵍ Some mss insert, "and certain *others* with them"

Luke 24:9 — Messiah at Emmaus

bered His sayings; ⁹and having returned from the tomb, *they* told all these things to the Eleven, and to all the remaining *ones*.

¹⁰And it was מִרְיָם הַמַּגְדָּלִית, Mir'yam HaMag'daliyt, and יוֹחָנָה, Yochanah, and מִרְיָם, Mir'yam the *mother* of יַעֲקֹב, Ya'aqov, and the other women with them who told these things to the emissaries. ¹¹And these sayings appeared in their sight as nonsense, and they were not believing them. ¹²But כֵּיפָא, Keifa,ᵃ having arisen, ran to the tomb. And having stooped down, he saw the linen clothes alone, and he went away to his own home in wonder at that which was come to pass.

¹³And look! two of them were going on during that day to a village seven milesᵇ distant from יְרוּשָׁלַיִם, Y'rushalayim (the name of which IS Emmaus), ¹⁴and they were conversing with one another about all these things that had happened.

¹⁵And in their conversing and reasoning together, it came to pass that יֵשׁוּעַ, Yeshua Himself, having come near, was going on with them; ¹⁶but their eyes were taken hold of, so as not to know *it was* Him. ¹⁷And He said to them, "What ARE these words that you exchange with one another, walking *along*?" And they stood *there* with a sad look,ᶜ ¹⁸and one by *the* name *of* Cleopas, answering, said to Him, "Are you alone such a stranger in יְרוּשָׁלַיִם, Y'rushalayim that you have not known *of* the things that came to pass in it in these days?" ¹⁹And He said to them, "What things?" And they said to Him, "The things about יֵשׁוּעַ הַנָּצְרָתִי, Yeshua HaNatz'ratiy, who became a man—a prophet—powerful in action and word before God and all the people—²⁰how also the chief כֹּהֲנִים, Ko'haniym and our rulers handed Him over to a judgment of death and crucified Him! ²¹And we were hoping that it is He who is about to redeem יִשְׂרָאֵל, Yis'rael. Not only (*along* with all these things) *is* this *the* third day passing since these things happened, ²²but also certain *ones* of our women astonished us: coming early to the tomb, ²³and not having found His body, they came *to us*, saying also to have seen a vision of Messengers who say He is alive. ²⁴And certain *ones* of those with us went away to the tomb and found *it* even as the women said, but Him they did not see."

²⁵And He said to them, "O unthinking and slow in heart to believe on all that the prophets spoke! ²⁶Was it not necessary for the Messiah to suffer these things, and to enter into His glory?" ²⁷And having begun from מֹשֶׁה, Mosheh, and from all the prophets, He expounded to them in all the Scriptures the things about Himself.

²⁸And they came near to the village where they were going, and He gave the impressionᵈ of going on further, ²⁹but they constrained Him, saying, "Remain with us, for it is toward evening, and the day has now declined," and He went in to stay with them.

³⁰And it came to pass in His reclining (at mealtime) with them, *that* having taken the *matzah* bread, He blessed *it*. And having broken *the matzah*, He was giving *it* to them, ³¹and their eyes were opened, and they recognized Him, and He became unseen byᵉ them. ³²And they said to one another, "Was not our heart burning within us as He was speaking to us on the road, as He was opening up the Scriptures to us?"

³³And having risen up that same hour, they returned to יְרוּשָׁלַיִם, Y'rushalayim and found the Eleven gathered together, and those with them, ³⁴saying, "The Master was really raised and was seen by שִׁמְעוֹן, Shim'on!" ³⁵And they were telling *about* the things on the road, and how He was made known to them in the breaking of the *matzah* bread.

ᵃ כֵּיפָא, Keifa—Gk: Πέτρος, Petros; see יוֹחָנָן Yn. 1:42
ᵇ "seven miles"—literally, "sixty stadia"
ᶜ "'walking *along*?' And they stood *there* with a sad look"—some mss say, "walking *along*, and you are sad?"
ᵈ "gave the impression"—Young's says, "made an appearance"
ᵉ "unseen by" or "invisible to"

The ascension.   **Acts 1:6**

36 And as they were speaking these things, He Himself stood in the middle of them and said to them, "שָׁלוֹם עֲלֵכֶם, Shalom 'alekhem." 37 And being amazed and becoming frightened, they were thinking themselves to *be* see*ing* a רוּחַ, ruach. 38 And He said to them, "Why are you troubled? And why do reasonings come up in your hearts? 39 See *by* My hands and My feet that I am He. Touch Me and see, because a רוּחַ, ruach does not have flesh and bones as you see Me having." 40 And having said this, He showed the hands and the feet to them.

41 And while they were not believing from the joy *of it all* and *were still* in wonder, He said to them, "Do you have anything here to eat?" 42 and they gave part of a broiled fish[a] to Him. 43 And having taken *it,* He ate *it* in their sight; 44 and He said to them, "These ARE My words that I spoke to you *while* still being with you, that it is necessary for all the things that are written about Me in the תּוֹרַת, Torah *of* מֹשֶׁה, Mosheh and the נְבִיאִים, N'viyiym and the תְּהִלִים, T'hiliym to be fulfilled."

[a] Some mss insert, "and of a honeycomb"

45 Then He opened up their understanding to understand the Scriptures. 46 And He said to them, "So it has been written:[b] the Messiah *is* to suffer, and to rise out of the dead the third day; 47 and reformation toward[c] release of sins *is* to be proclaimed in His Name to all *of* the world-ethnicities, beginning from יְרוּשָׁלַיִם, Y'rushalayim. 48 You are witnesses of these things.

49 "And look! I send the promise of My Father upon you, but you *are to* sit in the city until you are clothed with power from on high."

50 And He led them outside as far as to בֵּית־עֲנָיָה, Beit-An'yah, and having lifted up His hands, He blessed them. 51 And it came to pass in His blessing them *that* He was parted from them and was carried up to the heaven.

52 And they, having bowed before Him, returned to יְרוּשָׁלַיִם, Y'rushalayim with great joy, 53 and were continually in the Temple, blessing God.[d]

[b] Some mss insert, "and it was necessary *that* in this way"
[c] "toward"—some mss say, "and"
[d] "blessing God"—some mss say, "praising and blessing God. אָמֵן, Amen."

Acts

OF THE EMISSARIES

1

1 I, indeed, made the former account, O Theophilus, regarding all *the* things that יֵשׁוּעַ, Yeshua began both to do and to teach, 2 until the day in which He was taken up, *after* having given command through the רוּחַ הַקֹּדֶשׁ, Ruach HaQodesh to the emissaries whom He picked out, 3 to whom He also presented Himself alive after His suffering—in many convincing proofs, being seen by them through *the* forty days, and speaking the things regarding the Reign of God.

~ c. A.D. 30 ~

4 And being gathered together, He commanded them not to separate from יְרוּשָׁלַיִם, Y'rushalayim, but to wait for the promise of the Father, which, HE SAID, "you heard from Me; 5 because יוֹחָנָן, Yochanan, indeed, immersed with water, but you will be immersed with the רוּחַ הַקֹּדֶשׁ, Ruach HaQodesh—after not many days."

6 They, therefore, indeed, having come together, were asking Him, saying, "Master, do You at this time restore the Reign

to יִשְׂרָאֵל, Yis'rael?" ⁷And He said to them, "It is not yours to know times or seasons that the Father appointed in His own authority; ⁸but you will receive power at the coming upon you of the רוּחַ הַקֹּדֶשׁ, Ruach HaQodesh, and you will be My witnesses both in יְרוּשָׁלַיִם, Y'rushalayim, and in all יְהוּדָה, Y'hudah and שֹׁמְרוֹן, Shom'ron, and *even* to the end of the earth."

⁹And *after* having said these things, while they were looking, He was lifted up, and a cloud took Him up from their sight. ¹⁰And as they were fixing their gaze to the heaven in His going on, then look! two men in white clothing stood by them, ¹¹who also said, "Men, גְּלִילִים, G'liyliym, why do you stand looking into the heaven? This יֵשׁוּעַ, Yeshua, who was taken up from you into the heaven, will come in just the same way you saw Him going on to the heaven."

¹²Then they returned to יְרוּשָׁלַיִם, Y'rushalayim from the Mountain that is called "of Olives," that is near יְרוּשָׁלַיִם, Y'rushalayim, a שַׁבָּת, Shabat *day's* journey *away*. ¹³And when they came in, they went up to the upper room where *they* were staying—not only כֵּיפָא, Keifa[a] and יוֹחָנָן, Yochanan, but also יַעֲקֹב, Ya'aqov and Andrew, Philip and תּוֹמָא, Toma, בַּר־תַּלְמַי, Bar-Tal'mai and מַתִּתְיָהוּ, Matit'yahu, יַעֲקֹב, Ya'aqov *the son of* חַלְפַּי, Chal'fai and שִׁמְעוֹן, Shim'on the Zealot, and יְהוּדָה, Y'hudah *the son of* יַעֲקֹב, Ya'aqov. ¹⁴These were all continuing with one mind in prayer,[b] with *the* women, and מִרְיָם, Mir'yam the mother of יֵשׁוּעַ, Yeshua, and His brothers.

¹⁵And in these days, כֵּיפָא, Keifa, having risen up in the middle of the brothers[c] (the number of the names also at the same place was about a hundred and twenty), said, ¹⁶"Men, brothers, it is necessary *for* the Scripture to be fulfilled—which the רוּחַ הַקֹּדֶשׁ, Ruach HaQodesh spoke beforehand through the mouth of דָּוִד, David—regarding יְהוּדָה, Y'hudah (who became a guide to those who took יֵשׁוּעַ, Yeshua), ¹⁷because he was numbered among us, and received the share in this service."

¹⁸(This one, indeed, then, purchased a field out of the wages of unrighteousness; and, falling headlong, *he* burst apart in the middle, and all his bowels gushed out. ¹⁹And it became known to all those living in יְרוּשָׁלַיִם, Y'rushalayim, insomuch that that place is called—in their own dialect—חֲקַל־דְּמָא, 'Chaqal-D'ma; that is, Field of Blood.)

²⁰"For it has been written in the book of תְּהִלִּים, T'hiliym,

'Let his lodging-place become desolate, and let no one be living in it,'[d]

and,

'Let another take his *duty of* overseeing.'[e]

²¹It is therefore necessary *to choose* one of the men who came with us during the whole time that the Master יֵשׁוּעַ, Yeshua went in and went out among us, ²²beginning from the immersion of יוֹחָנָן, Yochanan, until the day in which He was received up from us—one of these *men is* to become a witness with us of His Rising Again."

²³And they set *forward* two *men*: יוֹסֵף, Yosef called בַּר־שַׁבָּא, Bar-Saba (who was *also* called Justus), and מַתִּתְיָה, Matit'yah. ²⁴And having prayed, they said, "You, ADONAI, who are knowing the heart of all, show *us* which one of these two you have chosen ²⁵to take the place[f] of this service and assignment as an emissary (from which יְהוּדָה, Y'hudah sidestepped,[g] to go on to his own place)." ²⁶And they gave lots to them, and the lot fell upon מַתִּתְיָה, Matit'yah, and he was numbered with the eleven emissaries.

---

[a] כֵּיפָא, Keifa—Gk: Πέτρος, Petros; see יוֹחָנָן *Yn.* 1:42; also throughout chapters 1 and 2
[b] Some mss insert, "and requests for help"
[c] "brothers"—some mss say, "disciples"
[d] תְּהִלִּים T'hiliym 69:26(25)
[e] תְּהִלִּים T'hiliym 109:8
[f] "place"—some mss say, "share"
[g] "sidestepped"—Young says, "by *his* sidestep, fell"

Filled with the Ruach HaQodesh.

2 ¹And in the day of the *Feast of* שָׁבֻעוֹת, Shavuot being fulfilled, they were all together[a] at the same place. ²And there came suddenly out of the heaven a sound as of a driving, violent breath, and it filled the whole House where they were sitting. ³And there appeared to them tongues *being* divided—as if of fire—and it sat upon each one of them. ⁴And they were all filled with the רוּחַ הַקֹּדֶשׁ, Ruach HaQodesh and began to speak with other languages,[b] as the רוּחַ, Ruach was giving them to declare.

⁵And *during the Feast*, there were יְהוּדִים, Y'hudiym living in יְרוּשָׁלַיִם, Y'rushalayim —God-fearing men *who traveled* from every nation of those under the heaven— ⁶and at the sound of this having come, the great number *of them* came together and were confounded, because they were each one hearing them speaking in his own dialect. ⁷And they were amazed and in wonder, saying, "Look! are not all these who are speaking גְּלִילִים, G'liyliym? ⁸And how do we hear *them*, each in our own dialect in which we were born? ⁹Parthians and Medes and Elamites and those living in Mesopotamia, also *those* in יְהוּדָה, Y'hudah and Cappadocia *and* Pontus and Asia, ¹⁰also *those in* Phrygia and Pamphylia *and* Egypt and the parts of Libya that ARE along Cyrene, and the visitors from Rome ¹¹(both יְהוּדִים, Y'hudiym and proselytes) *and* Cretes and Arabs—we heard them speaking in our languages the great things of God!"

¹²And they were all amazed and were in doubt, saying to one another, "What does this want to be?" ¹³And others, mocking, said, "They are full of sweet wine!" ¹⁴But כֵּיפָא, Keifa, having stood up with the Eleven, lifted up his voice and declared to them, "Men! יְהוּדִים, Y'hudiym! and all those living in יְרוּשָׁלַיִם, Y'rushalayim! let this be known to you, and receive my sayings into your ear, ¹⁵for these *here* are not drunk, as you take it up *in your mind*, for it is *only* the third hour of the day. ¹⁶But this is that which has been spoken through the prophet יוֹאֵל, Yoel:

¹⁷"'And it will be in the last days," says God, "I will pour out of My רוּחַ, Ruach upon all flesh, and your sons and your daughters will prophesy, and your young men will see visions, and your old men will dream dreams. ¹⁸And even upon My male slaves and upon My female slaves, in those days I will pour out of My רוּחַ, Ruach, and they will prophesy, ¹⁹and I will give wonders in the heaven above and signs upon the earth beneath—blood, fire, and vapor of smoke. ²⁰The sun will be turned to darkness, and the moon to blood, before the coming of the Day of ADONAI—the great and illustrious. ²¹And it will be *that* everyone who will call upon the Name of ADONAI— he will be saved."'[c]

²²"Men! יִשְׂרְאֵלִים, Yis'raeliym! hear these words: יֵשׁוּעַ הַנָּצְרָתִי, Yeshua HaNatz'ratiy— a man approved by God among you by powerful acts and wonders and signs that God did through Him in your midst (as you yourselves have known)——²³this *is* the One (being given over by the predetermined decision and foreknowledge of God, having *been* nailed to an execution stake by wrongdoing hands) *whom* you put to death, ²⁴*but* whom God raised up *from the dead*, having untied the pains of the death, because it was not possible for Him to be held by it. ²⁵For דָּוִד, David says in regard to Him:

'I foresaw ADONAI always before me, because He is at my right hand, so that I may not be shaken. ²⁶Because of this, my heart was *made to* rejoice, and my tongue was extremely joyful, and yet my flesh will also encamp on hope, ²⁷because You will not leave my soul to שְׁאוֹל, Sh'ol, nor will You give Your Undefiled One to see decay. ²⁸You *have*

---

[a] "together"—some mss say, "with one mind"
[b] "languages"—lit. "tongues"; also in verse 11
[c] יוֹאֵל *Yoel* 3:1-5 (2:28-32)

made known to me *the* paths of life; You will fill me with joy in Your presence.'ᵃ

²⁹"Men! Brothers! it is permitted to speak to you unhindered concerning the patriarch דָּוִד, David, that he both died and was buried, and his tomb is among us to this day. ³⁰Therefore, being a prophet—and knowing that GOD SWORE TO HIM WITH AN OATH *THAT* OUT OF THE FRUIT OF HIS LOINSᵇ *THERE WOULD BE ONE* TO SIT UPON HIS THRONEᶜ—³¹having foreseen *it*, he spoke concerning the Rising Again of the Messiah: that he WAS NOT LEFT TO שְׁאוֹל, SH'OL, NOR DID his flesh SEE DECAY.ᵈ

³²"This יֵשׁוּעַ, Yeshua God raised up, of which we are all witnesses. ³³Having been exalted, then, at the right hand of God—also having received from the Father the promise of the רוּחַ הַקֹּדֶשׁ, Ruach HaQodesh—He was pouring out this which you both see and hear.

³⁴"For דָּוִד, David did not go up to the heavens, yet he himself says,

'ADONAI says to my master, "Sit at my right hand, ³⁵until I make your enemies your footstool."'ᵉ

³⁶Therefore, let all the house of יִשְׂרָאֵל, Yis'rael know assuredly that God made Him both Master and Messiah—this יֵשׁוּעַ, Yeshua whom you crucified."

³⁷And having heard, they were pierced to the heart, *and* they also said to כֵּיפָא, Keifaᶠ and to the remainder of the emissaries, "What should we do, men? brothers?" ³⁸And כֵּיפָא, Keifa said to them, "Reform, and be immersed, each of you, in the Name of יֵשׁוּעַ, Yeshua *the* Messiah, to *the* release of your sins; and you will receive the gift of the רוּחַ הַקֹּדֶשׁ, Ruach HaQodesh. ³⁹Indeed, the promise is to you and to your children and to all those far off—as many as ADONAI our God will call." ⁴⁰Also, with many other words, he testified and was exhorting them, saying, "Be saved from this perverse generation!" ⁴¹Then those, indeed, who received his word were immersed, and there were added on that day about three thousand souls.

⁴²And they were continuing steadfastly in the teaching of the emissaries and in the sharing, in the breaking of the bread and in the prayers. ⁴³And *reverent* fear was coming on every soul, *for* many wonders, and also signs, were being done through the emissaries.

⁴⁴And all those believing were together and had all things *in* common, ⁴⁵and they were selling their properties and their possessions and were dividing them up to all, as anyone had need. ⁴⁶Also, continuing daily with one mind in the Temple and breaking bread from house to house,ᵍ they were sharing of food in rejoicing and simplicity of heart, ⁴⁷praising God and having favor with all the people. And every day, the Master was adding togetherʰ those being saved.

3 ¹And כֵּיפָא, Keifa and יוֹחָנָן, Yochanan were going up at the same time to the Temple, at the hour of the prayer (the ninth HOUR); ²and a certain man, being lame from his mother's womb, was being carried—*he* whom they were laying every day at the gate of the Temple (called *the* Beautiful *gate*) to ask *for* a charity from those entering into the Temple. ³And having seen כֵּיפָא, Keifa and יוֹחָנָן, Yochanan about to go into the Temple, he was begging to receive a charity. ⁴But כֵּיפָא, Keifa, having fixed his gaze toward him with יוֹחָנָן, Yochanan, said, "Look toward us!"

ᵃ תְּהִלִּים *T'hiliym* 16:8-11 (LXX)
ᵇ Some mss insert, "according to the flesh, to raise up the Messiah"
ᶜ תְּהִלִּים *T'hiliym* 132:11; שְׁמוּאֵל ב *Sh'muel Beit* 7:12f; תְּהִלִּים *T'hiliym* 89:4f(3f)
ᵈ תְּהִלִּים *T'hiliym* 16:10
ᵉ תְּהִלִּים *T'hiliym* 110:1
ᶠ כֵּיפָא, Keifa—Gk: Πέτρος, Petros; see יוֹחָנָן *Yn.* 1:42; also in verse 38, and throughout chapter 3
ᵍ "from house to house"—κατ' οἶκον, kat oikon—Young's says, "at every house"
ʰ "together"—some mss say, "to the Called-Forth (ἐκκλησία, ekklesia)"

⁵And he was paying close attention to them, looking to receive something from them. ⁶But כֵּיפָא, Keifa said, "Silver or gold I have none, but what I have, I give that to you: in the Name of יֵשׁוּעַ הַמָּשִׁיחַ הַנָּצְרָתִי, Yeshua HaMashiyach HaNatz'ratiy, rise up and be walking!"

⁷And having seized him by the right hand, he raised him up, and instantly his feet and ankles were strengthened. ⁸And, leaping up, he stood and was walking; and *he* entered with them into the Temple, walking and leaping and praising God.

⁹And all the people saw him walking and praising God, ¹⁰and they were knowing him, that he was the *one* who, for a charity, was sitting at the Beautiful gate of the Temple. And they were filled with wonder and amazement at what had happened to him. ¹¹And at his[a] holding כֵּיפָא, Keifa and יוֹחָנָן, Yochanan, all the people ran together to them in the colonnade called "of שְׁלֹמֹה, Sh'lomoh," *being* greatly amazed.

¹²And כֵּיפָא, Keifa, having seen, answered to the people, "Men! יִשְׂרָאֵלִים, Yis'raeliym! why are you in wonder at this? Or why do you fix your gaze on us, as if by our own power or godliness we have made him to walk? ¹³"The God of אַבְרָהָם, Av'raham and the God of יִצְחָק, Yitz'chaq and the God of יַעֲקֹב, Ya'aqov—the God of our fathers—glorified His servant יֵשׁוּעַ, Yeshua, whom you handed over and denied in the presence of Pilate when he had given judgment to release HIM. ¹⁴But you denied the Holy and Righteous One and *instead* desired a man— a murderer—to be given to you, ¹⁵and you killed the Prince[b] of the Life, whom God raised out of the dead, of which we are witnesses. ¹⁶And on the faith of His Name, His Name made this *lame* one (whom you see and have known) strong—even the faith that IS through Him gave to him this perfect soundness before you all.

¹⁷"And now, brothers, I have known that you did IT through ignorance (as also your leaders *did*), ¹⁸and what things God had announced beforehand through the mouth of all the prophets—that His Messiah should suffer—He fulfilled this way. ¹⁹Reform, therefore, and return, for *the* blotting out *of* your sins, ²⁰*so that* times of refreshing may come from the presence of ADONAI, and He may send *the one* who has been appointed[c] to you—Messiah יֵשׁוּעַ, Yeshua, ²¹whom, indeed, it is necessary *for* Heaven to receive until *the* times of the restoration of all things, of which God spoke through the mouth of His holy prophets from the age.

²²"מֹשֶׁה, Mosheh, indeed, said,[d] 'ADONAI YOUR GOD WILL RAISE UP TO YOU A PROPHET LIKE ME OUT OF YOUR BROTHERS. YOU MUST LISTEN TO HIM IN ALL THINGS,[e] as many as he may speak to you.' ²³And it will be: every soul that does not hear that prophet will be utterly destroyed out of the people. ²⁴And also, all the prophets— from שְׁמוּאֵל, Sh'muel and those following in order, as many as spoke—also proclaimed[f] these days. ²⁵You are the sons of the prophets and of the בְּרִית, b'riyt that God made to your fathers, saying to אַבְרָהָם, Av'raham, 'AND IN YOUR SEED WILL ALL THE FAMILIES OF THE EARTH BE BLESSED.'[g] ²⁶God, having raised up His servant,[h] sent Him to you first, blessing you in the turning away of each one from your evil ways."

4 ¹And as they were speaking to the people, the כֹּהֲנִים, Ko'haniym and the captain of the Temple and the צְדוּקִים, Tzaduqiym came to them—²being greatly annoyed because of their teaching the people and proclaiming in יֵשׁוּעַ, Yeshua the Rising Again out of the dead

---

[a] "at his"—some mss say, "at the lame man who was healed"
[b] "Prince" or "Author"; cf. Acts 5:31, עִבְרִים Iv'riym 2:10, 12:2
[c] "appointed"—some mss say, "proclaimed beforehand"
[d] Some mss insert, "to the fathers"
[e] דְּבָרִים D'variym 18:15,18
[f] "proclaimed"—some mss say, "foretold of"
[g] בְּרֵאשִׁית B'reshiyt 22:18
[h] Some mss insert, "יֵשׁוּעַ, Yeshua"

—³and they threw *their* hands on them and put them in custody until the next day, for it was already evening. ⁴But many of those hearing the word believed, and the number of the men became about five thousand.

⁵And it came to pass on the next day *that* their leaders and זְקֵנִים, Z'qeniym and סוֹפְרִים, Sof'riym were gathered together in יְרוּשָׁלַיִם, Y'rushalayim, ⁶and חָנָן, Chanan the כֹּהֵן הַגָּדוֹל, Kohen HaGadol and כֵּיפָא, Qayafa and יוֹחָנָן, Yochanan and Alexander and as many as were of the ancestry of the כֹּהֵן הַגָּדוֹל, Kohen HaGadol *were there also*. ⁷And having set *Keifa and Yochanan* in the middle *of them*, they were asking, "In what power, or in what name, did you do this?"

⁸Then כֵּיפָא, Keifa,ᵃ having been filled with the רוּחַ הַקֹדֶשׁ, Ruach HaQodesh, said to them, "Leaders of the people, and זְקֵנִים, Z'qeniym:ᵇ ⁹if we today are *being* examined concerning the good deed *done* to the weak man, *and* by whom he has been saved, ¹⁰be it known to all of you, and to all the people of יִשְׂרָאֵל, Yis'rael, that in the Name of יֵשׁוּעַ הַמָּשִׁיחַ הַנָּצְרָתִי, Yeshua Ha-Mashiyach HaNatz'ratiy, whom you crucified *and* whom God raised out of the dead —in Him has this one stood whole here in your presence! ¹¹This is THE STONE THAT WAS TREATED WITH CONTEMPT BY YOU, THE BUILDERS, THAT BECAME HEAD OF THE CORNER,ᶜ ¹²and there is not salvation in any other. Indeed, there is no other Name under the heaven that has been given among men in which we must be saved."

¹³And seeing the freedom in speech of כֵּיפָא, Keifa and יוֹחָנָן, Yochanan, and having perceived that they are uneducated and common men, they were in wonder. They were also taking note of them—that they had been with יֵשׁוּעַ, Yeshua. ¹⁴And seeing the man who had been healed standing with them, they had nothing to say against IT. ¹⁵And having commanded them to go away out of the Sanhedrin, they were taking counsel with one another, ¹⁶saying, "What should we do to these men? Because *of the fact* that, indeed, a notable sign has been done through them, *it is* known to all those living in יְרוּשָׁלַיִם, Y'rushalayim, and we are not able to deny IT. ¹⁷But so that it may spread no further toward the people, let us threaten them to no longer speak in this name to any man."

¹⁸And having called them, they commanded them not to speak at all—nor to teach—in the Name of יֵשׁוּעַ, Yeshua. ¹⁹But כֵּיפָא, Keifa and יוֹחָנָן, Yochanan, answering, said to them, "Whether it is righteous in the sight of God to listen to you rather than to God, you *be the* judge, ²⁰for we cannot *help* but speak what we saw and heard." ²¹And they, having further threatened THEM, let them go, finding nothing *justifiable for* how they might punish them, because of the people—since all were glorifying God for that which had been done ²²(for the man upon whom this sign of the healing had been done was above forty years of age).

²³And being let go, they went to their own friends and declared whatever the chief כֹּהֲנִים, Ko'haniym and the זְקֵנִים, Z'qeniym *had* said to them. ²⁴And they, having heard, lifted up the voice to God with one mind and said, "Sovereign One, You ARE He who MADE THE HEAVEN AND THE EARTH, THE SEA, AND ALL THAT ARE IN THEM,ᵈ ²⁵who by our father—through the רוּחַ הַקֹדֶשׁ, Ruach HaQodesh,ᵉ by the mouth of דָוִד, David Your servant—said,

'Why did *the* גּוֹיִם, Goyim rage, and *the* peoples plot empty things? ²⁶The kings of the earth stood up, and the leaders were gathered together against ADONAI and against His Messiah.'ᶠ

ᵃ כֵּיפָא, Keifa—Gk: Πέτρος, Petros; see יוֹחָנָן Yn. 1:42; also throughout chapters 4 and 5
ᵇ Some mss insert, "of יִשְׂרָאֵל, Yis'rael"
ᶜ תְּהִלִּים T'hiliym 118:22
ᵈ שְׁמוֹת Sh'mot 20:11; cf. תְּהִלִּים T'hiliym 146:6
ᵉ Some mss omit, "by our father—through the רוּחַ הַקֹדֶשׁ, Ruach HaQodesh"
ᶠ תְּהִלִּים T'hiliym 2:1-2

²⁷For both Herod and Pontius Pilate were gathered together in truth in this city[a] with גּוֹיִם, Goyim and peoples of יִשְׂרָאֵל, Yis'rael against Your holy servant יֵשׁוּעַ, Yeshua (whom You anointed), ²⁸to do whatever Your hand and Your purpose predetermined to come to pass. ²⁹And now, ADONAI, look on their threatenings and give to Your slaves to speak Your word with all freedom, ³⁰in the stretching out of Your hand, for healing and signs and wonders to come to pass through the Name of Your holy servant—יֵשׁוּעַ, Yeshua!"

³¹And when they had prayed, the place in which they were gathered together was shaken, and they were all filled with the רוּחַ הַקֹּדֶשׁ, Ruach HaQodesh and were speaking the word of God with freedom. ³²And of the great number of those who believed, *their* heart and soul were one. And not one *of them* was saying that anything of the things he had was his own, but all things were in common to them.

³³And with great power, the emissaries were giving the testimony to the Rising Again of the Master יֵשׁוּעַ, Yeshua, *and* great favor was also on them all, ³⁴for there was not anyone among them who lacked. For as many as were possessors of fields or houses were selling THEM *and* bringing the proceeds of the thing sold, ³⁵and *they* were laying them at the feet of the emissaries, and distribution was being made to each *person* as anyone had need.

³⁶And יוֹסֵף, Yosef—a לֵוִי, Leviy, of Cypress by birth, who was called בַּר־נַבָּא, Bar-Naba by the emissaries (which is, having been interpreted, "Son of Encouragement")—³⁷a field being his, having sold IT, brought the money and laid IT at the feet of the emissaries.

5 ¹And a certain man by *the* name חֲנַנְיָה, 'Chanan'yah, with שַׁפִּירָא, Shapiyra his wife, sold a property ²and kept back *some* of the proceeds (his wife also being aware *of it*). And having brought a certain part, he laid IT at the feet of the emissaries. ³And כֵּיפָא, Keifa said, "חֲנַנְיָה, 'Chanan'yah, why did הַשָּׂטָן, HaSatan fill your heart for you to lie to the רוּחַ הַקֹּדֶשׁ, Ruach HaQodesh and to keep back *some* of the proceeds of the place? ⁴While it remained *unsold*, did it not remain yours? And having been sold, were *the proceeds* not in your authority? Why IS it that you put this thing in your heart? You did not lie to men, but to God." ⁵And חֲנַנְיָה, 'Chanan'yah, hearing these words, having fallen down, breathed his last, and great fear came upon all who heard *of it*. ⁶And having risen, the younger men wrapped him up; and having carried *him* out, they buried HIM.

⁷And it came to pass, about three hours after, that his wife, not knowing what had happened, came in. ⁸And כֵּיפָא, Keifa answered to her, "Tell me if you sold the place for so much," and she said, "Yes, for so much." ⁹And כֵּיפָא, Keifa said to her, "How was it agreed by you to tempt the רוּחַ, Ruach of ADONAI? Look! the feet of those who buried your husband ARE at the door, and they will carry you out *also*." ¹⁰And she fell down instantly at his feet and breathed her last; and the young men, having come in, found her dead; and having carried *her* out, they buried HER by her husband. ¹¹And great fear came upon all the Called-Forth,[b] and on all who heard these things.

¹²And among the people, many signs and wonders were coming through the hands of the emissaries, and they were all with one mind in the colonnade of שְׁלֹמֹה, Sh'lomoh, ¹³but no one among the remainder was daring to join himself to them. Nevertheless, the people were magnifying them ¹⁴(and *all* the more were believers added to the Master—crowds of both men and women), ¹⁵such that *they* even *went* into the streets to bring out the weak and to lay THEM on cots and mats, so that at the coming of כֵּיפָא, Keifa, even HIS shadow might overshadow someone of them.

---

[a] Some mss omit, "in this city"

[b] "Called-Forth"—ἐκκλησίαν, ekklesian; see מַתִּתְיָהוּ Matit'yahu 16:18

¹⁶And also the people of the cities surrounding יְרוּשָׁלַיִם, Y'rushalayim were coming together carrying weak persons and those harassed by unclean רוּחוֹת, ruchot, who were all healed.

¹⁷And having risen, the כֹּהֵן הַגָּדוֹל, Kohen HaGadol and all those with him (being the sect of the צְדוּקִים, Tzaduqiym) were filled with jealousy ¹⁸and laid hands on the emissaries and put them in a public prison. ¹⁹But during the night, a Messenger of ADONAI, having opened the doors of the prison and having brought them out, said, ²⁰"Go on, and, standing in the Temple, speak to the people all the sayings of this Life." ²¹And having heard, they entered into the Temple at dawn and were teaching.

And the כֹּהֵן הַגָּדוֹל, Kohen HaGadol and those with him, having come, called together the Sanhedrin and the whole Senate of the sons of יִשְׂרָאֵל, Yis'rael, and they sent *word* to the prison to have them brought. ²²But the attendants, having come, did not find them in the prison; and having turned back, they told *them what had happened*, ²³saying, "We, indeed, found the prison shut in all safety, and the guards standing at the doors; but having opened *it*, we found no one within."

²⁴And as the captain of the Temple and the chief כֹּהֲנִים, Ko'haniym heard these words, they were uncertain about them *as* to what would come *of* this. ²⁵And coming near, a certain one told them, "Look! the men whom you put in prison are standing in the Temple and teaching the people." ²⁶Then the captain, having gone away with *his* attendants, was bringing them *back* without violence (for they were fearing the people, that they might be stoned). ²⁷And having brought them *back*, they set THEM in the Sanhedrin, and the כֹּהֵן הַגָּדוֹל, Kohen HaGadol questioned them, ²⁸saying, "Did we not strictly command you not to teach in this name? And look! you have filled יְרוּשָׁלַיִם, Y'rushalayim with your teaching, and you intend to bring the blood of this man upon us."

²⁹And כֵּיפָא, Keifa and the emissaries, answering, said, "*We* must obey God, rather than men. ³⁰The God of our fathers raised up יֵשׁוּעַ, Yeshua—whom you killed, having hung *Him* on a tree. ³¹God has exalted this One—a Prince and a Savior—with His right hand, to give reformation to יִשְׂרָאֵל, Yis'rael and forgiveness of sins. ³²And we are[a] witnesses of these sayings, *as* also *is* the רוּחַ הַקֹּדֶשׁ, Ruach HaQodesh, whom God gave to those obeying Him."

³³And *when* they had heard, *they* were cut TO THE HEART and were intending[b] to put them to death. ³⁴But a certain one, having risen up in the Sanhedrin—a פָּרוּשׁ, Parush by *the* name גַּמְלִיאֵל, Gam'liyel, a תּוֹרָה, Torah teacher honored by all the people—commanded *them* to put the men[c] outside *for* a little *while*.

³⁵And he said to them, "Men! יִשְׂרָאֵלִים, Yis'raeliym! be careful for yourselves regarding these men—what you are about to do. ³⁶For before these days, Theudas rose up saying that *he* himself was someone (to whom a number of men joined themselves—about four hundred who were put to death), and all, as many as were being persuaded by[d] him, were scattered, and *it* came to nothing. ³⁷After this one, יְהוּדָה, Y'hudah of the גָּלִיל, Galiyl rose up in the days of the enrollment and drew away[e] people after him, but that one was *also* destroyed, and all, as many as were being persuaded by him, were scattered. ³⁸And now I say to you: stay away from these men and leave them alone, because if this purpose or this action is of men, it will be overthrown. ³⁹But if it is of God, you will not be able to overthrow them; otherwise, you may also be found fighting against God."

---

[a] Some mss insert, "His"
[b] "intending"—some mss say, "considering *whether*"
[c] "men"—some mss say, "emissaries"
[d] "being persuaded by"—πείθω, peitho, most often translated "trust" or "persuade." Here, Young says "obeying." Also in next verse, and vs. 39 (where Young's says, "agreed").
[e] Some mss insert, "many"

And they were persuaded by him, ⁴⁰and having called the emissaries near, having beaten THEM, they commanded THEM not to speak in the Name of יֵשׁוּעַ, Yeshua and let them go.

⁴¹They, indeed, then went away from the presence of the Sanhedrin, rejoicing that they were counted worthy to suffer degradation for His Name. ⁴²And every day in the Temple, and from house to house,[a] they were not stopping teaching and proclaiming Good News—the Messiah יֵשׁוּעַ, Yeshua.

6 ¹And in those days, *with* the disciples multiplying, there came a murmuring among the Ἑλληνιστάς, Hellenistas toward the עִבְרִים, Iv'riym, because their widows were being overlooked in the daily service *of food*. ²And the Twelve, having called near a great number of the disciples, said, "It is not pleasing that we, having left *the service of* the word of God, *have to* serve at tables. ³So, brothers, look for seven men from *among* you who are well testified of *and* full of the רוּחַ, Ruach and wisdom, whom we might set over this necessity, ⁴and we will give ourselves continually to prayer and to the service of the word." ⁵And the thing was pleasing before all the great number *of them*, and they chose Stephen (a man full of faith and the רוּחַ הַקֹּדֶשׁ, Ruach HaQodesh) and Philip and Prochorus and Nicanor and Timon and Parmenas and Nicolas (a proselyte from Antioch), ⁶whom they set before the emissaries. And they, having prayed, laid THEIR hands on them.

~ c. A.D. 32 ~

⁷And the word of God increased, and the number of the disciples multiplied in יְרוּשָׁלַיִם, Y'rushalayim exceedingly. A great number of the כֹּהֲנִים, Ko'haniym also were obedient to the faith.

⁸And Stephen, full of *unmerited* favor[b] and power, was doing great wonders and signs among the people. ⁹And there arose certain of those of the synagogue called "of the Freedmen," and Cyrenians, and Alexandrians, and of those from Cilicia and Asia, disputing with Stephen, ¹⁰but they were not able to withstand the wisdom and the רוּחַ, ruach with which he was speaking. ¹¹Then they instigated men, *who were* saying, "We have heard him speaking evil sayings in regard to מֹשֶׁה, Mosheh and God." ¹²They also stirred up the people and the זְקֵנִים, Z'qeniym and the סוֹפְרִים, Sof'riym; and having come upon HIM, they caught him and brought HIM to the Sanhedrin. ¹³They also set up false witnesses, saying, "This one does not stop speaking sayings against this holy place and the תּוֹרָה, Torah, ¹⁴for we have heard him saying that this יֵשׁוּעַ הַנָּצְרָתִי, Yeshua HaNatz'ratiy will overthrow this place and will change the customs that מֹשֶׁה, Mosheh handed down to us." ¹⁵And fixing their gaze at him, all those sitting in the Sanhedrin saw his face as *if* it were the face of a Messenger.

7 ¹And the כֹּהֵן הַגָּדוֹל, Kohen HaGadol said, "Are these things so?" ²And he said, "Men! brothers and fathers! listen: the God of the glory appeared to our father אַבְרָהָם, Av'raham, being in Mesopotamia, before his living in חָרָן, Charan, ³and He said to him, 'GO OUT OF YOUR LAND, AND OUT OF YOUR RELATIVES, AND COME TO THE LAND THAT I WILL SHOW YOU.'[c] ⁴Then, having come out of the land of the כַּשְׂדִּים, Khas'diym, he lived in חָרָן, Charan; and from that place, after the death of his father, He removed him to this land in which you now live. ⁵And He gave him no inheritance in it, not even a footstep, but promised TO GIVE IT TO HIM FOR A POSSESSION, AND TO HIS SEED AFTER HIM,[d] *even though* he had no child. ⁶And God spoke this way: that his 'SEED WILL BE SOJOURNING IN A LAND BELONGING TO OTHERS, AND THEY

---

[a] "from house to house"—κατ' οἶκον, kat oikon— Young's says, "in every house"
[b] "*unmerited* favor"—some mss say, "faith"
[c] בְּרֵאשִׁית *B'reshiyt* 12:1
[d] בְּרֵאשִׁית *B'reshiyt* 12:7

WILL ENSLAVE AND DO EVIL *TO* IT *FOR* FOUR HUNDRED YEARS. ⁷AND THE גּוֹי, GOY, *TO* WHOM THEY WILL BE ENSLAVED, I WILL JUDGE,' God said, 'AND AFTER THESE THINGS, THEY WILL COME OUT, AND WILL SERVE ME IN THIS PLACE.'ª

⁸"And He gave to him the בְּרִית מִילָה, b'riyt miylah. And so he brought forth יִצְחָק, Yitz'chaq and circumcised him on the eighth day; and יִצְחָק, Yitz'chaq BROUGHT FORTH יַעֲקֹב, Ya'aqov; and יַעֲקֹב, Ya'aqov, the twelve patriarchs. ⁹And the patriarchs, having been moved with jealousy, sold יוֹסֵף, Yosef to מִצְרַיִם, Mitz'rayim. But God was with him, ¹⁰and delivered him out of all his oppressions, and gave him favor and wisdom in front of פַּרְעֹה, Par'oh, king of מִצְרַיִם, Mitz'rayim; and he set him *as* governor over מִצְרַיִם, Mitz'rayim and all his house.

¹¹"And there came a famine on all of מִצְרַיִם, Mitz'rayim and כְּנַעַן, K'na-an, and great oppression, and our fathers were not finding sustenance. ¹²But יַעֲקֹב, Ya'aqov, having heard that there was grain in מִצְרַיִם, Mitz'rayim, sent our fathers *there* a first time; ¹³and at the second time, יוֹסֵף, Yosef was made known to his brothers, and the ancestryᵇ of יוֹסֵף, Yosef became unconcealed to פַּרְעֹה, Par'oh. ¹⁴Then יוֹסֵף, Yosef, having sent *word*, called for יַעֲקֹב, Ya'aqov his father and all the relatives—with seventy-five souls *in all*—¹⁵and יַעֲקֹב, Ya'aqov went down to מִצְרַיִם, Mitz'rayim and died—himself and our fathers—¹⁶and they were carried over into שְׁכֶם, Sh'khem and were laid in the tomb that אַבְרָהָם, Av'raham bought for a price in money from the sons of חֲמוֹר, 'Chamor in שְׁכֶם, Sh'khem.

¹⁷"And as the time of the promise which God had professedᶜ to אַבְרָהָם, Av'raham was drawing near, the people increased and multiplied in מִצְרַיִם, Mitz'rayim, ¹⁸until another king arose over מִצְרַיִם, Mitz'rayim who had not known יוֹסֵף, Yosef. ¹⁹This one, having dealt craftily with our ancestry, did evil to our fathers (causing *them* to expose their babies, so that they would not live), ²⁰in whose time מֹשֶׁה, Mosheh was born. And he was beautiful to God, and he was brought up *for* three months in the house of his father, ²¹but when he had been abandoned, the daughter of פַּרְעֹה, Par'oh took him up and reared him to herself for a son. ²²And מֹשֶׁה, Mosheh was taught in all the wisdom of the מִצְרַיִם, Mitz'rayim, and he was powerful in his words and in actions.

²³"And when forty years were fulfilled to him, it came upon his heart to look in on his brothers, the sons of יִשְׂרָאֵל, Yis'rael. ²⁴And having seen a certain one suffering injustice, he defended *him* and did justice to the oppressed, having struck *down* the מִצְרִי, Mitz'riy. ²⁵And he was supposing his brothers *would come* to understand that God *was* giving them salvation through his hand, but they did not understand.

²⁶"On the succeeding day, he also showed himself to *his brothers—two of* them—as they were being combative, and *he* was *attempting to* reconcile them to peace, saying, 'Men, you are brothers—why do you do injustice to one another?'ᵈ ²⁷And he who was doing injustice to the neighbor pushed him away, saying, 'WHO SET YOU *AS* A RULER AND JUDGE OVER US? ²⁸DO YOU WANT TO KILL ME, AS YOU KILLED THE מִצְרִי, MITZ'RIY YESTERDAY?'ᵉ ²⁹And at this word, מֹשֶׁה, Mosheh fled and became a sojourner in the land of מִדְיָן, Mid'yan, where he brought forth two sons.

³⁰"And when forty *more* years had been fulfilled, A MESSENGER APPEARED TO HIM in the desert of הַר סִינַי, Har Siynai IN A FLAME OF FIRE IN A BUSH.ᶠ ³¹And מֹשֶׁה, Mosheh, having seen, was wondering at the sight. And *as he was* drawing near to look, there came a voice of

---

ª בְּרֵאשִׁית *B'reshiyt* 15:13-14
ᵇ "ancestry"—γένος, *genos*—race, family, nation, people; offspring, descendants; sort, kind; also in verse 18
ᶜ "had professed"—some mss say, "swore"
ᵈ cf. שְׁמוֹת *Sh'mot* 2:13
ᵉ שְׁמוֹת *Sh'mot* 2:14
ᶠ שְׁמוֹת *Sh'mot* 3:2

Stephen's address continues.   **Acts 7:52**

ADONAI, *saying,* [32]'I AM THE GOD OF YOUR FATHERS;

אֱלֹהֵי אַבְרָהָם אֱלֹהֵי יִצְחָק וֵאלֹהֵי יַעֲקֹב
'Elohei Av'raham,'Elohei Yitz'chaq, vElohei Ya'aqov.'[a]

And מֹשֶׁה, Mosheh, having become terrified, dared not look. [33]AND ADONAI SAID TO HIM, 'UNTIE THE SANDAL OF YOUR FEET, FOR THE PLACE ON WHICH YOU HAVE STOOD IS HOLY GROUND.[b] [34]SEEING, I HAVE SEEN THE MISTREATMENT OF MY PEOPLE THAT *ARE* IN מִצְרַיִם, MITZ'RAYIM, AND I HEARD THEIR GROANING, AND *I* CAME DOWN TO DELIVER THEM. AND NOW, COME—I WILL SEND YOU TO מִצְרַיִם, MITZ'RAYIM.'[c]

[35]"This מֹשֶׁה, Mosheh, whom they refused, saying, 'Who set you *as* both a ruler and a judge *over us?*'—God sent this one *as* a ruler and a redeemer, by the hand of a Messenger who appeared to him in the bush. [36]This one brought them out, having done wonders and signs in the land of מִצְרַיִם, Mitz'rayim, and in the יַם־סוּף, Yam-Suf, and *for* forty years in the desert. [37]This is the מֹשֶׁה, Mosheh who said to the sons of יִשְׂרָאֵל, Yis'rael, 'GOD WILL RAISE UP TO YOU A PROPHET LIKE ME OUT OF YOUR BROTHERS.'[d] [38]This is he who was in the קָהָל, qahal[e] in the desert with the Messenger who was speaking to him on the הַר סִינַי, Har Siynai, and who, with our fathers, received the living sayings to give to us. [39]*This is the one* to whom our fathers did not want to become obedient, but pushed *him* away and turned back in their hearts to מִצְרַיִם, Mitz'rayim, [40]SAYING TO אַהֲרֹן, A'HARON, 'MAKE GODS FOR US WHO WILL GO ON BEFORE US, FOR THIS מֹשֶׁה, MOSHEH, WHO BROUGHT US OUT OF THE LAND OF מִצְרַיִם, MITZ'RAYIM—WE HAVE NOT KNOWN WHAT HAPPENED TO HIM.'[f]

[41]"And they made a calf in those days, and brought a sacrifice to the idol, and were rejoicing in the actions of their hands. [42]And God turned *away* and gave them up to do service to the army of the heaven, as it has been written in the scroll of the prophets:

'Did you offer slain beasts and sacrifices to Me forty years in desert, O house of יִשְׂרָאֵל, Yis'rael? [43]And you took up the tent of מֶלֶךְ, Molekh, and the star of your god Rephan—the figures that you made *in order* to bow before them. And I will remove your dwelling beyond Babylon.'[g]

[44]"The Tent of the Testimony was *given* to our fathers in the desert (as He who was speaking to מֹשֶׁה, Mosheh directed, to make it according to the figure that he had seen), [45]which our fathers (having received *it* in succession) also brought in with יְהוֹשֻׁעַ, Y'hoshua, into the dispossession of the גּוֹיִם, Goyim whom God drove out from the presence of our fathers. *So it was* until the days of דָּוִד, David, [46]who found favor in God's sight and requested to find a dwelling for the God[h] of יַעֲקֹב, Ya'aqov, [47]but *it was* שְׁלֹמֹה, Sh'lomoh *who finally* built Him a House.

[48]"But the Most High does not live in *houses* made with *human* hands, as the prophet says:

[49]'The heaven IS My throne, and the earth My footstool; what house will you build to Me?'

says ADONAI; or,

'What IS My stopping-place? [50]Has not My hand made all these things?'[i]

[51]You stiff-necked and uncircumcised in hearts and in ears! You always resist the רוּחַ הַקֹּדֶשׁ, Ruach HaQodesh. As your fathers *were, so* also *are* you. [52]Which of the

---

[a] שְׁמוֹת *Sh'mot* 3:6, "the God of Abraham, the God of Isaac, and the God of Jacob"; cf. שְׁמוֹת *Shm.* 3:15-16
[b] שְׁמוֹת *Sh'mot* 3:5
[c] שְׁמוֹת *Sh'mot* 3:7-8,10
[d] דְּבָרִים *D'variym* 18:15; some mss insert, "you will hear him"
[e] "קָהָל, qahal"—Gk. ἐκκλησία, ekklesia
[f] שְׁמוֹת *Sh'mot* 32:1; cf. 32:33
[g] עָמוֹס *Amos* 5:25-27 (LXX)
[h] "God"—the earliest mss say, "house"
[i] יְשַׁעְיָהוּ *Y'sha'yahu* 66:1-2a

prophets did your fathers not persecute? And they killed those who announced beforehand about the coming of the Righteous One, of whom you have now become betrayers and murderers—⁵³*you* who received the תּוֹרָה, Torah by decree of Messengers, but did not guard IT."

⁵⁴And hearing these things, they were cut to the hearts and gnashed the teeth at him. ⁵⁵But being full of the רוּחַ הַקֹּדֶשׁ, Ruach HaQodesh, having fixed his gaze to the heaven, he saw the glory of God, and יֵשׁוּעַ, Yeshua standing at the right hand of God. ⁵⁶And he said, "Look! I see the heavens having been opened, and the Son of Man standing at the right hand of God!" ⁵⁷And they, having shouted out with a loud voice, stopped their ears and rushed upon him with one mind. ⁵⁸And having thrown him outside the city, they were stoning HIM (and the witnesses put down their garments at the feet of a young man called שָׁאוּל, Shaul). ⁵⁹And *as* they were stoning Stephen, *he was* calling and saying, "Master יֵשׁוּעַ, Yeshua, receive my רוּחַ, ruach!" ⁶⁰And having bowed the knees, he shouted with a loud voice, "Master! Do not lay this sin on them!" and having said this, he fell asleep.

8

¹And שָׁאוּל, Shaul was agreeing to his death. And there came in that day a massive persecution upon the Called-Forth[a] in יְרוּשָׁלַיִם, Y'rushalayim, and they were all scattered abroad throughout the regions of יְהוּדָה, Y'hudah and שֹׁמְרוֹן, Shom'ron, except the emissaries. ²And God-fearing men carried Stephen away and made great mourning over him; ³but שָׁאוּל, Shaul was ravaging the Called-Forth, entering into every house and dragging off *both* men and women—giving them up to prison. ⁴They then, indeed, having been scattered, went around proclaiming Good News—the word.

⁵And Philip, having gone down to the city of שֹׁמְרוֹן, Shom'ron, was proclaiming the Messiah to them. ⁶And the crowds were paying attention with one mind to the things spoken by Philip, while hearing and seeing the signs that he was doing. ⁷Indeed, unclean רוּחוֹת, ruchot came out from many who were possessed, crying out with a loud voice, and many who had been paralytic and lame were healed. ⁸And there was much joy in that city.

⁹And a certain man by *the* name שִׁמְעוֹן, Shim'on was previously in the city using magic and amazing the גּוֹיִם, Goyim of שֹׁמְרוֹן, Shom'ron, saying himself to be a certain great one, ¹⁰to whom they were all paying attention, from small to great, saying, "This one is the Power of God who is called Great." ¹¹And they were paying attention to him because of his having amazed them for a long time with deeds of magic. ¹²But when they believed Philip *as he was* proclaiming Good News regarding the Reign of God and the Name of יֵשׁוּעַ, Yeshua *the* Messiah, they were immersed—both men and women. ¹³And שִׁמְעוֹן, Shim'on himself also believed; and, having been immersed, he was continuing with Philip; *and* also seeing *the* signs and powerful acts being done, he was amazed.

¹⁴And the emissaries in יְרוּשָׁלַיִם, Y'rushalayim, having heard that שֹׁמְרוֹן, Shom'ron had received the word of God, sent to them כֵּיפָא, Keifa[b] and יוֹחָנָן, Yochanan, ¹⁵who, having come down, prayed regarding them, that they might receive the רוּחַ הַקֹּדֶשׁ, Ruach HaQodesh. ¹⁶For as yet, He was fallen upon none of them, and they had only been immersed to the Name of the Master יֵשׁוּעַ, Yeshua. ¹⁷Then they were laying hands on them, and they received the רוּחַ הַקֹּדֶשׁ, Ruach HaQodesh. ¹⁸And שִׁמְעוֹן, Shim'on, having seen that the רוּחַ, Ruach was given through the laying on of the hands of the emissaries, brought money before them, ¹⁹saying, "Give this authority to me also, so that on whoever I might lay the hands, he may receive the רוּחַ הַקֹּדֶשׁ, Ruach HaQodesh."

---

[a] "Called-Forth"—ἐκκλησίαν, ekklesian; also in vs 3; see מַתִּתְיָהוּ *Matit'yahu* 16:18

[b] כֵּיפָא, Keifa—Gk: Πέτρος, Petros; see יוֹחָנָן *Yn.* 1:42; also in verse 20

20And כֵּיפָא, Keifa said to him, "Your silver—*along* with you—may it be to destruction! because you thought to obtain the gift of God through money. 21You have neither a share nor portion in this thing, for your heart is not right before God. 22Therefore, reform from this, your wickedness, and implore ADONAI *to see* if the purpose of your heart may then be forgiven you. 23For I perceive you *as* being in the bile of bitterness and *the* bond of unrighteousness." 24And שִׁמְעוֹן, Shim'on, answering, said, "Implore to ADONAI for me, *so* that nothing of the things you have spoken may come upon me!"

25They therefore, indeed, having testified fully and spoken the word of ADONAI, were returning to יְרוּשָׁלַיִם, Y'rushalayim. And they were proclaiming Good News in many villages of the שֹׁמְרֹנִים, Shom'roniym.

26And a Messenger of ADONAI spoke to Philip, saying, "Arise, and go on toward the south, on the road that is going down from יְרוּשָׁלַיִם, Y'rushalayim to עַזָּה, Azah" (this *one* is deserted). 27And having arisen, he went on, and look! *there was* a man of Ethiopia—a eunuch, a ranking man of Candace the queen of the Ethiopians, who was *in charge* over all her treasure—who had come to worship in יְרוּשָׁלַיִם, Y'rushalayim. 28And he was returning and sitting on his chariot, and he was reading יְשַׁעְיָהוּ, Y'sha'yahu the prophet. 29And the רוּחַ, Ruach said to Philip, "Go near, and be joined to this chariot." 30And Philip, having run near, heard him reading יְשַׁעְיָהוּ, Y'sha'yahu the prophet and said, "Do you know, then, what you are reading?" 31And he said, "Indeed, how am I able, if someone does not guide me?" And he called Philip, having come up, to sit with him. 32And the portion of the Scripture that he was reading was this:

"As a sheep to slaughter he was led,
and as a lamb before his shearer, without sound,
so he does not open his mouth;

33In his humiliation his judgment was taken away;
his generation—who will declare?
because his life is taken from the earth."[a]

34And the eunuch, answering Philip, said, "I ask you: about whom does the prophet say this? about himself, or about some other one?" 35And Philip, having opened his mouth and having begun from this Scripture, proclaimed Good News to him —יֵשׁוּעַ, Yeshua.

36And as they were going on the road, they came upon a certain water, and the eunuch said, "Look! water! What forbids me from being immersed?"[b] 38And he commanded the chariot to stand still, and they both went down to the water—both Philip and the eunuch—and he immersed him.

39And when they came up out of the water, the רוּחַ, Ruach of ADONAI caught Philip away, and the eunuch saw him no more, for he was going on his way, rejoicing. 40And Philip was found at אַשְׁדּוֹד, Ash'dod; and passing through, he was proclaiming Good News to all the cities, until his coming to Cæsarea.

~ c.A.D. 33 ~

9 1And שָׁאוּל, Shaul, still breathing of threatening and slaughter to the disciples of the Master, having gone to the כֹּהֵן הַגָּדוֹל, Kohen HaGadol, 2asked *for* letters from him to דַּמֶּשֶׂק, Dameseq, to the synagogues, *so* that if he might find any *who were* being of the Way, both men and women, he could bring them bound to יְרוּשָׁלַיִם, Y'rushalayim.

3And while *he was* going, he came near to דַּמֶּשֶׂק, Dameseq, and suddenly, there shone around him a light from the heaven. 4And having fallen on the ground, he heard a voice saying to him, "שָׁאוּל שָׁאוּל, Shaul, Shaul, why do you persecute Me?"

[a] יְשַׁעְיָהוּ Y'sha'yahu 53:7-8
[b] Later mss include all or part of verse 37, "And Philip said, 'If you believe out of all the heart, it is permitted'; and he, answering, said, 'I believe יֵשׁוּעַ, Yeshua *the* Messiah to be the Son of God.'"

⁵And he said, "Who are you, Master?" And He[a] said, "I am יֵשׁוּעַ, Yeshua, whom you persecute.[b] ⁶But arise, and enter into the city, and it will be told to you what you must do." ⁷And the men who were journeying with him stood speechless, hearing indeed the voice, but seeing no one. ⁸And שָׁאוּל, Shaul arose from the ground, and *although* his eyes had been opened, he saw nothing. And leading him by the hand, they brought him to דַּמֶּשֶׂק, Dameseq, ⁹and he was three days without seeing, and he neither ate nor drank.

¹⁰And there was a certain disciple in דַּמֶּשֶׂק, Dameseq by *the* name *of* חֲנַנְיָה, 'Chanan'yah, and the Master said to him in a vision, "חֲנַנְיָה, 'Chanan'yah," and he said, "See me, Master." ¹¹And the Master SAID to him, "Having risen, go on to the street that is called Straight, and look in the house of יְהוּדָה, Y'hudah for ONE by *the* name *of* שָׁאוּל, Shaul of Tarsus. For look! he prays, ¹²and he saw in a vision a man by *the* name *of* חֲנַנְיָה, 'Chanan'yah, coming in and laying the hands on him *so that* he may see again." ¹³And חֲנַנְיָה, 'Chanan'yah answered, "Master, I have heard from many about this man, how he did many evils to Your קְדוֹשִׁים, Q'doshiym in יְרוּשָׁלַיִם, Y'rushalayim. ¹⁴And he has authority here from the chief כֹּהֲנִים, Ko'haniym to bind all *of* those calling on Your Name." ¹⁵And the Master said to him, "Be going on, because this one is a chosen instrument to Me—to carry My Name in the presence of not only גּוֹיִם, Goyim and kings, but also the sons of יִשְׂרָאֵל, Yis'rael. ¹⁶For I will show him how many things he must suffer for My Name."

¹⁷And חֲנַנְיָה, 'Chanan'yah went away and entered into the house and, having put HIS hands upon him, said, "שָׁאוּל, Shaul, brother, the Master has sent me—יֵשׁוּעַ, Yeshua, who appeared to you on the road in which you were coming—*so that* you might see again and might be filled with the רוּחַ הַקֹּדֶשׁ, Ruach HaQodesh." ¹⁸And immediately, something like scales fell from his eyes. He also saw again;[c] and having arisen, *he* was immersed; ¹⁹and having received nourishment, *he* was strengthened. And he was with the disciples in דַּמֶּשֶׂק, Dameseq *for a* certain *number of* days, ²⁰and immediately, in the synagogues, he was proclaiming יֵשׁוּעַ, Yeshua[d]—that He is the Son of God.

²¹And all those hearing *him* were amazed and said, "Is this not he who, in יְרוּשָׁלַיִם, Y'rushalayim, destroyed those calling on this Name, and *who* had come here for this intent: that he might bring them bound to the chief כֹּהֲנִים, Ko'haniym?" ²²And שָׁאוּל, Shaul was still more strengthened, and he was confounding the יְהוּדִים, Y'hudiym living in דַּמֶּשֶׂק, Dameseq, proving that this is the Messiah.

— c. A.D. 36 —

²³And when many days were fulfilled, the יְהוּדִים, Y'hudiym took counsel together *regarding how* to kill him, ²⁴but their plot against HIM was known to שָׁאוּל, Shaul. And they were also watching the gates both day and night, *so that* they could kill him; ²⁵but his disciples, having taken him, let him down by night through the wall, lowering *him* in a basket.

²⁶And having come to יְרוּשָׁלַיִם, Y'rushalayim, he tried to join himself to the disciples, but they were all afraid of him, not believing that he was a disciple. ²⁷But בַּר־נַבָּא, Bar-Naba, having taken him, brought HIM to the emissaries and described to them how he saw the Master on the road, and that He spoke to him, and how he was speaking boldly in דַּמֶּשֶׂק, Dameseq in the Name of יֵשׁוּעַ, Yeshua.

²⁸And he was with them, coming in and going out in יְרוּשָׁלַיִם, Y'rushalayim, speaking boldly in the Name of the Master. ²⁹He was both speaking and disputing with the Ἑλληνιστάς, Hellenistas, but they were taking in hand *efforts* to kill him. ³⁰But the brothers, having known, brought him

---

[a] "He"—some mss say, "the Master"
[b] Some mss insert, "'It is hard for you to kick at the goads.' ⁶Trembling also, and astonished, he said, 'Master, what do you want me to do?' And the Master SAID to him"
[c] Some mss insert, "instantly"
[d] "Yeshua"—some mss say, "the Messiah"

Taviyta raised to life.   **Acts 10:12**

down to Cæsarea and sent him out to Tarsus.

³¹ So, then, the Called-Forth[a] throughout all יְהוּדָה, Y'hudah and *the* גָּלִיל, Galiyl and שֹׁמְרוֹן, Shom'ron had peace, being built up. And going on in the fear of the Master and in the encouragement of the רוּחַ הַקֹדֶשׁ, Ruach HaQodesh, they were multiplied.

³² And it came to pass that כֵּיפָא, Keifa,[b] passing throughout all PARTS, came down also to the קְדוֹשִׁים, Q'doshiym who were living at לֹד, Lod, ³³ and he found there a certain man by *the* name *of* Æneas, who was *a* paralytic, laid upon a mat for eight years. ³⁴ And כֵּיפָא, Keifa said to him, "Æneas, יֵשׁוּעַ, Yeshua *the* Messiah heals you. Arise and spread *your* cot for yourself," and immediately he arose. ³⁵ And all those living at לֹד, Lod and שָׁרוֹן, Sharon saw him and turned to the Master.

³⁶ And in יָפוֹ, Yafo, there was a certain female disciple by *the* name *of* טְבִיתָא, Taviyta (which, translated, is called Dorcas). This woman was full of good actions and *the* charity that she was doing. ³⁷ And it came to pass in those days *that*, having become infirmed, she died. And having bathed her, they laid her in an upper room.

³⁸ And לֹד, Lod was near to יָפוֹ, Yafo, *so* the disciples, having heard that כֵּיפָא, Keifa was in that PLACE, sent two men to him, pleading with him, "Do not delay to come through to us." ³⁹ And כֵּיפָא, Keifa, having arisen, went with them. *When* they had come, they brought *him* into the upper room; and all the widows stood by him, weeping and showing *him* shirts and coats—as many as Dorcas made while she was with them.

⁴⁰ And כֵּיפָא, Keifa—having put them all outside, and having bowed the knees—prayed. And having turned to the body, he said, "טְבִיתָא, Taviyta, arise!" And she opened her eyes, and having seen כֵּיפָא, Keifa, she sat up. ⁴¹ And having given her HIS hand, he lifted her up; and having called the קְדוֹשִׁים, Q'doshiym and the widows, he presented her alive! ⁴² And it became known throughout all יָפוֹ, Yafo, and many believed in the Master. ⁴³ And it came to pass that he remained many days in יָפוֹ, Yafo with a certain one, שִׁמְעוֹן, Shim'on, a tanner.

~ c. A.D. 39 ~

10 ¹ And there was a certain man in Cæsarea by *the* name *of* Cornelius—a centurion from a regiment called "Italian"—² *who was* godly; and fearing God with all his house, *he was* doing many kind acts *of* charity to the people and imploring God always.

³ About the ninth hour of the day, he saw openly in a vision a Messenger of God coming in to him and saying to him, "Cornelius." ⁴ And having fixed his gaze on him, and becoming afraid, he said, "What is it, Master?" And he said to him, "Your prayers and your charity went up for a remembrance in front of God; ⁵ so now, send men to יָפוֹ, Yafo, and send for a certain one *named* שִׁמְעוֹן, Shim'on, who is called כֵּיפָא, Keifa. ⁶ This one is staying as a guest with a certain שִׁמְעוֹן, Shim'on (a tanner) whose house is by the sea."[c] ⁷ And when the Messenger who was speaking to him went away, having called two of the house servants and a godly soldier from those attending to him continually, ⁸ and having related all *the* things to them, he sent them to יָפוֹ, Yafo.

⁹ And on the next day, as these *three* were proceeding on the road and were drawing near to the city, כֵּיפָא, Keifa went up on the house-top to pray, about the sixth hour. ¹⁰ And he became very hungry, and wanted to eat. And while they were making *the* food ready, there came upon him a trance, ¹¹ and he saw the heaven opened and a certain thing descending, like a large *linen* sheet *being* let down upon the ground[d] at the four corners, ¹² in which were all the *kinds of* four-footed animals[e] and creep-

---

[a] "Called-Forth"—ἐκκλησία, ekklesia; see *Mt.* 16:18
[b] כֵּיפָא, Keifa—Gk: Πέτρος, Petros; see יוֹחָנָן *Yn.* 1:42; also throughout chapters 9 and 10
[c] Some mss insert, "This one will speak to you what you must do."
[d] Some mss insert, "and bound"
[e] Some mss insert, "and the wild beasts"

ing things of the earth, and the birds of the heaven.

¹³And a voice came to him: "Having risen, כֵּיפָא, Keifa,[a] kill and eat." ¹⁴And כֵּיפָא, Keifa said, "Not so, Master! because at no time did I *ever* eat anything unholy[b] and unclean."

¹⁵And THERE WAS a voice again a second time, *saying* to him, "What God cleansed, you *must* not declare unholy." ¹⁶And this was done three times; and immediately,[c] the thing was received up to the heaven.

¹⁷And as כֵּיפָא, Keifa was perplexed in himself *as to* what the vision that he saw might be, look! the men who had been sent by Cornelius (having made inquiry for the house of שִׁמְעוֹן, Shim'on) stood at the gate. ¹⁸And having called, they were asking if שִׁמְעוֹן, Shim'on who is called כֵּיפָא, Keifa stayed as a guest here. ¹⁹And while כֵּיפָא, Keifa *was still* thinking through the vision, the רוּחַ, Ruach said to him, "Look! three men are looking for you; ²⁰but having arisen, go down*stairs* and go on with them, doubting nothing, because I have sent them."

²¹And כֵּיפָא, Keifa, having come down to the men,[d] said, "Look! I am he whom you seek. What IS the reason for which you have come?" ²²And they said, "Cornelius—a centurion, a man righteous and fearing God, and well-testified to by the whole ethnic-group of the Jews—was divinely warned by a holy Messenger to send for you *to come* to his house, and to hear spoken words from you."

²³Therefore, having called them in, he accommodated them as *his* guests; and on the next day, having arisen, he went out with them (and certain *ones* of the brothers from יָפוֹ, Yafo went with him *as well*). ²⁴And on the next day, he entered into Cæsarea; and Cornelius was waiting for them, having called together his relatives and close friends.

²⁵And it came *to pass* that as כֵּיפָא, Keifa entered in, Cornelius, having met him *and* having fallen at HIS feet, bowed before HIM. ²⁶But כֵּיפָא, Keifa raised him *up*, saying, "Stand up! I myself am also a man."

²⁷And talking with him, he went in and found many having come together. ²⁸And he said to them, "You know how illicit it is for a man, a יְהוּדִי, Y'hudiy, to keep company with or to come to *visit* one of another nation. But God showed me not to call *any* man unholy or unclean. ²⁹For this reason, without even speaking against it, I came, having been sent for. I ask, therefore, for what matter did you send for me?"

³⁰And Cornelius said, "Four days ago until this hour, I was[e] praying in my house AT the ninth hour. And look! a man stood in my presence in bright clothing, ³¹and he said, 'Cornelius, your prayer was heard, and your kind acts *of charity* were remembered in God's sight. ³²Therefore, send to יָפוֹ, Yafo, and call for שִׁמְעוֹן, Shim'on, who is called כֵּיפָא, Keifa. This one stays as a guest in the house of שִׁמְעוֹן, Shim'on (a tanner) by the sea.'[f] ³³Therefore, I sent for you at once, *and* you also did well, having come. Now, therefore, we are all *here* in God's sight to hear all *the* things that have been commanded you by the Master."[g]

³⁴And כֵּיפָא, Keifa, having opened his mouth, said, "I take hold of the truth that God is no accepter of faces,[h] ³⁵but in every ethnic group, he who is fearing Him and is putting righteousness into action is acceptable to Him. ³⁶The word that He sent to the sons of יִשְׂרָאֵל, Yis'rael (proclaiming Good News *and* peace through יֵשׁוּעַ, Yeshua the Messiah—this One is Master of all), ³⁷you have known. *This is* the spoken word that came throughout all יְהוּדָה, Y'hudah, having begun from the גָּלִיל, Galiyl, after the immersion that יוֹחָנָן, Yochanan proclaimed. ³⁸יֵשׁוּעַ, Yeshua, who IS from

---

[a] כֵּיפָא, Keifa—Gk: Πέτρος, Petros; see יוֹחָנָן *Yn.* 1:42; also throughout chapters 10 and 11
[b] "unholy"—lit. "common"; also in vss. 15 & 28
[c] "immediately"—some mss say, "again"
[d] Some mss insert, "who had been sent to him from Cornelius"
[e] Some mss insert, "fasting and"
[f] Some mss insert, "who, having come, will speak to you"
[g] "the Master"—some mss say, "God"
[h] cf. דְּבָרִים *D'variym* 10:17, Romans 2:11; Young's says, "no respecter of persons"

Keifa's address at Cæsarea.   **Acts 11:17**

נָצְרַת, N'tzaret—*you know* how God anointed Him with the רוּחַ הַקֹּדֶשׁ, Ruach HaQodesh and power (*He* who went throughout *the* Land doing good and healing all those subjugated by the devil, because God was with Him).

³⁹"And we—we are witnesses of all *the* things that He did, both in the land of the יְהוּדִים, Y'hudiym and in יְרוּשָׁלַיִם, Y'rushalayim. *He* whom they also put to death, having hung *Him* upon a tree—⁴⁰this One God raised up on the third day, and gave Him to become seen ⁴¹(not to all the people, but to witnesses; to those having been chosen beforehand by God; to us who ate with *Him* and drank with Him after His rising out of the dead). ⁴²And He commanded us to proclaim to the people and to testify fully that this is the One who has been appointed by God *as* judge of *both* living and dead. ⁴³To this One all the prophets testify: that through His Name, everyone that is believing in Him receives release from sins."

⁴⁴While כֵּיפָא, Keifa was still speaking these sayings, the רוּחַ הַקֹּדֶשׁ, Ruach HaQodesh fell upon all those hearing the word, ⁴⁵and those of the believing Circumcision[a] were astonished—as many as came with כֵּיפָא, Keifa—because the gift of the רוּחַ הַקֹּדֶשׁ, Ruach HaQodesh had also been poured out upon the גּוֹיִם, Goyim, ⁴⁶for they were hearing them speaking with *other* languages[b] and magnifying God.

Then כֵּיפָא, Keifa answered, ⁴⁷"Is anyone *of us* able to forbid the water, that these may not be immersed—*these* who received the רוּחַ הַקֹּדֶשׁ, Ruach HaQodesh, even as we *did* also?" ⁴⁸And he commanded them to be immersed in the Name of יֵשׁוּעַ, Yeshua *the* Messiah.[c] Then they asked him to remain *a* certain *number of* days.

11

¹And the emissaries and the brothers who were in יְהוּדָה, Y'hudah heard that the גּוֹיִם, Goyim also received the word of God, ²so when כֵּיפָא, Keifa came up to יְרוּשָׁלַיִם, Y'rushalayim, those of the Circumcision were contending with him, saying, "You went in to uncircumcised men, and ate with them!"

⁴And כֵּיפָא, Keifa, having begun, explained to them in order, saying, ⁵"I was in the city of יָפוֹ, Yafo, praying, and in a trance I saw a vision: a certain thing coming down out of the heaven—like a large *linen* sheet being let down by four corners, and it came to me—⁶at which, having fixed my gaze, I was looking. And I saw the four-footed animals of the earth, and the wild beasts, and the creeping things, and the birds of the heaven; ⁷and I also heard a voice saying to me, 'Having arisen, כֵּיפָא, Keifa, kill and eat.' ⁸And I said, 'Not so, Master! because at no time has anything unholy[d] or unclean entered into my mouth.' ⁹And the voice answered a second time out of the heaven, 'What God cleansed, you *must* not declare unholy.' ¹⁰And this happened three times, and all was drawn up again to the heaven.

¹¹"And look! immediately, three men stood at the house in which we were, having been sent from Cæsarea to me; ¹²and the רוּחַ, Ruach said to me to go with them, doubting nothing—and these six brothers also went with me.

"And we entered into the house of the man, ¹³and he declared to us how he saw the Messenger standing in his house and saying, 'Send to יָפוֹ, Yafo, and call for שִׁמְעוֹן, Shim'on, who is called כֵּיפָא, Keifa, ¹⁴who will speak sayings by which you will be saved—you and all your house.' ¹⁵And in my beginning to speak, the רוּחַ הַקֹּדֶשׁ, Ruach HaQodesh fell upon them, even as also upon us in the beginning. ¹⁶And I remembered the saying of the Master, how He said, 'יוֹחָנָן, Yochanan indeed immersed with water, but you will be immersed with the רוּחַ הַקֹּדֶשׁ, Ruach HaQodesh.' ¹⁷If, then, God gave the equal gift to them as also to us, having believed upon the Master יֵשׁוּעַ, Yeshua *the* Messiah, who was I *to be* able to withstand God?"

---

[a] "Circumcision"—a reference to Jews
[b] "languages"—lit. "tongues"
[c] יֵשׁוּעַ, Yeshua *the* Messiah"—some mss say, "the Master"

[d] "unholy"—lit. "common"; also in vs. 9

¹⁸And they, having heard these things, were silent *of further contention*, and glorified God, saying, "Then God also gave the Reformation to Life to the גּוֹיִם, Goyim."

~ c. A.D. 40 ~
Ya'aqov writes his letter.

¹⁹Those, indeed, therefore, *who* had been scattered abroad from the oppression that came after Stephen, went through to Phoenicia and Cyprus and Antioch, speaking the word to none except to יְהוּדִים, Y'hudiym only. ²⁰And there were certain of them—men of Cyprus and Cyrene who, having come into Antioch, were speaking also to the Ἑλληνιστάς, Hellenistas, proclaiming Good News *of* the Master יֵשׁוּעַ, Yeshua, ²¹and the hand of ADONAI was with them. A great number also, having believed, turned to the Master.

²²And the account regarding them was heard in the ears of the Called-Forth[a] that is in יְרוּשָׁלַיִם, Y'rushalayim. And they sent out בַּר־נַבָּא, Bar-Naba to go through to Antioch, ²³who, having come and having seen the *unmerited* favor of God, was rejoicing and was exhorting all with purpose of heart to remain faithful to the Master. ²⁴For he was a good man, and full of the רוּחַ הַקֹּדֶשׁ, Ruach HaQodesh and of faith. And a great many were added to the Master.

~ c. A.D. 42 ~

²⁵And בַּר־נַבָּא, Bar-Naba went to Tarsus to look for שָׁאוּל, Shaul, ²⁶and having found him, he brought him to Antioch. And it also came to pass that they gathered together a whole year with[b] the Called-Forth[c] and taught a great many people. The disciples also were called[d] "Messiah-followers"[e] for the first time in Antioch.

~ c. A.D. 43 ~

²⁷And in those days, prophets came from יְרוּשָׁלַיִם, Y'rushalayim to Antioch. ²⁸And one of them, by *the* name *of* Agabus, having stood up, signified through the רוּחַ, Ruach *that* a great famine was about to be throughout all the world (which came to pass in the time of Claudius). ²⁹And the disciples determined *that* as any one *of them* was prospering, each of them *ought* to send *a* contribution for service to the brothers living in יְהוּדָה, Y'hudah, ³⁰which they also did, having sent *it* to the זְקֵנִים, z'qeniym by the hand of בַּר־נַבָּא, Bar-Naba and שָׁאוּל, Shaul.

12

¹And about that time, Herod the king put forth his hands to do evil to certain *ones* of those of the Called-Forth, ²and he killed יַעֲקֹב, Ya'aqov, the brother of יוֹחָנָן, Yochanan, with the sword. ³And having seen that it was pleasing to the יְהוּדִים, Y'hudiym, he proceeded to lay hold of כֵּיפָא, Keifa[f] also (and these were the days of *the* Feast of הַמַּצּוֹת, HaMatzot), ⁴whom also having seized, he put in prison, having handed HIM over to four squads of four soldiers to guard him, intending after the פֶּסַח, Pesach to bring him out to the people.

⁵Therefore, כֵּיפָא, Keifa, indeed, was kept in the prison, and prayer was fervently being made to God for him by the Called-Forth. ⁶And when Herod was about to bring him out—that same night—כֵּיפָא, Keifa, having been bound with two chains, was sleeping between two soldiers. Also, guards were in front of the door, watching the prison.

⁷And look! a Messenger of ADONAI *was* suddenly standing there, and a light shone in the buildings. And having struck כֵּיפָא, Keifa in the side, he woke him up, saying, "Rise in haste!" and his chains fell from off HIS hands. ⁸And the Messenger said to him, "Dress yourself and bind on your sandals," and he did so. And *the* Messenger said to

---

[a] "Called-Forth"—ἐκκλησίας, ekklesias; see מַתִּתְיָהוּ *Matit'yahu* 16:18; also in vss. 12:1&5
[b] "with"—ἐν, en—Young's says, "in"
[c] "Called-Forth"—ἐκκλησία, ekklesia; see מַתִּתְיָהוּ *Matit'yahu* 16:18
[d] "called"—Young's says, "divinely called"
[e] "Messiah-followers"—see א כֵּיפָא *1 Keifa* 4:16
[f] כֵּיפָא, Keifa—Gk: Πέτρος, Petros; see יוֹחָנָן *Yn.* 1:42; also throughout chapter 12

Calling of Bar-Naba and Shaul.

him, "Put your coat around *yourself* and be following me."

⁹And having gone forth, he was following him, though he did not know that it was truly *happening*—that which was done through the Messenger—and was thinking he was seeing a vision. ¹⁰And having passed through a first guard station and a second, they came to the iron gate that is leading to the city, which opened for them on its own! And having gone forth, they went on through one street, and immediately the Messenger went away from him. ¹¹And כֵּיפָא, Keifa, having come to himself, said, "Now I have known of the truth: that ADONAI sent His Messenger and delivered me from the hand of Herod, and *from* all the expectation of the people of the יְהוּדִים, Y'hudiym."

¹²And having realized *this*, he came to the house of מִרְיָם, Mir'yam (the mother of יוֹחָנָן, Yochanan, who is called Mark) where there were many gathered together and praying.

¹³And when he had knocked at the door of the entrance, a slave-girl by *the* name *of* Rhoda came to listen *for who it was*. ¹⁴And having known the voice of כֵּיפָא, Keifa, from the joy she did not open the entrance but, having run in, told of the standing of כֵּיפָא, Keifa in front of the entrance.

¹⁵And they said to her, "You are insane!" but she was confidently affirming IT to be so. And they were saying, "It is his Messenger."

¹⁶And כֵּיפָא, Keifa was continuing knocking; and having opened *the entrance*, they saw him and were astonished. ¹⁷And having rapidly waved to them with the hand to be silent, he described to them how ADONAI brought him out of the prison, and he said, "Declare these things to יַעֲקֹב, Ya'aqov and to the brothers." And having gone out, he went on to another place.

¹⁸And when day had come, there was no small stir among the soldiers *as to* what, then, had become of כֵּיפָא, Keifa. ¹⁹And having searched for him and not having found *him*, Herod, having examined the guards, commanded THEM to be led away to punishment. And having gone down from יְהוּדָה, Y'hudah to Cæsarea, he was staying THERE.

²⁰And he was highly displeased with the צֹרִים, Tzoriym and צִדֹנִים, Tzidoniym, and with one mind they came to him, and (having made a friend of Blastus, who IS *in charge* over the bedrooms of the king) they were asking *for* peace, because of their land *needing to* being nourished from the king's.

²¹And on a set day, Herod, having clothed himself in kingly clothing and having sat down on the tribunal *seat*, was making a public address to them—²²and the public was shouting, "The voice of a god, and not of a man!" ²³And instantly a Messenger of ADONAI struck him, because he did not give the glory to God; and having been eaten of worms, he breathed his last.

~ c. A.D. 45 ~

²⁴And the word of God grew and multiplied, ²⁵and בַּר־נַבָּא, Bar-Naba and שָׁאוּל, Shaul returned to יְרוּשָׁלַיִם, Y'rushalayim, having fulfilled the service, taking יוֹחָנָן, Yochanan with THEM—who was called Mark.

~ c. A.D. 46 ~

13

¹And there were certain prophets and teachers in Antioch among[a] the Called-Forth[b] there: not only בַּר־נַבָּא, Bar-Naba and שִׁמְעוֹן, Shim'on (who is called Niger) and Lucius the Cyrenian, but also Manaen (Herod the tetrarch's foster-brother) and שָׁאוּל, Shaul. ²And in their serving the Master and fasting, the רוּחַ הַקֹּדֶשׁ, Ruach HaQodesh said, "Separate to Me בַּר־נַבָּא, Bar-Naba and שָׁאוּל, Shaul to the work to which I have called them." ³Then, having fasted and having prayed and having laid the hands on them, they released THEM.

⁴They, indeed, then, having been sent forth by the רוּחַ הַקֹּדֶשׁ, Ruach HaQodesh,

---
[a] "among"—κατὰ, kata—Young's says, "in"
[b] "Called-Forth"—ἐκκλησίαν, ekklesian; see מַתִּתְיָהוּ *Matit'yahu* 16:18

went down to Seleucia. From that place, they also sailed to Cyprus; ⁵and having come to Salamis, they proclaimed the word of God in the synagogues of the יְהוּדִים, Y'hudiym (and they also had יוֹחָנָן, Yochanan AS an assistant).

⁶And having gone through the whole island to Paphos, they found a certain man —a magian,[a] a false prophet, a יְהוּדִי, Y'hudiy, whose name IS בַּר־יֵשׁוּעַ, Bar-Yeshua— ⁷who was with the proconsul Sergius Paulus (*himself* an intelligent man). This one, having called for בַּר־נַבָּא, Bar-Naba and שָׁאוּל, Shaul, desired to hear the word of God. ⁸But Elymas the magian (for so is his name interpreted) opposed them, seeking to pervert the proconsul from the faith.

⁹But שָׁאוּל, Shaul—who IS also Paul[b]— having been filled with the רוּחַ הַקֹּדֶשׁ, Ruach HaQodesh, having fixed his gaze on him, ¹⁰said, "O *you* full of all underhandedness and all unscrupulousness! son of the Accuser! enemy of all righteousness! Will you not stop perverting the right ways of the Master? ¹¹And now, look! a hand of the Master IS upon you, and you will be blind, not seeing the sun for a season!" And instantly, a mist and darkness fell on him; and he, going around, was looking for someone to lead HIM by the hand. ¹²Then the proconsul, having seen what had come to pass, believed, being astonished at the teaching of the Master.

¹³And those around Paul, having set sail from Paphos, came to Perga of Pamphylia. And יוֹחָנָן, Yochanan, having gone away from them, returned to יְרוּשָׁלַיִם, Y'rushalayim. ¹⁴And they, having gone through from Perga, came to Antioch of Pisidia. And having gone into the synagogue on יוֹם הַשַּׁבָּת, Yom HaShabat, they sat down. ¹⁵And after the reading from the תּוֹרָה, Torah and from the Prophets, the leading men of the synagogue sent *word* to them, saying, "Men, brothers, if there is in you a word of exhortation to the people—say on."

¹⁶And Paul, having arisen, and having rapidly waved with the hand, said, "Men, יִשְׂרְאֵלִים, Yis'raeliym, and those fearing God, listen: ¹⁷the God of this people יִשְׂרָאֵל, Yis'rael chose our fathers, and He exalted the people in their sojourning in the land of מִצְרַיִם, Mitz'rayim, and with an arm *uplifted* high, He brought them out of it. ¹⁸And *for* a period of about forty years, He put up with them in the desert. ¹⁹And having destroyed *the* seven ethnic-groups[c] in the land of כְּנַעַן, K'na-an, He distributed their land to them as an inheritance ²⁰(*this all took* about four hundred and fifty years). And after these things, He gave judges *to them* until שְׁמוּאֵל, Sh'muel the prophet. ²¹And thereafter, they asked for a king, and God gave to them שָׁאוּל, Shaul—son of קִישׁ, Qish, a man of the tribe of בִּנְיָמִין, Bin'yamiyn—for forty years. ²²And having removed him, He raised up to them דָּוִד, David for a king, to whom also, having testified, He said, 'I FOUND דָּוִד, DAVID, the SON of יִשַׁי, Yishai, A MAN ACCORDING TO MY HEART, who will do all My will.'[d] ²³Of this one's seed, God, according to His promise, brought[e] to יִשְׂרָאֵל, Yis'rael a Savior—יֵשׁוּעַ, Yeshua!

²⁴"Before His coming, יוֹחָנָן, Yochanan had first proclaimed an immersion of reformation to all the people of יִשְׂרָאֵל, Yis'rael. ²⁵But as יוֹחָנָן, Yochanan was fulfilling the course, he said, 'Whom do you suppose me to be? I am not HE, but look! He comes after me, of whom I am not worthy to untie the sandal of HIS feet.'

²⁶"Men, brothers, sons of the ancestry of אַבְרָהָם, Av'raham, and those among you fearing God—to us the word of this salvation was sent. ²⁷For those living in יְרוּשָׁלַיִם, Y'rushalayim, and their leaders—not having known this One, *or* even the voices of the prophets (which are being read every

---

[a] "magian"—μάγον, magon—astrologer, sorcerer, magician; also in vs. 8 (μάγος, magos)
[b] From this point forward, Luke refers to שָׁאוּל, Shaul by his Roman name, "Paul," that is, Παῦλος, Paulos. See note at 1 Timothy 1:1.
[c] cf. דְּבָרִים *D'variym* 7:1
[d] cf. שְׁמוּאֵל א *Sh'muel Alef* 13:14; תְּהִלִּים *T'hiliym* 89:21(20)
[e] "brought"—some mss say, "raised"

שַׁבָּת, Shabat)—having judged H*im*, fulfilled *them*. ²⁸And having found no reason for *a* death *sentence*, they asked of Pilate that He should be put to death. ²⁹And when they completed all the things written about Him, having taken H*im* down from the tree, they laid Him in a tomb. ³⁰But God raised Him out of the dead! ³¹And He was seen for many days by those who came up with Him from the גָּלִיל, Galiyl to יְרוּשָׁלַיִם, Y'rushalayim, who are now His witnesses to the people.

³²"And we proclaim Good News to you: that the promise made to the fathers— ³³this, God has completed to us (their children) in full, having raised up יֵשׁוּעַ, Yeshua, as also it has been written in the second Melody,

'You are My Son; today I have brought you forth.'ᵃ

³⁴And *as for the fact* that He raised Him up out of the dead, no more to return to decay, He has said this:

'I will give to you the faithful undefiledness of דָּוִד, David.'ᵇ

³⁵Therefore, also, in another *passage* He said,

'You will not give Your undefiled One to see decay.'ᶜ

³⁶For דָּוִד, David, indeed, having served his own generation by the will of God, fell asleep, and was added to his fathers, and saw decay; ³⁷but He whom God raised up did not see decay!

³⁸"Therefore, let it be known to you—men, brothers—that through this One the forgiveness of sins is proclaimed to you, and from all things from which you were unable to be declared righteous in the תּוֹרָה, Torah of מֹשֶׁה, Mosheh, ³⁹in this One, everyone who is believing is declared righteous. ⁴⁰Therefore, watch out! *so that* what has been spoken in the prophets may not come upon you:

⁴¹'See, you despisers, and wonder and perish, because I work a work in your days—a work in which you may not believe, though someone describes *it* to you.'"ᵈ

⁴²And having gone out,ᵉ *the people*ᶠ were pleading *with* them that these sayings *again* be spoken to them on the next שַׁבָּת, Shabat. ⁴³And when the synagogue had been dismissed, many of the יְהוּדִים, Y'hudiym and of the devout proselytes followed Paul and בַּר־נַבָּא, Bar-Naba, who, speaking to them, were persuading them to remain in the *unmerited* favor of God.

⁴⁴And on the coming שַׁבָּת, Shabat, almost all the city was gathered together to hear the word of Adonai;ᵍ ⁴⁵but the יְהוּדִים, Y'hudiym, having seen the crowds, were filled with jealousy and contradicted the things spoken by Paul,ʰ speaking evil. ⁴⁶And speaking boldly, Paul and בַּר־נַבָּא, Bar-Naba said, "It was necessary that the word of God be spoken first to you. Seeing *that* you thrust it away and do not judge yourselves worthy of the life age-enduring, look! we turn to the גּוֹיִם, Goyim. ⁴⁷For so has Adonai commanded us:

'I have set you as a light for *the* גּוֹיִם, Goyim—for your being for salvation to the end of the earth.'"ⁱ

⁴⁸And the גּוֹיִם, Goyim, hearing *this*, were rejoicing and were glorifying the word of Adonai, and *they* believed—as many as were appointed to life age-enduring— ⁴⁹and the word of Adonai was spread abroad through all the region.

⁵⁰And the יְהוּדִים, Y'hudiym stirred up the devout, respected women and the elite men of the city, and *they* raised persecution against Paul and בַּר־נַבָּא, Bar-Naba and put them out from their borders.

ᵃ תְּהִלִּים *T'hiliym* 2:7
ᵇ יְשַׁעְיָהוּ *Y'sha'yahu* 55:3
ᶜ תְּהִלִּים *T'hiliym* 16:10
ᵈ חֲבַקּוּק *'Chavaquq* 1:5
ᵉ Some mss insert, "of the synagogue of the יְהוּדִים, Y'hudiym"
ᶠ "*the people*"—some mss say, "גּוֹיִם, Goyim"
ᵍ "Adonai"—some mss say, "God"
ʰ Some mss insert, "contradicting and"
ⁱ יְשַׁעְיָהוּ *Y'sha'yahu* 49:6

⁵¹But having shaken off the dust of their feet against them, they came to Iconium, ⁵²and the disciples were filled with joy and the רוּחַ הַקֹּדֶשׁ, Ruach HaQodesh.

14

¹And it came to pass in Iconium, that they entered together into the synagogue of the יְהוּדִים, Y'hudiym, and spoke such that a great number of both יְהוּדִים, Y'hudiym and Greeks believed. ²But the unbelieving יְהוּדִים, Y'hudiym stirred up and poisoned[a] the souls of the גּוֹיִם, Goyim against the brothers. ³Therefore, indeed, they remained a long time, speaking boldly in the Master, who was testifying to the word of His *unmerited* favor *and* giving signs and wonders to come to pass through their hands.

⁴And the whole of the city was divided, and some were with the יְהוּדִים, Y'hudiym, and some with the emissaries. ⁵And when there was an onrush—both of the גּוֹיִם, Goyim and of the יְהוּדִים, Y'hudiym, with their leaders—to mistreat THEM and to stone them, ⁶they, having become aware, fled to the cities of Lycaonia, Lystra, and Derbe, and to the surrounding region, ⁷and there they were proclaiming Good News.

⁸And a certain man in Lystra was sitting *there*—disabled in the feet, lame from the womb of his mother, who had never walked. ⁹This one heard Paul speaking, who, having fixed his gaze on him and having seen that he had faith to be saved, ¹⁰said with a loud voice, "Stand up—upright on your feet!" And he leapt *up* and was walking. ¹¹And the crowds, having seen what Paul did, lifted up their voice in the speech of Lycaonia, saying, "The gods, having become like men, came down to us!" ¹²They were also calling בַּר־נַבָּא, Bar-Naba "Zeus," and Paul "Hermes," since he was the leader in speaking.

¹³And the priest of the *temple of* Zeus that is in front of the city, having brought oxen and garlands to the entrances, wanted to *offer a* sacrifice with the crowds. ¹⁴But having heard, the emissaries בַּר־נַבָּא, Bar-Naba and Paul, having torn their coats, sprang out into the crowd, shouting ¹⁵and saying, "Men! Why do you do these things? We are also men with *natural* affections like you, *yet* proclaiming Good News to you, *so that* from these useless things *you will* turn to the living God, WHO MADE THE HEAVEN AND THE EARTH AND THE SEA AND ALL THE THINGS IN THEM[b]—¹⁶who in the past generations allowed all the world-ethnicities to go on in their ways, ¹⁷though He did not leave Himself without witness, doing good from heaven *by* giving rains to you, and fruitful seasons, filling your hearts with food and gladness." ¹⁸But *even* saying these things, *it was* with difficulty *that* they stopped the crowds from sacrificing to them.

¹⁹And there came יְהוּדִים, Y'hudiym from Antioch and Iconium; and they, having persuaded the crowds and having stoned Paul, dragged him outside of the city, supposing him to be dead. ²⁰But with the disciples having surrounded him, he, having arisen, entered into the city; and on the next day, he went out with בַּר־נַבָּא, Bar-Naba to Derbe. ²¹Having proclaimed Good News also to that city, and having discipled many, they returned to Lystra and to Iconium and to Antioch, ²²strengthening the souls of the disciples, exhorting *them* to remain in the faith, and that "we must go through many oppressions to enter into the Reign of God." ²³And having handpicked[c] זְקֵנִים, z'qeniym for them among all[d] *the* Called-Forth,[e] having prayed with fastings, they committed them to the Master in whom they had believed.

²⁴And having passed through Pisidia, they came to Pamphylia; ²⁵and having spoken the word in Perga, they went down to Attalia, ²⁶and from that place sailed to Antioch, where they had been given (by the

---

[a] "poisoned"—Young's says, "made evil"

[b] תְּהִלִּים T'hiliym 146:6

[c] "handpicked"—Young's says, "appointed to them by vote"

[d] "among all"—κατ', kat—Young's says, "in every"

[e] "Called-Forth"—ἐκκλησίαν, ekklesian; see מַתִּתְיָהוּ Matit'yahu 16:18; also in vs. 27

Dissension about circumcision.   Acts 15:21

unmerited favor of God) for the work that they fulfilled. ²⁷And having come and gathered *all* the Called-Forth together, they were making known as many things as God had done with them, and that He opened a door of faith to the גּוֹיִם, Goyim. ²⁸And they stayed no small time with the disciples.

~ c. A.D. 50 ~

15 ¹And certain *ones*, having come down from יְהוּדָה, Y'hudah, were teaching the brothers: "If you are not circumcised according to the custom of מֹשֶׁה, Mosheh, *then* you are not able to be saved." ²But there having been no small standoff and contentious debate by Paul and בַּר־נַבָּא, Bar-Naba with them, they arranged for Paul and בַּר־נַבָּא, Bar-Naba and certain others of them to go up to יְרוּשָׁלַיִם, Y'rushalayim to the emissaries and זְקֵנִים, z'qeniym about this question. ³Then, indeed, having been sent on their way by the Called-Forth,ᵃ they were passing through both Phoenicia and שֹׁמְרוֹן, Shom'ron, describing the conversion of the גּוֹיִם, Goyim, and they were causing great joy among all the brothers.

⁴And having come to יְרוּשָׁלַיִם, Y'rushalayim, they were received by the Called-Forth and the emissaries and the זְקֵנִים, z'qeniym, *and* they also made known as many things as God had done with them. ⁵And there rose up certain of those of the sect of the פְּרוּשִׁים, P'rushiym who believed, saying *of the Goyim,* "It is necessary to circumcise them, *and* also to command them to keep the תּוֹרָה, Torah of מֹשֶׁה, Mosheh." ⁶And the emissaries and זְקֵנִים, z'qeniym were gathered together to see about this matter. ⁷And after there had been much contentious debate, כֵּיפָא, Keifa,ᵇ having risen up, said to them, "Men, brothers, you know that from former days, God chose *me from* among you, for the גּוֹיִם, Goyim to hear through my mouth the word of the Good News, and to believe. ⁸And the heart-knowing God testified to them, having given the רוּחַ הַקֹּדֶשׁ, Ruach HaQodesh (even as *He* also *gave* to us), ⁹and also put no difference between us and them, having purified their hearts by the faith. ¹⁰Now, therefore, why do you tempt God, *so as* to put a yoke on the neck of the disciples which neither our fathers nor we were able to bear? ¹¹But through the *unmerited* favor of the Master יֵשׁוּעַ, Yeshua,ᶜ we believe to be saved, even as they also *do*." ¹²And all the great number *of them* stopped talking, and were listening to בַּר־נַבָּא, Bar-Naba and Paul relating all *the* signs and wonders *that* God did among the גּוֹיִם, Goyim through them.

¹³And after they stopped talking, יַעֲקֹב, Ya'aqov answered, saying, "Men, brothers, listen to me. ¹⁴שִׁמְעוֹן, Shim'on at first related how God looked after the גּוֹיִם, Goyim to take out *from them* a people for His Name. ¹⁵And to this the words of the prophets agree, as it has been written:

¹⁶"'After these things I will return, and I will build again the סֻכָּה, Sukah of דָּוִד, David that is fallen down, and its ruins I will build again, and will set it upright, ¹⁷*so that* the remnant of men may seek after the Master, and all the גּוֹיִם, Goyim, upon whom My Name has been called," says ADONAI, who is doing these things'ᵈ

¹⁸known from the ages.ᵉ ¹⁹Therefore, I judge not to trouble those from *among* the גּוֹיִם, Goyim who turn to God; ²⁰rather, to write to them to abstain from the pollutions of the idols, and the sexual immorality, and the strangled thing, and the blood. ²¹For מֹשֶׁה, Mosheh, from former generations, in every city has those

---

ᵃ "Called-Forth"—ἐκκλησίας, ekklesias; see מַתִּתְיָהוּ Matit'yahu 16:18; also in vss. 4 & 41
ᵇ כֵּיפָא, Keifa—Gk: Πέτρος, Petros; see יוֹחָנָן Yn. 1:42
ᶜ Some mss insert, "Messiah"
ᵈ עָמוֹס *Amos* 9:11-12 (LXX). According to the Hebrew, "'In that day I *will* raise the סֻכָּה, Sukah of דָּוִד, David that is fallen—and I have repaired their breaches, and its ruins I raise up, and I have built it up as in days of old—so that *Yis'rael will* possess the remnant of אֱדוֹם, 'Edom, and all the גּוֹיִם, Goyim on whom My Name is called,' an affirmation of ADONAI—doer of this."
ᵉ Some mss insert, "to God are all His works"

proclaiming him, being read in the synagogues every שַׁבָּת, Shabat."

²²Then it seemed good to the emissaries and the זְקֵנִים, z'qeniym, with all the Called-Forth,[a] to send chosen men out from themselves to Antioch with Paul and בַּר־נַבָּא, Bar-Naba—יְהוּדָה, Y'hudah (called בַּר־שַׁבָּא, Bar-Saba) and סִילָא, Siyla, *who are* leading men among the brothers—²³having written through their hand:

"*From* the emissaries and the זְקֵנִים, z'qeniym, brothers; to those brothers in Antioch and Syria and Cilicia who ARE of the גּוֹיִם, Goyim: שָׁלוֹם, shalom.[b] ²⁴Since we have heard that certain *ones*—to whom we gave no command—having gone out from us, troubled you with words, subverting your souls,[c] ²⁵it seemed good to us, having come together with one mind, to send chosen men to you with our beloved בַּר־נַבָּא, Bar-Naba and Paul—²⁶men who have given up their lives for the Name of our Master יֵשׁוּעַ, Yeshua the Messiah.

²⁷"We have sent, therefore, יְהוּדָה, Y'hudah and סִילָא, Siyla, and they will be telling *you* by word the same things *we are writing now*.

²⁸"For it seemed good to the רוּחַ הַקֹּדֶשׁ, Ruach HaQodesh, and to us, to lay upon you no more burden except these necessary things: ²⁹to abstain from things offered to idols, and blood, and strangled things, and sexual immorality—keeping yourselves from which, you will do well. Be strong!"

³⁰Then, indeed, having been released, they went to Antioch and, having brought the great number *of them* together, delivered the letter. ³¹And having read *it*, they rejoiced for the encouragement. ³²And יְהוּדָה, Y'hudah and סִילָא, Siyla, themselves also being prophets, exhorted and strengthened the brothers through many words. ³³And having passed some time, they were released with peace from the brothers *back* to those having sent them.[d]

~ c. A.D. 51 ~
Paul writes his letter to the Galatians.

³⁵And Paul and בַּר־נַבָּא, Bar-Naba continued in Antioch, teaching and proclaiming Good News (with many others also)—the word of the Master. ³⁶And after *a* certain *number of* days, Paul said to בַּר־נַבָּא, Bar-Naba, "Having turned again, we should look after the brothers in every city in which we have proclaimed the word of the Master, *to see* how they are *doing*." ³⁷And בַּר־נַבָּא, Bar-Naba was intending to also take with THEM יוֹחָנָן, Yochanan, called Mark, ³⁸but Paul was not thinking it good to take him with them—*he* who went away from them from Pamphylia, and did not go with them to *do* the work.[e]

³⁹And there came a sharp contention, so that they were parted from one another; and בַּר־נַבָּא, Bar-Naba, having taken Mark, sailed to Cyprus; ⁴⁰and Paul, having chosen סִילָא, Siyla, went out, having been given up to the *unmerited* favor of the Master[f] by the brothers. ⁴¹And he went through Syria and Cilicia, strengthening the Called-Forth-Communities.[g]

16
¹And he also came to Derbe and to Lystra, and look! a certain disciple was there by *the* name *of* Timothy—son of a believing יְהוּדִי, Y'hudiy woman, but of a father, a Greek—²who was well testified to by the brothers in Lystra and Iconium. ³Paul wanted this one to go with him, and having taken HIM, he circumcised him, because of the יְהוּדִים, Y'hudiym who are in those places, for they all knew that his father was a Greek.

⁴And as they were going on through the cities, they were delivering to them the de-

---

[a] "Called-Forth"—ἐκκλησία, ekklesia; see מַתִּתְיָהוּ Matit'yahu 16:18
[b] "shalom"—see מַתִּתְיָהוּ Matit'yahu 26:49
[c] Some mss insert, "saying *it is necessary for you* to be circumcised and to keep the תּוֹרָה, Torah"
[d] Some mss continue with vs. 34, "but it seemed good to סִילָא, Siyla to still remain there."
[e] cf. Acts 13:13
[f] "the Master"—some mss say, "God"
[g] "Called-Forth-Communities"—ἐκκλησίας, ekklesias; see מַתִּתְיָהוּ Matit'yahu 16:18

Paul and Siyla at Philippi.   **Acts 16:27**

crees to keep that had been judged by the emissaries and זְקֵנִים, z'qeniym who ARE in יְרוּשָׁלַיִם, Y'rushalayim. ⁵Then, indeed, were the Called-Forth-Communities[a] made strong in the faith, and were abounding in number every day. ⁶And they went through Phrygia and the region of Galatia, having been forbidden by the רוּחַ הַקֹּדֶשׁ, Ruach HaQodesh to speak the word in Asia; ⁷and having gone toward Mysia, they were trying to go on into Bithynia, but the רוּחַ, Ruach of יֵשׁוּעַ, Yeshua[b] did not allow them. ⁸So, having passed by Mysia, they came down to Troas.

⁹And a vision appeared to Paul during the night: a certain man of Macedonia was standing and pleading with him, and saying, "Having passed through to Macedonia, help us!" ¹⁰And when he saw the vision, immediately we endeavored to go to Macedonia, assuredly putting together *in our minds* that God[c] had called us to proclaim Good News to them.

¹¹And having set sail from Troas, we came with a straight course to Samothracia, and on the next day to Neapolis, ¹²and from that place to Philippi, which is a principal city of the part of Macedonia *that is* a Roman colony. And we were remaining in this city *a* certain *number of* days.

¹³And on יוֹם הַשַּׁבָּת, Yom HaShabat, we went outside of the gate, by a river, where we were supposing *a place of* prayer to be. And having sat down, we were speaking to the women who came together; ¹⁴and a certain woman was listening, by *the* name *of* Lydia—a seller of purple *fabrics*, of the city of Thyatira, reverencing God—whose heart the Master opened to pay careful attention to the things spoken by Paul.

¹⁵And when she and her household were immersed, she appealed to us, saying, "If you have judged me to be faithful to the Master, having entered my house, stay!" and she constrained us.

¹⁶And it came to pass, in our going on to the *place of* prayer, *that* a certain slave-girl met us, having a רוּחַ, ruach of Python,[d] who brought much employment to her masters by predicting the future. ¹⁷She, following Paul and us, was shouting, saying, "These men are slaves of the Most High God, who proclaim to you a way of salvation!" ¹⁸And she was doing this for many days. But Paul, having been greatly annoyed, and having turned *to her*, said to the רוּחַ, ruach, "I command you, in the Name of יֵשׁוּעַ, Yeshua *the* Messiah, to come out from her!" and it came out the same moment.

¹⁹And her masters—having seen that the hope of their employment was gone—having caught Paul and סִילָא, Siyla, dragged THEM to the market-place, to the leaders. ²⁰And having brought them to the civil officers, they said, "These men, being יְהוּדִים, Y'hudiym, trouble our city exceedingly, ²¹and they proclaim customs that are not permitted for us to receive nor to do, being Romans." ²²And the crowd rose up together against *Paul and Siyla*. And the civil officers, having torn their garments from them, were giving orders to beat THEM with rods. ²³And *after* many wounds having *been* laid upon them, they threw them into prison, having commanded the jailer to guard them securely——²⁴who, having received such a command, put them into the inner prison, and made their feet secure in the stocks.

²⁵And at midnight, Paul and סִילָא, Siyla were praying *and* singing praises to God, and the prisoners were hearing them. ²⁶Then, suddenly, a massive earthquake came, so that the foundations of the prison were shaken, and all the doors were instantly opened, and the bonds of all *the prisoners* were loosened.

²⁷And the jailer, having come out of sleep and having seen the doors of the prison open, having drawn the sword, was about to kill himself, thinking the prisoners to

---

[a] "Called-Forth-Communities"—ἐκκλησίαι, ekklesiai; see מַתִּתְיָהוּ *Matit'yahu* 16:18
[b] Some mss omit, "of יֵשׁוּעַ, Yeshua"
[c] "God"—some mss say, "the Master"
[d] "Python"—a serpent slain by Apollo in Greek mythology

have fled. ²⁸But Paul called out with a loud voice, saying, "You should not do yourself any harm, for we are all here!"

²⁹And having asked for the lights, he sprang in; and trembling, he fell down before Paul and סִילָא, Siyla ³⁰and, having brought them out, said, "Sirs, what must I do—that I may be saved?" ³¹And they said *to him*, "Believe in the Master יֵשׁוּעַ, Yeshua,ᵃ and you will be saved—you and your house." ³²And they spoke the word of the Master to him, along with all those in his household.

³³And having taken them, in that time of the night, he bathed THEM from the wounds and was immersed at once— himself and all his *household*. ³⁴Having also brought them into the house, he set food before THEM, and *he* was glad with all the household, he having believed in God.

³⁵And when day had come, the civil officers sent the rod-bearers, saying, "Let those men go"; ³⁶and the jailer told these words to Paul: "The civil officers have sent *word* that you may be let go. Now, therefore, having gone out, go on in peace." ³⁷And Paul said to them, "Having beaten us publicly, uncondemned—*we* being men *who are* Roman *citizens*—they threw US into prison, and now privately they send us away! Why, no! but having come themselves, let them bring us out." ³⁸And the rod-bearers told these sayings to the civil officers, and they were afraid, having heard that they are Roman *citizens*. ³⁹And having come, they appealed to them; and having brought THEM out, they were asking THEM to go away from the city. ⁴⁰And they, having gone out from the prison, entered into THE HOUSE OF Lydia; and having seen the brothers, they encouraged them and went out.

17 ¹And having passed through Amphipolis and Apollonia, they came to Thessalonica, where *there* was a synagogue of the יְהוּדִים, Y'hudiym; ²and according to the custom of Paul, he went in to them; and for three שַׁבָּתוֹת, Shabatot, he reasoned with them from the Scriptures, ³opening *them up* and citing that "it was necessary *for* the Messiah to suffer and to rise again out of the dead," and that, "this is the Messiah: יֵשׁוּעַ, Yeshua, whom I proclaim to you." ⁴And certain *ones* of them believed and attached themselves to Paul and to סִילָא, Siyla—also a great number of the devout Greeks, and not a few of the elite women.

⁵And theᵇ יְהוּדִים, Y'hudiym—having been moved with envy, and having taken to themselves certain evil men of the *ones* lounging *around the marketplace*, and having made a crowd—were setting the city in an uproar. Having also assailed the house of Jason, they were looking for *Paul and Siyla* to bring THEM *out* into the public. ⁶And not having found them, they dragged Jason and *also* certain brothers to the city leaders, calling aloud, "These, having put the world in commotion, have also come here—⁷*these* whom Jason has received— and all these do contrary to the decrees of Cæsar, saying another *one* to be king: יֵשׁוּעַ, Yeshua." ⁸And they troubled the crowd and the city leaders *who were* hearing these things. ⁹And having taken *money as* security from Jason and the remainder *of them*, they let them go.

¹⁰And the brothers immediately, during the night, sent out to Berea both Paul and סִילָא, Siyla, who, having come, went to the synagogue of the יְהוּדִים, Y'hudiym. ¹¹And these were more noble than those in Thessalonica, *for* they received the word with all readiness of mind, every day examining the Scriptures *to find out* whether those things were so. ¹²Indeed, therefore, many of them believed, and *also* not a few of the respected Greek women and men. ¹³And when the יְהוּדִים, Y'hudiym from Thessalonica knew that the word of God was also proclaimed by Paul in Berea, they came

---

ᵃ Some mss insert, "Messiah."

ᵇ Some mss insert, "unbelieving."

Paul at Athens.

there also, agitating and troubling[a] the crowds. ¹⁴So, then, the brothers immediately sent Paul out to go on as far as to the sea, but both סִילָא, Siyla and Timothy remained there.

¹⁵And those escorting Paul brought him as far as Athens, and having received a command for סִילָא, Siyla and Timothy—that with all speed they might come to him—they departed. ¹⁶And while Paul *was* waiting for them in Athens, his רוּחַ, ruach was stirred in him, seeing the city wholly given to idolatry. ¹⁷Therefore, indeed, he was reasoning in the synagogue with the יְהוּדִים, Y'hudiym, and with the devout persons, and in the market-place every day with those who happened to be there.

¹⁸And also, certain *ones* of the Epicurean and Stoic philosophers were meeting together to see him, and some were saying, "What would this seed picker[b] want to say?" and others, "He seems to be a preacher of foreign demons," since he proclaimed יֵשׁוּעַ, Yeshua and the Rising Again as Good News.

¹⁹And having taken him, they brought HIM to the Areopagus, saying, "Are we able to know what this new teaching IS that is spoken by you? ²⁰For you bring certain foreign things to our ears. We want, then, to know what these things would want to be."

²¹Now all *the* Athenians and visiting foreigners were spending their time on nothing else but to say something *novel*, or to hear some newer thing. ²²And Paul, having stood in the middle of the Areopagus, said, "Men! Athenians! in all things I perceive you as over-religious, ²³for *while* passing through and contemplating your objects of reverence, I found also an elevated platform on which had been inscribed: 'To *an* unknown God,' whom, therefore, *though* not knowing, you reverence. This One I announce to you.

²⁴"God, who made the world and all things in it (this One, being Master of heaven and of earth), does not live in temples made with hands. ²⁵Neither by human hands is He served, *as if He was* needing anything—He *who*, to all, *is* giving life, and breath, and all things. ²⁶He also made from one *man*[c] every ethnic-group of men, to live upon all the face of the earth—having predetermined *their* appointed times, and the boundaries of their dwellings—²⁷*and* to seek God[d] (if perhaps they *would* feel around for[e] Him), and find *Him*; though, indeed, He is not far from each one of us. ²⁸For in Him we live, and move, and be, as also certain *ones* of your poets have said, 'For we are also His children.'

²⁹"Being, therefore, children of God, we ought not to think the Divine Being to be likened to gold, or silver, or stone—*an* engraving of art, and device of man. ³⁰Indeed, therefore, having overlooked the times of the ignorance, God now commands all men everywhere to reform, ³¹because He *has* set a day in which He is about to judge the world in righteousness by a Man whom He appointed, having given assurance to all *and* having raised Him out of the dead."

³²And having heard of the Rising Again of the dead, some, indeed, were mocking *him*, but others said, "We will also hear you again concerning this." ³³So Paul went out from among them, ³⁴and certain men, having stuck to him, believed, among whom IS also Dionysius the Areopagite, and a woman by *the* name *of* Damaris, and others with them.

18

¹After these things, having separated *himself* from Athens, he came to Corinth; ²and having found a certain יְהוּדִי, Y'hudiy by *the* name *of* Aquila (of Pontus by birth) and Priscilla his wife—*both* recently come from Italy because of Claudius having directed all

---

[a] Some mss omit, "and troubling"
[b] "seed picker"—fig. "a false teacher who picks up and passes on scraps of truth or information" (Friberg)
[c] "one *man*"—some mss say, "one blood"
[d] "God"—some mss say, "the Master"
[e] "around for"—Young's says, "after"

of the יְהוּדִים, Y'hudiym to separate *themselves* from Rome—he came to them. ³And because of being of the same trade, he stayed with them and was working, for they were *also* tent-makers by trade. ⁴And he was reasoning in the synagogue every שַׁבָּת, Shabat, persuading both יְהוּדִים, Y'hudiym and Greeks.

⁵And when both סִילָא, Siyla and Timothy had come down from Macedonia, Paul was *completely* occupied with the word,ᵃ testifying fully to the יְהוּדִים, Y'hudiym *that the* Messiah is יֵשׁוּעַ, Yeshua.

⁶But on their resisting and speaking evil, having shaken *out* HIS clothes, he said to them, "Your blood IS upon your head—I am clean; from now on, I will go to the גּוֹיִם, Goyim!"

⁷And having left from that place, he went into the house of a certain one by *the* name *of* Titiusᵇ Justus, a reverencer of God, whose house was next to the synagogue. ⁸And Crispus, the head of the synagogue, believed in the Master with all his house, and many of the Corinthians hearing *Paul* were believing, and they were being immersed.

⁹And in the night, through a vision, the Master said to Paul, "Be not afraid, but be speaking and do not be silent, ¹⁰because I am with you; and no one will lay *their* hands on you to do you evil, because I have many people in this city." ¹¹And he continued *for* a year and six months, teaching the word of God among them.

~ c. A.D. 52 ~

Paul writes his two letters to the Thessalonians.

¹²And when Gallio was proconsul of Achaia, the יְהוּדִים, Y'hudiym made an attack with one mind upon Paul, and brought him to the judgment seat, ¹³saying, "This one persuades men to reverence God *in ways* against the תּוֹרָה, Torah." ¹⁴And Paul being about to open HIS mouth, Gallio said to the יְהוּדִים, Y'hudiym, "If, indeed, it was anything unrighteous, or an act of wicked crime, O Jews, *then* I *would* have endured you according to reason. ¹⁵Rather, if it is questions concerning words and names and of your Law, look TO IT yourselves! I do not want to be a judge of these things." ¹⁶And he drove them from the judgment seat. ¹⁷And having taken Sosthenes, the head of the synagogue, they were allᶜ beating HIM in front of the judgment seat, and Gallio was not even caring about these things.

¹⁸And Paul, having further remained a good many days, having said good-bye to the brothers, was sailing to Syria—having sheared HIS head in Cenchrea, for he had *taken* a vow—and with him WERE Priscilla and Aquila. ¹⁹And they came down to Ephesus, and he left them there. And he himself, having entered into the synagogue, reasoned with the יְהוּדִים, Y'hudiym. ²⁰But when they had requested HIM to remain a longer time, he did not consent; ²¹but having said good-bye—also saying,ᵈ "I will return to you again, God willing"—he sailed from Ephesus; ²²and having come down to Cæsarea, having gone up and having greeted the Called-Forth,ᵉ he went down to Antioch.

~ c. A.D. 53 ~

²³And having stayed some time, he went out, going in order through the region of Galatia and Phrygia, strengthening all the disciples. ²⁴And a certain יְהוּדִי, Y'hudiy, Apollos by name—an Alexandrian by birth, a man of eloquence, being mighty in the Scriptures—came to Ephesus. ²⁵This one was instructed in the way of the Master and, being fervent in the רוּחַ, Ruach, was speaking and teaching the things about Yeshuaᶠ accurately,

---

ᵃ "word"—some mss say, רוּחַ, Ruach.

ᵇ "Titius" is omitted in some mss; one early ms says "Titus"

ᶜ "they were all"—some mss say, "all the Greeks were"

ᵈ Some mss insert, "It is necessary for me by all means to keep the coming Feast at יְרוּשָׁלַיִם, Y'rushalayim, and"

ᵉ "Called-Forth"—ἐκκλησίαν, ekklesian; see מַתִּתְיָהוּ Matit'yahu 16:18

ᶠ "Yeshua"—some mss say, "the Master"

yet knowing only the immersion of יוֹחָנָן, Yochanan. ²⁶This one also began to speak boldly in the synagogue; and Priscilla and Aquila, having heard of him, took him to THEMSELVES and more accurately explained to him the way of God.

²⁷And when he *was* intending to go through into Achaia, the brothers wrote to the disciples *there*, having exhorted them to receive him—who, having come, greatly helped them who have believed through the *unmerited* favor. ²⁸Indeed, he was powerfully refuting the יְהוּדִים, Y'hudiym publicly, showing through the Scriptures יֵשׁוּעַ, Yeshua to be the Messiah.

~ c. A.D. 54 ~
Paul writes his two letters to the Corinthians.

19 ¹And it came to pass during Apollos' being in Corinth, *that* Paul, having gone through the upper parts, came to Ephesus and found certain disciples. ²And he said to them, "Did you receive the רוּחַ הַקֹּדֶשׁ, Ruach HaQodesh, having believed?" And they said to him, "But we did not even hear whether there is any רוּחַ הַקֹּדֶשׁ, Ruach HaQodesh." ³And he said, "To what, then, were you immersed?" And they said, "To *the* immersion of יוֹחָנָן, Yochanan." ⁴And Paul said, "יוֹחָנָן, Yochanan immersed with an immersion of reformation, saying to the people that they should believe in Him who is coming after him—that is, in[a] יֵשׁוּעַ, Yeshua." ⁵And having heard, they were immersed—to the Name of the Master יֵשׁוּעַ, Yeshua. ⁶And when Paul laid HIS hands on them, the רוּחַ הַקֹּדֶשׁ, Ruach HaQodesh came upon them, and they were speaking with *other* languages[b] and prophesying. ⁷And there were, *in* all, about twelve men.

⁸And having gone into the synagogue, he was speaking boldly for three months, reasoning and persuading *about* the things concerning the Reign of God. ⁹And when certain *ones* were hardened and were disbelieving, speaking evil of the Way in front of the great number *of them*, having gone away from them, he set apart the disciples, reasoning every day in the school of Tyrannus. ¹⁰And this happened for two years, so that all those living in Asia heard the word of the Master[c]—both יְהוּדִים, Y'hudiym and Greeks.

¹¹Also, God was working uncommon, powerful acts through the hands of Paul, ¹²such that even handkerchiefs or aprons from his body were taken to the weak, and the sicknesses left from them, and the evil רוּחוֹת, ruchot went out.

¹³And certain *ones* of the יְהוּדִים, Y'hudiym, *who were* wandering exorcists, also took upon THEMSELVES to name the Name of the Master יֵשׁוּעַ, Yeshua over those having the evil רוּחוֹת, ruchot, saying, "I command you by יֵשׁוּעַ, Yeshua, whom Paul proclaims." ¹⁴And there were seven sons of a certain Sceva—a יְהוּדִי, Y'hudiy, a chief כֹּהֵן, kohen—doing this thing, ¹⁵and the evil רוּחַ, ruach, answering, said to them, "Indeed, יֵשׁוּעַ, Yeshua I know, and Paul I am acquainted with, but you—who are you?" ¹⁶And the man in whom was the evil רוּחַ, ruach leaped upon them and, having overcome all, prevailed against them, so that they fled out of that house naked and wounded.

¹⁷And this became known to all—both יְהוּדִים, Y'hudiym and Greeks—who were living at Ephesus, and fear fell upon them all, and the Name of the Master יֵשׁוּעַ, Yeshua was being magnified. ¹⁸Also, many of those who believed were coming, confessing and making their practices known; ¹⁹and many of those who had practiced the magic arts, having brought the books together, were burning THEM in front of all. And they counted together the prices of them and found *that* IT *came to* five *times* ten thousand pieces of silver. ²⁰In this way the word of the Master[d] was powerfully increasing and prevailing.

---

[a] Some mss insert, "the Messiah"
[b] "languages"—lit. "tongues"
[c] Some mss insert, "יֵשׁוּעַ, Yeshua"
[d] "the Master"—Young & KJV say "God"

Acts 19:21 — *Tumult at Ephesus.*

~ c. A.D. 56 ~
Paul writes his letter to the Romans.

21 And when these things were fulfilled, Paul purposed in the רוּחַ, Ruach, having gone through Macedonia and Achaia, to go on to יְרוּשָׁלַיִם, Y'rushalayim, saying, "After my being there, it is necessary for me also to see Rome." 22 And having sent two of those serving with him to Macedonia—Timothy and Erastus—he himself stayed a time in Asia.

23 And at that time, there came no small stir regarding the Way, 24 for a certain one, Demetrius by name—a worker in silver, making silver temples of Artemis—was bringing no small *amount of* business to the craftsmen. 25 *When* he had brought in together a crowd *of silver workers*, and those who worked around such things, he said, "Men, you know that by this work we have our wealth; 26 and you see and hear that not only at Ephesus, but almost in all Asia, this Paul, having persuaded *many*, turned away a great number, saying that they who are made by hands are not gods. 27 And *we are* in danger, not only *that* this—our department—is to come into disregard, but also that the temple of the great goddess Artemis is to be considered as nothing; and even her greatness, whom all Asia and the world worships, is about to be brought down."

28 And they, having heard and having become full of rage, were shouting, saying, "Great IS the Artemis of the Ephesians!" 29 And the city was filled with the confusion, *and* they rushed with one mind into the theater, having caught Gaius and Aristarchus (Macedonians), Paul's fellow-travelers.

30 And upon Paul's intending to enter into the public, the disciples were not allowing him. 31 And also certain *ones* of the chief men of Asia—being his friends, having sent word to him—were appealing to him not to venture himself into the theater.

32 Some indeed, therefore, were shouting out one thing, and some another, for the assembly[a] was confused, and the majority did not know for what *reason* they had come together. 33 And *some* out of the crowd united *around*[b] Alexander—the יְהוּדִים, Y'hudiym having thrust him forward—and Alexander, having rapidly waved with the hand, wanted to make a defense to the public. 34 But having known that he is a יְהוּדִי, Y'hudiy, one voice came out of *them* all for about two hours, shouting, "Great IS the Artemis of the Ephesians!"

35 And the public clerk, having quieted the crowd, said, "Men! Ephesians! who, indeed, is *there* of men that does not know that the city of the Ephesians is a devotee of the great Artemis, and of that which fell down from Zeus? 36 These things, then, not being *able* to be denied, it is necessary for you to be quiet and to do nothing rashly. 37 Indeed, you brought these men *here*, who are neither temple-robbers, nor speaking evil of our goddess. 38 So then, if Demetrius and the craftsmen with him have a matter with anyone, court DAYS are held, and there are proconsuls—let them accuse one another. 39 And if you search after anything further,[c] it will be determined in the legal assembly. 40 Indeed, we are also in jeopardy of being accused of insurrection in regard to this day, there being no occasion by which we will be able to give an account for this commotion." 41 And having said these things, he dismissed the assembly.

20

1 And after the stopping of the riot, Paul, having sent for the disciples, and having exhorted[d] *and* embraced THEM, went out to go on to Macedonia. 2 And having gone through those parts, and having exhorted them with many words, he came to Greece.

3 And having made three months' STAY —*because of* a plot of the יְהוּדִים, Y'hudiym having been *made* against him—and be-

---

[a] "assembly"—ἐκκλησία, ekklesia; also in vs. 39 & 41
[b] "united *around*"—some mss say, "put forward"
[c] "further"—some mss say, "concerning other matters"
[d] Some mss omit, "exhorted"

168

Recovery of Eutychus.

ing about to set out to Syria, he became of a mind to return through Macedonia. ⁴And accompanying him[a] were Sopater *son* of Pyrrhus[b] of Berea, and Aristarchus and Secundus of *the* Thessalonians, and Gaius of Derbe, and Timothy, and Tychicus and Trophimus of *the* Asiatics. ⁵And these, having gone ahead, waited for us in Troas; ⁶and we sailed from Philippi, after the days of *the Feast of* הַמַּצּוֹת, HaMatzot, and came to them to Troas in five days, where we stayed seven days.

⁷And on the first of the week,[c] when we[d] had been gathered together to break bread, Paul was discussing with them. *And being* about to depart on the next day, he was also continuing the words until midnight. ⁸And there were many *oil* lamps in the upper room where we were gathered together, ⁹and sitting by the window was a certain youth by *the* name *of* Eutychus—being brought down by a deep sleep as Paul *was* discussing at length. *And* he, having sunk down from the sleep, fell down from the third story and was lifted up dead. ¹⁰But Paul, having gone down, fell on him and, having embraced HIM, said, "Make no commotion, for his life is in him." ¹¹And having come up, and having broken the bread, and having tasted *of it*, having also talked for a long time, until daylight, in this way *Paul* went away. ¹²And they brought the boy *home* alive and were encouraged in no ordinary measure.

¹³And having gone ahead to the ship, we set sail for Assos, intending to take in Paul from that place (for he had so arranged, intending himself to go on foot); ¹⁴and when he met with us at Assos, having taken him up, we came to Mitylene. ¹⁵And having sailed from that place, on the next day we came opposite Chios, and the next day we arrived at Samos, and[e] on the following day we came to Miletus—

¹⁶for Paul had decided to sail past Ephesus so that there would not be a loss of time to him in Asia, for he hurried *in order* to be at יְרוּשָׁלַיִם, Y'rushalayim, if it were possible for him, on the day of the שָׁבֻעוֹת, Shavuot.

¹⁷And from Miletus, having sent *word* to Ephesus, he called for the זְקֵנִים, z'qeniym of the Called-Forth.[f] ¹⁸And when they had come to him, he said to them, "You—you know how, from the first day in which I came to Asia, I was with you at all times, ¹⁹serving the Master with all humility and tears and *ways of* testing that came on me by the plots of the יְהוּדִים, Y'hudiym against ME, ²⁰and how I kept back nothing of what things are good for you, not *failing* to make known to you and to teach you publicly and from house to house,[g] ²¹testifying fully—both to יְהוּדִים, Y'hudiym and Greeks—reformation toward God and faith toward our Master יֵשׁוּעַ, Yeshua.[h] ²²And now, look! I—bound by the רוּחַ, Ruach—go on to יְרוּשָׁלַיִם, Y'rushalayim not knowing the things that will meet with me in it, ²³except that the רוּחַ הַקֹּדֶשׁ, Ruach HaQodesh testifies fully to me in every city, saying that bonds and oppressions wait for me. ²⁴But by no account do I make life[i] precious to myself, so that I *will* finish my course[j] and the service that I received from the Master יֵשׁוּעַ, Yeshua, to testify fully *of* the Good News of the *unmerited* favor of God. ²⁵And now, look! I have known that you will no longer see my face—all you among whom I went proclaiming the Reign. ²⁶Therefore, I testify to you this day that I am clear from the blood of all, ²⁷for I did not keep back from declaring the whole purpose of God to you.

²⁸"Be careful for yourselves and for all the flock among which the רוּחַ הַקֹּדֶשׁ, Ru-

---

[a] Some mss insert, "to Asia"
[b] Some mss omit, "*son* of Pyrrhus"
[c] "week"—lit. σαββάτων, sabbaton, that is, שַׁבָּתוֹת, shabatot
[d] "we"—some mss say, "the disciples"
[e] Some mss insert, "having remained in Trogyllium"
[f] "Called-Forth"—ἐκκλησίας, ekklesias; see מַתִּתְיָהוּ *Matit'yahu* 16:18
[g] "from house to house"—κατ' οἴκους, kat oikous—Young's says, "in every house"
[h] Some mss insert, "Messiah"
[i] "by no account do I make life"—some mss say, "I make account of none of these, neither do I count my life"
[j] Some mss insert, "with joy"

ach HaQodesh *has* made you overseers, to feed the Called-Forth[a] of God that He acquired through His own blood. ²⁹I have known that after my departing, savage wolves will enter in to you, not sparing the flock; ³⁰and from your own selves there will arise men speaking distorted things, to draw away the disciples after them. ³¹Therefore, be awake, remembering that *for* three years, night and day, I did not stop warning each one with tears. ³²And now, I commit you[b] to God, and to the word of His *unmerited* favor that is able to build up and to give the inheritance among all those *who are* set apart. ³³The silver or gold or clothes of no one did I covet; ³⁴you yourselves know that to my *own* needs, and to those who were with me, these hands served. ³⁵*In* all things I showed you that, laboring this way, it is necessary for *us* to take part with the infirmed, and to be mindful of the words of the Master יֵשׁוּעַ, Yeshua that He Himself said: 'It is more blessed to give than to receive.'"

³⁶And having said these things, having knelt down,[c] he prayed with them all. ³⁷And there came a great weeping to all, and having fallen upon Paul's neck, they were kissing him, ³⁸deeply anguished most of all for the word that he had said: that they were about to see his face no more. And they were accompanying him to the ship.

21

¹And it came to pass at our sailing, having been parted from them, having run *a* direct *course, that* we came to Cos, and the next DAY to Rhodes, and from there to Patara. ²And having found a ship passing over to Phoenicia, having gone on board, we sailed. ³And having sighted Cyprus, but having left it on the left *side,* we were sailing to Syria and landed at צוֹר, Tzor, for there the ship was unloading the cargo.

⁴And having found out *where* the disciples *were,* we stayed there seven days. And they said to Paul, through the רוּחַ, Ruach, not to go up to יְרוּשָׁלַיִם, Y'rushalayim. ⁵But when it came *time* that we completed the days, having gone out, we went on our way, *with* all *the disciples* bringing *their* women and children with us to the outside of the city. And having knelt down on the shore *and* having prayed, ⁶we embraced one another and went onboard the ship, and they returned to their own friends.

⁷And having finished the voyage from צוֹר, Tzor, we came down to Ptolemais. And having greeted the brothers, we remained one day with them; ⁸and on the next day, departing, we[d] came to Cæsarea. And having entered into the house of Philip the proclaimer of Good News (being *one* of the Seven), we stayed with him; ⁹and this one had four daughters, virgins, *who were* prophesying.

¹⁰And remaining many more days, a certain one came down from יְהוּדָה, Y'hudah—a prophet by *the* name *of* Agabus. ¹¹And he, having come to us and having raised up Paul's belt, having bound his own feet and hands *with it,* said, "The רוּחַ הַקֹּדֶשׁ, Ruach HaQodesh says this: the man whose belt this is—so will the יְהוּדִים, Y'hudiym in יְרוּשָׁלַיִם, Y'rushalayim bind *him,* and they will hand HIM over to the hands of the גּוֹיִם, Goyim."

¹²And when we heard these things, we pleaded with PAUL—both we, and those of that place—not to go up to יְרוּשָׁלַיִם, Y'rushalayim. ¹³Then Paul answered *us,* "What *are* you doing, weeping and crushing my heart? For I am ready not only to be bound, but also to die at יְרוּשָׁלַיִם, Y'rushalayim for the Name of the Master יֵשׁוּעַ, Yeshua." ¹⁴And when he was not persuaded, we were silent, saying, "The will of the Master be done."

~ c. A.D. 57 ~

¹⁵And after these days, having gotten ready,[e] we were going up to יְרוּשָׁלַיִם, Y'ru-

---

[a] "Called-Forth"—ἐκκλησίαν, ekklesian; see מִתְתְיָהוּ Matit'yahu 16:18
[b] Some mss insert, "brothers"
[c] "knelt down"—Young's says, "bowed his knees" also in 21:5
[d] "we"—some mss say, "those in company with Paul"
[e] "gotten ready"—some mss say, "taken OUR things"

Paul's visit to Y'rushalayim.   **Acts 21:37**

shalayim, [16]and *some* of the disciples from Cæsarea also went *up* with us, bringing a certain Mnason of Cyprus, an aged[a] disciple with whom we would be staying as guests.

[17]And when we had come to יְרוּשָׁלַיִם, Y'rushalayim, the brothers gladly received us. [18]And on the next day, Paul was going in with us to יַעֲקֹב, Ya'aqov, *and* all the זְקֵנִים, z'qeniym also came. [19]And having greeted them, he was relating one by one each of the things God did among the גּוֹיִם, Goyim through his service; [20]and they, having heard, were glorifying God.[b]

They also said to him, "You see, brother, how many tens of thousands among the יְהוּדִים, Y'hudiym there are who have believed, and all are zealous for the תּוֹרָה, Torah. [21]But they are told about you, that you teach apostasy from מֹשֶׁה, Mosheh to all *the* יְהוּדִים, Y'hudiym *living* among the גּוֹיִם, Goyim, saying not to circumcise the children, nor to walk after the customs.

[22]"What is it, then? Certainly[c] they will hear that you have come. [23]Therefore, do this that we say to you: we have four men having a vow on themselves. [24]Having taken these *men*, be purified with them, and pay their expenses,[d] so that they will shave the head; and all will know that the things of which they have been told about you are nothing, but *that* you walk—yourself also—keeping the תּוֹרָה, Torah. [25]And concerning those of the גּוֹיִם, Goyim who have believed: we have written *to them*, having given judgment that they[e] guard themselves from both idol-sacrifices, and blood, and a strangled thing, and sexual immorality."

[26]Then Paul, having taken the men on the following day, *and* having purified himself with them, was entering into the Temple, announcing the fulfillment of the *seven* days of the purification until the offering was offered for each one of them.[f]

[27]But as the seven days were about to be fully ended, the יְהוּדִים, Y'hudiym from Asia, having seen him in the Temple, were stirring up all the crowd, and they threw *their* hands on him, [28]shouting, "Men! יִשְׂרָאֵלִים, Yis'raeliym! help! This is the man who is teaching all *men* everywhere against the people, and the תּוֹרָה, Torah, and this place! Also, he brought Greeks into the Temple, and has defiled this holy place!" [29](For they had previously seen Trophimus, the Ephesian, in the city with him—whom they were supposing that Paul had brought into the Temple.) [30]And so the whole city was moved, and there was a running together of the people. And having taken hold on Paul, they were dragging him out of the Temple, and immediately the doors were shut.

[31]And while they were looking to kill him, a rumor that all יְרוּשָׁלַיִם, Y'rushalayim had been thrown into confusion came to the chief captain of the *Roman* regiment, [32]who at once, having taken soldiers and centurions, ran down upon them. And they, having seen the chief captain and the soldiers, stopped beating Paul.

[33]Then the chief captain, having come near, took him and commanded *for* HIM to be bound with two chains, and was asking who he might be and what it was he had been doing.

[34]And some among the crowd were calling out one thing, and some another. And not being able to know the certainty because of the commotion, *the captain* commanded *for Paul* to be carried to the barracks. [35]And when he came upon the steps, it happened *that* he was carried by the soldiers because of the violence of the crowd, [36]for the crowd of the people was following after *them*, shouting, "Away with him!"

[37]And Paul, being about to be led into the barracks, said to the chief captain, "Is it per-

---

[a] "aged"—not necessarily "aged" as in "old"; perh. "early"
[b] "God"—some mss say, "the Master"
[c] Some mss insert, "it is necessary *for* the great number *of them* to come together, for"
[d] "pay their expenses"—Young's says, "be at expense with them"
[e] Some mss insert, "observe no such thing, except to"
[f] See בְּמִדְבַּר *B'mid'bar* 6:1-21

mitted for me to say anything to you?" and he said, "Do you know Greek? ³⁸Are you not, then, the Egyptian who before these days made an uprising and led the four thousand men of the assassins into the desert?" ³⁹And Paul said, "I, indeed, am a man, a יְהוּדִי, Y'hudiy of Tarsus of Cilicia, a citizen of no insignificant city; and I implore you: allow me to speak to the people." ⁴⁰And when he had given him permission, Paul, having stood upon the stairs, rapidly waived with the hand to the people; and when there was a great silence, he spoke to them in the Hebrew dialect, saying:

22

¹"Men! brothers and fathers! hear now my defense to you!" ²And they, having heard that he was speaking to them in the Hebrew dialect, gave *even* more silence. And he said, ³"I am a man, a יְהוּדִי, Y'hudiy, having been born in Tarsus of Cilicia, and brought up in this city at the feet of גַּמְלִיאֵל, Gam'liyel, having been taught according to the exactitude of the תּוֹרָה, Torah of the fathers, being zealous of God, *just* as you all are today. ⁴And I persecuted this Way to death, binding and handing over both men and women to prisons, ⁵as also the כֹּהֵן הַגָּדוֹל, Kohen HaGadol testifies of me, and all the Council of זְקֵנִים, Z'qeniym. And having received letters from them to the brothers, I was going on to דַּמֶּשֶׂק, Dameseq, to even bring those bound there to יְרוּשָׁלַיִם, Y'rushalayim, so that they might be punished.

⁶"And it came to pass in my going on and coming near to דַּמֶּשֶׂק, Dameseq, about noon, *that* suddenly out of the heaven a great light shone around me. ⁷I also fell to the ground, and I heard a voice saying to me, 'שָׁאוּל שָׁאוּל, Shaul, Shaul! Why do you persecute Me?' ⁸And I answered, 'Who are you, Master?' And He said to me, 'I am יֵשׁוּעַ הַנָּצְרָתִי, Yeshua HaNatz'ratiy, whom you persecute.' ⁹(And they who were with me indeed saw the light,ª but they heard not the voice of Him who was speaking to me.) ¹⁰And I said, 'What should I do, Master?' And the Master said to me, 'Having risen, go on to דַּמֶּשֶׂק, Dameseq, and there you will be told about all *the* things that have been appointed for you to do.' ¹¹And when I could not see from the glory of that light, being led by the hand by those who were with me, I came to דַּמֶּשֶׂק, Dameseq.

¹²"And a certain one, חֲנַנְיָה, 'Chanan'yah—a God-fearing man according to the תּוֹרָה, Torah, being testified to by all the יְהוּדִים, Y'hudiym living THERE—¹³having come to me and stood by ME, said to me, 'שָׁאוּל, Shaul, brother, look up *and see!*' and *at* the same moment I looked up to *see* him. ¹⁴And he said, 'The God of our fathers chose you beforehand to know His will, and to see the Righteous One, and to hear a voice out of His mouth, ¹⁵because you will be His witness to all men of what you have seen and heard. ¹⁶And now, why do you delay? Having arisen, immerse yourself and wash away your sins, calling on His Name.'ᵇ

¹⁷"And it came to pass *that* when I returned to יְרוּשָׁלַיִם, Y'rushalayim, and while I was praying in the Temple, I came into a trance, ¹⁸and I saw Him saying to me, 'Hurry and go out of יְרוּשָׁלַיִם, Y'rushalayim quickly, because they will not receive your testimony about Me.' ¹⁹And I said, 'Master, they themselves know that I was imprisoning and was beating in every synagogue those believing in You, ²⁰and when the blood of your witness Stephen was being poured out, I was also standing by and agreeing,ᶜ and guarding the coats of those *who were* putting him to death.' ²¹And He said to me, 'Go, because I will send you far off to *the* גּוֹיִם, Goyim.'"

²²And they were hearing him *up* until this word, and *then* they lifted up their voice, saying, "Away from the earth with such a one! For he is not fit to live!" ²³And as they were shouting and throwing off

---

ª Some mss insert, "and became afraid"

ᵇ "His Name"—some mss say, "the Name of the Master"

ᶜ Some mss insert, "to his death"

their coats and flinging dust into the air, ²⁴the chief captain commanded *for* him to be brought into the barracks, saying, "Let him be examined by flogging," so that he might know for what reason they were calling against him this way.

²⁵And as they were stretching him with the straps, Paul said to the centurion who was standing by, "Is it permitted to you to flog a man, a Roman, uncondemned?" ²⁶And the centurion, having heard, went near to the chief captain *and* told *him*, saying, "What are you about to do?ᵃ For this man is a Roman *citizen*!" ²⁷And the chief captain, having come near, said to him, "Tell me, are you a Roman *citizen*?" and he said, "Yes." ²⁸And the chief captain answered, "I obtained *my* citizenship with a great sum *of money*," and Paul said, "But I have been even born so."

²⁹Therefore, they who were about to examine him immediately went away from him, and the chief captain was also afraid (having learned that he is a Roman *citizen*, and because he had bound him). ³⁰And on the next day, intending to know the certainty *of* why he was accused by the יְהוּדִים, Y'hudiym, he untied himᵇ and commanded the chief כֹּהֲנִים, Ko'haniym and all the Sanhedrin to come together. And having brought Paul down, he set HIM before them.

23

¹And Paul, having fixed his gaze on the Sanhedrin, said, "Men, brothers, in all good conscience I have lived to God to this day." ²And the כֹּהֵן הַגָּדוֹל, Kohen HaGadol, חֲנַנְיָה, 'Chanan'yah, commanded those standing by him to strike him on the mouth. ³Then Paul said to him, "God is about to strike you, you white-washed wall! And you— you sit judging me according to the תּוֹרָה, Torah, yet violating תּוֹרָה, Torah, you order me to be struck!" ⁴And those who stood by said, "Do you speak evil of the כֹּהֵן הַגָּדוֹל, Kohen HaGadol of God?" ⁵And Paul said, "I did not know, brothers, that he is כֹּהֵן הַגָּדוֹל, Kohen HaGadol, for it has been written,

'You must not speak evil of the leader of your people.'"ᶜ

⁶And Paul, having known that the one part *of the Sanhedrin* are צַדּוּקִים, Tzaduqiym, and the other פְּרוּשִׁים, P'rushiym, was shouting in the Sanhedrin, "Men! brothers! I am a פָּרוּשׁ, Parush, *the* son of פְּרוּשִׁים, P'rushiym, *and* I am *being* judged regarding *the* hope and Rising Again of dead men!"

⁷And when he had said this, there came a standoff of the פְּרוּשִׁים, P'rushiym and צַדּוּקִים, Tzaduqiym, and the crowd was divided ⁸(for צַדּוּקִים, Tzaduqiym, indeed, say there is no Rising Again nor Messenger nor רוּחַ, ruach, but פְּרוּשִׁים, P'rushiym profess *them* all). ⁹And there came a great outcry, and some of the סוֹפְרִים, Sof'riym of the part *of the* פְּרוּשִׁים, P'rushiym, having arisen, were protesting violently, saying, "We find no evil in this man!" and "*What* if a רוּחַ, ruach spoke to him, or a Messenger?"ᵈ ¹⁰And when a huge standoff had come, the chief captain, having been afraid that Paul might be pulled to pieces by them, commanded the soldiers, having gone down, to take him by force out of the middle of them and to bring HIM to the barracks.

¹¹And on the following night, the Master, having stood by him, said, "Take courage,ᵉ for as you fully testified the things about Me at יְרוּשָׁלַיִם, Y'rushalayim, so it is necessary for you also to testify at Rome."

¹²And when day had come, the יְהוּדִים, Y'hudiym, having made a commotion, called down curses on themselves, saying to neither eat nor drink until they could kill Paul. ¹³And they were more than forty *men* who made this conspiracy by oath, ¹⁴who, having come near to the chief כֹּהֲנִים, Ko'haniym and to the זְקֵנִים, Z'qeniym, said, "With a solemn oath we bound curses on

---

ᶜ שְׁמוֹת Sh'mot 22:27(28)
ᵈ Some mss insert, "We should not fight against God."
ᵉ Some mss insert, "Paul"

ᵃ Some mss precede the question with, "Watch out!"
ᵇ Some mss insert, "from the bonds"

ourselves, to taste nothing until we have killed Paul. ¹⁵Now, therefore, you, with the Sanhedrin: signify to the chief captain that[a] he should bring *Paul* down to you, as if *you are* intending to decide the things regarding him more accurately. But we, before his coming near, are ready to put him to death."

¹⁶And the son of Paul's sister, having heard of the ambush, *and* having gone and entered into the barracks, told Paul. ¹⁷And Paul, having called near one of the centurions, said, "Lead this young man to the chief captain, for he has something to tell him." ¹⁸He, indeed, then, having taken him, brought him to the chief captain and said, "The prisoner Paul, having called me near, asked ME to bring this young man to you, *who* has something to say to you."

¹⁹And the chief captain, having taken him by the hand, and having gone away privately, asked *him*, "What is it that you have to tell me?" ²⁰and he said, "The יְהוּדִים, Y'hudiym agreed to ask you that tomorrow you would bring Paul down to the Sanhedrin—as if intending to ask something more accurately concerning him. ²¹You, therefore: may you not be persuaded by them, for there lie in wait for him more than forty of them—men who bound curses on themselves not to eat nor to drink until they kill him. And now they are ready, waiting for the consent from you."

²²The chief captain, then, indeed, let the young man go, having commanded HIM to "tell no one that you disclosed these things to me." ²³And having called near a certain two of the centurions, he said, "Make ready two hundred soldiers, and seventy horsemen, and two hundred spearmen, *so* that they may go on to Cæsarea from the third hour of the night. ²⁴Also provide beasts *of burden*, so that, having set Paul on *them*, they may bring him safe to Felix the governor"; ²⁵*and* he had written a letter having this pattern:

²⁶"*From* Claudius Lysias; to the most noble governor Felix: greetings. ²⁷This man *was* having been taken by the Jews and being about to be killed by them, *when*, having come with the soldiers, I rescued him, having learned that he is a Roman citizen. ²⁸And wanting to know the reason for which they were accusing him, I brought him down to their Sanhedrin, ²⁹*where* I found him accused regarding questions of their Law, but having no accusation worthy of death or bonds. ³⁰And *with* a plot against this man having been disclosed to me,[b] I sent *him* to you at once, also having given command to the accusers to say the things against him before you."[c]

³¹Then, indeed, the soldiers, according to that *which was* directed *to* them, having taken up Paul, brought him by night to Antipatris; ³²but on the next day, having allowed the horsemen to go on with him, they returned to the barracks. ³³Those having entered into Cæsarea and delivered the letter to the governor also presented Paul to him. ³⁴And[d] having read IT and inquired from what province he is, and having understood that HE IS from Cilicia, ³⁵he said, "I will hear you when your accusers also have come," having commanded him to be kept in the Prætorium[e] of Herod.

24

¹And after five days the כֹּהֵן הַגָּדוֹל, Kohen HaGadol, חֲנַנְיָה, 'Chanan'yah, came down with some זְקֵנִים, Z'qeniym and a certain orator, Tertullus, and they made apparent to the governor THE THINGS against Paul. ²And when he had been called, Tertullus began to accuse HIM, saying *to Felix*, "We have been enjoying much peace through you and *your* reforms[f] *that are* being done to this nation through your forethought. ³Also, always and everywhere, we receive it with all thankfulness, most noble Felix. ⁴But so that I may not be tedious to you further,

---

[a] Some mss insert, "tomorrow"
[b] Some mss insert, "about to be *perpetrated* by the Jews"
[c] Some mss close the letter with "Be strong."
[d] Some mss insert, "the governor"
[e] "Prætorium"—the governor's headquarters
[f] "reforms"—some mss say, "worthy deeds"

I appeal *to* you to hear us concisely in your gentleness. ⁵For *we* have found this man *to be* a pestilence and moving all the Jews throughout the world to insurrections—also a ringleader of the sect of the Nazarenes—⁶who even tried to profane the Temple, *and* whom we also took hold of.ᵃ ⁸Having examined *him* yourself, *then*, from him you may be able to know about all these things of which we accuse him." ⁹And the יְהוּדִים, Y'hudiym also joined in the attack,ᵇ professing these things to be so.

¹⁰And Paul answered (the governor having nodded to him to speak), "Knowing THAT you have been a judge to this ethnic-group for many years, the more confidently I answer the things regarding myself. ¹¹You are able to *verify and* know that it is not more than twelve days to me since I went up to worship in יְרוּשָׁלַיִם, Y'rushalayim, ¹²and neither did they find me reasoning with anyone in the Temple or making a contention of the crowd, nor in the synagogues, nor in the city—¹³nor are they able to prove to youᶜ the things concerning which they now accuse me. ¹⁴But I confess this to you: that, according to the Way (which they call a sect), I so serve the God of the fathers, believing all things that have been written in the תּוֹרָה, Torah and in the Prophets, ¹⁵having hope toward God—which they themselves also wait for—THAT there is about to be a Rising Again, both of righteous and unrighteous. ¹⁶And in this, I do my best to have a conscience always void of offense toward God and men.

¹⁷"And after many years, I came to do charity to my ethnic-group and *to make* offerings, ¹⁸in which *they* found me purified in the Temple, not with a crowd, nor with commotion. ¹⁹But *there were* certain יְהוּדִים, Y'hudiym from Asia who ought to be present *here* before you, and to accuse *me*, if they had anything against me. ²⁰Or, let these same *ones* say what unrighteousness they foundᵈ when I was standing before the Sanhedrin, ²¹except regarding this one voice in which I shouted, standing among them: 'I am judged today by you regarding the Rising Again of the dead!'"

²²And Felix delayed them (having known more accurately of the things regarding the Way), saying, "When Lysias the chief captain comes down, I will decide the things regarding you." ²³Having given a direction to the centurion to watch him, he also *said* to let HIM have *some* liberty, and to forbid none of his own friends to serveᵉ him.

²⁴And after *a* certain *number of* days, Felix, having come with Drusilla his wife (*she* being יְהוּדִיָה, Y'hudiyah), sent for Paul and heard him regarding the faith toward Messiah יֵשׁוּעַ, Yeshua.ᶠ ²⁵And he *was* reasoning about righteousness and self-control and the judgment that is coming. *And* Felix, having become afraid, answered, "Be going for now, and having gotten time, I will call for you"; ²⁶and at the same time, *he was* hoping that money would be given to him by Paul *as a bribe*.ᵍ Therefore, he was also sending for him frequently *and* conversing with him.

~ c. A.D. 59 ~
Paul writes his letter to the Colossians.

²⁷And two years having been fulfilled, Felix received a successor, Porcius Festus; *but* Felix, also wanting to lay *down* a favor on the יְהוּדִים, Y'hudiym, left Paul bound.

25

¹Festus, therefore, having come into the province, after three days went up to יְרוּשָׁלַיִם, Y'rushalayim from Cæsarea. ²And the chief כֹּהֲנִים, Ko'haniym and the principal men of the יְהוּדִים, Y'hudiym made apparent to

---

ᵃ Some mss insert, "and wanted to judge according to our Law, ⁷but Lysias the chief captain, having come near with much violence, took *him* away out of our hands, ⁸having commanded his accusers to come to you."
ᵇ "joined in the attack"—some mss say, "agreed"
ᶜ "to you"—some mss say, "against me"
ᵈ Some mss insert, "in me"
ᵉ Some mss insert, "or to come near to"
ᶠ Some mss omit, "יֵשׁוּעַ, Yeshua"
ᵍ Some mss insert, "*so that he would release him*"

him THE THINGS against Paul, and were calling on him, ³asking *for* a favor against *Paul, that he might send for him to be transferred to* יְרוּשָׁלַיִם, Y'rushalayim, *so that they could be* making an ambush on the road to put him to death.

⁴Then, indeed, Festus answered that Paul was *being* watched in Cæsarea, and he was about to go on THERE speedily himself. ⁵"Therefore, those able among you," he said, "having come down together, if there be anything in the man, let them accuse him."

⁶And having stayed among them not more than eight or ten[a] days, having gone down to Cæsarea, and on the next day having sat upon the judgment seat, he commanded Paul to be brought. ⁷And when he had come, the יְהוּדִים, Y'hudiym who had come down from יְרוּשָׁלַיִם, Y'rushalayim stood there around him, bringing many and weighty charges which they were not able to prove. ⁸*Then* Paul, making a defense, *said*, "Neither in regard to the תּוֹרָה, Torah of the יְהוּדִים, Y'hudiym, nor in regard to the Temple, nor in regard to Cæsar, did I commit any sin."

⁹And Festus, wanting to lay *down* a favor on the יְהוּדִים, Y'hudiym, answering Paul, said, "Are you willing, having gone up to יְרוּשָׁלַיִם, Y'rushalayim, to be judged there before me regarding these things?" ¹⁰And Paul said, "I am standing *now* at the judgment seat of Cæsar, where I ought to be judged. I did no unrighteousness to *the* יְהוּדִים, Y'hudiym, as you also very well know. ¹¹If indeed, then, I am unrighteous and have done anything worthy of death, I ask not to escape from dying. But if there is *truth in* none of the things of which these accuse me, no one is able to make a favor of me to them. I appeal to Cæsar!" ¹²Then Festus, having conferred with *his* council, answered, "To Cæsar you have appealed; to Cæsar you will go."

¹³And *a* certain *number of* days having passed, Agrippa the king and Bernice came down to Cæsarea, greeting Festus. ¹⁴And as they were continuing there *for* more days, Festus submitted to the king the things regarding Paul, saying, "There is a certain man, a prisoner, left by Felix, ¹⁵about whom the chief priests and the elders of the Jews made known *to me* (in my being at Jerusalem), asking *for* a conviction[b] against him—¹⁶to whom I answered that it is not a custom of Romans to make a favor of any man[c] before *such a time* that he who is accused may have the accusers face to face and receive a place of defense in regard to the charge laid against HIM. ¹⁷Therefore, when they had come together here, I—making no delay, having sat upon the judgment seat on the succeeding DAY— commanded the man to be brought, ¹⁸about whom the accusers, having stood up, were bringing no accusation of the evils[d] which I was thinking of. ¹⁹Rather, they had against him certain questions about their own religion and about a certain 'Yeshua' who was dead, whom Paul affirmed to be alive. ²⁰And I, doubting regarding the question about these things, asked if he would want to go on to Jerusalem and to be judged there regarding these things. ²¹But *upon* Paul having appealed to be watched until the decision of the Emperor, I commanded *for* him to be watched until I send him to Cæsar." ²²And Agrippa said to Festus, "I myself was also wanting to hear the man." He said, "Tomorrow you will hear him."

²³On the next day, therefore—on the coming of Agrippa and Bernice with much display, and they having entered into the audience room (with both the chief captains and the principal men of the city), and Festus having *so* ordered—Paul was brought forth. ²⁴And Festus said, "King Agrippa, and all men who are present with us: you see this one about whom all the great number of the Jews dealt with me, both in Jerusalem and here, crying out *that* he ought not to live any longer. ²⁵But

---

[a] "not more than eight or ten"—some mss say, "more than ten"
[b] "conviction"—some mss say, "decision"
[c] Some mss insert, "to die"
[d] Some mss omit, "the evils"

I found him to have done nothing worthy of death; and he himself having appealed to the Emperor, I decided to send him— ²⁶but regarding whom I have no certain thing to write to MY master. Therefore, I brought him forward before you—and especially before you, King Agrippa—so that when the examination has been made, I might have something to write; ²⁷for it does seem irrational to me, when sending a prisoner on, not to also signify the charges against him."

26 ¹And Agrippa said to Paul, "It is permitted to you to speak for yourself." Then Paul, having stretched forth the hand, was making a defense: ²"Regarding all the things of which I am accused by the יְהוּדִים, Y'hudiym, King Agrippa, I have thought myself happy, being about to make a defense before you today, ³especially knowing you to be acquainted with all things—both customs and questions—among the יְהוּדִים, Y'hudiym. Therefore, I implore you to hear me patiently.

⁴"So then, all the יְהוּדִים, Y'hudiym know the manner of my life from youth, which from the beginning was among my ethnic-group, and in יְרוּשָׁלַיִם, Y'rushalayim. ⁵They were knowing me beforehand from the first (if they are willing to testify), that according to the most exact sect of our religion, I lived as a פָּרוּשׁ, Parush. ⁶And now, I have stood judged for the hope in the promise made to our fathers by God, ⁷to which our twelve tribes, intently serving God night and day, hope to come. It is concerning this hope that I am accused by the יְהוּדִים, Y'hudiym, O king. ⁸Why is it judged incredible with you all if God raises the dead?

⁹"I, indeed, therefore, thought with myself that it was necessary for ME to do many things against the Name of יֵשׁוּעַ הַנָּצְרָתִי, Yeshua HaNatz'ratiy, ¹⁰which I also did in יְרוּשָׁלַיִם, Y'rushalayim. And I not only shut up many of the קְדוֹשִׁים, Q'doshiym in prison, having received the authority from the chief כֹּהֲנִים, ko'haniym, but also, when they were being put to death, I gave my vote against them. ¹¹And in every synagogue, often punishing them, I was compelling THEM to speak evil; and being exceedingly enraged against them, I was also persecuting THEM even to outside cities.

¹²"In the course of which things, as I was going on to דַּמֶּשֶׂק, Dameseq with authority and commission of the chief כֹּהֲנִים, ko'haniym, ¹³at mid-day, O king, I saw on the road—out of heaven, above the brightness of the sun—a light shining around me and those going on with me. ¹⁴And when we all had fallen to the ground, I heard a voice saying to me in the Hebrew dialect, 'שָׁאוּל שָׁאוּל, Shaul, Shaul, why do you persecute Me? It is hard for you to kick against the goads!' ¹⁵And I said, 'Who are you, Master?' and the Master said, "I am יֵשׁוּעַ, Yeshua, whom you persecute. ¹⁶But rise and stand on your feet, for I appeared to you for this: to appoint you as an attendant and a witness, both of the things in which you have seen Me, and of the things IN WHICH I will appear to you, ¹⁷delivering you from your people and from the גּוֹיִם, Goyim—to whom I am sending you, ¹⁸to open their eyes, in order to turn THEM from darkness to light and FROM the authority of הַשָּׂטָן, HaSatan to God, for their receiving forgiveness of sins and a portion among those having been set apart by faith that IS toward Me.'

¹⁹"Upon which, King Agrippa, I was not obstinate[a] toward the heavenly vision. ²⁰Rather—first to those in דַּמֶּשֶׂק, Dameseq, and also to those in יְרוּשָׁלַיִם, Y'rushalayim and all the region of יְהוּדָה, Y'hudah, and to the גּוֹיִם, Goyim—I was proclaiming their need to reform and to turn to God, doing actions worthy of reformation. ²¹Because of these things, the יְהוּדִים, Y'hudiym, having caught me in the Temple, were endeavoring to kill ME. ²²Therefore, having obtained help from God until this day, I have stood testifying both

---

[a] "obstinate"—ἀπειθής, apeithes, a negative of πείθω, peitho, which is most often translated "trust" or "persuade." Here, Young says "disobedient."

to small and to great, saying nothing besides the things that both the prophets and מֹשֶׁה, Mosheh spoke of as about to come: ²³that the Messiah is to suffer, *and* that *as the* first of a rising from the dead, He is about to proclaim light both to the Y'hudiy people and to the גּוֹיִם, Goyim."

²⁴And while he was making this defense, Festus, with a loud voice, said, "You are insane, Paul! Much learning has turned you crazy!" ²⁵And Paul said, "I am not insane, most noble Festus, but I speak out the sayings of truth and soundness of mind. ²⁶For the king (toward whom I also speak boldly) knows about these things, for I am persuaded *that* none of these things are hidden from him—indeed, this thing has not been done in a corner.

²⁷"King Agrippa, do you believe the prophets? I have known that you do believe!" ²⁸And Agrippa said to Paul, "In a little *time* you *will* persuade me, to make *me*[a] a 'Messiah-follower'!"[b] ²⁹And Paul said, "I would have prayed to God—both in a little *time* and in much—not only *for* you, but also *for* all those hearing me today, to become such as I also am, except *for* these bonds."

³⁰And[c] the king rose up, and the governor—Bernice also—and those sitting with them, ³¹and having gone away, they were speaking to one another, saying, "This man does nothing worthy of death or of bonds"; ³²and Agrippa said to Festus, "This man might have been released if he had not appealed to Cæsar."

~ c. A.D. 60 ~
Paul writes his letters to Philemon & the Ephesians.

27

¹And when our sailing to Italy was determined, they were handing over both Paul and certain others, prisoners, to a centurion by *the* name *of* Julius, of the regiment of the Emperor. ²And having embarked in a ship of Adramyttium (*it* being about to sail by the coasts of Asia), we set sail (there *also* being with us Aristarchus, a Macedonian of Thessalonica). ³And on the next DAY, we touched at צִידוֹן, Tziydon; and Julius, treating Paul courteously, allowed HIM, having gone on to *his* friends, to receive THEIR care.

⁴And from that place, having set sail, we sailed under Cyprus, because of the winds being against us; ⁵and having sailed over the sea by Cilicia and Pamphylia, we came to Myra of Lycia. ⁶And there the centurion, having found a ship of Alexandria sailing to Italy, put us into it; ⁷and having sailed slowly *for* many days, and coming by Cnidus with difficulty—the wind not allowing us—we sailed under Crete, by Salmone. ⁸And passing it with difficulty, we came to a certain place called "Fair Havens," near to which was the city OF Lasæa.

⁹And after much time being spent, and the sailing now being dangerous—also because of the Fast already being past—Paul was admonishing *them*, ¹⁰saying to them, "Men, I see that the voyage is about to be with hurt and much damage, not only of the cargo and of the ship, but also of our lives." ¹¹But the centurion gave more credence to the pilot and to the shipowner than to the things spoken by Paul. ¹²And *with* the harbor being unsuitable to winter in, the majority gave counsel to sail from there, if by any means they might be able, having reached Phoenix (WHICH IS a harbor of Crete looking to the southwest and north-west), to winter THERE. ¹³And *with* a south wind blowing softly, having thought they had obtained THEIR purpose, having lifted anchor, they sailed close by Crete. ¹⁴But not long after, there arose against her a tempestuous wind that is called Euraquilo,[d] ¹⁵and *with* the ship being caught and not being able to bear up against the wind, having given HER up, we were driven on. ¹⁶And having run under a certain little island called Cauda, we were hardly able to become masters of the

---
[a] "to make *me*"—some mss say, "to become"
[b] "Messiah-follower"—see כֵּיפָא א 1 Keifa 4:16
[c] Some mss insert, "when he had spoken these things"

[d] "Euraquilo"—some mss say, "Euroclydon"

His shipwreck at Malta. *Acts 27:44*

life-boat. ⁱ⁷And after having lifted it up, they were using supports undergirding the ship. And fearing that they would fall on the Syrtis, having let down the gear,ᵃ in this way they were driven on.

¹⁸And *with* us being exceedingly storm-tossed, *on* the next DAY they were throwing *the cargo* overboard.ᵇ ¹⁹And on the third DAY, they cast out the tackling of the ship with their own hands. ²⁰And *with* neither sun nor stars appearing for many days, and no small storm lying upon us, all the hope of our being saved was finally taken away.

²¹And there having been fasting *for a long time*, then Paul, having stood in the middle of them, said, "It was necessary for YOU, indeed, O men, having trusted my authority, not to set sail from Crete, and to save this hurt and damage. ²²But now I exhort you to take courage, for there will be no loss of life among you—only *loss* of the ship. ²³For there stood by me this night a Messenger of God—Whose I am, and Whom I serve—²⁴saying, 'Be not afraid, Paul. It is necessary for you to stand before Cæsar; and look! God has given to you all those sailing with you.' ²⁵Therefore, take courage, men! For I believe God that it will be so, even as it has been spoken to me. ²⁶But *first*, it is necessary for us to be cast *away* on a certain island."

²⁷And when the fourteenth night came, as we were being carried up and down in the Adriatic *Sea*, toward the middle of the night, the sailors were supposing that some land drew near to them. ²⁸And having sounded, they found twenty fathoms; and having gone a little farther, and again having sounded, they found fifteen fathoms. ²⁹And fearing that we might fall on rough places, having cast four anchors out of the stern, they were praying *for* day to come.

³⁰And *with* the sailors looking to flee out of the ship and having let down the life-boat to the sea (in pretense, as IF they were about to cast anchors out of the foreship), ³¹Paul said to the centurion and to the soldiers, "If these *men* do not remain in the ship, you are not able to be saved." ³²Then the soldiers cut off the ropes of the life-boat, and allowed it to fall off.

³³And until day*time* was about to be, Paul was calling upon all to share of *some* nourishment, saying, "Fourteen days today, waiting, you continue fasting, having taken nothing. ³⁴Therefore, I appeal to you to take nourishment, for this is for your safety. Indeed, a hair from the head of not one of you will be destroyed."

³⁵And having said these things, and having taken bread, he gave thanks to God in sight of *them* all; and having broken IT, he began to eat. ³⁶And all having taken courage, they themselves also took food ³⁷(and we were—all the souls in the ship—276). ³⁸And having eaten sufficient nourishment, they were lightening the ship, throwing the wheat out into the sea.

³⁹And when the day came, they were not recognizing the land but were seeing a certain bay having a beach, into which they were considering, if possible, to thrust the ship forward. ⁴⁰And having cast off the anchors, they were leaving THEM in the sea. At the same time, having loosened the ropes of the rudders and having hoisted up the mainsail to the wind, they were making for the shore. ⁴¹And having fallen into a place between two seas, they ran the ship aground, and the forepart, indeed, having stuck fast, remained immovable, but the rear was broken by the violence of the waves.

⁴²And the soldiers' decision was that they should kill the prisoners, so that no one, having swum out, should escape. ⁴³But the centurion, wanting to save Paul, prevented them from *going forward with* the decision and commanded those able to swim, having thrown themselves overboard first, to get to the land, ⁴⁴and the remainder *to follow*—some indeed *floating* on boards, and

---

ᵃ "gear"—possibly "sea anchor" or "sail"; Young says, "mast"

ᵇ "throwing... overboard"—Young's says, "making a clearing"

some *keeping afloat* upon certain things of the ship. And it came to pass this way that all came to the land safely.

28

¹And having been saved, then we *came to* know that the island was called Malta; ²and the βάρβαροι, Barbaroi were showing us no ordinary kindness, for having kindled a fire, they received us all, because of the pressing rain and because of the cold.

³But when Paul had gathered together a certain quantity of sticks and had laid THEM on the fire, a viper, having come out because of the heat, fastened on his hand. ⁴And when the βάρβαροι, Barbaroi saw the beast hanging from his hand, they said to one another, "Certainly this man is a murderer, whom, having been saved out of the sea, the justice did not allow to live." ⁵He then, indeed, having shaken off the beast into the fire, suffered no evil. ⁶And they were expecting him to be about to swell up or to suddenly fall down dead, but after expecting IT for a long time and seeing nothing uncommon happening to him, changing THEIR minds, they said he was a god.

⁷And in the *area* near that place were *the* grounds of the principal man of the island, by *the* name *of* Publius, who, having received us, courteously accommodated US as guests *for* three days. ⁸And it came to pass *that* the father of Publius *was* being pressed by feverish heats and dysentery to lie *in* bed. *And* Paul, having entered in to *see* him, having prayed and having laid HIS hands on him, healed him. ⁹And when this had been done, the others in the island *who were* having weaknesses were also coming and were healed, ¹⁰who also honored us with many honors. And *as* we *were* setting sail, they were loading US *up* with the things that were necessary.

¹¹And after three months, we set sail in a ship of Alexandria that had wintered in the island, *which was marked* with the sign *of* Dioscuri. ¹²And having landed at Syracuse, we remained *there for* three days. ¹³Having cast off from that place, we came to Rhegium; and after one day, when a south wind had sprung up, the second DAY we came to Puteoli ¹⁴where, having found brothers, we were called upon to remain with them seven days—and *in* this way we came to Rome. ¹⁵And from that place, the brothers, having heard the things about us, came to meet us—*from* as far as Appii Forum and Three Taverns—*and* Paul, having seen them *and* having given thanks to God, took courage.

¹⁶And when we came to Rome,ᵃ Paul was allowed to remain by himself, with the soldier guarding him. ¹⁷And it came to pass after three days *that* he called together those who are the principal men of the יהודים, Y'hudiym.

And when they had come together, he said to them, "Men! brothers! I, having done nothing contrary to the people or to the customs of the fathers, a prisoner from יְרוּשָׁלַיִם, Y'rushalayim, was handed over to the hands of the Romans ¹⁸who, having examined me, were wanting to release ME, because of there being no cause in me *deserving* of death. ¹⁹But when the יהודים, Y'hudiym had spoken against IT, I was compelled to appeal to Cæsar (not as *though I was* having anything to accuse my ethnic-group of). ²⁰For this reason, therefore, I called for you, to see and to speak with YOU, for because of the hope of יִשְׂרָאֵל, Yis'rael, with this chain I am bound."

²¹And they said to him, "We neither received letters about you from יְהוּדָה, Y'hudah, nor did any one of the brothers who came *here* declare or speak any evil about you. ²²But we think it good to hear from you what you think, for, indeed, concerning this sect it is known to us that it is spoken against everywhere."

²³And having appointed a day for him, they came to him—more of them—to the place where he was staying as a guest. To these he was expounding, testifying fully *to* the Reign of God, persuading them also about יֵשׁוּעַ, Yeshua, both from the תּוֹרָה, To-

---

ᵃ Some mss insert, "the centurion handed over the prisoners to the captain of the barrack, but"

rah of מֹשֶׁה, Mosheh and *from* the Prophets, from morning until evening. ²⁴And some, indeed, were believing the things spoken, and some were not believing.

²⁵And not being agreed with one another, they were going away, after Paul had spoken one *parting* word: "The רוּחַ הַקֹּדֶשׁ, Ruach HaQodesh spoke well through יְשַׁעְיָהוּ, Y'sha'yahu the prophet to your fathers, ²⁶saying,

'Go on to this people and say, "With hearing you will hear, but you will not understand, and seeing you will see, but you will not perceive," ²⁷for the heart of this people was made thick, and with the ears they heard heavily, and their eyes they closed; otherwise, they would see with the eyes, and with the heart would understand, and be turned back, and I would heal them.'ᵃ

²⁸Be it known to you, therefore, that this salvation of God was sent to the גּוֹיִם, Goyim; these also will hear it!"ᵇ

~ c. A.D. 61 ~
Paul writes letters to the Philippians, Titus & Timothy.

³⁰And Paul remained an entire two years in his own rented HOUSE and was receiving all those coming in to him, ³¹proclaiming the Reign of God, and teaching the things about the Master יֵשׁוּעַ, Yeshua *the* Messiah with all boldness—unforbidden.

ᵃ יְשַׁעְיָהוּ *Y'sha'yahu* 6:9-10 (LXX)
ᵇ Some mss continue with vs 29, "And when he had said these things, the יְהוּדִים, Y'hudiym went away, having much disputation among themselves."

PAUL'S LETTER TO THE

Galatians

1

¹From Paul,ᵃ an emissary—not *sent* from men, nor through man, but through יֵשׁוּעַ, Yeshua *the* Messiah and God the Father, who raised Him out of the dead—²and all the brothers with me; to the Called-Forth-Communitiesᵇ of Galatia: ³*unmerited* favor to you and peace from God our Father and the Master יֵשׁוּעַ, Yeshua *the* Messiah, ⁴who gave Himself for our sins, that He might deliver us out of the present evil age, according to the will of God—even our Father—⁵to Whom IS the glory to the ages of the ages. אָמֵן, Amen.

⁶I *am in* wonder that you are so quickly transferred from Him who called you in the *unmerited* favor of Messiah, to another Good News ⁷(which is not *really* another), except *that* there are certain *ones* who are troubling you and *are* wanting to pervert the Good News of the Messiah. ⁸But even if we or a Messenger out of Heaven should proclaim Good News to you different from what we proclaimed to you, let him be accursed! ⁹As we have said before and now say again: if anyone should proclaim to you Good News different from what you received, let him be accursed! ¹⁰Indeed, do I now persuade men, or God? Or do I look to please men? If I still pleased men, I would not be Messiah's slave.

¹¹For I make known to you, brothers, that the Good News that was proclaimed by me is not according to man, ¹²for I neither received it from man, nor was I taught IT, but *received it* through a revelation of יֵשׁוּעַ, Yeshua *the* Messiah. ¹³For you heard of

---
ᵃ "Paul"—Παῦλος, Paulos; see 1 Timothy 1:1
ᵇ "Called-Forth-Communities"—ἐκκλησίαις, ekklesiais; see מַתִּתְיָהוּ *Matit'yahu* 16:18

my behavior at one time in Judaism: that I was exceedingly persecuting the Called-Forth[a] of God and destroying her,[b] 14 and *that* I was *also* advancing in Judaism above many equals in age in my own ancestry, being more abundantly zealous for my fathers' traditions.

15But when God was well pleased (having set me apart since the womb of my mother, and having called ME through His *unmerited* favor) 16to reveal His Son in me, so that I would proclaim Good News *of* Him among the גּוֹיִם, Goyim, I did not immediately consult with flesh and blood, 17nor did I go up to יְרוּשָׁלַיִם, Y'rushalayim to those who were emissaries before me, but I went away to עֲרָב, 'Arav and again returned to דַמֶּשֶׂק, Dameseq. 18Then, after three years, I went up to יְרוּשָׁלַיִם, Y'rushalayim to get to know כֵּיפָא, Keifa and remained with him fifteen days, 19but I did not see any of the other emissaries, except יַעֲקֹב, Ya'aqov, the brother of the Master.[c] 20(And the things that I write to you, look! in God's sight, I do not lie.)

21Then I came to the regions of Syria and of Cilicia, 22and *I* was unknown by face to the Called-Forth-Communities[d] of יְהוּדָה, Y'hudah that ARE in Messiah. 23And they were only hearing that "he who was persecuting us then, now proclaims Good News—the faith that at one time he was destroying!" 24and they were glorifying God in me.

2 1Then, after fourteen years,[e] I again went up to יְרוּשָׁלַיִם, Y'rushalayim with בַּר־נַבָּא, Bar-Naba, having also taken Titus with me. 2And I went up by revelation and submitted to them the Good News that I proclaim among the גּוֹיִם, Goyim, but *I did so* privately to those *who were* esteemed, so that I might not run (or had not run) in emptiness. 3But not even Titus who WAS with me, being a Greek, was compelled to be circumcised—4and THAT *was only made an issue* because of the false brothers brought in under false pretenses (who slipped in to spy out our liberty that we have in Messiah יֵשׁוּעַ, Yeshua, so that they might bring us under bondage), 5to whom we did not even for a moment yield in submission, so that the truth of the Good News would remain to you.

6And from those who were esteemed to be something (whatever they were then, it makes no difference to me; God does not accept the face of man)—indeed, those esteemed *ones* added nothing to me. 7But on the contrary, having seen that I have been entrusted with the Good News of the Uncircumcision,[f] as כֵּיפָא, Keifa[g] *is entrusted* with THAT of the Circumcision[h] 8(for He who worked in כֵּיפָא, Keifa to the assignment as an emissary of the Circumcision also worked in me in regard to the גּוֹיִם, Goyim), 9and having known the *unmerited* favor that was given to me, יַעֲקֹב, Ya'aqov and כֵּיפָא, Keifa and יוֹחָנָן, Yochanan—who were esteemed to be pillars—gave to me and to בַּר־נַבָּא, Bar-Naba a right hand of partnership, so that we WOULD GO to the גּוֹיִם, Goyim, and they to the Circumcision. 10*They* only *asked* that we should be mindful of the poor, which I was also diligent—this very thing—to do.

11Yet when כֵּיפָא, Keifa *later* came to Antioch, I stood up against him to the face, because he was blameworthy. 12For before the coming of certain *ones* from יַעֲקֹב, Ya'aqov, he was eating with the גּוֹיִם, Goyim; but when they came, he was withdrawing and separating himself, fearing those of the Circumcision. 13And the other יְהוּדִים, Y'hudiym also joined in with his hypocrisy, so that even בַּר־נַבָּא, Bar-Naba was carried away by their hypocrisy.

14But when I saw that they were not walking uprightly to the truth of the Good News, I said to כֵּיפָא, Keifa in front

---

[a] "Called-Forth"—ἐκκλησίαν, ekklesian; see מַתִּתְיָהוּ Matit'yahu 16:18
[b] "her"—Young's says, "it"; cf. Ephesians 5:25-26
[c] See Acts 9:23ff
[d] "Called-Forth-Communities"—ἐκκλησίαις, ekklesiais; see מַתִּתְיָהוּ Matit'yahu 16:18
[e] See Acts 15:1ff

[f] "Uncircumcision"—that is, the Goyim
[g] כֵּיפָא, Keifa—Gk: Πέτρος, Petros; also verse 8 (but not verse 9, 11 or 14); see יוֹחָנָן Yn. 1:42
[h] "Circumcision"—that is, the Jews; also in vs. 12

Righteousness by faith.

of them all, "If you, being יְהוּדִי, Y'hudiy, live here in the manner of the גּוֹי, Goyim and not in the manner of the יְהוּדִים, Y'hudiym, how do you *come to* compel the גּוֹיִם, Goyim to live like יְהוּדִים, Y'hudiym? ¹⁵We *who are* יְהוּדִים, Y'hudiym by nature and not 'sinners of the גּוֹיִם, Goyim,' ¹⁶but *are* having known that a man is not declared righteous by actions of תּוֹרָה, Torah unless through the faith of יֵשׁוּעַ, Yeshua *the* Messiah—we also believed in Messiah יֵשׁוּעַ, Yeshua so that we would be declared righteous by the faith of Messiah, and not by actions of תּוֹרָה, Torah, since no flesh will be declared righteous by actions of תּוֹרָה, Torah.

¹⁷"And if, *while* looking to be declared righteous in Messiah, we ourselves were also found *to be* sinners, IS then Messiah a servant of sin? Let it not be! ¹⁸For if the things I *previously* threw down, these I build up again, *then* I set myself forth *as a* sidestepper *of Torah*. ¹⁹For through תּוֹרָה, Torah I died to תּוֹרָה, Torah[a] *that is based on actions,* so that I may live to God. With Messiah I have been crucified, ²⁰and I no longer live—but Messiah lives in me. And that which I now live in the flesh, I live in the faith of the Son of God, who loved me and gave Himself for me. ²¹I do not make void the *unmerited* favor of God, for if righteousness IS through תּוֹרָה, Torah, then Messiah died for nothing."

3 ¹O unthinking Galatians! Who bewitched you[b]—before whose eyes יֵשׁוּעַ, Yeshua *the* Messiah was previously described[c] *as* crucified? ²I only want to learn this from you: did you receive the רוּחַ, Ruach by actions of תּוֹרָה, Torah, or by the hearing of faith? ³You are so unthinking! Having begun in the רוּחַ, Ruach, do you now finish in the flesh? ⁴So many things you suffered in vain! (If, indeed, *it was* even in vain.)

⁵He, therefore, who is supplying the רוּחַ, Ruach to you and working powerful acts

Galatians 3:14

among you—IS IT by actions of תּוֹרָה, Torah, or by the hearing of faith? ⁶*Just as* אַבְרָהָם, Av'raham BELIEVED GOD, AND IT WAS CREDITED TO HIM—TO RIGHTEOUSNESS,[d] ⁷know, then, that those of faith—these are *also* sons of אַבְרָהָם, Av'raham.

⁸And the Scripture, having foreseen that God declares the גּוֹיִם, Goyim righteous by faith, proclaimed the Good News beforehand to אַבְרָהָם, Av'raham,[e]

"Blessed in you will be all the גּוֹיִם, Goyim,"[f]

⁹so that those of faith are blessed with the faithful אַבְרָהָם, Av'raham.

¹⁰For as many as are of actions of תּוֹרָה, Torah are under a curse, for it has been written,

"Cursed IS everyone who is not continuing all things that have been written in the Book of the תּוֹרָה, Torah—to do them."[g]

¹¹And *it* is evident that by תּוֹרָה, Torah, no one is declared righteous before God, because,

"The righteous will live by faith."[h]

¹²So the תּוֹרָה, Torah *that is based on actions* is not of faith; rather,

"The one who did them will live in them."[i]

¹³But Messiah redeemed us from the curse declared in[j] the תּוֹרָה, Torah, having become a curse for us (for it has been written,

"Cursed is everyone who is hung on a tree"[k]);

¹⁴so that the blessing of אַבְרָהָם, Av'raham may come to the גּוֹיִם, Goyim in Messiah

---

[d] בְּרֵאשִׁית *B'reshiyt* 15:6
[e] Young ends verse 8 and begins verse 9 here.
[f] בְּרֵאשִׁית *B'reshiyt* 12:3
[g] דְּבָרִים *D'variym* 27:26
[h] חֲבַקּוּק *'Chavaquq* 2:4
[i] "them," that is, "My statutes and My judgments," see וַיִּקְרָא *Vayiq'ra* 18:5
[j] "declared in"—Young's says, "of"
[k] דְּבָרִים *D'variym* 21:23

---

[a] "to תּוֹרָה, Torah" is missing from Young's
[b] Some mss insert, "not to be persuaded by the truth"
[c] Some mss insert, "among you"

Galatians 3:15 — *Heirship of believers.*

יֵשׁוּעַ, Yeshua, *and* so that we may receive the promise of the רוּחַ, Ruach through the faith.

15Brothers, as a man I say THIS: even a man's validated בְּרִית, b'riyt—no one makes void or adds to *it*. 16Now, the promises were spoken to אַבְרָהָם, Av'raham and to his seed. (He does not say, "And to seeds," as of many, but as of one, "And to your seed,"ᵃ which is Messiah.) 17And I say this: the תּוֹרָה, Torah that came after four hundred and thirty years *in Mitz'- rayim* does not set aside a בְּרִית, b'riyt validated beforehand by God,ᵇ to make void the promise. 18For if the inheritance IS by תּוֹרָה, Torah, IT IS no longer by promise, yet God gave IT to אַבְרָהָם, Av'raham through promise.

19Why, then, the תּוֹרָה, Torah? It was added on account of the sidestepping— until the Seed to which the promise had been made would come—having been set in order through Messengers in the hand of a mediator. 20Now the mediator is not of one *party only*, but God is one. 21The תּוֹרָה, Torah, then: *IS it* against the promises of God? Let it not be! For if a *command of* תּוֹרָה, Torah was given that was able to make *one* alive, truly by *actions of* תּוֹרָה, Torah there would have been the righteousness. 22But the Scripture has shut in the whole *world* under sin, so that the promise by faith in יֵשׁוּעַ, Yeshua the Messiah would be given to those believing.

23And before the coming of the faith, we Y'hudiym were being guarded under *the guardianship of* תּוֹרָה, Torah—*completely* shut in to the faith about to be revealed, 24so that the תּוֹרָה, Torah became our child-conductor,ᶜ *leading us* to Messiah, so that by faith we would be declared righteous. 25But *with* the faith having *now* come, we are no longer under *the guardianship of* a child-conductor, 26for you are all sons of God through the faith in Messiah יֵשׁוּעַ, Ye-shua. 27For as many as were immersed to Messiah clothed *themselves* in Messiah; 28there is not here יְהוּדִי, Y'hudiy or Greek, there is not here slave nor freeman, there is not here male and female, for you are all one in Messiah יֵשׁוּעַ, Yeshua. 29And if you ARE of Messiah, then you are seed of אַבְרָהָם, Av'raham—according to promise, heirs.

4 1And I say, *for* as long a time as the heir is a little child, he differs nothing from a slave (*although* being master of all *the house*), 2but is under guardians and managers until the appointed time of the father. 3So also we, when we were little children, were in slavery under the basic principles of the world. 4But when the fullness of time came, God sent forth His Son (having come from a woman), having come under *the guardianship of* תּוֹרָה, Torah, 5so that He would redeem those under *the guardianship of* תּוֹרָה, Torah, *and* so that we Y'hudiym would receive the adoption as sons. 6And because you are sons, God sent forth the רוּחַ, Ruach of His Son into our hearts, shouting, "אַבָּא, Abba! Father!" 7so that you are no longer a slave, but a son—and if a son, also an heir through God.ᵈ

8But then, indeed, not having known God, you *Goyim* were enslaved to those by nature not being gods. 9But now having known God— or rather, *now* being known by God—how do you turn again to the weak and poor basic principles to which you desire to be enslaved anew? 10You observe days, and months, and times, and years! 11I am afraid for you, that perhaps I labored toward you in vain.

12Become as I AM—because I AM also as you, brothers—I implore you. You did no hurt to me, 13and you have known that through *my* weakness of the flesh I proclaimed Good News to you at the first, 14and your testing that IS in my flesh you did not despise nor reject, but you re-

---

ᵃ See בְּרֵאשִׁית *B'reshiyt* 12:7, 13:15, 24:7
ᵇ Some mss insert, "to Messiah"
ᶜ "child-conductor"—a stern guardian of boys; see Thayer
ᵈ "heir through God"—some mss say, "heir of God through Messiah."

ceived me as a messenger of God—as Messiah יֵשׁוּעַ, Yeshua *Himself.* ¹⁵Where,ᵃ then, is your happiness? For I testify to you that if possible, having plucked out your eyes, you would have given *them* to me. ¹⁶Have I therefore become your enemy *by* speaking truth to you? ¹⁷They *who trouble you* are zealous for you, YET for no good purpose.ᵇ Rather, they want to shut youᶜ out, so that you may be zealous for them.

¹⁸(But IT IS good to be zealously regarded at all times in what is good, and not only in my being present with you. ¹⁹My little children, of whom I again suffer birth-pains until Messiah may be formed in you, ²⁰I was wanting, then, to be present with you now and to change my tone,ᵈ because I am in doubt about you.)

²¹Tell me, you who are wanting to be under *the guardianship of* תּוֹרָה, Torah: do you not hear the תּוֹרָה, Torah? ²²For it has been written that אַבְרָהָם, Av'raham had two sons, one by the slave-girl and one by the free-woman. ²³But he who IS of the slave-girl was born according to flesh, and he who IS of the free-woman *was born* through promise. ²⁴These things *may* be allegorized, for these are two בְּרִיתוֹת, b'riy-tot: one, indeed, from Mount סִינַי, Siynai —*the one* bringing forth *her child* to slavery—who is הָגָר, Hagar. ²⁵Now this הָגָר, Hagar is Mount סִינַי, Siynai in עֲרָב, 'Arav, and corresponds to the יְרוּשָׁלַיִם, Y'rushala-yim that EXISTS now, for she is in slavery with her children. ²⁶But the יְרוּשָׁלַיִם, Y'ru-shalayim above is the free-woman, who is our mother, ²⁷for it has been written,

> "Rejoice, O barren *one*, who is not bearing *children*; break forth and cry out, you who are not having labor pains, because many ARE the children of the desolate—more than of her *who is* having the husband."ᵉ

²⁸Now you, brothers—as יִצְחָק, Yitz'chaq —are children of promise; ²⁹but, as then, he who was born according to the flesh persecuted him *who was born* according to the רוּחַ, Ruach. So also now. ³⁰But what does the Scripture say?

"Cast out the slave-girl and her son, for the son of the slave-girl will not be heir with the son of the free-woman."ᶠ

³¹Therefore, brothers, we are not a slave-girl's children, but the free-woman's.

5 ¹For the freedom,ᵍ Messiah made you free—stand, then! and be not held fast again by a yoke of slavery. ²Look! I, Paul, say to you *Goyim* that if you become circumcised,ʰ Messiah will profit you nothing. ³And I testify again to every circumcised man that he is a debtor to do the whole תּוֹרָה, Torah. ⁴You were cut off from the Messiah, you who are *seeking to be* declared righteous by תּוֹרָה, Torah! You fell away from the *unmerited* favor. ⁵For by the רוּחַ, Ruach, by faith, we wait for a hope of righteousness. ⁶For in Messiah יֵשׁוּעַ, Ye-shua, neither circumcision nor uncircumcision is able to doⁱ anything, but *only* faith working through love.

⁷You were running well! Who hindered you, *so as* not to be persuaded byʲ the truth? ⁸The persuasion *they use* IS not of Him who is calling you! ⁹"A little leaven leavens the whole batch *of dough.*" ¹⁰However, I have confidence in regard to you in the Master, that you will think nothing otherwise;ᵏ and he who is troubling you will carry the judgment, whoever he may be. ¹¹But I, brothers—if I still proclaim circumcision, why am I still persecuted?

ᵃ "where"—some mss say, "what"
ᵇ "for no good purpose"—Young's says, "not well"
ᶜ "you"—Young's says, "us"
ᵈ "tone"—lit. "voice," as Young's says
ᵉ יְשַׁעְיָהוּ Y'sha'yahu 54:1
ᶠ בְּרֵאשִׁית B'reshiyt 21:10
ᵍ Some mss insert, "with which"
ʰ Paul personally had Timothy—who was Jewish —circumcised. See Acts 16:1-3.
ⁱ "is able to do"—Young's says, "availeth"
ʲ "be persuaded by"—πείθεσθαι, peithesthai, most often translated "trust" or "persuade." Young's says, "obey."
ᵏ "think nothing otherwise"—Young's says, "be none otherwise minded"

Then the stumbling-block of the *execution* stake has been done away. ¹²O *how I wish that even they who are unsettling you would just* castrateᵃ *themselves!* ¹³For you —to freedom you were called, brothers, only not the freedom for an occasion to *indulge* the flesh. Rather, through the love, serve one another, ¹⁴for the whole תּוֹרָה, Torah is fulfilled in one word—in this: "YOU MUST LOVE YOUR NEIGHBOR AS YOURSELF."ᵇ ¹⁵But if you bite and devour one another, watch out that you are not consumed by one another!

¹⁶But I say: walk in the רוּחַ, Ruach, and the desire of the flesh you will not bring to its goal. ¹⁷For the flesh desires contrary to the רוּחַ, Ruach, and the רוּחַ, Ruach contrary to the flesh, for these are opposed to one another, so that the things that you want—these you may not do. ¹⁸And if you are led by the רוּחַ, Ruach, you are not under *the guardianship of* תּוֹרָה, Torah.

¹⁹And the actions of the flesh are also unconcealed, which are: sexual immorality,ᶜ uncleanness, sensuality, ²⁰idolatry, φαρμακεία, pharmakeia,ᵈ hatred, infighting, fierce rivalry, fits of rage, selfish ambition, dissensions, sects, ²¹envyings,ᵉ drunkennesses, orgies, and such like— of which I tell you beforehand (as I said previously), that those doing such things will not inherit the Reign of God.

²²But the fruit of the רוּחַ, Ruach is: love, joy, peace, patience, kindness, goodness, faithfulness, ²³humility, *and* self-control —there is no תּוֹרָה, Torah against such things; ²⁴and those who are of Messiah יֵשׁוּעַ, Yeshua *have* crucified the flesh *along* with the passions and the desires. ²⁵If we will live in the רוּחַ, Ruach, in the רוּחַ, Ruach we will also walk. ²⁶Let us not become conceited, provoking one another, *and* envying one another!

ᵃ "castrate"—lit. "cut off"
ᵇ וַיִּקְרָא *Vayiq'ra* 19:18
ᶜ Some mss begin this list with "adultery"
ᵈ φαρμακεία, pharmakeia—usually "sorcery," or "witchcraft"
ᵉ Some mss insert, "murders"

6 ¹Brothers, if a man is also overtaken by any misstep, you who ARE spiritual *should* restore such a one in a רוּחַ, ruach of humility, paying attention to yourself; otherwise, you also may be tempted. ²Carry the burdens of one another, and in this way you will fill up the תּוֹרָה, Torah of the Messiah, ³for if anyone, being nothing, thinks HIMSELF to be something, he deceives himself. ⁴But let each one examine his own action, and then in regard to himself alone he will have the *reason for* boasting, and not in regard to another, ⁵for each one must carry his own load.

⁶And let him who is instructed in the word share in all good things with he who is instructing *him*. ⁷Be not led astray: God is not mocked; for what a man sows, that also he will reap, ⁸because he who is sowing to his own flesh, from the flesh will reap decay; and he who is sowing to the רוּחַ, Ruach, from the רוּחַ, Ruach will reap life age-enduring. ⁹And in the doing good, let us not be faint-hearted, for at the proper time we will reap——*if we are* not giving up. ¹⁰Therefore, then, as we have opportunity, let us do the good to all, and especially to those of the household of the faith.

¹¹See in how large letters I have written to you with my own hand! ¹²As many as are wanting to make a good showing in the flesh, these compel you *Goyim* to become circumcised, only so that they may not be persecuted for the *execution* stake of Messiah. ¹³For neither do those *who are* themselves circumcised guard the תּוֹרָה, Torah, but they want you to be circumcised, so that they may take pride in your flesh.

¹⁴And for me, let it not be—to take pride *in anything* except in the *execution* stake of our Master יֵשׁוּעַ, Yeshua *the* Messiah, through which the world has been crucified to me, and I to the world. ¹⁵Forᶠ nei-

ᶠ Some mss insert, "in Messiah יֵשׁוּעַ, Yeshua"

ther circumcision is[a] anything, nor uncircumcision, but a new creation; [16]and as many as walk by this rule—peace and *loving*-kindness upon them, and on the יִשְׂרָאֵל, Yis'rael of God!

[17]From now on, let no one give me trouble, for in my body I carry the scars of יֵשׁוּעַ, Yeshua. [18]The *unmerited* favor of our Master יֵשׁוּעַ, Yeshua *the* Messiah *is* with your רוּחַ, ruach, brothers! אָמֵן, Amen.

[a] "is"—some mss say, "is able *to do*"

PAUL'S FIRST LETTER TO THE THESSALONIANS

1 Thessalonians

1 [1]*From* Paul[a] and Silvanus[b] and Timothy; to the Called-Forth[c] of *the* Thessalonians in God the Father, and the Master יֵשׁוּעַ, Yeshua *the* Messiah: *unmerited* favor to you, and peace.[d]

[2]We give thanks to God always for all of you, making mention of you in our prayers, [3]unceasingly remembering your work of the faith and the labor of the love and the perseverance of the hope of our Master יֵשׁוּעַ, Yeshua *the* Messiah in front of our God and Father, [4]having known, beloved brothers, your chosenness by God [5](because our Good News did not come to you only in word, but also in power, and in the רוּחַ הַקֹּדֶשׁ, Ruach HaQodesh, and in much assurance), even as you have known what sort of *men* we became among you because of you. [6]And you—you became imitators of us and of the Master (having received the word in much oppression, with joy of the רוּחַ הַקֹּדֶשׁ, Ruach HaQodesh), [7]so that you became an example to all those believing in Macedonia and in Achaia. [8]For from you has the word of the Master sounded out—not only in Macedonia and in Achaia, but in every place has your faith toward God gone out—so that we have no need to say anything. [9]For they themselves declare about us what kind *of* entrance we had to you, and how you turned to God from the idols, to serve a living and true God [10]and to wait for His Son from the Heavens, whom He raised out of the dead—יֵשׁוּעַ, Yeshua, who is rescuing us from the wrath that is coming.

2 [1]For you yourselves have known, brothers, *about* our entrance to you —that it did not become empty. [2]But having suffered before and having been mistreated in Philippi (as you have known), we were bold in our God to speak the Good News of God to you in *a time of* much conflict. [3]For our exhortation *is* not out of deceit, nor out of uncleanness, nor in underhandedness; [4]but as we have been approved by God to be entrusted with the Good News, so we speak—not as *those* pleasing men, but *pleasing* God, who is examining our hearts. [5]For at no time did we come with speech of flattery (as you have known), nor in a pretext for covetousness (God *is* our witness!), [6]nor looking for glory from men (neither from you nor from others), [7]*despite*, as Messiah's emissaries, being able to be burdensome.

But we became gentle[e] among you, as a nursing *mother* cherishes her own chil-

[a] "Paul"—Παῦλος, Paulos; see 1 Timothy 1:1
[b] "Silvanus"—a variant of סִילָא, Siyla
[c] "Called-Forth"—ἐκκλησία, ekklesia; see מַתִּתְיָהוּ Matit'yahu 16:18
[d] Some mss insert, "from God our Father and the Master יֵשׁוּעַ, Yeshua *the* Messiah!"

[e] "gentle"—the earliest mss say, "little children"

dren. ⁸In this way, being desirous of you, we were well-pleased to impart to you not only the Good News of God, but also our own souls, because you became beloved to us. ⁹For you remember, brothers, our labor and hardship; working night and day so as not to be a burden upon any of you, we proclaimed to you the Good News of God. ¹⁰You ARE witnesses—as God is also—of how purely and righteously and blamelessly we became to you who believe, ¹¹just as you have also known how with each one of you—as a father does with his own children—¹²we are exhorting you and encouraging *you* and testifying *to you*, for your walking worthily of God, who is calling you to His own Reign and glory.

¹³And because of this, we also give thanks to God continually that, having received the word of hearing from us *that is* of God, you accepted *it*—not *as* the word of man, but as it truly is: the word of God, who also works in you who believe. ¹⁴For you became imitators, brothers, of the Called-Forth-Communities[a] of God in Messiah יֵשׁוּעַ, Yeshua that are in יְהוּדָה, Y'hudah, because you suffered such things—even you—from your own countrymen, as they also *did* from the יְהוּדִים, Y'hudiym, ¹⁵who *also* put to death both the Master יֵשׁוּעַ, Yeshua and the prophets, and *who* persecuted us. (And they are *also* not pleasing God, and ARE against all men, ¹⁶forbidding us to speak to the גּוֹיִם, Goyim—that they might be saved—so *as* to always fill up their sins. But the Wrath has come upon them—to the end!)

¹⁷And we, brothers, having been taken from you for the space of a moment (in presence, not in heart), hastened the more abundantly to see your face with much desire. ¹⁸Therefore, we wanted to come to you (I, indeed—Paul), both once and again, but הַשָּׂטָן, HaSatan hindered us. ¹⁹For what IS our hope or joy or crown of boasting? Is *it* not even you, in front of our Master יֵשׁוּעַ, Yeshua[b] at His *coming* presence? ²⁰For you are our glory and joy.

3 ¹Therefore, bearing with *it* no longer, we thought *it* good to be left alone in Athens, ²and *we* sent Timothy—our brother, and God's[c] fellow-workman in the Good News of the Messiah—to establish you and to encourage you for the sake of your faith, ³so that no one *will* be moved in these oppressions. For you yourselves have known that we are set *in place* for this. ⁴For even when we were with you, we said to you beforehand that we are about to suffer oppression (as it also came to pass, and you have known IT). ⁵Because of this, I, bearing with *it* no longer, also sent *Timothy* to know your faith; otherwise, he who is tempting *might* tempt you, and our labor might be in emptiness.

⁶And now Timothy *is* having come to us from you and *is* having declared good news to us of your faith and love, and that you have a good remembrance of us always, desiring much to see us, as we also *desire TO SEE* you. ⁷Because of this we were encouraged over you, brothers, in all our distress and oppression, through your faith, ⁸because now we live, if you stand fast in the Master. ⁹For what thanks are we able to repay to God for you, for all the joy with which we rejoice because of you in the presence of our God? ¹⁰Night and day *we are* exceedingly imploring *God* that we might see your face and restore the things lacking in your faith.

¹¹And may our God and Father Himself, and our Master יֵשׁוּעַ, Yeshua, direct our way to you, ¹²and may the Master cause you to increase and to abound in the love to one another and to all, even as we also *do* to you, ¹³to the stabilizing *of* your hearts *to be* blameless in holiness before our God and Father, in the presence of our Master

---

[a] "Called-Forth-Communities"—ἐκκλησιῶν, ekklesion; see מַתִּתְיָהוּ Matit'yahu 16:18

[b] Some mss insert, "*the* Messiah"; also in vss. 3:11 & 13

[c] "God's"—some mss say, "a servant of God, and our"

יֵשׁוּעַ, Yeshua, with all His קְדוֹשִׁים, Q'doshiym. אָמֵן, Amen.

4

¹As to the remainder, then, brothers, we ask you and call upon you in the Master יֵשׁוּעַ, Yeshua that as you received from us how it was necessary for you to walk and to please God—even as you do walk[a]—that you may abound *all* the more, ²for you have known what commands we gave you through the Master יֵשׁוּעַ, Yeshua.

³For this is the will of God: your holiness—that you abstain from the sexual immorality; ⁴that each of you know *how* to obtain his own thing in holiness and honor ⁵(not in the passion of lust, as also *do* the גּוֹיִם, Goyim that were not knowing God); ⁶*and* that no one go beyond and defraud his brother in the matter, because the Master IS an avenger of all these (as we also previously spoke and testified to you). ⁷For God did not call us for uncleanness, but into holiness. ⁸He, therefore, who is putting away *these commands* does not put away man, but God, who also gives His רוּחַ הַקֹּדֶשׁ, Ruach HaQodesh to you.

⁹And concerning the brotherly love, you have no need of OUR writing to you, for you yourselves are God-taught to love one another, ¹⁰for you do it also to all the brothers who ARE in all Macedonia. But we call upon you, brothers, to abound still more, ¹¹and *also* to make it your aim to live a quiet life,[b] and to tend to your own *things*,[c] and to work with your own hands (as we commanded you), ¹²so that you may walk respectably toward those outside, and may have lack of nothing.

¹³And we do not want you to be ignorant, brothers, about those who have fallen asleep, so that you may not grieve, as also the remainder *of people do*, who have no hope. ¹⁴For if we believe that יֵשׁוּעַ, Yeshua died and rose again, so also will God bring with Him those *fallen* asleep through יֵשׁוּעַ, Yeshua. ¹⁵For this we say to you in the word of the Master: that we who are living, who remain until the *coming* presence of the Master, may not precede those asleep, ¹⁶because the Master Himself—with a shout, with the voice of a Chief-Messenger, and with the שׁוֹפָר, shofar of God—will come down from heaven, and the dead in Messiah will rise first. ¹⁷Then we who are living, who are remaining, will be caught away in *the* clouds together with them to meet the Master in *the* air, and so we will be always with the Master. ¹⁸So then, encourage one another with these words.

5

¹And concerning the times and the seasons, brothers, you have no need of my writing to you, ²for *you* yourselves have known thoroughly that the Day of ADONAI will come in this way: as a thief in the night. ³When they say, "Peace and security," then sudden destruction stands by them—as the labor pains DO to her who is with child—and they will not escape. ⁴But you, brothers, are not in darkness, *such* that the Day would catch you as a thief, ⁵for you are all sons of light and sons of day. We are not of night nor of darkness. ⁶So, then, we should not sleep as the others, but *stay* awake and be sober. ⁷For those *who are* sleeping sleep by night, and those making themselves drunk are drunken by night. ⁸But we, being of day: let us be sober, putting on a breastplate of faith and love, and a helmet—a hope of salvation; ⁹because God did not appoint us to wrath, but to the acquiring of salvation through our Master יֵשׁוּעַ, Yeshua *the* Messiah, ¹⁰who died for us, so that whether we wake *or* whether we sleep, we may live together with Him. ¹¹Therefore, encourage one another, and *each* one build up the *other* one, even as you are doing.

¹²And we ask you, brothers, to know those laboring among you and leading you in the Master and admonishing you, ¹³and to esteem them very abundantly in

---
[a] Some mss omit, "even as you do walk"
[b] "live a quiet life"—Young's says, "be quiet"
[c] "tend to your own *things*"—Young's says, "do your own business"

love because of their work. Be at peace among yourselves. ¹⁴And we exhort you, brothers: admonish the disorderly; encourage the discouraged; support the weak; be patient to all. ¹⁵See that no one returns evil for evil to anyone, but always pursue that which is good, both to one another and to all.

¹⁶Always rejoice; ¹⁷continually pray; ¹⁸in everything give thanks—for this *is* the will of God in Messiah יֵשׁוּעַ, Yeshua in regard to you. ¹⁹Do not quench the רוּחַ, Ruach; ²⁰do not treat prophecies with contempt. ²¹Rather, examine all things; hold fast *to* that which is good; ²²abstain from every form of evil. ²³And may the God of the peace Himself wholly set you apart, and your whole רוּחַ, ruach and soul and body be preserved unblameably in the *coming* presence of our Master יֵשׁוּעַ, Yeshua *the* Messiah. ²⁴Faithful is He who is calling you, who also will do *it*.

²⁵Brothers, pray also for us; ²⁶greet all the brothers in a holy kiss.

²⁷I put you under oath BY the Master that this letter be read to all the[a] brothers. ²⁸The *unmerited* favor of our Master יֵשׁוּעַ, Yeshua *the* Messiah *is* with you![b]

---

[a] Some mss insert, "holy"
[b] Some mss conclude, "אָמֵן, Amen."

PAUL'S SECOND LETTER TO THE THESSALONIANS

2 Thessalonians

1

¹*From* Paul[a] and Silvanus[b] and Timothy; to the Called-Forth[c] of *the* Thessalonians in God our Father, and the Master יֵשׁוּעַ, Yeshua *the* Messiah: ²*unmerited* favor to you, and peace, from God our Father and the Master יֵשׁוּעַ, Yeshua *the* Messiah!

³We ought to give thanks to God always for you, brothers, as it is fitting, because your faith increases greatly, and the love of each one of you all abounds to one another. ⁴Therefore, we ourselves boast in you among[d] the Called-Forth-Communities[e] of God for your perseverance and faith in all your persecutions and oppressions that you endure.

⁵*These are* an indication of the righteous judgment of God, for your being counted worthy of the Reign of God (for which you also suffer), ⁶since IT IS a righteous thing with God *for Him* to give back trouble to those troubling you ⁷and, to you who are troubled, *to give* relief with us at the revelation of the Master יֵשׁוּעַ, Yeshua from Heaven, with Messengers of His power, ⁸in flaming fire, giving vengeance to those not knowing God, and to those not obeying the Good News of our Master יֵשׁוּעַ, Yeshua.[f]

⁹*It is these* who will suffer justice—destruction age-enduring—from the face of the Master and from the glory of His strength ¹⁰in that Day when He comes to be glorified in His קְדוֹשִׁים, Q'doshiym and, because our testimony was believed among you, to be wondered at in all those having believed. ¹¹To this *end* we also pray always for you, that our God may count you worthy of the calling, and may fulfill all the good pleasure of *His* goodness and the work of the faith in power, ¹²so that the

---

[a] "Paul"—Παῦλος, Paulos; see 1 Timothy 1:1
[b] "Silvanus"—a variant of סִילָא, Siyla
[c] "Called-Forth"—ἐκκλησία, ekklesia; see מַתִּתְיָהוּ Matit'yahu 16:18
[d] "among"—Young's says, "in"
[e] "Called-Forth-Communities"—ἐκκλησίαις, ekklesiais; see מַתִּתְיָהוּ Matit'yahu 16:18

[f] Some mss insert, "*the* Messiah"; also in vs. 12

Name of our Master יֵשׁוּעַ, Yeshua may be glorified in you, and you in Him, according to the *unmerited* favor of our God and Master יֵשׁוּעַ, Yeshua *the* Messiah.

2

¹And we ask you, brothers, in regard to the *coming* presence of our Master יֵשׁוּעַ, Yeshua *the* Messiah and of our gathering together to Him, ²that you not be quickly shaken in mind, nor be troubled—neither through *a* רוּחַ, ruach, nor through word *of mouth*, nor through letters *seeming* as *if they are coming* through us (as *if indicating* that the Day of the Master[a] has arrived). ³Let not anyone deceive you in any manner, because if the falling away does not come first and the man of misdeeds[b] be revealed (the son of the destruction ⁴who is opposing and raising himself up above all *things* called "god" or worshipped, so that he has sat down in the Temple of God,[c] showing himself off that he is "God"), THE DAY WILL NOT COME.

⁵Do you not remember that, still being with you, I said these things to you? ⁶And you have known what is now keeping *him* down, for his being revealed in his own time. ⁷Indeed, the mystery of the misdeeds *is* already *at* work. Only he who is now keeping *it* down WILL HINDER *it*, until he may be out of the way. ⁸And then the Wrongdoing[d] One will be revealed—whom the Master יֵשׁוּעַ, Yeshua will put to death[e] with the רוּחַ, ruach of His mouth and will destroy with the appearing of His *coming* presence—⁹HIM whose *coming* presence is according to the working of הַשָׂטָן, HaSatan in all power and signs and pseudo-wonders, ¹⁰and in all deceitfulness of unrighteousness to those being destroyed, because they did not receive the love of the truth for *the purpose of* their being saved. ¹¹And because of this, God sends to them a working of delusion, for *the purpose of* their believing the lie, ¹²so that they may be judged—all who did not believe the truth, but were well pleased in the unrighteousness.

¹³But we—we ought to give thanks to God always for you, brothers, beloved by the Master, that God chose you *as* a firstfruit[f] to salvation (in holiness of the רוּחַ, Ruach and belief of the truth), ¹⁴to which He also called you through our Good News, to the acquiring of the glory of our Master יֵשׁוּעַ, Yeshua *the* Messiah. ¹⁵So then, brothers, stand firm, and hold *to* the traditions *of orderly conduct*[g] that you were taught *by us*—whether through word *of mouth*,[h] or whether through our letter.

¹⁶And may our Master יֵשׁוּעַ, Yeshua *the* Messiah Himself, and God our Father (who loved us, and gave *us* encouragement age-enduring, and good hope in *unmerited* favor), ¹⁷encourage your hearts and establish you in every good word and action.

3

¹As to the remainder, brothers, pray concerning us, that the word of the Master may run *free* and may be glorified as also with you, ²and that we may be delivered from the unreasonable and evil men, for not all ARE of the faith. ³But faithful is the Master, who will stabilize you and will guard YOU from the evil. ⁴And we have confidence in the Master regarding you, that the things that we command, you both do and will do. ⁵And may the Master direct your hearts to the love of God, and to the perseverance of the Messiah.

⁶And we command you, brothers, in the Name of our Master יֵשׁוּעַ, Yeshua *the* Messiah, to withdraw yourselves from every brother *who is* walking disorderly and not *following* after the tradition *of orderly conduct* that you received from us. ⁷For you yourselves have known how necessary it is for YOU to imitate us, because we did not

---

[a] "the Master"—some mss say, "Messiah"

[b] "misdeeds" or "wickedness"—some mss say, "sin"; in this vs., and in vs. 7, the Greek is ἀνομίας, anomias

[c] Some mss insert, "as 'God'"

[d] "Wrongdoing"—ἄνομος, anomos

[e] "the Master יֵשׁוּעַ, Yeshua put to death"—some mss say, "the Master will consume"

[f] "*as* a first-fruit"—some mss say, "from the beginning"

[g] "traditions *of orderly conduct*"—see 3:6ff

[h] "word *of mouth*"—or perh. "*spoken* word"

act disorderly among you, ⁸nor did we eat anyone's bread for nothing; rather, in labor and in hardship, *we were* working by night and by day, *so as* not to be a burden to any of you ⁹(not because we do not have authority, but so that we might give ourselves to you *as* a pattern—to imitate us). ¹⁰For even when we were with you, we commanded you this: that if anyone is not willing to work, neither let him eat. ¹¹For we hear of certain *ones* walking disorderly among you, working *at* nothing, but working at the affairs of others.ᵃ ¹²But we command and exhort such *persons* in the Master יֵשׁוּעַ, Yeshua *the* Messiah, that, working with quietness, they eat their own bread. ¹³And you, *our* brothers—may you not be weary *of* doing good. ¹⁴And if any one does not obey our word through this letter, *take* note *of* this one, to keep no company with him, so that he may be ashamed; ¹⁵yet count HIM not as an enemy, but admonish HIM as a brother.

¹⁶And may the Master of the peace Himself give the peace to you always, *and* in every way. The Master IS with you all!

¹⁷The greeting by my hand (Paul), which is a sign in every letter, I write this way: ¹⁸the *unmerited* favor of our Master יֵשׁוּעַ, Yeshua *the* Messiah IS with you all!ᵇ

ᵃ "working at the affairs of others" or "being busybodies"; Young's says, "over working"
ᵇ Some mss conclude, "אָמֵן, Amen."

PAUL'S FIRST LETTER TO THE CORINTHIANS

1 Corinthians

1 ¹*From* Paul,ᵃ a called emissary of Messiah יֵשׁוּעַ, Yeshua through the will of God, and Sosthenes the brother; ²to the Called-Forthᵇ of God that is in Corinth—to those set apart in Messiah יֵשׁוּעַ, Yeshua, called קְדוֹשִׁים, Q'doshiym—with all those in every place calling upon the Name of our Master יֵשׁוּעַ, Yeshua *the* Messiah, *who is* theirs and ours: ³*unmerited* favor to you and peace from God our Father and the Master יֵשׁוּעַ, Yeshua *the* Messiah!

⁴I give thanks to my God always concerning you for the *unmerited* favor of God that was given to you in Messiah יֵשׁוּעַ, Yeshua: ⁵that in everything you were enriched in Him (in all *you* say and *in* all *your* knowledge) ⁶as the testimony of the Messiah was made firm in you, ⁷so that you are not *lagging* behind in any gift, waiting for the revealing of our Master יֵשׁוּעַ, Yeshua *the* Messiah, ⁸who will also make you firm to the end—unblameable in the Day of our Master יֵשׁוּעַ, Yeshua *the* Messiah. ⁹Faithful IS God, through whom you were called to the sharing *in the life* of His Son יֵשׁוּעַ, Yeshua *the* Messiah, our Master.

¹⁰And I call upon you, brothers, through the Name of our Master יֵשׁוּעַ, Yeshua *the* Messiah, that you all say the same thing, and there may not be divisions among you, and you may be perfectly united in the same mind and in the same judgment. ¹¹For it was made clear to me about you, my brothers, by those of Chloe, that infightings are among you. ¹²And I say this: that each one of you says, "I, indeed, am of Paul!"—"and I of Apollos!"—"and I of כֵּיפָא, Keifa!"—"and I of Messiah!" ¹³But has the Messiah been divided? was Paul crucified for you? or were you immersed to the Name of Paul? ¹⁴(I give thanks to

ᵃ "Paul"—Παῦλος, Paulos; see 1 Timothy 1:1
ᵇ "Called-Forth"—ἐκκλησία, ekklesia; see מַתִּתְיָהוּ Matit'yahu 16:18

The power and wisdom of God.

God that I immersed not one of you—except Crispus and Gaius—15so that no one can say that you were immersed to my own name. 16Oh, and I also immersed Stephanas' household—beyond that, I do not know if I immersed any other.)

17For Messiah did not send me to immerse, but to proclaim Good News—*though* not in *the* wisdom of words, so that the *execution* stake of the Messiah may not be made empty.[a] 18For the word of the *execution* stake is foolishness to those indeed being destroyed, but to us—those being saved—it is the power of God. 19For it has been written,

"I will destroy the wisdom of the wise, and the intelligence of the intelligent I will bring to nothing."[b]

20Where IS the wise? where *is* the סוֹפֵר, sofer? where *is* the debater of this age? Did not God make foolish the wisdom of the world? 21For since, in the wisdom of God, the world through its wisdom did not know God, it pleased God through the foolishness of the proclaiming *of the Good News* to save those *who are* believing.

22And since יְהוּדִים, Y'hudiym ask *for* signs and Greeks seek wisdom, 23we also—we proclaim Messiah crucified: to יְהוּדִים, Y'hudiym, indeed, a stumblingblock; and to גּוֹיִם, Goyim,[c] foolishness; 24but to those *who are* called (both יְהוּדִים, Y'hudiym and Greeks), Messiah *is* the power of God and the wisdom of God, 25because the foolishness of God is wiser than men, and the weakness of God is stronger than men. 26For see your calling, brothers: that not many ARE wise according to the flesh; not many *are* mighty; not many *are* noble. 27But God chose the foolish things of the world so that He might put the wise to shame; and God chose the weak things of the world so that He might put the strong to shame. 28And God chose the things of the world with no noble ancestry,[d] and the things despised—the things that are not—so that He might make useless the things that are, 29*such* that no flesh may boast before God.

30But you—you are of Him in Messiah יֵשׁוּעַ, Yeshua, who became wisdom from God to us (also righteousness, and holiness, and redemption), 31so that, as it has been written,

"He who is boasting, let him boast in ADONAI."[e]

2

1And I, having come to you, brothers, came—not in superiority of words or wisdom—proclaiming to you the mystery[f] of God, 2for I decided not to know anything among you except יֵשׁוּעַ, Yeshua *the* Messiah, and Him crucified. 3And I, in weakness and in fear and in much trembling, was with you; 4and my word and my proclaiming was not in persuasive words of[g] wisdom, but in demonstration of the רוּחַ, Ruach and of power, 5so that your faith may not be in the wisdom of men, but in the power of God.

6Yet we speak wisdom among the mature, but not wisdom of this age, nor of the rulers of this age—of those becoming useless. 7Rather, we speak the wisdom of God, hidden in a mystery that God predetermined before the ages to our glory, 8which none of the rulers of the age knew. For if they had known, they would not have crucified the Master of the glory. 9But as it has been written, "WHAT EYE DID NOT SEE, AND EAR DID NOT HEAR, AND UPON THE HEART OF MAN DID NOT ASCEND"[h]—*this is* what God prepared for those *who are* loving Him. 10But God revealed THEM to us through the רוּחַ, Ruach; for the רוּחַ, Ruach searches all things, even the depths of God. 11Indeed, who of men has known the things of the man, except the רוּחַ, ruach of the man that IS in him? So also no

---

[a] "empty"—Young's says, "of no effect"
[b] יְשַׁעְיָהוּ Y'sha'yahu 29:14
[c] Some mss say, "Greeks"
[d] "with no noble ancestry"—Young's says, "base"
[e] יִרְמְיָהוּ Yir'm'yahu 9:23(22)
[f] "mystery"—some mss say, "testimony"
[g] Some mss insert, "human"
[h] יְשַׁעְיָהוּ Y'sha'yahu 64:3(4); 65:17

one has known the things of God, except the רוּחַ אֱלֹהִים, Ruach 'Elohiym. ¹²And we did not receive the רוּחַ, ruach of the world, but the רוּחַ, Ruach that IS of God, so that we may know the things bestowed on us by God— ¹³things which we also speak, not in words taught by human wisdom, but in those taught by the רוּחַ, Ruach,[a] with spiritual things comparing[b] spiritual things. ¹⁴Now, the natural man does not receive the things of the רוּחַ אֱלֹהִים, Ruach 'Elohiym, for they are foolishness to him; and he is not able to know THEM, because they *need to* be spiritually examined. ¹⁵But he who is spiritual examines all things, yet he himself is examined by no one. ¹⁶For WHO HAS KNOWN THE MIND OF ADONAI, THAT HE WILL INSTRUCT HIM?[c] But we—we have the mind of Messiah.

3 ¹And I, brothers, was not able to speak to you as spiritual, but as fleshly—as to little children in Messiah. ²I fed you with milk, not with *solid* food, for you were not yet able *to take it*. But even now, you are still not able, ³for you are still fleshly! For where THERE IS envying among you, and infighting,[d] are you not fleshly and walking in the manner of men? ⁴For when one says, "I, indeed, am of Paul," and another, "I *am* of Apollos," are you not human?[e]

⁵Who, then, is Apollos; and who is Paul? *Merely* servants through whom you believed, and to each as the Master gave. ⁶I planted; Apollos watered; but God was giving growth, ⁷so that neither he who is planting is anything, nor he who is watering, but He who is giving growth: God. ⁸And he who is planting and he who is watering are one, and each one will receive his own wages, according to his own labor.

⁹For we are fellow-workmen of God; you are God's cultivated field—God's building.

¹⁰According to the *unmerited* favor of God that was given to me, I laid a foundation as a wise master-builder, and another builds on IT.[f] But each one, let him look at how he builds on *it*, ¹¹for no one is able to lay another foundation except that which is laid, which is יֵשׁוּעַ, Yeshua *the* Messiah. ¹²And if anyone builds upon the foundation—gold, silver, precious stones, wood, hay, straw—¹³the work of each *one* will become known, for the Day will make IT clear, because it is revealed in fire; and the work of each—what kind it is—the fire itself will test. ¹⁴If anyone's work that he built on IT remains, he will receive a wage; ¹⁵but if the work of anyone is burned up, he will suffer loss, and he himself will be saved, but just as *one escaping* through *a* fire.

¹⁶Have you not known that you are a temple of God, and *that* the רוּחַ אֱלֹהִים, Ruach 'Elohiym lives in you? ¹⁷If anyone ruins the temple of God, God will ruin him, for the temple of God is holy, which *is what* you are.

¹⁸Let no one deceive himself: if anyone seems to be wise among you in this age, let him become a fool, so that he may become wise. ¹⁹For the wisdom of this world is foolishness with God, for it has been written,

"*It is God* who is catching the wise in their craftiness";[g]

²⁰and again, "ADONAI KNOWS THE REASONINGS of the wise, THAT THEY ARE VAIN."[h] ²¹So then, let no one boast in men, for all things are yours, ²²whether Paul, or Apollos, or כֵּיפָא, Keifa, or the world, or life, or death, or things present, or things about to be—all are yours, ²³and you ARE Messiah's, and Messiah IS God's.

---

[a] "רוּחַ, Ruach"—some mss say, "רוּחַ הַקֹּדֶשׁ, Ruach HaQodesh"
[b] "with spiritual things comparing" or possibly, "to spiritual ones explaining"
[c] יְשַׁעְיָהוּ Y'sha'yahu 40:13
[d] Some mss insert, "and divisions"
[e] "human"—some mss say, "fleshly"
[f] The remainder of this verse is missing in Young's.
[g] אִיּוֹב Iyov 5:13
[h] תְּהִלִּים T'hiliym 94:11

4 ¹Let a man consider us in this way: as assistants of Messiah and stewards of the mysteries of God. ²In this case, moreover, it is required of the stewards that one must be found faithful, ³but to me, it is for a very little thing that I may be examined by you, or by man's day *of examination in court*. Indeed, I do not even examine myself ⁴(for I have been conscious of nothing to *hold against* myself, though I have not been declared right in this); rather, he who is examining me is the Master. ⁵So then, judge nothing before the time, until the Master comes, who will both bring to light the hidden things of the darkness, and reveal the purposes of the hearts. And then the praise will come to each *one* from God.

⁶And these things, brothers, I transferred to myself and to Apollos because of you, so that in us you would learn not *to go*[a] beyond what has been written, *and* so that you will not be puffed up, one for one against the other. ⁷Indeed, who makes you so different? And what do you have that you did not receive? And if you also received, why do you boast as *one* not having received? ⁸You are already having been filled! You were already *made* rich! Without us you *already* reigned *like kings!* (And indeed, I wish you did reign, so that we could also reign together with you.)

⁹For I think God set us forth last—the emissaries—as *those* appointed to death, because we became a spectacle to the world and to Messengers and to men. ¹⁰We ARE fools because of Messiah, but you *are* wise in Messiah; we ARE weak, but you *are* strong; you *are* glorious, but we *are* dishonored. ¹¹*Even* until the present time, we not only hunger and thirst, but are naked, and are beaten with fists, and wander about *homeless*, ¹²and labor, working with OUR own hands. Being reviled, we bless; being persecuted, we endure; ¹³being spoken evil of, we *make our* appeal. We became as *the* filth of the world—a scouring-off of all things—until now.

¹⁴I write these things not AS *a child-conductor*[b] putting you to shame, but warning *you* as my beloved children. ¹⁵Indeed, *even* if you have ten thousand child-conductors in Messiah, yet *you do* not *have* many fathers. For in Messiah יֵשׁוּעַ, Yeshua, through the Good News, I—I brought you forth. ¹⁶I call upon you, therefore: become imitators of me. ¹⁷Because of this, I sent Timothy to you (who is my child—beloved and faithful—in the Master) who will remind you of my ways in Messiah יֵשׁוּעַ, Yeshua,[c] as I teach everywhere among all *the* Called-Forth.[d]

¹⁸Now certain *ones of you* are puffed up, as if I were not coming to you; ¹⁹but I will come quickly to you (if the Master wills), and I will know not the word of those puffed up *ones*, but the power; ²⁰for the Reign of God is not in word, but in power. ²¹What do you want? Should I come to you with a rod, or in love and with a רוּחַ, ruach of humility?

5 ¹*Indeed*, sexual immorality is actually heard of among you—and such sexual immorality as is not even[e] among the world-ethnicities—such that one has the wife of his father! ²And you are having been puffed up, and did not rather mourn, *such* that he who did this action would be taken away[f] from among you. ³For I indeed (being absent *from you* as to the body, but present *with you* as to the רוּחַ, ruach) have already judged (as *if* being present *with you*) him who so worked this thing: ⁴you, being gathered together in the Name of our Master יֵשׁוּעַ, Yeshua[g] (also *with* my רוּחַ, ruach), with the power of our Master יֵשׁוּעַ, Yeshua, ⁵*are* to hand over such a one to הַשָּׂטָן, HaSatan for the destruction of the flesh, so that the

---

[a] "*to go*"—some mss say, "to think"
[b] "child-conductor"—a stern guardian of boys, see Thayer; also in next verse
[c] Some mss omit, "יֵשׁוּעַ, Yeshua"
[d] "Called-Forth"—ἐκκλησία, ekklesia; see מַתִּתְיָהוּ Matit'yahu 16:18
[e] Some mss insert, "named"
[f] "taken away"—some mss say, "removed"
[g] Some mss insert, "Messiah"; both times in this verse

רוּחַ, ruach may be saved in the Day of the Master.[a]

⁶Your boasting IS not good! Have you not known that a little leaven leavens the whole batch *of dough*? ⁷Clean out the old leaven, so that you may be a new batch *of dough*, because you are unleavened; for our פֶּסַח, Pesach—Messiah—was also sacrificed[b] ⁸so that we may keep the Feast, not with old leaven, nor with the leaven of evil and wickedness, but with *the* מַצָּה, matzah of purity and truth.

⁹I wrote to you in the letter not to keep company with *those who are* sexually immoral—¹⁰certainly not *meaning* with the sexually immoral of this world (or with the covetous and plunderers or idolaters), since you *would be* obligated then to go out from this world. ¹¹But now I write to you not to keep company with HIM (if *it is* anyone being named a brother), *who* may be sexually immoral, or covetous, or an idolater, or a slanderer, or a drunkard, or a plunderer—with such a one not even to eat together. ¹²For what *business* have I to judge those outside *the brothers*? Do you not judge those within; ¹³and those outside, God judges? "PUT AWAY THE EVIL FROM AMONG YOURSELVES."[c]

6 ¹Does any one of you dare, having a matter with the other, to go to be judged before the unrighteous and not before the קְדוֹשִׁים, Q'doshiym? ²Or have you not known that the קְדוֹשִׁים, Q'doshiym will judge the world? And if the world is judged by you, are you unworthy of *presiding over* the smaller *courts of* judgment? ³Have you not known that we will judge Messengers? Why not then the things of *this* life? ⁴Of the things of *this* life, indeed, then, if you have *courts of law for* judgment, cause these *men* to sit *in judgment of you*—even those despised among the Called-Forth.[d] ⁵I speak to shame you:

it cannot be so, *that* there is no one wise among you who will be able to discern in the middle of his brothers! ⁶But brother goes to be judged with brother—and this before unbelievers!

⁷Already, then, indeed, there is actually defeat for you, that you have lawsuits with one another. Why do you not rather suffer injustice? Why not rather be defrauded? ⁸But you—you do injustice, and you defraud, and *you do* this *to your* brothers!

⁹Have you not known that the unrighteous will not inherit the Reign of God? Be not led astray: neither *the* sexually immoral, nor idolaters, nor adulterers, nor *the* effeminate,[e] nor men who practice homosexual acts, ¹⁰nor thieves, nor *the* covetous, nor drunkards, nor slanderers, nor plunderers will inherit the Reign of God. ¹¹And certain *ones* of you were these! But you were washed; but you were set apart; but you were declared righteous in the name of the Master יֵשׁוּעַ, Yeshua *the* Messiah,[f] and in the רוּחַ, Ruach of our God!

¹²"All things are permitted for me," but not all things are profitable; "all things are permitted for me," but I—I will not be put under authority by anything. ¹³"The foods ARE for the belly, and the belly for the foods," but God will make useless both this and these. And the body IS not for sexual immorality, but for the Master; and the Master for the body. ¹⁴And God both raised *up* the Master, and will *also* raise us up through His power.

¹⁵Have you not known that your bodies are members of Messiah? Having taken, then, the members of the Messiah, should I make THEM members of a prostitute? Let it not be! ¹⁶Have you not known that he who is joined to the prostitute is one body *with her*? "FOR THEY WILL BE," He says, "THE TWO FOR ONE FLESH."[g] ¹⁷But he who is joined to the Master is one רוּחַ, ruach *with Him*. ¹⁸Flee the sexual immorality! Every sin—whatever a man commits—is outside the body, but he who is

---

[a] Some mss insert, "יֵשׁוּעַ, Yeshua"
[b] Some mss insert, "for us"
[c] דְּבָרִים D'variym 13:6(5), 17:7, 21:21, 22:21
[d] "Called-Forth"—ἐκκλησία, ekklesia; see מַתִּתְיָהוּ Matit'yahu 16:18
[e] "effeminate" or "male prostitute"
[f] Some mss omit, "Messiah"
[g] בְּרֵאשִׁית B'reshiyt 2:24

Instructions concerning marriage. **1 Corinthians 7:25**

committing sexual immorality sins *also* against his own body. ¹⁹Have you not known that your body is a temple of the רוּחַ הַקֹּדֶשׁ, Ruach HaQodesh in you, which you have from God? And you are not your own, ²⁰for you were bought with a price. *So then,* glorify God in your body.[a]

7 ¹Now concerning the things of which you wrote: *IT IS* good for a man not to touch a woman, ²but because of the sexual immorality, let each man have his own wife, and let each woman have her own husband. ³To the wife, let the husband return what is due,[b] and likewise also the wife to the husband. ⁴The wife does not have authority over her own body; rather, the husband *does*. And likewise also, the husband does not have authority over his own body; rather, the wife *does*. ⁵Do not deprive one another, except by *mutual* consent for a time, so that you may be free for[c] prayer, but again may come together, so that הַשָּׂטָן, HaSatan may not tempt you because of your lack of self-control. ⁶And this I say by way of concession, not of command, ⁷but I want all men to be even as I myself *AM*. But each has his own gift of God—one indeed this way, and *another* one that.

⁸And I say to the unmarried and to the widows: it is good for them if they remain *unmarried* even as I *AM*; ⁹but if they do not have self-control, let them marry, for it is better to marry than to burn *with desire*. ¹⁰And to the married I command—not I, but the Master: let a wife not separate from a husband ¹¹(but even if she separates, let her remain unmarried, or let her be reconciled to the husband), and let a husband not send away a wife *in divorce*.

¹²And to the rest I speak *this*—I, not the Master: if any brother has an unbelieving wife, and she is pleased to live with him, let him not send her away *in divorce*; ¹³and if any woman has an unbelieving husband, and this one is pleased to live with her, let her not send the husband away *in divorce*; ¹⁴for the unbelieving husband has been set apart in the wife, and the unbelieving wife has been set apart in the husband;[d] otherwise, your children are unclean, but now they are holy. ¹⁵But if the unbelieving *one* separates himself, let him separate himself. The brother or the sister is not under bondage in such *CASES*, and God has called you *to live* in peace. ¹⁶For what have you known, O wife, whether you will save the husband? or what have you known, O husband, whether you will save the wife?

¹⁷Otherwise, as the Master apportioned to each *person, and* as God has called each *person*, in this way let him walk.

And in all the Called-Forth-Communities,[e] in this way do I direct: ¹⁸was anyone called, being circumcised? Let him not become uncircumcised. Has anyone been called in uncircumcision? Let him not be circumcised. ¹⁹The circumcision is nothing, and the uncircumcision is nothing, but *what matters is* a keeping of the commands of God.

²⁰Each *one*, in the calling in which he was called—in this, let him remain. ²¹Were you called *as* a slave? Be not anxious (but if you are also able to become free, rather *make use of IT*), ²²for he who *IS* in the Master, *though* having been called *as* a slave, is the Master's freedman. Likewise, he *who is* having been called *as* the free man is a slave of Messiah.

²³You were bought with a price, *so* become not slaves of men. ²⁴*Rather,* brothers—each *one*: in that in which he was called, in this *condition* let him remain with God.

²⁵Now concerning the virgins, a command of the Master I have not, but I give judgment as *one* having obtained *loving-*

---

[a] Some mss insert, "and in your רוּחַ, ruach, which are God's"
[b] "what is due"—some mss say, "the due good-will"
[c] Some mss insert, "fasting and"
[d] "husband," lit. "brother"
[e] "Called-Forth-Communities"—ἐκκλησίαις, ekklesiais; see מַתִּתְיָהוּ *Matit'yahu* 16:18

kindness from the Master to be faithful. ²⁶I think, therefore, this to be good because of the present necessity: that IT IS good for a man to[a] be this way. ²⁷Have you been bound to a wife? Seek not to be freed. Have you been released from a wife? Seek not a wife. ²⁸But even if you do marry, you did not sin; and if the virgin marries, she did not sin; but such *ones* will have oppression in the flesh, and I *am trying to* spare you.

²⁹And this I say, brothers: the time from now on is having been shortened, so that both those having wives will be as not having; ³⁰and those weeping, as not weeping; and those rejoicing, as not rejoicing; and those buying, as not possessing; ³¹and those using the world, as not using IT up—for the *outward* appearance of this world is passing away.

³²And I want you to be without anxiety. The unmarried *man* is anxious for the things of the Master (how he may please the Master), ³³but the married *man* is anxious for the things of the world (how he may please the wife), ³⁴and he has been divided. *Likewise*, both the unmarried woman and the virgin are[b] anxious for the things of the Master (that she may be holy, both in the body and the רוּחַ, ruach), but the married *woman* is anxious for the things of the world (how she may please the husband).

³⁵And this I say for your own profit, *and* not so that I may throw a noose upon you, but for the good order and devotedness to the Master, undistractedly. ³⁶And if anyone thinks IT to be unbecoming to his virgin *daughter* (if she is beyond the bloom of age *for marrying*, and *he feels* it ought to be so), let him do what he wants; he does not sin—*he may* let them marry. ³⁷But he who has stood steadfast in his heart (not having obligation), and has authority over his own will, and has decided this in his own heart—to *continue to* watch over his own virgin *daughter*—will do well. ³⁸So, both he who is giving his virgin *daughter* in marriage does well, and he who is not giving in marriage does better.

³⁹A wife is bound[c] *in marriage for* as long a time as her husband lives; but if her husband sleeps *in death*, she is free to be married to whom she wants, *though* only in the Master. ⁴⁰But according to my judgment, she is happier if, *unmarried*, she so remains (and I think I also have the רוּחַ אֱלֹהִים, Ruach 'Elohiym).

8 ¹Now concerning the things sacrificed to idols: we have known that we all have knowledge. Knowledge puffs up, but love builds up. ²If anyone thinks to know anything, he has not yet known as HE ought to know; ³but if anyone loves God, this one has been known by Him.

⁴Concerning the eating, then, of the things sacrificed to idols: we have known that an idol IS nothing in the world, and that there is no[d] God except One. ⁵For even if there are those called "gods"—whether in heaven or upon earth, as there are many "gods" and many "masters"— ⁶yet to us *there* IS one God, the Father (from whom ARE all the things, and we *are* to Him), and one Master, יֵשׁוּעַ, Yeshua *the* Messiah (through whom ARE all the things, and we *are* through Him).

⁷But the knowledge *of this* is not in all men. And certain *ones*, until now being accustomed to[e] *sacrificing food to* the idol, *continue to* eat IT as *if it were still* a thing sacrificed to an idol; and their conscience, being weak, is defiled. ⁸But foods will not bring us near to God. We are neither lacking if we do not eat; nor, if we do eat, are we in abundance.[f]

⁹But watch out, so that this privilege of yours may not become a stumbling-block

---

[a] "to"—Young says, "that the matter"
[b] "and he has been divided. *Likewise*, both the unmarried woman and the virgin are"—some mss say, "The wife and the virgin have *also* been divided: the unmarried *woman* is"
[c] Some mss insert, "by תּוֹרָה, Torah"
[d] Some mss insert, "other"
[e] "being accustomed to"—some mss say, "with consciousness of"
[f] "in abundance"—Young's says, "in advance"

Rights of an emissary.

to the weak. ¹⁰For if anyone sees you, the *one* having "knowledge," in an idol's temple reclining (at mealtime), will not his conscience—he being weak—be emboldened to eat the things sacrificed to idols? ¹¹For the weak *one* is destroyed by your "knowledge"—the brother because of whom Messiah died. ¹²And *by* sinning this way in regard to the brothers, and striking their weak conscience, you sin in regard to Messiah. ¹³Therefore, if foods cause my brother to stumble, I will eat no meat—to the age—so that I will not cause my brother to stumble.

9 ¹Am I not free? Am I not an emissary? Have I not seen יֵשׁוּעַ, Yeshua,[a] our Master? Are you not my work in the Master? ²*Even* if I am not an emissary to others, yet doubtless I am to you, for you are the seal of my assignment as an emissary in the Master.

³My defense to those who examine me is this: ⁴have we no right[b] to eat and to drink? ⁵have we no right to lead about a *believing* sister—a wife—as also the other emissaries, and the brothers of the Master, and כֵּיפָא, Keifa? ⁶or do only we—I and בַּר־נַבָּא, Bar-Naba—have no right not to work? ⁷Who, at any time, serves as a soldier at his own expense? Who plants a vineyard, but does not eat the fruit of it? Or who feeds a flock, but does not eat of the milk of the flock? ⁸Do I speak these things according to man? or does not the תּוֹרָה, Torah also say these things? ⁹For in the תּוֹרָה, Torah of מֹשֶׁה, Mosheh it has been written,

"You must not muzzle an ox threshing out grain."[c]

Does God care for the oxen? ¹⁰or does He say *this* by all means because of us? Yes, because of us it was written, because the plower ought to plow in hope, and he who is threshing in hope *ought*[d] to share *in* his harvest.

¹¹If we sowed to you the spiritual things, *is it* too great *a thing* if we reap your material things? ¹²If others share of this right over you, do we not more? But we did not use this right; rather, we bear *with* all things, so that we may give no hindrance to the Good News of the Messiah. ¹³Have you not known that those working around the things of the Temple *also* eat *the food* of the Temple? and those attending to the altar are sharers with *the offerings made on* the altar? ¹⁴So also did the Master direct those *who are* proclaiming the Good News: to live *by means* of the Good News.

¹⁵But I have used none of these things, nor did I write these things so that it may be done this way in my case. For *it is* good for me rather to die, than that anyone make my boasting empty. ¹⁶For if I proclaim Good News, it is no boasting for me, for obligation is laid upon me, for אוֹי, oy! *it* is to me if I do not proclaim *the* Good News. ¹⁷For if I do this willingly, I have a reward; but if unwillingly, I have *nevertheless* been entrusted with a stewardship! ¹⁸What, then, is my reward? That *in* proclaiming *the* Good News, I will make the Good News[e] *available* without charge, *so as* not to abuse my authority in the Good News.

¹⁹ For *though* being free from all men, to all men I made myself a slave, so that I might gain *some, all* the more.
²⁰ And I became to the *unbelieving* יְהוּדִים, Y'hudiym as an *unbelieving* יְהוּדִי, Y'hudiy, so that I might gain יְהוּדִים, Y'hudiym.

To those under *the guardianship of* תּוֹרָה, Torah,[f] *I became* as *one* under *the guardianship of* תּוֹרָה, Torah, so that I might gain those under *the guardianship of* תּוֹרָה, Torah (myself not being under *the guardianship of* תּוֹרָה, Torah).[g]

---

[a] Some mss insert, "Messiah"
[b] "right" or "authority"; also in verses 5, 6 and 12
[c] דְּבָרִים *D'variym* 25:4
[d] Some mss insert, "of his hope"
[e] Some mss insert, "of the Messiah"
[f] "under *the guardianship of* תּוֹרָה, Torah"—cf. Galatians 3:23
[g] Some mss omit, "(myself not being under *the guardianship of* תּוֹרָה, Torah)"

1 Corinthians 9:21 — Admonitions & warnings.

21 To those without תּוֹרָה, Torah, *I became* as *one* without תּוֹרָה, Torah, so that I might gain those without תּוֹרָה, Torah (*myself* not being without *the* תּוֹרָה, Torah of God, but within *the* תּוֹרָה, Torah of Messiah).

22 I became[a] weak to the weak, so that I might gain the weak—to all men I have become all things, so that by all means I may save some.

23 And all things I do because of the Good News, so that I may become a fellow-sharer of it.

24 Have you not known that those running in a race all indeed run, but *only* one receives the prize? Run this way, so that you may obtain *it*! 25 Now, everyone who is striving *for the prize* is self-controlled in all things. These indeed *do this*, then, so that they may receive a crown *that is* perishable, but we *strive for* an immortal *crown!* 26 I, therefore, run this way: not as *one running* uncertainly. I fight this way: not as *one* beating air. 27 Rather, I beat down my body and bring IT into slavery; otherwise, having proclaimed to others, I myself may become disqualified.

10 ¹For I do not want you to be ignorant, brothers, that our fathers were all under the cloud, and all passed through the sea, ²and all were immersed to מֹשֶׁה, Mosheh in the cloud and in the sea, ³and all ate the same spiritual food, ⁴and all drank the same spiritual drink (for they were drinking of a spiritual rock *that was* following them, and the rock was the Messiah). ⁵But in the majority of them, God was not well-pleased, for their bodies were scattered in the desert. ⁶And those things became patterns for us, for our not *being ones who* passionately desire evil things, as these *fathers* also desired.

⁷Do not become idolaters, as certain *ones* of them *did*, as it has been written,

"The people sat down to eat and to drink, and stood up to play."[b]

⁸Nor may we commit sexual immorality, as certain *ones* of them committed sexual immorality, and there fell in one day twenty-three thousand.[c] ⁹Nor may we test the Messiah, as also certain *ones* of them tempted *God*, and were being destroyed by the serpents.[d] ¹⁰Nor grumble, as some of them grumbled and were destroyed by the Destroyer.[e]

¹¹And these things happened to those people as patterns, and they were written for our warning, to whom the end of the ages has come, ¹²so that he who is thinking *he will be able* to stand—let him watch out, so that he may not fall.

¹³No way of testing has taken *hold of* you, except *that which is* human, and God —who will not allow you to be tempted above what you are able—is faithful. And with the way of testing, He will also make the way out, for your being able to bear IT.

¹⁴Therefore, my loved ones, flee from the idolatry. ¹⁵I speak as to wise men— judge what I say: ¹⁶the cup of the blessings that we bless—is it not the sharing of the blood of the Messiah? *And* the bread that we break—is it not the sharing of the body of the Messiah? ¹⁷Because *there is* one bread, we, the many, are one Body, for we all share of the one bread.

¹⁸Look at the people of יִשְׂרָאֵל, Yis'rael![f] Are not those eating the sacrifices sharers of the altar? ¹⁹What, then, do I say? that a sacrifice offered to an idol is anything? or that an idol is anything? ²⁰No, but that the things which they[g] sacrifice, they sacrifice to demons, and not to God; and I do not want you to become sharers of the demons! ²¹You are not able to drink *both* the cup of the Master and the cup of demons; you are not able to share of *both* the table

---

[a] Some mss insert, "as"
[b] שְׁמוֹת Sh'mot 32:6
[c] בְּמִדְבַּר B'mid'bar 25:1-9
[d] בְּמִדְבַּר B'mid'bar 21:1-9
[e] בְּמִדְבַּר B'mid'bar 17:6ff(16:41ff)
[f] "the people of יִשְׂרָאֵל, Yis'rael"—lit. "יִשְׂרָאֵל, Yis'rael according to the flesh"
[g] "they"—some mss say, "the גּוֹיִם, Goyim," indicating a probable interpretation for "they"

Covered and uncovered.

of the Master and the table of demons. ²²Do we provoke the Master to jealousy? Are we stronger than He? ²³"All things are permitted,"ᵃ but not all things are profitable. "All things are permitted," but not all things build up. ²⁴Let no one seek his own, but *one* another's.

²⁵Whatever is sold in the meat-market, eat, not examining *it* because of the conscience, ²⁶FOR THE EARTH *IS* ADONAI'S, AND ITS FULLNESS.ᵇ ²⁷If anyone of the Unbelieving calls you *to a meal*, and you want to go, eat all that is set before you, examining nothing because of the conscience. ²⁸But if anyone says to you, "This is a thing sacrificed,"ᶜ do not eat, for the sake of the one who showed IT, and of the conscience.ᵈ ²⁹(And *by* "conscience," I do not mean of yourself, but of the other *person*, for why IS IT that my liberty *should* be judged by another's conscience? ³⁰If I thankfully share *in the meal*, why am I spoken evil of for that for which I give thanks?)

³¹Whether, then, you eat, or drink, or do anything, do *it* all to the glory of God. ³²Become offenseless, both to יְהוּדִים, Y'hudiym and Greeks, and to the Called-Forthᵉ of God, ³³as I also in all things please all —not seeking my own profit, but that of many, so that they may be saved.

11
¹Become imitators of me, as I also AM of Messiah. ²And I commend youᶠ that in all things you remember me, and *that* you keep the traditions *of orderly conduct*ᵍ as I delivered *them* to you. ³But I want you to know that the Messiah is the head of every man, and the head of a woman is the husband,ʰ and the head of the Messiah is God.

⁴*Therefore*, every man praying or prophesying having *something* down from the headⁱ dishonors his head, ⁵and every woman praying or prophesying with the head uncoveredʲ dishonors her head—for it is one and the same thing with her *head* being shaven. ⁶For if a woman's *head* is not covered,ᵏ then let her *head* be shorn; but since IT IS a shame for a woman to be shorn or shaven, let her *head* be covered. ⁷For a man, indeed, ought not to cover the head,ˡ *he* being the image and glory of God; but the woman is the glory of a man. ⁸For the man is not from the woman, but the woman *is* from the man; ⁹and the man also was not created because of the woman, but the woman because of the man. ¹⁰Because of this, the woman ought to have A SIGN of authority on the head, because of the Messengers. ¹¹(But neither IS a woman *set* apart from a man, nor a man *set* apart from a woman, in the Master. ¹²For as the woman IS from the man, so also IS the man *born* because of the woman, and all the things ARE from God.)

¹³*So* judge in your own selves: is it fitting for a woman uncoveredᵐ to pray to God? ¹⁴Does not even nature itself teach you that if a man indeed has long hair, it is a dishonor to him, ¹⁵but a woman, if she has long hair, it is a glory to her, because the hair has been given to her forⁿ a covering? ¹⁶But if anyone thinks to be contentious, we have no such custom—neither *do* the Called-Forth-Communitiesᵒ of God.

ᵃ Some mss insert, "for me"; also later in verse
ᵇ תְּהִלִּים T'hiliym 24:1
ᶜ "sacrificed"—some mss say, "sacrificed to an idol"
ᵈ Some mss end this verse by repeating verse 26.
ᵉ "Called-Forth"—ἐκκλησία, ekklesia; see מַתִּתְיָהוּ Matit'yahu 16:18
ᶠ Some mss insert, "brothers"
ᵍ "traditions *of orderly conduct*"; cf. 2Thes. 2:15, 3:6-7
ʰ "husband" or "man"

ⁱ "having *something* down from the head" or "having *long hair like a woman's* down from the head" (cf. vs. 14); or possibly "having *a veil* down from the head"; Young's says, "having the head covered"
ʲ "uncovered" or "uncovered *by not having long hair*" (cf. vs. 15); or possibly, "uncovered *by not having a veil*"
ᵏ "covered" or "covered *by her long hair*"; or possibly, "covered *by a veil*"; also at end of verse
ˡ "cover the head" or "cover the head *with long hair like a woman's*"; or poss., "cover the head *with a veil*"
ᵐ "uncovered" or "uncovered, *by virtue of not having long hair*" (cf. vs. 15); or possibly, "uncovered, *by virtue of not having a veil*"
ⁿ "for"—Young's says, "instead of"
ᵒ "Called-Forth-Communities"—ἐκκλησίαι, ekklesiai; see מַתִּתְיָהוּ Matit'yahu 16:18

1 Corinthians 11:17

¹⁷And *in* this command, I give *you* no praise, because not for the better, but for the worse, do you come together. ¹⁸For first, indeed, when you *are* coming together in a Called-Forth-Gathering,ᵃ I hear of divisions being among you — and partly, I believe IT ¹⁹(for different sidesᵇ ought to also be among you, so that those approved may also become known among you). ²⁰Therefore, when you *are* coming together at the same place, it is not to eat the Master's meal, ²¹for in the eating, each *one* takes his meal before *the other*, and, *as a result*, one is hungry and another is drunk. ²²Why? Have you not *your own* houses to eat and to drink in? Or do you despise the Called-Forthᶜ of God, and shame those not having *anything*? What can I say to you? Should I praise you in this? I do not praise *you*!

²³For I — I received from the Master that which I also delivered to you: that the Master יֵשׁוּעַ, Yeshua, on the night in which He was handed over, took *matzah* bread, ²⁴and having given thanks, he broke *it* and said,ᵈ "This is My body, that is for you;ᵉ do this to the remembrance of Me."ᶠ ²⁵He did likewise also *with* the cup after the eating, saying, "This cup is the בְּרִית הַחֲדָשָׁה, B'riyt Ha'Chadashah in My blood;ᵍ do this, as often as you drink IT, to the remembrance of Me." ²⁶For as often as you eat this bread and drink the cup, you proclaim the death of the Master until He comes.

²⁷Therefore, whoever eats the bread or drinks the cup of the Master unworthily will be guilty of the body and the blood of the Master. ²⁸And let a man be examining himself, and in this way let him eat of the bread, and let him drink of the cup.

²⁹For he who is eating and drinkingʰ eats and drinks judgment to himself *if he is* not discerning the body.ⁱ ³⁰Because of this, many among you ARE weak and infirmed, and many sleep; ³¹but if we ourselves were discerning, we would not be being judged. ³²But being judged by the Master, we are disciplined, so that with the world we may not be condemned.

³³So then, my brothers, *when you are* coming together to eat, wait for one another. ³⁴If anyone is hungry, let him eat at home, so that you may not come together to judgment.

And the remaining *things*, whenever I come, I will arrange.

12

¹And concerning the spiritual things, brothers, I do not want you to be ignorant. ²You have known that whenʲ you were *pagan* גּוֹיִם, Goyim, as you were led *astray, you were* being carried away to the idols *that are* without a voice. ³Therefore, I make known to youᵏ that no one speaking in the רוּחַ אֱלֹהִים, Ruach 'Elohiym says, "יֵשׁוּעַ, Yeshua IS accursed," and no one is able to say, "יֵשׁוּעַ, Yeshua IS Master," except in the רוּחַ הַקֹּדֶשׁ, Ruach HaQodesh.

⁴Now there are diverse varieties of gifts, but the same רוּחַ, Ruach; ⁵and there are diverse varieties of service, but the same Master; ⁶and there are diverse varieties of workings, but it is the same God who is working them all in all *people*.

⁷And to each *individual* the manifestation of the רוּחַ, Ruach has been given for *the* common good. ⁸For to one (through the רוּחַ, Ruach) has been given a word of wisdom; and to another, a word of knowledge (according to the same רוּחַ, Ruach); ⁹to another, faith (in the same רוּחַ, Ruach); and to another, gifts of healings (in the oneˡ רוּחַ, Ruach); ¹⁰and to another,

---

ᵃ "Called-Forth-Gathering"— ἐκκλησία, ekklesia
ᵇ "different sides"—Young's says, "sects"
ᶜ "Called-Forth"—ἐκκλησίας, ekklesias; see מַתִּתְיָהוּ Matit'yahu 16:18
ᵈ Some mss insert, "Take, eat"; cf. מַתִּתְיָהוּ Mt. 26:26, Mark 14:22
ᵉ Some mss insert, "being broken"
ᶠ cf. Luke 22:19
ᵍ cf. Luke 22:20

ʰ Some mss insert, "unworthily"
ⁱ Some mss insert, "of the Master"
ʲ Some mss omit, "when"
ᵏ "make known to you"—Young says, "give you to understand"
ˡ "one"—some mss say, "same"

Praise of love.

in-workings of powerful acts;[a] and to another, prophecy; and to another, discernings of רוּחוֹת, ruchot; to another, DIFFERENT kinds of languages;[b] and to another, interpretation of languages—¹¹and the one and the same רוּחַ, Ruach works all these, dividing to each *person* individually as He intends.

¹²For even as the body is one and has many members, and all the members of the body (being many) are one body, so also IS the Messiah. ¹³Indeed, in one רוּחַ, Ruach we were all also immersed to one body—whether יְהוּדִים, Y'hudiym or Greeks, whether slaves or freemen—and[c] one רוּחַ, Ruach all were made to drink, ¹⁴for the body is also not one member, but many.

¹⁵If the foot says, "Because I am not a hand, I am not *part* of the body," it is not, because of this, not *part* of the body. ¹⁶And if the ear says, "Because I am not an eye, I am not *part* of the body," it is not, because of this, not *part* of the body.

¹⁷If the whole body IS an eye, where *is* the hearing? If the whole *body is* hearing, where *is* the smelling? ¹⁸But now, God set the members—each one of them—in the body as He willed. ¹⁹But if all are one *and the same* member, where *is* the body? ²⁰And now, indeed, *there* ARE many members, but one body; ²¹and the eye is not able to say to the hand, "I have no need of you," nor again, the head to the feet, "I have no need of you."

²²But the members of the body which seem to be more weak are much more necessary; ²³and those *parts* of the body that we think to be less honorable, we put more abundant honor around these; and our unbecoming things have more abundant decency, ²⁴but our presentable things have no *such* need. Rather, God mixed the body together, having given more abundant honor to the lacking part,

²⁵so that there may be no division in the body, but that the members may have the same anxiety for one another. ²⁶And if one member suffers, all the members suffer with IT; or *if* one member is glorified, all the members rejoice with IT. ²⁷And you are the body of Messiah—and, in particular, *its* members.

²⁸And some, indeed, God set among the Called-Forth:[d] first emissaries, secondly prophets, thirdly teachers, afterwards *workers of* powers, afterwards *those with* gifts of healings, helpings, governings, *and those who speak in* different kinds of languages.[e] ²⁹ARE all emissaries? ARE all prophets? ARE all teachers? ARE all *workers of* powers? ³⁰have all the gifts of healings? do all speak with *different kinds of* languages? do all interpret? ³¹But eagerly desire the greater[f] gifts; and yet, a far *more* excellent way do I show to you:

13

¹If I speak with the languages of men and of Messengers, but have not love, I have become sounding brass, or a clanging cymbal.

²And if I have *the gift of* prophecy, and know all the mysteries and all the knowledge, and if I have all the faith—so as to remove mountains—but have not love, I am nothing.

³Even if I give away all my possessions to feed others, and I give up my body so that I may boast,[g] but have not love, I am benefitted nothing.

⁴The love is patient; it is kind. The love does not envy; it[h] does not boast *of* itself. *It* is not puffed up, ⁵does not act unbecomingly, does not seek its own things, is not provoked, does not *keep* count *of* wrong, ⁶rejoices not over the unrighteousness, but rejoices with the truth. ⁷It bears all things; it believes all things; it hopes all things; it endures all things. ⁸The love never fails;

---

[a] "powerful acts" or "miracles"
[b] "languages"—lit. "tongues"; both times in this verse
[c] Some mss insert, "into"
[d] "Called-Forth"—ἐκκλησία, ekklesia; see מַתִּתְיָהוּ Matit'yahu 16:18
[e] "languages"—lit. "tongues"; also in 12:30, 13:1, 13:8
[f] "greater"—some mss say, "better"
[g] "boast"—some mss say, "be burned"
[h] "it"—some mss say, "the love"

but if THERE ARE prophecies, they will become useless; if languages, they will stop; if knowledge, it will become useless. ⁹For in part we know, and in part we prophesy; ¹⁰but when that which is perfect comes, that which IS in part will become useless.

¹¹When I was a little child, I was speaking as a little child; I was thinking as a little child; I was reasoning as a little child. When I became a man, I made useless the childish things. ¹²For we see now through a mirror obscurely, but then, face to face; now I know in part, but then I will know fully, as I was also known. ¹³And now there remains these three: faith, hope *and* love. But the greatest of these IS love.

14 ¹Pursue the love, and eagerly desire*ᵃ* the spiritual things, but *desire* more that you may prophesy. ²For he who is speaking in an UNKNOWN language*ᵇ* does not speak to men, but to God, for no one listens *with understanding*, and in *his* רוּחַ, ruach he speaks mysteries. ³On the other hand, he who is prophesying to men speaks up-building, and exhortation, and encouragement. ⁴He who is speaking in an UNKNOWN language builds up himself, but he who is prophesying builds up the Called-Forth.*ᶜ*

⁵Now, I want you all to speak with *unknown* languages, but *I want* more that you may prophesy; and greater is he who is prophesying than he who is speaking with *unknown* languages (except one *who* may *also* interpret, so that the Called-Forth may receive building up).

⁶And now, brothers, if I come to you speaking *unknown* languages, what will I benefit you, unless I *also* speak to you either in revelation, or in knowledge, or in prophesying, or in teaching? ⁷Yet *even* the things without life-giving sound, whether flute or harp—if they do not give a difference in the sounds, how will that which is fluted or that which is harped be known? ⁸For if a שׁוֹפָר, shofar also gives an uncertain sound, who will prepare himself for battle? ⁹So also you: unless through the *unknown* language you give speech *that is* easily understood, how will that which is spoken be known? Indeed, you will be speaking to air.

¹⁰There are, it may be, so many kinds of voices in the world, and none is without meaning. ¹¹If, then, I do not know the power *in the meaning* of the voice, I will be a βάρβαρος, Barbaros to him who is speaking, and he who is speaking is a βάρβαρος, Barbaros to me. ¹²So *it is* also *with* you: since you are zealous for spiritual gifts, seek that you may abound *in them* for the building up of the Called-Forth. ¹³Therefore, he who is speaking in an UNKNOWN language—let him pray that he may interpret. ¹⁴For if I pray in an UNKNOWN language, my רוּחַ, ruach prays, but my understanding is unfruitful.

¹⁵What is it, then? I will pray with the רוּחַ, ruach, and I will pray also with the understanding; I will sing melodies with the רוּחַ, ruach, and I will sing melodies with the understanding. ¹⁶Otherwise, if you bless with the רוּחַ, ruach, how will he who is filling the place of the unlearned*ᵈ* say "אָמֵן, Amen" at your giving thanks, since he has not known what you say? ¹⁷For you, indeed, give thanks well, but the other *person* is not built up! ¹⁸I give thanks to God *that* I speak more than you all with *unknown* languages—¹⁹but in a Called-Forth-Gathering,*ᵉ* I want to speak five words with my understanding, rather than tens of thousands of words in an UNKNOWN language, so that I may also instruct others.

²⁰Brothers, do not become children in the thinking, but be little children in the evil, and in the thinking become mature. ²¹In the תּוֹרָה, Torah it has been written that,

---

ᵃ "desire"—Young's says, "seek"

ᵇ "language," lit. "tongue"; also throughout chapter 14

ᶜ "Called-Forth"—ἐκκλησίαν, ekklesian; see מַתִּתְיָהוּ Matit'yahu 16:18; also in vs. 5 (ἐκκλησία, ekklesia) and vs. 12 (ἐκκλησίας, ekklesias)

ᵈ "unlearned"—ἰδιώτου, idiotou; also in vs. 24

ᵉ "Called-Forth-Gathering"—ἐκκλησία, ekklesia; also in vss. 28 & 35; "Called-Forth" in verse 23

Orderly gatherings.

"With other languages and with other speech[a] I will speak to this people, but not even so will they hear Me,"[b] says ADONAI. ²²Therefore, the *unknown* languages are for a sign, not to the believing *ones*, but to the unbelieving; and the prophecy IS not for the unbelieving, but for the believing.

²³If, therefore, the whole Called-Forth comes together, to the same place, and all speak with *unknown* languages, and there come in *some who are* unlearned or unbelievers, will they not say that you are insane? ²⁴But if all prophesy, and anyone comes in—an unbeliever or *someone who is* unlearned—he is convicted by all, *and* he is examined by all. ²⁵The secrets of his heart become unconcealed, and so, having fallen upon HIS face, he will bow before God, declaring that God really is among you.

²⁶What is it, then, brothers? Whenever you come together, each has a melody, has a teaching, has a revelation, has an *unknown* language, has an interpretation? Let all things be for building up. ²⁷If anyone speaks an UNKNOWN language, *it should be done* by two—or at the most, by three—and in turn; and let one interpret. ²⁸But if there is no interpreter, let him *with the unknown language* stop talking[c] *aloud* in a Called-Forth-Gathering, and let him speak to himself and to God.

²⁹And prophets—let two or three speak, and let the others discern *what is said*; ³⁰but if ANYTHING is revealed to another *one who is* sitting *down*, let the first *one sit down and* stop talking. ³¹For you are all able to prophesy one by one, so that all may learn and all may be exhorted; ³²but the spiritual gift of prophets are submitted to prophets, ³³for God is not A GOD of disorder, but of peace, as in all the Called-Forth-Gatherings[d] of the קְדוֹשִׁים, Q'doshiym.

³⁴The women—let them stop talking *the way they do* in the Called-Forth-Gatherings, for it is not permitted for them to speak *the way they do*; but let them be submitted *to their husbands*, as the תּוֹרָה, Torah also says.[e] ³⁵So if they want to learn anything, let them ask their own husbands at home, for it is shameful for a woman to speak *the way they do* in a Called-Forth-Gathering.

³⁶Did the word of God come forth from you? or did it only come to you? ³⁷If anyone thinks *himself* to be a prophet, or spiritual, let him acknowledge the things that I write to you—that it is a command of the Master; ³⁸but if anyone is ignorant *of these*, he is ignored.[f] ³⁹Therefore, my brothers, earnestly desire to prophesy, and do not forbid *each other* to speak with *unknown* languages, ⁴⁰but let all things be done decently and in *an* order*ly manner*.

15 ¹And I make known to you, brothers, the Good News that I proclaimed to you, which you also received, in which you also have stood, ²*and* through which you are also being saved (if you hold fast to what word I proclaimed *as* Good News to you—unless you believed in vain). ³For I delivered to you first what I also received: that Messiah died for our sins according to the Scriptures, ⁴and that He was buried, and that He has risen on the third day according to the Scriptures, ⁵and that He appeared to כֵּיפָא, Keifa, then to the Twelve. ⁶Afterwards, He appeared to more than five hundred brothers at once (of whom the majority remain until now, but certain *ones* fell asleep). ⁷Afterwards, He appeared to יַעֲקֹב, Ya'aqov, *and* then to all the emissaries.

⁸And last of all, as to the *one of* untimely birth, He appeared also to me, ⁹for I am the least of the emissaries, who is not worthy to be called an emissary, because I per-

---

[a] "speech"—lit. "lips"
[b] יְשַׁעְיָהוּ *Y'sha'yahu* 28:11-12
[c] "stop talking"—most trans., incl. Young's, "be silent" or similar; also in verses 30 and 34
[d] "Called-Forth-Gatherings"—ἐκκλησίαις, ekklesiais; see מַתִּתְיָהוּ *Matit'yahu* 16:18; also in verse 34
[e] cf. בְּרֵאשִׁית *B'reshiyt* 3:16
[f] "he is ignored"—some mss say, "let him be ignorant"

secuted the Called-Forth[a] of God. ¹⁰But by the *unmerited* favor of God, I am what I am, and His *unmerited* favor that *is* toward me came not in emptiness. Rather, I labored more abundantly than they all did; yet not I, but the *unmerited* favor of God that *is* with me. ¹¹Whether, then, *it was* I or they, in this way we proclaim, and in this way did you believe.

¹²And if Messiah is proclaimed—that He has risen out of the dead—how *can* certain *ones* among you say that there is no Rising Again of dead persons? ¹³But if there is no Rising Again of dead persons, neither has Messiah risen. ¹⁴And if Messiah has not risen, then both our proclaiming *is* empty, and your faith *is* empty, ¹⁵and we are also found *to be* false witnesses of God, because we testified of God that He raised up the Messiah (whom He did not raise if dead persons then do not rise— ¹⁶for if dead persons do not rise, neither has Messiah risen). ¹⁷And if Messiah has not risen, your faith is vain, *and* you are still in your sins; ¹⁸then, also, those having fallen asleep in Messiah *are* destroyed. ¹⁹If we have hope in Messiah in this life only, we are to be most pitied of all men!

²⁰But now, Messiah has risen out of the dead—the first-fruit of those sleeping! ²¹For since death *came* through *a* man, also through *a* man *came* the Rising Again of the dead.

²²For even as in אָדָם, Adam all die, so also in the Messiah all will be made alive, ²³but each in his own order: the first-fruit, Messiah; afterwards, those who are the Messiah's in his *coming* presence; ²⁴then, the end, when he hands over the Reign to the God and Father—when He will have made useless all rule, and all authority and power—²⁵for he must reign until he has put all the enemies under his feet, ²⁶*and* the last enemy is done away *with*: death. ²⁷For HE PUT ALL THINGS IN SUBMISSION UNDER HIS FEET[b] (and when one says that all things have been put in submission, *it is* evident that *God* —He who put all the things in submission to him—is excepted; ²⁸and when all the things are put in submission to him, then the Son himself will also be put in submission to Him who put all the things in submission to him, *such* that God will be the all in all).

²⁹Otherwise, what will they who are immersed for the dead do, if the dead do not rise at all? Why also are they immersed for them?[c] ³⁰Why also do we stand in jeopardy every moment? ³¹Every day do I die —*I swear to this*, brothers, by the pride in you that I have in Messiah יֵשׁוּעַ, Yeshua our Master. ³²If I fought with wild beasts in Ephesus according to the manner of a man, what *is* the advantage to me if the dead do not rise? "LET US EAT AND DRINK, FOR TOMORROW WE DIE!"[d]

³³Be not led astray: "Evil associations corrupt good character." ³⁴Wake up *from your stupor*, as is right, and sin not; for certain *ones* have an ignorance of God (I say THIS to you for shame).

³⁵But someone will say, "How do the dead rise? And with what kind of body do they come?"[e] ³⁶You unwise! What you sow is not brought to life unless it dies! ³⁷And that which you sow, you do not sow the body that will be, but bare grain—it may be of wheat, or of some kind of the other *grains*, ³⁸but God gives a body to it as He willed, and to each of the seeds its own body.

³⁹All flesh *is* not the same flesh, but there is one of men, and another flesh of beasts, and another flesh of birds, and another of fishes; ⁴⁰and THERE ARE heavenly bodies and earthly bodies. But the glory of the heavenly *is* one *kind*, and that of the earthly *is* another; ⁴¹one glory of sun, and another glory of moon, and another glory of stars —for star differs from star in glory.

---

[a] "Called-Forth"—ἐκκλησίαν, ekklesian; see מַתִּתְיָהוּ *Matit'yahu* 16:18

[b] תְּהִלִּים *T'hiliym* 8:7(6)

[c] "them"—some mss say, "the dead"

[d] יְשַׁעְיָהוּ *Y'sha'yahu* 22:13

[e] This sentence is missing from Young's.

⁴²So also IS the Rising Again of the dead: it is sown in decay, it is raised in *the* imperishable; ⁴³it is sown in dishonor, it is raised in glory; it is sown in weakness, it is raised in power; ⁴⁴it is sown a natural body, it is raised a spiritual body. If there is a natural body, there is also a spiritual body. ⁴⁵So also it has been written, "The first MAN, אָדָם, Adam, BECAME A LIVING SOUL";ᵃ the last אָדָם, Adam IS for a life-giving רוּחַ, ruach. ⁴⁶But that which is spiritual IS not first; rather, that which WAS natural—*and then* afterwards, that which IS spiritual. ⁴⁷The first man IS from the earth, made of earth; the second man ISᵇ from Heaven. ⁴⁸As the *man* made of earth IS, such ARE also the *men* made of earth; and as the heavenly *man* IS, such ARE also the heavenly *men*. ⁴⁹And as we have borne the image of the *man* made of earth, we will also bear the image of the heavenly *man*.

⁵⁰And this I say, brothers: that flesh and blood are not able to inherit the Reign of God, nor does the decay inherit the imperishable. ⁵¹Look! I tell you a mystery: we will not all sleep, but we will all be changed ⁵²in a moment, in the twinkling of an eye, in the last שׁוֹפָר, shofar. For it will sound, and the dead will be raised undecaying, and we—we will be changed.

⁵³For this perishable *thing* must put on *the* imperishable, and this mortal *thing is* to put on immortality. ⁵⁴And when this perishable *thing* has put on *the* imperishable, and this mortal *thing* has put on immortality, then the word that has been written will be brought to pass: "THE DEATH WAS SWALLOWED UP—TO VICTORY!ᶜ ⁵⁵WHERE, O DEATH, IS YOUR victory? WHERE, O Death,ᵈ IS YOUR STING?"ᵉ ⁵⁶And the sting of the death IS the sin, and the power of the sin *is* the תּוֹרָה, Torah.ᶠ ⁵⁷But to God—thanks *be* to Him who is giving us the victory through our Master יֵשׁוּעַ, Yeshua *the* Messiah! ⁵⁸Therefore, my beloved brothers, become steadfast, unmovable, abounding in the work of the Master at all times, knowing that your labor is not empty in the Master.

16

¹And concerning the *money* collection that IS for the קְדוֹשִׁים, Q'doshiym: as I directed to the Called-Forth-Communitiesᵍ of Galatia, so also *should* you do. ²On every first DAY of the week,ʰ let each one of you lay *something aside* by himself, treasuring up whatever he may have prospered, so that when I come, then collections may not be made. ³And whenever I come, whomever you approve, these I will send through letters *of introduction* to carry your favor to יְרוּשָׁלַיִם, Y'rushalayim; ⁴but if it is fitting for me also to go, they will go with me.

⁵And I will come to you when I pass through Macedonia (for I am passing through Macedonia), ⁶and it may be *that* I will stay with you, or even *spend the* winter, so that you may send me forward wherever I go ⁷(for I do not want to see you now *just* in the passing, for I hope to remain a certain *amount of* time with you, if the Master permits). ⁸But I will remain in Ephesus until the שָׁבֻעוֹת, Shavuot, ⁹for a door has been opened to me—great and effectual—and *the* opposers ARE many.

¹⁰And if Timothy comes, see that he is with you without fear, for he works the work of the Master, even as I *do*. ¹¹No one, then, may despise him. And send him forward in peace, so that he will come to me, for I expect him with the brothers. ¹²And concerning Apollos our brother: I appealed to him much that he should come to you with the brothers, but it was not at all HIS will that he may come now; rather, he will come when he has opportunity.

¹³*Stay* awake; stand in the faith; be men; be strong; ¹⁴let all your things be done in love.

ᵃ בְּרֵאשִׁית B'reshiyt 2:7
ᵇ Some mss insert, "the Master"
ᶜ יְשַׁעְיָהוּ Y'sha'yahu 25:8
ᵈ "Death"—some mss say, שְׁאוֹל, Sh'ol," which is what it says in the text of Hoshea being quoted
ᵉ הוֹשֵׁעַ Hoshea 13:14
ᶠ cf. Romans 5:12-21; 7:7-25

ᵍ "Called-Forth-Communities"—ἐκκλησίαις, ekklesiais; see מַתִּתְיָהוּ Matit'yahu 16:18
ʰ "week"—lit. σαββάτου, sabbatou, that is, שַׁבָּת, shabat

¹⁵And I appeal to you, brothers (you have known the household of Stephanas, that it is the first-fruit of Achaia, and *that* they set themselves to the service to the קְדוֹשִׁים, Q'doshiym), ¹⁶that you also be submitted to such, and to everyone who is working with us and laboring. ¹⁷And I rejoice over the presence of Stephanas and Fortunatus and Achaicus, because these filled up your lack, ¹⁸for they refreshed my רוּחַ, ruach and yours. Acknowledge, therefore, those who ARE such.

¹⁹The Called-Forth-Communities[a] of Asia greet you; Aquila and Prisca, *along* with the Called-Forth[b] in their house, *also* greet you much in the Master. ²⁰All the brothers greet you. Greet one another in a holy kiss.

²¹*Here is* the greeting of ME, Paul, with my *own* hand.

²²If anyone does not love the Master,[c] let him be accursed! מָרָנָא תָא, Marana ta! ²³The *unmerited* favor of the Master יֵשׁוּעַ, Yeshua[d] IS with you; ²⁴my love IS with you all in Messiah יֵשׁוּעַ, Yeshua.[e]

---

[a] "Called-Forth-Communities"—ἐκκλησίαι, ekklesiai; see מַתִּתְיָהוּ Matit'yahu 16:18
[b] "Called-Forth"—ἐκκλησία, ekklesia; see מַתִּתְיָהוּ Matit'yahu 16:18
[c] Some mss insert, "יֵשׁוּעַ, Yeshua *the* Messiah"
[d] Some mss insert, "the Messiah"
[e] Some mss conclude, "אָמֵן, Amen."

Paul's Second Letter to the Corinthians

2 Corinthians

1

¹*From* Paul,[a] an emissary of Messiah יֵשׁוּעַ, Yeshua through the will of God, and Timothy the brother; to the Called-Forth[b] of God that is in Corinth, with all the קְדוֹשִׁים, Q'doshiym who are in all Achaia: ²*unmerited* favor to you, and peace from God our Father, and the Master יֵשׁוּעַ, Yeshua *the* Messiah!

³Blessed IS the God and Father of our Master יֵשׁוּעַ, Yeshua *the* Messiah, the Father of the mercies and God of all encouragement, ⁴who is encouraging us in all our oppression, for *the purpose of* our being able to encourage those in any oppression through the encouragement with which we ourselves are encouraged by God, ⁵because as the sufferings of the Messiah abound to us, so through the Messiah does our encouragement also abound. ⁶So then, if we are oppressed, IT IS for your encouragement and salvation; if we are encouraged, IT IS for your encouragement,[c] which is worked in the enduring of the same sufferings that we also suffer. ⁷And our hope IS steadfast for you, knowing that even as you are sharers of the sufferings, so also *are you sharers* of the encouragement.

⁸For we do not want you to be ignorant, brothers, of our oppression that happened in Asia—that we were exceedingly burdened above OUR power, so that we despaired even of life. ⁹But we ourselves have had the sentence of the death in ourselves, so that we may not be trusting on ourselves but on God, who is raising the dead, ¹⁰who delivered—and will deliver—us out of so great a death, *and* in whom we have hoped that even yet He will deliver. ¹¹You *are* also working together for us by your request *to God* for help, so that the gift *given* to us through many persons may be thankfully acknowledged for us through many.

---

[a] "Paul"—Παῦλος, Paulos; see 1 Timothy 1:1
[b] "Called-Forth"—ἐκκλησία, ekklesia; see מַתִּתְיָהוּ Matit'yahu 16:18
[c] Some mss insert, "and salvation"

¹²For our boasting is this: the testimony of our conscience, that we conducted ourselves in the world (and more abundantly toward you) in simplicity and *the* sincerity of God, and not in fleshly wisdom, but in the *unmerited* favor of God. ¹³For we write to you no other things, but *only* what you either read or even acknowledge; and I hope that you will acknowledge *it* to the end, ¹⁴as you also acknowledged us in part—that we are your boasting, even as you also ARE ours, in the Day of our Master יֵשׁוּעַ, Yeshua. ¹⁵And in this confidence I was intending to come to you beforehand so that you might have a second favor, ¹⁶and to pass through you to Macedonia, and to come to you again from Macedonia, and by you to be sent forward to יְהוּדָה, Y'hudah.

¹⁷Intending this, therefore, did I then use the lightness *of levity*? Or the things that I consider—do I consider *them* according to the flesh, so that it may be with me *both* "Yes, yes" and "No, no"? ¹⁸But God IS faithful, *such* that our word to you is not "Yes" and "No." ¹⁹For the Son of God, יֵשׁוּעַ, Yeshua *the* Messiah, having been proclaimed among you through us (through me and Silvanus[a] and Timothy), did not become "Yes" and "No," but in Him it has become "Yes!" ²⁰For as many as ARE promises of God, in Him ARE the "Yes"; therefore, also through[b] Him *is* the "אָמֵן, Amen," for *the* glory to God through us. ²¹And He who is making you firm with us into Messiah—and *who* anointed us—IS God, ²²who also sealed us and gave the down-payment of the רוּחַ, Ruach in our hearts.

²³And I call on God for a witness upon my soul, that *for the purpose of* sparing you I did not yet come to Corinth ²⁴(not that we are lords over your faith, but we are workers together with your joy, for by the faith you stand).

2

¹For I decided this to myself: not to come to you again in grief. ²For if I make you grieve, then who is he who is making me rejoice, except he who is made to grieve by me? ³And I wrote this same thing, so that having come, I may not have grief from them of whom I ought to have joy, having confidence in you all that my joy is of you all. ⁴For out of much oppression and pressure of heart I wrote to you through many tears, not so that you might be made to grieve, but so that you might know the love that I have more abundantly toward you.

⁵And if anyone has caused grief, he has not caused grief to me, but in part (so that I may not *be a* burden) *to* you all. ⁶This punishment that IS by the majority is sufficient for such a one, ⁷so that, on the contrary, IT IS instead for you to forgive and to encourage; otherwise, such a one may be swallowed up by overabundant grief. ⁸Therefore, I call upon you to confirm love to him; ⁹for to this *end* I also wrote, so that I might know the proof of you—whether you are obedient in regard to all things.

¹⁰And to whom you forgive anything, I also *forgive it*. For what I also have forgiven—if I have forgiven anything—*I FORGIVE IT* because of you in the presence of Messiah, ¹¹so that we may not be overreached by הַשָּׂטָן, HaSatan, for of his devices, we are not ignorant.

¹²And having come to Troas for the Good News of the Messiah, and a door having been opened to me in the Master, ¹³I *nevertheless* have not had rest to my רוּחַ, ruach, on *account of* my not finding Titus my brother. But having taken leave of them, I went to Macedonia.

¹⁴Yet thanks ARE to God, who at all times is leading us in triumph in the Messiah, and is revealing the fragrance of His knowledge through us in every place. ¹⁵Because of Messiah, we are a sweet smell to God *both* among those being saved, and among those being destroyed—¹⁶to the one, indeed, a fragrance from death to death; and to the other, a fragrance from life to life. And for these things, who is sufficient? ¹⁷For we are not as the many *who are* adulterating the word of God *by* ped-

---

[a] "Silvanus"—a variant of סִילָא, Syla
[b] "therefore, also through"—some mss say, "and in"

dling it for profit. But as *ones* of purity—but as *ones* of God—in the presence of God, we speak in Messiah.

3 ¹Do we begin again to prove ourselves? or do we need (as some *do*) letters of recommendation to you, or from you? ²You are our letter, having been written in our hearts, known and read by all men. ³*It is* revealed that you are a letter of Messiah served by us, written not with ink, but with the רוּחַ, Ruach of the living God, not in the tablets of stone, but in tablets of the heart of flesh. ⁴And such *is the* confidence we have through the Messiah toward God: ⁵not that we are sufficient of ourselves to think *of* anything as from ourselves; but our sufficiency IS from God, ⁶who also made us sufficient TO BE servants of a בְּרִית חֲדָשָׁה, B'riyt 'Chadashah (not of letter, but of רוּחַ, Ruach; for the letter kills, but the רוּחַ, Ruach makes alive).

⁷But if the service of the death, engraved in letters in stones, came in glory, so that the sons of יִשְׂרָאֵל, Yis'rael were not able to fix their gaze to the face of מֹשֶׁה, Mosheh because of the glory of his face (which was being made useless), ⁸how will the service of the רוּחַ, Ruach not be in more glory? ⁹For if the service of the condemnation IS in glory, *then* the service of the righteousness abounds in much more glory, ¹⁰since also even that which has been glorious has—in this respect—not been glorious, because of the superior glory. ¹¹For if that which is being made useless IS through glory, *then* that which is remaining IS in much more glory.

¹²Having such hope, then, we use much freedom in speech ¹³and ARE not as מֹשֶׁה, Mosheh, who was putting a veil upon his face for the sons of יִשְׂרָאֵל, Yis'rael, *for their* not fixing their gaze to the end of that which is being made useless. ¹⁴Nevertheless, their minds were hardened. For to this very day, at the reading of the בְּרִית הַיְשָׁנָה, B'riyt HaY'shanah, the same veil—that in Messiah is being made useless—remains unwithdrawn. ¹⁵Yes, until today, whenever מֹשֶׁה, Mosheh is read, a veil lies upon their heart; ¹⁶but whenever one turns to the Master,ᵃ the veil is taken away. ¹⁷Now, the Master is the רוּחַ, Ruach, and where the רוּחַ, Ruach of the Master IS, there IS liberty. ¹⁸And we all, with unveiled face, seeing the glory of the Master *as* in a mirror, are being transformed to the same image, from glory to glory, even as by the Master, the רוּחַ, Ruach.ᵇ

4 ¹Because of this—having this service, as we received *loving*-kindness—we do not lose heart; ²but *we* renounced for ourselves the hidden things of shame, not walking in cunning, nor deceitfully using the word of God, but *instead* proving ourselves by the manifestation of the truth to every conscience of men, in *the* sight of God. ³And if also our Good News is veiled, it is veiled in those being destroyed—⁴in whom the god of this age blinded the minds of the unbelieving, so that there does not shine forth the enlightening of the Good News of the glory of the Messiah, who is the image of God. ⁵For we proclaim not ourselves, but Messiah יֵשׁוּעַ, Yeshua *as* Master, and ourselves *as* your slaves because of יֵשׁוּעַ, Yeshua, ⁶because IT IS God—who said light will shine out of darknessᶜ—who shone in our hearts for the enlightening of the knowledge of the glory of God in the face of יֵשׁוּעַ, Yeshua *the* Messiah.

⁷But we have this treasure in earthen containers, so that the excellency of the power is of God, and not of us: ⁸being pressed on every side, but not compressed; perplexed, but not in despair; ⁹persecuted, but not abandoned; struck down, but not destroyed; ¹⁰at all times carrying around in the body the dying ofᵈ יֵשׁוּעַ, Yeshua, so that the life of יֵשׁוּעַ, Yeshua may also be revealed in our body. ¹¹For we who are living are always handed over to death because of יֵשׁוּעַ, Yeshua, so that the life of יֵשׁוּעַ, Yeshua

---

ᵃ "the Master" or "ADONAI" (κύριος, kurios); also in vss. 17-18

ᵇ "the Master, the רוּחַ, Ruach" or "the רוּחַ, Ruach of the Master"

ᶜ cf. בְּרֵאשִׁית *B'reshiyt* 1:3, יוֹחָנָן *Yochanan* 1:4-5

ᵈ Some mss insert, "the Master"

The service of reconciliation.

may also be revealed in our dying flesh. ¹²Therefore the death works in us, but the life in you.

¹³And having the same רוּחַ, ruach of the faith according to that which has been written,

"I believed; therefore, I spoke,"[a]

we also believe; therefore, we also speak, ¹⁴knowing that He who raised up the Master יֵשׁוּעַ, Yeshua will also raise us up with[b] יֵשׁוּעַ, Yeshua and will bring *us* near with you. ¹⁵For all the things ARE because of you, so that the *unmerited* favor, having been multiplied because of the thanksgiving of the many, may abound to the glory of God.

¹⁶Therefore, we do not lose heart. Rather, if our outward man also decays, yet our inward *man* is renewed day by day. ¹⁷For the momentary *and* light matter of our oppression more and more exceedingly accomplishes an age-enduring weight of glory for us—¹⁸we *who are* not looking to the things *that are* seen, but to the things not seen; for the things seen ARE temporary, but the things not seen ARE age-enduring.

5 ¹For we have known that if our earthly house of the tent is thrown down, we have a building from God—a house not made with hands, *but* age-enduring in the Heavens. ²For in this we also groan, earnestly desiring to clothe ourselves with our dwelling *place* that is from Heaven. ³If that be so, having unclothed[c] ourselves, we will not be found naked, ⁴for we who are in the tent also groan, being burdened, in that we want not to unclothe ourselves, but to clothe ourselves, so that the mortal may be swallowed up by the Life.

⁵Now, He who brought us about to this self-same thing IS God, who gave to us the down-payment of the רוּחַ, Ruach. ⁶Having courage, then, at all times, and knowing that being at home in the body *means that* we are away from home from the Master ⁷(for we walk through faith, not through

2 Corinthians 5:21

sight), ⁸we have courage and are well-pleased rather to be away from the home of the body, and to be at home with the Master.

⁹Therefore, we are also ambitious, whether at home or away from home, to be well-pleasing to Him. ¹⁰For it is necessary for all of us to be revealed in front of the judgment seat of the Messiah, so that each one may receive *what is due for* the things DONE through the body, in reference to the things that he did, whether good or evil. ¹¹Having known, therefore, the fear of the Master, we persuade men; but to God we are revealed (and I hope to have been revealed also in our consciences). ¹²Not again do we prove ourselves to you, but we are giving occasion to you for boasting about us, so that you may have SOMETHING in reference to those boasting in face, and not in heart. ¹³For if we were beside ourselves, IT WAS to God, *and* if we are of sound mind, IT IS to you. ¹⁴For the love of the Messiah compels us, having judged this: that One died for all, therefore all died. ¹⁵And He died for all, so that those living may no longer live to themselves, but to Him who died for them and was raised again.

¹⁶Therefore, from now on we have known no one according to the flesh (and if we have known Messiah according to the flesh, yet now we no longer know Him *this way*). ¹⁷Therefore, if anyone IS in Messiah, HE IS a new creature; the old things *have* passed away; look! he has[d] become new! ¹⁸And all the things ARE of God, who reconciled us to Himself through[e] Messiah and gave to us the service of the reconciliation, ¹⁹such that God was reconciling the world to Himself in Messiah, not counting their missteps against[f] them, and has put in us the word of the reconciliation. ²⁰For the sake of Messiah, then, we are ambassadors; as if God were calling through us, we implore *you* for the sake of Messiah: "Be reconciled to God." ²¹God made

---

[a] תְּהִלִּים T'hiliym 116:10
[b] "with"—some mss say, "through"
[c] "unclothed"—some mss say, "clothed"
[d] "he has"—some mss say, "all the things have"
[e] Some mss insert, "יֵשׁוּעַ, Yeshua"
[f] "against"—Young's says, "to"

211

Him who did not know sin *to be* sin for our sake, so that we may become the righteousness of God in Him.

6 ¹And working together *with Him*, we also call upon YOU, that you not receive the *unmerited* favor of God in emptiness. ²For He says,

"In an acceptable time, I heard you; and in a day of salvation, I helped you."ᵃ

Look! now IS "a well-accepted time." Look! now *is* "a day of salvation." ³In nothing *are we* giving any cause of offense, so that the service *of the reconciliation* may not be blamed. ⁴Rather, in everything *we are* proving ourselves as God's servants: in much perseverance, in oppressions, in needs, in distresses, ⁵in wounds, in imprisonments, in uprisings, in labors, in sleeplessness, in *forced* fastings, ⁶in pureness, in knowledge, in patience, in kindness, in the רוּחַ הַקֹּדֶשׁ, Ruach HaQodesh, in love unfeigned, ⁷in the word of truth, in the power of God, through the weapons of the righteousness, on the right and on the left, ⁸through glory and dishonor, through evil report and good report; *regarded* as leading astray, yet true; ⁹as unknown, yet recognized; as dying, and look! we live; as disciplined, yet not put to death; ¹⁰as sorrowful, yet always rejoicing; as poor, yet making many rich; as having nothing, yet possessing all things.

¹¹Our mouth has been open to you, O Corinthians; our heart has been made large! ¹²You are not *being* compressed by us, and *yet* you are compressed *toward us* in your OWN inward parts. ¹³Nevertheless, AS a reward of the same kind *you received from us* (I say THIS as to children), be made large *in heart toward us* also!

¹⁴Do not become unequally yoked withᵇ unbelievers, for what partnership IS THERE between righteousness and wickedness? or what does light share with darkness? ¹⁵and what agreement has Messiah with בְּלִיַּעַל, B'liya-al? or what part does a believer *have in common* with an unbeliever? ¹⁶and what agreement has the Temple of God with idols? For we are a temple of the living God, as God said,

"I will live in them, and will walk among THEM, and I will be their God, and they will be My people."ᶜ

¹⁷Therefore, "COME FORTH OUT FROM THE MIDDLE OF THEM, AND BE SET APART," says ADONAI, and "DO NOT TOUCH AN UNCLEAN THING,ᵈ and I—I will receive you." ¹⁸And "I WILL BE TO YOU FOR A FATHER, AND YOU— YOU WILL BE TO ME FOR SONS AND DAUGHTERS,"ᵉ says יהוה צְבָאוֹת, ADONAI Tz'vaot.

7 ¹Having these promises, then, loved ones, let us cleanse ourselves from every pollution of flesh and רוּחַ, ruach, perfecting holiness in the fear of God. ²Make room for us, *for* we did no one wrong; we corrupted no one; we exploited no one. ³I say THIS not to condemn you, for I have said before that you are in our hearts—to die with *you* and to live with *you*. ⁴Indeed, my freedom in speech to you IS great; my boasting on your behalf *is* great. I have been filled with the encouragement, *and* I overabound with the joy above all our oppression. ⁵For *since* we have also come to Macedonia, our flesh has had no relaxation, but on every side we are oppressed: outside *there* ARE fightings, inside—fears. ⁶But He who is encouraging the downcast—God—He encouraged us by the presence of Titus, ⁷and not only by his presence, but also by the encouragement with which he was encouraged over you (making known to us your longing desire, your mourning, *and* your zeal for me), so that I rejoiced *all* the more. ⁸For even if in the *previous* letter I made you grieve, I do not regret *it* (although I did re-

---

ᵃ יְשַׁעְיָהוּ *Y'sha'yahu* 49:8
ᵇ "unequally yoked with"—Young's says, "yoked with others—"
ᶜ שְׁמוֹת *Sh'mot* 29:45; וַיִּקְרָא *Vayiq'ra* 26:12
ᵈ יְשַׁעְיָהוּ *Y'sha'yahu* 52:11
ᵉ שְׁמוּאֵל ב *Sh'muel Beit* 7:14 (א) דִּבְרֵי־הַיָּמִים *Div'rei HaYamiym Alef* 17:13); יְשַׁעְיָהוּ *Y'sha'yahu* 43:6; הוֹשֵׁעַ *Hoshea* 2:1(1:10)

Effect of godly grief.

gret *it*), for I see that the letter did make you grieve (although *only* for a moment). ⁹*But* now I rejoice, not that you were made to grieve, but that you were made to grieve to *the point of* reformation. For you were made to grieve toward God so that you might receive damage from us in nothing. ¹⁰For the grieving toward God enacts reformation to salvation without regret, but the grieving of the world brings about death. ¹¹For look! this same thing (being made to grieve toward God), how much diligence it brings about in you! Rather, *verbal* defense! rather, indignation! rather, fear! rather, longing desire! rather, zeal! rather, vengeance! In everything you proved yourselves to be pure in the matter.

¹²When I also wrote to you, then, *it was* not for his sake who did wrong, nor for his sake who suffered wrong, but for your diligence for our sake being revealed to you before God.

¹³Because of this, we have been encouraged; and in our encouragement, we rejoiced *all* the more abundantly in the joy of Titus, that his רוּחַ, ruach has been refreshed from you all ¹⁴(because if I have boasted anything to him for your sake, I was not put to shame; but *just* as we spoke to you all things in truth, so our boasting before Titus also became truth); ¹⁵and his tender affection is more abundantly toward you, remembering the obedience of you all, *and* how you received him with fear and trembling. ¹⁶I rejoice that I have confidence in you in everything.

8 ¹And we make known to you, brothers, the *unmerited* favor of God that has been given in the Called-Forth-Communities[a] of Macedonia, ²because in much trial of oppression, the abundance of their joy and their deep poverty abounded to the riches of their generosity; ³because I testify *that* according to THEIR power (and *even* above THEIR pow-

er) they were *giving* of their own accord, ⁴with much exhortation imploring of us *for* the favor and the sharing of the service to the קְדוֹשִׁים, Q'doshiym. ⁵And not as we expected, but they gave themselves first to the Master, and *then* to us, through the will of God, ⁶so that we exhorted Titus that as he began before, so also he may finish this favor to you as well. ⁷But even as you abound in everything — in faith, and word, and knowledge, and all diligence, and in our love to you[b] — *see* that you may also abound in this *unmerited* favor. ⁸I do not speak in regard to a command, but through the diligence of others, also proving the genuineness of your love. ⁹For you know the *unmerited* favor of our Master יֵשׁוּעַ, Yeshua *the* Messiah: that, *though* being rich, because of you He became poor, so that by that poverty, you would become rich.

¹⁰And a judgment I give in this, for this IS good for you, who a year ago began before not only to do *this*, but also to want *it*: ¹¹now, then, also finish doing IT, so that even as THERE IS the readiness of the will, so also *is there* the finishing, out of what you have. ¹²For if the willing mind is present, it is well-accepted in regard to what anyone has, not in regard to what he has not. ¹³For *I* SPEAK not so that others *may have* relief and you *may be* pressured, but, by *way of* equality, ¹⁴your abundance at the present time *is enough* for their need, so that also their abundance may be for your need, *such* that there may be equality. ¹⁵As it has been written,

"He who GATHERED much had nothing over, and he who GATHERED little had no lack."[c]

¹⁶And thanks to God, who is putting the same diligence for you into the heart of Titus, ¹⁷because he indeed accepted the exhortation and, being more diligent, he went out to you of his own accord.

---

[a] "Called-Forth-Communities"—ἐκκλησίαις, ekklesiais; see מַתִּתְיָהוּ Matit'yahu 16:18

[b] "our love to you"—some mss say, "your love to us"

[c] שְׁמוֹת Sh'mot 16:18

¹⁸And we sent with him the brother whose praise in *regard to* the Good News *is* sung through all the Called-Forth-Communities,ᵃ ¹⁹and not only so, but who was also handpickedᵇ by the Called-Forth-Communities *to be* our fellow-traveler with this favor that is served by us, to the glory of the Master Himself, and our willing mind— ²⁰avoiding this,ᶜ so that no one may blame us in this abundance that is served by us. ²¹For we are providing right things, not only in *the* sight of the Master, but also in *the* sight of men. ²²And we sent with them our brother, whom we examined in many things many times, *and found* being diligent (and now *being* much more diligent by the great confidence that is toward you). ²³So, if *anyone asks* about Titus, *he is* my partner and fellow-worker towards you; *and if anyone asks about* our brothers, *they are* emissaries of *the* Called-Forth-Communities, *a* glory of Messiah. ²⁴Therefore, *regarding* the proof of your love, and of our boasting on your behalf: *be* proving *these* to them in the face of the Called-Forth-Communities.

9 ¹For, indeed, regarding the service that *is* for the קְדוֹשִׁים, Q'doshiym, it is superfluous for me to write to you ²for I have known your readiness of mind, which for your sake I boast of to *the* Macedonians, *saying* that "Achaia has been prepared a year ago"; and your zeal stirred up the majority *of them*. ³But I sent the brothers so that our boasting on your behalf may not be made empty in this respect, *but* that, as I said, you may be ready. ⁴Otherwise, if *the* Macedonians come with me and find you unprepared, we will be put to shame (*and* that *is* not saying *anything of* you) in this same confidence.ᵈ ⁵Therefore, I thought IT necessary to exhort the brothers, so that they may go ahead to you and prepare beforehand your formerly announced blessing, *such* that this *will* be ready as a blessing, and not as covetousness. ⁶But *know* this: He who is sowing sparingly will also reap sparingly, and he who is sowing in blessings will also reap in blessings. ⁷Each one *should act* as he purposes in *his* heart, not out of grief or out of obligation, for God loves a cheerful giver.

⁸And God is able to cause all *unmerited* favor to abound to you, so that in everything, always having all sufficiency, you abound to every good action. ⁹As it has been written,

"He dispersed abroad; he gave to the poor; his righteousness remains to the age."ᵉ

¹⁰And He who is supplying seed to the sower and bread for food will supply and multiply your seed sown, and increase the fruits of your righteousness, ¹¹being enriched in everything to all generosity, which, through us, brings about thanksgiving to God. ¹²For the administration of this service is not only supplying the needs of the קְדוֹשִׁים, Q'doshiym, but is also abounding through many thanksgivings to God. ¹³Through the proof of this service, *they will be* glorifying God (for the submission of your confession to the Good News of the Messiah, and FOR the generosity of the sharing to them and to all); ¹⁴and by their requests for help for your sake, *they will be* longing after you because of the exceeding, *unmerited* favor of God upon you. ¹⁵Thanks to God for His indescribable gift!

10 ¹And I myself, Paul, call upon you through the humility and gentleness of the Messiah (I, who in *bodily* presence, indeed, AM lowly among you, and being *physically* absent, have courage toward you) ²and I implore YOU that, being present, I may not *need to* have courage with the confidence with which I consider *it necessary* to be bold against certain

---

ᵃ "Called-Forth-Communities"—ἐκκλησιῶν, ekklesion; also in verses 19, 23 and 24
ᵇ "handpicked"—Young's says, "appointed by vote"
ᶜ "this" may be referring to unwarranted criticism for how the "favor" and "abundance" are handled
ᵈ Some mss insert, "of boasting"
ᵉ תְּהִלִּים *T'hiliym* 112:9

Paul's authority.

ones who are considering us as walking according to the flesh. ³For *though we may be* walking in the flesh, we do not war according to the flesh, ⁴for the weapons of our warfare ARE not fleshly, but powerful to God for *the* bringing down of strongholds — ⁵bringing down reasonings and every high thing lifted up against the knowledge of God; and bringing into captivity every thought to the obedience of the Messiah, ⁶and being in readiness to avenge every disobedience, whenever your obedience may be fulfilled.

⁷Do you *only* see the things according to *bodily* presence? If anyone has trusted in himself to be Messiah's, let him consider this again concerningᵃ himself: that as he is Messiah's, so also ARE we.ᵇ ⁸For even if I boast somewhat more abundantly about our authority that the Master gave for building up and not for tearing you down, I will not be ashamed, ⁹so that I do not seem as if I would terrify you through the letters *I send*. ¹⁰"Because the letters, indeed," says *a certain* one, "ARE weighty and strong, but *his* bodily presence *is* weak, and *his* speech *is* contemptible." ¹¹This one—let him consider this: that such as we are in word through *our* letters, being *physically* absent, such also, being present *in body*, ARE WE in action.

¹²For we do not make *ourselves* bold *in order* to rank or to compare ourselves with certain of those commending themselves. But they, *when* measuring themselves among themselves, and comparing themselves with themselves, are not wise. ¹³And we will not boast *of* ourselves in regard to the unmeasured things, but according to the measure of the area that the God of measure appointed to us, to reach even to you. ¹⁴For we do not stretch ourselves overmuch as *if* not reaching to you, for we even came to you in the Good News of the Messiah, ¹⁵not boasting of the things *we have* not measured (*that is*, in other men's labors), but having hope

(as your faith increases) to be enlarged in you, according to our area (into abundance), ¹⁶*in order* to proclaim Good News in the PLACES beyond you, *and* not to boast in regard to the things made ready in another's area. ¹⁷And HE WHO IS BOASTING—LET HIM BOAST IN ADONAI;ᶜ ¹⁸for *it is* not he who is commending himself *who* is proven, but he whom ADONAI commends.

11 ¹O that you were enduring with me a little bit of foolishness (but you do indeed endure with me), ²for I am jealous for you with *the* jealousy of God, for I betrothed you to one husband — a pure virgin to present to Messiah. ³But I fear that perhaps as the serpent deceived חַוָּה, Chavah in his cunning, your minds may be corrupted *and kept* from *knowing* the simplicity and the purenessᵈ that IS in the Messiah. ⁴For if, indeed, he who is coming *to you* proclaims another יֵשׁוּעַ, Yeshua whom we did not proclaim *to you*, or you receive another רוּחַ, ruach which you did not *previously* receive, or another Good News which you did not *previously* accept, you tolerate IT *all too* well! ⁵For I consider that I have been behind the most eminent emissaries *in* nothing. ⁶But even if *I am* unlearned in word, yet *I am* not *so* in knowledge, but in everything we have made *this* evident to you in all things.

⁷Did I do the sin *by* humbling myself so that you would be exalted, because I freely proclaimed the Good News of God to you? ⁸I robbed other Called-Forth-Communities,ᵉ having taken wages *from them, so that I could give myself freely* for your service. ⁹Yet being present with you and having been in need, I was burdensome to no one, for the brothers supplied my need (having come from Macedonia), and in everything I kept myself burdenless to you—and will keep *myself so*.

ᵃ "concerning"—some mss say, "from"
ᵇ Some mss insert, "Messiah's"
ᶜ יִרְמְיָהוּ *Yir'm'yahu* 9:23(24)
ᵈ Some mss omit, "and the pureness"
ᵉ "Called-Forth-Communities"—ἐκκλησίαις, ekklesiais; see מַתִּתְיָהוּ *Matit'yahu* 16:18

¹⁰The truth of Messiah is in me, because this boasting in regard to me will not be stopped in the regions of Achaia. ¹¹Why? Because I do not love you? God has known *that I do!* ¹²But what I do *with regard to boasting*, I will also *continue to* do, so that I may cut off the occasion of those wanting an occasion *to claim* that, in that which they boast, they may also be found *the same* as we. ¹³For those such *men* ARE false emissaries, deceitful workers, disguising themselves as emissaries of Messiah. ¹⁴And no wonder! for even הַשָּׂטָן, Ha-Satan disguises himself as a Messenger of light. ¹⁵*It is* no great thing, then, if his servants also disguise themselves as servants of righteousness—whose end will be according to their actions.

¹⁶Again I say, let no one think me to be a fool; if otherwise, then receive me even as a fool, so that I also may boast a little. ¹⁷(That which I speak, I speak not according to the Master, but as in foolishness—in this, the confidence of boasting.) ¹⁸Since many boast according to the flesh, I also will boast. ¹⁹For gladly do you tolerate the fools—*you being so "wise"*—²⁰for you tolerate *it* if anyone is bringing you under bondage, if anyone devours *you*, if anyone takes away *from you*, if anyone exalts himself, *or* if anyone strikes you on the face ²¹(I *must* say, in reference to dishonor, that we have been weak). But in whatever respect anyone is bold—in foolishness I say THIS—I also am bold:

²²Are they עִבְרִים, Iv'riym? I *am* also! Are they יִשְׂרְאֵלִים, Yis'raeliym? I *am* also! Are they seed of אַבְרָהָם, Av'raham? I *am* also! ²³Are they servants of Messiah? (I speak as *if I am* out of my mind!ᵃ) I *am* more *so:* in labors more abundantly, in prisons more frequently, in wounds above measure, in *brushes with* death many times— ²⁴five times from *the* יְהוּדִים, Y'hudiym, I received forty LASHES save one, ²⁵three times I was beaten with rods, once I was stoned, three times I was shipwrecked, I have spent a night and a day in the deep *of the sea*—²⁶on journeys many times, *in* dangers of rivers, dangers of robbers, dangers from *my* kindred, dangers from *the* גּוֹיִם, Goyim, dangers in *the* city, dangers in *the* desert, dangers in *the* sea, dangers among false brothers, ²⁷in laboriousness and painfulness, in sleeplessness many times, in hunger and thirst, in *forced* fastings many times, in cold and nakedness.

²⁸Apart from the external things, *there is also* the pressure that is upon me daily: the concern for all the Called-Forth-Communities.ᵇ ²⁹(Who is weak, and I am not weak? Who is stumbled *into sin*, and I do not burn?)

³⁰If it is necessary to boast, I will boast of the things of my weakness; ³¹the God and Father of the Master יֵשׁוּעַ, Yeshuaᶜ—who is blessed to the ages—has known that I do not lie! ³²In דַּמֶּשֶׂק, Dameseq, the governor of Aretas the king was watching the city of the דַּמֶּשְׂקִיִּים, Dames'qiyiym, to seize me, ³³but I was let down in a rope basket through a window through the wall, and fled out of his hands.ᵈ

12 ¹It is necessary to boast, though itᵉ is not profitable, but *now* I will come to visions and revelations of the Master:

²I have known a man in Messiah... fourteen years ago (whether in the body, I have not known, or out of the body, I have not known; *only* God has known), such a one was taken away to the third heaven. ³And I have known such a man (whether in the body, or apart fromᶠ the body, I have not known; *only* God has known)—⁴that he was taken away to the Paradise and heard unutterable sayings that it is not permitted for man to speak. ⁵Of such a one I will boast, but of myself I will not boast, except in weaknesses. ⁶Indeed, if I want to boast, I will not be a fool, for I will say truth. But

---

ᵃ "out of my mind"—Young's says, "beside myself"
ᵇ "Called-Forth-Communities"—ἐκκλησιῶν, ekklesion; see מַתִּתְיָהוּ *Matit'yahu* 16:18
ᶜ Some mss insert, "*the* Messiah"
ᵈ see Acts 9:23-25
ᵉ "It is necessary to boast, though it"—some mss say, "To boast, really"
ᶠ "apart from"—some mss say, "out of"

Extraordinary revelations.

I refrain, so that no one in regard to me may think anything above what he sees *in* me, or anything *he* hears from me, ⁷even in the exceeding greatness of the revelations. Therefore, in order that I will not be exalted overmuch, there was given to me a thorn in the flesh—a messenger of הַשָּׂטָן, HaSatan, so that he might beat me with fists—so that I will not be exalted overmuch.

⁸Concerning this thing, three times I appealed to the Master that it would go away from me, ⁹but He said to me, "My *unmerited* favor is sufficient for you, for power is brought to its goal[a] in weakness." Most gladly, therefore, will I instead boast in my weaknesses, so that the power of the Messiah may rest on me. ¹⁰Therefore, I am well pleased *to endure* in weaknesses, in damages, in needs, in persecutions and distresses for *the sake of* Messiah; for whenever I am weak, then I am strong.

¹¹I have become a fool,[b] *but* you compelled me; for I ought to have been commended by you, for in nothing was I behind the most eminent emissaries—even if I *myself* am nothing. ¹²The signs of the emissary, indeed, were worked among you in all perseverance, both in signs and wonders and mighty deeds; ¹³for what *aspect* is there in which you are inferior to the rest of the Called-Forth-Communities,[c] except that I myself was not a burden to you? Forgive me this injustice!

¹⁴Look! I am ready to come to you this third time, and I will not be a burden, for I seek not *what is* yours, but you! For the children ought not to store up for the parents, but the parents for the children, ¹⁵and I most gladly will spend and be entirely spent for your souls. If[d] *I am* loving you more abundantly, am I *to be* loved less?

¹⁶And be it so, I did not burden you—but being cunning, *perhaps* I took you with underhandedness! ¹⁷Any one of those whom I have sent to you—by him, did I take advantage of you? ¹⁸I appealed to Titus and sent the brother with HIM. Did Titus take advantage of you? Did we not walk in the same רוּחַ, ruach? did we not *walk* in the same steps?

¹⁹All this time,[e] do you think that we are making *a* defense *of ourselves* to you? In the presence of God in Messiah we speak, and all the things, loved ones, ARE for your up-building. ²⁰For I fear that perhaps, having come, I may find you not such as I want, and I myself may be found by you such as you do not want—that perhaps there *will* be infighting, fierce rivalry, fits of rage, *selfish* ambitions, evil-speakings, gossip, puffings-up, *and* uprisings, ²¹such that when I again have come, my God may humble me in regard to you, and I might mourn many of those having sinned beforehand and not having reformed concerning the uncleanness and sexual immorality and sensuality that they practiced.

13 ¹This third time I come to you; BY THE MOUTH OF TWO OR THREE WITNESSES WILL EVERY WORD[f] BE ESTABLISHED.[g] ²I have said before, and I say IT beforehand (as being present *in body* the second time, and being *physically* absent now), to those having sinned beforehand, and to all the remaining *ones:* that if I come again, I will not spare *anyone,* ³since you seek a proof of the Messiah speaking in me, who toward you is not weak, but is powerful in you. ⁴For He also[h] was crucified from weakness, yet He lives from the power of God; for we also are weak in Him, but we will live with Him from the power of God toward you.

⁵Test yourselves *to see* if you are in the faith; examine yourselves. Do you yourselves not recognize that יֵשׁוּעַ, Yeshua *the* Messiah is in you, unless, in some respect, you are failing the test? ⁶And I hope that

---

[a] "brought to its goal"—some mss say, "perfected"
[b] Some mss insert, "*in my* boasting"
[c] "Called-Forth-Communities"—ἐκκλησίας, ek-klesias; see מַתִּתְיָהוּ *Matit'yahu* 16:18
[d] "if"—some mss say, "even if"
[e] "All this time"—some mss say, "Again"
[f] "word"—Young's says, "saying"
[g] דְּבָרִים *D'variym* 19:15
[h] "For He also"—some mss say, "For even if He"

you will know that we—we are not failing the test. ⁷And we pray before God that you *will* do no evil—not so that we may appear proven, but that you may do what is right, even *if we appear to* be as failing the test. ⁸For we are not able to do anything against the truth, but *only* for the truth; ⁹for we rejoice when we are weak, but you are strong. And this we pray for: your perfection! ¹⁰Because of this, I write these things, being *physically* absent, so that, being present *bodily*, I may not treat ANYone sharply, according to the authority that the Master gave me for building up and not for tearing down.

¹¹As to the remainder, brothers: rejoice. Be made perfect, be encouraged, be of the same mind, be at peace; and the God of the love and peace will be with you. ¹²Greet one another in a holy kiss; ¹³all the קְדוֹשִׁים, Q'doshiym greet you.

¹⁴The *unmerited* favor of the Master יֵשׁוּעַ, Yeshua *the* Messiah, and the love of God, and the sharing of the רוּחַ הַקֹּדֶשׁ, Ruach HaQodesh IS with you all!ᵃ

ᵃ Some mss conclude, "אָמֵן, Amen."

PAUL'S LETTER TO THE

Romans

1

¹*From* Paul,ᵃ a slave of Messiah יֵשׁוּעַ, Yeshua, a called emissary, having been separated to the Good News of God ²(which He announced before through His prophets in *the* sacred Scriptures) ³concerning His Son (who, according to the flesh, has come of the seed of דָּוִד, David; ⁴who, according to the רוּחַ, ruach of holiness, is designated as *the* Son of God in power by the Rising Again from the dead), יֵשׁוּעַ, Yeshua *the* Messiah, our Master ⁵(through whom we received *unmerited* favor and assignment as an emissary, for obedience of faith among all the גּוֹיִם, Goyim for *the* sake of His Name, ⁶among whom are you also—the Called of יֵשׁוּעַ, Yeshua *the* Messiah); ⁷to all who are in Rome, loved ones of God, called קְדוֹשִׁים, Q'doshiym: *unmerited* favor to you, and peace from God our Father and FROM the Master יֵשׁוּעַ, Yeshua *the* Messiah!

⁸First, indeed, I thank my God through יֵשׁוּעַ, Yeshua *the* Messiah for you all, that your faith is proclaimed in the whole world. ⁹For God is my witness (whom I serve in my רוּחַ, ruach in the Good News of His Son), how unceasingly I make mention of you, ¹⁰always imploring in my prayers *that* somehow now, at last, I will prosper, by the will of God, *so as* to come to you. ¹¹For I long to see you, so that I may impart to you some spiritual gift, that you may be stabilized—¹²and that is, *for me* to be encouraged together with you, through the faith *we see* in one another, both yours and mine.

¹³And I do not want you to be ignorant, brothers, that many times I purposed to come to you—and was hindered until the present time—so that I might also have some fruit among you, even as also among the other ethnic groups. ¹⁴Both to Greeks and to βαρβάροι, Barbaroi, both to wise and to thoughtless, I am a debtor. ¹⁵So, as much as is in me, I am ready also *to come* to you who ARE in Rome to proclaim Good News.

¹⁶For I am not ashamed of the Good News,ᵇ for it is the power of God to salva-

ᵃ "Paul"—Παῦλος, Paulos; see 1 Timothy 1:1

ᵇ Some mss insert, "of the Messiah"

The invisible things.   Romans 2:8

tion to everyone who is believing, both to יְהוּדִי, Y'hudiy first, and to Greek. ¹⁷For in it the righteousness of God is revealed from faith to faith, as it has been written, "AND THE RIGHTEOUS ONE WILL LIVE BY FAITH."ᵃ ¹⁸For the wrath of God is revealed from Heaven upon all ungodliness and unrighteousness of men, *who are* holding down the truth in unrighteousness, ¹⁹because that which is known of God is evident among them, for God made IT evident to them.

²⁰For from the creation of the world, the invisible things of Him—being understood by *way of* the *visible* things *that have been* made—are plainly seen (both His eternal power and divine nature), so that they are without excuse; ²¹because *despite* having known God, they did not glorify HIM as God, nor gave Him thanks, but *instead* were made empty in their reasonings, and their uncomprehending heart was darkened. ²²Claiming to be wise, they were made fools, ²³and they changed the glory of the immortal God into the likeness of an image of mortal man, and of birds and four-footed animals and reptiles. ²⁴For this reason, God gave them up in the lusts of their hearts to uncleanness, to degrade their bodies among themselves —²⁵*those* who changed the truth of God into a falsehood, and honored and served the created-thing rather than the Creator, who is blessed to the ages. אָמֵן, Amen.

²⁶Because of this, God gave them up to degrading affections, for even their females changed the natural use into that *which is* against nature; ²⁷and likewise the males (having left the natural use of the female) also burned in the longing toward one another—males with males working shame*ful acts,* and in themselves receiving the reward that was fit for their error.

²⁸And, as they did not approve of having God in *their* knowledge, God gave them up to a failed mind, to do what ought not to be done.ᵇ ²⁹Having been filled with all unrighteousness,ᶜ wickedness, covetousness, *and* hateful feelings,ᵈ *they are* full of envy, murder, infighting, deceit, *and* maliciousness;ᵉ *they are* gossips, ³⁰evil-speakers, God-haters, insulting, arrogant, boasters, inventors of evil things, obstinateᶠ toward parents, ³¹uncomprehending, faithless, without natural affection,ᵍ *and* unmerciful *ones* ³²who, *despite* having known the righteous judgment of God—that those practicing such things are worthy of death —not only do them, but also have delight with those practicing them.

2

¹Therefore, you are inexcusable, O man—every one *of you* who is judging *the other.* For in that in which you judge the other, you condemn yourself, for you who are judging practice the same things. ²And we have known that the judgment of God upon those practicing such things is according to truth.

³So, do you think this, O man (*you* who are judging those who are practicing such things, but are doing them *yourself*): that you will escape the judgment of God? ⁴Or do you despise the riches of His goodness and tolerance and patience, not knowing that the goodness of God leads you to reformation?!

⁵But according to your hardness and unreformed heart, you store up wrath to yourself in the Day of wrath and of the revelation of the righteous judgment of God, ⁶who will REWARD EACH *ONE* ACCORDING TO HIS ACTIONS:ʰ ⁷to those, indeed, who in perseverance of good actions seek glory and honor and immortality, *He will give* life age-enduring; ⁸but to those *who are* self-seeking and unpersuaded byⁱ the truth, but being per-

---

ᵃ חֲבַקּוּק *'Chavaquq* 2:4
ᵇ "what ought not to be done"—Young's says, "the things not seemly"
ᶜ some mss insert, "sexual unfaithfulness"
ᵈ "hateful feelings"—Young's says, "malice"
ᵉ "maliciousness"—Young's says, "evil dispositions"
ᶠ "obstinate"—ἀπειθής, apeithes, a negative of πείθω, peitho ("trust"). Here, Young says "disobedient."
ᵍ some mss insert, "unappeasable"
ʰ תְּהִלִּים *T'hiliym* 62:13(12), מִשְׁלֵי *Mish'lei* 24:12
ⁱ "unpersuaded by"—ἀπειθέω, apeitheo, a negative of πείθω, peitho ("trust" or "persuade"). Here, Young says "disobedient to."

suaded by[a] the unrighteousness, *there will be* wrath and rage. [9]*There will be* oppression and distress upon every soul of man that is working the evil (both of יְהוּדִי, Y'hudiy first, and of Greek), [10]but glory, and honor, and peace to everyone who is working the good (both to יְהוּדִי, Y'hudiy first, and to Greek).

[11]Indeed, there is no acceptance of faces[b] with God. [12]For as many as have sinned without *having* תּוֹרָה, Torah[c] also will be destroyed without *being judged by* תּוֹרָה, Torah; and as many as have sinned in תּוֹרָה, Torah[d] will be judged through תּוֹרָה, Torah. [13]For *it is* not the hearers of תּוֹרָה, Torah *who* ARE righteous before God, but the doers of תּוֹרָה, Torah *who* will be declared righteous. [14]For when גּוֹיִם, Goyim (who do not have the תּוֹרָה, Torah) naturally do the *righteous* things[e] of the תּוֹרָה, Torah, these *Goyim* (*though* not having the תּוֹרָה, Torah) are a תּוֹרָה, torah to themselves—[15]*these* who show the action of the תּוֹרָה, Torah written in their hearts, *with* their conscience also bearing witness with them, and the thoughts, between one another, *either* accusing or else defending *them* [16]in the Day when (according to my Good News) God judges the secrets of men through Messiah יֵשׁוּעַ, Yeshua.

[17]But if you are named יְהוּדִי, Y'hudiy,[f] and rest upon תּוֹרָה, Torah, and boast in God, [18]and know the will *of God*, and approve the distinctions[g] (being instructed out of the תּוֹרָה, Torah), [19]and have confidence that you yourself are a leader of blind ones (a light for those in darkness, [20]an instructor of foolish ones, a teacher of little children), having in the תּוֹרָה, Torah the embodiment[h] of the knowledge and of the truth——[21]you, then, who are teaching *one* another: do you not teach yourself? [22]You who are proclaiming NOT TO STEAL[i]—do you steal? You who are saying NOT TO COMMIT ADULTERY[j] —do you commit adultery? You who are abhorring the idols[k]—do you defile the holy things?[l] [23]You who boast in the תּוֹרָה, Torah—do you dishonor God through the sidestepping of the תּוֹרָה, Torah? [24]For,

"Because of you, the Name of God is spoken of *as* evil among the גּוֹיִם, Goyim,"[m]

just as it has been written.

[25]For circumcision,[n] indeed, benefits *you* if you practice תּוֹרָה, Torah; but if you are a sidestepper of תּוֹרָה, Torah, your circumcision has become uncircumcision.[o] [26]If, therefore, the Uncircumcision[p] keep the righteousness of the תּוֹרָה, Torah,[q] will not his uncircumcision be counted as circumcision?[r] [27]And the Uncircumcision, naturally fulfilling the תּוֹרָה, Torah, will judge

---

[a] "being persuaded by"—πείθω, peitho, most often translated "trust" or "persuade." Here, Young says "obeying."
[b] "acceptance of faces"—that is, favoritism
[c] "without *having* תּוֹרָה, Torah"—that is, without the *written* Torah. This is a reference to the Goyim (also in vs. 14).
[d] "in Torah"—that is, according to the *written* Torah (also in vss. 17-25). This is referring to the Jew.
[e] cf. vss. 2:26-27
[f] Paul is addressing Jewish believers here. This is not an invitation for Gentiles to call themselves spiritual Jews.
[g] "distinctions" possibly between right and wrong, or good and evil, or things that are more important than others, or of being Jewish, etc.

[h] "embodiment"—Young's says, "form"
[i] שְׁמוֹת *Sh'mot* 20:13(15), דְּבָרִים *D'variym* 5:17(19)
[j] שְׁמוֹת *Sh'mot* 20:13(14), דְּבָרִים *D'variym* 5:17(18)
[k] שְׁמוֹת *Sh'mot* 20:4, דְּבָרִים *D'variym* 5:8
[l] "defile the holy things"—lit. "rob temples"
[m] יְחֶזְקֵאל *Y'chez'qel* 36:22
[n] "circumcision"—not merely the physical mark, this is a reference to being a Jew
[o] "your circumcision has become uncircumcision" —that is, when a Jew fails to practice Torah, he loses his covenantal advantage and becomes like the Goy (uncircumcised)
[p] "Uncircumcision"—a reference to the Goyim
[q] "the righteousness of the תּוֹרָה, Torah" can be kept by the Goyim, despite the fact that they "do not have the [written] תּוֹרָה, Torah." They are "a תּוֹרָה, torah to themselves... [since] the תּוֹרָה, Torah [is] written in their hearts" (vss. 14-15).
[r] "his uncircumcision be counted as circumcision" —that is, the Gentile who keeps *the righteousness of the Torah* has the same *righteous standing* before God as the Jew. The phrase does not mean that Gentiles become Jews (or Israelites)—spiritual or otherwise.

Depravity of all. Romans 3:25

you who, through *the* letter *of the written Torah* and circumcision, ARE a sidestepper of תּוֹרָה, Torah. ²⁸For one is not יְהוּדִי, Y'hudiy who is *only so* outwardly; neither IS circumcision that which is *only* outward in *the* flesh. ²⁹But one IS יְהוּדִי, Y'hudiy who is *also so* inwardly, and *whose* circumcision IS *also* of the heart—in the רוּחַ, ruach, not *only* in letter—for which the praise is not of men, but of God.

3 ¹What, then, IS the superiority of the יְהוּדִי, Y'hudiy? or what *is* the advantage gained from the circumcision? ²Much in every way! For first, indeed, that they were entrusted with the sayings of God. ³Indeed, what if certain *ones* were faithless? will their faithlessness make useless the faithfulness of God? ⁴Let it not be! and let God become true, and every man false, as it has been written,

"that You may be declared righteous in Your words, and will overcome in Your being judged."ᵃ

⁵And if our unrighteousness establishes God's righteousness, what will we say? "Is God, who is inflicting the wrath, unrighteous?" (I speak according to the manner of a man.) ⁶Let it not be! Otherwise, how will God judge the world? ⁷But *we will* say, "If the truth of God abounded more to His glory in my falsehood, why am I still also judged as a sinner?" ⁸And *why* not *say* (as we are spoken evil of, and as certain *ones*—whose condemnation is righteous—affirm us to *be* saying), "We may do the evil things, so that the goodᵇ may come"?

⁹What then? Are we better? Not at all! For we charged beforehand both יְהוּדִים, Y'hudiym and Greeks—all—with being under sin, ¹⁰as it has been written,

"There is none righteous, not even one. ¹¹There is none who is understanding; there is none who is seeking after God.

¹²All turned aside;ᶜ together they became worthless. There is none doing good; there is not even one."ᵈ

¹³"Their throat IS an opened tomb; with their tongues, they used deceit."ᵉ

"*The* poison of asps IS under their lips—ᶠ

¹⁴*those* whose mouth is full of cursing and bitterness."ᵍ

¹⁵"Swift ARE their feet to shed blood. ¹⁶Ruin and misery ARE in their paths, ¹⁷and they did not know the path of peace."ʰ

¹⁸"There is no fear of God before their eyes."ⁱ

¹⁹And we have known that as many things as the תּוֹרָה, Torah says, it speaks to those *who are* in the תּוֹרָה, Torah, so that every mouth may be stopped, and all the world will become answerable to God. ²⁰Therefore, no flesh may be declared righteous in His sight by actions of תּוֹרָה, Torah, for through תּוֹרָה, Torah is a knowledge of sin.

²¹But now, the righteousness of God has been revealed apart from תּוֹרָה, Torah (testified to by the תּוֹרָה, Torah and the Prophets) ²²and the righteousness of God IS through the faith of יֵשׁוּעַ, Yeshua *the* Messiah to allʲ those believing (indeed, there is no difference——²³for all sinned and are come short of the glory of God), ²⁴being declared righteous without *paying a* cost, by His *unmerited* favor through the redemption that IS in Messiah יֵשׁוּעַ, Yeshua ²⁵(whom, through the faith in His blood, God set forth *as a* כַּפֹּרֶת, Kaporet for the showing of His righteousness, because of the passing over of the past sins

---

ᵃ תְּהִלִּים T'hilim 51:6(4) (LXX)
ᵇ "good"—Young's says, "good ones"
ᶜ "turned aside"—Young's says, "went out of the way"
ᵈ תְּהִלִּים T'hiliym 14:1-3; 53:1-4(3)
ᵉ תְּהִלִּים T'hiliym 5:10(9)
ᶠ תְּהִלִּים T'hiliym 140:4(3)
ᵍ תְּהִלִּים T'hiliym 10:7
ʰ יְשַׁעְיָהוּ Y'sha'yahu 59:7-8
ⁱ תְּהִלִּים T'hiliym 36:2(1)
ʲ Some mss insert, "and upon all"

²⁶in the forbearance of God—for the showing of His righteousness in the present time, for His being righteous, and declaring him righteous who IS of the faith of יֵשׁוּעַ, Yeshua).

²⁷Where, then, IS the boasting? It was excluded. By what תּוֹרָה, Torah? of actions? No, but by a תּוֹרָה, torah of faith, ²⁸for we consider a man to be declared righteous by faith, apart from actions of תּוֹרָה, Torah. ²⁹Is HE only the God of יְהוּדִים, Y'hudiym? Is He not also of גּוֹיִם, Goyim? Yes, also of גּוֹיִם, Goyim, ³⁰since God IS one, who will declare the Circumcision righteous by faith, and also the Uncircumcision through the same faith.ᵃ

³¹Do we then make תּוֹרָה, Torah useless through the faith? Let it not be! Rather, we make תּוֹרָה, Torah stand.

4 ¹What then will we say אַבְרָהָם, Av'raham (our forefather according to the flesh) to have found? ²For if אַבְרָהָם, Av'raham was declared righteous by actions, then he has something to boast about—but not before God. ³For what does the Scripture say?

"And אַבְרָהָם, Av'raham believed God, and it was credited to him—to righteousness."ᵇ

⁴Now to him who is working, the wage is not credited to him out of unmerited favor, but paid out of a debt due. ⁵But to him who is not working, yet is believing upon Him who is declaring righteous the ungodly, his faith is credited to him to righteousness, ⁶even as דָּוִד, David also speaks of the happiness of the man to whom God credits righteousness apart from actions:

⁷"Happy are they whose misdeeds were forgiven, and whose sins were covered. ⁸Happy is the man whose sin ADONAI does not credit to him."ᶜ

⁹Is this happiness, then, only upon the Circumcision, or also upon the Uncircumcision? For we say, "The faith was credited to אַבְרָהָם, Av'raham—to righteousness." ¹⁰How, then, was it credited? he being in circumcision? or in uncircumcision? Not in circumcision, but in uncircumcision! ¹¹And he received the sign of circumcision—a seal of the righteousness of the faith—while he was in the uncircumcision, for his being the father of all those believing through uncircumcision (for the righteousness also being credited to them), ¹²and father of circumcision to those who are not only of circumcision, but who also walk in the steps of the faith of our father אַבְרָהָם, Av'raham while he was in uncircumcision.

¹³For the promise to אַבְרָהָם, Av'raham, or to his seed, of his being heir of the world IS not through תּוֹרָה, Torah, but through the righteousness of faith. ¹⁴For if only they who are of תּוֹרָה, Torah ARE heirs, then the faith has been made empty, and the promise has been made useless, ¹⁵for the תּוֹרָה, Torah brings about wrath. And where תּוֹרָה, Torah is not, neither IS there sidestepping.

¹⁶Because of this, the promise IS of faith, that IT MAY BE according to unmerited favor, for IT being made sure to all the seed—not only to that which IS of the תּוֹרָה, Torah, but also to that which IS of the faith of אַבְרָהָם, Av'raham, ¹⁷who is father of us all (as it has been written, "I HAVE SET YOU AS A FATHER OF MANY ETHNIC-GROUPS"ᵈ) in the sight of Him whom he believed: God, who is bringing the dead to life, and is calling the things not being as being.

¹⁸Av'raham, in hope against hope, believed for his becoming the father of many ethnic-groups according to that which was spoken: "SO WILL YOUR SEED BE."ᵉ ¹⁹And not having been weak in the faith, he lookedᶠ to his own body—having already become as good as dead, being about a hundred years old—and the deadness of the womb of שָׂרָה, Sarah. ²⁰But at the prom-

---

ᵃ "Circumcision/Uncircumcision"—that is, Jews and Gentiles, respectively
ᵇ בְּרֵאשִׁית B'reshiyt 15:6; also in verse 22
ᶜ תְּהִלִּים T'hiliym 32:1-2
ᵈ בְּרֵאשִׁית B'reshiyt 17:5
ᵉ בְּרֵאשִׁית B'reshiyt 15:5
ᶠ Some mss insert, "not"

Reconcilation by Messiah.

ise of God, he did not stagger in unbelief, but was strengthened in faith, having given glory to God ²¹and having been fully persuaded that what He has promised He is also able to do. ²²Therefore, IT WAS ALSO CREDITED TO HIM TO RIGHTEOUSNESS.

²³And it was not written that "it was credited to him" on his account alone, ²⁴but also on ours, to whom it is about to be credited—to us believing on Him who raised up יֵשׁוּעַ, Yeshua our Master out of the dead, ²⁵who was handed over because of our missteps, and was raised up because of our being declared righteous.

5 ¹Therefore, having been declared righteous by faith, we have peace toward God through our Master יֵשׁוּעַ, Yeshua *the* Messiah, ²through whom we also have the access, by the faith, into this *unmerited* favor in which we have stood. And we boast on the hope of the glory of God.

³And not only *so*, but we also boast in the oppressions, knowing that the oppression brings about perseverance; ⁴and perseverance, proof *of character*; and proof *of character*, hope. ⁵And the hope does not make *us* ashamed, because the love of God has been poured out in our hearts through the רוּחַ הַקֹּדֶשׁ, Ruach HaQodesh that has been given to us.

⁶For in our still being weak, Messiah—in due time—died for the ungodly. ⁷For with difficulty will anyone die for a righteous man; indeed, for the good man, perhaps someone even dares to die. ⁸But God proves His own love to us: that, in our still being sinners, Messiah died for us. ⁹*How* much more, then, having now been declared righteous in His blood, will we be saved through Him from the wrath! ¹⁰For if, being enemies, we have been reconciled to God through the death of His Son, *then how* much more, having been reconciled, will we be saved in His life!

¹¹And not only *so*, but we are also boasting in God through our Master יֵשׁוּעַ, Yeshua *the* Messiah, through whom we have now received the Reconciliation. ¹²Because of this, even as through one man the sin entered into the world, and through the sin, the death, so the death also passed through to all men, in that all sinned. ¹³For until תּוֹרָה, Torah, sin was in the world. But sin is not charged *to one's account* when there is no תּוֹרָה, Torah. ¹⁴*And yet*, death reigned from אָדָם, Adam until מֹשֶׁה, Mosheh, even upon those not having sinned in the likeness of the side-stepping of אָדָם, Adam (who is a pattern of Him who is coming).

¹⁵But the free gift IS not also like the misstep. For if, by the misstep of the one *man*, the many died, *how* much more did the *unmerited* favor of God—and the free gift in *unmerited* favor of the one man, יֵשׁוּעַ, Yeshua *the* Messiah—abound to the many. ¹⁶And the free gift IS not as through *the* one who sinned. For the judgment indeed IS of one *man's misstep leading* to condemnation, but the gift IS *forgiveness* of *our* many missteps *leading* to a declaration of "Righteous." ¹⁷For if by the misstep of the one *man* the death reigned through the one *man, how* much more will those who are receiving the abundance of the *unmerited* favor and the free gift of the righteousness, reign in life through the One—יֵשׁוּעַ, Yeshua *the* Messiah.

¹⁸So, then, as through one misstep IT IS to condemnation to all men, so also through one declaration of "Righteous" IT IS a declared righteousness[a] of life to all men. ¹⁹For as through the disobedience of the one man the many were made sinners, so also through the obedience of the One will the many be made righteous.

²⁰And תּוֹרָה, Torah came in so that the misstep might abound; but where the sin abounded, the *unmerited* favor overabounded, ²¹so that even as the sin reigned in the death, so also the *unmerited* favor may reign through righteousness to life age-enduring through יֵשׁוּעַ, Yeshua *the* Messiah, our Master.

---
[a] "declared righteousness"—Young's says, "justification"

Romans 6:1 — *Use of the Torah.*

6 ¹What, then, will we say? should we continue in the sin so that the *unmerited* favor may abound? ²Let it not be! We who died to the sin—how will we still live in it? ³Are you ignorant that we—as many as were immersed into Messiah יֵשׁוּעַ, Yeshua—were immersed into His death? ⁴Therefore, we were buried together with Him through the immersion into the death, so that even as Messiah was raised up out of the dead, through the glory of the Father, so also we might walk in newness of life.

⁵For if we have become planted together to the likeness of His death, *so* also will we be of the Rising Again, ⁶knowing this: that our old man[a] was crucified with *HIM*, so that the body of the sin may be made useless, for *the purpose of* our no longer serving the sin—⁷for he who has died has been set free from the sin.

⁸And if we died with Messiah, we believe that we also will live with Him, ⁹knowing that Messiah, having been raised up out of the dead, no longer dies—death no longer has dominion over Him. ¹⁰For in that He died, He died once to the sin; and in that He lives, He lives to God. ¹¹So also you: consider yourselves to be dead indeed to the sin, and living to God in Messiah יֵשׁוּעַ, Yeshua.[b]

¹²Therefore, let not the sin reign in your mortal body, to obey[c] its lusts. ¹³Neither present your members to the sin *as* instruments of unrighteousness, but present yourselves to God as living *ones*, having risen out of the dead, and your members *as* instruments of righteousness to God. ¹⁴For sin will not have dominion over you, for you are not under *the guardianship of* תּוֹרָה, Torah,[d] but under *unmerited* favor.

¹⁵What then? should we sin because we are not under *the guardianship of* תּוֹרָה, Torah, but under *unmerited* favor? Let it not be! ¹⁶Have you not known that to whom you present yourselves *as* slaves for obedience, you are slaves to whom you obey—whether of sin to death, or of obedience to righteousness? ¹⁷But thanks to God that you were *once* slaves of the sin and were obedient from the heart to the form of teaching to which you were handed over, ¹⁸but *now*, having been freed from the sin, you became slaves to the righteousness!

¹⁹I speak in the manner of men because of the weakness of your flesh. For even as you presented your members *as* slaves to the uncleanness and to the wickedness[e]—*leading* to the *increasing* wickedness—so now present your members *as* slaves to the righteousness—*leading* to holiness. ²⁰For when you were slaves of the sin, you were free from the righteousness. ²¹What fruit, therefore, were you having then, in the things of which you are now ashamed? For the end *result* of those *is* death.

²²But now, having been freed from the sin and having become slaves to God, you have your fruit *leading* to holiness, and the end *result is* life age-enduring. ²³For the wages of the sin *is* death, but the gift of God *is* life age-enduring in Messiah יֵשׁוּעַ, Yeshua our Master.

7 ¹Are you ignorant, brothers—for I speak to those knowing תּוֹרָה, Torah—that the תּוֹרָה, Torah has dominion over the man as long as he lives? ²For the married woman has been bound by תּוֹרָה, Torah to the living husband, but if the husband dies, she has been *set* free from the תּוֹרָה, Torah of the husband. ³So then, *with* the husband being alive, she will be called an adulteress if she becomes another man's. But if the husband dies, she is free from the תּוֹרָה, Torah, so as not to be an adulteress, having become another man's.

⁴Therefore, my brothers, you also were made dead to the תּוֹרָה, Torah through the body of the Messiah—for your becoming another's—who was raised up out of the dead, so that we might bear fruit to God. ⁵For when we were in the flesh, the pas-

---

[a] "our old man," that is, "our old self"
[b] Some mss insert, "our Master"
[c] Some mss insert, "it in"
[d] "under *the guardianship of* תּוֹרָה, Torah"—cf. Galatians 3:23
[e] "wickedness"—Gk. ἀνομίαν, anomian

sions of the sins that ARE *made known* through the תּוֹרָה, Torah were working in our members to bear fruit to the death. ⁶But now, being dead to that in which we were held, we have ceased from the תּוֹרָה, Torah, so that we may serve in newness of רוּחַ, ruach, and not in oldness of letter.

⁷What, then, will we say? *that* the תּוֹרָה, Torah IS sin? Let it not be! Rather, I did not know the sin except through תּוֹרָה, Torah. Indeed, I also *would* not have known *what* the covetousness *was* if the תּוֹרָה, Torah had not said, "YOU MUST NOT COVET."ᵃ ⁸But the sin, having received an opportunity through the command, brought about all covetousness in me—for apart from תּוֹרָה, Torah, sin is dead.

⁹And I was once alive apart from תּוֹרָה, Torah, but when the command had come, the sin revived, and I died. ¹⁰And the command that IS for life—this was found by me for death.ᵇ ¹¹For the sin, having received an opportunity through the command, deceived me and, through it, killed ME.

¹²Therefore, the תּוֹרָה, Torah, indeed, IS holy, and the command *is* holy and righteous and good. ¹³That which is good, then —has it become death to me? Let it not be! But the sin, so that it might be shown *to be* sin, through the good *was* bringing about death to me, so that the sin might become exceedingly sinful through the command. ¹⁴For we have known that the תּוֹרָה, Torah is spiritual, but I am of flesh, sold under the sin. ¹⁵For that which I bring about, I do not understand. Indeed, what I do not want, this I practice; but what I hate, this I do.

¹⁶And if what I do not want *to do*, this I do, I consent to the תּוֹרָה, Torah that IT IS good; ¹⁷and now it is no longer I that bring it about, but the sin living in me. ¹⁸For I have known that there does not live in me (that is, in my flesh) good; for to want *to do good* is present with me, but *the ability* to bring about that which is right is not.ᶜ ¹⁹For the good that I want *to do*, I do not, but the evil that I do not want *to do*, this I practice. ²⁰And if what I do not want *to do*, this I do, it is no longer I that bring it about, but the sin that is living in me.

²¹I find, then, the תּוֹרָה, torah, that when I desire to do what is right, the evil is present with me. ²²For I delight in the תּוֹרָה, Torah of God according to the inward man, ²³but I see another תּוֹרָה, torah in my members, warring against the תּוֹרָה, Torah of my mind—and bringing me into captivity in the תּוֹרָה, torah of the sin that IS in my members. ²⁴I AM a wretched man! Who will deliver me out of this body of death?ᵈ ²⁵And thanks *are* to God, through יֵשׁוּעַ, Yeshua *the* Messiah our Master! So then, I myself indeed serve the תּוֹרָה, Torah of God with the mind, but with the flesh, *I serve* the תּוֹרָה, torah of sin.

8

¹Therefore, there is now no condemnation to those in Messiah יֵשׁוּעַ, Yeshua.ᵉ ²For the תּוֹרָה, torah of the רוּחַ, Ruach of the life in Messiah יֵשׁוּעַ, Yeshua set youᶠ free from the תּוֹרָה, torah of the sin and of the death. ³For what the תּוֹרָה, Torah was not able to do, in that it was weak through the flesh *of men*, God, having sent His own Son in the likeness of sinful flesh —and for *a* sin *offering*—condemned the sin in the flesh *of men*, ⁴so that the righteousness of the תּוֹרָה, Torah may be fulfilled in us who do not walk according to the flesh, but according to the רוּחַ, Ruach.

⁵For those who are according to the flesh *set their* mind *on* the things of the flesh, but those *who are* according to the רוּחַ, Ruach *set their* mind *on* the things of the רוּחַ, Ruach. ⁶For the mind of the flesh IS death, but the mind of the רוּחַ, Ruach *is* life and peace, ⁷because the mind of the flesh IS hostility to God. Indeed, it does not submit itself to the תּוֹרָה, Torah of God, for neither is it able *to do so*; ⁸and those who are in the flesh are not able to please God.

ᵃ שְׁמוֹת Sh'mot 20:14(17); דְּבָרִים D'variym 5:18(21)
ᵇ "found by me for death" or possibly, "found for death to me"
ᶜ "is not"—some mss say, "I do not find"
ᵈ "this body of death" or "the body of this death"
ᵉ Some mss insert, "who walk not according to the flesh, but according to the רוּחַ, Ruach"
ᶠ "you"—some mss say, "me"

⁹However, you are not in the flesh, but in the רוּחַ, Ruach, if indeed the רוּחַ אֱלֹהִים, Ruach 'Elohiym lives in you. But if anyone does not have the רוּחַ, Ruach of Messiah, this one is not His. ¹⁰But if Messiah IS in you, the body indeed IS dead because of sin, but the רוּחַ, Ruach IS life because of righteousness. ¹¹And if the רוּחַ, Ruach of Him who raised up יֵשׁוּעַ, Yeshua out of the dead lives in you, *then* He who raised up Messiah out of the dead will also bring your dying bodies to life through His רוּחַ, Ruach living in you.

¹²So then, brothers, we are debtors, *but* not to the flesh, to live according to the flesh; ¹³for if you live according to the flesh, you are about to die. But if, by the רוּחַ, Ruach, you put to death the deeds of the body, you will live. ¹⁴For as many as are led by the רוּחַ אֱלֹהִים, Ruach 'Elohiym— these are the sons of God. ¹⁵For you did not receive a רוּחַ, ruach of bondage again to fear, but you received a רוּחַ, ruach of adoption *as sons* in which we shout, "אַבָּא, Abba, Father!" ¹⁶The רוּחַ, Ruach Himself testifies with our רוּחַ, ruach that we are children of God, ¹⁷and if *we are* children, *we are* also heirs—heirs, indeed, of God, and heirs together of Messiah, if, indeed, we suffer together *with Him*, so that we may also be glorified together *with Him*.

¹⁸For I consider that the sufferings of the present time ARE not worthy TO BE COM- PARED with the glory about to be revealed in us, ¹⁹for the eager expectation of the creation waits for the revealing of the sons of God. ²⁰Indeed, the creation was submitted to futility—not of its *own* will, but because of Him who submitted IT—in hope ²¹that the creation itself will also be set free from the slavery of the decay, to the liberty of the glory of the children of God. ²²For we have known that all the creation groans together and suffers together *as in the* pain *of childbirth* until now.

²³And not only *SO*, but also we ourselves, having the first-fruit of the רוּחַ, Ruach— even we ourselves groan in ourselves, wait- ing for *our* adoption *as sons*, the redemption of our body, ²⁴for we were saved in hope. But hope seen is not hope; for who hopes for what he *already* sees? ²⁵And if we hope for what we do not see, through perseverance, we wait for IT.

²⁶And likewise, the רוּחַ, Ruach also helps our weakness. For we have not known (as it is necessary for *US*) what we might pray for, but the רוּחַ, Ruach Himself makes pleading[a] with groanings unutterable.[b] ²⁷And He who is searching the hearts has known what the mind of the רוּחַ, Ruach IS, because according to God He intercedes for קְדוֹשִׁים, Q'doshiym.

²⁸And we have known that to those loving God, all things work together for good to those who are called according to *His* purpose, ²⁹because *those* whom He foreknew, He also predetermined *to be* conformed to the image of His Son, so that He would be first-born among many brothers. ³⁰And *those* whom He predetermined, He also called; and *those* whom He called, He also declared righteous; and *those* whom He declared righteous, He also glorified.

³¹What then will we say to these things? If God IS for us, who IS against us? ³²He who indeed did not spare His own Son, but handed Him over for us all—how will He not also, with Him, give to us all the things?

³³Who will lay a charge against the chosen ones of God? God IS He that is declaring righteous——³⁴who IS he that is condemning? Messiah יֵשׁוּעַ, Yeshua[c] IS He that died (and more, was raised up), who is also at the right hand of God, who also intercedes for us.

³⁵Who will separate us from the love of the Messiah? Oppression? or distress? or persecution? or famine? or nakedness? or danger? or sword? ³⁶(as it has been written, "FOR YOUR SAKE WE ARE PUT TO DEATH ALL THE DAY LONG; WE

---

[a] Some mss insert, "for us"
[b] "unutterable" or "inexpressible in words"
[c] Some mss omit, יֵשׁוּעַ, Yeshua

WERE COUNTED AS SHEEP FOR SLAUGHTER."ᵃ) ³⁷But in all these, we more than conquer through Him who loved us. ³⁸For I am persuaded that neither death, nor life, nor Messengers, nor rulers, nor things present, nor things about to be, nor powers, ³⁹nor height, nor depth, nor any other created thing will be able to separate us from the love of God that IS in Messiah יֵשׁוּעַ, Yeshua, our Master.

9 ¹I say the truth in Messiah—I do not lie, my conscience bearing testimony with me in the רוּחַ הַקֹּדֶשׁ, Ruach HaQodesh—²that I have great grief and unceasing pain in my heart. ³For I was praying to be accursed—I myself—from the Messiah for *the sake of* my brothers, my relatives according to the flesh, ⁴who are יִשְׂרְאֵלִים, Yis'raeliym; whose IS the adoption *as sons*, and the glory, and the בְּרִיתוֹת, b'riytot, and the תּוֹרָה, Torah-giving, and the עֲבֹדָה, 'avodah, and the promises; ⁵also whose ARE the fathers; and of whom, according to the flesh, IS the Messiah—who is over all, God blessed to the ages,ᵇ אָמֵן, amen!

⁶But it is not possible that the word of God has failed, for not all these who ARE of יִשְׂרָאֵל, Yis'rael are יִשְׂרָאֵל, Yis'rael, ⁷nor because they are seed of אַבְרָהָם, Av'raham ARE *they* all *his* children, but "IN יִצְחָק, YITZ'CHAQ WILL A SEED BE CALLED TO YOU;"ᶜ ⁸that is, the children of the flesh—these ARE not children of God. Rather, the children of the promise are counted as seed. ⁹For the word of promise IS this: "ACCORDING TO THIS TIME I WILL COME, AND THERE WILL BE TO שָׂרָה, SARAH A SON."ᵈ

¹⁰And not only *so*, but *consider* also רִבְקָה, Riv'qah, having conceived *two* by one *seed*—*by* יִצְחָק, Yitz'chaq our father. ¹¹For they being not yet born, nor having done anything good or evil (so that the purpose of God would remain according to *His* choice—¹²not *of their* actions, but of Him who is calling), it was said to her, "THE GREATER IN AGE WILL SERVE THE LESSER IN AGE,"ᵉ ¹³as it has been written,

"יַעֲקֹב, Ya'aqov I loved, but עֵשָׂו, Esav I hated."ᶠ

¹⁴What, then, will we say? *Is* unrighteousness with God? Let it not be! ¹⁵For to מֹשֶׁה, Mosheh He says,

"I will do *loving*-kindness to whom I do *loving*-kindness, and I will have compassion on whom I have compassion."ᵍ

¹⁶So, then, *it is* not of him who is willing, nor of him who is running, but of God who is doing *loving*-kindness. ¹⁷For the Scripture says to פַּרְעֹה, Par'oh,

"I raised you up for this very thing, *so* that I would prove My power in you, and that My Name would be publicized in all the earth."ʰ

¹⁸So then, to whom He wants, He does *loving*-kindness, and whom He wants *to harden*, He hardens.

¹⁹You will say to me, then, "Why does He still find fault? for who has resisted His will?" ²⁰No. Rather, O man, who are you that are answering backⁱ to God? Will the formed thing say to Him who formed IT, "Why did you make me this way?" ²¹Has not the potter authority over the clay, to make out of the same lump the one thing for honor and the *other* one for dishonor?

²²But *what if* God, wanting to prove the wrath and to make His power known, endured in much patience objects of wrath prepared for destruction? ²³And *this was*

ᵃ תְּהִלִּים T'hiliym 44:23(22)
ᵇ "who is over all, God blessed to the ages" or "who is over all, God blessed to the ages" or "who is over all God, blessed to the ages" or "who is over all (God *be* blessed to the ages)"
ᶜ בְּרֵאשִׁית B'reshiyt 21:12
ᵈ בְּרֵאשִׁית B'reshiyt 18:10
ᵉ בְּרֵאשִׁית B'reshiyt 25:23
ᶠ מַלְאָכִי Mal'akhiy 1:2-3
ᵍ שְׁמוֹת Sh'mot 33:19
ʰ שְׁמוֹת Sh'mot 9:16
ⁱ "answering back" or "answering again"

Romans 9:24 — *A goal of the Torah.*

so that He would make known the riches of His glory on objects of *loving*-kindness that He prepared beforehand for glory, ²⁴whom He also called—us—not only out of *the* יְהוּדִים, Y'hudiym, but also out of *the* גּוֹיִם, Goyim, ²⁵as in הוֹשֵׁעַ, Hoshea He also says,

"I will call what IS not My people, 'My people,' and her *who is* not loved, 'Loved.'" ²⁶"And it will be, in the place where it was said to them, 'You ARE not My people'—there they will be called sons of the living God."ᵃ

²⁷And יְשַׁעְיָהוּ, Y'sha'yahu *also* shouts concerning יִשְׂרָאֵל, Yis'rael,

"Even if the number of the sons of יִשְׂרָאֵל, Yis'rael may be as the sand of the sea, *only* the remnant will be saved. ²⁸For He is finishing a matter, and is cutting *it* short;ᵇ ADONAI will do *it* upon the land *of the earth.*"ᶜ

²⁹And as יְשַׁעְיָהוּ, Y'sha'yahu says before,

"Unless יהוה צְבָאוֹת, ADONAI Tz'vaot had left a seed to us, we would have become as סְדֹם, S'dom, and we would have been made like to עֲמֹרָה, 'Amorah."ᵈ

³⁰What, then, will we say? that גּוֹיִם, Goyim, who are not pursuing righteousness, attained to righteousness—even righteousness that IS of faith—³¹but יִשְׂרָאֵל, Yis'rael, pursuing a תּוֹרָה, Torah of righteousness, did not arrive at תּוֹרָה, Torah.ᵉ ³²Why? Because *it was pursued* not by faith, but as by actions.ᶠ For they stumbled at the stone of stumbling, ³³as it has been written,

"Look! I place in צִיּוֹן, Tziyon a stone of stumbling and a rock of offense, and *he* who is believing thereon will not be ashamed."ᵍ

10

¹Brothers, the pleasure of my heart, indeed, and my request for help to God for יִשְׂרָאֵל, Yis'rael,ʰ is—for salvation. ²For I bear them testimony that they have a zeal for God, but not according to knowledge. ³For not knowing the righteousness of God, and looking to establish their own righteousness, they did not submit to the righteousness of God. ⁴For a goal of תּוֹרָה, Torah is Messiah, for righteousness to everyone who is believing. ⁵Indeed, מֹשֶׁה, Mosheh describes the righteousness that IS of the תּוֹרָה, Torah—that,

"The man who did them will live in them."ⁱ

⁶But the righteousness of faith speaks this way: "You should not say in your heart, 'WHO WILL GO UP TO THE HEAVEN?'"ʲ (that is, to bring Messiah down), ⁷"or, 'Who will go down to the abyss?'" (that is, to bring up Messiah out of the dead). ⁸But what does it say?

"The word is near you, in your mouth and in your heart—"ᵏ

that is, the word of the faith that we proclaim: ⁹that if you confess with your mouth, "יֵשׁוּעַ, Yeshua *is* Master,"ˡ and believe in your heart that God raised Him out of the dead, you will be saved. ¹⁰For with the heart ONE believes, *leading* to righteousness; and with the mouth confession is made, *leading* to salvation. ¹¹For the Scripture says,

"Everyone who is believing on Him will not be ashamed."ᵐ

¹²For there is no difference between יְהוּדִי, Y'hudiy and Greek, for the same Master of all IS rich to all those calling upon Him. ¹³For,

"Everyone—whoever will call upon the Name of ADONAI, he will be saved."ⁿ

ᵃ הוֹשֵׁעַ *Hoshea* 2:25(23), 2:1(1:10)
ᵇ Some insert, "in righteousness, because a matter cut short"
ᶜ יְשַׁעְיָהוּ *Y'sha'yahu* 10:22-23
ᵈ יְשַׁעְיָהוּ *Y'sha'yahu* 1:9
ᵉ Some mss insert, "of righteousness"
ᶠ Some mss insert, "of תּוֹרָה, Torah"
ᵍ יְשַׁעְיָהוּ *Y'sha'yahu* 8:14, 28:16 (LXX)
ʰ יִשְׂרָאֵל, Yis'rael"—earlier mss say, "them"
ⁱ וַיִּקְרָא *Vayiq'ra* 18:5
ʲ דְּבָרִים *D'variym* 30:12
ᵏ דְּבָרִים *D'variym* 30:14
ˡ "Master" or "ADONAI"; see Philippians 2:10-11
ᵐ יְשַׁעְיָהוּ *Y'sha'yahu* 28:16
ⁿ יוֹאֵל *Yoel* 3:5(2:32)

¹⁴How, then, may they call upon HIM in whom they did not believe? and how may they believe ON HIM of whom they did not hear? and how may they hear apart from one proclaiming? ¹⁵and how may they proclaim, if they are not sent? As it has been written,

"How beautiful *are* the feet of those proclaiming Good News[a] of the good things!"[b]

¹⁶But they were not all obedient to the Good News. For יְשַׁעְיָהוּ, Y'sha'yahu says,

"ADONAI, who gave credence to *the* report *they heard* from us?"[c]

¹⁷So then, the faith *is* by *hearing* a report, and the report *is heard* through a spoken word of Messiah.[d] ¹⁸But I say, "Did they not hear?" Yes, indeed,

"their voice went forth to all the earth, and their spoken words to the ends of the habitable world."[e]

¹⁹But I say, "Did יִשְׂרָאֵל, Yis'rael not understand?" First, מֹשֶׁה, Mosheh says,

"I will provoke you to jealousy by THAT WHICH IS not a people; by an uncomprehending גּוֹי, Goy I will anger you";[f]

²⁰and יְשַׁעְיָהוּ, Y'sha'yahu is very bold, and says,

"I was found by those not looking for Me; I became seen to those not asking about Me."[g]

²¹But to יִשְׂרָאֵל, Yis'rael He says,

"All the day I stretched out My hands to a people unbelieving and contradictory."[h]

---

[a] Some mss insert, "of peace, of those proclaiming Good News"
[b] יְשַׁעְיָהוּ Y'sha'yahu 52:7
[c] יְשַׁעְיָהוּ Y'sha'yahu 53:1 (LXX)
[d] "Messiah"—some mss say, "God"
[e] תְּהִלִּים T'hiliym 19:5(4)
[f] דְּבָרִים D'variym 32:21; "people" and גּוֹי, Goy are both ἔθνει, ethnei here in the Greek, but they are different in the Hebrew.
[g] יְשַׁעְיָהוּ Y'sha'yahu 65:1
[h] יְשַׁעְיָהוּ Y'sha'yahu 65:2

---

11 ¹I say *this*, then: "Did God push away His people?" Let it not be! Indeed, I also am a יִשְׂרְאֵלִי, Yis're'liy, of the seed of אַבְרָהָם, Av'raham, of the tribe of בִּנְיָמִין, Bin'yamiyn. ²God did not push away His people whom He knew beforehand. Have you not known—in *reference to* אֵלִיָּהוּ, Eliyahu—what the Scripture says? how he pleads with God regarding יִשְׂרָאֵל, Yis'rael:

³"ADONAI, they killed your prophets, they dug down your altars, and I was left alone, and they seek my life."[i]

⁴But what *did* the Divine Answer say to him?

"I left to Myself seven thousand men who did not bow a knee to בַּעַל, Ba-al."[j]

⁵So then, also in the present time, there has been a remnant according to the choice of *unmerited* favor ⁶(and if by *unmerited* favor, then *it is* no longer by actions; otherwise, the *unmerited* favor becomes *unmerited* favor no longer).[k] ⁷What then? What יִשְׂרָאֵל, Yis'rael searches after, this it did not obtain, but the chosen did obtain *it*, and the remaining were hardened, ⁸as it has been written,

"God gave to them a רוּחַ, ruach of deep sleep, eyes not to see, and ears not to hear, to this very day."[l]

⁹And דָּוִד, David says,

"Let their table become to them for a snare, and for a trap, and for a stumbling-block, and for a retribution. ¹⁰Let their eyes be darkened, to not see, and *make* their back always bend down."[m]

¹¹I say *this*, then: "Did they stumble so that they might fall?" Let it not be! But by their misstep, the salvation IS *come* to the גּוֹיִם, Goyim to arouse *Yis'rael* to jealousy.

---

[i] מְלָכִים א M'lakhiym Alef 19:10&14
[j] מְלָכִים א M'lakhiym Alef 19:18
[k] Some mss insert, "But if *it is* by actions, *then* it is no longer *unmerited* favor; otherwise, the action is no longer action."
[l] דְּבָרִים D'variym 29:3(4); יְשַׁעְיָהוּ Y'sha'yahu 29:10
[m] תְּהִלִּים T'hiliym 69:23-24(22-23)

¹²And if their misstep IS the riches of the world, and their diminishing *is* the riches of *the* גּוֹיִם, Goyim, how much more *will* their fullness *be*? ¹³But I speak to you—to the גּוֹיִם, Goyim—inasmuch, then, as I am indeed an emissary of גּוֹיִם, Goyim: I *will* glorify my service ¹⁴if by any means I will arouse to jealousy *those of* my own flesh, and will save some of them. ¹⁵For if their rejection IS a reconciliation of the world, what *will* their reception *be* if not life out of the dead? ¹⁶And if the first-fruit *from the dough* IS holy, *then the whole* batch *is* also;ᵃ and if the root IS holy, *then* the branches *are* too.

¹⁷But if certain *ones* of the branches were broken off, and you *Goyim*, being *of* a wild olive tree, were grafted in among them and became a fellow-sharer of the root of the richness of the olive tree, ¹⁸do not boast against the branches. But if you do boast, *remember that* you do not carry the root, but the root *carries* you! ¹⁹You will say then, "Branches were broken off, so that I might be grafted in." ²⁰Right! by unbelief they were broken off, but you have stood by faith. *Therefore*, be not high-minded, but be fearing, ²¹for if God did not spare the natural branches, otherwise, He will also not spare you.

²²See, then, *the* kindness and severity of God: upon those indeed who fell, severity; and upon you, God's kindness—if you remain in the kindness (otherwise, you will also be cut off). ²³And those also—if they do not remain in unbelief—will be grafted *back* in, for God is able to graft them in again. ²⁴For if you, *Goyim*, were cut out from the olive tree *that is* wild by nature, and contrary to nature were grafted into a cultivated olive tree, how much more will they who ARE according to nature be grafted into their own olive tree?

²⁵For I do not want you to be ignorant of this mystery, brothers, so that you may not be wise in your own conceits: that hardness in part has happened to יִשְׂרָאֵל, Yis'rael until the fullness of the גּוֹיִם, Goyim comes in; ²⁶and so all יִשְׂרָאֵל, Yis'rael will be saved, as it has been written,

"There will come forth out of צִיּוֹן, Tziyon he who is delivering; he will turn away ungodliness from יַעֲקֹב, Ya'aqov. ²⁷And this IS the בְּרִית, b'riyt from Me to them, when I take away their sins."ᵇ

²⁸Regarding the Good News, indeed, THEY ARE enemies on account of you, but regarding the chosenness, *they are* beloved on account of the fathers; ²⁹for unregretted-of ARE the gifts and the calling of God. ³⁰Indeed, as you *Goyim* once did not believe in God, and now find *loving-*kindness by the unbelief of these *Y'hudiym*, ³¹so also these *Y'hudiym* now do not believe, so that in *the loving-*kindness *given* to you, they may also now find *loving-*kindness. ³²For God shut up together the whole *world* to unbelief, so that to the whole *world* He might do *loving-*kindness.

³³O, *the* depth of *the* riches and wisdom and knowledge of God! How unsearchable *are* His judgments, and untraceable His ways! ³⁴For

"Who has known the mind of ADONAI? or who became His counselor?"ᶜ

³⁵or

"Who gave first to Him, that it should be given back to him again?"ᵈ

³⁶Because from Him, and through Him, and to Him ARE all the things. To Him IS the glory—to the ages. אָמֵן, Amen.

12

¹I therefore appeal to you, brothers, through the compassions of God, to present your bodies *as* a sacrifice: living, holy, acceptable to God—your logicalᵉ עֲבֹדָה, 'avodah. ²And be not conformed to this age, but be transformed by the renewing of the mind for your ex-

---

ᵃ see בְּמִדְבַּר *B'mid'bar* 15:17-21

ᵇ יְשַׁעְיָהוּ *Y'sha'yahu* 59:20-21; cf. יִרְמְיָהוּ *Yir'm'yahu* 31:33-34
ᶜ יְשַׁעְיָהוּ *Y'sha'yahu* 40:13 (LXX)
ᵈ אִיּוֹב *Iyov* 41:3(11)
ᵉ "logical" or "reasonable"—λογικὴν, logiken; Young's says, "intelligent," that is, "to have understanding" (archaic definition)

Obedience to civil power.   Romans 13:9

amining what *is* the will of God—the good and acceptable and perfect *will*. ³For I say through the *unmerited* favor that was given to me, to everyone who is among you, not to think *of yourselves* above what *you* ought to think, but to think *in such a way* so as to think soundly, *just* as God dealt to each *of you* a measure of faith. ⁴For as in one *individual's* body we *each* have many members, and all the members do not have the same function, ⁵so we, the many, are one body in Messiah, and each one members of one another.

⁶And *since we are* having different gifts according to the *unmerited* favor that was given to us: if prophecy, "*Use it* according to the proportion of faith!" ⁷or service, "*Use it* in the serving!" or he who is teaching, "*Use it* in the teaching!" ⁸or he who is exhorting, "*Use it* in the exhortation!" He who is giving, "In generosity!" He who is leading, "In diligence!" He who is doing *loving*-kindness, "In cheerfulness."

⁹The love unfeigned *is this:* abhorring the evil; sticking to the good; ¹⁰tenderly loving[a] one another in the love of brothers; going before[b] one another in *showing* the honor; ¹¹in the diligence, not sluggish; in the רוּחַ, ruach, fervent; *in* the Master, serving; ¹²in the hope, rejoicing; in the oppression, enduring; in the prayer, steadfastly continuing; ¹³to the needs of the קְדוֹשִׁים, Q'doshiym, contributing; the hospitality *to strangers,* pursuing.

¹⁴Bless those *who are* persecuting you—bless, and not curse. ¹⁵*You are* to rejoice with the rejoicing *ones,* and to weep with the weeping *ones.* ¹⁶Be of the same mind one toward another, not thinking the high things; but going along with the humble-minded *ones,* become not wise in your own conceit. ¹⁷*Be* giving back to no one evil for evil, providing right things in the sight of all men.

¹⁸If possible—so far as *it* is in you—*be* living in peace with all men, ¹⁹not avenging yourselves, loved ones, but give place to the wrath *of God*, for it has been written, "VENGEANCE *IS* MINE; I WILL REPAY," says ADONAI. ²⁰"BUT IF YOUR ENEMY HUNGERS, FEED HIM; IF HE THIRSTS, GIVE HIM DRINK. FOR *IN* DOING THIS, YOU WILL HEAP COALS OF FIRE ON HIS HEAD."[c] ²¹Be not overcome by the evil, but overcome the evil with the good.

13 ¹Let every soul be submitted to the higher authorities, for there is no authority except by God, and those existing authorities are appointed by God, ²so that he who is setting himself against the authority has resisted against God's decree. And those *who are* resisting will receive judgment to themselves.

³For those *who are* ruling are not a terror to *your* good actions, but to the evil *actions*. And do you want to not be afraid of the authority? That which is good, be doing, and you will be commended for it, ⁴for it[d] is a servant of God to you for good. But if you do that which is evil, be fearing, for it does not bear the sword in vain. For it is a servant of God—an avenger for wrath to him who is doing that which is evil.

⁵Therefore, it is necessary to be submitted *to the rulers*, not only because of the wrath, but also because of the conscience. ⁶Indeed, because of this, you also pay taxes, for they are servants of God, attending continually to this very thing. ⁷Return to all *people* THEIR dues: to whom taxes *are due,* the taxes; to whom customs,[e] the customs; to whom fear, the fear; to whom honor, the honor.

⁸Owe nothing to anyone, except to love one another; for he who is loving the other—he has fulfilled תּוֹרָה, Torah. ⁹For, "YOU MUST NOT COMMIT ADULTERY," "YOU MUST DO NO MURDER," "YOU MUST NOT STEAL,"[f] "YOU MUST NOT

---

[a] "tenderly loving"—Young's says, "kindly affectioned to"
[b] "going before" or "outdoing"
[c] דְּבָרִים *D'variym* 32:35; מִשְׁלֵי *Mish'lei* 25:21-22
[d] "it"—that is, "the authority" (see verse 3)
[e] "customs," as in import customs, duty taxes
[f] Some mss insert, "you must not give false testimony"

COVET,"ᵃ and if there is any other command, it is summed up in this word—in this: "YOU MUST LOVE YOUR NEIGHBOR AS YOURSELF."ᵇ ¹⁰The love does no evil to the neighbor. Therefore, the love IS the fullness of תּוֹרָה, Torah.

¹¹And *consider* this, knowing the time: that the hour IS already *come* for you to be aroused out of sleep, for nearer IS our salvation now than when we *first* believed. ¹²The night has advanced, and the day comes near. Let us lay aside, therefore, the actions of the darkness, and let us put on the armor of the light. ¹³As in daytime, let us walk respectably—not in orgies and drunkennesses, not in bedroom liaisonsᶜ and sensuality, not in infighting and fierce rivalry. ¹⁴But put on the Master יֵשׁוּעַ, Yeshua *the* Messiah, and make no provision for the flesh—for *satisfying its* lusts.

14

¹And receive him who is weak in the faith, *but* not to *make* determinations of *his* reasonings. ²One believes that he may eat all things, but he who is weak eats *only* herbs *and vegetables.* ³Let him who is eating *all things* not despise him who is not eating *all things;* and let him who is not eating *all things* not judge him who is eating *all things,* for God has received him.

⁴*And* you—who are you that are judging another's house servant? To his own master he stands or falls, and he will be made to stand, for the Masterᵈ is able to make him stand.

⁵For one judges one day above another, and another judges every day ALIKE. Let each in his own mind be fully assured. ⁶He who is regarding the day—he regards IT to *honor* the Master.ᵉ He who is eating *all things*—he eats to *honor* the Master, for he gives thanks to God. And he who is not eating *all things*—to *honor* the Master, he does not eat, and gives thanks to God.

⁷For none of us lives to himself, and none dies to himself. ⁸Indeed, both if we live, we live to the Master, and if we die, we die to the Master. *So* then, both if we live and if we die, we are the Master's; ⁹for because of this, Messiah diedᶠ and lived again, so that of both *the* dead and *the* living, He may be *the* Master.

¹⁰And you—why do you judge your brother? or again, you—why do you treat your brother with contempt? For we will all stand at the judgment seat of God,ᵍ ¹¹for it has been written, "'I live!' says ADONAI. 'TO ME EVERY KNEE WILL BOW, AND EVERY TONGUE WILL CONFESS TO GOD.'"ʰ ¹²So, then, each of us will give *an* accounting to God concerning himself. ¹³No longer, therefore, may we judge one another, but rather, judge this: not to put a stumbling-stone or a trapping-stickⁱ before the brother.

¹⁴I have known, and am persuaded in the Master יֵשׁוּעַ, Yeshua, that nothing IS impureʲ of itself, except to him who is considering anything to be impure—to that one, IT IS impure. ¹⁵For if your brother is grieved through foods, you no longer walk according to love. With your foods, do not destroy that one for whom Messiah died!

¹⁶Let not, then, your good *thing* be spoken evil of, ¹⁷for the Reign of God is not *a matter of* eating and drinking, but *of* righteousness and peace and joy in the רוּחַ הַקֹּדֶשׁ, Ruach HaQodesh. ¹⁸For he who in this thing is enslaved to the Messiah IS acceptable to God and approved of *by* men.

ᵃ שְׁמוֹת Sh'mot 20:13ff; דְּבָרִים D'variym 5:17ff
ᵇ וַיִּקְרָא Vayiq'ra 19:18
ᶜ "bedroom liaisons"—κοίταις, koitais; Young's says, "chamberings"
ᵈ "the Master"—some mss say, "God"
ᵉ Some mss insert, "and he who is not regarding the day, he does not regard IT to *honor* the Master"
ᶠ Some mss insert, "and rose again"
ᵍ "God"—some mss say, "the Messiah"
ʰ יְשַׁעְיָהוּ Y'sha'yahu 45:23 (LXX)
ⁱ "trapping-stick"—σκάνδαλον, skandalon; Young's says, "offence"
ʲ "impure"—lit. "common" (κοινὸν, koinon), all three times in this verse. Young's (and nearly all other translations) says, "unclean." While the passage may partially relate to foods that are *ritually* "clean" and "unclean," Paul is not saying that Leviticus 11 "unkosher" foods should no longer be considered "unclean." On the contrary, this whole section points to verse 21.

¹⁹So then, let us pursue the things of peace, and the things of building up one another. ²⁰Do not throw down the work of God for the sake of foods! All things, indeed, ARE pure, but evil IS to the man who is eating through that which causes stumbling. ²¹IT IS not right to eat meat, nor to drink wine, nor to DO ANYTHING in which your brother stumbles.ᵃ

²²You have faith *in such matters! but* have that *just* to yourself in the sight of God. Happy is he who is not judging himself by what he approves. ²³But he who is wavering,ᵇ if he eats, has been condemned, because IT IS not of faith, and all that IS not of faith is sin.

15 ¹And we ought—we who are strong—to carry the weaknesses of the weak, but not to please ourselves. ²Let each one of us please the neighbor for *the sake of* good, toward building *him* up. ³For even the Messiah did not please Himself, but, as it has been written,

"The disgraces of those denouncing You fell upon me."ᶜ

⁴For as many things as were previously written were writtenᵈ for our instruction, so that through the perseverance and through the exhortation of the Scriptures, we might have the hope.

⁵And may the God of the perseverance and of the exhortation give to you to have the same mind toward one another, according to Messiah יֵשׁוּעַ, Yeshua, ⁶so that with one mind—with one mouth—you may glorify the God and Father of our Master יֵשׁוּעַ, Yeshua *the* Messiah. ⁷Therefore, receive one another, as also the Messiah received you, to the glory of God.

⁸For I say:ᵉ Messiah has become a servant of *the* Circumcision for the truth of God, to confirm the promises *made* to the fathers, ⁹and *for* the גּוֹיִם, Goyim—for *loving*-kindness to glorify God. As it has been written,

"Because of this I will confess to You among *the* גּוֹיִם, Goyim, and to Your Name I will sing melodies."ᶠ

¹⁰and again it says,

"Rejoice, you גּוֹיִם, Goyim, with His people!"ᵍ

¹¹and again,

"Praise ADONAI, all you גּוֹיִם, Goyim! and commend Him, all the peoples!"ʰ

¹²and again, יְשַׁעְיָהוּ, Y'sha'yahu says,

"There will be the root of יִשַׁי, Yishai, and he who is rising *up* to rule גּוֹיִם, Goyim—upon him will גּוֹיִם, Goyim hope."ⁱ

¹³And the God of the hope will fill you with all joy and peace in the believing, for your abounding in the hope in *the* power of the רוּחַ הַקֹּדֶשׁ, Ruach HaQodesh.

¹⁴And I am persuaded regarding you, my brothers—I myself also—that you yourselves are also full of goodness, having been filled with all the knowledge, *and* also able to warn one another. ¹⁵Additionally, I wrote to you the more boldly,ʲ as reminding you in part, because of the *unmerited* favor that is given to me by God ¹⁶for my being a servant of *the* Messiah יֵשׁוּעַ, Yeshua to the גּוֹיִם, Goyim—acting as כֹּהֵן, kohen in the Good News of God—so that the offering up of the גּוֹיִם, Goyim may become acceptable, set apart by the רוּחַ הַקֹּדֶשׁ, Ruach HaQodesh.ᵏ

¹⁷I have, then, the boasting in Messiah יֵשׁוּעַ, Yeshua in the things pertaining to

---

ᵃ Some mss insert, "or is made to fall, or is weak"
ᵇ "wavering"—Young says, "making a difference"
ᶜ תְּהִלִּים T'hiliym 69:10(9)
ᵈ "written"—some mss say, "previously written"
ᵉ Some mss insert, "יֵשׁוּעַ, Yeshua"
ᶠ תְּהִלִּים T'hiliym 18:50(49); שְׁמוּאֵל ב Sh'muel Beit 22:50
ᵍ דְּבָרִים D'variym 32:43
ʰ תְּהִלִּים T'hiliym 117:1
ⁱ יְשַׁעְיָהוּ Y'sha'yahu 11:10
ʲ Some mss insert, "brothers"
ᵏ Paul shows that, as a Messianic Jew, he is fulfilling the ancient calling and purpose of Yis'rael, according to שְׁמוֹת Sh'mot 19:3-6 (cf. 1Ke.2:19). See also Acts 13:44-49.

God. ¹⁸For I will not dare to speak anything of the things that *are* not *what the* Messiah accomplished through me, to *the* obedience of *the* גּוֹיִם, Goyim—by word and action, ¹⁹in power of signs and wonders, in power of the רוּחַ אֱלֹהִים, Ruach 'Elohiym—so that I, from יְרוּשָׁלַיִם, Y'rushalayim, and in a circle as far as Illyricum, have fully proclaimed the Good News of the Messiah. ²⁰And so, *I was* making it *my* aim to proclaim Good News not where Messiah was *already* named (so that I would not build upon another's foundation), ²¹but as it has been written,

"To whom it was not told about him, they will see; and they who have not heard will understand."ᵃ

²²*This is* why I was also hindered many times from coming to you. ²³But now—no longer having a place in these regions, and having a longing for many years to come to you—²⁴when I go on to Spain,ᵇ I hope, then, in going through, to see you and to be sent by you on my way there, when I have first been filled of you for a while.ᶜ

²⁵And now, I am going on to יְרוּשָׁלַיִם, Y'rushalayim, serving the קְדוֹשִׁים, Q'doshiym, ²⁶for it pleased Macedonia and Achaia well to make a certain contribution for the poor of the קְדוֹשִׁים, Q'doshiym who ARE in יְרוּשָׁלַיִם, Y'rushalayim. ²⁷Indeed, it pleased *them* well, *as* also they are their debtors—for if the גּוֹיִם, Goyim participated in their spiritual things, they ought also to serve them in the material things. ²⁸Having finished this, then, and having sealed this fruit to them, I will return to Spain through you. ²⁹And I have known that, coming to you, I will come in the fullness of the blessingᵈ of Messiah.

³⁰And I call upon you, brothers, through our Master יֵשׁוּעַ, Yeshua *the* Messiah and through the love of the רוּחַ, Ruach, to strive together with me in the prayers for me to God, ³¹so that I may be delivered from those in יְהוּדָה, Y'hudah *who are* not believing, and that my service for יְרוּשָׁלַיִם, Y'rushalayim may become acceptable to the קְדוֹשִׁים, Q'doshiym, ³²so that in joy, coming to you through the will of God, I may be refreshed with you. ³³And the God of the peace IS with you all. אָמֵן, Amen.

16 ¹And I commend you to Phoebe our sister (*who is* also being a servant of the Called-Forthᵉ that IS in Cenchrea) ²that you may receive her in the Master, in a manner worthy ofᶠ *the* קְדוֹשִׁים, Q'doshiym, and assist her in whatever matter she may have need of you—for she also became a matriarchᵍ of many, and of myself.

³Greet Prisca and Aquila, my fellow-workers in Messiah יֵשׁוּעַ, Yeshua, ⁴who laid down their own neck for my life, *and* to whom not only I give thanks, but also all the Called-Forth-Communitiesʰ of the גּוֹיִם, Goyim; ⁵and *greet* the Called-Forthⁱ at their house. Also greet Epænetus, my beloved *friend*, who is *the* first-fruit of Asiaʲ to Messiah.

⁶Greet מִרְיָם, Mir'yam, who labored much for you;ᵏ ⁷*and* greet Andronicus and Junias, my relatives and my fellow-captives, who are of note among the emissaries, who also have been in Messiah before me.

⁸Greet Ampliatus, my beloved *friend* in the Master; ⁹greet Urbanus, our fellow-worker in Messiah, and Stachys my beloved *friend*; ¹⁰greet Apelles, the proven in Messiah; greet those of the HOUSEHOLD of Aristobulus; ¹¹greet Herodion, my relative; greet those of the HOUSEHOLD of Narcissus, who are in the Master; ¹²greet Try-

---

ᵃ יְשַׁעְיָהוּ *Y'sha'yahu* 52:15
ᵇ Some mss insert, "I will come to you"
ᶜ "for a while"—lit. "in part"
ᵈ Some mss insert, "of the Good News"

ᵉ "Called-Forth"—ἐκκλησίας, ekklesias; see מַתִּתְיָהוּ *Matit'yahu* 16:18; also in verse 23
ᶠ "in a manner worthy of"—Young's says, "as *it* becomes"
ᵍ "matriarch" or "benefactor" or "patroness"; Young says "leader"
ʰ "Called-Forth-Communities"—ἐκκλησίαι, ekklesiai; also v. 16
ⁱ "Called-Forth"—ἐκκλησίαν, ekklesian
ʲ "Asia"—some mss say, "Achaia"
ᵏ "you"—some mss say, "us"

phena and Tryphosa, who are laboring in the Master; greet Persis, the beloved *friend*, who labored much in the Master.

¹³Greet Rufus, the chosen one in the Master, and his mother and mine; ¹⁴greet Asyncritus, Phlegon, Hermes, Patrobas, Hermas, and the brothers with them; ¹⁵greet Philologus and Julia, Nereus and his sister, and Olympas, and all the קְדוֹשִׁים, Q'doshiym with them; ¹⁶greet one another in a holy kiss. All the Called-Forth-Communities of Messiah greet you.

¹⁷And I call upon you, brothers, to watch out *for* those who are causing the divisions and the stumbling-blocks—contrary to the teaching that you learned—and *to* turn away from them. ¹⁸Indeed, such *people* do not serve our Master,[a] Messiah, but their own belly, and through the smooth word and flattering speech, they deceive the hearts of the innocent. ¹⁹For *word of* your obedience reached to *them* all; regarding you, therefore, I rejoice. And I want you to be wise as to the good, but innocent as to the evil. ²⁰And the God of the peace will quickly shatter הַשָׂטָן, HaSatan under your feet; the *unmerited* favor of our Master יֵשׁוּעַ, Yeshua[b] IS with you.[c]

²¹Timothy, my fellow-worker, and my relatives Lucius and Jason and Sosipater greet you. ²²(I, Tertius, who wrote *down* this letter, greet you in the Master.) ²³Gaius my host, and *that* of the whole Called-Forth, greets you. Erastus (the steward of the city) and Quartus the brother greet you.[d]

²⁵And to Him who is able to stabilize you according to my Good News and the proclaiming of יֵשׁוּעַ, Yeshua *the* Messiah, according to the revelation of the mystery (having been kept silent in the times of the ages, ²⁶but now having been made evident, also, through *the* prophetic Scriptures, according to a command of the age-enduring God), having been made known to all the גּוֹיִם, Goyim for obedience of faith—²⁷to the only wise God, through יֵשׁוּעַ, Yeshua *the* Messiah, to Him IS glory to the ages! אָמֵן, Amen.

---

[a] Some mss insert, "יֵשׁוּעַ, Yeshua"
[b] Some mss insert, "Messiah"
[c] Some mss insert, "אָמֵן, Amen!"
[d] Some mss continue with verse 24, "The *unmerited* favor of our Master יֵשׁוּעַ, Yeshua *the* Messiah, IS with you all. אָמֵן, Amen."

PAUL'S LETTER TO THE

Colossians

1 ¹From Paul,[a] an emissary of Messiah יֵשׁוּעַ, Yeshua through the will of God, and Timothy the brother; ²to the קְדוֹשִׁים, Q'doshiym in Colossæ, and to the faithful brothers in Messiah: *unmerited* favor to you, and peace from God our Father![b]

³We give thanks to God, Father of our Master יֵשׁוּעַ, Yeshua *the* Messiah, *and are* always praying for you, ⁴having heard of your faith in Messiah יֵשׁוּעַ, Yeshua and of the love which you have to all the קְדוֹשִׁים, Q'doshiym ⁵because of the hope that is laid up for you in the Heavens. *This is that* which you heard of beforehand in the word of the truth of the Good News ⁶which is come to you, as also in all the world is bearing fruit and growing[c]—as also in you, from the day in which you

---

[a] "Paul"—Παῦλος, Paulos; see 1 Timothy 1:1
[b] Some mss insert, "and the Master יֵשׁוּעַ, Yeshua, Messiah"
[c] Some mss omit, "and growing"

heard and knew the *unmerited* favor of God in truth, ⁷as you learned from Epaphras, our beloved fellow-slave, who is a faithful servant of the Messiah for you, ⁸who also declared to us your love in the רוּחַ, Ruach. ⁹Because of this, from the day in which we heard, we also do not stop praying for you and asking that you may be filled with the full knowledge of His will in all wisdom and spiritual understanding, ¹⁰to walk worthily in the Master *so as to be* all pleasing, being fruitful in every good action and increasing in the knowledge of God, ¹¹*and* being made strong in all power according to the strength of His glory—to all perseverance and patience with joy—*and* ¹²giving thanks to the Father, who made you[a] sufficient for the sharing of the inheritance of the קְדוֹשִׁים, Q'doshiym in the light.

¹³*It is He* who rescued us out of the authority of the darkness and transferred *us* into the Reign of the Son of His love ¹⁴(in whom we have the redemption[b]—the forgiveness of the sins), ¹⁵who is the image of the invisible God, first-born of all creation, ¹⁶because in Him were all the things created in the heavens and upon the earth: those visible, and those invisible. Whether thrones or dominions or rulers or authorities, all things have been created through Him and for Him, ¹⁷and He Himself is before all, and all the things have held together in Him.

¹⁸And He Himself is the head of the Body—the Called-Forth[c]—who is the beginning, the first-born out of the dead, so that He Himself would become first in all THINGS, ¹⁹because in Him it pleased all the fullness *of the Deity*[d] to dwell ²⁰and, through Him, to reconcile all the things to Himself, having made peace through the blood of His *execution* stake; *all are reconciled* through Him, whether the things on the earth or the things in the heavens.

²¹And you, once being alienated and enemies in the mind, *engaged* in the evil actions; ²²yet now He reconciled *you* in the body of His flesh through the death, *in order* to present you *as* holy and unblemished and unblameable before Himself, ²³if *only* you also remain in the faith, being founded and settled and not moved away from the hope of the Good News which you heard (*that* which was proclaimed in all creation that IS under the heaven, of which I became —I, Paul—a servant).

²⁴I now rejoice in the sufferings *I endure* for you, and fill up the things of the oppressions of the Messiah *that are* lacking in my flesh for *the sake of* His Body, which is the Called-Forth,[e] ²⁵of which I became a servant according to the stewardship of God that was given to me for you, to fulfill the word of God, ²⁶the mystery that has been hidden from the ages and from the generations but now is revealed to His קְדוֹשִׁים, Q'doshiym, ²⁷to whom God wanted to make known what ARE the riches of the glory of this mystery among the גּוֹיִם, Goyim— which is Messiah in you, the hope of the glory, ²⁸whom we proclaim, warning every man and teaching every man in all wisdom, so that we may present every man perfect in Messiah.[f] ²⁹*It is this* for which I also labor, striving according to His working that is working in me in power.

2 ¹For I want you to know how great a conflict I have for you, and *for* those in Laodicea, and *for* as many as have not seen my face in the flesh: ²that their hearts may be encouraged, being united in love and to all riches of the full assurance of the understanding, *leading* to the full knowledge of the mystery of God—*that is*, of Messiah,[g] ³in whom are hidden all the treasures of the wisdom and knowledge.

⁴I say this so that no one may deceive you in persuasive words ⁵(for even if I am absent in the flesh, I am yet with you in the רוּחַ, ruach, rejoicing and seeing your order and the steadfastness of your faith in re-

---

[a] "you"—some mss say, "us"
[b] Some mss insert, "through His blood"
[c] "Called-Forth"—ἐκκλησίας, ekklesias; see *Mt.* 16:18
[d] cf. Colossians 2:9
[e] "Called-Forth"—ἐκκλησία, ekklesia; see *Mt.* 16:18
[f] Some mss insert, "יֵשׁוּעַ, Yeshua"
[g] "mystery of... Messiah"—some mss say, "mystery of the God and Father, and of the Messiah"

Spiritual life.

gard to Messiah): ⁶as, then, you received Messiah יֵשׁוּעַ, Yeshua the Master, in Him, walk! ⁷being rooted and built up in Him, and made firm in the faith (as you were taught), abounding[a] in thanksgiving.

⁸See that no one will be carrying you away as plunder through the philosophy and empty deceit according to the tradition of men—according to the basic principles of the world—and not according to Messiah, ⁹because in Him all the fullness of the Deity dwells bodily, ¹⁰and you are made full in Him who is the head of all rule and authority, ¹¹in whom you were also circumcised with a circumcision not made with hands (in the putting-off of the body[b] of the flesh in the circumcision of the Messiah), ¹²being buried with Him in the immersion (in which you also rose with HIM through the faith of the working of God, who raised Him from the dead).

¹³And you being dead in the missteps and the uncircumcision of your flesh, He made you alive together with Him, having forgiven us all the missteps, ¹⁴*and* having blotted out the handwriting in the decrees that is against us (that was opposed to us); and He has taken it out of the way, having nailed it to the *execution* stake. ¹⁵Having stripped the rulers and the authorities, he made a spectacle of them openly, having triumphed over them in it.

¹⁶So then, let no one judge you in eating and in drinking, or in respect to a חַג, chag, or of a חֹדֶשׁ, chodesh, or of שַׁבָּתוֹת, shabatot, ¹⁷which are a shadow of the coming things; but the body IS of the Messiah. ¹⁸Let no one cheat you of your prize *through* delighting in the humble-mindedness,[c] and IN worship of the Messengers, delving into the things he has[d] seen, being vainly puffed up by the mind of his flesh, ¹⁹and not holding *onto* the Head, from which the whole body—through the joints and ligaments being supplied and knit together—may increase with the increase of God.

²⁰If you died with Messiah from the basic principles of the world, *then* why, as *if you are still* living in the world, are you submitted to *its* decrees? ²¹"Do not touch! nor taste! nor handle!" ²²(which are all *decrees leading* to destruction with the using *of them*) according to the commands and teachings of men—²³which are, indeed, having an appearance of wisdom in self-imposed religion[e] and humble-mindedness and *severe* neglecting of *the* body, *but these are* not of any value, *except* to a satisfying of the flesh.

3

¹If, then, you were raised with the Messiah, look for the things above, where the Messiah is seated at the right hand of God. ²Have in mind the things above, not the things upon the earth, ³for you died, and your life has been hidden with the Messiah in God. ⁴Then, when the Messiah—your[f] life—is revealed, we will also be revealed with him in glory.

⁵Put to death, then, the members that ARE upon the earth—sexual immorality, uncleanness, *lustful* passion, evil desire, and the covetousness (which is idolatry)—⁶because of which things the wrath of God comes upon the sons of the obstinance,[g] ⁷*and* in which you also once walked when you lived in these. ⁸But now, even you, put off the whole *of* wrath, rage, wickedness, evil-speaking, *and* filthy talking out of your mouth.

⁹Do not lie to one another, having put off the old man[h] with his practices, ¹⁰and having put on the new, which is renewed in regard to knowledge according to the image of Him who created him, ¹¹where there is not Greek and יְהוּדִי, Y'hudiy, Circumcision and Uncircumcision,[i] βάρβαρος, Bar-

---

[a] Some mss insert, "in it"
[b] Some mss insert, "of the sins"
[c] "humble-mindedness"—in this context, possibly asceticism, or other form of self-abasement; also in vs. 23
[d] Some mss insert, "not"
[e] "self-imposed religion"—Young's: "will-worship"
[f] "your"—some mss say, "our"
[g] Some early mss omit, "upon the sons of the obstinance"
[h] "the old man," that is, "the old self"
[i] "Circumcision and Uncircumcision"—that is, Jew and Gentile

baros, Scythian, slave, freeman—but the all and in all: Messiah.

¹²Therefore, as chosen ones of God, holy and loved, put on *the* inward parts of compassion, kindness, humble-mindedness, humility, *and* patience, ¹³bearing with one another and forgiving each other if anyone may have a complaint with anyone. And as the Master[a] forgave you, so also *should* you *forgive*. ¹⁴But above all these things, HAVE love, which is a bond of the perfection. ¹⁵And let the peace of the Messiah[b] rule in your hearts, to which you were also called in one Body, and become thankful.

¹⁶Let the word of Messiah live in you richly, teaching and warning each other in all wisdom, singing in melodies, praises, and spiritual songs, with the *unmerited* favor[c] in your hearts to God.[d] ¹⁷And all *things*—whatever you do in word or in action—DO all things in the Name of the Master עֵשׁוּיַ, Yeshua, giving thanks to God the Father through Him.

¹⁸The wives! be submitted to the husbands, as is fitting in the Master.

¹⁹The husbands! love the wives, and be not bitter with them.

²⁰The children! obey the parents in all things, for this is well-pleasing to the Master.

²¹The fathers! do not stir up your children *to resentment*, so that they *will* not become discouraged.

²²The slaves! obey in all things those who are *your* masters according to the flesh. *Do this* not just when the master has his eye on you[e]—as men-pleasers—but in simplicity of heart, fearing the Master.[f] ²³Whatever you do, do *it* out of *your* soul, as to the Master and not to men, ²⁴having known that from the Master you will receive the payment of the inheritance—*it is* the Master, Messiah, you serve. ²⁵For he who is doing unrighteously will receive *back for* what he did unrighteously, and there is no acceptance of persons.[g]

4

¹The masters! give that which is righteous and equal to the slaves, having known that you also have a Master in the Heaven.

²Continue *steadfastly* in the prayer, *staying* awake in it in thanksgiving, ³praying at the same time for us also, that God may open a door to us for the word, to speak the mystery of the Messiah (because of which I also have been bound)—⁴that I may *make* it evident, as I ought to speak.

⁵Walk in wisdom toward those *who are* outside *the community*, redeeming the time, ⁶*with* your word always in *unmerited* favor—being seasoned with salt—to know how you ought to answer each one.

⁷Tychicus, the beloved brother and faithful servant and fellow-slave in the Master, will make known to you all the things about me—⁸*he* whom I sent to you for this very thing, so that you might know the things about us,[h] and he might encourage your hearts. ⁹With *him will be* Onesimus, the faithful and beloved brother, who is of you. They will make known to you all *the* things that ARE happening here.

¹⁰Aristarchus my fellow-captive greets you, as does Mark (the cousin[i] of בַּר־נָבָא, Bar-Naba, concerning whom you received commands—if he comes to you, receive him) ¹¹and עֵשׁוּיַ, Yeshua (who is called Justus): these alone, who are of the Circumcision, ARE fellow-workers for the Reign of God who became a comfort to me.

¹²Epaphras greets you, who IS of you, a slave of Messiah עֵשׁוּיַ, Yeshua,[j] always striving for you in the prayers, so that you may stand perfect and fully assured[k] in all the will of God. ¹³For I testify of him, that he

---

[a] "Master"—some mss say, "Messiah"
[b] "the Messiah"—some mss say, "God"
[c] "teaching and warning..., singing in melodies..., with the *unmerited* favor" or "teaching and warning... in melodies..., singing with the *unmerited* favor"
[d] "God"—some mss say, "the Master"
[e] "not just when the master has his eye on you"— literally, "not in eye-service"
[f] "the Master"—some mss say, "God"

[g] "acceptance of persons"—that is, favoritism
[h] "you... us"—some mss say, "he... you"
[i] "cousin"—Young's says, "nephew"
[j] Some mss omit, "עֵשׁוּיַ, Yeshua"
[k] "fully assured"—some mss say, "made full"

No longer a slave.

has much pain[a] for you, and those in Laodicea, and those in Hierapolis.

[14]Luke the beloved physician greets you, *as* also *does* Demas.

[15]Greet those brothers in Laodicea, and *also* Nymphas, and the Called-Forth[b] in her[c] house. [16]And when this letter is read among you, see[d] that it is also read among the Called-Forth[e] of the Laodiceans, and that the LETTER from Laodicea you may also read. [17]And say to Archippus, "See to the service that you received in the Master, that you may fulfill it."

[18]The greeting by the hand of me (Paul) —remember my bonds: the *unmerited* favor IS with you.[f]

---

[a] "pain" or "labor"—some mss say, "zeal"
[b] "Called-Forth"—ἐκκλησίαν, ekklesian; see *Mt.* 16:18
[c] "her"—some mss say, "his"
[d] "see"—Young's says, "cause"
[e] "Called-Forth"—ἐκκλησία, ekklesia; see מַתִּתְיָהוּ *Matit'yahu* 16:18
[f] Some mss conclude, "אָמֵן, Amen."

PAUL'S LETTER TO

Philemon

[1]*From* Paul,[a] a prisoner of Messiah יֵשׁוּעַ, Yeshua, and Timothy the brother; to Philemon, our beloved and fellow-worker, [2]and Apphia our sister,[b] and Archippus our fellow-soldier, and the Called-Forth[c] in your house: [3]*unmerited* favor to you, and peace from God our Father and the Master יֵשׁוּעַ, Yeshua *the* Messiah!

[4]I give thanks to my God, always making mention of you in my prayers, [5]*because I am* hearing of your love and faith that you have toward the Master יֵשׁוּעַ, Yeshua, and toward all the קְדוֹשִׁים, Q'doshiym.

[6]*And I pray* that the sharing of your faith *together* may become active in the full knowledge of every good thing that IS in us[d] toward Messiah.[e] [7]For I had much joy and encouragement in your love, because the inward parts of the קְדוֹשִׁים, Q'doshiym have been refreshed through you, *my* brother.

[8]Therefore, having much boldness in Messiah to command you *to do* that which is fitting, [9]*yet* because of the love, I *would* rather appeal (being such a one as Paul the aged, and now also a prisoner of Messiah יֵשׁוּעַ, Yeshua): [10]I appeal to you concerning my child—whom I became father to[f] in the bonds—Onesimus, [11]who was once worthless to you, but now is useful both to me and to you. [12]*It is he* whom I sent again to you, and he[g] (who is my own inward parts) [13]whom I wanted to retain to myself, so that for your sake he might serve me in the bonds of the Good News. [14]But apart from your mind, I wanted to do nothing, so that your good deed may not be of obligation, but of willingness. [15]For perhaps because of this he separated *from you* for a time, so that you would have him *back* age-enduringly, [16]no longer as a slave, but above a slave—a beloved brother (especially to me, and how much more to you), both in the flesh and in the Master!

[17]If, then, you have sharing with me, receive him as me. [18]And if he hurt you, or owes anything, be charging this to me. [19]I, Paul, wrote *this* with my hand: I—I will re-

---

[a] "Paul"—Παῦλος, Paulos; see 1 Timothy 1:1
[b] "sister"—some mss say, "beloved"
[c] "Called-Forth"—ἐκκλησία, ekklesia; see *Mt.* 16:18
[d] "us"—some mss say, "you"
[e] Some mss insert, "יֵשׁוּעַ, Yeshua"
[f] "became father to"—lit. "brought forth"
[g] "he"—some mss say, "him receive"

pay *you* (so that I may not say to you that you even owe yourself to me). ²⁰Yes, brother, I may have benefit of you in the Master; refresh my inward parts in Messiah.ᵃ ²¹Having been confident in your obedience, I wrote to you, having known that you will do even above what I may say. ²²And at the same time, also prepare a place for me where I may stay as a guest,

ᵃ "Messiah"—some mss say, "the Master"

for I hope that through your prayers I will be given to you.

²³Epaphras, my fellow-captive in Messiah יֵשׁוּעַ, Yeshua, greets you, *as do* ²⁴Mark, Aristarchus, Demas, *and* Luke, my fellow-workmen!

²⁵The *unmerited* favor of the Master יֵשׁוּעַ, Yeshua *the* Messiah *is* with your רוּחַ, ru-ach!ᵇ

ᵇ Some mss conclude, "אָמֵן, Amen."

PAUL'S LETTER TO THE

Ephesians

1

¹*From* Paul,ᵃ an emissary of Messiah יֵשׁוּעַ, Yeshua through the will of God; to the קְדוֹשִׁים, Q'doshiym who are in Ephesus, and to the faithful in Messiah יֵשׁוּעַ, Yeshua: ²*unmerited* favor to you, and peace from God our Father and the Master יֵשׁוּעַ, Yeshua *the* Messiah!

³Blessed *is* the God and Father of our Master יֵשׁוּעַ, Yeshua *the* Messiah, who *has* blessed us with every spiritual blessing in the Heavenly places in Messiah, ⁴as He chose us in Him before the foundation of the world (for our being holy and unblemished before Him). In love, ⁵He has predetermined us to the adoption as sons through יֵשׁוּעַ, Yeshua *the* Messiah to Himself (according to the good pleasure of His will), ⁶to the praise of the glory of His *unmerited* favor, of which He made us favored in the *One being* loved. ⁷*This is He* in whom we have the redemption through His blood *and* the release from *our* missteps, according to the riches of His *unmerited* favor, ⁸in which He abounded toward us in all wisdom and insight. ⁹He has made known to us the mystery of His will according to His good pleasure, which He purposed in Himself ¹⁰in regard to the stewardship of the fullness of the times: to bring into one *thing* the whole *thing* in the Messiah—the things in the Heavens and the things upon the earth *brought together* in Him.

¹¹*This is He* in whom we also obtained an inheritance, being predetermined according to the purpose of Him who is working all the things according to the purpose of His will, ¹²for our being to the praise of His glory—EVEN those who first hoped in the Messiah. ¹³*This is He* in whom you also *believed*, having heard the word of the truth (the Good News of your salvation), *and* in whom also, having believed, you were sealed with the רוּחַ הַקֹּדֶשׁ, Ruach Ha-Qodesh of the promise ¹⁴(who is a downpayment of our inheritance, towards the redemption of *that* acquired possession), to the praise of His glory.

¹⁵Because of this, I also (having heard of your faith in the Master יֵשׁוּעַ, Yeshua, and *your* love to all the קְדוֹשִׁים, Q'doshiym) ¹⁶do not stop giving thanks for you *and* making mention of you in my prayers, ¹⁷asking that the God of our Master יֵשׁוּעַ, Yeshua *the* Messiah—the Father of the glory—may give to you a רוּחַ, ruach of wisdom and revelation in the recognition of Him.

ᵃ "Paul"—Παῦλος, Paulos; see 1 Timothy 1:1

The household of God.

¹⁸I pray that the eyes of your heart[a] *are* being enlightened for your knowing what the hope of His calling is, what the riches of the glory of His inheritance in the קְדוֹשִׁים, Q'doshiym *are*, ¹⁹and what the exceeding greatness of His power *is* to us who are believing, according to the working of the strength of His might, ²⁰which He worked in the Messiah (having raised him *up* out of the dead, and having set HIM at His right hand in the heavenly PLACES, ²¹far above all rule and authority and power and dominion and every name named—not only in this age, but also in the coming one). ²²And He put all things under his feet, and gave him *as* head over all things to the Called-Forth,[b] ²³which is his Body—the fullness of Him who is filling *up* all the *things* in all *ways*.

2 ¹You also *were* being dead in your missteps and the sins ²in which you once walked according to the age of this world (according to the ruler of the authority of the air, of the רוּחַ, ruach that is now working in the sons of obstinance,[c] ³among whom we all also once walked in the lusts of our flesh—doing the wants of the flesh and of the thoughts) and were by nature children of wrath, as the others *are* also.

⁴But God, being rich in *loving*-kindness (because of His great love with which He loved us—⁵even *while we were* being dead in the missteps), made us alive together with the Messiah (by *unmerited* favor you are having been saved), ⁶and raised US up together, and seated US together in the heavenly PLACES in Messiah יֵשׁוּעַ, Yeshua, ⁷so that in the ages that are coming, He might show the exceeding riches of His *unmerited* favor in kindness toward us in Messiah יֵשׁוּעַ, Yeshua. ⁸For by *unmerited* favor you are having been saved, through faith, and this not of *something* you did—

it is the gift of God, ⁹not of *your* actions—so that no one may boast. ¹⁰For we are His workmanship, created in Messiah יֵשׁוּעַ, Yeshua for good actions, which God prepared beforehand, so that in them we may walk.

¹¹Therefore, remember that at one time, you,[d] the גּוֹיִם, Goyim in the flesh (who are called Uncircumcision by those called Circumcision[e]—in the flesh, made by hands) —¹²that you were at that time apart from Messiah, having been alienated from the citizenship of יִשְׂרָאֵל, Yis'rael, and strangers to the בְּרִיתוֹת, b'riytot of the promise, having no hope and without God in the world. ¹³But now, in Messiah יֵשׁוּעַ, Yeshua, you—being at one time far off—became near in the blood of the Messiah.

¹⁴For He is our peace, who made *the* both one, and broke down the middle wall of the enclosure ¹⁵(having made useless[f] the hostility in His flesh, the תּוֹרָה, torah of the commands in decrees[g]), so that in Him He might create the two into one new man, making peace, ¹⁶and might reconcile both in one body to God through the *execution* stake, having killed the hostility by it. ¹⁷And having come, He proclaimed Good News: peace to you—the Far-off—and peace to the Near, ¹⁸for through Him we have the access to the Father—we both—in one רוּחַ, Ruach.

¹⁹Then, therefore, you are no longer strangers and sojourners, but you are fellow-citizens of the קְדוֹשִׁים, Q'doshiym and of the household of God, ²⁰being built upon the foundation of the emissaries and prophets —Messiah יֵשׁוּעַ, Yeshua Himself being *the* chief corner-STONE, ²¹in whom the whole

---

[a] "heart"—some mss say, "understanding"
[b] "Called-Forth"—ἐκκλησία, ekklesia; see מַתִּתְיָהוּ Matit'yahu 16:18
[c] "obstinance"—ἀπείθεια, apeitheia, a negative of πείθω, peitho, which is most often translated "trust" or "persuade." Here, Young says, "disobedience."
[d] following "you," Young adds "WERE"
[e] "Circumcision"—that is, Jews
[f] "made useless"—Young's says, "done away *with*"
[g] "The תּוֹרָה, torah of the commands in decrees" does not simply mean "the תּוֹרָה, Torah" monolithically, as such an understanding would put Paul in conflict with himself (cf. 1Ti. 1:8, Ro. 7:12). The phrase may be referring to either the Oral Law, or the commands of Torah that erect a "middle wall" between Israel and foreigners, indicating that its "breaking down" results in "a change of the תּוֹרָה, Torah" (עִבְרִים Iv'riym 7:12).

building, fitted together, increases to *become* a holy temple in ADONAI ²²(in whom you are also built together, for a home of God in the רוּחַ, Ruach).

3 ¹For this reason, I, Paul, *am* the prisoner of Messiah יֵשׁוּעַ, Yeshua for you, the גּוֹיִם, Goyim ²(if, indeed, you heard of the stewardship of the *unmerited* favor of God that was given to me in regard to you): ³that by a revealing, the mystery was made known to me, as I wrote before in *a* few WORDS ⁴(in regard to this, reading IT, you are able to understand my insight into the mystery of the Messiah, ⁵which in other generations was not made known to the sons of men, as it was *only* now revealed to His holy emissaries and prophets in the רוּחַ, Ruach), ⁶*namely,* that the גּוֹיִם, Goyim are fellow-heirs, and of the same Body, and sharers of the promise in Messiah יֵשׁוּעַ, Yeshuaª through the Good News ⁷(of which I became a servant, according to the gift of the *unmerited* favor of God that was given to me, according to the working of His power).

⁸This favor was given to me (the less-than-the-least of all קְדוֹשִׁים, Q'doshiym): to proclaim Good News—the untraceable riches of the Messiah—to the גּוֹיִם, Goyim, ⁹and to cause all to see what IS the stewardshipᵇ of the mystery that has been hidden from the ages in God (who created all the thingsᶜ), ¹⁰so that the multifold wisdom of God might be made known now, through the Called-Forth,ᵈ to the rulers and the authorities in the heavenly PLACES. ¹¹This *was* according to a purpose of the ages, which He made in Messiah יֵשׁוּעַ, Yeshua our Master, ¹²in whom we have the freedom in speech and access in confidence through the faith in Him. ¹³I therefore ask YOU not to lose heart in my oppressions for you, which is your glory.

¹⁴For this reason I bow my knees to the Fatherᵉ ¹⁵(of whom the whole family in the Heavens and on earth is named): ¹⁶so that He may give to you according to the riches of His glory, to be strengthened with power through His רוּחַ, Ruach in regard to the inner man, ¹⁷*in order for* the Messiah to dwell through the faith in your hearts (having been rooted and founded in love), ¹⁸so that you may be able in strength to comprehend (with all the קְדוֹשִׁים, Q'doshiym) what IS the breadth, and length, and height, and depth *of*—¹⁹*and* also to know—the love of the Messiah that is exceeding the knowledge, so that you may be filled to all the fullness of God. ²⁰And to Him who is able to do exceedingly abundantly above all things that we ask or think (according to the power that is working in us)—²¹to Him IS the glory in the Called-Forthᶠ and in Messiah יֵשׁוּעַ, Yeshua, to all the generations of the age of the ages! אָמֵן, Amen.

4 ¹I, then, the prisoner of the Master, call upon you to walk worthily of the calling with which you were called, ²with all humble-mindedness and humility, with patience, bearing with one another in love, ³being diligent to keep the unity of the רוּחַ, Ruach in the bond of the peace—⁴one Body and one רוּחַ, Ruach (as you were also called in one hope of your calling), ⁵one Master, one faith, one immersion, ⁶one God and Father of all, who IS over all, and through all, and inᵍ all.

⁷But to each one of you was given the *unmerited* favor, according to the measure of the gift of Messiah. ⁸Therefore, He said,

"Having gone up on high, he led captive *your* captives; he gave gifts to men."ʰ

⁹(And that "he went up"—what is it *meaning* except that he also went downⁱ to the

---

ª Some mss omit, "יֵשׁוּעַ, Yeshua"
ᵇ "stewardship"—some mss say, "sharing"
ᶜ Some mss insert, "through Messiah יֵשׁוּעַ, Yeshua."
ᵈ "Called-Forth"—ἐκκλησία, ekklesia; see מַתִּתְיָהוּ Matit'yahu 16:18
ᵉ Some mss insert, "of our Master יֵשׁוּעַ, Yeshua *the* Messiah"
ᶠ "Called-Forth"—ἐκκλησία, ekklesia; see מַתִּתְיָהוּ Matit'yahu 16:18
ᵍ Some mss insert, "you"
ʰ תְּהִלִּים T'hiliym 68:19(18)
ⁱ Some mss insert, "first"

lower parts of the earth? ¹⁰He who went down is the same who also went up far above all the heavens, so that He may fill all things.) ¹¹And He gave some AS emissaries, and some AS prophets, and some AS proclaimers of Good News, and some AS shepherds and teachers, ¹²toward the equipping of the קְדוֹשִׁים, Q'doshiym for the work of service—for the building up of the Body of the Messiah——¹³until we all may come to the unity of the faith and of the recognition of the Son of God, to a perfect man*hood, and* to the *whole* measure of maturity of the fullness of the Messiah, ¹⁴so that we may no longer be little children, tossed and carried about by every wind of the teaching (by the sleight *of hand* of men; by craftiness, toward the scheme of leading *us* astray), ¹⁵but speaking the truth in love, may we grow up IN all things into Him who is the head—Messiah——¹⁶from whom the whole Body *grows* (being fitted together and united, through the support of every joint, according to the proper working[a] of each single part). The growing up of the Body produces the building up of itself in love.

¹⁷This, then, I say, and I testify in the Master: you are to walk no longer as the *unbelieving*[b] גּוֹיִם, Goyim walk in the futility of their mind ¹⁸(being darkened in the understanding, being alienated from the life of God because of the ignorance that is in them, because of the hardness of their heart), ¹⁹who, having become insensitive, gave themselves up to the sensuality, for the working of all uncleanness in greediness. ²⁰But you did not learn the Messiah this way. ²¹If indeed you heard Him and were taught in Him (as truth is in יֵשׁוּעַ, Yeshua), ²²you are to put off the old man[c] (concerning the former behavior that is corrupt according to the lusts of the deceit), ²³and to be renewed in the רוּחַ, ruach of your mind, ²⁴and to put on the new man[d] (which, according to God, was created in righteousness and undefiledness of the truth).

²⁵Therefore, putting away the lying, let each *of you* speak truth with his neighbor, because we are members one of another. ²⁶BE ANGRY AND DO NOT SIN;[e] let not the sun go down upon your anger, ²⁷and do not give place to the Accuser. ²⁸*The* one who is stealing—let him steal no longer, but rather let him labor (working with his own hands the thing that is good), so that he may have *something* to impart to him *who is* having need. ²⁹Let no rotten word go out of your mouth, but what is good to the needful building up *of others*, so that it may give favor to the hearers. ³⁰And do not make sorrowful the רוּחַ הַקֹּדֶשׁ, Ruach HaQodesh of God (in whom you were sealed to a day of redemption).

³¹Let all bitterness and rage and wrath and clamor and evil-speaking be put away from you (*along* with all hateful feelings[f]), ³²and become kind to one another, tenderhearted, forgiving one another as also God in Messiah forgave you.

5

¹Become, then, imitators of God (as beloved children) ²and walk in love, as also the Messiah loved us and gave Himself for us—an offering and a sacrifice to God for a fragrance of a sweet smell. ³But sexual immorality, and all uncleanness or covetousness—let it not even be named among you, as is fitting for קְדוֹשִׁים, Q'doshiym. ⁴Also, *let there be no* obscenity and foolish talking, or crude joking—which are not fitting—but rather thanksgiving. ⁵Indeed, this you know: that everyone *who is* sexually immoral, or unclean, or covetous—who is an idolater—has no inheritance in the Reign of the Messiah and God.

⁶Let no one deceive you with empty words, for because of these things the wrath of God comes upon the sons of the obstinance.[g] ⁷Do not, then, become sharers

---

[a] "proper working"—Young's says, "working in the measure"
[b] *"unbelieving"*—some mss say, "other"
[c] "the old man," that is, "the old self"
[d] "the new man," that is, "the new self"
[e] cf. תְּהִלִּים T'hiliym 4:5(4) (LXX)
[f] "hateful feelings"—Young's says, "malice"
[g] "obstinance"—ἀπείθεια, apeitheia, a negative of

with them, ⁸for at one time you were Darkness, but now *you are* Light in the Master.

As children of Light, walk ⁹(for the fruit of the Light[a] IS in all goodness and righteousness and truth, ¹⁰proving what is well-pleasing to the Master), ¹¹and have no partnership with the unfruitful actions of the Darkness, but rather even refute *them*. ¹²For it is shameful even to speak of the things done in secret by them, ¹³and all the things rebuked by the Light are revealed, ¹⁴for everything that is revealed is Light. Therefore it[b] says, "Awaken yourself, you who are sleeping, and arise out of the dead, and the Messiah will shine upon you."

¹⁵Look diligently, then, at how you walk —not as unwise but as wise, ¹⁶redeeming the time, because the days are evil. ¹⁷Because of this, do not become fools, but understand what the will of the Master IS.

¹⁸And do not be drunk with wine, in which is reckless living, but be filled in the רוּחַ, Ruach— ¹⁹speaking to each other in melodies and praises and spiritual songs; singing and making melody with *all* your heart to the Master; ²⁰giving thanks always for all things to the God and Father, in the Name of our Master יֵשׁוּעַ, Yeshua *the* Messiah; ²¹*and* submitting yourselves to one another in the fear of Messiah.[c]

²²The wives! submit yourselves[d] to your own husbands, as to the Master, ²³because the husband is head of the wife, as also the Messiah IS head of the Called-Forth[e]—He is savior of the Body. ²⁴But as the Called-Forth is submitted to Messiah, so also ARE the wives *submitted* to the husbands in everything.

²⁵The husbands! love the wives, as the Messiah also loved the Called-Forth and gave Himself for her,[f] ²⁶so that He might set her apart (having cleansed HER with the bathing of the water with[g] the spoken word), ²⁷so that He might present her to Himself—the glorious Called-Forth—not having spot or wrinkle, or any of such things, but that she may be holy and unblemished. ²⁸In this *same* way the husbands also ought to love their own wives as their own bodies (he who is loving his own wife loves himself, ²⁹for no one ever hated his own flesh, but nourishes and cherishes it), as the Messiah[h] also *loves* the Called-Forth, ³⁰since we are members of His Body.[i]

³¹"For this reason will a man leave his father and mother, and will be joined to his wife; and they—the two—will be for one flesh."[j]

³²This mystery is great, but I speak in regard to Messiah and to the Called-Forth. ³³But also, let each *and* every one *of* you in this way love his own wife as himself. And the wife—*see* that she respects[k] the husband.

6
¹ The children! obey your parents in the Master, for this is righteous. ²"HONOR YOUR FATHER AND MOTHER," which is the first command with a promise: ³"THAT IT WILL BE WELL WITH YOU, AND YOU WILL LIVE A LONG TIME UPON THE LAND."[l]

⁴And the fathers! do not provoke your children *to anger*, but nourish them in the instruction and warning of the Master.

⁵The servants! obey those *who are* your masters according to the flesh with fear and trembling, in the simplicity of your heart, as *you would be obedient* to the Mes-

---

πείθω, peitho, usually "trust" or "persuade." Here, Young says, "disobedience."

[a] "Light"—some mss say, "רוּחַ, Ruach"
[b] "it"—Young's says, "he"
[c] "Messiah"—some mss say, "God"
[d] "submit yourselves" is not in earlier mss, but in addition to the immediate context; cf. 1 Keifa 3:1, Colossians 3:18 and Titus 2:5
[e] "Called-Forth"—ἐκκλησία, ekklesia; see מַתִּתְיָהוּ Matit'yahu 16:18; throughout chapter 5

[f] "her"—Young's says, "it"; also occurs in verses 26 & 27
[g] "with"—Young's says, "in"
[h] "Messiah"—some mss say, "Master"
[i] Some mss insert, "of His flesh, and of His bones"
[j] בְּרֵאשִׁית B'reshiyt 2:24
[k] "respects"—φοβῆται, phobetai—"to fear"; Young's says, "reverence"
[l] שְׁמוֹת Sh'mot 20:12, דְּבָרִים D'variym 5:16

The whole Armor of God.

siah. ⁶*Do this* not as men-pleasers (only when the master has his eye on you[a]) but as slaves of Messiah, doing the will of God out of *your* soul ⁷(serving with good-will as to the Master, and not to men), ⁸having known that whatever good thing each one may do, this he will receive *back* from the Master, whether slave or freeman.

⁹And the masters! do the same things to them. Stop sending threats, having known that the Master—both theirs and yours—is in the Heavens, and favoritism is not with Him.

¹⁰As for the rest *of you,*[b] be strong in the Master, and in the strength of His might. ¹¹Put on the whole Armor of God, for your being able to stand against the schemes of the Accuser ¹²(because we do not have the wrestling with blood and flesh, but with the rulers, with the authorities, with the world-forces of this darkness,[c] *and* with the spiritual things of the evil in the heavenly places.) ¹³Because of this, take up the whole Armor of God, so that you may be able to resist in the Day of the evil, and—*after* having done all things—to stand.

¹⁴Stand, therefore, having your waist wrapped around with Truth,[d] and having put on the Breast-plate of the Righteousness,[e] ¹⁵and having bound under your feet the preparation of the Good News of the Peace.[f] ¹⁶In all, having taken up the Shield of the Faith (by which you will be able to extinguish all the flaming arrows of the evil one), ¹⁷also receive the Helmet of the Salvation[g] and the Sword of the רוּחַ, Ruach (which is the spoken word of God), ¹⁸through all prayer and requests for help, praying at all times in the רוּחַ, Ruach, and in regard to the same *thing*, being alert in all perseverance and requests for help for all the קְדוֹשִׁים, Q'doshiym.

¹⁹And for my sake, *also pray* that a word in the opening of my mouth may be given to me—unhindered—to make known the mystery of the Good News ²⁰(for which I am an ambassador in a chain), *and* that I may speak freely in it, as I must speak.

²¹And so that you may know—you also—the things about me (how I am doing), Tychicus (the beloved brother and faithful servant in the Master) will make all things known to you——²²he whom I sent to you for this very thing: so that you might know the things about us, and he might encourage your hearts.

²³Peace to the brothers, and love with faith from God the Father, and the Master יֵשׁוּעַ, Yeshua *the* Messiah! ²⁴The *unmerited* favor *is* with all those loving our Master יֵשׁוּעַ, Yeshua *the* Messiah—undecayingly![h]

---

[a] "only when the master has his eye on you"—literally, "with eye-service"
[b] Some mss insert, "my brothers"
[c] "this darkness"—some mss say, "the darkness of this age"
[d] cf. יְשַׁעְיָהוּ *Y'sha'yahu* 11:5
[e] cf. יְשַׁעְיָהוּ *Y'sha'yahu* 59:17
[f] cf. יְשַׁעְיָהוּ *Y'sha'yahu* 52:7
[g] cf. יְשַׁעְיָהוּ *Y'sha'yahu* 59:17
[h] Some mss conclude, "אָמֵן, Amen."

PAUL'S LETTER TO THE

Philippians

1

¹*From* Paul[a] and Timothy, slaves of Messiah יֵשׁוּעַ, Yeshua; to all the קְדוֹשִׁים, Q'doshiym in Messiah יֵשׁוּעַ, Yeshua who are in Philippi, *together* with *the* overseers and servers: ²*unmerited* favor to you, and peace from God our Father, and the Master יֵשׁוּעַ, Yeshua *the* Messiah.

---

[a] "Paul"—Παῦλος, Paulos; see 1 Timothy 1:1

³I give thanks to my God upon all the remembrance of you—⁴always, in every request of mine for help for you all, making the request for help with joy—⁵for your sharing in the Good News from the first day until now, ⁶having been confident of this very thing: that He who began a good work in you will finish IT until the Day of Messiah יֵשׁוּעַ, Yeshua ⁷(as it is righteous for me to think this about you all, because of my having you in the heart, both in my bonds and IN the defense and confirmation of the Good News, all of you being fellow-sharers of *unmerited* favor with me).

⁸For God is my witness, how I long for you all in the inward parts of Messiah יֵשׁוּעַ, Yeshua. ⁹And this I pray: that your love may yet abound more and more in full knowledge and all perception, ¹⁰for your examining the things that differ, so that you may be pure and offenseless until the Day of Messiah, ¹¹being filled with the fruit of righteousness that IS through יֵשׁוּעַ, Yeshua the Messiah, to the glory and praise of God.

¹²And I want you to know, brothers, that the *difficult* things regarding me have instead come to an advancement of the Good News, ¹³such that my bonds have become known in Messiah in the whole Prætorium,ᵃ and to all the other places; ¹⁴and the majority of the brothers in the Master, having confidence by my bonds, are more abundantly bold to fearlessly speak the word.

¹⁵Certain *ones*, indeed, even through envy and infighting, and certain *others* also through good-will, proclaim the Messiah. ¹⁶The one, indeed, *does so* out of love, having known that I am set *in place* for a defense of the Good News; ¹⁷but the other proclaims the Messiah *out of selfish* ambition, not purely, supposing to stir upᵇ affliction *for me* in my bonds.ᶜ ¹⁸What then? except that in every way, whether in pretense or in truth, Messiah is proclaimed (and in this I rejoice—yes, and will rejoice).

¹⁹For I have known that this will turn out to me for salvation—through *both* your requests for help, and the help of the רוּחַ, Ruach of יֵשׁוּעַ, Yeshua *the* Messiah—²⁰*and* according to my eager expectation and hope, that I will be ashamed in nothing. Rather, in all freedom—as always, also now—Messiah will be magnified in my body, whether through *my* life, or through *my* death. ²¹For to me, to live IS Messiah, and to die, gain.

²²But if *I am* to live in the *physical* flesh, this IS a fruitful action to me. And what will I choose? I do not know, ²³but I am pressed by the two, having the desire to depart and to be with Messiah (for it is far better). ²⁴But *it* is more necessary to remain in the flesh on your account. ²⁵And being persuaded of this, I have known that I will remain and continue with you all, to your advancement and joy of the faith, ²⁶so that your boasting may abound in Messiah יֵשׁוּעַ, Yeshua in me, through my presence *that is coming* again to you.

²⁷*So then*, conduct yourselves only worthily of the Good News of the Messiah, so that, whether having come and seen you or being absent, I may hear of the things regarding you: that you stand fast in one רוּחַ, ruach, with one soul, striving together for the faith of the Good News, ²⁸and not terrified in anything by those *who are* opposing *you* (which is a sign of destruction to them, but to you, of your salvation—and that from God), ²⁹because to you it was given, on behalf of Messiah, not only to believe in Him, but also to suffer on behalf of Him, ³⁰having the same conflict such as you saw in me, and now hear of in me.

2 ¹If, then, any exhortation IS in Messiah, if any encouragement of love, if any sharing of רוּחַ, ruach, if any inward parts and compassion, ²*then* fulfill my joy: that you may think the same thing—having the same love, *being* of one soul, thinking the one thing—³*doing* nothing in *selfish* ambition or in conceit, but in humility of mind, counting one another higher than yourselves—⁴each *of* you not look-

---

ᵃ "Prætorium"—the governor's headquarters
ᵇ "stir up"—some mss say, "add"
ᶜ Some mss reverse the content of verses 16 and 17.

ing to your own *things*, but each also to the things of others.

⁵Let this thinking be in you that IS also in Messiah יֵשׁוּעַ, Yeshua, ⁶who, being in God's form,ᵃ thought to be equal to God not a thing to hold onto.ᵇ ⁷But He emptied Himself, having taken a slave's formᶜ— having been made in the likeness of men —⁸and in appearance having been found as a man, He humbled Himself, having become obedient to death—death even of an *execution* stake. ⁹Therefore, also, God highly exalted Him and gave to Him the Name that IS above every name, ¹⁰so that atᵈ the Name of יֵשׁוּעַ, Yeshua, EVERY KNEE WILL BOW (of those of heaven, and those of earth, and those under the earth) ¹¹AND EVERY TONGUE WILL CONFESSᵉ that יֵשׁוּעַ, Yeshua *the* Messiah IS ADONAI,ᶠ to the glory of God the Father.

¹²Therefore, my loved ones, as you always obey (not only as in my presence, but now much more in my absence), work out your own salvation with fear and trembling, ¹³for it is God who is working in you, both to will and to work, for His good pleasure.

¹⁴Do all things without murmurings and reasonings, ¹⁵so that you may become blameless and innocent children of God, unblemished in the middle of a crooked and perverse generation, among whom you are shown to be as lights in the world, ¹⁶holding out the word of life. *This is* for rejoicing to me in regard to the Day of Messiah, that I did not run in emptiness, nor in emptiness did I labor. ¹⁷But if I am also poured out *as a drink offering* upon the sacrifice and service of your faith, *then* I *myself* rejoice, and *I* also rejoice with you all. ¹⁸Because of this, you *yourselves should* also rejoice, and rejoice with me.

¹⁹And I hope in the Master יֵשׁוּעַ, Yeshua to send Timothy to you quickly (so that I also may be encouraged, having known the things regarding you), ²⁰for I have no one *else* like-minded, who will care sincerely for the things regarding you ²¹(for they all seek their own things, not the things of Messiah יֵשׁוּעַ, Yeshua); ²²but you know the proof of him: that as a child SERVES a father, he served with me in regard to the Good News. ²³Indeed, I therefore hope to send him immediately, when I see the things through concerning me. ²⁴And I trust in the Master that I myself will also come quickly.

²⁵And I thought IT necessary to send to you Epaphroditus—my brother and fellow-workman and fellow-soldier, and your emissary and servant to my need—²⁶since he was longing after you all, and *was* in heaviness because you heard that he ailed ²⁷(for he also ailed near to death, but God dealt kindly with him—and not only with him, but also with me, so that I might not have grief upon grief).

²⁸Therefore, *all* the more eagerly I sent him, so that having seen him again you may rejoice, and I may be *all* the less grieved. ²⁹Therefore, receive him in the Master with all joy, and hold such *men* in honor, ³⁰since on account of the work of Messiah he drew near to death, having risked the life so that he might fill up your deficiency of service to me.

3 ¹As to the remainder, my brothers, rejoice in the Master! To write the same things to you *again* indeed is not tiresome to me, but IS *done* for you *to be* sure.ᵍ

²Watch out for the dogs; watch out for the evil-doers; watch out for the Mutilation! ³For we are the Circumcision, who, by the רוּחַ, Ruach of God, are servingʰ and glorying in Messiah יֵשׁוּעַ, Yeshua, and having no confidence in *the* flesh—⁴though,

---

ᵃ "God's form"—μορφῇ θεοῦ, morphe theou; Young's says, "the form of God"
ᵇ "to hold onto" or "to be seized" or "to be grasped"—Young's says, "robbery"
ᶜ "a slave's form"— μορφὴν δούλου, morphen doulou; Young's says, "the form of a servant"
ᵈ "at" or "in"—Young's says, "in"
ᵉ יְשַׁעְיָהוּ Y'sha'yahu 45:23
ᶠ "ADONAI," given the context of the cited verse; Gk. κύριος, kurios

ᵍ "sure" or "secure"
ʰ "by the רוּחַ, Ruach of God are serving"—some mss say, "by the רוּחַ, Ruach, are serving God"

I also have CAUSE FOR confidence even in *the* flesh.

Indeed, if any other one thinks to have confidence in *the* flesh, I *have* more: ⁵circumcision on the eighth day! of the ancestry of יִשְׂרָאֵל, Yis'rael! of the tribe of בִּנְיָמִין, Bin'yamiyn! עִבְרִי מִן הָעִבְרִים, Iv'riy min Ha-Iv'riym!ᵃ in regard to תּוֹרָה, Torah, a פָּרוּשׁ, Parush! ⁶in regard to zeal, persecuting the Called-Forth!ᵇ in regard to righteousness that is in תּוֹרָה, Torah, becoming blameless!

⁷But what things were gains to me, these I have counted *to be* loss because of the Messiah. ⁸Yes, indeed, and I count all things to be loss because of the excellency of *having* a knowledge of Messiah יֵשׁוּעַ, Yeshua my Master—because of whom I suffered the loss of all things, and consider them to be excrement—so that I may gain Messiah ⁹and be found in Him, not having my *own* righteousness which IS of תּוֹרָה, Torah, but that which IS through faith of Messiah (the righteousness that is of God *which comes* by the faith), ¹⁰in order to know Him and the power of His Rising Again and the sharing of His sufferings, being conformed to *Him in* His death, ¹¹if somehow I may attain to the Rising Again from the dead.

¹²Not that I *have* already obtained *this,* or have already been perfected, but I pursue *it,* if I also might lay hold of that for which I was also laid hold of by Messiah יֵשׁוּעַ, Yeshua. ¹³Brothers, I do not consider myself to have laid hold *of it,* but *rather this* one thing: forgetting, indeed, the things behind, and stretching forth to the things in front of *me,* ¹⁴I pursue *it* to the mark for the prize of the high calling of God in Messiah יֵשׁוּעַ, Yeshua.

¹⁵As many *of us,* therefore, as ARE mature, let us think this *same thing* (and if IN anything you think otherwise, this also God will reveal to you); ¹⁶moreover, to what we have come, *let us* walk by the same standard.ᶜ ¹⁷Together, brothers, become imitators of me, and pay attention to those walking this *same* way, because you have us *as* a pattern. ¹⁸For many walk (of whom I told you many times, and now, even weeping, *I tell you again*) who *are* the enemies of the *execution* stake of the Messiah, ¹⁹whose end IS destruction, whose god IS the belly, and whose glory IS in their shame—who are thinking *only of* the things on earth.

²⁰For our citizenship is in the Heavens, from where we also await a Savior—the Master יֵשׁוּעַ, Yeshua *the* Messiah—²¹who will change the figure of the body of our humiliation to its becoming conformed to the body of His glory, according to the working of His power, even to subject all the things to Himself.

4

¹So then, my brothers—beloved and longed for, my joy and crown—in this way, stand in the Master, loved ones.

²I exhort Euodia and I exhort Syntyche to be of the same mind in the Master. ³Yes, I also ask you, genuine yoke-fellow, *to* be assisting those women who strived along with me in the Good News (also with Clement and the others, my fellow-workers, whose names ARE in the book of life).

⁴Rejoice in the Master always—again, I will say: rejoice! ⁵Let your gentleness be known to all men. The Master IS near.

⁶Be anxious for nothing, but in everything—by prayer and by asking for help, with thanksgiving—let your requests be made known to God. ⁷And the peace of God, which is surpassing all understanding, will guard your hearts and your thoughts in Messiah יֵשׁוּעַ, Yeshua.

⁸As to the remainder, brothers: as many things as are true, as many as ARE serious, as many as ARE righteous, as many as ARE pure, as many as ARE lovely, as many as ARE of good report—if *there is* any moral excellence, and if any *are* commendable—think upon these things. ⁹The things that you also learned and received and heard and saw in me—do those, and the God of the peace will be with you.

ᵃ translated, "a Hebrew of Hebrews"; could possibly imply, as Stern says, "a Hebrew speaker, with Hebrew-speaking parents"

ᵇ "Called-Forth"—ἐκκλησίαν, ekklesian; see מַתִּתְיָהוּ Matit'yahu 16:18

ᶜ Some mss insert, "think the same thing"

¹⁰And I rejoiced greatly in the Master that now at length you flourished again in caring for me (for which you were also *previously* caring, but lacked opportunity), ¹¹not that I say THIS because of want. For I *have* learned to be content in the things in which I am: ¹²I have both known *what it is* to be humiliated *in hardship*, and known *what it is* to have abundance. I have been initiated in everything and in all things: both to be full and to be hungry, both to have abundance and to be in want. ¹³I have strength for all things in Him *who is*ᵃ strengthening me.

¹⁴But you did well, having shared with my oppression; ¹⁵and you have known—even you Philippians—that in the beginning of *my proclaiming* the Good News, when I went out from Macedonia, no Called-Forth-Communityᵇ contributed with me in regard to giving and receiving except you only ¹⁶(because also in Thessalonica, both once and again you sent *a gift* to *meet* my need—¹⁷not that I seek after the gift, but I seek after the fruit that is overflowing to your account).

¹⁸But *now* I have all things, and abound. I am filled, having received from Epaphroditus the things from you—an aroma of a sweet smell, a sacrifice acceptable *and* well-pleasing to God. ¹⁹And my God will supply all your need according to His riches in glory in Messiah יֵשׁוּעַ, Yeshua; ²⁰and to God, even our Father, IS the glory—to the ages of the ages. אָמֵן, Amen.

²¹Greet every holy one in Messiah יֵשׁוּעַ, Yeshua; the brothers with me greet you; ²²all the קְדוֹשִׁים, Q'doshiym greet you, and especially those of Cæsar's house. ²³The *unmerited* favor of the Master יֵשׁוּעַ, Yeshua the Messiah IS with your רוּחַ, ruach.ᶜ

ᵃ "Him *who is*"—some mss say, "Messiah's"
ᵇ "Called-Forth-Community"—ἐκκλησία, ekklesia; see מַתִּתְיָהוּ *Matit'yahu* 16:18
ᶜ "your רוּחַ, ruach"—some mss say, "you all. אָמֵן, Amen."

PAUL'S LETTER TO

Titus

1 ¹*From* Paul,ᵃ a slave of God and an emissary of יֵשׁוּעַ, Yeshua *the* Messiah, according to the faith of the chosen ones of God and an acknowledging of truth that IS according to godliness, ²*based* upon *the* hope of life age-enduring, which God—who does not lie—promised before *the* times of *the* ages ³(but in *its* own times, He revealed His word in *the* proclaiming, with which I was entrusted, according to a command of God our Savior); ⁴to Titus, a true child according to a common faith: *unmerited* favor andᵇ peace from God the Father, andᶜ Messiah יֵשׁוּעַ, Yeshua, our Savior!

⁵For this reason I left you in Crete: so that you might arrange the things *that were* left unfinished and might set in order זְקֵנִים, z'qeniym in every city, as I appointed to you—⁶*namely*, if anyone is above reproach, a husband of one wife, *and* having faithfulᵈ children *who are* not under accusation of riotous or out-of-control living.

⁷Indeed, the overseer must be above reproach as God's manager: not self-pleasing, not quick-tempered, not given to wine, not violent, not given to dishonest gain, ⁸but a lover of strangers, a lover of good,ᵉ of sound mind, righteous, undefiled, self-

---

ᵃ "Paul"—Παῦλος, Paulos; see 1 Timothy 1:1
ᵇ "and"—some mss say, "*loving*-kindness"
ᶜ Some mss insert, "the Master"
ᵈ "faithful" or "believing"
ᵉ Some translations, including Young's, insert "men" or "things"

controlled, ⁹holding *firmly*—according to the teaching—to the faithful word, so that he may be able to also exhort *others* in the sound teaching, and to refute the contradictors.

¹⁰For there are many *who are* both out-of-control, empty-talkers, and mind-deceivers (especially those of the Circumcision) ¹¹whose mouth must stop—who overturn whole households *by* teaching what things *they* ought not, for dishonest gain's sake.

¹²A certain one of them, a prophet of their own, said, "Cretans! always liars, evil beasts, lazy bellies!" ¹³This testimony is true, for which reason *you must* refute them sharply, so that they may be sound in the faith, ¹⁴not paying attention to Jewish myths and commands of men, turning themselves away from the truth. ¹⁵To the clean *one*, all things ARE clean, but to the defiled and faithless, nothing IS clean; and of them, even the mind and the conscience ARE defiled. ¹⁶They profess to know God, but in the actions they deny HIM, being detestable and obstinate[a] and disqualified *as* to every good action.

2 ¹And you—be speaking what is fitting for the sound teaching: ²older men to be sober-minded, serious, of sound mind, *and* sound in the faith, in the love, *and* in the perseverance; ³older women, likewise, in demeanor as is appropriate *for* sacred persons—not false accusers, not enslaved to much wine, teachers of good things—⁴so that they may train the young women in sound-mindedness, to be lovers of THEIR husbands, lovers of THEIR children, ⁵of sound mind, pure, homemakers,[b] good, *and* submitted to their own husbands, so that the word of God may not be spoken evil of.

⁶Likewise, be exhorting the younger men to be of sound mind ⁷regarding all things, showing yourself *to be* a pattern of good actions—incorruptibility in the teaching, seriousness,[c] ⁸*and* sound words beyond reproach—so that he who is against *us* may be ashamed, having nothing evil to say about us.[d]

⁹Slaves ARE to be submitted to their own masters, to be well-pleasing in all things, not talking back, ¹⁰not pilfering, but showing all good faithfulness, so that they will adorn the teaching of God our Savior in all things.

¹¹For the *unmerited*, saving favor of God was made apparent to all men, ¹²instructing us, so that *while* denying the ungodliness and the worldly lusts, we may live soberly and righteously and *in a* godly manner in the present age, ¹³waiting for the blessed hope and appearing of the glory of our great God and Savior,[e] יֵשׁוּעַ, Yeshua *the* Messiah, ¹⁴who gave Himself for us so that He could ransom us from all misdeeds and cleanse to Himself a people treasured *as His own*,[f] zealous for good actions. ¹⁵Be speaking these things and exhorting and refuting with all authority—let no one disregard you!

3 ¹Remind them to be submitted to rulers and authorities; to trust authority;[g] to be ready toward every good action; ²to speak evil of no one; not to be quarrelsome, *but* gentle, showing all humility to all men. ³For we—we also—were once unthinking, obstinate, led astray, serving various lusts and pleasures, living in wickedness and envy, hated *and* hating one another. ⁴But when the kindness of God our Savior and *His* love toward men appeared, ⁵He saved us (not by actions that we did that ARE in righteousness, but according to His *loving*-kindness) through a bathing of regeneration and a renewing of the רוּחַ הַקֹּדֶשׁ, Ruach HaQodesh ⁶(which He

---

[a] "obstinate"—ἀπειθεῖς, apeitheis, see footnote at 2 Timothy 3:2. Here, Young says, "disobedient." Also in verse 3:3.

[b] "homemakers"—οἰκουργοὺς, oikourgous—lit., "house-workers"; some mss say, "keepers of THEIR OWN houses"

[c] Some mss insert, "uncorruptedness"

[d] "us"—some mss say, "you"

[e] or "the great God, and our Savior"

[f] cf. דְּבָרִים D'variym 7:6, 14:2, 26:18; שְׁמוֹת Sh'mot 19:5

[g] "trust authority"—πειθαρχεῖν, peitharchein, related to πείθω, peitho; see footnote at 2 Timothy 3:2. Here, Young's says, "obey rule."

poured upon us richly, through יֵשׁוּעַ, Yeshua *the* Messiah our Savior), ⁷so that having been declared righteous by His *unmerited* favor, we may become heirs to the hope of life age-enduring.

⁸Faithful IS the word; and regarding these things, I counsel you to affirm *them* fully so that they who have believed God may be mindful to be leading *others* in good actions. These are good and profitable things to men.

⁹But stand away from foolish *intentionally polarizing* questions, and genealogies, and infightings, and battles about תּוֹרָה, Torah, for they are unprofitable and vain. ¹⁰After a first and second warning, be rejecting a divisive man, ¹¹having known that he who IS such has been turned inside out and sins, being self-condemned.

¹²When I send Artemas or Tychicus to you, be diligent to come to me to Nicopolis, for I have determined to winter there. ¹³Bring Zenas the תּוֹרָה, Torah-expert[a] and Apollos diligently on their way, so that nothing may be lacking to them. ¹⁴And also let those *who are* ours learn to be leading *others* in good actions to *meet* the necessary needs, so that they may not be unfruitful.

¹⁵All those with me greet you. Greet those loving us in *the* faith.

The *unmerited* favor IS with you all![b]

[a] "Torah-expert"—νομικὸν, nomikon
[b] Some mss conclude, "אָמֵן, Amen."

הַמִּכְתָּב הַשֵּׁנִי מִן כֵּיפָא THE SECOND LETTER FROM KEIFA

2 Keifa כֵּיפָא ב

1

¹From שִׁמְעוֹן כֵּיפָא, Shim'on Keifa,[a] a slave and an emissary of יֵשׁוּעַ, Yeshua *the* Messiah; to those who obtained an equally precious faith with us in the righteousness of our God and Savior, יֵשׁוּעַ, Yeshua *the* Messiah: ²*unmerited* favor to you, and peace be multiplied in the acknowledgement of God and of יֵשׁוּעַ, Yeshua our Master!

³As *with* all things, His divine power has given to us the things pertaining to life and godliness through the acknowledgement of Him who called us to His own[b] glory and moral excellence, ⁴through which the precious and greatest promises have been given to us, so that through these, you may become sharers of a divine nature, having escaped from the decay in the world *that is* in lust.

⁵And also *for* this same *reason*, having brought in alongside all diligence, superadd in your faith the moral excellence; and in the moral excellence, the knowledge; ⁶and in the knowledge, the self-control; and in the self-control, the perseverance; and in the perseverance, the godliness; ⁷and in the godliness, the brotherly love; and in the brotherly love, the love. ⁸For these things, being and abounding to you, make YOU neither inactive nor unfruitful in regard to the acknowledging of our Master יֵשׁוּעַ, Yeshua *the* Messiah; ⁹for he with whom these things are not present is blind—short-sighted—having become forgetful of the cleansing of his old sins. ¹⁰Therefore, *all* the more, brothers, be diligent to make your calling and chosenness reliable, for *by* doing these things, you will never stumble—¹¹for *in* this way, the entrance into the age-enduring Reign of our Master and Savior יֵשׁוּעַ,

[a] כֵּיפָא, Keifa—Gk: Πέτρος, Petros; see יוֹחָנָן Yn. 1:42
[b] "to His own" or "by His own"—some mss say, "through"

Yeshua *the* Messiah will be richly super-added to you.

¹²Therefore, I will always intend[a] to remind you regarding these things, though *you are* having known them, and having been stabilized in the truth *that* has come. ¹³But I think *it is* right, as long as I am in this tent *of my body*, to stir you up in reminding YOU, ¹⁴having known that soon is the laying aside of my tent, even as our Master יֵשׁוּעַ, Yeshua *the* Messiah also made clear to me. ¹⁵And I will also be diligent *so* that at every time after my out-going, you *will* have power to make remembrance of these things.

¹⁶Indeed, not having followed skillfully devised myths, we made known to you the power and *coming* presence of our Master יֵשׁוּעַ, Yeshua *the* Messiah—rather, having become eye-witnesses of His majesty.

¹⁷For having received honor and glory from God the Father, such a voice *was* being brought to Him by the excellent glory, *saying*, "This is My Son—My Beloved, in whom I delighted."[b]

¹⁸And this voice, brought out of heaven, we—we heard, being with Him on the holy mountain. ¹⁹And we have the prophetic word *made* more firm, to which you do well *to be* paying attention—as to a lamp shining in a dark place, until day dawns, and a morning star arises in your hearts —²⁰knowing this first: that no prophecy of the Scripture comes *out* of personal interpretation. ²¹For not by *the* will of man did prophecy ever come, but, driven by the רוּחַ הַקֹּדֶשׁ, Ruach HaQodesh, men spoke from God.[c]

2 ¹And there also came false prophets among the people, *just as there* will also be false teachers among you who will secretly bring in destructive heresies—even denying the Sovereign *One* who bought them—bringing quick destruction to themselves. ²And many will follow their sensuality,[d] because of whom the Way of the Truth will be spoken evil of. ³And, in covetousness, with molded words, they (whose condemnation of old is not fruitless) will make merchandise *out* of you—and their destruction does not fall asleep.

⁴Indeed, if God did not spare Messengers who sinned (rather, with chains[e] of thick gloom, having thrown THEM down to בְּאֵר שַׁחַת, B'er Shachat, *He* handed THEM over to *the* condemnation being reserved *for them*); ⁵and *if*—having brought a Flood on the world of the ungodly—*He* did not spare the ancient world, but guarded the *ark's* eighth person, נֹחַ, Noach, a proclaimer of righteousness; ⁶and *if*, having turned the cities of סְדֹם, S'dom and עֲמֹרָה, 'Amorah to ashes, *He* condemned *them* with an overthrow (having set THEM *as* an example of *what is* coming to the[f] ungodly); ⁷and *if* He rescued righteous לוֹט, Lot, worn down by the conduct in sensuality of the unprincipled *people* ⁸(for the righteous man—in seeing and hearing *the conduct*, living among them day by day with *their* wrongful[g] actions—was tormenting *his* righteous soul), ⁹then ADONAI has known *how* to rescue godly ones out of *ways of* testing, and to watch over unrighteous ones to a Day of Judgment, being punished—¹⁰but especially those going after the flesh in lust of defilement, and despising *His* dominion.

Presumptuous *and* self-pleasing, they are not afraid to speak evil of *the* glorious majesties, ¹¹whereas Messengers, being greater in strength and power, do not bring an evil-speaking judgment against them before ADONAI. ¹²But these, as irrational animals, born according to nature for capture and destruction—speaking evil in what things they are ignorant of— will also be destroyed in their destruction, ¹³suffering wrong *as the* wage of unrighteousness, counting *as* pleasures the

---

[a] "intend"—some mss say, "not be careless"
[b] מַתִּתְיָהוּ *Matit'yahu* 3:17, 17:5
[c] "men spoke from God"—some mss say, "holy men of God spoke"
[d] "sensuality"—some mss say, "destructive ways"
[e] "chains"—other mss say, "pits"
[f] "of *what is* coming to the"—some mss say, "to those about to be"
[g] "wrongful"—Gk. ἀνόμοις, anomois

Certainty of judgment. כֵּיפָא ב 2 Keifa 3:14

luxury in the day*time. They are* spots and blemishes, luxuriating in their deceits *as they are* feasting with you. ¹⁴Having eyes full of adultery, and unable to cease from sin, *they go about* enticing unstable souls; having a heart trained in covetousness, *they become* children of a curse. ¹⁵Abandoning a right way, they went astray, having followed in the way of בִּלְעָם, Bil'am the SON of בְּעוֹר, B'or, who loved the wage of unrighteousness, ¹⁶but had a rebuke of his own wrongdoing: a donkey without sound—having spoken in a man's voice —restrained the insanity of the prophet.

¹⁷These are wells without water and mists driven by a storm; the thick gloom of the darkness has been kept for them.ᵃ ¹⁸For, speaking overswellings of futility, they entice in *the* lusts of the flesh—*in* sensuality—those barelyᵇ escaping from those conducting themselves in error. ¹⁹*They are* promising to them liberty, themselves being slaves of the decay.

For by whom anyone has been overcome, to this one he has been brought to slavery. ²⁰For if—having escaped from the pollutions of the world in the acknowledging of our Master and Savior יֵשׁוּעַ, Yeshua *the* Messiah, and being entangled by these again—they have been overcome, the last things have become worse to them than the first. ²¹For it would have been better for them not to have acknowledged the way of the righteousness, than, having *once* acknowledged IT, to turn back from the holy command handed down to them. ²²That of the true adage has happened to them: "A DOG RETURNED TO HIS OWN VOMIT,"ᶜ and "A sow, having bathed herself, *went back* to rolling in the mud."

3 ¹This *is* now, loved ones, a second letter I write to you, in *both of* which I stir up your pure mind in reminding YOU ²to be mindful of the sayings said previously by the holy prophets, and of the command of your emissariesᵈ of the Master and Savior, ³knowing this first: that in the eventual end of the days, there will come scoffers with *their* scoffing going on according to their own lusts ⁴and saying, "Where is the promise of His *coming* presence? For, *ever* since the fathers fell asleep, all things remain this way from the beginning of the creation." ⁵For this is willingly unobserved by them: that the heavens were of old, and the ground *was* standing together out of water and through water by the word of God, ⁶through which the then-world was destroyed, having been deluged by water; ⁷and *that*—by the same word—the present heavens and the earth are stored up for fire, being kept for a day of judgment and destruction of the ungodly men.

⁸But let this one thing not be unobserved by you, loved ones: that one day with ADONAI IS as a thousand years, and a thousand years as one day.ᵉ ⁹ADONAI is not slow in regard to the promise (as certain *ones* count slowness), but is patient toward you,ᶠ not wanting any to be lost, but all to pass on to reformation. ¹⁰And it will come—the Day of ADONAI—as a thief,ᵍ in which the heavens will pass away with a rushing noise, and the elements *will* be dissolved with burning heat, and *the* earth and the actions in it will be found out.ʰ

¹¹With all these being dissolved in this way, what kind of people ought you to be in holy behavior and godly acts? ¹²*The* kind who *are* waiting for and hastening the *coming* presence of the Day of God, by which the heavens, being on fire, will be dissolved, and the elements will melt with burning heat. ¹³But we wait for new heavens and a new earth according to His promise, in which righteousness lives. ¹⁴Therefore, loved ones, *while* waiting for

---

ᵃ Some mss insert, "to the age"
ᵇ "barely"—some mss say, "truly"
ᶜ מִשְׁלֵי Mish'lei 26:11
ᵈ "of your emissaries"—some mss say, "of us, the emissaries"
ᵉ cf. תְּהִלִּים T'hiliym 90:4
ᶠ "you"—some mss say, "us"
ᵍ Some mss insert, "in the night"
ʰ "found out"—some mss say, "burnt up"

these things, be diligent, spotless and unblameable, to be found by Him in peace. ¹⁵And the patience of our Master: count *it as* salvation, as also our beloved brother Paul[a] wrote to you, according to the wisdom given to him—¹⁶as *he* also *writes* in all *his* letters, speaking in them about these things (among which certain things are hard to be understood, which the untaught and unstable twist, as *they* also *do* the other Scriptures, to their own destruction).

¹⁷You, then, loved ones, knowing *this* beforehand, be on guard; otherwise, being led away together with the error of the unprincipled, you may fall from your own stability. ¹⁸But increase in *unmerited* favor and in the knowledge of our Master and Savior יֵשׁוּעַ, Yeshua *the* Messiah. To Him *is* the glory, both now and to the Day of the age! אָמֵן, Amen.

---

[a] "Paul"—Παῦλος, Paulos; see 1 Timothy 1:1

הַמִּכְתָּב מִן THE LETTER FROM

יְהוּדָה Y'hudah

¹*From* יְהוּדָה, Y'hudah, a slave of יֵשׁוּעַ, Yeshua *the* Messiah, and brother of יַעֲקֹב, Ya'aqov; to those called—loved[a] in God the Father, and kept in יֵשׁוּעַ, Yeshua *the* Messiah: ²*loving*-kindness to you, and peace and love be multiplied!

³Loved ones, using all diligence to write to you about our common salvation, I had need to write to you, exhorting *you* to exert intense effort[b] for the faith once delivered to the קְדוֹשִׁים, Q'doshiym. ⁴For certain men came in unnoticed, having long ago been previously written for this judgment—ungodly *men*, perverting the *unmerited* favor of our God to sensuality, and denying our only Sovereign[c] and Master, יֵשׁוּעַ, Yeshua *the* Messiah. ⁵Now I intend to remind you—*though* you are knowing all things—that ADONAI, once[d] having saved a people out of the land of מִצְרַיִם, Mitz'rayim, secondly destroyed those who did not believe. ⁶Also, Messengers—who did not keep their own rule, but left their own dwelling *place*—He has kept in everlasting bonds, under darkness, to a judgment of a great Day, ⁷as סְדֹם, S'dom and עֲמֹרָה, 'Amorah and the cities around them (like these, having given themselves to sexual promiscuity, and gone after other flesh), *which* have been set before *us as* an example of fire age-enduring, suffering justice.

⁸Likewise, nevertheless, those dreaming *ones* indeed also defile the flesh, and they put away *His* dominion, and they speak evil of glorious majesties. ⁹Yet מִיכָאֵל, Miykhael, the leading Messenger, when contending with the Accuser (he was disputing about the body of מֹשֶׁה, Mosheh), did not dare to bring up an evil-speaking judgment, but said, "ADONAI rebuke you!"[e] ¹⁰But these *people*, indeed, speak evil of as many things as they have not known *and understood*. And as many things as they understand naturally (as the irrational animals), in these they are corrupted. ¹¹אוֹי, Oy! to them, because they went on in the way of קַיִן, Qayin, and they rushed to the error of בִּלְעָם, Bil'am, and they were

---

[a] "loved"—some mss say, "set apart"
[b] "exert intense effort"—Young's says, "agonize"
[c] Some mss insert, "God"
[d] "*though* you are knowing all things—that ADONAI, once"—some mss say, "you once knowing this—that ADONAI"
[e] Verse 9 may be referencing a legendary elaboration of the account of Moshe's death from the *Testament of Moses*, a Jewish writing from the first century.

destroyed in the opposition of קֹרַח, Qorach.

¹²These are jagged rocks in your love-feasts, feasting together with you, shepherding themselves without fear. *They are clouds without water, carried away by winds; autumnal trees without fruit, twice dead, rooted up;* ¹³*wild waves of a sea, foaming out their own shames; stars going astray, to whom the gloom of the darkness has been watched over to the age.*

¹⁴And the seventh from אָדָם, Adam—חֲנוֹךְ, 'Chanokh—also prophesied to these, saying, "Look! ADONAI came with His holy tens of thousands ¹⁵to do judgment against all, and to refute all their ungodly ones regarding all their actions of ungodliness that they did godlessly, and regarding all the harsh things that ungodly sinners spoke against Him."ᵃ

¹⁶These are grumblers *and* complainers, walking according to their lusts, and their mouth speaks great swellings, giving admiration to people for the sake of gaining advantage.

¹⁷But you, loved ones: remember the sayings previously spoken by the emissaries of our Master יֵשׁוּעַ, Yeshua *the* Messiah, ¹⁸that they said to you that in the Last Time there will be scoffers going on after their own lusts of ungodlinesses. ¹⁹These are those causing divisions,ᵇ naturalistic men, not having the רוּחַ, Ruach.

²⁰But you, loved ones: building yourselves up in your most holy faith *and* praying in the רוּחַ הַקֹּדֶשׁ, Ruach HaQodesh, ²¹watch over yourselves in the love of God, waiting for the *loving*-kindness of our Master יֵשׁוּעַ, Yeshua *the* Messiah, to life age-enduring. ²²And be kind to some, *who are* doubting;ᶜ ²³and save others, snatching *them* out of the fire; and show others *loving*-kindnessᵈ in fear, hating even the clothes polluted from the flesh.

²⁴And to Him who is able to guard you fromᵉ stumbling, and to set YOU in the presence of His glory unblemished, in extreme joy; ²⁵to the onlyᶠ God, our Savior, through יֵשׁוּעַ, Yeshua *the* Messiah, our Master,ᵍ IS glory and greatness, power and authority, before all the age,ʰ both now and to all the ages! אָמֵן, Amen.

ᵃ 1 Enoch 1:9, of the *Pseudepigrapha* (see Glossary)

ᵇ "causing divisions"—some mss say, "setting themselves apart"

ᶜ "*who are* doubting"—Young says, "judging thoroughly"

ᵈ Some mss omit, "and show others *loving*-kindness"

ᵉ "from"—Young's says, "not"

ᶠ Some mss insert, "wise"

ᵍ Some mss omit, "through יֵשׁוּעַ, Yeshua *the* Messiah, our Master"

ʰ Some mss omit, "before all the age"

THE GOOD NEWS OF YESHUA ACCORDING TO בְּשׂוֹרַת יֵשׁוּעַ עַל־פִּי

יוֹחָנָן Yochanan

1 ¹In the beginning was the Word, and the Word was with God, and the Word was God; ²this One was in the beginning with God. ³All things happened through Him, and without Him not even one thing happened that has happened. ⁴In Him was Life, and the Life was the Light of men. ⁵And the Light shines in the darkness, but the darkness did not perceive it.

⁶There came a man, having been sent from God, whose name *was* יוֹחָנָן, Yochanan. ⁷This one came for *giving* testimony, so that he could testify about the Light, so that all might believe through him. ⁸That one was not the Light, but *he came* so that he could testify about the Light.

⁹He *who was* coming to the world was the true Light, which enlightens every man. ¹⁰He was in the world, and the world was made through Him, but the world did not know Him; ¹¹He came to His own things, but His own people did not receive Him. ¹²Yet as many as did receive Him—to those believing in His Name—to them He gave authority to become children[a] of God, ¹³who were brought forth not of blood, nor of the will of flesh, nor of the will of man, but of God.

¹⁴And the Word became flesh and dwelt among us, and we looked upon His glory—glory as of the one and only[b] of a father, full of *unmerited* favor and truth. ¹⁵יוֹחָנָן, Yochanan testifies about Him, and has shouted, saying, "This was He of whom I said, 'He who is coming after me has come in front of me, for before me, He was.'"

¹⁶For we all received out of His fullness, even *unmerited* favor over-against *unmerited* favor. ¹⁷For the תּוֹרָה, Torah was given through מֹשֶׁה, Mosheh; the *unmerited* favor and the truth came through יֵשׁוּעַ, Yeshua *the* Messiah. ¹⁸No one has ever seen God. The one and only *of* God,[c] who is in the arms of the Father—he explained *Him*.

¹⁹And this is the testimony of יוֹחָנָן, Yochanan, when the יְהוּדִים, Y'hudiym sent to him כֹּהֲנִים, Ko'haniym and לְוִיִם, L'viyim out of יְרוּשָׁלַיִם, Y'rushalayim, so that they might question him, "Who are you?" ²⁰And he confessed and did not deny, but confessed, "I am not the Messiah." ²¹And they questioned him, "What then? Are you אֵלִיָּהוּ, Eliyahu?" And he said, "I am not." "Are you the Prophet?" and he answered, "No." ²²Then they said to him, "*Tell us* who you are, so that we may give an answer to those sending us. What do you say about yourself?" ²³*And* he said, "I AM A VOICE OF ONE CALLING, 'IN THE DESERT, MAKE STRAIGHT THE WAY OF ADONAI!' as יְשַׁעְיָהוּ, Y'sha'yahu the prophet said."[d]

²⁴And those sent were from the פְּרוּשִׁים, P'rushiym, ²⁵and they questioned him and said to him, "Why, then, do you immerse, if you are not the Messiah, nor אֵלִיָּהוּ, Eliyahu, nor the Prophet?" ²⁶יוֹחָנָן, Yochanan answered them, saying, "I immerse with

---

[a] "children"—Young's says, "sons"
[b] "one and only" or "only begotten" (μονογενοῦς, monogenous)—lit. "one-of-a-kind"; also in vs 18 (μονογενὴς, monogenes)
[c] "*of* God" cf. 1:14; or simply "God"—some mss say, "Son"
[d] יְשַׁעְיָהוּ Y'sha'yahu 40:3

water; He whom you have not known has stood in *the* middle of you—²⁷this One who *is* coming after me,ᵃ of whom I am not worthy that I may untie the strap of His sandal."

²⁸These things came to pass in בֵּית־עֲנָיָה, Beit-An'yah,ᵇ beyond the יַרְדֵּן, Yar'den, where יוֹחָנָן, Yochanan was immersing. ²⁹On the next day, he saw יֵשׁוּעַ, Yeshua coming to him, and said, "Look! the Lamb of God, who is taking away the sin of the world! ³⁰This is He about whom I said, 'After me comes a man who has come in front of me, because before me, He was.' ³¹But I knew Him not; rather, because of this—so that He would be revealed to יִשְׂרָאֵל, Yis'rael—I came immersing with water."

³²And יוֹחָנָן, Yochanan testified, saying, "I have seen the רוּחַ, Ruach coming down, as a dove out of heaven, and it remained on him. ³³And I did not know him, but He who sent me to immerse with water, He said to me, 'On whomever you see the רוּחַ, Ruach coming down and remaining on him, this is he who is immersing with the רוּחַ הַקֹּדֶשׁ, Ruach HaQodesh.' ³⁴And I have seen, and have testified, that this is the Son of God!"

³⁵On the next day, again, יוֹחָנָן, Yochanan was standing, and two of his disciples *were* with him. ³⁶And having looked on יֵשׁוּעַ, Yeshua *as* He was walking, he said, "Look! the Lamb of God!" ³⁷And the two disciples heard him speaking, and they followed יֵשׁוּעַ, Yeshua.

³⁸And יֵשׁוּעַ, Yeshua, having turned, and having noticed them following *Him*, said to them, "What are you looking for?" And they said to Him, "רַבִּי, Rabiy"—which is, being translated, "Teacher"—"where are You staying?" ³⁹*And* He said to them, "Come, and you will see." So they came and saw where He stayed, and they stayed with Him that day (the hour was about the tenth).

⁴⁰Andrew, the brother of שִׁמְעוֹן כֵּיפָא, Shim'on Keifa,ᶜ was one of the two who heard from יוֹחָנָן, Yochanan and followed Yeshua. ⁴¹This one first finds his own brother שִׁמְעוֹן, Shim'on, and says to him, "We have found the מָשִׁיחַ, Mashiyach!" (which is, being translated, "Anointed One"). ⁴²He brought him to יֵשׁוּעַ, Yeshua. Having looked upon him, יֵשׁוּעַ, Yeshua said, "You are שִׁמְעוֹן, Shim'on, the son of יוֹחָנָן, Yochanan.ᵈ You will be called כֵּיפָא, Keifa" (which is translated, "a rock"ᵉ).

⁴³On the next day, He wanted to go to the גָּלִיל, Galiyl, and He found Philip. And יֵשׁוּעַ, Yeshua said to him, "Be following Me." ⁴⁴And Philip was from בֵּית־צַיְדָה, Beit-Tzai'dah, of the city of Andrew and כֵּיפָא, Keifa. ⁴⁵Philip found נְתַנְאֵל, N'tan'el and said to him, "Him of whom מֹשֶׁה, Mosheh wrote in the תּוֹרָה, Torah—and the prophets *also*—we have found: יֵשׁוּעַ, Yeshua, son of יוֹסֵף, Yosef, who *is* from נְצֶרֶת, N'tzaret!" ⁴⁶And נְתַנְאֵל, N'tan'el said to him, "Is any good thing able to be out of נְצֶרֶת, N'tzaret?" Philip said to him, "Come and see."

⁴⁷יֵשׁוּעַ, Yeshua saw נְתַנְאֵל, N'tan'el coming to Him, and He said about him, "Look! truly a יִשְׂרְאֵלִי, Yis'r'eliy, in whom underhandedness is not." ⁴⁸נְתַנְאֵל, N'tan'el said to Him, "From where do you know me?" יֵשׁוּעַ, Yeshua answered him, "Before Philip's calling you—you being under the figtree—I saw you." ⁴⁹נְתַנְאֵל, N'tan'el answered him, "רַבִּי, Rabiy, you are the Son of God! You are the King of יִשְׂרָאֵל, Yis'rael!" ⁵⁰יֵשׁוּעַ, Yeshua answered and said to him, "Because I said to you, 'I saw you under the fig-tree,' you believe; you will see *even* greater things than these." ⁵¹And He said to him, "אָמֵן אָמֵן, Amen, amen, I say to you: you will see the Heaven opened, and the Messengers of God going up and coming downᶠ upon the Son of Man."

ᵃ "this One coming after me"—some mss say, "it is this One coming after me, who has been before me"

ᵇ "בֵּית־עֲנָיָה, Beit-An'yah"—some mss say, "בֵּית־עֲבָרָה, Beit-'Avarah"

ᶜ "כֵּיפָא, Keifa—actually, Πέτρος, Petros; see verse 42; also in verse 44

ᵈ "יוֹחָנָן, Yochanan"—some mss say, "יוֹנָה, Yonah"; cf. מַתִּתְיָהוּ *Matit'yahu* 16:17

ᵉ "a rock," that is, "Πέτρος, Petros"

ᶠ cf. בְּרֵאשִׁית *B'reshiyt* 28:12

יוֹחָנָן Yochanan 2:1 — *Water turned into wine.*

2 ¹And *on* the third day, a wedding happened in קָנָה, Qanah of the גָּלִיל, Galiyl, and the mother of יֵשׁוּעַ, Yeshua was there, ²and also יֵשׁוּעַ, Yeshua was called (and His disciples) to the wedding.

³And when *the supply of* wine had failed, the mother of יֵשׁוּעַ, Yeshua said to Him, "They have no wine." ⁴And יֵשׁוּעַ, Yeshua said to her, "What do you *want* with Me,ᵃ woman? My time is not yet come." ⁵His mother said to the servants, "Whatever He says to you, do."

⁶And there were six stone water-jugs there, placed according to the purifying *customs* of the יְהוּדִים, Y'hudiym, each *capable of* holding two or three measures.ᵇ ⁷יֵשׁוּעַ, Yeshua said to them, "Fill the water-jugs with water," and they filled them to the brim. ⁸And He said to them, "Now draw *some* out and bring *it* to the table-master." So they brought *it*.

⁹And as the table-master tasted the water *that had* become wine—and knew not where it was from (but the servants who had drawn the water knew)—the table-master called the bridegroom ¹⁰and said to him, "Every man, at first, sets out the good wine, and when they have *all* drunk freely, then the inferior. You kept the good wine until now!"

¹¹This, *the* beginning of the signs, יֵשׁוּעַ, Yeshua did in קָנָה, Qanah of the גָּלִיל, Galiyl, and revealed His glory, and His disciples believed in Him. ¹²After this, He went down to כְּפַר־נַחוּם, K'far-Nachum—He, and His mother, and His brothers, and His disciples—and there they remained not many days.

¹³And the פֶּסַח, Pesach of the יְהוּדִים, Y'hudiym was near, and יֵשׁוּעַ, Yeshua went up to יְרוּשָׁלַיִם, Y'rushalayim ¹⁴and found in the Temple those selling oxen and sheep and doves, and the money-changers sitting *at their tables*. ¹⁵And having made a whip of small cords, He drove *them* all out of the Temple—both the sheep, and the oxen— and He poured out the coins of the money-changers, and He overturned the tables. ¹⁶And to those selling the doves He said, "Take these things from here! Do not make the House of my Father a house of business!"

¹⁷His disciples remembered that it is written,

"The zeal of Your House will eat me up."ᶜ

¹⁸The יְהוּדִים, Y'hudiym then answered and said to Him, "What sign do you show to us that *gives* you *authority to* do these things?" ¹⁹יֵשׁוּעַ, Yeshua answered and said to them, "Destroy this Temple, and in three days I will raise it up." ²⁰The יְהוּדִים, Y'hudiym, therefore, said, "Building this Temple *took* forty and six years! and you will raise it up in three days?" ²¹(But He was speaking about the temple of His body. ²²When, then, He was raised out of the dead, His disciples remembered that He said this, and they believed the Scripture, and the word that יֵשׁוּעַ, Yeshua had said.)

²³And as He was in יְרוּשָׁלַיִם, Y'rushalayim during the פֶּסַח, Pesach, during the Feast, many believed in His Name, seeing His signs that He was doing. ²⁴But יֵשׁוּעַ, Yeshua Himself was not *entrusting* Himself to them, because of His knowing all MEN, ²⁵and because He had no need that any should testify about man, for He Himself was knowing what was in man.

3 ¹And there was a man of the פְּרוּשִׁים, P'rushiym—Nicodemus *was* his name, a leader of the יְהוּדִים, Y'hudiym. ²This one came to Him by night and said to Him, "רַבִּי, Rabiy, we have known that you—a teacher—have come from God, for no one is able to do these signs that you do if God is not with him." ³יֵשׁוּעַ, Yeshua answered and said to him, "אָמֵן אָמֵן, Amen, amen, I say to you: if anyone is not born *again* from above, he is not able to see the Reign of God." ⁴Nicodemus said to Him, "How is a man able to be born,

---

ᵃ "What do you *want* with Me"—lit., "what to Me and to you"; cf. Mark 5:7 and Luke 8:28

ᵇ twenty or thirty gallons

ᶜ תְּהִלִּים T'hiliym 69:10(9)

Discourse with Nicodemus.

being old? Is he able to enter into the womb of his mother a second time, and to be born?"

⁵יֵשׁוּעַ, Yeshua answered, "אָמֵן אָמֵן, Amen, amen, I say to you: if anyone is not born of water and the רוּחַ, Ruach, he is not able to enter into the Reign of God. ⁶That which has been born of the flesh is flesh, and that which has been born of the רוּחַ, Ruach is רוּחַ, ruach. ⁷Do not wonder that I said to you, 'You need to be born *again* from above.' ⁸The רוּחַ, Ruach[a] blows where he wants, and you hear his voice, but you have not known where he comes from, and where he goes. So is everyone who has been born of the רוּחַ, Ruach."

⁹Nicodemus answered and said to Him, "How are these things able to happen?" ¹⁰יֵשׁוּעַ, Yeshua answered and said to him, "You are the teacher of יִשְׂרָאֵל, Yis'rael, and these things you do not know!

¹¹"אָמֵן אָמֵן, Amen, amen, I say to you: we speak what we have known, and we testify *to* what we have seen, and our testimony you do not receive. ¹²If I said to you the earthly things, and you do not believe, how, if I will say to you the heavenly things, will you believe? ¹³And no one has gone up to the Heaven except He who came down out of the Heaven: the Son of Man.[b]

¹⁴"And as מֹשֶׁה, Mosheh lifted up the serpent in the desert, so it is necessary *for* the Son of Man to be lifted up, ¹⁵so that everyone who is believing in Him[c] may have life age-enduring.

¹⁶"For God so loved the world, that the Son—the one and only[d]—He gave, so that everyone who is believing in Him may not be destroyed, but may have life age-enduring.

¹⁷"For God did not send the Son to the world so that He might judge the world, but so that the world might be saved through Him. ¹⁸He who is believing in Him is not judged, but he who is not believing has been judged already, because he has not believed in the Name of the one and only Son of God.

¹⁹"And this is the judgment: that the light has come to the world, and men loved the darkness rather than the light, for their actions were evil. ²⁰For everyone who is doing wicked things hates the light, and does not come into the light, so that his actions will not be detected. ²¹But he who is doing the truth comes to the light, so that his actions may be revealed—that they are having been done in God."

²²After these things, יֵשׁוּעַ, Yeshua and His disciples came to the land of יְהוּדָה, Y'hudah, and He stayed there with them and was immersing. ²³And יוֹחָנָן, Yochanan was also immersing in עֵנוֹן, Enon, near to שָׁלֵם, Shalem, because there were many waters there. And *people* were coming and were being immersed ²⁴(for יוֹחָנָן, Yochanan was not yet thrown into the prison). ²⁵Then, from the disciples of יוֹחָנָן, Yochanan, there arose a question with a *certain* יְהוּדִי, Y'hudiy about purifying, ²⁶and they came to יוֹחָנָן, Yochanan and said to him, "רַבִּי, Rabiy, he who was with you beyond the יַרְדֵּן, Yar'den, to whom you testified—look! this one is immersing, and all are coming to him."

²⁷יוֹחָנָן, Yochanan answered and said, "A man is not able to receive anything if it has not been given him from the Heaven. ²⁸You yourselves testify to me that I said I am not the Messiah, but that I am having been sent in front of Him. ²⁹He who is having the bride is *the* bridegroom, but the friend of the bridegroom, who is standing and hearing him, rejoices with joy because of the voice of the bridegroom. This, then—my joy—has been fulfilled.

³⁰"It is necessary *for* Him to increase, and *for* me to become less. ³¹He who is coming from above is above all; he who is from the earth, he is from the earth, and from the earth he speaks. *But* He who is coming from the Heaven is above all.

³²"What He has seen and heard, *to* this

---

[a] "רוּחַ, Ruach" or "wind"
[b] Some mss insert, "who is in the Heaven"
[c] Some mss insert, "may not be destroyed, but"
[d] "one and only" or "only begotten"—literally, "one-of-a-kind"; μονογενῆ, monogene; also in verse 18 (μονογενοῦς, monogenous)

He testifies, and no one receives His testimony. ³³He who is receiving His testimony certifies that God is true, ³⁴for He whom God sent speaks the sayings of God, for He[a] gives the רוּחַ, Ruach without measure. ³⁵The Father loves the Son and has given all things into His hand. ³⁶He who is believing in the Son has life age-enduring, but he who is not believing the Son will not see life, but the wrath of God remains on him."

4 ¹Therefore, when יֵשׁוּעַ, Yeshua[b] knew that the פְּרוּשִׁים, P'rushiym heard that יֵשׁוּעַ, Yeshua made and immersed more disciples than יוֹחָנָן, Yochanan ²(though, indeed, יֵשׁוּעַ, Yeshua Himself was not immersing, but rather His disciples), ³He left יְהוּדָה, Y'hudah and went away again to the גָּלִיל, Galiyl, ⁴and it was necessary for Him to go through שֹׁמְרוֹן, Shom'ron.

⁵So He came to a city of שֹׁמְרוֹן, Shom'ron called סוּכָר, Sukhar, near to the place that יַעֲקֹב, Ya'aqov had given to his son יוֹסֵף, Yosef, ⁶and there was a well of יַעֲקֹב, Ya'aqov there. So יֵשׁוּעַ, Yeshua, having been weary from the journey, was sitting this way on the well (it was about the sixth hour), ⁷and there came a woman out of שֹׁמְרוֹן, Shom'ron to draw water.

יֵשׁוּעַ, Yeshua said to her, "Give Me *something* to drink," ⁸for His disciples were gone away to the city so that they could buy food. ⁹Then the שֹׁמְרוֹנִית, Shom'roniyt woman said to Him, "How do you, being a יְהוּדִי, Y'hudiy, ask *for* a drink from me, being a שֹׁמְרוֹנִית, Shom'roniyt woman?" (for יְהוּדִים, Y'hudiym have no dealing with *the* שֹׁמְרוֹנִים, Shom'roniym).

¹⁰יֵשׁוּעַ, Yeshua answered and said to her, "If you had known the gift of God, and who it is who is saying to you, 'Give Me *something* to drink,' you would have asked Him, and He would have given you living water." ¹¹The woman said to Him, "Sir, you do not even have a bucket for drawing *water*, and the well is deep. From where, then, do you have the living water? ¹²Are you greater than our father יַעֲקֹב, Ya'aqov, who gave us the well, and drank out of it himself, and *also* his sons, and his cattle?"

¹³יֵשׁוּעַ, Yeshua answered and said to her, "Everyone who is drinking of this water will thirst again, ¹⁴but whoever drinks of the water that I will give him will not thirst—to the age. And the water that I will give him will become in him a well of water, springing up to life age-enduring."

¹⁵The woman said to Him, "Sir, give me this water, that I may not thirst, nor come *back* here to draw *water*." ¹⁶He said to her, "Go, call your husband, and come *back* here."

¹⁷The woman answered and said to Him, "I do not have a husband." יֵשׁוּעַ, Yeshua said to her, "You said *it* well, 'I do not have a husband,' ¹⁸for you have had five husbands, and now, he whom you have is not your husband. This you have said truly."

¹⁹The woman said to Him, "Sir, I see that you are a prophet. ²⁰Our fathers worshipped on this mountain, but you—you say that in יְרוּשָׁלַיִם, Y'rushalayim is the place where it is necessary to worship." ²¹יֵשׁוּעַ, Yeshua said to her, "Believe Me, woman, that there comes a time when neither on this mountain nor in יְרוּשָׁלַיִם, Y'rushalayim will you worship the Father. ²²You worship what you have not known; we worship what we have known, because the salvation is of the יְהוּדִים, Y'hudiym.

²³"But there comes a time, and it is now, when the true worshippers will worship the Father in רוּחַ, ruach and truth, for the Father also looks for such to worship Him. ²⁴God *is* a רוּחַ, Ruach, and it is necessary for those worshipping Him to worship in רוּחַ, ruach and truth." ²⁵The woman said to Him, "I have known that מָשִׁיחַ, Mashiyach (who is called Messiah) comes. When that One comes, He will tell us all things." ²⁶יֵשׁוּעַ, Yeshua said to her, "I am *he*, who is speaking to you."

²⁷And His disciples came upon this and were in wonder that He was speaking with a woman. (No one, however, said, "What are you looking for?" or "Why do You speak

---

[a] "He"—some mss say, "God"
[b] יֵשׁוּעַ, Yeshua—some mss say, "the Master"

Disabled man encounters Yeshua. יוֹחָנָן Yochanan 5:6

with her?") ²⁸The woman then left her water-jug, and went away to the city, and said to the men, ²⁹"Come, see a man who told me all things—as many as I did. Is this the Messiah?" ³⁰They went out of the city and were coming toward Him.

³¹Meanwhile, His disciples were asking Him, saying, "רַבִּי, Rabiy, eat." ³²But He said to them, "I have food to eat that you have not known." ³³The disciples then said one to another, "Did anyone bring Him anything to eat?" ³⁴יֵשׁוּעַ, Yeshua said to them, "My food is that I may do the will of Him who sent Me, and may finish His work. ³⁵Do not say that it is four more months, and *then* the harvest comes. Look! I say to you: lift up your eyes and see the fields, that they are white toward harvest already.

³⁶"He who is reaping receives a wage and gathers fruit to life age-enduring, so that he who is sowing and he who is reaping may rejoice together. ³⁷For in this the saying is true: that one is the sower and another the reaper. ³⁸I sent you to reap that on which you have not labored. Others labored, and you have entered into their labor."

³⁹And many of the שֹׁמְרֹנִים, Shom'roniym from that city believed in Him because of the word of the woman testifying, "He told me all the things that I did." ⁴⁰So when the שֹׁמְרֹנִים, Shom'roniym came to Him, they were asking Him to remain with them; and He remained there two days, ⁴¹and many more believed because of His word. ⁴²And they said to the woman, "We no longer believe *simply* because of your speaking, for we ourselves have heard and known that this is truly the Savior of the world!"ᵃ

⁴³And after the two days He went from there to the גָּלִיל, Galiyl, ⁴⁴for יֵשׁוּעַ, Yeshua Himself testified that a prophet in his own homeland will not have honor. ⁴⁵Then, when He came to the גָּלִיל, Galiyl, the גְּלִילִים, G'liyliym received Him, having seen all *the* things—as many as He did in יְרוּשָׁלַיִם, Y'rushalayim during the Feast (for they also went to the Feast).

ᵃ Some mss insert, "—the Messiah!"

⁴⁶Then He came again to קָנָה, Qanah of the גָּלִיל, Galiyl (where He made the water *into* wine), and there was a certain royal official, whose son was infirmed in כְּפַר־נַחוּם, K'far-Nachum. ⁴⁷*When* he heard that יֵשׁוּעַ, Yeshua had come out of יְהוּדָה, Y'hudah to the גָּלִיל, Galiyl, he went away to Him, and was asking that He may come down and heal his son, for he was about to die. ⁴⁸יֵשׁוּעַ, Yeshua then said to him, "Unless you see signs and wonders, you will not believe." ⁴⁹The royal official said to Him, "Sir, come down before my child dies." ⁵⁰יֵשׁוּעַ, Yeshua said to him, "Be going on—your son lives." The man believed the word that יֵשׁוּעַ, Yeshua said to him, and was going on. ⁵¹And *as he was* now going down, his slaves met him, saying that his child lives. ⁵²Then he asked of them the hour in which he had become better. Then they said to him, "Yesterday at the seventh hour the fever left him." ⁵³Then the father knew that IT WAS in that hour in which יֵשׁוּעַ, Yeshua said to him, "Your son lives"; and he himself believed, and his whole house.

⁵⁴And this, again, *is* a second sign יֵשׁוּעַ, Yeshua did, having come out of יְהוּדָה, Y'hudah to the גָּלִיל, Galiyl.

5

¹After these things there was a Feast of the יְהוּדִים, Y'hudiym, and יֵשׁוּעַ, Yeshua went up to יְרוּשָׁלַיִם, Y'rushalayim. ²Now, there is in יְרוּשָׁלַיִם, Y'rushalayim, by the sheep-GATE, a pool that in Hebrewᵇ is called, "בֵּית־חַסְדָּא, Beit-Chas'da," having five colonnades. ³In these were lying a great number of the infirmed, blind, lame, *and* withered.ᶜ

⁵And there was a certain man there, being in his ailment *for* thirty and eight years; ⁶*and* יֵשׁוּעַ, Yeshua, having seen him lying *there*, and having known that he had already *been there* a long time, said to him, "Do you want to become whole?"

ᵇ "Hebrew"—technically, Aramaic
ᶜ Some mss insert, "waiting for the moving of the water. ⁴(For a Messenger at a set time was going down in the pool, and was disturbing the water; then the first *one* having gone in after the disturbing of the water became whole of whatever sickness he was held *by*.)"

⁷The ailing man answered Him, "Sir, I have no man, that when the water is disturbed, he may put me into the pool. And while I am coming *to get in*, another goes down in front of me." ⁸יֵשׁוּעַ, Yeshua said to him, "Rise, lift up your mat, and be walking." ⁹And immediately, the man became whole, and he lifted up his mat, and was walking.

Now, it was a שַׁבָּת, Shabat on that day. ¹⁰Then the יְהוּדִים, Y'hudiym said to him who had been healed, "It is a שַׁבָּת, Shabat, and it is not permitted for you to lift up your mat." ¹¹But he answered them, "He who made me whole—that one said to me, 'Lift up your mat, and be walking.'" ¹²They questioned him, "Who is the man who is saying to you, 'Lift *it* up and be walking'?" ¹³But he who was healed had not known who He was, for יֵשׁוּעַ, Yeshua moved away, there being a crowd in the place.

¹⁴After these things, יֵשׁוּעַ, Yeshua found him in the Temple and said to him, "Look! you have become whole. Sin no longer; otherwise, something worse may happen to you." ¹⁵The man went away and told the יְהוּדִים, Y'hudiym that it was יֵשׁוּעַ, Yeshua who made him whole, ¹⁶and because of this the יְהוּדִים, Y'hudiym were persecuting יֵשׁוּעַ, Yeshua,ᵃ because He was doing these things on a שַׁבָּת, Shabat. ¹⁷And יֵשׁוּעַ, Yeshua answered them, "My Father works until now, and *so* I work."

¹⁸Because of this, then, the יְהוּדִים, Y'hudiym were looking to kill him *all* the more, because not only was He "breaking the שַׁבָּת, Shabat,"ᵇ but He was also calling God His own Father, making Himself equal to God.

¹⁹So יֵשׁוּעַ, Yeshua responded and was saying to them, "אָמֵן אָמֵן, Amen, amen, I say to you: the Son is not able to do anything of himself, if he does not see the Father doing anything. For whatever things He does— these also the Son likewise does. ²⁰For the Father loves the Son, and shows to him all things that He Himself does.

"And He will show him greater acts than these, so that you may *be in* wonder. ²¹For, as the Father raises the dead and makes alive, so also the Son makes alive whom he wills. ²²For neither does the Father judge anyone, but He has given all the judgment to the Son, ²³so that all may honor the Son as they honor the Father. He who is not honoring the Son does not honor the Father who sent him.

²⁴"אָמֵן אָמֵן, Amen, amen, I say to you: he who is hearing my word and is believing Him who sent me has life age-enduring, and he does not come into judgment, but has passed out of the death into the life. ²⁵אָמֵן אָמֵן, Amen, amen, I say to you: there comes a time, and it now is, when the dead will hear the voice of the Son of God, and those having heard will live. ²⁶Indeed, as the Father has life in Himself, so also He gave to the Son to have life in himself. ²⁷And He gave him authority to do judgment, because he is *the* Son of Man.

²⁸"Marvel not at this, because there comes a time in which all those in the tombs will hear his voice, ²⁹and they will come out— those who did the good things to a Rising Again of life, but those who practiced the evil things to a Rising Again of judgment.

³⁰"I am unable to do anything of myself. I judge as I hear, and my judgment is righteous, because I seek not my own will, but the will of Himᶜ who sent me.

³¹"If I *alone* testify about myself, my testimony is not true. ³²*But* there is another who is testifying about me, and I have known that the testimony that he testifies about me is true. ³³You have sent to יוֹחָנָן, Yochanan, and he has testified to the truth ³⁴(but I do not receive testimony from man; rather, I say these things so that you may be saved). ³⁵He was the burning and shining lamp, and you wanted to be extremely joyful for a moment in his light.

³⁶"But I have the testimony greater than *that* of יוֹחָנָן, Yochanan. Indeed, the acts that the Father has given me so that I might complete them (the acts themselves that I do), they testify about me—that the Father

---

ᵃ Some mss insert, "and looking to kill Him"
ᵇ "breaking the שַׁבָּת, Shabat" according to the man-made traditions of the יְהוּדִים, Y'hudiym

ᶜ "Him"—some mss say, "the Father"

He walks on the water. יוֹחָנָן **Yochanan 6:20**

has sent me. ³⁷And the Father who sent me—He has testified about me. You have neither heard His voice at any time, nor have you seen His form, ³⁸and His word you do not have remaining in you, because you do not believe him whom He sent.

³⁹"You search the Scriptures because you think to have life age-enduring in them. But these are they that are testifying about me— ⁴⁰and you do not want to come to me so that you may have life.

⁴¹"I do not receive glory from man, ⁴²but I have known you: that you do not have the love of God in yourselves.

⁴³"I have come in the Name of my Father, but you do not receive me. *But if another comes in his own name, him you will receive.* ⁴⁴You—how are you able to believe, receiving glory from one another, but you do not seek the glory that IS from God alone? ⁴⁵Do not think that I will accuse you to the Father. There is *one* who is *already* accusing you: מֹשֶׁה, Mosheh, in whom you have hoped.

⁴⁶Indeed, if you were believing מֹשֶׁה, Mosheh, you would have been believing me, for he wrote about me. ⁴⁷But if you do not believe his writings, how will you believe my sayings?"

6 ¹After these things, יֵשׁוּעַ, Yeshua went away beyond the sea of the גָּלִיל, Galiyl (of Tiberias), ²and there was a large crowd following Him because they were seeing the signs that He was doing on the infirmed. ³And יֵשׁוּעַ, Yeshua went up to the mountain, and He was sitting there with His disciples, ⁴and the פֶּסַח, Pesach was near—the Feast of the יְהוּדִים, Y'hudiym.

⁵יֵשׁוּעַ, Yeshua then, having lifted up HIS eyes and having seen that a large crowd was coming to Him, said to Philip, "From where may we buy loaves *of bread,* so that these *people* may eat?" ⁶(And He said this, testing him; for He Himself had known what He was about to do.)

⁷Philip answered Him, "Two hundred days' wages[a] worth of loaves are not sufficient to *feed* them, *such* that each may receive some little *bit.*"

⁸One of His disciples—Andrew, the brother of שִׁמְעוֹן כֵּיפָא, Shim'on Keifa[b]—said to Him, ⁹"There is a little boy here who has five barley loaves and two fishes; but these—what are they to so many *people?*"

¹⁰יֵשׁוּעַ, Yeshua said, "Make the men to sit down." And there was much grass in the place, so the men sat down—about five thousand in number. ¹¹Then יֵשׁוּעַ, Yeshua took the loaves, and having given thanks, He distributed *them*[c] to those reclining. Likewise also of the little fishes—as much as they wanted. ¹²And when they were filled, He said to His disciples, "Gather together the broken pieces that are *left* over, so that nothing may be lost." ¹³Then they gathered together and filled twelve handbaskets with broken pieces from the five barley loaves that were *left* over by those having eaten.

¹⁴Then the men, having seen the sign that He did, said, "This is truly the Prophet[d] who is coming to the world." ¹⁵יֵשׁוּעַ, Yeshua, therefore, having known that they were about to come and to take Him by force so that they could make Him king, withdrew again to the mountain, Himself alone.

¹⁶And when evening came, His disciples went down to the sea; ¹⁷and having entered into a boat, they were going over the sea to כְּפַר־נַחוּם, K'far-Nachum. And darkness had already come, and יֵשׁוּעַ, Yeshua had not yet come to them. ¹⁸The sea also—a great wind blowing—was being raised. ¹⁹Having pushed onwards, then, about three or four miles,[e] they saw יֵשׁוּעַ, Yeshua walking on the sea, and coming near to the boat! And they were afraid, ²⁰but He said to them, "I am HE—be not

---

[a] "days' wages"—lit. "denaries"
[b] כֵּיפָא, Keifa—actually, Πέτρος, Petros; see יוֹחָנָן *Yn.* 1:42; also vs. 68
[c] Some mss insert, "to the disciples, and the disciples"
[d] see דְּבָרִים *D'variym* 18:15-19
[e] "three or four miles"—lit. "twenty-five or thirty stadia"

afraid." ²¹Then they were willing to receive Him into the boat, and immediately the boat came to the ground to which they were going.

²²On the next day, the crowd that was standing on the other side of the sea saw that there was no other little boat there except one,[a] and that יֵשׁוּעַ, Yeshua had not gone in with His disciples into the boat, but His disciples went away alone. ²³Other little boats came from Tiberias, near the place where they ate the bread *and* the Master had given thanks; ²⁴therefore, when the crowd saw that יֵשׁוּעַ, Yeshua was not there, nor His disciples, they themselves entered into the little boats and came to כְּפַר-נַחוּם, K'far-Nachum looking for יֵשׁוּעַ, Yeshua.

²⁵And having found Him on the other side of the sea, they said to Him, "רַבִּי, Rabiy, when did You come here?" ²⁶יֵשׁוּעַ, Yeshua answered them and said, "אָמֵן אָמֵן, Amen, amen, I say to you: you look for Me, not because you saw signs, but because you ate of the loaves *of bread* and were satisfied. ²⁷Work not for the food that is perishing, but for the food that is remaining to life age-enduring, which the Son of Man will give to you. For the Father certified him— EVEN God."

²⁸Then they said to him, "What should we do so that we may do the works of God?" ²⁹יֵשׁוּעַ, Yeshua answered and said to them, "This is the work of God: that you may believe in him whom He sent." ³⁰Then they said to him, "What sign, then, do you do, so that we may see and believe you? What work do you do? ³¹Our fathers ate the מָן, mahn in the desert, as it is having been written, 'HE GAVE THEM BREAD OUT OF THE HEAVEN TO EAT.'"[b]

³²יֵשׁוּעַ, Yeshua, therefore, said to them, "אָמֵן אָמֵן, Amen, amen, I say to you: מֹשֶׁה, Mosheh did not give you the bread out of the heaven, but my Father gives you the true bread out of the Heaven. ³³Indeed, the bread of God is that which is coming down out of the Heaven, and giving life to the world." ³⁴Then they said to him, "Sir, always give us this bread."

³⁵יֵשׁוּעַ, Yeshua said to them, "I am the bread of the Life; he who is coming to me will not hunger, and he who is believing in me will not thirst—at any time. ³⁶But I said to you that you also have seen me, and you do not believe. ³⁷All that the Father gives to me will come to me, and he who is coming to me, I will never ever drive away, ³⁸because I have come down from the Heaven, not so that I may do my will, but the will of Him who sent me. ³⁹And this is the will of Him[c] who sent me: that all that He has given to me, I may not lose *any* of it, but raise it up in the last day. ⁴⁰For this is the will of my Father:[d] that everyone who is seeing the Son, and is believing in him, may have life age-enduring, and I will raise him up in the last day."

⁴¹The יְהוּדִים, Y'hudiym, therefore, were grumbling at Him, because He said, "I am the bread that came down out of the Heaven." ⁴²And they said, "Is this not יֵשׁוּעַ, Yeshua, the son of יוֹסֵף, Yosef, whose father and mother we have known? How does He now say, 'Out of the Heaven I have come down'?"

⁴³יֵשׁוּעַ, Yeshua answered and said to them, "Grumble not with one another. ⁴⁴No one is able to come to me, if the Father who sent me does not draw him; and I will raise him up in the last day. ⁴⁵It is having been written in the Prophets:

'And they will all be taught by God.'[e]

Everyone who heard and learned from the Father comes to me ⁴⁶(not that anyone has seen the Father, except he who is from God—he has seen the Father).

⁴⁷"אָמֵן אָמֵן, Amen, amen, I say to you: he who is believing[f] has life age-enduring. ⁴⁸I am the bread of the Life. ⁴⁹Your fathers ate the מָן, mahn in the desert, and they died, ⁵⁰*but* this is the bread that is coming down

---

[a] Some mss insert, "that *one* into which His disciples entered"
[b] תְּהִלִּים T'hiliym 78:24, 105:40; שְׁמוֹת Sh'mot 16:4; נְחֶמְיָה N'chem'yah 9:15
[c] "Him"—some mss say, "the Father"
[d] "my Father"—some mss say, "Him who sent me"
[e] יְשַׁעְיָהוּ Y'sha'yahu 54:13; cf. יִרְמְיָהוּ Yir'm'yahu 31:34
[f] Some mss insert, "in Me"

out of the Heaven, so that anyone may eat of it, and not die. ⁵¹I am the living bread that came down out of the Heaven. If anyone eats of this bread, he will live—to the age. And the bread indeed[a] is my flesh that I will give for the life of the world."

⁵²The יְהוּדִים, Y'hudiym, therefore, were being combative with one another, saying, "How is this one able to give us his flesh to eat?" ⁵³ יֵשׁוּעַ, Yeshua, therefore, said to them, "אָמֵן אָמֵן, Amen, amen, I say to you: if you do not eat the flesh of the Son of Man and do not drink His blood, you have no life in yourselves. ⁵⁴He who is eating My flesh and is drinking My blood has life age-enduring, and I will raise him up in the last day. ⁵⁵For My flesh is true food, and My blood is true drink.[b] ⁵⁶He who is eating My flesh, and is drinking My blood, remains in Me, and I in him.

⁵⁷"As the living Father sent Me (and I live because of the Father), he who is also eating Me—that one also will live because of Me. ⁵⁸This is the bread that came down out of the Heaven, not as your fathers ate[c] and died. He who is eating this bread will live—to the age." ⁵⁹(He said these things in a synagogue, teaching in כְּפַר-נַחוּם, K'far-Nachum.)

⁶⁰Then many of His disciples, having heard, said, "This word is hard. Who is able to listen to it?" ⁶¹And יֵשׁוּעַ, Yeshua, having known in Himself that His disciples were grumbling about this, said to them, "Does this stumble you? ⁶²Then *what* if you see the Son of Man going up *to* where He was before? ⁶³It is the רוּחַ, Ruach that is giving life; the flesh does not benefit anything. The sayings that I have spoken to you are רוּחַ, ruach, and they are life, ⁶⁴but there are certain *ones* of you who do not believe"—for יֵשׁוּעַ, Yeshua had known from the beginning who they were who were not believing, and who he was who would hand Him over. ⁶⁵And He said, "Because of this I have said to you that no one is able to come to Me if it has not been given him from the Father." ⁶⁶*And* from this TIME, many of His disciples went away backward, and were walking with Him no more.

⁶⁷So יֵשׁוּעַ, Yeshua said to the Twelve, "Do you also want to go away?" ⁶⁸שִׁמְעוֹן כֵּיפָא, Shim'on Keifa answered Him, "Master, to whom would we go? You have *the* sayings of life age-enduring; ⁶⁹and we have believed, and we have known, that You are the Holy One of[d] God!" ⁷⁰ יֵשׁוּעַ, Yeshua answered them, "Did I not choose you, the Twelve? And *yet* one of you is an accuser." ⁷¹He spoke of יְהוּדָה, Y'hudah, SON of שִׁמְעוֹן, Shim'on, אִישׁ-קְרִיּוֹת, Iysh-Q'riyot, for he (one of the Twelve) was about to hand Him over.

7

¹And after these things, יֵשׁוּעַ, Yeshua was walking in the גָּלִיל, Galiyl (for He did not want to walk in יְהוּדָה, Y'hudah, since the יְהוּדִים, Y'hudiym were looking to kill Him), ²and the Feast of the יְהוּדִים, Y'hudiym was near—that of סֻכּוֹת, Sukot.

³So His brothers said to Him, "Leave from here and go away to יְהוּדָה, Y'hudah, so that your disciples also will see your acts that you do. ⁴For no one does anything in secret, and *yet* himself looks to be *known* in public. If you do these things, reveal yourself to the world"—⁵for not even His brothers were believing in Him.

⁶So יֵשׁוּעַ, Yeshua said to them, "My time is not yet come, but your time is always ready. ⁷The world is not able to hate you, but it does hate Me, because I testify about it—that its actions are evil. ⁸You—you go up to the Feast. I do not yet[e] go up to this Feast, because my time has not yet been fulfilled." ⁹And having said these things, He remained in the גָּלִיל, Galiyl.

¹⁰And when His brothers had gone up to the Feast, then He Himself also went up—not openly, but as in secret. ¹¹The יְהוּדִים, Y'hudiym, then, were looking for

---

[a] Some mss insert, "that I will give"
[b] "is true food… is true drink"—some mss say, "truly is food… truly is drink"
[c] Some mss insert, "the מָן, mahn"
[d] "Holy One of"—some mss say, "Messiah, the Son of the living"
[e] Earlier mss omit, "yet"

Him at the Feast, and said, "Where is that one?" ¹²And there was much grumbling about Him among the crowd. Some indeed said, "He is good"; and others said, "No—rather, he leads the many astray." ¹³No one, however, was speaking freely about Him, through fear of *the authorities of* the יְהוּדִים, Y'hudiym.

¹⁴And it being now the middle of the Feast, יֵשׁוּעַ, Yeshua went up to the Temple, and He was teaching. ¹⁵The יְהוּדִים, Y'hudiym, then, were in wonder, saying, "How has this one known *the letters of Scripture*, not having learned *them formally*?" ¹⁶Then יֵשׁוּעַ, Yeshua answered them and said, "My teaching is not mine, but His who sent me. ¹⁷If anyone wants to do His will, he will know about the teaching—whether it is of God, or *whether* I speak from myself. ¹⁸He who is speaking from himself seeks his own glory, but he who is seeking the glory of Him who sent him—this one is true, and unrighteousness is not in him. ¹⁹Has not מֹשֶׁה, Mosheh given you the תּוֹרָה, Torah? And *yet* none of you does the תּוֹרָה, Torah! Why do you look to kill Me?"

²⁰The crowd answered, "You have a demon! Who is looking to kill you?" ²¹יֵשׁוּעַ, Yeshua answered and said to them, "I did one act, and you all marvel. ²²Because of this—*that* מֹשֶׁה, Mosheh has given you the circumcision (not that it is of מֹשֶׁה, Mosheh, but of the fathers)—you circumcise a man even on a שַׁבָּת, Shabat. ²³If a man receives circumcision on a שַׁבָּת, Shabat, so that the תּוֹרָה, Torah of מֹשֶׁה, Mosheh may not be broken, *why* are you angered with Me, that I made an entire man whole on a שַׁבָּת, Shabat? ²⁴Judge not according to appearance; rather, judge *according to* the righteous judgment."

²⁵Then certain *ones* of the יְרוּשָׁלַיִם, Y'rushalamiym said, "Is this not he whom they are looking to kill? ²⁶And look! he speaks freely, and they say nothing to him. Perhaps the leaders truly know that this is[a] the Messiah? ²⁷But this one—we have known where he is from; and the Messiah, when he comes, no one knows where he is from."

²⁸Then יֵשׁוּעַ, Yeshua shouted in the Temple, teaching and saying, "You have both known Me, and you have known where I am from! And I have not come of Myself, but He who sent Me is true——*He* whom you have not known! ²⁹I have known Him, because I am from Him, and He sent Me."

³⁰Then they were looking to seize Him, but no one laid the hand on Him, because His time had not yet come.

³¹And many out of the crowd believed in Him, and said, "The Messiah, when he comes—will he do more signs than this one did?" ³²The פְּרוּשִׁים, P'rushiym heard the crowd murmuring these things about Him, and the chief כֹּהֲנִים, Ko'haniym and the פְּרוּשִׁים, P'rushiym sent *their* attendants so that they might take Him.

³³יֵשׁוּעַ, Yeshua, therefore, said, "*For* a little time I am still with you, and *then* I go away to Him who sent Me. ³⁴You will look for Me, but you will not find Me, and where I am, you are not able to come." ³⁵Then the יְהוּדִים, Y'hudiym said among themselves, "Where is this one about to go that we will not find him? Is he about to go to the Dispersion of the Greeks, and to teach the Greeks? ³⁶What is this word that he said, 'You will look for me, but you will not find me, and where I am, you are not able to come'?"

³⁷And on the last day of the Feast—the loudest[b]—יֵשׁוּעַ, Yeshua stood and shouted, saying, "If anyone thirsts, let him come to Me and drink! ³⁸He who is believing in Me, as the Scripture said—out of his belly will flow rivers of living water!" ³⁹(And He said this about the רוּחַ, Ruach which those having believed in Him were about to receive, for the רוּחַ, Ruach[c] was not yet, because יֵשׁוּעַ, Yeshua was not yet glorified.)

⁴⁰Then many out of the crowd, having heard these words, said, "This is truly the Prophet!" ⁴¹Others said, "This is the Messiah!" And others said, "Why? does the Mes-

---

[a] Some mss insert, "truly"

[b] "loudest" or "great"

[c] "Some mss insert, "הַקֹּדֶשׁ, HaQodesh"

The light of the world. יוֹחָנָן Yochanan 8:19

siah come out of the גָלִיל, Galiyl? ⁴²Did not the Scripture say that the Messiah comes out of the seed of דָוִד, David, and from בֵּית־לֶחֶם, Beit-Lechem—the village where דָוִד, David was?"

⁴³Therefore, a division arose among the crowd because of Him, ⁴⁴and certain *ones* of them were wanting to seize Him, but no one threw *their* hands on Him.

⁴⁵Then the attendants came to the chief כֹּהֲנִים, Ko'haniym and פְּרוּשִׁים, P'rushiym, and they said to them, "Why did you not bring him?" ⁴⁶The attendants answered, "Never has a man spoken this way.ᵃ" ⁴⁷The פְּרוּשִׁים, P'rushiym, then, answered them, "Have you also been led astray? ⁴⁸Did anyone from the leaders believe in him? or from the פְּרוּשִׁים, P'rushiym? ⁴⁹Rather, this crowd that is not knowing the תּוֹרָה, Torah is accursed!"

⁵⁰Then Nicodemus (he who came to Him beforeᵇ) said to them (being one of them), ⁵¹"Does our תּוֹרָה, Torah judge the man if it does not hear from him first, and know what he does?" ⁵²They answered and said to him, "Are you also from the גָלִיל, Galiyl? Search and see that a prophet does not rise out of the גָלִיל, Galiyl."

The most reliable early manuscripts do not have Yochanan 7:53-8:11.

⁵³And each one went on to his house.

8 ¹Now יֵשׁוּעַ, Yeshua went on to the Mountain of the Olives, ²and at dawn, He came again to the Temple, and all the people were coming to Him. And having sat down, He was teaching them, ³and the סוֹפְרִים, Sof'riym and the פְּרוּשִׁים, P'rushiym brought a woman having been caught in adultery. And having set her in the middle *of the courtyard*, ⁴they said to Him, "Teacher, this woman has been caught in the very act *of* committing adultery, ⁵and in the תּוֹרָה, Torah, מֹשֶׁה, Mosheh commanded us to stone such *women*. You, therefore—what do you say?" ⁶(And they said this, testing Him, so that they might have grounds to accuse Him.)

But יֵשׁוּעַ, Yeshua, having stooped down, was writing on the ground with the finger. ⁷And when they continued asking Him, He straightened Himself up and said to them, "The sinless among you—let him throw the stone at her first." ⁸And again, having stooped down, He was writing on the ground.

⁹And having heard,ᶜ they were going out one by one, having begun from the older ones. And He was left alone, and the woman was in the middle *of the courtyard*.

¹⁰And יֵשׁוּעַ, Yeshua, having straightened Himself up,ᵈ said to her, "Woman, where are they?ᵉ Did no one pass sentence on you?" ¹¹And she said, "No one, sir." And יֵשׁוּעַ, Yeshua said, "Neither do I pass sentence on you. Be going on, and from now on,ᶠ sin no more."

---

¹²Then יֵשׁוּעַ, Yeshua again spoke to them, saying, "I am the light of the world. He who is following Me will not walk in the darkness, but He will have the light of the life."

¹³Then the פְּרוּשִׁים, P'rushiym said to Him, "You testify of yourself; your testimony is not true."

¹⁴יֵשׁוּעַ,Yeshua answered and said to them, "Even if I testify of Myself, My testimony is true, because I have known where I came from, and where I go. But you—you have not known where I come from, or where I go. ¹⁵You judge according to the flesh; I do not judge anyone. ¹⁶But even if I do judge, My judgment is true, because I am not *judging* alone, but I and the Father who sent Me. ¹⁷And it has also been written in your תּוֹרָה, Torah that the testimony of two men is true.ᵍ ¹⁸I am ONE who is testifying of Myself, and the Father who sent Me testifies of Me *also*."

¹⁹Then they said to Him, "Where is your father?" יֵשׁוּעַ, Yeshua answered, "You have known neither Me nor My Father. If you had known Me, My Father you also *would* have known."

ᵃ Some mss insert, "—as this man"
ᵇ "before"—some mss say, "by night"

ᶜ Some mss insert, "and being convicted by their conscience"
ᵈ Some mss insert, "and having seen no one but the woman"
ᵉ Some mss insert, "—your accusers?"
ᶠ Some mss omit, "from now on"
ᵍ cf. דְּבָרִים D'variym 17:6, 19:15

²⁰He spoke *all* these sayings in the Treasury, teaching in the Temple, and no one seized Him, because His time had not yet come.

²¹Then He said again to them, "I *will* go away, and you will look for Me, and in your sin you will die. Where I go away, you are not able to come."

²²Then the יְהוּדִים, Y'hudiym said, "Will he kill himself? For he said, 'Where I go away, you are not able to come.'" ²³And He said to them, "You are from below; I am from above. You are of this world; I am not of this world. ²⁴Therefore, I said to you that you will die in your sins—for if you do not believe that I am HE, you will die in your sins."

²⁵Then they said to Him, "You—who are you?" יֵשׁוּעַ, Yeshua said to them, "Even what I spoke of to you at the beginning. ²⁶I have many things to speak and to judge regarding you. But He who sent Me is true, and I—what things I heard from Him, these I say to the world."

²⁷They knew not that He spoke to them of the Father. ²⁸Then יֵשׁוּעַ, Yeshua said to them, "When you lift up the Son of Man, then you will know that I am HE; and I do nothing of Myself, but as the Father taught Me, I speak these things. ²⁹And He who sent Me is with Me; He did not leave Me alone, because I always do the things pleasing to Him."

³⁰As He was speaking these things, many believed in Him. ³¹יֵשׁוּעַ, Yeshua, therefore, said to the יְהוּדִים, Y'hudiym who believed in Him, "If you remain in My word, you are truly my disciples, ³²and you will know the truth, and the truth will make you free."

³³They answered Him, "We are seed of אַבְרָהָם, Av'raham, and we have been slaves to no one at any time. How *then* can you say, 'You will become free'?"

³⁴יֵשׁוּעַ, Yeshua answered them, "אָמֵן אָמֵן, Amen, amen, I say to you: everyone who is committing sin is a slave of the sin. ³⁵Now the slave does not remain to the age in the *family's* house, *but* the son remains to the age. ³⁶If, then, the Son makes you free, in reality, you will be free.

³⁷"I have known that you are seed of אַבְרָהָם, Av'raham, but you look to kill Me, because My word has no place in you. ³⁸I speak that which I have seen with the Father; and you, therefore—that which you have heard from[a] your[b] father, you do."

³⁹They answered and said to Him, "Our father is אַבְרָהָם, Av'raham."

יֵשׁוּעַ, Yeshua said to them, "If you are children of אַבְרָהָם, Av'raham, you would have been doing the acts of אַבְרָהָם, Av'raham. ⁴⁰But now, you look to kill Me—a man who has spoken to you the truth I heard from God. אַבְרָהָם, Av'raham did not do this; ⁴¹you do the acts of your father."

Then they said to Him, "We have not been born *out* of sexual unfaithfulness. We have one Father—God!"

⁴²יֵשׁוּעַ, Yeshua said to them, "If God were your father, you would have been loving Me, for I came forth from God—and am come. Indeed, neither have I come of Myself; rather, He sent Me.

⁴³"Why do you not understand my speech? Because you are not able to hear my word. ⁴⁴You are of the father—the Accuser—and you want to do the lusts of your father. He was a murderer from the beginning, and he has not stood in the truth, because there is no truth in him. When one speaks the lie, he speaks his own *nature*, because he is a liar—*as* also his father. ⁴⁵And because I say the truth, you do not believe Me. ⁴⁶Who of you convicts Me of sin? If I speak truth, why do you not believe Me? ⁴⁷He who is of God hears the sayings of God. Because of this, you do not hear: because you are not of God."

⁴⁸The יְהוּדִים, Y'hudiym answered and said to Him, "Do we not say *it* well, that you are a שֹׁמְרוֹנִי, Shom'roniy, and have a demon?"

⁴⁹יֵשׁוּעַ, Yeshua answered, "I do not have a demon, but I honor My Father, and you dishonor Me. ⁵⁰But I do not seek My own glory. There is *One* who is seeking and is

---

[a] "heard from"—some mss say, "seen with"
[b] "your"—the earliest manuscripts say "the"; cf. verse 41

judging. ⁵¹אָמֵן אָמֵן, Amen, amen, I say to you: if anyone keeps My word, he will not see death—to the age."

⁵²The יְהוּדִים, Y'hudiym, therefore, said to Him, "Now we know that you have a demon! אַבְרָהָם, Av'raham died, and the prophets, but you say, 'If anyone keeps my word, he will not taste death—to the age.' ⁵³Are you greater than our father אַבְרָהָם, Av'raham, who died? And the prophets died. Whom do you make yourself *to be*?"

⁵⁴יֵשׁוּעַ, Yeshua answered, "If I glorify Myself, My glory is nothing. It is My Father (of whom you say, 'He is our God') who is glorifying Me. ⁵⁵And you have not known Him, but I have known Him. And if I say that I have not known Him, I will be like you, speaking falsely. But I have known Him, and I keep His word. ⁵⁶אַבְרָהָם, Av'raham your father was extremely joyful that he would see My day; and he saw, and rejoiced."

⁵⁷The יְהוּדִים, Y'hudiym, therefore, said to Him, "You are not yet fifty years old, and you have seen אַבְרָהָם, Av'raham?"

⁵⁸יֵשׁוּעַ, Yeshua said to them, "אָמֵן אָמֵן, Amen, amen, I say to you: before אַבְרָהָם, Av'raham became—I am."

⁵⁹Therefore, they raised up stones so that they could throw *them* at Him, but יֵשׁוּעַ, Yeshua hid Himself and went out of the Temple.ª

9

¹And passing by, He saw a man blind from birth, ²and His disciples asked Him, saying, "רַבִּי, Rabiy, who sinned —this one, or his parents—that he should be born blind?"

³יֵשׁוּעַ, Yeshua answered, "Neither did this one sin, nor his parents, but so that the acts of God might be revealed in him. ⁴It is necessary for usᵇ to be doing the acts of Him who sent Me while it is day, *for* night comes, when no one is able to work. ⁵While I am in the world, I am a light of the world."

⁶Saying these things, He spat on the ground, and made clay *out* of the saliva, and rubbed the clay on his eyes, and said to him, ⁷"Go away, *and* wash at the pool of שִׁלֹחַ, Shiloach"—which is, interpreted, "Sent."

He went away, therefore, and washed, and came *away* seeing! ⁸Then the neighbors and those seeing him beforehand— that he was a beggarᶜ—said, "Is this not he who is *always* sitting and begging?" ⁹Others said, "This is he"; *still* others said, "No, but he resembles him." *Yet* he himself said, "I am *he*."

¹⁰Then they said to him, "Then how were your eyes opened?" ¹¹He answered, "The man called יֵשׁוּעַ, Yeshua made *some* clay, and rubbed *it on* my eyes, and said to me, 'Go away toᵈ שִׁלֹחַ, Shiloach and wash.' Then having gone away, and having washed, I received sight!" ¹²And they said to him, "Where is that one?" He said, "I do not know."

¹³They brought him who once WAS blind to the פְּרוּשִׁים, P'rushiym. ¹⁴Now it was a שַׁבָּת, Shabat on the day יֵשׁוּעַ, Yeshua made the clay and opened his eyes. ¹⁵Therefore, the פְּרוּשִׁים, P'rushiym were again also asking him how he received *his* sight, and he said to them, "He put clay on my eyes, and I washed, and *now* I see."

¹⁶Then certain *ones* of the פְּרוּשִׁים, P'rushiym said, "This man is not from God, because he does not keep the שַׁבָּת, Shabat." But others said, "How is a man—a sinful one—able to do such signs?" And there was a division among them.

¹⁷Then they said again to the blind man, "You—what do you say of him, since he opened your eyes?" and he said, "He is a prophet."

¹⁸The יְהוּדִים, Y'hudiym, therefore, did not believe *what was being said* about him— that he was blind and received sight—until *the time* that they called the parents of him who received sight. ¹⁹And they asked them, saying, "Is *this* your son, of whom you say that he was born blind? How then does he now see?"

ª Some mss insert, "going through the middle of them, and so passed by"
ᵇ "us"—some mss say, "Me"
ᶜ "a beggar"—some mss say, "blind"
ᵈ Some mss insert, "the pool of"

²⁰Then his parents answered and said, "We have known that this is our son, and that he was born blind, ²¹but how he now sees, we have not known—or who opened his eyes, we have not known. Ask him! He is of age. He himself will speak about himself." ²²(His parents said these things because they were afraid of the יְהוּדִים, Y'hudiym, for the יְהוּדִים, Y'hudiym had already agreed together that if anyone professes Him *to be* Messiah, he would be put out of the synagogue. ²³Because of this his parents said, "He is of age, ask him.")

²⁴So for a second time they called the man who was blind, and they said to him, "Give glory to God. We have known that this man is a sinner." ²⁵Then he answered, "If he is a sinner, I have not known. One thing I have known: that being blind, now I see."

²⁶Then they said to him, "What did he do to you? How did he open your eyes?" ²⁷He answered them, "I told you already, and you did not hear. Why do you want to hear *it* again? Do you also want to become his disciples?"

²⁸And they spoke evil of him and said, "You are his disciple, but we are disciples of מֹשֶׁה, Mosheh! ²⁹We have known that God has spoken to מֹשֶׁה, Mosheh, but this one—we have not known where he is from."

³⁰The man answered and said to them, "Indeed, in this is a thing of marvel: that you have not known where he is from, yet he opened my eyes! ³¹We have known that God does not hear sinners, but if anyone is a worshipper of God, and does His will, He hears him. ³²From the age it was not heard that anyone opened *the* eyes of one who has been born blind. ³³If this one were not from God, he would not *be* able to do anything!"

³⁴They answered and said to him, "You were born completely in sins, and you *dare to* teach us!" and they threw him out.

³⁵יֵשׁוּעַ, Yeshua heard that they threw him out, and having found him, He said, "Do you believe in the Son of Man?"[a] ³⁶He answered and said, "And who is he, sir, that I may believe in him?" ³⁷יֵשׁוּעַ, Yeshua said to him, "You have both seen Him, and He who is speaking with you is He." ³⁸And he said, "I believe, sir," and bowed before Him.

³⁹And יֵשׁוּעַ, Yeshua said, "I came to this world for judgment, so that those not seeing may see, and those seeing may become blind." ⁴⁰Those of the פְּרוּשִׁים, P'rushiym who were with Him heard these things, and they said to Him, "Are we also blind?" ⁴¹יֵשׁוּעַ, Yeshua said to them, "If you were blind, you would *be as* not having had sin. But now *that* you say, 'we see,' your sin remains.

10 ¹"אָמֵן אָמֵן, Amen, amen, I say to you: he who is not entering through the door to the courtyard of the sheep, but is going up *the wall* from another side—that one is a thief and a robber. ²But he who is entering through the door is shepherd of the sheep; ³the doorkeeper opens to this one, and the sheep hear his voice, and he calls his own sheep by name and leads them forth.

⁴"When he sends out all his own, he goes on in front of them, and the sheep follow him because they have known his voice. ⁵But they will not follow a stranger; rather, they will flee from him, because they have not known the voice of strangers."

⁶יֵשׁוּעַ, Yeshua spoke this allegory to them, but they did not understand what the things were that He was speaking to them.

⁷יֵשׁוּעַ, Yeshua, then, said again, "אָמֵן אָמֵן, Amen, amen, I say to you: I am the door of the sheep. ⁸All—as many as came before Me—are thieves and robbers, but the sheep did not hear them. ⁹I am the door. If anyone comes in through Me, he will be saved, and he will come in and go out and find pasture. ¹⁰The thief does not come, except that he may steal, and kill, and destroy. I came so that they may have life, and may have *it* abundantly.

¹¹"I am the good shepherd. The good shepherd lays down his life for the sheep.

---

[a] "Son of Man"—some mss say, "Son of God"

Safety of the sheep. יוֹחָנָן **Yochanan 11:3**

¹²The *one* being a hired hand and not a shepherd, whose own the sheep are not, sees the wolf coming, and leaves the sheep, and flees—and the wolf catches them and scatters *them*ᵃ— ¹³because he is a hired hand and is not caring for the sheep.

¹⁴"I am the good shepherd, and I know My SHEEP and My sheep know Me, ¹⁵as the Father knows Me and I know the Father. And I lay down My life for the sheep. ¹⁶And I have other sheep that are not of this courtyard; it is necessary for Me to bring these also. And they will hear My voice, and there will become one flock—one shepherd.

¹⁷"Because of this the Father loves Me: because I lay down My life, so that I may take it *up* again. ¹⁸No one takes it from Me, but I lay it down of Myself. I have authority to lay it down, and I have authority to take it *up* again. This command I received from My Father."

¹⁹There again was a division among the יְהוּדִים, Y'hudiym because of these words, ²⁰and many of them said, "He has a demon, and is insane! Why do you listen to him?" ²¹Others said, "These sayings are not those of a demon-possessed *man*. Is a demon able to open blind men's eyes?"

²²Then the *feast of* Dedication in יְרוּשָׁלַיִם, Y'rushalayim came. It was winter, ²³and יֵשׁוּעַ, Yeshua was walking in the Temple, in the colonnade of שְׁלֹמֹה, Sh'lomoh. ²⁴The יְהוּדִים, Y'hudiym, therefore, came around Him and said to Him, "Until when will you hold our soul in suspense? If you are the Messiah, tell us freely."

²⁵יֵשׁוּעַ, Yeshua answered them, "I told you, but you do not believe. The acts that I do in the Name of My Father—these testify about Me. ²⁶But you do not believe, because you are not of My sheep.ᵇ ²⁷My sheep hear My voice, and I know them, and they follow Me, ²⁸and life age-enduring I give to them. And they will not be destroyed—to the age—and no one will snatch them out of My hand. ²⁹What My Fatherᶜ has given to Me is greater than all, and no one is able to snatch out of the hand of the Father. ³⁰I and the Father are one."

³¹Again the יְהוּדִים, Y'hudiym took up stones so that they could stone Him. ³²יֵשׁוּעַ, Yeshua answered them, "I showed you many good acts from the Father. Because of which of those acts do you stone Me?" ³³The יְהוּדִים, Y'hudiym answered Him, "We do not stone you for a good act, but for evil speaking, and because you (being a man) make yourself God."

³⁴יֵשׁוּעַ, Yeshua answered them, "Is it not having been written in your תּוֹרָה, Torah, 'I SAID, YOU ARE GODS'ᵈ? ³⁵If He called them gods to whom the word of God came (and the Scripture is not able to be broken), ³⁶how do you say of him whom the Father set apart and sent to the world, 'You speak evil'? Because I said I am *the* Son of God? ³⁷If I do not do the acts of My Father, do not believe Me; ³⁸but if I do, even if you may not believe Me, believe the acts, so that you may know and be knowingᵉ that the Father IS in Me, and I in the Father."

³⁹Therefore, they were looking again to seize Him, and He went forth out of their hand, ⁴⁰and went away again to the other side of the יַרְדֵּן, Yar'den (to the place where יוֹחָנָן, Yochanan was immersing at first) and remained there. ⁴¹And many came to Him and said, "יוֹחָנָן, Yochanan, indeed, did no sign, yet all things—as many as יוֹחָנָן, Yochanan said about this One—were true"; ⁴²and many believed in Him there.

11 ¹Now there was a certain one *who was* infirmed—אֶלְעָזָר, El'azar, from בֵּית־עַנְיָה, Beit-An'yah, of the village of מִרְיָם, Mir'yam and מַרְתָּא, Mar'ta her sister ²(and it was *this* מִרְיָם, Mir'yam who anointed the Master with ointment, and wiped His feet with her hair, whose brother—אֶלְעָזָר, El'azar was infirmed); ³therefore, the sisters sent *word* to Him, saying, "Mas-

---
ᵃ "scatters *them*"—some mss say, "scatters the sheep. And the hired hand flees"
ᵇ Some mss insert, "as I said to you"
ᶜ "What My Father"—some mss say, "My Father, who"
ᵈ תְּהִלִּים *T'hiliym* 82:6
ᵉ "be knowing"—some mss say, "believe"

ter, look! he whom you love is infirmed." ⁴And יֵשׁוּעַ, Yeshua, having heard, said, "This ailment is not to death, but for the glory of God, so that the Son of God may be glorified through it."

⁵And יֵשׁוּעַ, Yeshua was loving מָרְתָא, Mar'ta and her sister and אֶלְעָזָר, El'azar. ⁶Therefore, when He heard that he was infirmed, then, indeed, He remained in the place in which He was *for* two days— ⁷then after this, He said to the disciples, "Let us go to יְהוּדָה, Y'hudah again." ⁸The disciples said to Him, "רַבִּי, Rabiy, *just* now the יְהוּדִים, Y'hudiym were looking to stone You, and again You go there?"

⁹יֵשׁוּעַ, Yeshua answered, "Are there not twelve hours in the day? If anyone walks in the day, he does not stumble, since he sees the light of this world; ¹⁰but if anyone walks in the night, he does stumble, because the light is not in him." ¹¹He said these things, and after this He said to them, "אֶלְעָזָר, El'azar our friend has fallen asleep, but I go on so that I may awaken him." ¹²Therefore, the disciples said to Him, "Master, if he has fallen asleep, he will be saved *from his illness*."

¹³Now יֵשׁוּעַ, Yeshua had spoken about El'azar's death, but they thought that He spoke about the *natural* resting of sleep. ¹⁴So then יֵשׁוּעַ, Yeshua said to them freely, "אֶלְעָזָר, El'azar has died, ¹⁵but I rejoice for your sake, that you may believe, since I was not there. But let us go to him."

¹⁶Then תּוֹמָא, Toma (who is called Didymus), said to the fellow-disciples, "Let us go—we also—so that we may die with Him."[a]

¹⁷יֵשׁוּעַ, Yeshua, therefore, having come, found him having been four days already in the tomb. ¹⁸And בֵּית־עֲנְיָה, Beit-An'yah was near to יְרוּשָׁלַיִם, Y'rushalayim, about two miles[b] off, ¹⁹and many of the יְהוּדִים, Y'hudiym had come to מָרְתָא, Mar'ta and מִרְיָם, Mir'yam, so that they might comfort them concerning their brother. ²⁰מָרְתָא, Mar'ta, therefore, when she heard that יֵשׁוּעַ, Yeshua was coming, met Him. And מִרְיָם, Mir'yam kept sitting in the house.

²¹Then מָרְתָא, Mar'ta said to יֵשׁוּעַ, Yeshua, "Master, if You had been here, my brother would not have died. ²²But even now, I have known that whatever You ask of God, God will give to You." ²³יֵשׁוּעַ, Yeshua said to her, "Your brother will rise again."

²⁴מָרְתָא, Mar'ta said to Him, "I have known that he will rise again, in the Rising Again in the Last Day." ²⁵יֵשׁוּעַ, Yeshua said to her, "I am the Rising Again, and the Life. He who is believing in Me, even if he dies, will live. ²⁶And everyone who is living and believing in Me will not die—to the age. Do you believe this?" ²⁷She said to Him, "Yes, Master, I have believed that You are the Messiah, the Son of God, who is coming to the world."

²⁸And having said this, she went away and privately called מִרְיָם, Mir'yam her sister, saying, "The Teacher has come, and calls *for* you." ²⁹And when she heard *this*, she rose up quickly and was coming to Him.

³⁰And יֵשׁוּעַ, Yeshua had not yet come to the village, but was still in the place where מָרְתָא, Mar'ta met Him.

³¹Then the יְהוּדִים, Y'hudiym who were with her in the house and were comforting her, having seen מִרְיָם, Mir'yam (that she rose up quickly and went out), followed her, having thought,[c] "She goes away to the tomb, so that she may weep there."

³²Therefore, when she came where יֵשׁוּעַ, Yeshua was, having seen Him, מִרְיָם, Mir'yam fell at His feet, saying to Him, "Master, if You had been here, my brother would not have died." ³³Then, when He saw her weeping, and the יְהוּדִים, Y'hudiym who came with her weeping, יֵשׁוּעַ, Yeshua was intensely moved in the רוּחַ, ruach, and troubled Himself. ³⁴And He said, "Where have you laid him?" They said to Him, "Master, come and see." ³⁵יֵשׁוּעַ, Yeshua wept.

³⁶The יְהוּדִים, Y'hudiym, therefore, said, "Look! how He was loving him!" ³⁷And cer-

---

[a] "Him," meaning Yeshua (cf. 11:8), or, "him," meaning El'azar

[b] "two miles"—lit. "fifteen stadia"

[c] "having thought"—some mss say, "saying"

The rising again of El'azar.

tain *ones* of them said, "Was not this one, who opened the eyes of the blind man, also able to cause *it* so that this one might not have died?"

³⁸יֵשׁוּעַ, Yeshua, therefore, again intensely moved in Himself, came to the tomb. And it was a cave, and a stone was lying upon *the entrance of* it. ³⁹יֵשׁוּעַ, Yeshua said, "Take away the stone." The sister of him who had died—מָרְתָא, Mar'ta—said to Him, "Master, he already smells *bad*, for he is four days dead." ⁴⁰יֵשׁוּעַ, Yeshua said to her, "Did I not say to you that if you believe, you will see the glory of God?"

⁴¹Therefore, they took away the stone,ᵃ and יֵשׁוּעַ, Yeshua lifted His eyes upwards and said, "Father, I thank You that You heard me, ⁴²but I knew that You always hear me. Rather, because of the crowd that is standing by, I said *IT*, so that they may believe that You sent me."

⁴³And saying these things, with a loud voice He shouted out, "אֶלְעָזָר, El'azar! Come outside!" ⁴⁴He who died came out, *his* feet and hands being bound with grave-clothes, and his face bound about with a piece of cloth. יֵשׁוּעַ, Yeshua said to them, "Untie him, and allow him to go."

⁴⁵Therefore, many of the יְהוּדִים, Y'hudiym who came to מִרְיָם, Mir'yam, and saw what He did, believed in Him. ⁴⁶But certain *ones* of them went away to the פְּרוּשִׁים, P'rushiym and told them what יֵשׁוּעַ, Yeshua did. ⁴⁷Then the chief כֹּהֲנִים, Ko'haniym and the פְּרוּשִׁים, P'rushiym gathered together a Sanhedrin and said, "What should we do? For this man does many signs. ⁴⁸If we leave him alone *to go on* this way, all will believe in him, and the Romans will come and will take away both our place and ethnic-group."

⁴⁹And a certain one of them, קַיָּפָא, Qayafa (being כֹּהֵן גָּדוֹל, Kohen Gadol of that year), said to them, "You have not known anything, ⁵⁰nor considered that it is good for youᵇ that one man dies for the people,

and the whole ethnic-group not be destroyed." ⁵¹(And this he said not of himself, but being כֹּהֵן גָּדוֹל, Kohen Gadol of that year, he prophesied that יֵשׁוּעַ, Yeshua was about to die for *their* ethnic-group— ⁵²and not for *their* ethnic-group only, but also that He may gather together into one the children of God who have been scattered abroad.) ⁵³Therefore, from that day, they took counsel together that they might kill Him.

⁵⁴Therefore, יֵשׁוּעַ, Yeshua was no longer freely walking among the יְהוּדִים, Y'hudiym, but went away from there to the region near the desert, to a city called אֶפְרַיִם, Ef'rayim, and He stayed there with the disciples.

⁵⁵And the פֶּסַח, Pesach of the יְהוּדִים, Y'hudiym was near, and many went up to יְרוּשָׁלַיִם, Y'rushalayim from the countryside before the פֶּסַח, Pesach, that they might purify themselves.

⁵⁶Then they were looking for יֵשׁוּעַ, Yeshua and, standing in the Temple, said one with another, "What do you think?ᶜ that He may not come to the Feast?" ⁵⁷And the chief כֹּהֲנִים, Ko'haniym and the פְּרוּשִׁים, P'rushiym had given commands, that if anyone might know where He is, he should show *IT*, that they may seize Him.

12 ¹יֵשׁוּעַ, Yeshua, therefore, six days before the פֶּסַח, Pesach, came to בֵּית־עַנְיָה, Beit-An'yah, where אֶלְעָזָר, El'azar was (whom יֵשׁוּעַ, Yeshua raised out of the dead). ²Therefore, they made Him a meal there, and מָרְתָא, Mar'ta was serving, and אֶלְעָזָר, El'azar was one of those reclining together (at mealtime) with Him. ³מִרְיָם, Mir'yam, therefore, having taken a pound of ointment of spikenard, of great price, anointed the feet of יֵשׁוּעַ, Yeshua and wiped His feet with her hair. And the house was filled from the fragrance of the ointment.

⁴And יְהוּדָה אִישׁ־קְרִיּוֹת, Y'hudah Iysh-Q'riyotᵈ—one of His disciples, who was about

---
ᵃ Some mss insert, "where the dead was laid"
ᵇ "you"—some mss say, "us"
ᶜ "What do you think?"—Young's says, "What does *it* appear to you?"
ᵈ Some mss insert, "of שִׁמְעוֹן, Shim'on"

to hand Him over *in betrayal*—said, ⁵"Why was this ointment not sold for three hundred days' wages,ᵃ and given to the poor?" ⁶(And he said this, not because he was caring for the poor, but because he was a thief; and having *charge of* the *money* bag, what things were put in, he was carrying *off*.)

⁷Therefore יֵשׁוּעַ, Yeshua said, "Let her be, that she may keep it for the day of my burial preparation. ⁸For you *will* always have the poor with yourselves, but you *will* not always have Me."

⁹Then the large crowd of the יְהוּדִים, Y'hudiym knew that He was there, and they came, not only because of יֵשׁוּעַ, Yeshua, but also so that they may see אֶלְעָזָר, El'azar, whom He raised out of the dead. ¹⁰So the chief כֹּהֲנִים, Ko'haniym took counsel that they might also kill אֶלְעָזָר, El'azar, ¹¹since on account of him, many of the יְהוּדִים, Y'hudiym were going away and were believing in יֵשׁוּעַ, Yeshua.

¹²On the next day, the large crowd that came to the Feast, having heard that יֵשׁוּעַ, Yeshua was coming to יְרוּשָׁלַיִם, Y'rushalayim, ¹³took the branches of the palm *trees* and went out to meet Him, and *they* were shouting, "הוֹשַׁע־נָא, Hosha-na! BLESSED IS HE WHO IS COMING IN THE NAME OF ADONAIᵇ—even the King of יִשְׂרָאֵל, Yis'rael!" ¹⁴And יֵשׁוּעַ, Yeshua, having found a young donkey, sat upon it, as it is written,

¹⁵"Fear not, daughter of צִיּוֹן, Tziyon. Look! your king comes, sitting on a donkey's colt."ᶜ

¹⁶(His disciples did not know these things at the first, but when יֵשׁוּעַ, Yeshua was glorified, then they remembered that these things were having been written about Him, and *that* they did these things to Him.)

¹⁷Then the crowd who was with Him was testifying that He called אֶלְעָזָר, El'azar out of the tomb and raised him out of the dead. ¹⁸Also because of this, the crowd met Him—because they heard of His having done this sign. ¹⁹Therefore, the פְּרוּשִׁים, P'rushiym said among themselves, "You see that you do not gain anything? Look! the *whole* world went after him."

²⁰And there were certain Greeks from *among* those coming up *to* Y'rushalayim so that they might worship at the Feast; ²¹then these came near to Philip (who IS from בֵּית־צָיְדָה, Beit-Tzai'dah of the גָּלִיל, Galiyl) and were asking him, saying, "Sir, we want to see יֵשׁוּעַ, Yeshua." ²²Philip came and told Andrew; Andrew and Philip came and told יֵשׁוּעַ, Yeshua.

²³And יֵשׁוּעַ, Yeshua responded to them, saying, "The time has come that the Son of Man may be glorified. ²⁴אָמֵן אָמֵן, Amen, amen, I say to you: if the grain of the wheat, having fallen to the ground, does not die, it remains alone; but if it does die, it bears much fruit. ²⁵He who is loving his life losesᵈ it, and he who is hating his life in this world, to life age-enduring will keep it. ²⁶If anyone serves Me, let him follow Me; and where I am, there My servant will also be. If anyone serves Me, the Father will honor him.

²⁷"Now My soul has been troubled, and what? will I say, 'Father, save me from this moment'? Rather, because of this, I came to this moment. ²⁸Father, glorify Your Name."

Then there came a voice out of the heaven, "I both glorified, and again I will glorify IT." ²⁹The crowd, therefore, having stood and heard, were saying that there had been thunder. Others said, "A Messenger has spoken to Him."

³⁰יֵשׁוּעַ, Yeshua answered and said, "This voice has not come because of Me, but because of you. ³¹Now is a judgment of this world; now the ruler of this world will be thrown out. ³²And I, when I am lifted up from the earth, will draw all men to Myself." ³³And He said this signifying by what *sort of* death He was about to die.

³⁴Then the crowd answered Him, "We heard out of the תּוֹרָה, Torah that the Mes-

---

ᵃ "days' wages"—lit. "denaries"
ᵇ תְּהִלִּים T'hiliym 118:26
ᶜ זְכַרְיָה Z'khar'yah 9:9

ᵈ "loses"—ἀπόλλυμι, apollumi, meaning "to kill or destroy"

siah remains to the age. But how do You say that it is necessary for the Son of Man to be lifted up? Who is this—the Son of Man?"

35 יֵשׁוּעַ, Yeshua, therefore, said to them, "A little time longer is the Light among you; walk while you have the Light, so that darkness may not overtake you. And he who is walking in the darkness has not known where he goes. 36While you have the Light, believe in the Light, so that you may become sons of Light."

יֵשׁוּעַ, Yeshua spoke these things, and having gone away, He was hidden from them. 37Yet *even though* He had done so many signs in front of them, they were not believing in Him, 38so that the word of יְשַׁעְיָהוּ, Y'sha'yahu the prophet would be fulfilled, which he said:

"ADONAI, who gave credence to our report? and the arm of ADONAI—to whom was it revealed?"[a]

39Because of this, they were not able to believe, *such* that again יְשַׁעְיָהוּ, Y'sha'yahu said,

40"He has blinded their eyes and hardened their heart, so that they would not see with the eyes and understand with the heart and turn back, and I would heal them."[b]

41יְשַׁעְיָהוּ, Y'sha'yahu said these things because[c] he saw His glory, and spoke of Him. 42Still, however, many out of the leaders also believed in Him, but because of the פְּרוּשִׁים, P'rushiym, they were not professing *it*, so that they might not be put out of the synagogue 43(indeed, they loved the glory of men more than the glory of God). 44And יֵשׁוּעַ, Yeshua shouted and said, "He who is believing in Me does not believe in Me, but in Him who sent Me! 45And he who is looking at Me, looks at Him who sent Me! 46I have come—a light to the world—so that everyone who is believing in Me may not remain in the darkness.

47And if anyone hears My sayings and does not guard them,[d] I do not judge him (for I came not so that I would judge the world, but so that I would save the world). 48He who is rejecting Me and not receiving My sayings has one who is judging him: the word that I spoke, which will judge him in the Last Day. 49For I spoke not from Myself, but the Father who sent Me—He has given Me a command (what I would say, and what I would speak), 50and I have known that His command is life age-enduring. So then, what I speak—as the Father has said to Me, I so speak."

13 1And before the Feast of פֶּסַח, Pesach, יֵשׁוּעַ, Yeshua *was* knowing that His time had come—that He would pass over out of this world to the Father. Having loved His own who ARE in the world, He loved them to the end.

2And when *the* meal had come (the Accuser already having put IT into the heart of יְהוּדָה, Y'hudah *son* of שִׁמְעוֹן, Shim'on, אִישׁ־קְרִיּוֹת, Iysh-Q'riyot, that he would hand Him over *in* betrayal), 3*Yeshua* (knowing that the Father gave all things to Him into HIS hands, and that He came forth from God, and He goes to God) 4rose from the meal and laid down his clothes. And having taken a towel, he wrapped *it* around Himself. 5Afterward, He put water into the basin, and began to wash the feet of His disciples, and to wipe *them* with the towel with which He was being wrapped around.

6Then He came to שִׁמְעוֹן כֵּיפָא, Shim'on Keifa,[e] *who* said to Him, "You, Master—do You wash my feet?" 7יֵשׁוּעַ, Yeshua answered and said to him, "You have not known now that which I do, but after these things, you will understand." 8כֵּיפָא, Keifa said to Him, "You must not wash my feet—to the age." יֵשׁוּעַ, Yeshua answered him, "If I do not wash you, you have no part with Me." 9שִׁמְעוֹן כֵּיפָא, Shim'on Keifa said to Him, "Master, not only my feet, *then*, but also the hands and the

---

[a] יְשַׁעְיָהוּ Y'sha'yahu 53:1
[b] יְשַׁעְיָהוּ Y'sha'yahu 6:10
[c] "because"—some mss say, "when"

[d] "does not guard them"—some mss say, "and does not believe"
[e] כֵּיפָא, Keifa—actually, Πέτρος, Petros; here, and throughout chapter 13; see יוֹחָנָן Yn. 1:42

head." ¹⁰יֵשׁוּעַ, Yeshua said to him, "He who has been bathed has no need, except to wash his feet; rather, he is altogether clean. And you are clean, but not all *of you*," ¹¹for He knew *of* him who was handing Him over *in betrayal*. Because of this He said, "Not all *of you* are clean."

¹²When, therefore, He had washed their feet and taken *up* His clothes, and reclined (at mealtime) again, He said to them, "Do you know what I have done to you? ¹³You call Me 'The Teacher' and 'The Master,' and you speak well, for I am. ¹⁴If, then, I—the Master and the Teacher—washed your feet, so also you ought to wash one another's feet. ¹⁵For I gave an example to you, so that as I did to you, you also may do.

¹⁶"אָמֵן אָמֵן, Amen, amen, I say to you: a slave is not greater than his master, nor an emissary greater than he who sent him. ¹⁷If you have known these things, you are happy—if you do them. ¹⁸I do not speak about all *of* you; I have known whom I chose for Myself. But *it is* so that the Scripture may be fulfilled: HE WHO IS EATING MY BREAD LIFTED UP HIS HEEL AGAINST ME.ᵃ

¹⁹"From this *present* time I tell you *this*, before its coming to pass, so that when it comes to pass, you will believe that I am HE. ²⁰אָמֵן אָמֵן, Amen, amen, I say to you: he who is receiving whoever I send receives Me, and he who is receiving Me receives Him who sent Me."

²¹Having said these things, יֵשׁוּעַ, Yeshua was troubled in the רוּחַ, ruach, and *He* testified and said, "אָמֵן אָמֵן, Amen, amen, I say to you that one of you will hand Me over *in betrayal*." ²²The disciples were looking at one another, uncertain about whom He spoke. ²³One of His disciples, whom יֵשׁוּעַ, Yeshua loved, was reclining (at mealtime) in the arms of יֵשׁוּעַ, Yeshua. ²⁴שִׁמְעוֹן כֵּיפָא, Shim'on Keifa then nodded to this one to ask, "Who is he?" regarding whom He speaks. ²⁵Then that one, having leaned back this way on the chest of יֵשׁוּעַ, Yeshua, said to Him, "Master, who is it?" ²⁶יֵשׁוּעַ, Yeshua answered, "It is that one to whom I will dip the piece *of matzah*, and will give it to him." Then, having dipped the piece *of matzah*, He took *it* and gave IT to יְהוּדָה, Y'hudah *son* of שִׁמְעוֹן, Shim'on, אִישׁ־קְרִיּוֹת, Iysh-Q'riyot.

²⁷And after the piece *of matzah*, then הַשָּׂטָן, HaSatan entered into that one. יֵשׁוּעַ, Yeshua therefore said to him, "What you *are going to* do, do quickly," ²⁸but none of those reclining (at mealtime) knew for what intent He said this to him. ²⁹Indeed, certain *ones* were thinking (since יְהוּדָה, Y'hudah had the *money* bag) that יֵשׁוּעַ, Yeshua said to him, "Buy what we have need of for the Feast," or that he should give something to the poor. ³⁰Therefore, having received the piece *of matzah*, that one immediately went out; and it was night.

³¹Then, when he went out, יֵשׁוּעַ, Yeshua said, "Now was the Son of Man glorified, and God was glorified in him. ³²If God was glorified in him, God also will glorify him in Himself; yes, He will glorify him immediately.

³³"Little children, I am with you *only for* a little longer. You will look for Me, but—as I said to the יְהוּדִים, Y'hudiym—where I am going, you are not able to come. I also say IT to you now.

³⁴"A new command I give to you: that you love one another—as I loved you, that you also love one another. ³⁵In this will all know that you are My disciples: if you have love one to another."

³⁶שִׁמְעוֹן כֵּיפָא, Shim'on Keifa said to Him, "Master, where are you going?" יֵשׁוּעַ, Yeshua answered him, "Where I am going, you are not able to follow Me now, but afterward you will follow."

³⁷כֵּיפָא, Keifa said to Him, "Master, why am I not able to follow You now? I will lay down my life for You." ³⁸יֵשׁוּעַ, Yeshua answered, "You will lay down your life for Me! אָמֵן אָמֵן, Amen, amen, I say to you: a rooster will not crow until you deny Me three times.

ᵃ תְּהִלִּים *T'hiliym* 41:10(9)

The way, the truth, and the life.   יוֹחָנָן **Yochanan 14:30**

14 ¹"Let not your heart be troubled; believe in God; also believe in Me. ²In the house of My Father are many residences; and if not, I would have told you, because I go on to prepare a place for you. ³And if I go on and prepare a place for you, I will come again and will receive you to Myself, so that where I am, you may be also. ⁴And where I am going,ᵃ you have known the way."

⁵תּוֹמָא, Toma said to Him, "Master, we have not known where You are going; how are we able to know the way?" ⁶יֵשׁוּעַ, Yeshua said to him, "I am the way, and the truth, and the life; no one comes to the Father unless through Me. ⁷If you have known Me, you will also knowᵇ My Father. But from this time *on*, you have known Him, and have seen Him."

⁸Philip said to Him, "Master, show us the Father, and it is enough for us." ⁹יֵשׁוּעַ, Yeshua said to him, "For so long a time I am with you, and you have not known Me, Philip? He who has seen Me has seen the Father. How do you say, 'Show the Father to us?' ¹⁰Do you not believe that I AM in the Father, and the Father is in Me? The sayings that I say to you, I speak not from Myself, and the Father who is staying in Me does His acts. ¹¹Believe Me *when I say* that I AM in the Father, and the Father *is* in Me. But if not, believe because of the acts themselves.

¹²"אָמֵן אָמֵן, Amen, amen, I say to you: he who is believing in Me—that one will also do the acts that I do, and greater than these he will do, because I go on to the Father. ¹³And whatever you ask in My Name, I will do, so that the Father will be glorified in the Son; ¹⁴if you ask Meᶜ anything in My Name, I will do IT.

¹⁵"If you love Me, you willᵈ pay attention to My commands, ¹⁶and I will ask the Father, and He will give *to* you another Advocate, so that He may be with you—to the age: ¹⁷the רוּחַ הָאֱמֶת, Ruach Ha'Emet, whom the world is not able to receive, because it does not look for Him, nor know Him. You know Him because He remains with you, and will be in you. ¹⁸I will not leave you orphaned; I come to you.

¹⁹"*Only* a little *while* longer, and *then* the world will see Me no more; but you see Me, because I live, and you will live. ²⁰In that day, you will know that I AM in My Father, and you in Me, and I in you. ²¹He who is having My commands, and is paying attention to them—it is that one who is loving Me. And he who is loving Me will be loved by My Father, and I will love him, and will disclose Myself to him."

²²יְהוּדָה, Y'hudah (not the אִישׁ־קְרִיּוֹת, Iysh-Q'riyot) said to Him, "Master, and what has come to pass, *such* that You are about to disclose Yourself to us, and not to the world?"

²³יֵשׁוּעַ, Yeshua answered and said to him, "If anyone loves Me, he will pay attention to My word, and My Father will love him, and we will come to him, and we will make *our* residence with him. ²⁴He who is not loving Me does not pay attention to My words—and the word that you hear is not Mine, but the Father's who sent Me.

²⁵"These things I have spoken to you while *I am* remaining with you, ²⁶but the Advocate—the רוּחַ הַקֹּדֶשׁ, Ruach HaQodesh, whom the Father will send in My Name—He will teach you all things, and remind you of all things that I said to you.

²⁷"Peace I leave to you; My peace I give to you, *though* I do not give to you as the world gives. Let not your heart be troubled, nor let it be afraid. ²⁸You heard that I said to you, 'I go away, and *then* I come to you.' If you loved Me, you would have rejoiced thatᵉ I go on to the Father, because the Father is greater than I *am*.

²⁹"And now I have said IT to you before it comes to pass, so that when it comes to pass, you may believe. ³⁰I will no longer

---

ᵃ "where I am going"—some mss say, "you have known where I am going, and"
ᵇ "If you have known Me, you will also know"— some mss say, "If you had known Me, you would have also known"
ᶜ Some mss omit, "Me"
ᵈ Some mss omit, "you will"
ᵉ Some mss insert, "I said"

talk much with you (for the ruler of the world comes, and in Me he has nothing). ³¹But so that the world may know that I love the Father, even as the Father commanded Me, so I do.

"Arise. Let us go from here."

15 ¹"I am the true vine, and My Father is the farmer. ²Every branch in Me not bearing fruit, He takes it away; and every one bearing fruit, He cleans by pruning it, so that it may bear more fruit. ³You are already clean because of the word that I have spoken to you. ⁴Remain in Me, and I in you. As the branch is not able to bear fruit of itself if it does not remain in the vine, so neither *will* you, if you do not remain in Me.

⁵"I am the vine; you *are* the branches. He who is remaining in Me, and I in him— this one bears much fruit, because apart from Me you are not able to do anything. ⁶If anyone does not remain in Me, he is thrown forth outside as the branch, and is withered; and they gather and throw them into the fire, and they are burned. ⁷If you remain in Me, and My sayings remain in you, ask whatever you want, and it will be done to you.

⁸"My Father was glorified in this so that you may bear much fruit, and you may become My disciples. ⁹As the Father loved Me, I also loved you. Remain in My love. ¹⁰If you pay attention to My commands, you will remain in My love, as I have paid attention to the commands of My Father, and remain in His love. ¹¹I have spoken these things to you so that My joy may be in you, and your joy may be full.

¹²"This is My command: that you love one another, as I loved you. ¹³No one has greater love than this: that anyone may lay down his life for his friends. ¹⁴You are My friends if you do what I command you. ¹⁵I no longer call you slaves, because the slave has not known what his master does; but I have called you friends, because all *of the* things that I heard from My Father, I made known to you.

¹⁶"You did not select Me, but I selected you and appointed you, that you might go away, and might bear fruit, and your fruit might remain, so that whatever you ask of the Father in My Name, He may give you. ¹⁷"These things I command you, that you love one another.

¹⁸"If the world hates you, know that it has hated Me before you. ¹⁹If you were of the world, the world would have been loving its own, but because you are not of the world—rather, I selected *you* out of the world—because of this, the world hates you.

²⁰"Remember the word that I said to you: 'A slave is not greater than his master.' If they persecuted Me, they will also persecute you. If they paid attention to My word, they will also pay attention to yours. ²¹But they will do all these things to you because of My Name—because they have not known Him who sent Me. ²²If I had not come and spoken to them, they would not have sin, but now they have no pretext for their sin.

²³"He who is hating Me also hates My Father. ²⁴If I did not do among them the acts that no other did, they would not have sin, but now they have both seen and hated both Me and My Father. ²⁵Rather, so that the word that was written in their תּוֹרָה, Torah might be fulfilled, 'THEY HATED ME WITHOUT A CAUSE.'ᵃ

²⁶"When the Advocate comes, whom I will send to you from the Father—the רוּחַ הָאֱמֶת, Ruach Ha'Emet, who comes forth from the Father—He will testify of Me. ²⁷And you also testify, because from the beginning you are with Me.

16 ¹"I have spoken these things to you so that you may not be stumbled. ²They will put you out of the synagogues—but a time comes when everyone who has killed you will think *it was* to offer עֲבֹדָה, 'avodah to God. ³And they will do these things because they did not know the Father, nor Me.

⁴"But I have spoken these things to you so that when their time comes, you may

---

ᵃ תְּהִלִּים *T'hiliym* 35:19, 69:5(4)

The Advocate.

remember them—that I said THEM to you. And I did not say these things to you from the beginning because I was with you. ⁵And now I go away to Him who sent Me, yet none of you asks Me, 'Where do you go?' ⁶But because I have said these things to you, the grief has filled your heart.

⁷"But I tell you the truth: it is better for you that I go away, for if I do not go away, the Advocate will not come to you; but if I go on, I will send Him to you. ⁸And having come, He will convict the world regarding sin, and regarding righteousness, and regarding judgment. ⁹Indeed, regarding sin, because they do not believe in Me; ¹⁰and regarding righteousness, because I go away to the Father, and you *will* see me no more; ¹¹and regarding judgment, because the ruler of this world has been judged.

¹²"I still have many things to say to you, but you are not able to carry THEM now. ¹³But when He comes—the רוּחַ הָאֱמֶת, Ruach Ha'Emet—He will guide you into all the truth, for He will not speak from Himself, but He will speak as many things as He will hear, and He will tell you the coming things. ¹⁴He will glorify Me, because He will take of *what is* Mine and will tell *it* to you. ¹⁵All things—as many as the Father has—are Mine (because of this I said that He takes of *what is* Mine, and will tell *it* to you).

¹⁶"After a little while, you will no longer see Me; and again after a little while, you will see Me."ᵃ ¹⁷Then SOME of His disciples said to one another, "What is this that He says to us? 'After a little while, you will not see Me; and again after a little while, you will see Me'? and 'Because I go away to the Father'?" ¹⁸Then they said, "What is this He says? the 'little while'? We do not know what He is speaking *about*."

¹⁹יֵשׁוּעַ, Yeshua knew that they were wanting to ask Him *about it, and so* He said to them, "Do you look with one another regarding this because I said, 'After a little while, you will not see Me; and again after

Yochanan יוֹחָנָן *16:33*

a little while, you will see Me'? ²⁰אָמֵן אָמֵן, Amen, amen, I say to you that you will weep and mourn, and the world will rejoice; you will be grieved, but your grief will become joy.

²¹"The woman, when she brings forth *a child*, has grief, because her time has come. But when she brings forth the child, she no longer remembers the anguish, because of the joy that a human beingᵇ was born into the world.

²²"And you, therefore, indeed, have grief now, but again I will see you, and your heart will rejoice, and no one *will* take your joy from you. ²³And in that day, you will question Me nothing. אָמֵן אָמֵן, Amen, amen, I say to you: whatever you ask of the Father in My Name, He will give you. ²⁴Until now, you asked nothing in My Name. Ask, and you will receive, so that your joy may be full.

²⁵"I have spoken these things to you in allegories; but there comes a time when I will speak to you no longer in allegories, but will tell you freely of the Father. ²⁶In that day, you will make a request in My Name, but I do not say to you that I will ask the Father for you. ²⁷For the Father Himself loves you, because you have loved Me and you have believed that I came forth from God. ²⁸I came forth from the Father, and have come to the world; I leave the world again, and go on to the Father."

²⁹His disciples said, "Look! now You speak freely, and You no *longer* speak *in* allegory. ³⁰Now we have known that You have known all things, and have no need that anyone question You. In this, we believe that You came forth from God."

³¹יֵשׁוּעַ, Yeshua answered them, "Now do you believe? ³²Look! there comes a time— and it has come—that you will be scattered, each to his own things, and you will leave Me *all* alone. But I am not alone, because the Father is with Me. ³³I have spoken these things to you, so that in Me you may have peace. In the world, you will have

---

ᵃ Some mss insert, "because I go away to the Father."

ᵇ "human being" or "man," as it says in Young's

oppression, but take courage: I have overcome the world."

17 ¹יֵשׁוּעַ, Yeshua spoke these things and, lifting up His eyes to the Heaven, said, "Father, the time has come. Glorify Your Son, so that the Son may glorify You, ²as You gave authority to him over all flesh, so that—all that You have given to him—he may give to them life age-enduring. ³And this is the life age-enduring: that they may know You—the only true God—and him whom You sent —יֵשׁוּעַ, Yeshua *the* Messiah. ⁴I glorified You on the earth, having finished the work that You have given me so that I may do IT. ⁵And now, glorify me, Father, *along* with Yourself, with the glory that I had with You before the world was.

⁶"I revealed Your Name to the men whom You gave to me out of the world. They were Yours, and You gave them to me, and they have paid attention to Your word. ⁷Now they have known that all things, as many as You have given to me, are from You, ⁸because the sayings that You gave to me, I have given to them, and they themselves received *them*, and have known truly that I came forth from You, and they believed that You sent me. ⁹I ask in regard to them.

"Not in regard to the world do I ask, but in regard to those whom You have given to me, because they are Yours, ¹⁰and all mine are Yours, and Yours ARE mine, and I have been glorified in them. ¹¹And I am no longer in the world, but they are *still* in the world, and I come to You. Holy Father, watch over them in Your Name, which[a] You have given to me, that they may be one as we *are one.* ¹²When I was with them,[b] I was watching over them in Your Name, which You have given to me; and I guarded *them,*[c] and none of them was destroyed, except the son of the destruction, so that the Scripture would be fulfilled.[d]

¹³"And now I come to You, and I speak these things in the world, so that they may have my joy fulfilled in themselves. ¹⁴I have given Your word to them, and the world hated them, because they are not of the world, as I am not of the world. ¹⁵I do not ask that You take them out of the world, but that You keep them out of the evil.

¹⁶"They are not of the world, as I am not of the world. ¹⁷Set them apart in the[e] truth; Your word is truth. ¹⁸As You sent me to the world, I also sent them to the world; ¹⁹and I set myself apart for them, that they themselves may also be set apart in truth.

²⁰"And I do not ask in regard to these alone, but also in regard to those believing in me through their word, ²¹that they all may be one, as You, Father, ARE in me, and I in You—that they also may be[f] in us, so that the world may believe that You sent me.

²²"And the glory that You have given to me, I have given to them, so that they may be one as we are one——²³I in them, and You in me, so that they may be perfected into one——so that the world may know that You sent me, and loved them as You loved me.

²⁴"Father, that which You have given to me, I want that where I am, they also may be with me, so that they may see my glory that You have given to me, because You loved me before the foundation of the world. ²⁵Righteous Father, the world also did not know You, but I knew You, and these have known that You sent me. ²⁶And I made Your Name known to them, and will make *it* known, so that the love with which You loved me may be in them, and I in them."

18 ¹Having said these things, יֵשׁוּעַ, Yeshua went out with His disciples beyond the brook of קִדְרוֹן, Qid'ron, where there was a garden into which He entered—Himself and His dis-

---

[a] "which"—some mss say, "whom"
[b] Some mss insert, "in the world"
[c] "Your Name, which You have given to me; and I guarded *them*"—some mss say, "Your Name. I have guarded those whom You have given to me"
[d] See תְּהִלִּים T'hiliym 41:10(9)
[e] "the"—some mss say, "Your"
[f] Some mss insert, "one"

Arrest in the garden. יוֹחָנָן **Yochanan 18:27**

ciples. ²And יְהוּדָה, Y'hudah (who handed Him over *in betrayal*) also had known the place, because יֵשׁוּעַ, Yeshua had assembled there many times with His disciples.

³יְהוּדָה, Y'hudah, therefore, having taken the *Roman* battalion and attendants from the chief כֹּהֲנִים, Ko'haniym and from the פְּרוּשִׁים, P'rushiym, came there with torches and lanterns and weapons.

⁴יֵשׁוּעַ, Yeshua, therefore, knowing all *the* things that were coming upon Him, went out and said to them, "Who are you looking for?" ⁵They answered Him, "יֵשׁוּעַ הַנָּצְרָתִי, Yeshua HaNatz'ratiy." He said to them, "I am He." (And יְהוּדָה, Y'hudah, who handed Him over *in betrayal*, was standing with them.) ⁶Then, when He said to them, "I am He," they moved[a] away backward and fell to the ground.

⁷Again, therefore, He questioned them, "Who are you looking for?" and they said, "יֵשׁוּעַ הַנָּצְרָתִי, Yeshua HaNatz'ratiy." ⁸יֵשׁוּעַ, Yeshua answered, "I said to you that I am He. If, then, you are looking for Me, allow these *others* to go away." ⁹(*This was* so that the word that He said would be fulfilled: "those whom You have given to Me—I did not lose even one of them.")

¹⁰שִׁמְעוֹן כֵּיפָא, Shim'on Keifa,[b] having a sword, then drew it and struck the slave of the כֹּהֵן הַגָּדוֹל, Kohen HaGadol, and cut off his right ear (and the name of the slave was Malchus). ¹¹Then יֵשׁוּעַ, Yeshua said to כֵּיפָא, Keifa, "Put the sword into the sheath. The cup that the Father has given to Me—will I not drink it?"

¹²Then the battalion and the captain and the attendants of the יְהוּדִים, Y'hudiym took hold on יֵשׁוּעַ, Yeshua and bound Him, ¹³and they led Him away to חָנָן, Chanan first, for he was *the* father-in-law of קַיָּפָא, Qayafa, who was כֹּהֵן הַגָּדוֹל, Kohen HaGadol of that year. ¹⁴(And קַיָּפָא, Qayafa was he who gave counsel to the יְהוּדִים, Y'hudiym, that it is good for one man to die for the people.)

---

[a] "moved"—Young's says, "went"
[b] כֵּיפָא, Keifa—actually, Πέτρος, Petros; here, and throughout chapter 18; see יוֹחָנָן *Yn.* 1:42

¹⁵And כֵּיפָא, Shim'on Keifa was following יֵשׁוּעַ, Yeshua, *as was* also another disciple. And that disciple was known to the כֹּהֵן הַגָּדוֹל, Kohen HaGadol, and he entered with יֵשׁוּעַ, Yeshua into the courtyard of the כֹּהֵן הַגָּדוֹל, Kohen HaGadol—¹⁶but כֵּיפָא, Keifa was standing at the door outside. The other disciple (the one known to the כֹּהֵן הַגָּדוֹל, Kohen HaGadol) then went out, and he spoke to the female watching the door, and brought כֵּיפָא, Keifa in.

¹⁷Then the slave-girl watching the door said to כֵּיפָא, Keifa, "Are you also of the disciples of this man?" He said, "I am not." ¹⁸And the slaves and the attendants were standing *there*, having made a fire of coals because it was cold, and they were warming themselves. כֵּיפָא, Keifa was also standing with them and warming himself.

¹⁹So the כֹּהֵן הַגָּדוֹל, Kohen HaGadol questioned יֵשׁוּעַ, Yeshua about His disciples and about His teaching. ²⁰יֵשׁוּעַ, Yeshua answered him, "I have spoken freely to the world—I always taught in a synagogue, and in the Temple where the יְהוּדִים, Y'hudiym all come together—and I spoke nothing in secret. ²¹Why do you question Me? Question those having heard what I spoke to them. Look! These have known what I said."

²²And when He had said these things, one of the attendants standing nearby gave יֵשׁוּעַ, Yeshua a slap, saying, "Do you answer the כֹּהֵן הַגָּדוֹל, Kohen HaGadol this way?" ²³יֵשׁוּעַ, Yeshua answered him, "If I spoke wrongly, testify regarding the wrong. But if *I* spoke rightly, why do you hit Me?" ²⁴So חָנָן, Chanan sent Him bound to קַיָּפָא, Qayafa the כֹּהֵן הַגָּדוֹל, Kohen HaGadol.

²⁵And כֵּיפָא, Shim'on Keifa was standing and warming himself. Then they said to him, "Are you also *one* of his disciples?" He denied *it* and said, "I am not." ²⁶One of the slaves of the כֹּהֵן הַגָּדוֹל, Kohen HaGadol—being a relative of him whose ear כֵּיפָא, Keifa cut off—said, "Did I not see you in the garden with him?" ²⁷Then כֵּיפָא, Keifa denied *it* again, and immediately a rooster crowed.

²⁸Then they led יֵשׁוּעַ, Yeshua from קָיָפָא, Qayafa to the Prætorium,ᵃ and it was early. And they themselves did not enter into the Prætorium, so that they might not be defiled, but might eat the פֶּסַח, Pesach.ᵇ ²⁹So Pilate went outside to them and said, "What accusation do you bring against this man?" ³⁰They answered and said to him, "If he were not an evildoer, we would not have handed him over to you."

³¹Pilate, therefore, said to them, "You take him—you—and judge him according to your law." The יְהוּדִים, Y'hudiym said to him, "It is not permitted for us to put anyone to death." ³²(*This was* so that the word of יֵשׁוּעַ, Yeshua, which He said, would be fulfilled, signifying by what *kind of* death He was about to die.)

³³Pilate, therefore, entered into the Prætorium again, and called יֵשׁוּעַ, Yeshua, and said to Him, "Are you the King of the Jews?" ³⁴יֵשׁוּעַ, Yeshua answered, "Do you say this from yourself? or did others say it to you about Me?"

³⁵Pilate answered, "Am I a Jew? Your ethnic group and the chief priests handed you over to me. What did you do?" ³⁶יֵשׁוּעַ, Yeshua answered, "My kingdom is not of this world. If My kingdom were of this world, My attendants would have struggled so that I would not be handed over to *the* יְהוּדִים, Y'hudiym. But now My kingdom is not from here."

³⁷Pilate, therefore, said to Him, "Are you a king, then?" יֵשׁוּעַ, Yeshua answered, "*As* you say IT, thatᶜ I am a king. For this I have been born, and for this I have come to the world, so that I may testify to the truth. Everyone who is of the truth hears My voice."

³⁸Pilate said to Him, "What is truth?" and having said this, he went out to the יְהוּדִים, Y'hudiym again and said to them, "I find no fault in him. ³⁹Now, you have a custom that I will release *some*one to you during the Passover. Do you want, therefore, THAT I should release to you the king of the Jews?" ⁴⁰Then they shouted out again, saying, "Not this one, but בַּר־אַבָּא, Bar-Aba!" (And בַּר־אַבָּא, Bar-Aba was a robber.)

19 ¹So Pilate then took יֵשׁוּעַ, Yeshua and punished *HIM*; ²and the soldiers, having braided a crown of thorns, placed IT on His head; and they put a purple garment around Him, ³and were coming to Him andᵈ saying, "Hail! the king of the Jews!" and were giving Him slaps.

⁴And Pilate again went outside and said to them, "Look! I am bringing him outside to you, so that you may know that I find no fault in him."

⁵Then יֵשׁוּעַ, Yeshua came outside, wearing the thorny crown and the purple garment, and *Pilate* said to them, "Look! the man!"

⁶Then, when the chief כֹּהֲנִים, Ko'haniym and the attendants saw Him, they shouted, saying, "Crucify! Crucify!" Pilate said to them, "You take him and you crucify *him*, for I find no fault in him." ⁷The יְהוּדִים, Y'hudiym answered him, "We have a law, and according to that law he ought to die, for he made himself Son of God."

⁸So when Pilate heard this word, he was afraid *all* the more, ⁹and *he* entered again into the Prætorium and said to יֵשׁוּעַ, Yeshua, "Where are you from?" and יֵשׁוּעַ, Yeshua gave him no answer.

¹⁰Pilate, therefore, said to him, "Do you not speak to me? Have you not known that I have *the* authority to release you, and I have *the* authority to crucify you?" ¹¹יֵשׁוּעַ, Yeshua answered him, "You would have no authority against Me if it had not been given you from above. Because of this, he who has handed Me over to you has greater sin."

ᵃ "Prætorium"—the governor's headquarters

ᵇ If the meal of chapter 13 is the same as the פֶּסַח, Pesach meal of מַתִּתְיָהוּ Matit'yahu 26, Mark 14 and Luke 22, then here, "פֶּסַח, Pesach" may be referring to the additional sacrifices (or *chagigah*) associated with "חַג הַמַּצּוֹת, Chag HaMatzot, which is *also* widely called פֶּסַח, Pesach" (Luke 22:1)— the seven-day feast that would have begun that morning; cf. דִּבְרֵי הַיָּמִים ב Div'rei HaYamiym Beit 30:21-22.

ᶜ "that"—Young says, "because"

ᵈ Some mss omit, "coming to Him and"

¹²From this TIME on, Pilate was looking to release Him, but the יְהוּדִים, Y'hudiym shouted, saying, "If you release this one, you are not a friend of Cæsar! Everyone making himself a king speaks against Cæsar!"

¹³Pilate, then, having heard this word, brought יֵשׁוּעַ, Yeshua outside, and he sat down on the judgment seat at a place called "Pavement" (but *it is* "גַּבְּתָא, Gab'ta" in Hebrew[a]). ¹⁴And it was the Preparation Day of the פֶּסַח, Pesach,[b] about the sixth hour, and he said to the יְהוּדִים, Y'hudiym, "Look! Your king!" ¹⁵Then they shouted, "Take *him* away! Take *him* away! Crucify him!" Pilate said to them, "Should I crucify your king?" The chief כֹּהֲנִים, Kohaniym answered, "We have no king except Cæsar." ¹⁶Then, therefore, he handed Him over to them so that He could be crucified.

Then they took יֵשׁוּעַ, Yeshua,[c] ¹⁷and, carrying His execution stake, He went out to the place called "PLACE of a Skull" (which is called גֻּלְגָּלְתָּא, Gal'gal'ta in Hebrew), ¹⁸where they crucified Him and two others with Him—*one* on this side, and *one* on that side, and יֵשׁוּעַ, Yeshua in the middle.

¹⁹And Pilate also wrote a title and put IT on the execution stake, and it was written,

יֵשׁוּעַ הַנָּצְרָתִי מֶלֶךְ הַיְּהוּדִים
Yeshua HaNatz'ratiy,
Melekh HaY'hudiym[d]

²⁰Therefore, many of the יְהוּדִים, Y'hudiym read this title, because the place where יֵשׁוּעַ, Yeshua was crucified was near to the city, and it was having been written in Hebrew, in Latin, *and* in Greek. ²¹The chief כֹּהֲנִים, Ko'haniym of the יְהוּדִים, Y'hudiym then said to Pilate, "Write not 'The king of the יְהוּדִים, Y'hudiym,' but that '*This* one said, "I am king of the יְהוּדִים, Y'hudiym."'" ²²Pilate answered, "What I have written, I have written."

²³Then the soldiers, when they crucified יֵשׁוּעַ, Yeshua, took His garments and made four parts, *giving* a part to each soldier, *and* also the shirt. But the shirt was seamless, woven from the top throughout; ²⁴therefore, they said to one another, "Let us not split it, but cast a lot for it, *to determine* whose it will be." (*This was* so that the Scripture that is saying, "THEY DIVIDED MY GARMENTS TO THEMSELVES, AND UPON MY CLOTHES THEY CAST A LOT"[e] would be fulfilled.) Then the soldiers, indeed, did these things.

²⁵And by the *execution* stake of יֵשׁוּעַ, Yeshua stood His mother, and His mother's sister, מִרְיָם, Mir'yam *wife* of Clopas, and מִרְיָם הַמַּגְדָּלִית, Mir'yam HaMag'daliyt. ²⁶יֵשׁוּעַ, Yeshua, therefore, having seen HIS mother, and the disciple whom He loved standing nearby, said to HIS mother, "Woman, look! your son." ²⁷Afterward, He said to the disciple, "Look! your mother," and from that time, the disciple took her to his own HOME.

²⁸After this, יֵשׁוּעַ, Yeshua—knowing that all things have now been finished—said, "I thirst." (*This was* so that the Scripture would be fulfilled.)[f] ²⁹A container was placed *there* full of *wine* vinegar, so having put a sponge full of *wine* vinegar on a hyssop stalk, they held IT up to His mouth. ³⁰Then, when יֵשׁוּעַ, Yeshua received the *wine* vinegar, He said, "It has been finished." And having bowed the head, He gave up the רוּחַ, ruach.

³¹Then the יְהוּדִים, Y'hudiym (since it was the Preparation *Day*), so that the bodies would not remain on the *execution* stake on the שַׁבָּת, Shabat (for that שַׁבָּת, Shabat day was a great one),[g] asked of Pilate that

---

[a] "Hebrew"—technically, Aramaic; also in verse 17
[b] "the Preparation *Day* of the פֶּסַח, Pesach"—that is, the day of preparation for the seventh-day שַׁבָּת, Shabat during the Week of מַצָּה, Matzah; cf. Mark 15:42, Luke 23:54 (and Luke 22:1)
[c] Some mss insert, "and led HIM away"
[d] "Yeshua the Nazarene, King of the Jews"
[e] תְּהִלִּים T'hiliym 22:19(18)
[f] תְּהִלִּים T'hiliym 69:22(21)
[g] It was a "great" שַׁבָּת, Shabat because it was the seventh-day שַׁבָּת, Shabat during the week of מַצָּה, Matzah, and therefore, a special or "great" שַׁבָּת, Shabat. Neither פֶּסַח, Pesach nor the first day of

their legs may be broken, and they be taken away. ³²Then the soldiers came, and they, indeed, broke the legs of the first, and of the other who was crucified with Him. ³³But having come to יֵשׁוּעַ, Yeshua, when they saw Him already having been dead, they did not break His legs. ³⁴Rather, one of the soldiers pierced His side with a spear, and immediately blood and water came out. ³⁵And he who has seen has testified—and his testimony is true, and that one has known that he speaks true things—so that you also may believe.

³⁶For these things came to pass, so that the Scripture would be fulfilled,

"A bone of him will not be broken."ᵃ

³⁷And again, another Scripture says,

"They will look to him whom they pierced."ᵇ

³⁸And after these things, יוֹסֵף מִן־הָרָמָתַיִם, Yosef Min-HaRamatayim—being a disciple of יֵשׁוּעַ, Yeshua, but concealed because of *his* fear of the יְהוּדִים, Y'hudiym—asked of Pilate that he may take the body of יֵשׁוּעַ, Yeshua away, and Pilate gave permission.

He came, then, and took His body away, ³⁹and Nicodemus also came (who came to Him by night at the first) bearing a mixture of myrrh and aloes—about a hundred *Roman* pounds.ᶜ

⁴⁰Then they took the body of יֵשׁוּעַ, Yeshua and bound it with linen clothes with the spices, as it was the custom of the יְהוּדִים, Y'hudiym to prepare for burial. ⁴¹And there was a garden in the place where He was crucified, and in the garden a new tomb in which no one was yet laid. ⁴²Therefore, because of the Preparation *Day* of the יְהוּדִים, Y'hudiym, since the tomb was near, they laid יֵשׁוּעַ, Yeshua there.

ᵃ חַג הַמַּצּוֹת, Chag HaMatzot are called שַׁבָּתוֹת, Shabatot according to תּוֹרָה, Torah.
ᵃ תְּהִלִּים T'hiliym 34:21(20); cf. שְׁמוֹת Sh'mot 12:46; בְּמִדְבַּר B'mid'bar 9:12
ᵇ זְכַרְיָה Z'khar'yah 12:10
ᶜ "a hundred *Roman* pounds"—about seventy-five pounds

20

¹Now on the first of the weekᵈ—there still being darkness—מִרְיָם הַמַּגְדָּלִית, Mir'yam HaMag'daliyt came early to the tomb, and she saw the stone having been taken away from the tomb. ²Then she ran, and came to שִׁמְעוֹן כֵּיפָא, Shim'on Keifaᵉ and to the other disciple whom יֵשׁוּעַ, Yeshua loved, and said to them, "They took the Master away out of the tomb, and we have not known where they laid Him!"

³Then כֵּיפָא, Keifa and the other disciple went out, and they were coming to the tomb. ⁴And the two were running together, but the other disciple ran forward more quickly than כֵּיפָא, Keifa and came first to the tomb. ⁵And having stooped down, he saw the linen clothes lying *there*, yet, indeed, he did not enter.

⁶Then שִׁמְעוֹן כֵּיפָא, Shim'on Keifa also came, following him, and he entered into the tomb and saw the linen clothes lying *there*, ⁷and the piece of cloth that was upon His head not lying with the linen clothes, but apart, having been folded up in one place.

⁸Then, therefore, the other disciple who came first to the tomb also entered, and he saw and believed, ⁹for they did not yet understand the Scripture, that it was necessary for Him to rise again out of the dead.

¹⁰Then the disciples went away again to their own,ᶠ ¹¹but מִרְיָם, Mir'yam was standing near the tomb, weeping outside. Then, as she was weeping, she stooped down to the tomb ¹²and saw two Messengers in white, sitting, one at the head and one at the feet, where the body of יֵשׁוּעַ, Yeshua had been laid.

¹³And they said to her, "Woman, why do you weep?" She said to them, "Because they took away my Master, and I have not known where they laid Him." ¹⁴Having

---

ᵈ "week"—lit. σαββάτων, sabbaton, that is, שַׁבָּתוֹת, shabatot; cf. מַתִּתְיָהוּ Matit'yahu 28:1
ᵉ כֵּיפָא, Keifa—actually, Πέτρος, Petros; here, and throughout chapter 20 and 21; see יוֹחָנָן Yn. 1:42
ᶠ Young inserts "friends," while other trans. insert "homes," although the text does not specify.

He appears to His disciples. יוֹחָנָן Yochanan 21:6

said these things, she turned backward, and saw יֵשׁוּעַ, Yeshua standing *there*, but she had not known that it was יֵשׁוּעַ, Yeshua. ¹⁵יֵשׁוּעַ, Yeshua said to her, "Woman, why do you weep? Whom do you seek?" She, supposing that He was the gardener, said to Him, "Sir, if you carried Him away, tell me where you laid Him, and I will take Him away." ¹⁶יֵשׁוּעַ, Yeshua said to her, "מִרְיָם, Mir'yam!" Having turned, she said to Him in Hebrew,[a] "רַבִּי, Rabiy!"[b]—that is to say, "Teacher."

¹⁷יֵשׁוּעַ, Yeshua said to her, "Be not touching Me, for I have not yet ascended to the Father, but be going on to my brothers and say to them *that* I ascend to My Father and your Father, and to My God and your God." ¹⁸מִרְיָם הַמַּגְדָּלִית, Mir'yam Ha-Mag'daliyt came, telling the disciples, "I have seen the Master," and THAT He said these things to her.

¹⁹Therefore, it being evening on that day, the first of the week,[c] and the doors having been shut where the disciples were,[d] for fear of the יְהוּדִים, Y'hudiym, יֵשׁוּעַ, Yeshua came and stood in the middle *of them*, and said to them, "שָׁלוֹם עֲלֵכֶם, Shalom 'alekhem"; ²⁰and having said this, He showed them His hands and side. The disciples, therefore, rejoiced, having seen the Master.

²¹יֵשׁוּעַ, Yeshua, therefore, said to them again, "שָׁלוֹם עֲלֵכֶם, Shalom 'alekhem. As the Father has sent Me, I also send you." ²²And having said this, He breathed on THEM and said to them, "Receive the רוּחַ הַקֹּדֶשׁ, Ruach HaQodesh. ²³If you release the sins of anyone, they have been released from them; if you retain *the sins* of anyone, they have been retained."

²⁴Now תּוֹמָא, Toma, one of the Twelve (who is called Didymus), was not with them when יֵשׁוּעַ, Yeshua came. ²⁵Then the other disciples said to him, "We have seen the Master!" And he said to them, "If I do not see in His hands the mark of the nails, and put my finger to the mark of the nails, and put my hand to His side, I will not believe."

²⁶And after eight days, again His disciples were inside, and תּוֹמָא, Toma *was* with them. יֵשׁוּעַ, Yeshua came (*despite* the doors having been shut), and He stood in the middle *of them* and said, "שָׁלוֹם עֲלֵכֶם, Shalom 'alekhem." ²⁷Then He said to תּוֹמָא, Toma, "Bring your finger here, and see My hands; and bring your hand, and put IT to My side; and become not unbelieving, but believing."

²⁸תּוֹמָא, Toma answered and said to Him, "My Master and my God." ²⁹יֵשׁוּעַ, Yeshua said to him, "Because you have seen Me, you have believed. Happy *are* those not having seen, but having believed."

³⁰Then, indeed, יֵשׁוּעַ, Yeshua also did many other signs in *the* sight of His disciples that are not written in this book, ³¹but these have been written so that you may believe that יֵשׁוּעַ, Yeshua is the Messiah—the Son of God—and that, believing, you may have life in His Name.

21

¹After these things, יֵשׁוּעַ, Yeshua again revealed Himself to the disciples on the sea of Tiberias, and He revealed Himself this way:

²שִׁמְעוֹן כֵּיפָא, Shim'on Keifa, and תּוֹמָא, Toma (who is called Didymus), and נְתַנְאֵל, N'tan'el from קָנָה, Qanah of the גָּלִיל, Galiyl, and the SONS of זַבְדִּי, Zav'diy, and two others of His disciples were together. ³שִׁמְעוֹן כֵּיפָא, Shim'on Keifa said to them, "I am going away to fish." They said to him, "We also—we *will* go with you."

They went out and entered into the boat, but on that night they caught nothing.

⁴And morning now being come, יֵשׁוּעַ, Yeshua stood at the shore, yet, indeed, the disciples did not know that it was יֵשׁוּעַ, Yeshua.

⁵Then יֵשׁוּעַ, Yeshua said to them, "Young ones, do you have any fish for eating?" ⁶They answered Him, "No," and He said

---

[a] Some mss omit, "in Hebrew"
[b] "רַבִּי, Rabiy"—the Gk says ῥαββουνί, rabbouni
[c] "week"—lit. σαββάτων, sabbaton, that is, שַׁבָּתוֹת, shabatot
[d] Some mss insert, "gathered"

to them, "Cast the net at the right side of the boat, and you will find *some*." Then they cast *it*, but they were no longer able to draw it *up*, from the great number of the fishes.

⁷Therefore, that disciple whom יֵשׁוּעַ, Yeshua loved said to כֵּיפָא, Keifa, "It is the Master!" Then שִׁמְעוֹן כֵּיפָא, Shim'on Keifa, having heard it was the Master, wrapped around the outer garment (for he was undressed *for work*), and threw himself into the sea.

⁸And the other disciples came *to shore* by the little boat (for they were not far from the land, but about one hundred yards[a] off), dragging the net of the fishes.

⁹Then, when they came to the land, they saw a fire of coals lying *there*, and a fish lying on it, and bread. ¹⁰יֵשׁוּעַ, Yeshua said to them, "Bring *some* from the fishes that you caught *just* now." ¹¹So שִׁמְעוֹן כֵּיפָא, Shim'on Keifa went up and drew the net to the land, full of large fishes—a hundred and fifty-three—and though they were so many, the net was not split.

¹²יֵשׁוּעַ, Yeshua said to them, "Come, eat." And none of the disciples were venturing to ask Him, "Who are you?" knowing that it was the Master. ¹³יֵשׁוּעַ, Yeshua came and took the bread and gave *some* to them, and likewise the fish. ¹⁴(This WAS now a third time *that* יֵשׁוּעַ, Yeshua was revealed to the disciples *since* having been raised from the dead.)

¹⁵Then, when they had eaten, יֵשׁוּעַ, Yeshua said to שִׁמְעוֹן כֵּיפָא, Shim'on Keifa, "שִׁמְעוֹן, Shim'on SON of יוֹחָנָן, Yochanan,[b] do you love Me more than these?" He said to Him, "Yes, Master—You have known that I dearly love You." He said to him, "Feed My lambs."

¹⁶He said to him again, a second time, "שִׁמְעוֹן, Shim'on SON of יוֹחָנָן, Yochanan, do you love Me?" He said to Him, "Yes, Master—You have known that I dearly love You." He said to him, "Tend My sheep."

¹⁷He said to him the third time, "שִׁמְעוֹן, Shim'on SON of יוֹחָנָן, Yochanan, do you dearly love Me?" כֵּיפָא, Keifa was grieved that He said to him the third time, "Do you dearly love Me?" and he said to Him, "Master, you have known all things. You know that I dearly love You." יֵשׁוּעַ, Yeshua said to him, "Feed My sheep. ¹⁸אָמֵן אָמֵן, Amen, amen, I say to you: when you were younger, you were dressing yourself and walking where you wanted, but when you are old, you will stretch out your hands, and another will dress you and carry YOU where you do not want." ¹⁹And He said this, signifying by what death *Keifa* would glorify God. And having said this, He said to him, "Be following Me."

²⁰כֵּיפָא, Keifa, having turned around, saw following *them* the disciple whom יֵשׁוּעַ, Yeshua loved (who also reclined on His chest during the meal, and said, "Master, who is he who is handing You over *in betrayal?*"). ²¹Then כֵּיפָא, Keifa, having seen this one, said to יֵשׁוּעַ, Yeshua, "Master, and what of this one?" ²²יֵשׁוּעַ, Yeshua said to him, "If I want him to remain until I come, what *is it* to you? You, be following Me."

²³This word, therefore, went out to the brothers, that that disciple would not die. Yet יֵשׁוּעַ, Yeshua did not say to him that he would not die, but, "If I want him to remain until I come, what *is it* to you?"

²⁴This is the disciple who is testifying concerning these things, and who is having written these things—and we have known that his testimony is true. ²⁵And there are also many other things that יֵשׁוּעַ, Yeshua did, which, if they were written *down* one by one, I think not even the world itself to have room for the books that could be written.[c]

---

[a] "one hundred yards"—lit. "two hundred cubits"
[b] יוֹחָנָן, Yochanan"—some mss say, "יוֹנָה, Yonah"; cf. מַתִּתְיָהוּ *Matit'yahu* 16:17; also in verses 16 and 17

[c] Some mss conclude, "אָמֵן, Amen."

הַמִּכְתָּב הָרִאשׁוֹן מִן יוֹחָנָן THE FIRST LETTER FROM YOCHANAN

יוֹחָנָן א 1 Yochanan

1

¹That which was from the beginning, that which we have heard, that which we have seen with our eyes, that which we looked upon and our hands handled, regarding the Word of the Life: ²and the Life was revealed; and we have seen, and testify, and declare to you the age-enduring Life, which was with the Father, and was revealed to us. ³That which we have seen and heard, we declare also to you, so that you also may have sharing with us; and our sharing IS with the Father, and with His Son יֵשׁוּעַ, Yeshua *the* Messiah. ⁴And we write these things so that our[a] joy may be full.

⁵And this is the message that we have heard from Him and announce to you: that God is light, and in Him darkness is not at all. ⁶If we say, "We have sharing with Him," but walk in the darkness, we lie, and do not do the truth. ⁷But if we walk in the light, as He is in the light, we have sharing one with another, and the blood of יֵשׁוּעַ, Yeshua,[b] His Son, cleanses us from every sin. ⁸If we say, "We have no sin," we lead ourselves astray, and the truth is not in us. ⁹*But* if we confess our sins, He is faithful and righteous that He will forgive us the sins and cleanse us from every unrighteousness. ¹⁰If we say, "We have not sinned," we make Him a liar, and His word is not in us.

2

¹My little children, I write these things to you so that you may not sin. But if anyone sins, we have an advocate with the Father: יֵשׁוּעַ, Yeshua *the* Messiah, a righteous one. ²And He Himself is an appeasement for our sins (and not only for ours, but also for the whole world). ³And in this we know that we have known Him: if we pay attention to His commands. ⁴He who is saying, "I have known Him," but is not paying attention to His command—he is a liar, and the truth is not in him. ⁵But whoever pays attention to His word, in him the love of God has truly been perfected. In this we know that we are in Him. ⁶He who is saying he stays in Him ought himself also to walk in this way, as He walked.

⁷Loved ones,[c] I write to you not a new command, but an old command that you had from the beginning; the old command is the word that you heard.[d] ⁸*Then* again, a new command I write to you, which thing is true in Him and in you, because the darkness passes away and the true light now shines. ⁹He who is saying he is in the light, but is hating his brother, is in the darkness until now. ¹⁰He who is loving his brother remains in the light, and there is not a stumbling-block in him; ¹¹but he who is hating his brother is in the darkness, and he walks in the darkness, and he has not known where he goes, because the darkness blinded his eyes.

¹²I write to you, little children, because the sins have been forgiven you through His Name. ¹³I write to you, fathers, because you have known Him who IS from the beginning. I write to you, young men, because you have overcome the evil.

¹⁴I wrote to you, young ones, because you have known the Father. I wrote to you, fathers, because you have known Him who IS from the beginning. I wrote to you, young men, because you are strong, and the word of God remains in you, and you have overcome the evil.

---

[a] "our"—some mss say, "your"
[b] Some mss insert, "*the* Messiah"
[c] "loved ones"—some mss say, "brothers"
[d] Some mss insert, "from the beginning"

¹⁵Love not the world, nor the things in the world. If anyone loves the world, the love of the Father is not in him, ¹⁶because all that *is* in the world—the lust of the flesh, and the lust of the eyes, and the arrogance of the life—is not of the Father, but of the world. ¹⁷And the world passes away, and the lust of it, but he who is doing the will of God remains—to the age.

¹⁸Young ones, it is the final time, and even as you heard that the anti-messiah comes, even now, anti-messiahs have become many; therefore, we know that it is the final time. ¹⁹They went out from us, but they were not of us, for if they had been of us, they would have remained with us. Rather, *they went out* so that they would be revealed that they all are not of us.

²⁰And you have an anointing from the Holy One, and have known all things. ²¹I did not write to you because you have not known the truth, but because you have known it, and because no lie is of the truth. ²²Who is the liar, except he who is denying that יֵשׁוּעַ, Yeshua is the Messiah? This one who is denying the Father and the Son is the anti-messiah. ²³Everyone who is denying the Son does not have the Father, *but* he who is professing the Son has the Father also.ᵃ

²⁴You—that which you heard from the beginning, let it remain in you. If that which you heard from the beginning remains in you, you will also remain in the Son and in the Father. ²⁵And this is the promise that He promised us: the age-enduring Life.

²⁶I wrote these things to you about those leading you astray. ²⁷And you—the anointing that you received from Him, it remains in you, and you have no need that anyone teach you. But as His anointing teaches you regarding all—and is true, and is not a lie, and even as *it* was taught *to* you—remain in Him.

²⁸And now, little children, remain in Him so that when He is revealed, we may have boldness, and not be ashamed before Him in His *coming* presence. ²⁹If you know that He is righteous, know also that everyone *who is* doing the righteousness has been born of Him.

3

¹See what love the Father has given to us, so that we may be called children of God—and we are! Because of this, the world does not know us: because it did not know Him.

²Loved ones, we are now children of God, and it is not yet revealed what we will be. We have known that if He is revealed, we will be like Him, because we will see Him as He is. ³And everyone who is having this hope on Him purifies himself, even as He is pure.

⁴Everyone who is doing the sin also does the wickedness,ᵇ and the sin is the wickedness.ᶜ ⁵And you have known that He was revealed so that He might take awayᵈ sins, but sin is not in Him. ⁶Everyone who is remaining in Him does not sin, *but* everyone who is sinning has not seen Him, nor *has he* known Him.

⁷Little children, let no one lead you astray. He who is doing the righteousness is righteous, even as He is righteous. ⁸He who is doing the sin is of the Accuser, because the Accuser sins from the beginning. The Son of God was revealed for this: that He may break up the actions of the Accuser. ⁹Everyone who has been born of God does not sin, because *God's* seed remains in him; and he is not able to sin, because he has been born of God.

¹⁰In this are the children of God and the children of the Accuser known. Everyone who is not doing righteousness is not of God—even he who is not loving his brother—¹¹because this is the message that you heard from the beginning: that we should love one another. ¹²(Not as קַיִן, Qayin, *for* he was of the evil one, and he slaughtered his brother. And why did he slaughter him?

ᵃ Some mss omit, "*but* he who… Father also"
ᵇ "wickedness"—ἀνομίαν, anomian and ἀνομία, anomia resp. in this verse
ᶜ "the sin is the wickedness"—cf. 5:17
ᵈ Some mss insert, "our"

Because his *own* actions were evil, and those of his brother *were* righteous.)

¹³And do not marvel, brothers, if the world hates you. ¹⁴We have known that we have passed out of the death to the life, because we love the brothers. He who is not loving[a] remains in the death. ¹⁵Anyone who is hating his brother—he is a murderer, and you have known that no murderer has life age-enduring remaining in him. ¹⁶In this we have known the love: because he laid down His life for us—and we ought to lay down *our* lives for the brothers. ¹⁷And whoever has the life-*things* of the world, and views his brother having need, but shuts up his inward parts from him—how does the love of God remain in him?

¹⁸Little children, let us not love in word nor in the talk,[b] but in action and in truth! ¹⁹And in this we will know that we are of the truth, and we will persuade our heart in front of Him: ²⁰that *even* if our heart condemns *us*, that God is greater than our heart, and He knows all things.

²¹Loved ones, if our heart does not condemn us, we have boldness in speech toward God. ²²And whatever we ask, we receive from Him, because we pay attention to His commands, and we do the things pleasing in His sight. ²³And this is His command: that we believe in the Name of His Son—יֵשׁוּעַ, Yeshua *the* Messiah—and love one another, even as He gave *the* command to us. ²⁴And he who is keeping His commands remains in Him, and He in him. And in this we know that He remains in us: from the רוּחַ, Ruach that He gave us.

4 ¹Loved ones, do not believe every רוּחַ, ruach, but examine the רוּחוֹת, ruchot *to see* if they are of God, since many false prophets have gone out to the world. ²In this you *will* know the רוּחַ אֱלֹהִים, Ruach 'Elohiym: every רוּחַ, ruach that professes יֵשׁוּעַ, Yeshua *the* Messiah having come in the flesh is of God, ³but every רוּחַ, ruach that does not profess יֵשׁוּעַ, Yeshua[c] is not of God (and this is that of the anti-messiah, which you heard that it comes, and now it is already in the world).

⁴You—you are of God, little children, and you have overcome them, because greater is He who *is* in you than he who is in the world. ⁵They—they are of the world, because they speak this from the world, and the world hears them. ⁶We—we are of God. He who is knowing God hears us, *and* he who is not of God does not hear us. From this we know the רוּחַ, ruach of the truth and the רוּחַ, ruach of the error.

⁷Loved ones, let us love one another, because the love is of God, and everyone who is loving has been born of God, and knows God. ⁸He who is not loving did not know God, because God is love. ⁹The love of God was revealed in us in this: because His Son—the one and only[d]—God sent to the world, so that we may live through Him. ¹⁰In this is the love: not that we loved God, but that He loved us, and sent His Son *as* an appeasement for our sins.

¹¹Loved ones, if God loved us this way, we also ought to love one another. ¹²No one has ever seen God, *but* if we love one another, God remains in us, and His love is having been perfected in us. ¹³In this we know that we remain in Him, and He in us: because of His רוּחַ, Ruach He has given us.

¹⁴And we have seen and testify that the Father has sent the Son *to be* Savior of the world. ¹⁵Whoever professes that יֵשׁוּעַ, Yeshua is the Son of God—God remains in him, and he in God. ¹⁶And we have known and believed the love that God has in us. God is love, and he who is remaining in the love remains in God, and God remains in him.

¹⁷In this the love has been made perfect with us, so that we may have boldness in speech in the Day of the Judgment, because

---

[a] Some mss insert, "the brother"
[b] "the talk"—lit. "the tongue"
[c] Some mss insert, "*the* Messiah having come in the flesh"
[d] "one and only" or "only begotten"—lit. "one-of-a-kind"; μονογενὴς monogenes

even as He is, we — we also are in this world. ¹⁸Fear is not in the love; rather, the perfect love throws out the fear, because the fear has punishment — and he who is fearing has not been made perfect in the love. ¹⁹We — we love,ᵃ because He — He first loved us. ²⁰If anyone says, "I love God," but he hates his brother, he is a liar, for he who is not loving his brother (whom he has seen) is not ableᵇ to love God (whom he has not seen). ²¹And this *is* the command we have from Him: that he who is loving God should also love his brother.

5 ¹Everyone who is believing that יֵשׁוּעַ, Yeshua is the Messiah has been born of God, and everyone who is loving *the Father* who brought Him forth also loves him who is born of Him. ²In this we know that we love the children of God: when we love God and doᶜ His commands. ³For this is the love of God: that we pay attention to His commands. And His commands are not burdensome, ⁴because everyone who is born of God overcomes the world. And this is the victory that overcame the world: our faith. ⁵Who is he who is overcoming the world, if not he who is believing that יֵשׁוּעַ, Yeshua is the Son of God?

⁶This One is He who came through water and blood — יֵשׁוּעַ, Yeshua the Messiah — not in the water only, but in the water and in the blood. And it is the רוּחַ, Ruach that is testifying, because the רוּחַ, Ruach is the truth, ⁷for there are three who are testifying:ᵈ ⁸the רוּחַ, Ruach, and the water, and the blood — and *the* three are into the one.

⁹If we receive the testimony of men, the testimony of God is greater, because this is the testimony of God: that He has testified about His Son. ¹⁰He who is believing in the Son of God has the testimony in himself, *but* he who is not believing God has made Him a liar, because he has not believed in the testimony that God has testified about His Son. ¹¹And this is the testimony: that God gave to us life age-enduring, and this — the Life — is in His Son. ¹²He who is having the Son has the Life; he who is not having the Son of God does not have the Life.

¹³I wrote these things to you who are believing in the Name of the Son of God, so that you may know that you have life age-enduring.ᵉ ¹⁴And this is the boldness in speech that we have toward Him: that if we ask anything according to His will, He hears us, ¹⁵and if we have known that He hears us, whatever we ask, we have known that we have the request*ed* thin*gs* that we have requested of Him.

¹⁶If anyone sees his brother sinning a sin not *leading* to death, he will ask *God*, and He will give to him life — to those sinning not to death. (There is sin *leading* to death; I do not say that he may ask regarding it. ¹⁷All unrighteousness is sin, but there is sin not *leading* to death.) ¹⁸We have known that everyone who has been born of God does not sin, but he who was born of God watches over him,ᶠ and the evil one does not touch him. ¹⁹We have known that we are of God, and *that* the whole world lies in the evil *one's* hands. ²⁰But we have known that the Son of God has come, and has given us a mind, so that we may know Him who is true. And we are in Him who is true — in His Son יֵשׁוּעַ, Yeshua *the* Messiah. This One is the true God, and life age-enduring! ²¹Little children, guard yourselves from the idols!ᵍ

ᵃ Some mss insert, "Him"
ᵇ "is not able" — some mss say, "how is he able"
ᶜ "do" — some mss say, "pay attention to"
ᵈ Late mss insert, "in the Heaven — the Father, the Word, and the רוּחַ הַקֹּדֶשׁ, Ruach HaQodesh — and these, the three, are one; and *there* are three who are testifying in the earth:"
ᵉ Some mss insert, "and that you may believe in the Name of the Son of God"
ᶠ "him" — some mss say, "himself"
ᵍ Some mss conclude, "אָמֵן, Amen."

הַמִכְתָּב הַשֵׁנִי מִן יוֹחָנָן THE SECOND LETTER FROM YOCHANAN

יוֹחָנָן ב 2 Yochanan

¹*From* הַזָקֵן, HaZaqen; to the chosen Kyria[a] and to her children, whom I love in truth (and not I only, but also all those having known the truth): ²because of the truth that is remaining in us, and will be with us to the age, ³there will be *unmerited favor, loving-kindness, and* peace with you from God the Father and from[b] יֵשׁוּעַ, Yeshua *the* Messiah, the Son of the Father, in truth and love.

⁴I rejoiced exceedingly that I have found *some* of your children walking in truth, just as we received a command from the Father. ⁵And now I ask you, Kyria—not as *if* writing a new command to you, but *one* which we had from the beginning—that we love one another. ⁶And this is the love: that we walk according to His commands. This is the command, just as you heard from the beginning, so that you walk in it, ⁷because many *who are* leading astray went out into the world—*those* who are not professing יֵשׁוּעַ, Yeshua *the* Messiah

---
[a] "Kyria"—most trans. say "lady"; also in verse 5
[b] Some mss insert, "the Master"

coming in *the* flesh. This one is he who is leading astray, and the anti-messiah.

⁸See to yourselves, so that you do not lose the things that we worked *for*, but receive a full reward. ⁹Everyone who is going on ahead,[c] and is not remaining in the teaching,[d] does not have God; *but* he who is remaining in the teaching of the Messiah, this one has both the Father and the Son. ¹⁰If anyone comes to you and does not bring this teaching, do not receive him into *your* house, and do not say "שָׁלוֹם, Shalom!"[e] to him, ¹¹for he who is saying "שָׁלוֹם, Shalom" to him shares with his evil actions.

¹²Having many things to write to you, I did not intend *to do so* through paper and ink, but I hope to come to you and speak mouth to mouth, so that our joy may be full. ¹³The children of your chosen sister greet you.[f]

---
[c] "going on ahead"—some mss say, "sidestepping"
[d] Some mss insert, "of the Messiah"
[e] "shalom"—see note at מַתִּתְיָהוּ *Matit'yahu* 26:49
[f] Some mss conclude, "אָמֵן, Amen."

הַמִכְתָּב הַשְׁלִישִׁי מִן יוֹחָנָן THE THIRD LETTER FROM YOCHANAN

יוֹחָנָן ג 3 Yochanan

¹*From* הַזָקֵן, HaZaqen; to Gaius the beloved, whom I love in truth: ²loved one, regarding all things, I pray *for* you to prosper and be in health, even as your soul prospers, ³for I rejoiced exceedingly when *the* brothers *were* coming and testifying of the truth in you, even as you walk in truth. ⁴I have no joy greater than these things: that I hear of my children walking in the truth.

⁵Loved one, you faithfully do whatever you enact *with regard* to the brothers, even these *who are* foreigners, ⁶who testified of your love in *the* sight of *the* Called-Forth[a]

---
[a] "Called-Forth"—ἐκκλησίας, ekklesias; see מַתִּתְיָהוּ *Matit'yahu* 16:18; also in verse 10

and by whom you will do well, having sent them forward worthily of God. ⁷Because they went forth for H*IS* Name, receiving nothing from the *foreign* ethnic-groups, ⁸we, then, ought to support[a] such *men*, so that we may become fellow-workers to the truth.

⁹I wrote something to the Called-Forth,[b] but he who is loving the first place among them—Diotrephes—does not receive us. ¹⁰Because of this, if I come, I will cause him to remember his actions that he does, prattling against us with evil words. And not satisfied with these *actions*, neither does he himself receive the brothers, and he forbids those intending *to do so*, and he expels *them* out of the Called-Forth.

¹¹Loved one, be not following that which is evil, but that which is good. He who is doing good is of God; he who is doing evil has not seen God.

¹²Testimony to Demetrius has been given by all, and by the truth itself. And we also—we testify, and you have known that our testimony is true.

¹³I had many things to write to you, but I do not want to write to you through ink and pen. ¹⁴Rather, I hope to see you soon, and *then* we will speak mouth to mouth.

¹⁵Peace to you! The friends *here* greet you. Be greeting the friends *there* by name.

---

[a] "support"—some mss say, "receive"
[b] "Called-Forth"—ἐκκλησία, ekklesia; see מַתִּתְיָהוּ *Matit'yahu* 16:18

Revelation

OF YESHUA THE MESSIAH

¹A revelation of יֵשׁוּעַ, Yeshua *the* Messiah that God gave to Him, to show to His slaves what things are necessary to come to pass quickly. And He signified IT, having sent *it* through His Messenger to His slave יוֹחָנָן, Yochanan, ²who testified *to* the word of God and *to* the testimony of יֵשׁוּעַ, Yeshua *the* Messiah—as many things as he saw. ³Happy is he who is reading (and those *who are* hearing) the words of the prophecy and paying attention to the things written in it—for the time is near!

⁴From יוֹחָנָן, Yochanan; to the seven Called-Forth-Communities[a] that ARE in Asia: unmerited favor to you, and peace, from Him who is, and who was, and who is coming; and from the Seven רוּחוֹת, Ruchot that are in the presence of His throne; ⁵and from יֵשׁוּעַ, Yeshua *the* Messiah—the faithful witness, the first-born of the dead, and the ruler of the kings of the earth.

To Him who loves us, and untied[b] us from our sins by His blood, ⁶and made us a kingdom[c]—כֹּהֲנִים, ko'haniym to His God and Father—to Him IS the glory and the power to the ages of the ages! אָמֵן, Amen.

⁷LOOK! HE COMES WITH THE CLOUDS,[d] and every eye will see Him —even those who pierced Him[e]—and all the tribes of the Land will wail *in mourning* because of Him.[f] Yes! אָמֵן, Amen!

⁸"I am the א and the ת,"[g] says יהוה אֱלֹהִים, ADONAI 'Elohiym,[h] "who is, and who was, and who is coming; צְבָאוֹת, Tz'vaot."

---

[a] "Called-Forth-Communities"—ἐκκλησίαις, ekklesiais; ἐκκλησιῶν, ekklesion; or ἐκκλησίαι, ekklesiai; here, in verse 11, and throughout chapter 2; see מַתִּתְיָהוּ *Matit'yahu* 16:18
[b] "untied"—some mss say, "bathed"
[c] "a kingdom"—some mss say, "kings and"
[d] דָּנִיֵּאל *Daniyel* 7:13
[e] cf. זְכַרְיָה *Z'khar'yah* 12:10
[f] cf. זְכַרְיָה *Z'khar'yah* 12:10, 14
[g] "א and the ת"—that is, אָלֶף, alef and תָו, tav; lit. "A, alpha and the Ω, omega," the first and last letters in the Hebrew and Greek alphabets, respectively; some mss insert, "beginning and end"
[h] Some mss do not have "אֱלֹהִים, 'Elohiym"

Address to Ephesus.   **Revelation 2:10**

⁹I, יוֹחָנָן, Yochanan — your brother and fellow-partner in the oppression and reign and perseverance in יֵשׁוּעַ, Yeshua[a] — was on the island that is called Patmos, because of the word of God and the testimony of יֵשׁוּעַ, Yeshua. ¹⁰I was in the רוּחַ, Ruach on the Day of ADONAI,[b] and I heard behind me a loud voice, as of a שׁוֹפָר, shofar, saying,[c] ¹¹"What you see, write in a scroll, and send *it* to the seven Called-Forth-Communities:[d] to Ephesus, and to Smyrna, and to Pergamus, and to Thyatira, and to Sardis, and to Philadelphia, and to Laodicea."

¹²And I turned to see the voice that was speaking with me, and having turned, I saw seven golden מְנֹרוֹת, m'norot. ¹³And in the middle of the מְנֹרוֹת, m'norot *was* ONE like a son of man, clothed to the foot, and bound at the chest with a golden belt, ¹⁴and His head and hairs *were* white, as if white wool — as snow — and His eyes as a flame of fire, ¹⁵and His feet like burnished bronze — as in a furnace having been fired — and His voice as a sound of many waters. ¹⁶And *He was* having in His right hand seven stars, and out of His mouth a sharp two-edged sword was proceeding, and His face WAS as the sun shining in *all* its power.

¹⁷And when I saw Him, I fell at His feet as *if I were* dead, and He placed His right hand on me, saying, "Be not afraid. I am the First, and the Last, ¹⁸and He who is living. And I became dead, but look! I am living to the ages of the ages![e] And I have the keys of the death and of the שְׁאוֹל, Sh'ol.

¹⁹"So write the things that you have seen, and the things that are, and the things that are about to come after these things. ²⁰*This is* the mystery of the seven stars that you have seen upon My right hand, and the seven golden מְנֹרוֹת, m'norot: the seven stars are Messengers of the seven Called-Forth-Communities, and the seven מְנֹרוֹת, m'norot[f] are *the* seven Called-Forth-Communities.

2 ¹"To the Messenger of the Called-Forth[g] in Ephesus, write, 'He who is holding the seven stars in His right hand, who is walking in the middle of the seven מְנֹרוֹת, m'norot — the golden *ones* — says these things: ²I have known your actions and your labor and perseverance, and that you are not able to bear *with* evil ones, and that you have tested those saying themselves to be emissaries but are not, and have found them liars; ³and you have persevered and carried *on* because of My Name,[h] and have not been weary.

⁴"'But I have *this* against you: that you left your first love! ⁵Remember, then, from where you have fallen, and reform, and do the actions *you did at* first. But if not, I *will* come to you[i] and will remove your מְנוֹרָה, m'norah from its place — if you do not reform. ⁶But *at least* you have this: that you hate the actions of the Nicolaitans, which I also hate. ⁷He who is having an ear, let him hear what the רוּחַ, Ruach says to the Called-Forth-Communities: to him who is overcoming, I will give to him to eat of the tree of life that is in[j] the Paradise of God.'

⁸"And to the Messenger of the Called-Forth in Smyrna, write, 'The First and the Last, who became dead and lived, says these things: ⁹I have known your[k] oppression and poverty — but you are rich — and the evil-speaking by those saying themselves to be יְהוּדִים, Y'hudiym, and are not, but ARE a synagogue of הַשָּׂטָן, HaSatan.

¹⁰"'Be not afraid of the things you are about to suffer. Look! the Accuser is about to throw *some* of you into prison, so that you may be tested, and you will have oppression *for* ten days. Become faithful until

---

[a] Some mss insert, "*the* Messiah"; both instances in this verse
[b] "Day of ADONAI" — most translations, including Young's, say, "Lord's Day"
[c] Some mss insert, "'I am the א and the ת, the First and the Last,' and"
[d] Some mss insert, "that ARE in Asia"
[e] Some mss insert, "אָמֵן, amen"
[f] Some mss insert, "that you have seen"
[g] "Called-Forth" — ἐκκλησίας, ekklesias; see מַתִּתְיָהוּ Matit'yahu 16:18; also in vss 8, 12 and 18
[h] Some mss insert, "and have toiled,"
[i] Some mss insert, "quickly"
[j] Some mss insert, "the middle of"
[k] Some mss insert, "actions, and"

Revelation 2:11 — Address to Pergamus.

death, and I will give you the crown of the life. ¹¹He who is having an ear, let him hear what the רוּחַ, Ruach says to the Called-Forth-Communities: he who is overcoming may not be injured by the second death.'

¹²"And to the Messenger of the Called-Forth in Pergamus, write, 'He who is having the sharp two-edged sword says these things: ¹³I have known[a] where you live—where the throne of הַשָּׂטָן, HaSatan *IS*—and you hold fast *to* My Name, and you did not deny My faith, even in the days Antipas *WAS* My witness—My faithful *one*—who was put to death beside you, where הַשָּׂטָן, HaSatan lives.

¹⁴"'But I have a few things against you: that you have those there holding *to* the teaching of בִּלְעָם, Bil'am, who taught בָּלָק, Balaq to throw a stumbling-block before the sons of יִשְׂרָאֵל, Yis'rael, to eat idol-sacrifices, and to commit sexual immorality. ¹⁵Like this, you—even you—have those holding *to* the teaching of the Nicolaitans in the same way.[b]

¹⁶"'So, reform! and if not, I come to you quickly and will fight against them with the sword of my mouth. ¹⁷He who is having an ear, let him hear what the רוּחַ, Ruach says to the Called-Forth-Communities: to him who is overcoming, I will give to him the hidden מָן, mahn, and will give to him a white stone, and a new name written upon the stone that no one has known except him who is receiving *IT*.'

¹⁸"And to the Messenger of the Called-Forth in Thyatira, write, 'The Son of God, who is having His eyes as a flame of fire and His feet resembling burnished bronze, says these things: ¹⁹I have known your actions and love and faith and service, and your perseverance, and *that* your actions—the latest[c]—*ARE* more than the first.

²⁰"'But I have this[d] against you: that you allow the woman אִיזֶבֶל, Iyzevel—who is calling herself a prophetess—*to go unhindered*, and she teaches and leads My slaves astray to commit sexual immorality and to eat idol-sacrifices. ²¹And I gave a time to her so that she might reform, but she did not want to reform from her sexual immorality. ²²Look! I will throw her onto a bed, and those committing adultery with her into great oppression, if they do not reform from her[e] actions. ²³And her children I will kill in death, and all the Called-Forth-Communities[f] will know that I am He who is searching innermost parts and hearts. And I will give to you—to each *one*—according to your actions.

²⁴"'And I say to you, the remainder who are in Thyatira, as many as do not have this teaching, who did not know the depths of הַשָּׂטָן, HaSatan, as they say: I do not put upon you *any* other burden; ²⁵but *to* that which you have, hold fast until I come. ²⁶And he who is overcoming, and who is watching My actions until the end—I will give authority to him over the world-ethnicities ²⁷(AND HE WILL RULE THEM WITH A ROD OF IRON; AS THE CONTAINERS OF THE POTTER, THEY WILL BE BROKEN[g]) ²⁸as I have also received *authority* from My Father, and I will *also* give to him the morning star. ²⁹He who is having an ear, let him hear what the רוּחַ, Ruach says to the Called-Forth-Communities.'

3 ¹"And to the Messenger of the Called-Forth[h] in Sardis, write, 'He who is having the Seven רוּחוֹת, Ruchot of God, and the seven stars, says these things: I have known your actions, and that you have a reputation[i] that you live, but you are dead. ²Become awake, and strengthen the remainder of the things that

---

[a] Some mss insert, "your actions and"
[b] "in the same way"—some mss say, "which thing I hate"
[c] "latest" or "last"
[d] "*this*"—some mss say, "a few things"
[e] "her"—some mss say, "their"
[f] "Called-Forth-Communities"—ἐκκλησίαις, ekklesiais; ἐκκλησιῶν, ekklesion; or ἐκκλησίαι, ekklesiai; here, in verse 29, and throughout chapter 3
[g] תְּהִלִּים, T'hiliym 2:9
[h] "Called-Forth"—ἐκκλησίας, ekklesias; see מַתִּתְיָהוּ Matit'yahu 16:18; also in vss 3:1 & 3:14
[i] "reputation"—lit. "name"

are about to die, for I have not found your actions fulfilled in My God's sight.

³"'Remember, then, how you have received and heard, and be paying attention to *it*, and reform. If, then, you do not awake, I will come[a] as a thief, and you will not know what hour I will come upon you. ⁴But you have a few names in Sardis who did not defile their garments, and they will walk with Me in white, because they are worthy. ⁵He who is overcoming in this way will be wrapped around in white garments, and I will not blot out his name from the scroll of the life, and I will profess his name in the presence of My Father, and in the presence of His Messengers. ⁶He who is having an ear, let him hear what the רוּחַ, Ruach says to the Called-Forth-Communities.'

⁷"And to the Messenger of the Called-Forth in Philadelphia, write, 'He who is holy, He who is true, He who is having the key of דָּוִד, David, He who is opening and no one will shut, and is shutting and no one opens, says these things: ⁸I have known your actions. Look! I have set in your sight a door—opened—which no one is able to shut, since you have a little power, and paid attention to My word, and did not deny My Name. ⁹Look! *See what* I make of the synagogue of הַשָּׂטָן, HaSatan—those saying themselves to be יְהוּדִים, Y'hudiym, and are not, but lie. Look! I will make them so that they will come and bow before your feet, and may know that I loved you.

¹⁰"'Because you watched over the word of My perseverance, I also will watch over you from the time of the testing that is about to come upon all the world, to test those living upon the earth. ¹¹I come quickly; be holding fast *to* that which you have, so that no one may take your crown. ¹²*And* He who is overcoming—I will make him a pillar in the Temple of My God, and He may not go outside *it* any more. And I will write upon him the name of my God, and the name of the city of my God—יְרוּשָׁלַיִם הַחֲדָשָׁה, Y'rushalayim Ha'Chadashah, that is coming down out of the Heaven from My God, *and* also My new name. ¹³He who is having an ear, let him hear what the רוּחַ, Ruach says to the Called-Forth-Communities.'

¹⁴"And to the Messenger of the Called-Forth in Laodicea, write, 'The אָמֵן, Amen, the faithful and true witness, the beginning of God's creation, says these things: ¹⁵I have known your actions, that you are neither cold nor hot; I wish you were *either* cold or hot. ¹⁶So, because you are lukewarm, and neither hot nor cold, I am about to vomit you out of My mouth.

¹⁷"'Because you say, "I am rich, and have grown rich, and have no need"—and have not known that you are the wretched, and pitiful, and poor, and blind, and naked—¹⁸I counsel you to buy from Me gold fired by fire (that you may be rich), and white garments (that you may be wrapped around, and the shame of your nakedness may not be revealed), and eye-salve to anoint your eyes (that you may see).

¹⁹"'As many as I love, I refute and discipline—be zealous, then, and reform. ²⁰Look! I have stood at the door, and I knock. If anyone hears My voice and opens the door, indeed, I will come in to him, and will eat with him, and he with Me. ²¹He who is overcoming—I will give to him to sit with Me in My throne, as I also overcame, and sat down with My Father in His throne. ²²He who is having an ear, let him hear what the רוּחַ, Ruach says to the Called-Forth-Communities.'"

4 ¹And after these things, look! I saw a door opened in the heaven, and the first voice that I heard WAS as of a שׁוֹפָר, shofar speaking with me, saying, "Come up here, and I will show you what must come to pass after these things." ²Immediately, I was in the רוּחַ, Ruach, and look! a throne was set in the heaven, and ONE is sitting upon the throne. ³And the one sitting is in appearance like a stone—jasper and sardius—and a rainbow is around the throne in appearance like an emerald.

---

[a] Some mss insert, "upon you"

Revelation 4:4 — *Vision of the throne.*

⁴And around the throne ARE twenty-four *other* thrones and[a] twenty-four זְקֵנִים, Z'qeniym sitting upon the thrones, clothed in white garments, and upon their heads *are* crowns of gold. ⁵And out of the throne come lightnings and voices and thunders. And seven torches of fire are burning in sight of the throne, which are the Seven רוּחוֹת, Ruchot of God. ⁶And in sight of the throne IS something like a sea of glass like crystal—and in the middle of the throne and around the throne ARE four living creatures, full of eyes in front and behind. ⁷And the first living creature IS like a lion, and the second living creature IS like a calf, and the third living creature has the face as of a man, and the fourth living creature IS like an eagle flying.

⁸And the four living creatures—each one[b] of them having six wings—around and within are full of eyes; and they have no rest day and night, saying,

> "קָדוֹשׁ קָדוֹשׁ קָדוֹשׁ יהוה אֱלֹהֵי צְבָאוֹת
> Qadosh, qadosh, qadosh,
> ADONAI 'Elohei Tz'vaot;

who was, and who is, and who is coming." ⁹And when the living creatures give glory and honor and thanks to Him who is sitting upon the throne—who is living to the ages of the ages—¹⁰the twenty-four זְקֵנִים, Z'qeniym will fall down before Him who is sitting upon the throne, and will bow *in worship* before Him who is living to the ages of the ages. And they will throw their crowns before the throne, saying, ¹¹"Worthy are You, our Master and God,[c] to receive the glory and the honor and the power, because You—You created all the things, and because of Your will they are, and they were created."

5 ¹And I saw, upon the right hand of Him who is sitting upon the throne, a scroll written within and on the back, sealed with seven seals. ²And I saw a strong Messenger proclaiming with a loud voice, "Who is worthy to open the scroll, and to release its seals?" ³But no one in the heaven, nor upon the earth, nor under the earth, was able to open the scroll, nor to look at it.

⁴And I was weeping greatly, since no one was found worthy to open[d] the scroll, nor to look at it. ⁵And one of the זְקֵנִים, Z'qeniym said to me, "Weep not. Look! the Lion, who is of the tribe of יְהוּדָה, Y'hudah, the Root of דָּוִד, David, overcame to open the scroll and[e] the seven seals of it."

⁶And I saw in the middle of the throne and of the four living creatures—and in the middle of the זְקֵנִים, Z'qeniym—stood a Lamb, as *if* it had been slaughtered, having seven horns and seven eyes (which are the Seven רוּחוֹת, Ruchot of God, sent to all the earth), ⁷and he came and took the scroll out of the right hand of Him who is sitting upon the throne. ⁸And when he took the scroll, the four living creatures and the twenty-four זְקֵנִים, Z'qeniym fell before the Lamb—each one having a harp and golden bowls full of incenses, which are the prayers of the קְדוֹשִׁים, Q'doshiym—⁹and they sang a new song, saying, "Worthy are you to take the scroll and open its seals, because you were slaughtered, and *you* redeemed[f] to God in your blood *those* out of every nation, and language,[g] and people, and ethnicity, ¹⁰and *you* have made them a kingdom[h] and כֹּהֲנִים, ko'haniym to our God, and they[i] will reign upon the earth."

¹¹And I saw, and I heard the voice of many Messengers around the throne, and the living creatures, and the זְקֵנִים, Z'qeniym—and the number of them was ten thousands of ten thousands, and thousands of thousands—¹²saying with a loud voice, "Worthy is the Lamb that was slaughtered, to receive the power and wealth and wis-

---

[a] Some mss insert, "I saw the"
[b] "one"—lit. "one according to one"
[c] "our Master and God"—some mss say, "O Master"
[d] Some mss insert, "and to read"
[e] Some mss insert, "to release"
[f] Some mss insert, "us"
[g] "language"—lit. "tongue"
[h] "them a kingdom"—some mss say, "us kings"
[i] "they"—some translations say, "we"

Opening of the seals.

dom and strength and honor and glory and blessing!"

¹³And I heard every creature that is in the heaven, and upon the earth, and under the earth, and the things that are upon the sea, and all the things in them, saying, "To Him who is sitting upon the throne, and to the Lamb, IS the blessing and the honor and the glory and the power—to the ages of the ages!" ¹⁴And the four living creatures said, "אָמֵן, Amen!" and the[a] זְקֵנִים, Z'qeniym fell down and they worshipped.[b]

6 ¹And I saw when the Lamb opened one of the seven[c] seals, and I heard one of the four living creatures saying as *if* it were a voice of thunder, "Come!"[d] ²And I saw, and look! a white horse! And he who is sitting upon it is having a bow, and there was given to him a crown, and he went forth overcoming, and so that he may overcome.

³And when he opened the second seal, I heard the second living creature saying, "Come!" ⁴And there went out another horse—red—and to him who is sitting upon it, there was given to him *authority* to take the peace from the land, so that *the people* will also slaughter one another; and there was given to him a huge sword.

⁵And when he opened the third seal, I heard the third living creature saying, "Come!" And I saw, and look! a black horse! and he who is sitting upon it is having a pair of scales in his hand. ⁶And I heard something like[e] a voice in the middle of the four living creatures, saying, "A measure of wheat for a day's wage,[f] and three measures of barley for a day's wage," and "You may not injure the oil and the wine."

⁷And when he opened the fourth seal, I heard the voice of the fourth living creature, saying, "Come!" ⁸And I saw, and look! a pale horse! And he who is sitting upon him—his name is Death, and שְׁאוֹל, Sh'ol was following with him. And authority was given to them over the fourth part of the land, to kill with sword and with hunger and with death and by the beasts of the land.

⁹And when he opened the fifth seal, I saw under the altar the souls of those slaughtered because of the word of God, and because of the testimony that they held. ¹⁰And they shouted with a loud voice, saying, "Until when—O Sovereign, the Holy and True—do You not judge and take vengeance of our blood from those dwelling upon the land?" ¹¹And a white robe was given to them—to each—and it was said to them that they will rest themselves a little time longer, until also may be fulfilled *the number of* their fellow-slaves and their brothers who are about to be killed—even as they *had been*.

¹²And I saw when he opened the sixth seal; and a massive earthquake came, and the sun became black as sackcloth *made* of hair, and the whole[g] moon became as blood, ¹³and the stars of the heaven fell to the earth (like a fig-tree being shaken by a great wind throws her winter figs). ¹⁴And the heaven departed as a scroll rolled up, and every mountain and island—out of their places they were moved.

¹⁵And the kings of the earth, and the great men, and the leaders of thousands, and the rich, and the mighty, and each slave and freeman hid themselves in the caves and in the rocks of the mountains, ¹⁶and they said to the mountains and to the rocks, "Fall upon us, and hide us from the face of Him who is sitting upon the throne, and from the wrath of the Lamb!" ¹⁷because the great Day of their[h] wrath came, and who is able to stand?

---

[a] Some mss insert, "twenty-four"
[b] "worshipped"—some mss say, "bowed before Him who is living to the ages of the ages"
[c] Some mss omit, "seven"
[d] "Come!"—some mss say, "Come and look!"; also in vss 3, 5 & 7
[e] Some mss omit, "something like"
[f] "day's wage"—lit. "denary"; both times in this vs

[g] Some mss omit, "whole"
[h] "their"—some mss say, "His"

7 ¹After this, I saw four Messengers standing upon the four corners of the land, holding *back* the four winds of the land, so that the wind would not blow upon the land, nor upon the sea, nor upon any tree. ²And I saw another Messenger going up from the rising of the sun, having a seal of the living God. And he shouted with a loud voice to the four Messengers to whom it was given to injure the land and the sea, saying, ³"Do not injure the land, nor the sea, nor the trees, until we have sealed the slaves of our God upon their foreheads."

⁴And I heard the number of those sealed (144,000 were sealed out of all the tribes of the sons of יִשְׂרָאֵל, Yis'rael):

⁵12,000 of the tribe of יְהוּדָה, Y'hudah were sealed;
12,000 of the tribe of רְאוּבֵן, R'uven;ᵃ
12,000 of the tribe of גָּד, Gad;
⁶12,000 of the tribe of אָשֵׁר, Asher;
12,000 of the tribe of נַפְתָּלִי, Naf'taliy;
12,000 of the tribe of מְנַשֶּׁה, M'nasheh;
⁷12,000 of the tribe of שִׁמְעוֹן, Shim'on;
12,000 of the tribe of לֵוִי, Leviy;
12,000 of the tribe of יִשָּׂשכָר, Yisakhar;
⁸12,000 of the tribe of זְבֻלוּן, Z'vulun;
12,000 of the tribe of יוֹסֵף, Yosef;
12,000 of the tribe of בִּנְיָמִין, Bin'yamiyn were sealed.

⁹After these things, I saw, and look! a large crowd which no one was able to number, out of all world-ethnicities and nations and peoples and languages,ᵇ standing in the presence of the throne and in the presence of the Lamb, wrapped around in white robes, and *branches of* palms in their hands. ¹⁰And they shouted with a loud voice, saying, "The salvation IS to our God—to Him who is sitting upon the throne—and to the Lamb!"

¹¹And all the Messengers were standing around the throne, and *around* the זְקֵנִים, Z'qeniym and the four living creatures, and they fell upon their faces and bowed before God *in worship*, saying,

¹²"אָמֵן, Amen! the blessing, and the glory, and the wisdom, and the thanksgiving, and the honor, and the power, and the strength ARE to our God—to the ages of the ages! אָמֵן, Amen!"

¹³And one of the זְקֵנִים, Z'qeniym answered, saying to me, "These who have been wrapped around with the white robes: who are they, and where did they come from?" ¹⁴And I said to him, "Sir, you have known." And he said to me, "These are those who are coming out of the great oppression, and they washed their robes and made them white in the blood of the Lamb. ¹⁵Because of this, they are in the presence of the throne of God, and they do service to Him day and night in His Temple. And He who is sitting upon the throne will dwell over them. ¹⁶They will not hunger anymore, nor thirst anymore,ᶜ nor may the sun fall upon them, nor any heat, ¹⁷because the Lamb that IS in the middle of the throne will feed them and will lead them to fountains of waters of life, and God will wipe away every tear from their eyes."

8 ¹And when he opened the seventh seal, there came silence in the heaven *for* about half-an-hour. ²And I saw the seven Messengers who have stood before God, and there were given to them seven שׁוֹפָרוֹת, shofarot. ³And another Messenger came, and he stood at the altar, having a golden frankincense-holder, and there was much incense given to him, so that he will give IT to the prayers of all the קְדוֹשִׁים, Q'doshiym upon the golden altar that IS before the throne. ⁴And the smoke of the incenses went up to the prayers of the קְדוֹשִׁים, Q'doshiym out of the hand of the Messenger, before God. ⁵And the Messenger took the frankincense-holder and filled it out of the fire of the altar and threw IT to the earth, and there came thunders, and voices, and lightnings, and an earthquake.

⁶And the seven Messengers, who are having the seven שׁוֹפָרוֹת, shofarot, prepared themselves so that they could sound *them*.

ᵃ Some mss insert "were sealed" after each tribe
ᵇ "languages"—lit. "tongues"

ᶜ "nor thirst anymore" is missing from Young's

The oy! of locusts.

⁷And the first sounded *his*, and there came hail and fire, mingled with blood, and it was thrown to the land, and a third of the land was burned up,ª and a third of the trees were burned up, and all the green grass was burned up.

⁸And the second Messenger sounded *his*, and something like a great mountain burning with fire was thrown into the sea, and a third of the sea became blood, ⁹and a third of the creatures that ARE in the sea died (those having soulsᵇ), and a third of the ships were destroyed.

¹⁰And the third Messenger sounded *his*, and a huge star fell out of the heaven, burning as a torch, and it fell upon a third of the rivers and upon the fountains of the waters. ¹¹And the name of the star is called Wormwood. And a third of the waters became wormwood, and many of the men died of the waters, because they were made bitter.

¹²And the fourth Messenger sounded *his*, and a third of the sun was struck, and a third of the moon, and a third of the stars, so that a third of them would be darkened, and the day*light*—a third of it—would not shine; and the night likewise.

¹³And I saw and I heard one eagle,ᶜ flying in the mid-heaven, saying with a loud voice, "אוֹי אוֹי אוֹי, Oy! Oy! Oy! to those living upon the land because of the remaining voices of the שׁוֹפָר, shofar of the three Messengers who are about to *make* theirs sound!"

9 ¹And the fifth Messenger sounded *his*, and I saw a star out of the heaven having fallen to the earth, and there was given to it the key of the pit of the abyss. ²And he opened the pit of the abyss, and a smoke came up out of the pit like smoke of a large furnace, and the sun and the air were darkened from the smoke of the pit.

³And out of the smoke, locusts came forth to the earth, and there was given to them authority, as scorpions of the earth have authority. ⁴And it was said to them that they would not injure the grass of the earth, nor any green thing, nor any tree, but only the men who do not have the seal of God on the foreheads.

⁵And it was given to them that they may not kill them, but that they would be tormented *for* five months. And their torment IS *to be* as the torment of a scorpion, when it strikes a man. ⁶And in those days, men will look for the death, but they will not find it—and they will desire to die, but the death flees from them.

⁷And the likenesses of the locusts ARE like horses made ready to battle, and something like crowns resembling gold *are* upon their heads, and their faces *were* as faces of men, ⁸but they had hair as hair of women, and their teeth were as THOSE of lions, ⁹and they had breastplates as breastplates of iron, and the noise of their wings IS as the noise of chariots of many horses running into battle, ¹⁰and they have tails like scorpions, and stings, and in their tails IS their authority to injure men *for* five months. ¹¹They have a king over them—the Messenger of the Abyss. *The* name to him in Hebrew IS אֲבַדּוֹן, 'Avadon, and in the Greek he has a name: Ἀπολλύων, Apollyon. ¹²The first אוֹי, oy! *is* gone away. Look! there come yet a second and third אוֹי, oy!ᵈ after these things.

¹³And the sixth Messenger sounded *his shofar*, and I heard a voice out of the four horns of the altar of gold that is before God, ¹⁴saying to the sixth Messenger who is having the שׁוֹפָר, shofar, "Untie the four Messengers who are bound at the great river פְּרָת, P'rat," ¹⁵and the four Messengers who have been made ready for the hour and day and month and year were untied, so that they would kill a third of mankind. ¹⁶And the number of the forc-

---

ª Some mss omit, "and a third of the land was burned up"
ᵇ "souls"—ψυχὰς, psuchas—Young's and other translations say, "life"
ᶜ "eagle"—some mss say, "Messenger"
ᵈ "a second and third אוֹי, oy!"—lit. "two woes"

es of the horsemen WAS two tens of thousands of tens of thousands—and I heard the number of them.

¹⁷And I saw the horses this way in the vision, and those sitting upon them: having breastplates *the color* of fire and hyacinth and sulfur. And the heads of the horses ARE as heads of lions, and out of their mouths come fire and smoke and sulfur. ¹⁸By these three plagues[a] were a third of mankind killed: from the fire and the smoke and the sulfur that is coming out of their mouths, ¹⁹for the authority of the horses is in their mouth and in their tails, for their tails ARE like serpents, having heads, and with them they injure. ²⁰And the remainder of mankind who were not killed in these plagues did not reform from the actions of their hands, *such* that they would not bow *any longer* before the demons and the idols—those of gold, and those of silver, and those of brass, and those of stone, and those of wood—that are able neither to see, nor to hear, nor to walk. ²¹Yes, they did not reform from their murders, nor from their φαρμάκων, pharmakon,[b] nor from their sexual immoralities, nor from their thefts.

10

¹And I saw another strong Messenger coming down from the heaven, wrapped around with a cloud, and the rainbow upon his head, and his face as the sun, and his feet as pillars of fire, ²and having in his hand a little opened scroll. And he placed his right foot upon the sea and the left upon the land, ³and he shouted with a loud voice —as a lion roars—and when he shouted, the seven thunders spoke out their voices. ⁴And when the seven thunders spoke,[c] I was about to write, but I heard a voice out of the heaven saying, "Seal the things that the seven thunders spoke," and "You may not write them."

⁵And the Messenger whom I saw standing upon the sea and upon the land lifted up his right[d] hand to the heaven, ⁶and swore in Him who lives to the ages of the ages—who created the heaven and the things in it, and the land and the things in it, and the sea and the things in it—that time will no longer be, ⁷but in the days of the voice of the seventh Messenger, when he is about to sound *his shofar,* also the mystery of God has been finished, as He declared to His slaves, the prophets.

⁸And the voice that I heard out of the heaven is again speaking with me, and saying, "Go, take the scroll that is open in the hand of the Messenger who has been standing upon the sea and upon the land." ⁹And I went away to the Messenger, saying to him to give me the little scroll. And he said to me, "Take, and eat it up, and it will make your belly bitter, but in your mouth it will be sweet like honey." ¹⁰And I took the little scroll from the hand of the Messenger, and ate it up, and it was in my mouth as honey—sweet. But when I ate it, my belly was made bitter, ¹¹and they said to me, "You must prophesy again about many peoples and world-ethnicities and languages[e] and kings."

11

¹And a reed like a rod was given to me,[f] saying, "Rise, and measure the Temple of God, and the altar, and those worshipping in it, ²but leave out the courtyard that is outside the Temple and do not measure it, because it was given to the גּוֹיִם, Goyim, and they will trample the holy city under foot *for* forty-two months.

³"And I will give to my two witnesses, and they will prophesy a thousand, two hundred *and* sixty days, wrapped around with sackcloth. ⁴These are the two olive TREES, and the two מְנֹרוֹת, m'norot that stand in the presence of the Master[g] of the earth. ⁵And if anyone wants to injure them, fire comes out of their mouth and devours their enemies; and if anyone wants to injure them, he must be killed

---

[a] Some mss omit, "plagues"
[b] φαρμάκων, pharmakon—usually "sorcery" or "witchcraft"
[c] Some mss insert, "their voices"
[d] Some mss omit, "right"
[e] "languages"—lit. "tongues"; also in 11:9
[f] Some mss insert, "and the Messenger stood"
[g] Some mss say, "God"

this way. ⁶These have the authority to shut the heaven so that it may not rain rain in the days of their prophecy, and they have authority over the waters to turn them to blood, and to strike the land with every plague, as often as they want.

⁷"And when they finish their testimony, the beast that is coming up out of the abyss will make war with them, and will overcome them and kill them, ⁸and their dead bodies WILL BE laid upon the street of the great city (that, spiritually, is called סְדֹם, S'dom and מִצְרַיִם, Mitz'rayim—where their[a] Master was also crucified). ⁹And they see —they of the peoples and nations and languages and world-ethnicities—their dead bodies *for* three and a half days, and they do not allow their dead bodies to be put into tombs. ¹⁰And those living upon the land rejoice over them and celebrate, and they will send gifts to one another, because these—the two prophets—tormented those living upon the land."

¹¹But after the three and a half days, a רוּחַ, ruach of life from God entered into them, and they stood upon their feet, and great fear fell upon *all* those seeing them. ¹²And they heard a loud voice out of the heaven saying to them, "Come up here," and they went up to the heaven in the cloud, and their enemies saw them.

¹³And in that moment came a massive earthquake, and a tenth of the city fell. And killed in the earthquake were seven thousands *of the* names of men, but the rest became frightened, and they gave glory to the God of the heaven.

¹⁴The second אוֹי, oy! is gone away. Look! The third אוֹי, oy! comes quickly.

¹⁵And the seventh Messenger sounded *his shofar*, and there came loud voices in the heaven, saying, "The kingdom[b] of the world became THAT of our Master and of His Messiah, and He will reign to the ages of the ages!" ¹⁶And the twenty-four זְקֵנִים, Z'qeniym, who are sitting in the presence of God upon their thrones, fell upon their faces and bowed before God, ¹⁷saying, "We give thanks to You, יהוה אֱלֹהֵי צְבָאוֹת, ADONAI 'Elohei Tz'vaot, who is, and who was,[c] because You have taken Your great power, and reigned. ¹⁸And the world-ethnicities were angry; and Your wrath came, and *also* the time of the dead to be judged and to give the reward to Your slaves (to the prophets, and to the קְדוֹשִׁים, Q'doshiym, and to those fearing Your Name—the small and the great), and to destroy those who are destroying the land."

¹⁹And the Temple of God which is in the heaven was opened, and the אֲרוֹן בְּרִיתוֹ, 'Aron B'riyto was seen in His Temple, and there came lightnings and voices and thunders and an earthquake and massive hail.

12

¹And a great sign was seen in the heaven: a woman wrapped around with the sun, and the moon under her feet, and upon her head a crown of twelve stars; ²and being with child, she also shouted, suffering birth-pains and being tormented to bring *it* forth.

³And another sign was seen in the heaven, and look! a huge red dragon having seven heads and ten horns, and upon his head *are* seven crowns, ⁴and his tail drags a third of the stars of the heaven, and he throws them to the earth. And the dragon stood before the woman who is about to bring forth *her child*, so that when she brings forth her child, he may devour *it*. ⁵And she brought forth a male child who is about to rule all the world-ethnicities with a rod of iron. And her child was taken away to God and to His throne, ⁶and the woman fled to the desert, where she has a place there made ready from God, that they may nourish her there *for* a thousand, two hundred *and* sixty days.

⁷And there came war in the heaven: מִיכָאֵל, Miykhael and his Messengers to war against the dragon. And the dragon and his messengers warred, ⁸but they did not prevail—nor was their place found any-

---

[a] "their"—some mss say, "our"
[b] "kingdom"—some mss say, "kingdoms"
[c] Some mss insert, "and who is coming"

more in the heaven—⁹and the huge dragon was thrown down. The ancient serpent who is called "Accuser" and "הַשָּׂטָן, Ha-Satan"—who is leading the whole world astray—he was thrown down to the earth, and his messengers were thrown down with him.

¹⁰And I heard a loud voice in the heaven saying, "Now comes the salvation and the power and the reign of our God, and the authority of His Messiah, because the accuser of our brothers, who is accusing them before our God day and night, was thrown down. ¹¹And they overcame him because of the blood of the Lamb, and because of the word of their testimony, and they did not love their life— *even* until death. ¹²Rejoice because of this, you heavens, and those who dwell in them. אוֹי, Oy! *to you*,ᵃ the land and the sea, because the Accuser went down to you—having great rage— having known that he has little time."

¹³And when the dragon saw that he was thrown down to the earth, he pursued the woman who had brought forth the male *child*. ¹⁴And there were given to the woman the two wings of the great eagle, so that she could fly to the desert— to her place where she is nourished *for* a time, and times, and half a time— *away* from the face of the serpent. ¹⁵And the serpent threw water out of his mouth as a river *chasing* after the woman, so that he might cause her to be carried away by the river. ¹⁶But the land helped the woman, and the land opened its mouth and swallowed up the river that the dragon threw out of his mouth.

¹⁷And the dragon was angry against the woman, and went away to make war with the remainder of her seed—those keeping the commands of God, and having the testimony of יֵשׁוּעַ, Yeshua.ᵇ ¹⁸And he stood upon the sand of the sea.ᶜ

13 ¹And I saw out of the sea a beast coming up, having ten horns and seven heads, and ten crowns upon its horns, and names of evil-speaking upon its heads. ²And the beast that I saw resembled a leopard, and its feet *were* as of a bear, and its mouth as the mouth of a lion. And the dragon gave to it his power, and his throne, and great authority. ³And one of its heads *looked* like *it had been* slaughtered to death, but its deadly wound was healed, and all the earth marveled after the beast. ⁴And they bowed *in worship* to the dragon, because he gave the authority to the beast; and they bowed to the beast, saying, "Who IS like the beast? And who is able to war with it?"

⁵And there was given to it a mouth *for* speaking great things and evil-speakings, and authority was given to it to make war *for* forty-two months. ⁶And it opened its mouth for evil-speakings toward God, to speak evil of His name and His מִשְׁכָּן, mish'kanᵈ—those who dwell in the heaven. ⁷And there was given to it to make war with the קְדוֹשִׁים, Q'doshiym, and to overcome them; and there was given to it authority over every nation and people and languageᵉ and world-ethnicity.

⁸And all who are living upon the land will bow before it—*any* whose name has not been written in the scroll of the life of the Lamb that was slaughtered from the foundation of the world. ⁹If anyone has an ear, let him hear: ¹⁰if anyone *is to go into*ᶠ captivity, he goes away into captivity; if anyone *is* to be killedᵍ by *the* sword, he is to be killed by *the* sword.ʰ Here is the perseverance and the faith of the קְדוֹשִׁים, Q'doshiym.

¹¹And I saw another beast coming up out of the land, and it had two horns, like a lamb, but it was speaking as a dragon. ¹²And it does all the *acts of* authority of the

---

ᵃ "*to you*"—some mss say, "to those inhabiting"
ᵇ Some mss insert, "*the* Messiah"
ᶜ "And... sea"—some mss say, "I" instead of "he," and place this phrase at the beginning of 13:1

ᵈ Some mss insert, "and of"
ᵉ "language"—lit. "tongue"; also in 14:6
ᶠ "*is to go into*"—some mss say, "gathers a"
ᵍ "*is* to be killed"—some mss say, "kills"
ʰ cf. יִרְמְיָהוּ *Yir'm'yahu* 15:2, 43:11

first beast in its presence; and it makes the land and those living in it *such* that they will bow *in worship* before the first beast (whose deadly wound was healed); ¹³and it does massive signs, *such* that it also makes fire to come down from the heaven to the earth in the sight of men; ¹⁴and it leads astray those living on the land, because of the signs that were given it to do in the presence of the beast, telling those living upon the land to make an image to the beast (*the one* that has the wound of the sword, yet lived); ¹⁵and there was given to it to give a רוּחַ, ruach to the image of the beast, so that the image of the beast may also speak, and may cause that as many as will not bow *in worship* to the image of the beast may be killed.

¹⁶And it makes all *people become marked* —the small, and the great, and the rich, and the poor, and the freemen, and the slaves—*such* that they give to them a mark upon their right hand or upon their forehead, ¹⁷and *such* that no one is able to buy or sell, except he who is having the mark[a] —the name of the beast, or the number of his name.

¹⁸Here is the wisdom! He who is having understanding, let him count the number of the beast, for it is the number of a man —and its number IS 666.

14 ¹And I saw, and look! the Lamb is having stood upon the Mount צִיּוֹן, Tziyon, and a hundred *and* forty-four thousands with Him, having His name and[b] the name of His Father written upon their foreheads. ²And I heard a voice out of the heaven—as a voice of many waters, and as a voice of loud thunder—and the voice which I heard *was* like *that* of harpists harping with their harps, ³and they sang *something* like a new song before the throne and before the four living creatures and the זְקֵנִים, Z'qeniym, but no one was able to learn the song except the hundred *and* forty-four thousands who have been bought from the earth. ⁴These are they who were not defiled with women, for they are virgins. These who are following the Lamb wherever He goes, these were bought from among men *as* a firstfruit to God and to the Lamb, ⁵and in their mouth there was found no lie; they are unblemished.[c]

⁶And I saw another Messenger flying in mid-heaven, having age-enduring Good News to proclaim to those living upon the earth, and to every world-ethnicity and nation and language and people, ⁷saying in a loud voice, "Fear God, and give glory to Him, for the time of His judgment has come; and bow *in worship* before Him who made the heaven, and the land, and sea, and fountains of waters."

⁸And another Messenger, a second, followed, saying, "Fall, fall, did Babylon the Great, who has given of the wine of the rage of her sexual immorality to all the world-ethnicities to drink."

⁹And another Messenger, a third, followed them, saying in a loud voice, "If anyone bows *in worship* before the beast and his image, and receives a mark upon his forehead or upon his hand, ¹⁰he also will drink of the wine of the rage of God that has been mingled unmixed in the cup of his wrath. And he will be tormented in fire and sulfur in the presence of holy Messengers, and in the presence of the Lamb, ¹¹and the smoke of their torment *will* go up to ages of *the* ages. And they who are bowing before the beast and his image—also if any receives the mark of his name—*will* have no rest day and night. ¹²Here is the perseverance of the קְדוֹשִׁים, Q'doshiym[d]— those keeping the commands of God, and the faith of יֵשׁוּעַ, Yeshua."

¹³And I heard a voice out of the heaven saying,[e] "Write, 'Happy are the dead who in the Master are dying from this time *on!* "Yes," says the רוּחַ, Ruach, "so that they will rest from their labors, for their actions follow them!"'"

---

[a] Some mss insert, "or"
[b] Some mss omit, "His name and"
[c] Some mss insert, "before the throne of God"
[d] Some mss insert, "here *are*"
[e] Some mss insert, "to me"

¹⁴And I saw, and look! a white cloud! And sitting upon the cloud, ONE resembling a son of man, having a golden crown on his head and a sharp sickle in his hand. ¹⁵And another Messenger came forth out of the Temple, shouting in a loud voice to him who is sitting upon the cloud, "Send forth your sickle and reap, for the time to reap has come,ᵃ because the harvest of the earth has been ripe!" ¹⁶And he who is sitting upon the cloud put forth his sickle upon the earth, and the earth was reaped.

¹⁷And another Messenger came forth out of the Temple that IS in the heaven (he also was having a sharp sickle), ¹⁸and another Messenger came forth out of the altar (the one having authority over the fire). And he called with a loud voiceᵇ to him having the sharp sickle, saying, "Send forth your sharp sickle, and gather the clusters of the vine of the earth, because her grapes have come to perfection!" ¹⁹And the Messenger put forth his sickle to the earth, and gathered the vine of the earth, and threw IT to the great winepress of the rage of God. ²⁰And the winepress was trampled outside the city, and blood came forth out of the winepress—up to *the height of* the bridles of the horses—*for a distance of* two hundred miles.ᶜ

15 ¹And I saw another sign in the heaven, great and wonderful: seven Messengers having the seven last plagues, because in these the rage of God was completed. ²And I saw *something* like a sea of glass mingled with fire; and those who gain the victory over the beast, and his image,ᵈ AND the number of his name, *were* standing by the sea of the glass—having harps of God. ³And they sang the song of מֹשֶׁה, Mosheh—the slave of God—and the song of the Lamb, saying, "Great and wonderful ARE Your acts, יהוה אֱלֹהֵי צְבָאוֹת, ADONAI 'Elohei Tz'vaot;

ᵃ Some mss insert, "to you"
ᵇ "voice"—some mss say, "outcry"
ᶜ "two hundred miles"—lit. "a thousand, six hundred stadia"
ᵈ Some mss insert, "and his mark"

righteous and true ARE Your ways, O King of גּוֹיִם, Goyim.ᵉ ⁴Who will not fear,ᶠ O Master, and glorify Your Name? For You alone ARE undefiled, because ALL THE גּוֹיִם, GOYIM WILL COME AND BOW BEFORE YOU,ᵍ because Your righteous acts were revealed."

⁵And after these things, I saw, and the Temple of the מִשְׁכָּן, Mish'kan of the Testimony in the heaven was opened, ⁶and those having the seven plagues—the seven Messengers—came out from the Temple clothed in pure, shining linen, and their chests wrapped around with golden belts.

⁷And one of the four living creatures gave to the seven Messengers seven golden bowls full of the rage of God (who is living to the ages of the ages), ⁸and the Temple was filled with smoke from the glory of God and from His power, and no one was able to enter the Temple until the seven plagues of the seven Messengers were finished.

16 ¹And I heard a loud voice out of the Temple saying to the seven Messengers, "Go away, and pour out the seven bowls of the rage of God to the earth."

²And the first went away and poured out his bowl to the land, and there came a bad and painful sore upon those men having the mark of the beast, and those bowing to his image.

³And the second poured out his bowl to the sea, and there came blood as of ONE dead, and every living soul in the sea died.

⁴And the third poured out his bowl to the rivers and the well-springs of the waters, and there came blood. ⁵And I heard the Messenger of the waters, saying, "Righteousʰ are You who is and who was—the Holy Oneⁱ—because You judged these things, ⁶since they poured out *the* blood of

---
ᵉ "גּוֹיִם, Goyim"—some mss say, "קְדוֹשִׁים, Q'doshiym"; other mss say "ages"
ᶠ Some mss insert, "You"
ᵍ תְּהִלִּים T'hiliym 86:9; cf. יְשַׁעְיָהוּ Y'sha'yahu 66:23
ʰ Some mss insert, "O Master"
ⁱ "the Holy One"—Young says, "and who will be"

קְדוֹשִׁים, Q'doshiym and prophets, and You have given blood to them to drink. They are worthy *of it.*" ⁷And I heard[a] the altar saying, "Yes, יהוה אֱלֹהֵי צְבָאוֹת, Adonai 'Elohei Tz'vaot, true and righteous ARE Your judgments."

⁸And the fourth poured out his bowl upon the sun, and there was given to him to scorch mankind with fire. ⁹And men were scorched with great heat, and they spoke evil of the Name of God (who has the authority over these plagues), and they did not reform *so as* to give glory to Him.

¹⁰And the fifth poured out his bowl upon the throne of the beast, and his kingdom became darkened, and *people* were gnawing their tongues from the pain. ¹¹And from their pains, and from their sores, they spoke evil of the God of the heaven, and they did not reform from their actions.

¹²And the sixth poured out his bowl upon the great river, the פְּרָת, P'rat, and its water was dried up, so that the road of the kings who are from *the direction of* the rising of the sun may be made ready. ¹³And I saw COME out of the mouth of the dragon, and out of the mouth of the beast, and out of the mouth of the false prophet, three unclean רוּחוֹת, ruchot, like frogs—¹⁴for they are רוּחוֹת, ruchot of demons, doing signs—which go out to the kings[b] of the whole world, to bring them together to the battle of the great Day of אֱלֹהֵי צְבָאוֹת, 'Elohei Tz'vaot. ¹⁵("Look! I come as a thief. Happy IS he who is staying awake and keeping his clothes *on*, so that he may not walk naked, and they see the shame of his nakedness.") ¹⁶And they brought them together to the place that in Hebrew is called, "הַר מְגִדּוֹ, Har M'gido."

¹⁷And the seventh poured out his bowl upon the air, and there came forth a loud voice out of the Temple[c] from the throne, saying, "It has come!" ¹⁸And there came lightnings and voices and thunders, and a massive earthquake came, such as had not come since men came upon the earth—so terrible an earthquake, *and* so massive! ¹⁹And the great city came *apart* into three parts, and the cities of the גּוֹיִם, Goyim, fell, and Babylon the Great was remembered before God, to give to her the cup of the wine of the rage of His wrath, ²⁰and every island fled away, and mountains were not found *anymore,* ²¹and huge hail *stones*—about a hundred pounds[d] *each*—came down out of the heaven upon men. And mankind spoke evil of God because of the plague of the hail, because its plague was very massive.

17

¹And one of the seven Messengers who were having the seven bowls came and spoke with me, saying, "Come, I will show to you the judgment of the great prostitute, who is sitting upon many waters, ²with whom the kings of the earth committed sexual immorality, and those inhabiting the earth were made drunk from the wine of her sexual immorality."

³And he carried me away in the רוּחַ, Ruach to a desert, and I saw a woman sitting upon a scarlet-colored beast, full of names of evil-speaking, having seven heads and ten horns. ⁴And the woman was wrapped around with purple and scarlet-color, and adorned with gold and precious stone and pearls, having a golden cup in her hand full of abominations and the uncleanness of her sexual immorality. ⁵And upon her forehead was written a name: "Mystery, Babylon the Great, the Mother of the Prostitutes and the Abominations of the Earth."

⁶And I saw the woman drunken from the blood of the קְדוֹשִׁים, Q'doshiym, and from the blood of the witnesses of יֵשׁוּעַ, Yeshua; and having seen her, I marveled with great wonder. ⁷And the Messenger said to me, "Why did you marvel? I will tell you the mystery of the woman and of the beast that IS carrying her, which has the seven heads and the ten horns.

⁸"The beast that you saw: it was, and it is not, and it is about to come up out of the abyss and go away to destruction. And

---

[a] Some mss insert, "another from"
[b] Some mss insert, "of the earth, and"
[c] Some mss insert, "of the heaven"

[d] "a hundred pounds"—lit. "of talent weight"

those living upon the earth whose name has not been written upon the scroll of the life from the foundation of the world will marvel, looking at the beast that was, and is not, and will come.[a]

9 "Here IS the mind that is having wisdom: the seven heads are seven mountains upon which the woman sits. And there are seven kings: 10the five fell, the one is, *and* the other did not yet come, but when he comes, he must remain *for* a little time. 11And the beast that was, yet is not—he is also *an* eighth, and he is out of the seven, and he goes away to destruction.

12 "And the ten horns that you saw are ten kings who did not yet receive a kingdom, but receive authority as kings *at* the same time with the beast. 13These have one mind, and will give their power and authority to the beast. 14These will make war with the Lamb, but the Lamb will overcome them, because he is Master of masters and King of kings, and those with him are called, and chosen, and faithful."

15And he said to me, "The waters you saw, where the prostitute sits, are peoples and crowds and world-ethnicities and languages.[b] 16And the ten horns that you saw, and the beast—these will hate the prostitute, and will make her desolate and naked, and will eat her flesh, and will burn her in fire 17(for God gave into their hearts to do its mind, and to make *them* one mind, and to give their kingdom to the beast until the words of God will be brought to a goal). 18And the woman that you saw is the great city that is having reign over the kings of the land."

18

1 After these things, I saw another Messenger coming down out of the heaven, having great authority, and the earth was giving off light from his glory. 2And with a strong[c] voice, he shouted, saying, "Fall! Fall did Babylon the Great! And she became a home of demons, and a lair of every unclean רוּחַ, ruach, and a lair of every unclean and hateful bird, 3because all the world-ethnicities have drunk of the wine of the rage of her sexual immorality, and the kings of the earth committed sexual immorality with her, and merchants of the earth were made rich from the power of her sensual luxury."

4And I heard another voice out of the heaven, saying, "Come forth out of her, my people, so that you may not share with her sins, and so that you may not receive of her plagues, 5because her sins *are* piled up[d] to the heaven, and God remembered her unrighteousness. 6Give back to her as she also gave back,[e] and double the[f] doubles according to her actions—mingle to her double in the cup that she mingled.

7 "As much as she glorified herself and lived in sensual luxury, give to her *just* as much torment and mourning, because in her heart she says, 'I sit *here* a queen, and I am not a widow, and I will not see mourning.' 8Because of this, her plagues—death, and mourning, and famine—will come in one day, and she will be utterly burned in fire (because יהוה אֱלֹהִים, Adonai 'Elohiym, who is having judged her, IS strong). 9And the kings of the earth, who committed sexual immorality and lived in sensual luxury with her, will weep and will strike themselves *in mourning* for her when they see the smoke of her burning, 10having stood from afar (because of the fear of her torment), saying, 'אוֹי, Oy! Oy! The great city! Babylon—the strong city! because in one moment came your judgment.'

11 "And the merchants of the earth will weep and mourn over her, because no one buys their cargo anymore: 12cargo of gold, and silver, and precious stone, and pearls, and fine linen, and purple, and silk, and scarlet, and all scented wood, and every object of ivory, and every object of most precious wood, and brass, and iron, and

---

[a] "and will come"—some mss say, "although it is"
[b] "languages"—lit. "tongues"
[c] "with a strong"—some mss say, "in strength *with* a great"
[d] "*are* piled up"—some mss say, "followed *her*"
[e] Some mss insert, "to you"
[f] "the"—some mss say, "to her"

marble, ¹³and cinnamon, and spice,ᵃ and incense, and ointment, and frankincense, and wine, and *olive* oil, and fine flour, and wheat, and cattle, and sheep, and *cargo* of horses, and of chariots, and of bodies and souls of men.

¹⁴"And the fruit of your soul's lust went away from you, and all things—the delicate and the bright—went away from you, and no longer will you find them at all. ¹⁵*And* the merchants of these things, who were made rich by her, will stand far off (because of the fear of her torment), weeping and mourning, ¹⁶saying, 'אוֹי אוֹי, Oy! Oy! The great city that was wrapped around with fine linen, and purple, and scarlet, and adorned in gold, and precious stone, and pearl! ¹⁷because in one moment so many riches were made waste.'

"And every shipmaster, and all *those* sailing to a place,ᵇ and sailors, and as many as work the sea, stood far off. ¹⁸And they were shouting, seeing the smoke of her burning, saying, 'What CITY IS like the great city?' ¹⁹And they threw dust upon their heads, and were shouting, weeping and mourning, saying, 'אוֹי אוֹי, Oy! Oy! The great city! in which all *those* having the ships in the sea were made rich out of her wealth! for in one moment she was made waste.'

²⁰"Rejoice over her, O heaven, and you קְדוֹשִׁים, Q'doshiym and emissariesᶜ and prophets, because God judged your judgment of her!"

²¹And one strong Messenger raised up a stone like a huge millstone, and threw *it* into the sea, saying, "In this *same* way, with violence will Babylon the great city be thrown down, and will not be found at all any longer—²²and *the* voice of harpists and musicians and flute players and trumpeters will not be heard at all in you any longer, and any artisan of any art will not be found at all in you any longer, and *the* noise of a millstone will not be heard at all in you any longer, ²³and light from a lamp will not shine at all in you any longer, and *the* voice of bridegroom and of bride will not be heard at all in you any longer, for your merchants were the great ones of the earth, because in your φαρμακεία, pharmakeiaᵈ all the world-ethnicities were led astray. ²⁴And in her was found *the* blood of prophets and of קְדוֹשִׁים, Q'doshiym, and of all those who have been slaughtered on the earth."

19

¹After these things, I heard *something* like a loud voice of a great many in the heaven, saying, "הַלְלוּ יָהּ, Hal'lu Yah! The salvation, and the glory,ᵉ and the power IS toᶠ our God, ²because TRUE AND RIGHTEOUS ARE HIS JUDGMENTS,ᵍ because He judged the great prostitute who corrupted the earth in her sexual unfaithfulness, and HE AVENGED THE BLOOD OF HIS SLAVESʰ at her hand." ³And a second time they said, "הַלְלוּ יָהּ, Hal'lu Yah!" and "Her SMOKE GOES UP—TO THE AGES OF THE AGES!"ⁱ ⁴And the זְקֵנִים, Z'qeniym fell down—the twenty-four—and the four living creatures, and they bowed *in worship* before God who was sitting upon the throne, saying, "אָמֵן, Amen, הַלְלוּ יָהּ, Hal'lu Yah!"

⁵And a voice came out from the throne, saying, "Praise our God, all you His slaves, and those fearing Him—the small and the great." ⁶And I heard *something* like the voice of a great many, and like the voice of many waters, and like the voice of severe thunderings, saying, "הַלְלוּ יָהּ, Hal'lu Yah! because אֱלֹהֵינוּ יהוה צְבָאוֹת, 'Eloheinu ADONAI Tz'vaot reigns! ⁷Let us rejoice, and rejoice extremely, and give the glory to Him, for the marriage of the Lamb came, and his wife made herself ready.

ᵃ Some mss omit, "and spice"
ᵇ "all *those* sailing to a place"—some mss say, "all the company on the ships"
ᶜ "קְדוֹשִׁים, Q'doshiym and emissaries"—some mss say, "holy emissaries"
ᵈ φαρμακεία, pharmakeia—usually "sorcery," or "witchcraft"
ᵉ Some mss insert, "and the honor"
ᶠ Some mss insert, "ADONAI"
ᵍ תְּהִלִּים T'hiliym 19:10(9)
ʰ דְּבָרִים D'variym 32:43
ⁱ יְשַׁעְיָהוּ Y'sha'yahu 34:10

Revelation 19:8

⁸And there was given to her that she may be wrapped around with fine linen, shining and clean, for the fine linen is the righteous acts of the קְדוֹשִׁים, Q'doshiym."

⁹And he said to me, "Write, 'Happy ARE they who have been called to the *celebration* meal of the marriage of the Lamb.'" And he said to me, "These ARE the true words of God." ¹⁰And I fell in front of his feet to bow before him *in worship*, and he said to me, "Watch out *and do* not! I am a fellow-slave of you and of your brothers —those having the testimony of יֵשׁוּעַ, Yeshua. Bow before God *in worship*, for the testimony of יֵשׁוּעַ, Yeshua is the רוּחַ, ruach of the prophecy."

¹¹And I saw the heaven having been opened, and look! a white horse! and He who is sitting upon it is called Faithful and True, and in righteousness He judges and makes war, ¹²and His eyes ARE as a flame of fire, and upon His head ARE many crowns—having a name written that no one has known, except Himself. ¹³And He is wrapped around with a garment covered with blood, and His name is called The Word of God.

¹⁴And the armies in the heaven were following Him upon white horses, clothed in fine linen—white and clean—¹⁵and out of His mouth comes a sharp sword, so that with it He may strike the world-ethnicities, and He will rule them with a rod of iron. And He tramples the winepress of the rage of the wrath of אֱלֹהֵי צְבָאוֹת, 'Elohei Tz'vaot, ¹⁶and He has a name written on His garment and on His thigh: "King of kings, and Master of masters."

¹⁷And I saw one Messenger standing in the sun, and he shouted in a loud voice, saying to all the birds that are flying in the mid-heaven, "Come, be gathered together to the great meal of God,ᵃ ¹⁸so that you may eat *the* flesh of kings, and *the* flesh of leaders of thousands, and *the* flesh of strong men, and *the* flesh of horses and of those sitting upon them, and the flesh of all—both freemen and slaves; both small and great."

¹⁹And I saw the beast, and the kings of the earth, and their armies, having been gathered together to make the war with Him who is sitting upon the horse, and with His army. ²⁰And the beast was taken, and with him the false prophet who did the signs in his presence, in which he led astray those who received the mark of the beast, and those who bowed before his image. The two—*still* living—were thrown into the lake of the fire that is burning with sulfur, ²¹and the rest were killed with the sword of Him who is sitting on the horse—*the* SWORD which was coming out of His mouth. And from their flesh, all the birds were filled.

20 ¹And I saw a Messenger coming down out of the heaven, having the key of the abyss, and a huge chain over his hand, ²and he took hold of the dragon, the ancient serpent, who is *the* Accuser and הַשָּׂטָן, HaSatan, and bound him *for* a thousand years. ³And he threw him into the abyss, and shut and sealed *it* above him, so that he could not lead the world-ethnicities astray any longer, until the thousand years are finished. (After these *things*, he must be released *for* a little time.)

⁴And I saw thrones, and they sat upon them, and judgment was given to them— even the souls of those who have been beheaded because of the testimony of יֵשׁוּעַ, Yeshua and because of the word of God, and who did not bow before the beast nor his image, and did not receive the mark upon their forehead and upon their hand— and they lived and reigned with the Messiah *for* a thousand years ⁵(the remainder of the dead did not live again until the thousand years were finished).

This IS the first Rising Again. ⁶Happy and holy IS he who is having part in the first Rising Again. The second death has no authority over these. Rather, they will be כֹּהֲנִים, ko'haniym of God and of the

---

ᵃ "the great meal of God"—some mss say, "the meal of the great God"

New heaven and earth.   **Revelation 21:12**

Messiah, and will reign with him *for* the thousand years.

⁷And when the thousand years are finished, הַשָּׂטָן, HaSatan will be released out of his prison, ⁸and he will go out to lead astray the world-ethnicities that are in the four corners of the earth (גּוֹג, Gog and מָגוֹג, Magog) to gather them together to the war, of whom their number *is* as the sand of the sea. ⁹And they went up over the breadth of the land, and surrounded the camp of the קְדוֹשִׁים, Q'doshiym and the beloved city, but there came down fireᵃ out of the heaven and devoured them. ¹⁰And the Accuser, who was leading them astray, was thrown into the lake of fire and sulfur (where also the beast and the false prophet ARE), and they will be tormented day and night—to the ages of the ages.

¹¹And I saw a great white throne, and Him who is sitting upon it—from whose face the earth and the heaven fled away, and a place was not found for them. ¹²And I saw the dead—the great and the small —standing in the presence of the throne,ᵇ and scrolls were opened.

And another scroll was opened, which is that of the Life, and the dead were judged out of the things written in the scrolls—according to their actions. ¹³And the sea gave up those dead *ones* in it, and the death and the שְׁאוֹל, Sh'ol gave up the dead in them, and they were judged, each one according to their actions. ¹⁴And the death and the שְׁאוֹל, Sh'ol were thrown into the lake of the fire. This is the second death—the lake of fireᶜ—¹⁵and if anyone was not found written in the Scroll of the Life, he was thrown into the lake of the fire.

21

¹And I saw a new heaven and a new earth—for the first heaven and the first earth wentᵈ away, and the sea is not anymore. ²And Iᵉ saw the holy city—יְרוּשָׁלַיִם הַחֲדָשָׁה, Y'rushalayim Ha'Chadashah—coming down out of the heaven from God, made ready as a bride arranged for her husband. ³And I heard a loud voice from the throne,ᶠ saying, "Look! the מִשְׁכָּן, mish'kan of God *is* with men, and He will dwell with them, and they will be His peoples, and God Himself will be with them *and be* their God,ᵍ ⁴and Heʰ will wipe away every tear from their eyes, and death will not be anymore, nor mourning, nor crying, nor will there be any more pain, because the first things went away."

⁵And He who is sitting upon the throne said, "Look! I make all things new." And He says,ⁱ "Write, because these words are faithful and true." ⁶And He said to me, "It has been done! I am the א and the ת,ʲ the Beginning and the End. To him who is thirsting, I will give of the well-spring of the water of the life without cost. ⁷He who is overcoming will inherit these things, and I will be God to him, and he will be a son to Me. ⁸But to the fearful, and faithless, and detestable, and murderers, and sexually immoral, and φαρμάκοις, pharmakois,ᵏ and idolaters, and all the liars—their part *is* in the lake that is burning with fire and sulfur, which is the second death."

⁹And there came one out of the seven Messengers (who have the seven bowls that are full of the seven last plagues), and he spoke with me, saying, "Come. I will show you the bride—the wife of the Lamb." ¹⁰And he carried me away in the רוּחַ, Ruach to a massive and high mountain, and showed to me the holy city, יְרוּשָׁלַיִם, Y'rushalayim,ˡ coming down out of the heaven from God; ¹¹having the glory of God, her light *is* like a most precious stone, as a jasper stone, clear as crystal; ¹²having a massive and high wall; having twelve gates

---

ᵃ Some mss insert, "from God"
ᵇ "the throne"—some mss say, "God"
ᶜ Some mss omit, "the lake of fire"
ᵈ "went"—some mss say, "passed"
ᵉ Some mss insert, "יוֹחָנָן, Yochanan"

ᶠ "throne"—some mss say, "heaven"
ᵍ cf. וַיִּקְרָא *Vayiq'ra* 26:11-12
ʰ "He"—some mss say, "God"
ⁱ Some mss insert, "to me"
ʲ "א and the ת"—see note at 1:8
ᵏ φαρμάκοις, pharmakois—usually "sorcerers" or "ones who practice witchcraft"
ˡ Some mss say, "the great city, the holy יְרוּשָׁלַיִם, Y'rushalayim"

and twelve Messengers at the gates, and names written thereon, which are the names of the twelve tribes of the sons of יִשְׂרָאֵל, Yis'rael—13three gates at the east, and three gates at the north, and three gates at the south, and three gates at the west—14and the wall of the city had twelve foundations, and on them *the* twelve names of the twelve emissaries of the Lamb.

15And he who was speaking with me had a measure—a golden reed—so that he could measure the city, and its gates, and its wall. 16And the city lies square, and the length of it is as much as the breadth. And he measured the city with the reed: twelve thousand stadia[a]—the length and breadth and height of it are equal. 17And he measured its wall, a hundred forty-four cubits[b] *thick, according to* the measure of a man (that is, *also* of the Messenger).

18And the building material of its wall was jasper, and the city WAS pure gold—resembling pure glass. 19The foundations of the wall of the city have been arranged with every precious stone: the first foundation, jasper; the second, sapphire; the third, chalcedony; the fourth, emerald; 20the fifth, sardonyx; the sixth, sardius; the seventh, chrysolite; the eighth, beryl; the ninth, topaz; the tenth, chrysoprase; the eleventh, jacinth; *and* the twelfth, amethyst.

21And the twelve gates WERE twelve pearls—each one of the individual gates was *made* of one pearl. And the street of the city WAS pure gold, like transparent glass.

22And I did not see a Temple in *the city,* for its Temple is יהוה אֱלֹהֵי צְבָאוֹת, ADONAI 'Elohei Tz'vaot and the Lamb. 23And the city has no need of the sun nor the moon, that they may shine on it, for the glory of God gives off its light, and the lamp of it IS the Lamb. 24And the world-ethnicities[c] will walk by its light, and the kings of the earth will bring their glory[d] into it, 25and its gates will not be shut at all by daytime, for there will be no night. 26And they will bring the glory and honor of the world-ethnicities into it; 27and not at all will there enter into it anything impure, or he who is doing a detestable thing, or a lie, but *only* those written in the Scroll of the Life of the Lamb.

22

1And he showed me a[e] river of *the* water of life, bright as crystal, going forth out of the throne of God and of the Lamb. 2In the middle of its street, and on this side and on that *side* of the river, IS a tree of life, yielding twelve *kinds of* fruit, returning its fruits in each month. And the leaves of the tree ARE for the therapy of the world-ethnicities.

3And there will not be any curse anymore, and the throne of God and of the Lamb will be in it, and His slaves will serve Him, 4and they will see His face, and His name WILL BE upon their foreheads.

5And there will not be night, and they *will* not have need of light of a lamp and light of a sun, because יהוה אֱלֹהִים, ADONAI 'Elohiym will give them light. And they will reign to the ages of the ages.

6And he said to me, "These words ARE faithful and true." And ADONAI, God of the רוּחוֹת, ruchot of the[f] prophets, sent His Messenger to show to His slaves the things that must soon take place:[g]

> 7"And look! I come quickly! Happy IS he who is paying attention to the words of the prophecy of this scroll."

8And I, יוֹחָנָן, Yochanan, am he who is hearing and seeing these things. And when I heard and saw, I fell down to bow *in worship* before the feet of the Messenger who was showing me *all* these things, 9and he said to me, "Watch out *and do* not! I am a fellow-slave of you and of your brothers

---

[a] "twelve thousand stadia"—about fifteen hundred miles
[b] "a hundred forty-four cubits"—about seventy-two yards
[c] Some mss insert, "of the saved"
[d] Some mss insert, "and honor"
[e] Some mss insert, "pure"
[f] "רוּחוֹת, ruchot of the"—some mss say, "holy"
[g] "soon take place"—some mss say, "come quickly"

Invitation and warning.

the prophets, and of those paying attention to the words of this scroll. Bow *in worship* before God."

¹⁰And he said to me, "You may not seal *up* the words of the prophecy of this scroll, for the time is near. ¹¹He who is unrighteous—let him still be unrighteous; and he who is filthy—let him still be filthy; and he who is righteous—let him still do righteousness;ᵃ and he who is set apart—let him still be set apart."

¹²"Look! I come quickly, and My reward IS with Me, to return to each as his action is. ¹³I am the א and the ת ᵇ—the First and the Last—the Beginning and the End.

¹⁴"Happy are those *who are* washing their robes,ᶜ so that the authority to the tree of the life will be theirs, and they may enter into the city by the gates. ¹⁵Outside ARE the dogs, and the φάρμακοι, pharmakoi,ᵈ and the sexually immoral, and the murderers, and the idolaters, and everyone loving and doing a lie.

¹⁶"I, יֵשׁוּעַ, Yeshua, sent My Messenger to testify to you *about* these things regarding the Called-Forth-Communities.ᵉ I am the root and the descendant of דָּוִד, David, the bright morning star!

¹⁷"And the רוּחַ, Ruach and the Bride say, 'Come!'

"And he who is hearing *this*, let him say, 'Come!'

"And he who is thirsting, let him come; he who is wanting, let him take the water of life without cost.

¹⁸"I testify to everyone *who is* hearing the words of the prophecy of this scroll: if anyone adds to these, God will add to him the plagues that have been written in this scroll; ¹⁹and if anyone takes away from the words of the scroll of this prophecy, God will take away his part from the treeᶠ of the life and out of the holy city—the things that have been written in this scroll.

²⁰"He who is testifying *to* these things says, 'Yes, I come quickly!'"

אָמֵן, Amen!ᵍ Be coming, Master יֵשׁוּעַ, Yeshua! ²¹The *unmerited* favor of the Master יֵשׁוּעַ, Yeshuaʰ IS with all.ⁱ

ᵃ "do righteousness"—some mss say, "be declared righteous"
ᵇ "א and the ת"—see note at 1:8
ᶜ "washing their robes"—some mss say, "doing His commands"
ᵈ φάρμακοι, pharmakoi—see note at 21:8
ᵉ "Called-Forth-Communities"—ἐκκλησίαις, ekklesiais; see מַתִּתְיָהוּ *Matit'yahu* 16:18
ᶠ "tree"—some mss say, "scroll"
ᵍ Some mss insert, "Yes"
ʰ Some mss insert, "*the* Messiah"
ⁱ "all"—some mss say, "you all. אָמֵן, Amen."; other mss say, "the קְדוֹשִׁים, Q'doshiym"

Glossary

OF TRANSLITERATED TERMS

This glossary is alphabetized according to transliterated English. For simplicity's sake, punctuation has been ignored as far as alphabetizing is concerned.

Each entry includes the Hebrew or Greek word, followed by its transliteration (as found throughout the body of the MJLT), followed either by the anglicized form of the word in parentheses, or, when warranted, by English translation or definition.

Pronunciation Guide. The chart below lists the English transliteration of each Hebrew consonant. Most pronunciations sound like their transliterations, such as בּ (beit) = "b". That said, ח (cheit) deserves special mention. Represented in the transliteration as "ch," ח is sounded not in the front of the mouth (as in "much" or "church"), but gutturally, in the back of the throat (as in "Bach" or "loch")— not a sound normally heard in the English language. Similarly, the sound for כ (khaf), represented by "kh," is virtually identical to the guttural ח.

HEBREW	TRANSLITERATION	HEBREW	TRANSLITERATION	HEBREW	TRANSLITERATION
בּ	b	כ or ך	kh	ס or שׂ	s
ח	ch	ל	l	שׁ	sh
ד	d	מ or ם	m	ט or ת	t
פ	f	נ or ן	n	צ or ץ	tz
ג	g	פּ	p	ב or ו	v
ה	h	ק	q*	י	y
כּ	k	ר	r	ז	z

pronounced like "k"

Additionally, vowels in Hebrew are represented primarily according to a vowel pointing system; that is, a series of dashes and dots in proximity to the letters. Vowel points may appear in relation to any letter of the alphabet. In the following chart, the א is used as an example, though the א (as also the ע) has no associated sound by itself. The vowels are therefore pronounced and represented in the transliteration as follows:

HEBREW	TRANSLITERATION	PRONUNCIATION
אָ or אַ	a	"ah"
אֵ or אֶ	e	"eh"
אִ	i	"ee"
אֹ or וֹ	o	"oh"
אֻ or וּ	u	"oo"
אַי or אָי	ai	"ah-ee"
אֵי or אֶי	ei	"eh-ee"
אִי	iy	"ee"
א	'	~ stop ~

Glossary of Transliterated Terms (A - B)

A

אַבָּא, **Abba**
   an informal way to say "father"

אָחָז, **Achaz** (Ahaz)

אָדָם, **Adam** (Adam)

אַדִּי, **Adiy** (Addi)

אֲדֹנָי, **'Adonai**
   my master; a reference to God

ADONAI
   In small capital letters, this represents יהוה, known as the tetragrammaton, and commonly referred to as God's sacred name. In English, יהוה is often represented as YHVH, or YHWH. Many English bibles render it as "the LORD" in small capital letters, and sometimes, "Jehovah."

יהוה אֱלֹהֵי צְבָאוֹת, **ADONAI 'Elohei Tz'vaot**
   the LORD God of Hosts/Armies

יהוה אֱלֹהִים, **ADONAI 'Elohiym**
   the LORD God

יהוה צְבָאוֹת, **ADONAI Tz'vaot**
   the LORD of Hosts/Armies

אַהֲרֹן, **A'haron** (Aaron)

א, **Alef**
   first letter of the Hebrew alphabet, "first"

אָמֵן, **amen** (amen)

עַמִּינָדָב, **Amiynadav** (Amminadab)

אָמוֹן, **Amon**
   found in the genealogy of יֵשׁוּעַ, Yeshua (see מְלָכִים M'lakhiym Beit 21:18-25) in מַתִּתְיָהוּ Matit'yahu 1:10; earlier mss say, "אָמוֹץ, Amotz"

עֲמֹרָה, **'Amorah** (Gomorrah)

אָמוֹס, **Amos** (Amos)

אָמוֹץ, **Amotz** (Amos)

Ἀπολλύων, **Apollyon**
   destroyer

עֲרָב, **'Arav** (Arab)

אֲרוֹן בְּרִיתוֹ, **'Aron B'riyto**
   (the) ark of His covenant

אֲרוֹן הַבְּרִית, **'Aron HaB'riyt**
   ark of the covenant

אַרְפַּכְשַׁד, **Ar'pakh'shad** (Arphaxad)

אָסָא, **Asa** (Asa)

אַשְׁדּוֹד, **Ash'dod** (Azotus)

אָשֵׁר, **Asher** (Asher)

אֲבַדּוֹן, **'Avadon** (Abaddon)

אֲבִיָּה, **'Aviyah** (Abijah)

אֲבִיהוּד, **'Aviyhud** (Abihud)

עֲבֹדָה, **'avodah**
   service (of the Temple), rite, ceremony

אַבְרָהָם, **Av'raham** (Abraham)

עַזָּה, **Azah** (Gaza)

עַזּוּר, **Azur** (Azor)

B

בַּעַל, **Ba-al** (Baal)

בַּעַל־זְבוּב, **Ba-al–Z'vuv** (Beelzebub)

בָּלָק, **Balaq** (Balak)

בַּר־אַבָּא, **Bar-Aba** (Barabbas)

בַּר־נַבָּא, **Bar-Naba** (Barnabas)

בַּר־שַׁבָּא, **Bar-Saba** (Barsabbas)

בַּר־תַּלְמַי, **Bar-Tal'mai** (Bartholomew)

בַּר־יֵשׁוּעַ, **Bar-Yeshua** (Barjesus)

בָּרָק, **Baraq** (Barak)

βάρβαροι, **Barbaroi**
   barbarians

βάρβαρος, **Barbaros**
   barbarian

בַּרְטִימַי, **Bar'tiymai** (Bartimaeus)

Glossary of Transliterated Terms (B-D)

בּ, **Beit**
second letter of the Hebrew alphabet, "second"

בֵּית־עַנְיָה, **Beit-An'yah** (Bethany)
בֵּית־עֲבָרָה, **Beit-'Avarah** (Bethabara)
בֵּית־חַסְדָּא, **Beit-Chas'da** (Bethesda)
בֵּית־לֶחֶם, **Beit-Lechem** (Bethlehem)
בֵּית־פַּגֵּי, **Beit-Pagei** (Bethphage)
בֵּית־צַיְדָה, **Beit-Tzai'dah** (Bethsaida)
בֶּן־אֵל עֶלְיוֹן, **Ben-El El'yon**
Son of God Most High

בְּאֵר שַׁחַת, **B'er Shachat**
pit of ruin or destruction, "Tartarus"; may be theologically related to גֵּיהִנֹּם, Geihinom

בְּרֶכְיָה, **Berekh'yah** (Berachiah)
בִּלְעָם, **Bil'am** (Balaam)
בִּנְיָמִין, **Bin'yamiyn** (Benjamin)
בְּלִיַּעַל, **B'liya-al** (Belial)
בְּמִדְבַּר, **B'mid'bar**
in the wilderness, "Numbers"

בְּנֵי־רַגֶשׁ, **B'nei Ragesh**
"Boanerges"; the Greek is apparently rendering Aramaic for "Sons of Thunder"

בֹּעַז, **Boaz** (Boaz)
בְּעוֹר, **B'or** (Beor)
בְּרֵאשִׁית, **B'reshiyt**
in the beginning, "Genesis"

בְּרִית, **b'riyt**
covenant

בְּרִית חֲדָשָׁה, **B'riyt 'Chadashah**
New Covenant

בְּרִית הַחֲדָשָׁה, **B'riyt Ha'Chadashah**
(the) New Covenant

בְּרִית הַיְשָׁנָה, **B'riyt HaY'shanah**
Old Covenant

בְּרִית מִילָה, **b'riyt miylah**
covenant of circumcision

בְּרִית רִאשֹׁנָה, **b'riyt rishonah**
first covenant

בְּרִיתוֹת, **b'riytot**
covenants

C

חֲדָשָׁה, **'chadashah**
new

חַג, **chag**
feast

חַג הַמַּצּוֹת, **Chag HaMatzot**
the Feast of Unleavened Bread

חַגַּי, **Chagai** (Haggai)
חַלְפַי, **Chal'fai** (Alphaeus)
חֲמוֹר, **'Chamor** (Hamor)
חַנָּה, **Chanah** (Anna)
חָנָן, **Chanan** (Annas)
חֲנַנְיָה, **'Chanan'yah** (Ananias)
חֲנוֹךְ, **'Chanokh** (Enoch)
חֲקַל־דְּמָא, **'Chaqal-D'ma** (Akeldama)
חָרָן, **Charan** (Haran)
חַוָּה, **Chavah** (Eve)
חֲבַקּוּק, **'Chavaquq** (Habakkuk)
חֶסְלִי, **Ches'liy** (Esli)
חֶצְרוֹן, **Chetz'ron** (Hezron)
חִזְקִיָּהוּ, **Chiz'qiyahu** (Hezekiah)
חֹדֶשׁ, **chodesh**
new moon

D

דַּמֶּשֶׂק, **Dameseq** (Damascus)
דַּמְשְׂקִיִּים, **Dames'qiyiym** (Damascenes)
דָּנִיֵּאל, **Daniyel** (Daniel)
דָּוִד, **David** (David)
דִּבְרֵי הַיָּמִים, **Div'rei HaYamiym**
Accounts of the Days, "Chronicles"

Glossary of Transliterated Terms (D-H)

דְּבָרִים, **D'variym**
words, "Deuteronomy"

E

אֱדוֹם, **'Edom** (Idumea)
אֶפְרַיִם, **Ef'rayim** (Ephraim)
אֶלְעָזָר, **El'azar** (Eleazar *or* Lazarus)
עֵלִי, **Eliy** (Eli)
אֵלִיָּהוּ, **Eliyahu** (Elijah)
אֱלִיעֶזֶר, **'Eliyezer** (Eliezer)
אֱלִיהוּד, **'Eliyhud** (Eliud)
אֱלִישֶׁבַע, **'Eliysheva** (Elizabeth)
אֶלְמוֹדָם, **El'modam** (Elmadam)
אֱלֹהֵי, **'Elohei**
"God of"

אֱלֹהֵי צְבָאוֹת, **'Elohei Tz'vaot**
God of Hosts/Armies

אֱלֹהִים, **'Elohiym**
God

אֶלְיָקִים, **El'yaqiym** (Eliakim)
עֵנוֹן, **Enon** (Ænon)
אֱנוֹשׁ, **'Enosh** (Enosh)
עֵר, **Er** (Er)
עֵשָׂו, **Esav** (Esau)
אֶתְפַּתַח, **Et'patach**
"Ephphatha"; the Greek is apparently rendering Aramaic for "be opened"

עֵבֶר, **Ever** (Eber)
אֶבְיָתָר, **Ev'yatar** (Abiathar)

G

גַּבְּתָא, **Gab'ta** (Gabbatha)
גָּד, **Gad** (Gad)
גַּדְרִיִּים, **Gad'riyiym** (Gadarenes)
גָּלְגָּלְתָּא, **Gal'gal'ta** (Golgotha)
גָּלִיל, **Galiyl** (Galilee)
גַּמְלִיאֵל, **Gam'liyel** (Gamaliel)

גַּת־שְׁמָנֶה, **Gat-Sh'menah** (Gethsemane)
גַּבְרִיאֵל, **Gav'riyel** (Gabriel)
גְּדִלִים, **g'diliym**
fringes (see דְּבָרִים *D'variym* 22:12)

גֵּיהִנֹּם, **Geihinom**
"Gehenna"; that is, "hell"

גֵּרְזִיִּים, **Geraziyiym** (Gerasenes)
גִּדְעוֹן, **Gid'on** (Gideon)
גְּלִילִי, **G'liyliy** (Galilean)
גְּלִילִים, **G'liyliym** (Galileans)
גְּנֵיסָרֶת, **G'neisaret** (Gennesaret)
גּוֹג, **Gog** (Gog)
גּוֹי, **Goy**
person of non-Jewish ethnicity; people-group; "Gentile"

גּוֹיִם, **Goyim**
people of non-Jewish ethnicity; people-groups; "Gentiles"

H

הַבְּרִית הַחֲדָשָׁה, **HaB'riyt Ha'Chadashah**
the New Covenant

הַחֲדָשָׁה, **Ha'Chadashah**
the New

הַגָּלִילִי, **HaGaliyliy**
the Galilean

הָגָר, **Hagar** (Hagar)
הַכֹּהֵן, **HaKohen**
the Priest

הַלֵּל, **Halel**
Praise

הַלְלוּ יָהּ, **Hal'lu Yah**
Praise Yah; יָהּ is a shortened form of יהוה; "Hallelujah"

Glossary of Transliterated Terms (H-L)

הַמַּצּוֹת, **HaMatzot**
(the Feast of) the Unleavened Bread

הַנָּצְרָתִי, **HaNatz'ratiy**
the Nazarene

הַר מְגִדּוֹ, **Har M'gido** (Armageddon)
הַר סִינַי, **Har Siynai** (Mount Sinai)
הַר צִיּוֹן, **Har Tziyon** (Mount Zion)
הָרָמָתַיִם, **HaRamatayim** (Arimathea)

הַשָּׂטָן, **HaSatan**
the Adversary, "Satan"

הַזָּקֵן, **HaZaqen**
the Elder

Ἑλληνιστάς, **Hellenistas**
Jews under the influence of Greek culture; "Hellenists"

הֶבֶל, **Hevel** (Abel)

הוֹשַׁע־נָא, **Hosha-na**
"Hosanna"; the Greek is apparently rendering an Aramaic phrase meaning, "Save *us*, please!"

הוֹשֵׁעַ, **Hoshea** (Hosea)

I

עִמָּנוּאֵל, **Imanuel** (Immanuel)

עִבְרִים, **Iv'riym**
Hebrews, as in, the Hebrew (Jewish) people; Hebrew-speaking Jews

אִישׁ־קְרִיּוֹת, **Iysh-Q'riyot**
Man (from) Keriot, "Iscariot"

אִיּוֹב, **Iyov** (Job)
אִיזֶבֶל, **Iyzevel** (Jezebel)

K

כָּנָף, **kanaf**
the outermost edge or border of the garment where one is to make the צִיצִת, tziytzit and גְּדִלִים, g'diliym.

כַּפֹּרֶת, **Kaporet**
the atonement cover on the ark of the testimony, "mercy seat"

כֵּיפָא, **Keifa** (Cephas; that is, Peter)

כְּפַר־נַחוּם, **K'far-Nachum** (Capernaum)
כַּשְׂדִּים, **Khas'diym** (Chaldeans)
כְּהֻנָּה, **K'hunah**
Priesthood

כְּהֻנַּת קֹדֶשׁ, **K'hunat Qodesh**
Holy Priesthood

כְּנַעַן, **K'na-an** (Canaan)
כְּנַעֲנִית, **K'na'aniyt** (Canaanite, *female*)
כֹּהֲנִים, **Ko'haniym**
Priests

כֹּהֲנִים גְּדוֹלִים, **Ko'haniym G'doliym**
High Priests

כֹּהֲנִים הַגְּדוֹלִים, **Ko'haniym HaG'doliym**
the High Priests

כֹּהֵן, **kohen**
priest

כֹּהֵן גָּדוֹל, **Kohen Gadol**
High Priest

כֹּהֵן הַגָּדוֹל, **Kohen HaGadol**
the High Priest

כֹּהֵן לְאֵל עֶלְיוֹן, **Kohen l'El El'yon**
Priest to God Most High

כְּרֻבִים, **K'ruviym** (cherubim)
כּוּזָא, **Kuza** (Cuza *or* Chuza)

L

לַבַּי, **Labai** (Lebbeus)
לֶמֶךְ, **Lamekh** (Lamech)

Glossary of Transliterated Terms (L-N)

לֶחֶם הַפָּנִים, **Lechem HaPaniym**
Bread of the Presence; lit. "Bread of the Faces"

לֵוִי, **Leviy** (Levi)

לֵוִי בֶּן־חַלְפַּי, **Leviy Ben-Chal'fai**
Levi son of Alphaeus

לֹד, **Lod** (Lydda)

לוֹט, **Lot** (Lot)

לְוִיִּם, **L'viyim** (Levites)

M

מַחַת, **Machat** (Maath)

מְגָדוֹן, **Magadon** (Magadan)

מַגְדָּלִית, **Mag'daliyt** (Magdalene)

מָגוֹג, **Magog** (Magog)

מַהֲלַלְאֵל, **Ma'halal'el** (Mahalaleel)

מָן, **mahn** (manna)

מַלְאָכִי, **Mal'akhiy** (Malachi)

מַלְכִּי, **Mal'kiy** (Melchi)

מַלְכִּי־צֶדֶק, **Mal'kiy-Tzedeq** (Melchizedek)

מַלְיָא, **Mal'ya** (Melea)

מָרָנָא תָא, **marana ta**
"maranatha"; the Greek is apparently rendering an Aramaic phrase meaning, "Our Master, come!"

מַרְתָּא, **Mar'ta** (Martha)

מָשִׁיחַ, **Mashiyach** (Messiah)

מַתָּן, **Matan** (Matthan)

מַתָּת, **Matat** (Matthat)

מַתָּתָה, **Matatah** (Mattatha)

מַתִּתְיָה, **Matit'yah** (Mattathias)

מַתִּתְיָהוּ, **Matit'yahu** (Matthew)

מַצָּה, **matzah**
unleavened bread

מֶלֶךְ שָׁלֵם, **Melekh Shalem**
King of Salem, King of Peace

מִדְיָן, **Mid'yan** (Midian)

מִרְיָם, **Mir'yam** (Miriam or Mary)

מִרְיָם הַמַּגְדָּלִית, **Mir'yam HaMag'daliyt**
Miriam of the Magdala, "Mary Madalene"

מִשְׁכָּן, **mish'kan** (tent or tabernacle)

מִשְׁלֵי, **Mish'lei**
"Proverbs"

מִצְרַיִם, **Mitz'rayim** (Egypt)

מִצְרִי, **Mitz'riy** (Egyptian)

מִיכָאֵל, **Miykhael** (Michael)

מִיכָה, **Miykhah** (Micah)

מִינָא, **Miyna** (Menna)

מְלָכִים, **M'lakhiym**
kings

מְנַשֶּׁה, **M'nasheh** (Manasseh)

מְנוֹרָה, **m'norah**
menorah, "lampstand"

מְנֹרוֹת, **m'norot**
menorah, pl. (see מְנוֹרָה, m'norah)

מֹלֶךְ, **Molekh** (Molech or Moloch)

מֹשֶׁה, **Mosheh** (Moses)

מְתוּשֶׁלַח, **M'tushelach** (Methuselah)

N

נָחוֹר, **Nachor** (Nahor)

נַחְשׁוֹן, **Nach'shon** (Nahshon)

נַחוּם, **Nachum** (Nahum)

נַפְתָּלִי, **Naf'taliy** (Naphtali)

נַגַּי, **Nagai** (Naggai)

נַעִין, **Naiyn** (Nain)

נָתָן, **Natan** (Nathan)

נָצְרָתִי, **Natz'ratiy** (Nazarene)

נְחֶמְיָה, **N'chem'yah** (Nehemiah)

נֵרִי, **Neriy** (Neri)

נִינְוֵה, **Niyn'veh** (Nineveh)

Glossary of Transliterated Terms (N-R)

נֹחַ, **Noach** (Noah)
נְתַנְאֵל, **N'tan'el** (Nathanael)
נָצְרַת, **N'tzaret** (Nazareth)
נְבִיאִים, **N'viyiym**
 Prophets

O

עוֹבֵד, **Oved** (Obed)
אוֹי, **oy!** (woe!)

P

פַּרְעֹה, **Par'oh** (Pharaoh)
פָּרוּשׁ, **Parush**
 Pharisee
פֶּלֶג, **Peleg** (Peleg)
פֶּרֶץ, **Peretz** (Perez)
פֶּסַח, **Pesach**
 Passover
פְּנוּאֵל, **P'nuel** (Phanuel)
פְּרָת, **P'rat**
 Euphrates
פְּרוּשִׁים, **P'rushiym**
 Pharisees

Pseudepigrapha
 any of various pseudonymous or anonymous Jewish religious writings of the period 200 B.C. to A.D. 200; not included in any canon of biblical Scripture (Merriam-Webster)

Q

קָדוֹשׁ, **qadosh**
 holy
קָהָל, **qahal**
 the assembly of Israel
קָנָה, **Qanah** (Cana)
קַיָּפָא, **Qayafa** (Caiaphas)

קַיִן, **Qayin** (Cain)
קְדוֹשִׁים, **Q'doshiym**
 holy ones, "saints"
קֵינָן, **Qeinan** (Cainan)
קְהִלָּה, **q'hilah**
 see קָהָל, qahal
קִדְרוֹן, **Qid'ron** (Kidron)
קִישׁ, **Qish** (Kish)
קֹדֶשׁ הַקֳּדָשִׁים, **Qodesh HaQodashiym**
 Holy of Holies, Most Holy Place
קֹרַח, **Qorach** (Korah)
קָרְבָּן, **qor'ban** (corban *or* korban)
קוֹסָם, **Qosam** (Cosam)
קְרִיּוֹת, **Q'riyot** (Keriot)

R

רַבִּי, **Rabiy** (Rabbi)
רָחָב, **Rachav** (Rahab)
רָחֵל, **Rachel** (Rachel)
רָם, **Ram** (Ram)
רָמָה, **Ramah** (Ramah)
רְחַבְעָם, **R'chav'am** (Rehoboam)
רֵישָׁא, **Reisha** (Rhesa)
רִאשֹׁנָה, **rishonah**
 first
רִבְקָה, **Riv'qah** (Rebecca)
רְעוּ, **R'u** (Reu)
רוּחַ, **Ruach**
 Spirit
רוּחַ אֲדֹנָי, **Ruach 'Adonai**
 (the) Spirit of the Lord
רוּחַ אֱלֹהִים, **Ruach 'Elohiym**
 (the) Spirit of God
רוּחַ הָאֱמֶת, **Ruach Ha'Emet**
 (the) Spirit of Truth

Glossary of Transliterated Terms (R-S)

רוּחַ הַקֹּדֶשׁ, **Ruach HaQodesh**
the Holy Spirit

רוּחַ הַטֻּמְאָה, **ruach ha-tum'ah**
(the) unclean spirit

רוּחוֹת, **ruchot**
spirits

רוּת, **Rut** (Ruth)

רְאוּבֵן, **R'uven** (Reuben)

S

שַׁלְמוֹן, **Sal'mon** (Salmon)
שָׂרָה, **Sarah** (Sarah)
שָׂטָן, **Satan**
Adversary

סְדֹם, **S'dom** (Sodom)
שַׁבָּת, **Shabat**
Sabbath

שַׁבָּתוֹת, **Shabatot**
Sabbaths

שֶׁלַח, **Shalach** (Shelah)
שָׁלֵם, **Shalem** (Salem)
שָׁלוֹם, **Shalom**
peace (εἰρήνη, eirene); or, when used as a greeting, it is an appropriate Hebrew equivalent for χαῖρω, chairo, which means "rejoice" or "be well."

שָׁלוֹם עֲלֵכֶם, **Shalom 'alekhem**
"Peace to you" or "Peace be with you"

שָׁלוֹם לְךָ, **Shalom l'kha**
"Peace to you"

שְׁאַלְתִּיאֵל, **Sh'al'tiyel** (Shealtiel)
שַׁפִּירָא, **Shapiyra** (Sapphira)
שָׁרוֹן, **Sharon** (Sharon)
שָׁאוּל, **Shaul** (Saul)

שָׁבוּעוֹת, **Shavuot**
(the Feast of) Weeks

שֵׁם, **Shem** (Shem)
שֶׁקֶל, **sheqel** (shekel)
שֵׁת, **Shet** (Seth)
שִׁלֹחַ, **Shiloach** (Siloam)
שִׁמְעִי, **Shim'iy** (Semein)
שִׁמְעוֹן, **Shim'on** (Simon)
שִׁמְעוֹן בַּר־יוֹנָה, **Shim'on Bar-Yonah**
Simon son of Jonah

שִׁמְעוֹן הַקַּנַּי, **Shim'on HaQanai**
"Simon the Zealot"

שִׁמְעוֹן כֵּיפָא, **Shim'on Keifa**
Simon Cephas; that is, Simon Peter

שִׁמְשׁוֹן, **Shim'shon** (Samson)
שְׁכֶם, **Sh'khem** (Shechem)
שְׁלִיחִים, **sh'liychiym**
emissaries, apostles

שְׁלֹמִית, **Sh'lomiyt** (Salome)
שְׁלֹמֹה, **Sh'lomoh** (Solomon)
שְׁמוֹת, **Sh'mot**
names, "Exodus"

שְׁמוּאֵל, **Sh'muel** (Samuel)
שׁוֹפָר, **shofar**
ram's horn

שׁוֹפָרוֹת, **shofarot**
ram's horns

שְׁאוֹל, **Sh'ol**
the grave, "Sheol" or "Hades"

שֹׁמְרוֹן, **Shom'ron** (Samaria)
שֹׁמְרוֹנִי, **Shom'roniy** (Samaritan)
שֹׁמְרוֹנִים, **Shom'roniym** (Samaritans)
שֹׁמְרוֹנִית, **Shom'roniyt** (Samaritan, female)

שׁוֹשַׁנָּה, **Shoshanah** (Susanna)
סִילָא, **Siyla** (Silas)

Glossary of Transliterated Terms (S-Y)

סִינַי, **Siynai** (Sinai)

סוֹפֵר, **Sofer**
Scribe

סוֹפְרִים, **Sof'riym**
Scribes

שְׂרוּג, **S'rug** (Serug)

סֻכָּה, **sukah**
hut, temporary dwelling

סוּכַר, **Sukhar** (Sychar)

סֻכּוֹת, **sukot**
plural of סֻכָּה, sukah

T

תַּדַּי, **Tadai** (Thaddaeus)

טַלְיְתָא קוּמִי, **Tal'y'ta qumiy** (Talitha cumi)

תָּמָר, **Tamar** (Tamar)

Targum Pseudo-Jonathan
From Judaism, a targum (paraphrase/interpretation) of the Torah

טָבִיתָא, **Taviyta** (Tabitha)

תֶּרַח, **Terach** (Terah)

תְּפִלִּין, **t'filiyn**
phylacteries

תְּהִלִּים, **T'hiliym**
melodies, "Psalms"

טִימַי, **Tiymai** (Timaeus)

תּוֹמָא, **Toma** (Thomas)

תּוֹרָה, **Torah**
instruction, "Law," five books of Moses; exclusive of the Talmud or Rabbinic traditions of Judaism

צָדוֹק, **Tzadoq** (Zadok)

צְדוּקִים, **Tzaduqiym** (Sadducees)

צָרְפַת, **Tzar'fat** (Zarephath)

צְפַנְיָה, **Tz'fan'yah** (Zephaniah)

צִידוֹן, **Tziydon** (Sidon)

צִדֹנִים, **Tzidoniym** (Sidonians)

צִיּוֹן, **Tziyon** (Zion)

צִיצִת, **tziytzit**
tassels (see בְּמִדְבַּר B'mid'bar 15:38-39)

צוֹר, **Tzor** (Tyre)

צֹרִים, **Tzoriym** (Tyrians)

צְבָאוֹת, **Tz'vaot**
Hosts/Armies

U

אוּרִיָה, **Uriyah** (Uriah)

עֻזִיָּהוּ, **Uziyahu** (Uzziah)

V

וַיִּקְרָא, **Vayiq'ra**
and he called; "Leviticus"

Y

יַעֲקֹב, **Ya'aqov** (Jacob or "James")

יַעֲקֹב בֶּן־זַבְדִּי, **Ya'aqov Ben-Zav'diy**
Jacob son of Zebedee

יָפוֹ, **Yafo** (Joppa)

יָאִיר, **Yaiyr** (Jairus)

יָכִין, **Yakhiyn** (Achim)

יַם־הַגָּלִיל, **Yam HaGaliyl**
the Sea of Galilee

יַם־סוּף, **Yam-Suf**
(the) Red Sea

יַנַּי, **Yanai** (Jannai)

יַרְדֵּן, **Yar'den** (Jordan)

יְחֶזְקֵאל, **Y'chez'qel** (Ezekiel)

יֶרֶד, **Yered** (Jared)

יֵשׁוּעַ, **Yeshua**
salvation, anglicized as "Jesus"

יְהוֹרָם, **Y'horam** (Joram or Jehoram)

Glossary of Transliterated Terms (Y-Z)

יְהוֹשָׁפָט, **Y'hoshafat** (Jehoshaphat)

יְהוֹשֻׁעַ, **Y'hoshua** (Joshua)

יְהוּדָה, **Y'hudah** (Judah or Judas or Judea)

יְהוּדָה אִישׁ־קְרִיּוֹת, **Y'hudah Iysh-Q'riyot** Judah (the) man (from) Keriot, "Judas Iscariot"

יְהוּדִי, **Y'hudiy** (Jew or Jewish)

יְהוּדִיָה, **Y'hudiyah** (Jewish, *female*)

יְהוּדִים, **Y'hudiym** (Jews)

יִפְתָּח, **Yif'tach** (Jephthah)

יִרְמְיָהוּ, **Yir'm'yahu** (Jeremiah)

יִשָּׂשכָר, **Yisakhar** (Issachar)

יִשַׁי, **Yishai** (Jesse)

יִשְׂרָאֵל, **Yis'rael** (Israel)

יִשְׂרְאֵלִי, **Yis'r'eliy** (Israelite)

יִשְׂרְאֵלִים, **Yis'raeliym** (Israelites)

יִצְחָק, **Yitz'chaq** (Isaac)

יְכָנְיָהוּ, **Y'khan'yahu** (Jeconiah)

יוֹחָנָן, **Yochanan** (John or Joanan)

יוֹדָה, **Yodah** (Joda)

יוֹם הַשַׁבָּת, **Yom HaShabat** the Sabbath Day

יוֹאֵל, **Yoel** (Joel)

יוֹנָה, **Yonah** (Jonah)

יוֹנָם, **Yonam** (Jonam)

יוֹרֶה וּמַלְקוֹשׁ, **Yoreh uMal'qosh** early rain and later rain

יוֹרִים, **Yoriym** (Jorim)

יוֹסֵף, **Yosef** (Joseph)

יוֹסֵף מִן־הָרָמָתַיִם, **Yosef Min-HaRamatayim** Joseph of Arimathea

יוֹסֵי, **Yosei** (Joses)

יֹאשִׁיָהוּ, **Yoshiyahu** (Josiah)

יוֹתָם, **Yotam** (Jotham)

יְרִיחוֹ, **Y'riycho** (Jericho)

יְרוּשָׁלְמִים, **Y'rushalamiym** (Jerusalemites)

יְרוּשָׁלַיִם, **Y'rushalayim** (Jerusalem)

יְרוּשָׁלַיִם הַחֲדָשָׁה, **Y'rushalayim Ha'-Chadashah** the New Jerusalem

יְשַׁעְיָהוּ, **Y'sha'yahu** (Isaiah)

Z

זַכַּי, **Zakai** (Zacchaeus)

זָקֵן, **zaqen** an older person, "elder"

זַבְדִי, **Zav'diy** (Zebedee)

זֶרַח, **Zerach** (Zerah)

זְכַרְיָה, **Z'khar'yah** (Zacharias or Zechariah)

זְקֵנִים, **z'qeniym** a group of older persons who carry weight with and responsibility for the community; "elders"; leaders of Israel (Z'qeniym) as compared to leaders of the Called-Forth (z'qeniym)

זְרֻבָּבֶל, **Z'rubavel** (Zerubbabel)

זְבֻלוּן, **Z'vulun** (Zebulun)

About the Editor

KEVIN GEOFFREY, born Kevin Geoffrey Berger, is the firstborn son of a first-generation American, non-religious, Jewish family. Ashamed of his lineage from childhood, he deliberately attempted to hide his identity as a Jew, legally changing his name as a young adult. After experiencing an apparently miraculous healing from an incurable disease, however, Kevin began to search for God. Eventually, in 1988, he accepted Yeshua as Messiah, a decision which would ultimately lead him to be restored to his Jewish heritage. Today, Kevin is a strong advocate for the restoration of all Jewish believers in Yeshua to their distinct calling and identity as the faithful remnant of Israel.

Kevin has been licensed by the International Alliance of Messianic Congregations and Synagogues (IAMCS), and ordained by Jewish Voice Ministries International (JVMI). He has taught in live seminars and conferences throughout the United States, as well as multiple Messianic congregations and synagogues. He has also served in congregational leadership, as well as been involved in such endeavors as congregational planting and leadership development. Kevin is best known as an author, having published seven books to date, including the *Messianic Daily Devotional*, *The Messianic Life: Being a Disciple of Messiah*, and *Bearing the Standard: A Rallying Cry to Uphold the Scriptures*. In addition to writing about uniquely Messianic Jewish topics, Kevin's clear and impassioned teachings focus on true discipleship, radical life-commitment to Yeshua, and championing the Scriptures as God's perfect word.

Kevin is a husband, a father, and also the principal laborer of Perfect Word Ministries, a Messianic Jewish equipping ministry. He currently resides in Phoenix, Arizona, with his wife Esther and their four cherished sons, Isaac, Josiah, Hosea and Asher.

To learn more, order copies, or support the publication of the Messianic Jewish Literal Translation, please visit:

mjlt.org

A ministry of Perfect Word Ministries

resources.perfectword.org
1-888-321-PWMI